Compensation

Eighth Edition

George T. Milkovich
Cornell University

Jerry M. Newman
State University of New York—Buffalo

**With the assistance
of Carolyn Milkovich**

McGraw-Hill
Irwin

Boston   Burr Ridge, IL   Dubuque, IA   Madison, WI   New York   San Francisco   St. Louis
Bangkok   Bogotá   Caracas   Kuala Lumpur   Lisbon   London   Madrid   Mexico City
Milan   Montreal   New Delhi   Santiago   Seoul   Singapore   Sydney   Taipei   Toronto

 **McGraw-Hill Irwin**

COMPENSATION

Published by McGraw-Hill/Irwin, a business unit of The McGraw-Hill Companies, Inc., 1221 Avenue of the Americas, New York, NY, 10020. Copyright © 2005, 2002, 1999, 1996, 1993, 1990, 1987, 1984 by The McGraw-Hill Companies, Inc. All rights reserved. No part of this publication may be reproduced or distributed in any form or by any means, or stored in a database or retrieval system, without the prior written consent of The McGraw-Hill Companies, Inc., including, but not limited to, in any network or other electronic storage or transmission, or broadcast for distance learning.

Some ancillaries, including electronic and print components, may not be available to customers outside the United States.

This book is printed on acid-free paper.

domestic   2 3 4 5 6 7 8 9 0 DOC/DOC 0 9 8 7 6 5 4
international   1 2 3 4 5 6 7 8 9 0 DOC/DOC 0 9 8 7 6 5 4

ISBN   0-07-287543-7

Vice president and editor-in-chief: *Robin J. Zwettler*
Editorial director: *John E. Biernat*
Executive editor: *John Weimeister*
Editorial coordinator: *Trina Hauger*
Executive marketing manager: *Ellen Cleary*
Producer, Media technology: *Mark Molsky*
Lead project manager: *Pat Frederickson*
Freelance project manager: *Stacey C. Sawyer, Sawyer & Williams*
Production supervisor: *Debra R. Sylvester*
Lead designer: *Matthew Baldwin*
Supplement producer: *Betty Hadala*
Supplement author: *Jana Kuzmicki*
Senior digital content specialist: *Brian Nacik*
Cover design: *Krista Lehmkuhl*
Typeface: *10/12 Times Roman*
Compositor: *Shepherd, Inc.*
Printer: *R. R. Donnelley*

Library of Congress Cataloging-in-Publication Data
Milkovich, George T.
    Compensation / George T. Milkovich, Jerry M. Newman ; with the assistance of Carolyn Milkovich.—8th ed.
        p. cm.
    Includes bibliographical references and index.
    ISBN 0-07-287543-7 (alk. paper)
    1. Compensation management. I. Newman, Jerry M. II. Milkovich, Carolyn. III. Title.
HF5549.5.C67M54 2005
658.3'2—dc22   2003068855

www.mhhe.com

Table of Contents

PART THREE
EMPLOYEE CONTRIBUTIONS: DETERMINING INDIVIDUAL PAY

Chapter 9
Pay for Performance: The Evidence   257

Chapter 10
Pay-for-Performance Plans   285

Preface

Want to go for a walk? In space? If you are a Russian cosmonaut, you can earn a bonus of $1,000 for every space walk, up to three, per space trip. A contract listing specific tasks to be done on a space mission permits you to earn up to $30,000 above the $20,000 you earn while you are on the ground. In contrast, if you are a Microsoft engineer, the only thing you had to do for a recent pay increase was show up for work. A lackluster stock market eliminated the value of the astronomical stock options Microsoft had routinely doled out to employees. Employees were grumbling; top recruits were going elsewhere. What to do? Microsoft decided that its stock options were too risky, so it offered employees the chance to trade them in for actual shares of stock. Increase the value of people's pay and reduce the risk they face, and you get happier, more expensive people. And you can hire more. No word yet on improved performance, customer satisfaction, or even quality of new hires. Conclusion: *Pay matters.*

Many years ago, when Green Giant discovered too many insect parts in the pea pack from one of its plants, it designed a bonus plan that paid people for finding insect parts. Green Giant got what it paid for: insect parts. Innovative Green Giant employees brought insect parts from home to add to the peas just before they removed them and collected the bonus.

And speaking of bugs: A well-known software house designed a bonus plan that paid software engineers to find bugs in software code. Plan designers failed to realize that the people who found the bugs were the very same ones who wrote the buggy software code in the first place. Engineers joked about "writing me an SUV." Such problems are global. A British telephone information company paid a cash bonus based on how fast operators completed requests for information. Some operators discovered that the fastest way was to give out a wrong number or—even faster—just hang up on the caller. "We're actually looking at a new bonus scheme," says an insightful company spokesperson. Conclusion: *It matters what you pay for.*

Motorola trashed its old-fashioned pay system that employees said guaranteed a raise every six months if you were still breathing. The company replaced it with a system that paid for learning new skills and working in teams. Sounded good. Wasn't. Employees resented those team members who went off for six weeks of training at full pay while remaining team members picked up their work. Motorola was forced to trash its new-fashioned system, too. Conclusion: *It matters how you pay.*

We live in interesting times. Anywhere you look on the globe today, economic and social pressures are forcing managers to rethink how people get paid and what difference it makes. Traditional approaches to compensation are being questioned. But what is being achieved by all this experimentation and change? We have lots of fads and fashions, but is it all folderol? Where are the results?

In this book, we strive to cull beliefs from facts, wishful thinking from demonstrable results, and opinions from research. Yet when all is said and done, managing compensation is an art. As with any art, not everything that can be learned can be taught.

ABOUT THIS BOOK

This book is based on the strategic choices in managing compensation. We introduce these choices, which confront managers in the United States and around the world, in the total compensation model in Chapter 1. This model provides an integrating framework that is used throughout the book. Major compensation issues are discussed in the context of current theory, research, and practice. The practices illustrate new developments as well as established approaches to compensation decisions.

Each chapter contains at least one *Cybercomp* to point you to some of the vast compensation information on the Internet. Real-life *Your Turn* exercises ask you to apply the concepts and techniques discussed in each chapter. For example, the Your Turn in Chapter 10 takes you through several exercises designed to explain how stock options work and how to value them. It also allows you to connect to real-time stock prices for up-to-date stock option valuations.

The authors also publish *Cases in Compensation,* an integrated casebook designed to provide additional practical skills that apply the material in this book. The casebook is available directly from the authors (telephone: 310-450-5301; e-mail: gtm1@cornell.edu). Completing the integrated case will help you develop skills readily transferable to future jobs and assignments. Instructors are invited to phone for more information on how *Cases in Compensation* can help translate compensation research and theory into practice and build competencies for on-the-job decisions.

But *caveat emptor!* "Congress raises the executive minimum wage to $565.15 an hour," reads the headline in the satirical newspaper *The Onion* (www.onion.com) ("America's Finest News Source"). The article says that the increase will help executives meet the federal standard-of-easy-living. "Our lifestyles are expensive to maintain," complains one manager. While the story in *The Onion* may clearly be fiction, sometimes it is more difficult to tell. One manager told us that when she searched for this textbook in her local bookstore, store personnel found the listing in their information system—under fiction!

WHAT'S NEW

All chapters of this edition have been completely revised. This edition gives greater emphasis to the importance of total compensation and its relevance for achieving sustainable competitive advantage. It reinforces our conviction that beyond how much people are paid, *how* they are paid, really matters. Managing pay means ensuring that the right people get the right pay for achieving objectives in the right way. Chapter 2 explains how to craft a total compensation strategy and examines the research on best practices. New chapters on performance-based pay dig into all forms of variable pay such as stock options, profit sharing, gain sharing, and team-based approaches. Person-based plans are compared to job-based plans, including recent developments in skill and competency approaches. Changes in competitive market analysis caused by outsourcing and global competition are covered, as well as the increased use of market pricing and broad banding. Employee benefits, always changing and always important, are covered in two chapters. Chapter 14 broadens its discussion of board-of-director compensation, executive compensation, and sales compensation. We have always used international examples in every section; we also have a completely revised chapter on global compensation. Software to aid both employees and manager decisions is covered, along with a renewed focus on measuring the value gained from pay systems. Ethical issues and the paucity of standards of conduct are discussed. Each chapter has links to interesting Internet sites discussing compensation and benefit issues.

Research and surveys about compensation are flourishing. We have included the best and most relevant of them, along with a reader's guide on how to be an informed consumer of this material.

ACKNOWLEDGMENTS

In addition to our bookstore shopper, many people have contributed to our understanding of compensation and to the preparation of this textbook. We owe a special, continuing debt of gratitude to our students. In the classroom, they motivate and challenge us, and as returning seasoned managers, they try mightily to keep our work relevant.

Renae Broderick
Broderick Group

Joseph Bruno
Kodak

Ilene Butensky
Eaton

Federico Castellanos
IBM EMEA

Cindy Cohen
Impac

John Cross
Decisis

Frank Cummings
Gillette

Tom Cummings
Eaton

Matt Daniels
Merck

Andrew Doyle
Merrill Lynch Asia Pacific

Mark Englizian
Microsoft

Sally Fanning
Praxair

Thomas Fleming
IBM

Beth Florin
Clark Consulting

Richard Frings
Johnson & Johnson

Takashi Fujiwara
Mitsubishi

Yuichi Funada
Toshiba

Thomas Gresch
General Motors Acceptance Corporation

Steve Gross
W.W. Mercer

Lada Hruba
Bristol Meyers Squibb

Peder Jacobsen
Medtronic

Ann Killian
TRW

Dae-Ki Kim
SK Group

Tae-Jin Kim
SK Group

Sharon Knight
Phillip Morris

Hiroshi Kurihara
Fuji Xerox

Terrance Langley
IBM Japan

Glenn Leak
Harlequin Books

Christian LeBreton
IBM EMEA

Mitch Linnick
IBM

Rich Lodato
Bristol Meyers Squibb

Julio Mantilla
Gillette

Tony Marchak
IBM EMEA

Masaki Matsuhashi
Toshiba

Randy McDonald
IBM

Matt Milkovich
Registry Nursing

Michael Milkovich
West Publishing

Harvey Minkoff
TRW

Kate Mrozak
Cigna

David Ness
Medtronic

Erinn Newman
Accenture

Kelly Newman
Supplemental HealthCare

Terrie Newman
HR Foundations

Susan Podlogar
Johnson & Johnson

Joseph Rich
Clark Consulting

Jason Sekanina
Artesyn

Diana Southall
HR Foundations

Elke Stadelmann
Adam Opel AG

Tina Stenhouse
Moog, Inc.

Rick Steinberg
Praxair

Masanori Suzuki
General Electric China

Ichiro Takemura
Toshiba

Richard Their
Xerox

Jan Tichy
Merck

Andrew Thompson
Link Group Consultants

David Wazeter
*National Educational
Association*

Robert White
TRW China

Our universities, Cornell and Buffalo, provide forums for the interchange of ideas among students, experienced managers, and academic colleagues. We value this interchange. Other academic colleagues also provided helpful comments on this edition of the book. We particularly thank:

Tom Arnold
*Westmoreland
Community College*

Lubica Bajzikova
*Comenius University,
Bratislava*

Stuart Basefsky
Cornell University

Melissa Barringer
University of Massachusetts

Matt Bloom
University of Notre Dame

James T. Brakefield
Western Illinois University

Wayne Cascio
University of Colorado

Lee Dyer
Cornell University

Allen D. Engle Sr.
Eastern Kentucky University

Barry Gerhart
*University of Wisconsin,
Madison*

Luis Gomez-Mejia
Arizona State University

Robert Heneman
Ohio State University

Peter Hom
Arizona State University

Greg Hundley
Purdue

Edward Jenss
*University of Alabama,
Huntsville*

W. Roy Johnson
Iowa State University

Jiri Kamenicek
*Charles University,
Prague*

John G. Kilgour
*California State
University, Hayward*

Frank Krzystofiak
SUNY Buffalo

David I. Levine
Berkeley

Janet Marler
SUNY Albany

Thomas A. Mahoney
Vanderbilt University

Sarah Milkovich
Brown University

Ed Montemayer
University of Redlands

Atul Mitra
Northern Iowa University

Michael Moore
Michigan State University

J. Randall Nutter
Geneva College

Dane Partridge
*University of Southern
Indiana*

Richard Posthuma
*University of Texas
at El Paso*

Janez Prasnikar
University of Ljubljana

Vlado Pucik
IMD

Hesan Ahmed Quazi
Nanyang Business School

Sara Rynes
University of Iowa

Robin Remick
Cornell University

Yoko Sano
Keio University

Michael Sturman
Cornell University

Ningyu Tang
Shanghai Jiao Tong University

Charlie Tharp
Rutgers University

Charlie Trevor
University of Wisconsin, Madison

Zhong-Ming Wang
Zhejiang University

Yoshio Yanadori
Cornell University

Nada Zupan
University of Ljubljana

Chapter One

The Pay Model

Chapter Outline

A friend of ours writes that she is in one of the touring companies of the musical *Cats.* In the company are two performers called "swings" who sit backstage during each performance. Each swing must learn five different lead roles in the show. During the performance, the swing sits next to a rack with five different costumes and makeup for each of the five roles. Our friend, who has a lead in the show, once hurt her shoulder during a dance number. She signaled to someone offstage, and by the time she finished her number, the swing was dressed, in makeup, and out on stage for the next scene.

Our friend is paid $2,000 per week for playing one of the cats in the show. She is expected to do a certain number of performances and a certain number of rehearsals per week. She gets paid for the job she does. The swing gets paid $2,500 per week, whether she performs 20 shows that week or none. She is paid for knowing the five roles, whether she plays them or not.

Think of all the other employees, in addition to the performers, required for putting on a performance of *Cats*. Electricians, trombonists, choreographers, dressers, janitors, nurses, vocal coaches, accountants, stagehands, payroll supervisors, ushers, lighting technicians, ticket sellers—the list goes on. Consider the array of wages paid to these employees. Why does the swing get paid more than other performers? Why does the performer get paid more (or less) than the trombonist? How are these decisions made, and who is involved in making them? Whether the pay is our own or someone else's, compensation questions engage our attention.

Does the compensation received by all the people connected with *Cats* matter? Most employers believe that how people are paid affects people's behaviors at work, which affect an organization's chances of success. Compensation systems can help an organization achieve and sustain competitive advantage.[1]

COMPENSATION: DEFINITION, PLEASE?

What image does the word "compensation" bring to mind? It does not mean the same thing to everyone. Yet how people view compensation affects how they behave at work. Thus, we begin by recognizing different perspectives.

Society

Some people see pay as a measure of justice. For example, a comparison of earnings of women with those of men highlights what many consider inequities in pay decisions. The gender pay gap in the United States, after adjustment for differences in education, experience, and occupation, narrowed from 36 percent in 1980 to 12 percent in 2003. But this measure masks tremendous variations. When educational choices are taken into account, women's earnings are 94 percent of those of men. For people age 21 to 35 who live alone and have no children, the gap is close to zero. (Of course, this constitutes a very small segment of the labor force.)[2] The gap even varies by cities. Most people were surprised when 2000 census data showed that women in Wichita, Kansas, earn about half of what men earn but that women in Oakland, California, earn more than men.[3]

Sometimes differences in compensation among countries are listed as a cause of loss of jobs from more developed, higher-wage economies to less developed ones. As Exhibit 1.1 reveals, labor costs in Mexico are about 12 percent of those in the United States. However,

---

[1]E. Lawler III, *Rewarding Excellence* (San Francisco: Jossey-Bass, 2000); Patricia Zingheim and J. R. Schuster, *Pay People Right!* (San Francisco: Jossey-Bass, 2000); B. Gerhart, "Pay Strategy and Firm Performance," in *Compensation in Organizations: Current Research and Practice,* eds. S. L. Rynes and B. E. Gerhart (San Francisco: Jossey-Bass, 2000); B. E. and Mark Huselid, "High Performance Work Systems and Firm Performance: A Synthesis of Research and Management Implications," in *Research in Personnel and Human Resources,* ed. G. Ferris (Greenwich, CT: JAI Press, 1998); Barry Gerhart and Sara Rynes *Compensation: Theory, Evidence, and Strategic Implications* (Thousand Oaks, CA: Sage, 2003).

[2]H. J. Cummins, "Mommy Wage Gap: It's Real, but Is It Fair?" *Minneapolis Star & Tribune,* May 11, 2003; Genaro C. Armas, "White Men Still Outearn Other Groups," Associated Press, March 21, 2003; F. Blau, and L. Kahn, "Analyzing the Gender Pay Gap," *Quarterly Review of Economics and Finance* 39 (1999), pp. 625–646; Francine D. Blau and Lawrence M. Kahn, "Understanding International Differences in the Gender Pay Gap," NBER Working Paper W8200, Cambridge, MA, April 2001.

[3]Laurent Belsie, "Gender Pay Gap Varies by City," *Christian Science Monitor,* December 12, 2001.

EXHIBIT 1.1

Hourly Compensation Costs for Production Workers in Manufacturing in U.S. Dollars

Source: Bureau of Labor Statistics, April 2003

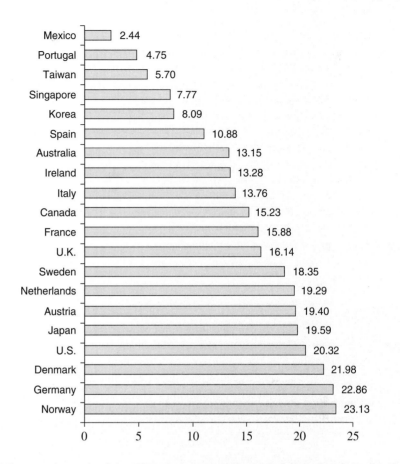

Mexico	2.44
Portugal	4.75
Taiwan	5.70
Singapore	7.77
Korea	8.09
Spain	10.88
Australia	13.15
Ireland	13.28
Italy	13.76
Canada	15.23
France	15.88
U.K.	16.14
Sweden	18.35
Netherlands	19.29
Austria	19.40
Japan	19.59
U.S.	20.32
Denmark	21.98
Germany	22.86
Norway	23.13

when differences in productivity (the relative output for each dollar of pay) are factored in, the wage advantage of Mexico, Korea, and Taiwan disappears. Therefore, understanding productivity differences among international locations is crucial.

Voters may see compensation, pensions, and health care for public employees as the cause of increased taxes. Public policymakers and legislators may view changes in average pay as guides for adjusting eligibility for social services (medical assistance, food stamps, and the like).

Some consumers may view increases in compensation as the cause of price increases. They may not believe that higher labor costs are to their benefit. Other consumers have lobbied universities to insist on higher wages for laborers in Guatemala who sew shirts and caps bearing the university logo.[4] All these differing perspectives are represented within a society and among individuals. After all, public employees, faculty, and students are also taxpayers and consumers. And they vote.

[4]U.S. Department of Labor, Bureau of Labor Statistics, "International Comparisons of Hourly Compensation Costs for Production Workers in Manufacturing, 2001," *www.bls.gov/fls/flsichcc.pdf;* Timothy Aeppel, "Manufacturers Spent Much Less Abroad Last Year," *Wall Street Journal,* May 9, 2003, p. A8; S. Greenhouse, "Anti-Sweatshop Movement Is Achieving Gains Overseas," *New York Times,* January 26, 2000, p. A10. Websites of interest on the movement include *www.maquilasolidarity.org/* and *www.geocities.com/whydoyoukeepdeletingme/ASSLLeague.html.*

Stockholders

To stockholders, executive pay is of special interest. Linking executive pay to company performance is supposed to increase stockholders' wealth. Unfortunately, this does not always happen. In the midst of a recent economic downturn in the United States, total shareholder returns were down by 22 percent, while the median CEO pay rose by 14 percent to $13.2 million.[5] Robert Nugent led Jack-in-the-Box to a 19 percent decline in shareholder value for which he received a 53 percent increase in his pay. And Walt Disney shareholders experienced an 18 percent reduction in their returns in 2002, while the total pay of the company's CEO, Michael Eisner, increased by 498 percent.

All is not goofy in the magic kingdom of executive compensation. Contrast the higher pay–lower performance at Jack-in-the-Box and Disney with the low performance–low pay at Eli Lilly, maker of Prozac and other drugs. Sidney Taurel's pay fell 49 percent to $11.2 million as Eli Lilly's performance declined.[6] There are even a few instances of higher pay for higher performance. At Silicon Graphics, the pay of CEO Robert Bishop increased 46.3 percent, reflecting a 111.5 percent improvement in total shareholder value.[7]

Managers

For managers, compensation influences their success in two ways. First, it is a major expense. Competitive pressures, both internationally and domestically, force managers to consider the affordability of their compensation decisions. Labor costs can account for more than 50 percent of total costs. In some industries, such as financial or professional services or public employment such as education and government, this figure is even higher. However, even within an industry, labor costs as a percent of total costs vary among individual firms. Exhibit 1.2 shows the range of labor costs as a percent of revenue within the airline industry. The big airlines have much higher labor costs than many of the smaller, low-fare operators.

In addition to treating pay as an expense, a manager also uses it to influence employee behaviors and improve organization performance. The way people are paid affects the quality of their work; their attitude toward customers; their willingness to be flexible,

---

[5] Graef Crystal, "Bloomberg Report," April 14, 2003, *www.bloomberg.com/news/commentary/gcrystal.html;* B. Hall, "What You Need to Know about Stock Options," *Harvard Business Review,* March–April 2000, pp. 121–129.

[6] Jerry Useem, "Have They No Shame?" *Fortune,* April 28, 2003, pp. 57–64; Janice Revell, "CEO Pensions: The Latest Way to Hide Millions," *Fortune,* April 28, 2003, pp. 68–70. *Fortune* publishes articles on executive pay every April. However, be cautious about using these isolated anecdotes to decide if executive compensation is related to firm performance. There is a wealth of research informing us on this issue. You will read about it in the chapter on special groups.

[7] "The Boss's Pay: The WSJ/Mercer 2002 CEO Compensation Survey," *Wall Street Journal,* April 14, 2003, pp. R6–R10; Joann S. Lublin, "Why the Get-Rich-Quick Days May Be Over," *Wall Street Journal,* April 14, 2003, pp. R1–R3; Brent M. Longnecker, *Stock Option Alternatives: A Strategic and Technical Guide to Long-Term Incentives* (Scottsdale, AZ: WorldatWork, 2003). For more discussion on executive pay, see Bruce Ellig, *The Complete Guide to Executive Compensation* (New York: McGraw-Hill, 2002); and Peter T. Chingos, *Paying for Performance: A Guide to Compensation Management* (New York: Wiley, 2002).

EXHIBIT 1.2
Labor Costs
as a
Percentage of
Revenues,
Airline
Industry

Source: The
companies.

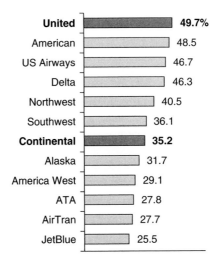

United	**49.7%**
American	48.5
US Airways	46.7
Delta	46.3
Northwest	40.5
Southwest	36.1
Continental	**35.2**
Alaska	31.7
America West	29.1
ATA	27.8
AirTran	27.7
JetBlue	25.5

learn new skills, or suggest innovations. People may become interested in unions or legal action against their employer based on how they get paid. This potential to influence employees' behaviors, and subsequently the productivity and effectiveness of the organization, makes the study of compensation worth your time.[8]

Employees

The pay individuals receive in return for the work they perform is usually the major source of their financial security. Hence, pay plays a vital role in a person's economic and social well-being. Employees may see compensation as a *return in an exchange* between their employer and themselves, as an *entitlement* for being an employee of the company, or as a *reward* for a job well done. Compensation can be all of these things, although how many employees see their pay as a reward remains an open question.

Describing pay as a reward may sound farfetched to anyone who has reluctantly rolled out of bed to go to work. Even though writers and consultants use that term, do people really say, "They just gave me a reward increase," or "Here is my weekly reward check?" Sounds silly, doesn't it? Yet if people see their pay as a return for their contributions and investments rather than as a reward, and if writers and consultants persist in trying to convince them that pay is a reward, there is a disconnect that misleads both employees and managers. Employees invest in education and training; they contribute their time and energy at the workplace. Compensation is their return on those investments and contributions.[9]

[8]K. Bartol and E. Locke, "Incentives and Motivation," chap. 4 in *Compensation in Organizations,* eds. S. Rynes & B. Gerhart (San Francisco: Jossey-Bass, 2000), pp. 104–150; Mary Graham et al., "In the Land of Milk and Money: One Dairy Farm's Strategic Compensation System," *Journal of Agribusiness,* 15(2) (1997), pp. 171–188.

[9]E. E. Lawler, *Rewarding Excellence* (San Francisco: Jossey-Bass, 2000); Steven E. Gross and Haig R. Nalbantian, "Looking at Rewards Holistically," *WorldatWork Journal* 11(2) (Second Quarter 2002).

Global Views—*Vive la différence*

In English, "compensation" means something that counterbalances, offsets, or makes up for something else. However, if we look at the origin of the word in different languages, we get a sense of the richness of the meaning, which can combine entitlement, return, and reward.[10]

In China, the traditional characters for the word "compensation" are based on the symbols for logs and water; compensation provides the necessities in life. In the recent past, the state owned all enterprises and compensation was treated as an entitlement. In today's China, compensation takes on a more subtle meaning. A new word, *dai yu,* is used. It refers to how you are being treated—your wages, benefits, training opportunities, and so on. When people talk about compensation, they ask each other about the *dai yu* in their companies. Rather than assuming that everyone is entitled to the same treatment, the meaning of compensation now includes a broader sense of returns, and rewards, as well as entitlement.

"Compensation" in Japanese is *kyuyo,* which is made up of two separate characters (*kyu* and *yo*), both meaning "giving something." *Kyu* is an honorific used to indicate that the person doing the giving is someone of high rank, such as a feudal lord, an emperor, or a samurai leader. Traditionally, compensation is thought of as something given by one's superior. Today, business consultants in Japan try to substitute the word *hou-syu,* which means "reward" and has no associations with notions of superiors. The many allowances that are part of Japanese compensation systems translate as *teate,* which means "taking care of something." *Teate* is regarded as compensation that takes care of employees' financial needs. This concept is consistent with the family, housing, and commuting allowances that are still used in many Japanese companies.[11]

These contrasting ideas about compensation—multiple views (societal, stockholder, managerial, employee, and even global) and multiple meanings (returns, rewards, entitlement)—add richness to the topic. But they can also cause confusion unless everyone is talking about the same thing. So let's define what we mean by "compensation" or "pay" (the words are used interchangeably in this book):

Compensation refers to all forms of financial returns and tangible services and benefits employees receive as part of an employment relationship.

---

[10]G. T. Milkovich and M. Bloom, "Rethinking International Compensation: From National Cultures to Markets and Strategic Flexibility," *Compensation and Benefits Review,* January 1998, pp. 1–10; Atul Mitra, Matt Bloom, and George Milkovich, "Crossing a Raging River: Seeking Far-Reaching Solutions to Global Pay Challenges," *WorldatWork Journal* 22(2) (Second Quarter 2002); Mark Fenton-O'Creevy, "HR Practice: Vive la Différence," *Financial Times,* October 2002, pp. 6–8; M. Mendenhall and Gary Oddou, *Readings and Cases in International Human Resource Management* (Cincinnati: South-Western College Publishing, 2000); Anne Tsui and Chung-Ming Lau, *The Management of Enterprises in the People's Republic of China* (Boston: Kluwer Academic, 2002); Morley Gunderson, "The Evolution and Mechanics of Pay Equity in Ontario," *Canadian Public Policy* 28, suppl. 12 (2002); Francine Blau and Lawrence M. Kahn, "Understanding International Differences in the Gender Pay Gap," NBER Working Paper W8200, National Bureau of Economic Research, Cambridge, MA, April 2001).

[11]Participants in an international compensation seminar at Cornell University provided the information on various meanings of compensation.

EXHIBIT 1.3   Total Returns for Work

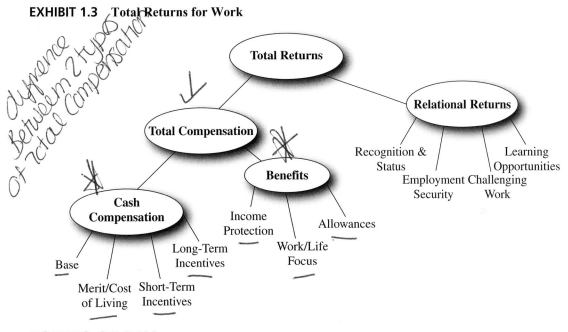

difference between 2 types of total compensation

FORMS OF PAY

Exhibit 1.3 shows the variety of returns people receive from work. They are categorized as *total compensation* and *relational returns.* The relational returns (learning opportunities, status, challenging work, and so on) are psychological.[12]

Total compensation returns are more transactional. They include pay received directly as cash (e.g., base, merit, incentives, cost-of-living adjustments) and indirectly as benefits (e.g., pensions, medical insurance, programs to help balance work and life demands, brightly colored uniforms).[13] Programs to pay people can be designed in a wide variety of ways, and a single employer typically uses more than one.

Cash Compensation: Base

Base wage is the cash compensation that an employer pays for the work performed. Base wage tends to reflect the value of the work or skills and generally ignores differences attributable to individual employees. For example, the base wage for machine operators may be $20 an hour. However, some individual operators may receive more because of their experience and/or performance. Some pay systems set base wage as a function of the skill or education an employee possesses; this is common for engineers and school-teachers.[14]

[12]D. Rousseau, *Psychological Contracts in Organizations* (Thousand Oaks, CA: Sage, 1995).

[13]"Brightly Colored Uniforms Boost Employee Morale," *The Onion* 36(43) (November 30, 2000).

[14]A. Milanowski, "The Varieties of Knowledge and Skill-Based Pay Design: A Comparison of Seven New Pay Systems for K-12 Teachers," Working Paper TC-01-2, University of Wisconsin–Madison, Wisconsin Center for Education Research, Consortium for Policy Research in Education, (2001).

A distinction is often made in the United States between wage and salary, with *salary* referring to pay for employees who are *exempt* from regulations of the Fair Labor Standards Act (FLSA) and hence do not receive overtime pay.[15] Managers and professionals usually fit this category. Their pay is calculated at an annual or monthly rate rather than hourly, because hours worked do not need to be recorded. In contrast, workers who are covered by overtime and reporting provisions of the Fair Labor Standards Act—*nonexempts*—have their pay calculated as an hourly wage. Some organizations, such as IBM, Eaton, and Wal-Mart, label all base pay as "salary." Rather than dividing employees into separate categories of salaried and wage earners, they believe that an "all-salaried" workforce reinforces an organization culture in which all employees are part of the same team. However, merely changing the terminology does not negate the need to comply with the FLSA.

Cash Compensation: Merit Pay/Cost-of-Living Adjustments

Periodic adjustments to base wages may be made on the basis of changes in what other employers are paying for the same work, changes in the overall cost of living, or changes in experience or skill.

According to surveys, 90 percent of U.S. firms use merit pay increases.[16] *Merit increases* are given as increments to the base pay in recognition of *past* work behavior. Some assessment of past performance is made, with or without a formal performance evaluation program, and the size of the increase is varied with performance. Thus, outstanding performers could receive an 8 to 10 percent merit increase 8 months after their last increase, whereas an average performer may receive, say, a 3 to 4 percent increase after 12 or 15 months. In contrast to merit pay, *cost-of-living adjustments* give the same percent increase across the board to everyone, regardless of performance.

Cash Compensation: Incentives

Incentives tie pay increases directly to performance. However, incentives differ from merit adjustments. First, incentives do not increase the base wage, and so must be re-earned each pay period. Second, the potential size of the incentive payment will generally be known beforehand. Whereas merit pay programs evaluate past performance of an individual and then decide on the size of the increase, the performance objective for incentive payments is called out very specifically ahead of time. For example, a Toyota dealer knows the commission on a Land Cruiser versus a Corolla prior to making the sale. Although both merit pay and incentives try to influence performance, incentives try to influence future behavior whereas merit recognizes (rewards) past behavior. The incentive-reward distinction is a matter of timing.

Incentives can be tied to the performance of an individual employee, a team of employees, a total business unit, or some combination of individual, team, and unit. The performance objective may be expense reduction, volume increases, customer satisfaction, revenue growth, return on investments, or increases in total shareholder value—the possi-

---

[15]U.S. Department of Labor, Employment Standards Administration, Wage and Hour Division. See Chapter 17 for greater detail on the FLSA and pay.

[16]Robert Heneman, *Merit Pay: Linking Pay Increases to Performance Ratings* (Reading, MA.: Addison-Wesley, 1992); Robert J. Greene, "Improving Merit Pay Plan Effectiveness," *ACA News* 41(4) (April 1998,).

bilities are endless.[17] Prax Air, for example, uses return on capital (ROC). For every quarter that a 6 percent ROC target is met or exceeded, Prax Air awards bonus days of pay. An 8.6 percent ROC means two extra days of pay for that quarter for every employee covered by the program. A ROC of 15 percent means eight and a half extra days of pay.

Because incentives are one-time payments, they do not have a permanent effect on labor costs. When performance declines, incentive pay automatically declines, too. Consequently, incentives are frequently referred to as *variable pay*.

Long-Term Incentives

Incentives may be short- or long-term. Long-term incentives are intended to focus employee efforts on multiyear results. Typically they are in the form of stock ownership or options to buy stock at specified, advantageous prices. Stock options straddle the categories of cash compensation and benefits. Some argue that they are not compensation at all, that they are more accurately described as an ownership share granted by owners to employees.[18]

The idea behind stock options is that employees with a financial stake in the organization will focus on long-term financial objectives: return on investment, market share, return on net assets, and the like. Bristol-Myers Squibb grants shares of stock to selected "Key Contributors" who make outstanding contributions to the firm's success. Some companies extend stock ownership beyond the ranks of managers and professionals. Sun Microsystems, Yahoo, PepsiCo, Wal-Mart, and Starbucks offer stock options to all their employees.[19]

Benefits: Income Protection

Exhibit 1.3 shows that benefits, including income protection, work/life balance services, and allowances, are also part of total compensation. Some income protection programs are legally required. In the United States, employers must pay into a fund that provides income replacement for workers who become disabled or unemployed. Employers also make half the contributions to social security. (Employees pay the other half.) Different countries have different lists of mandatory benefits.

Medical insurance, retirement programs, life insurance, and savings plans are common benefits. They help protect employees from the financial risks inherent in daily life. Often

[17]Steve Kerr, "The Best Laid Incentive Plans," *Harvard Business Review,* January 2003; Michael C. Sturman and J. C. Short, "Lump-Sum Bonus Satisfaction: Testing the Construct Validity of a New Pay Satisfaction Dimension," *Personnel Psychology* 53(200), pp. 673–700.

[18]Some believe greater stock ownership motivates performance; others argue that the link between individual job behaviors and the vagaries of the stock market are tenuous at best. S. Rodrick, *The Stock Options Book of 1998* (Oakland, CA: National Center for Employee Ownership, 1998) (see also the center's website at *www.nceo.org*); D. Kruse and J. Blasi, "Employee Ownership, Employee Attributes and Firm Performance," *Journal of Employee Ownership, Law and Finance,* April 2000, pp. 37–48; testimony of Dr. Douglas Kruse before the Committee on Education and the Workforce, February 13, 2002, *edworkforce.house.gov/hearings/107th/eer/enronthree21302/kruse.htm.*

[19]C. Rosen and E. Carberry, "Ownership Matters!" *Workspan,* October 2002, pp. 29–32; Ben Dunford, John Boudreau, and Wendy Boswell, "When Stock Options Fail to Motivate," CAHRS Working Paper 02-04, Ithaca, NY.

companies can provide these protections to employees cheaper than employees can obtain them for themselves. Because the cost of providing benefits has been rising (for example, employers pay nearly half the nation's health care bills, and health care expenditures have recently been increasing at annual rates around 15 to 20 percent), they are an increasingly important form of pay.[20] General Motors spends so much for benefits that it has been called a pension and health care provider that also makes cars. In a Gallup poll, people claimed they would require $5,000 more in extra pay to choose a job without pension, health care, and life insurance.

Benefits: Work/Life Focus

Programs that help employees better integrate their work and life responsibilities include time away from work (vacations, jury duty), access to services to meet specific needs (drug counseling, financial planning, referrals for child and elder care), and flexible work arrangements (telecommuting, nontraditional schedules, nonpaid time off). Responding to the changing demographics of the workforce (two-income families who demand employer flexibility so that family obligations can be met), many U.S. employers are giving a higher priority to these benefit forms. Medtronic, for example, touts its Total Well-Being program that seeks to provide "resources for growth—mind, body, heart, and spirit" for each employee. Health and wellness, financial rewards and security, individual and family well-being, and a fulfilling work environment are part of this "total well-being." Medtronic believes that this program permits employees to be "fully present" at work and less distracted by conflicts between their work and nonwork responsibilities.

Benefits: Allowances

Allowances often grow out of whatever is in short supply. In Vietnam and China, housing (dormitories and apartments) and transportation allowances are frequently part of the pay package.[21] Sixty years after the end of World War II–induced food shortages, some Japanese companies still continue to offer a "rice allowance" based on the number of an employee's dependents.[22] Almost all foreign companies in China discover that housing, transportation, and other allowances are expected. Companies that resist these allowances must come up with other ways to attract and retain talented employees. In many European countries, managers assume that a car will be provided—what make and model are negotiable.[23]

[20]Employee Benefits Research Institute's website, *www.ebri.org.* See also the EBRI's *Fundamentals of Employee Benefits* (Washington, DC: EBRI, 1997) and *EBRI Health Benefits Databook* (1999); Margaret L. Williams, Stanley B. Malos, and David K. Palmer, "Benefit System and Benefit Level Satisfaction: An Expanded Model of Antecedents and Consequences," *Journal of Management* 28(2) (2002), pp. 195–212.

[21]Anne Tsui and Chung-Ming Lau, *The Management of Enterprises in the People's Republic of China* (Boston: Kluwer Academic, 2002).

[22]Yoshio Yanadori and George Milkovich, "Minimizing Wage Competition? Entry-Level Compensation in Japanese Firms," working paper, Center for Advanced HR Studies, Ithaca, NY, 2003.

[23]The websites for the International Labour Organization (*www.ilo.org*) and the European Industrial Relations Observatory On-Line (*www.eiro.eurofound.ie*) publish news of developments in HR in Europe.

Total Earnings Opportunities: Present Value of a Stream of Earnings

Up to this point we have treated compensation as something paid or received at a moment in time. But compensation decisions have a temporal effect. Say you have a job offer of $50,000. If you stay with the firm five years and receive an annual increase of 4 percent, in five years you will be earning $60,833 a year. The expected cost commitment of the decision to hire you turns out to be $331,649 in cash. If you add in an additional 25 percent for benefits, the decision to hire you implies a commitment of over $400,000 from your employer. Will you be worth it? You will be after this course.

A present-value perspective shifts the comparison of today's initial offers to consideration of future bonuses, merit increases, and promotions. Sometimes a company will tell students that its relatively low starting offers will be overcome by larger future pay increases. In effect, the company is selling the present value of the future stream of earnings. But few students apply that same analysis to calculate the future increases required to offset the lower initial offers. Hopefully, all students who get through Chapter 1 will now do so.

Relational Returns from Work

Why does Bill Gates still show up for work every morning? Why do Microsoft millionaires continue to write code? Why does Andy Borowitz write the funniest satirical news site on the web (*www.borowitzreport.com*) for free? There is no doubt that nonfinancial returns from work have a substantial effect on employees' behavior. Exhibit 1.3 includes such relational returns from work as recognition and status, employment security, challenging work, and opportunities to learn. Other relational forms might include personal satisfaction from successfully facing new challenges, teaming with great co-workers, receiving new uniforms, and the like.[24] Such factors are part of the total return, which is a broader umbrella than total compensation.

The Organization as a Network of Returns

Sometimes it is useful to think of an organization as a network of returns created by all these different forms of pay, including total compensation and relational returns. The challenge is to design this network so that it helps the organization to succeed. As in the case of rowers pulling on their oars, success is more likely if all are pulling in unison rather than working against one another. In the same way, the network of returns is more likely to be useful if bonuses, development opportunities, and promotions all work together.

So the next time you walk in an employer's door, look beyond the cash and health care offered to search for all the returns that create the network. Even though this book focuses on total compensation, let's not forget that compensation is only one of many

---

[24]Austin Collins, "Pay in Theoretical Physics," *California Institute of Technology Newspaper,* May 23, 1997, p. 3; Richard P. Feynman, *The Pleasure of Finding Things Out* (Cambridge, MA: Helix Books, 1999); "Brightly Colored Uniforms Boost Employee Morale," *The Onion* 36(43) (November 30, 2000).

factors affecting people's decisions about work, as songwriter Roger Miller made clear in this 1960s tune:

> Got a letter just this morning, it was postmarked Omaha.
> It was typed and neatly written offering me a better job,
> Better job and higher wages, expenses paid, and a car.
> But I'm on TV here locally, and I can't quit, I'm a star.
> I come on TV a grinnin', wearin' pistols and a hat,
> It's a kiddie show and I'm the hero of the younger set.
> I'm the number one attraction in every supermarket parking lot.
> I'm the king of Kansas City. No thanks, Omaha, thanks a lot.
> Kansas City Star, that's what I are . . .

THE EMPLOYMENT RELATIONSHIP COMBINES TRANSACTIONAL AND RELATIONAL RETURNS

We have already described compensation as a return received in exchange for people's efforts and ideas at their workplace. Exchange is a key part of the relationship. For most people, many of the terms and conditions of their employment exchanges are left unstated, forming an implicit contract.[25]

> An **implicit contract** is an unwritten understanding between employers and employees over their reciprocal obligations and returns; employees contribute toward achieving the goals of the employer in exchange for returns given by the employer and valued by the employee.

Compensation is an important part of this employment relationship. Unanticipated changes in compensation often breach this implicit understanding. Replacing annual pay increases with incentives, raising the deductibles on health care insurance, or tinkering with pension plans may have a negative effect on employee behavior that is out of proportion to the financial impact of the change if employees feel the implicit contract has been breached.

Variations in Transactional and Relational Expectations

These reciprocal obligations and expectations vary among employers and employees. The implicit contract offered—the deal—at one organization is not the same as the one offered at another. It is possible to categorize employment relationships in terms of their emphasis on transactional returns (total cash and benefits), relational returns (sociopsychological returns), or both.

Exhibit 1.4 shows a grid with transactional returns on one axis and relational returns on the other. In the grid, organizations that pay low cash compensation and offer low relational returns are in the "workers as commodity" category. These organizations view

[25]M. Bloom, "The New Deal: Understanding Compensation in the Employment Relationship," *ACA Journal* 8(4), (1999), pp. 58–67; A. S. Tsui, J. L. Pearce, L. W. Porter, and J. P. Hite, "Choice of Employee-Organization Relationships," in *Research in Personnel and Human Resource Management,* ed. G. R. Ferris (Greenwich, CT: JAI Press, 1995); and Marvin H. Kosters, "New Employment Relationships and the Labor Market," *Journal of Labor Research* 18(4) (Fall 1997), pp. 551–559.

EXHIBIT 1.4   **Framework for Analyzing Employment Relationships**

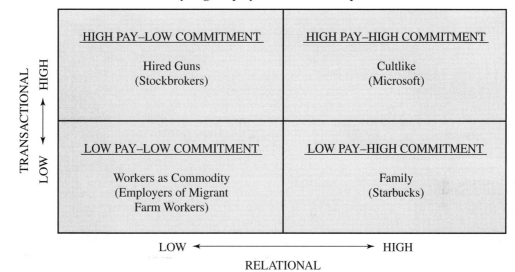

labor as input into the production process. In the United States, employers of migrant workers may offer this type of deal.

Organizations that offer both high compensation and high relational returns may be characterized as cultlike. Microsoft, Medtronic, and Toyota are examples. The strong commitment to the organization shows in the words and actions of employees: "being at the center of technology, having an impact on the work, working with smart people, the sheer volume of opportunities, shipping winning products, beating competition."[26]

Some organizations offer a family relationship: high relational and low transactional returns. Starbucks is an example; one writer calls it the "touchy-feely coffee company."[27] SAS Institute is another. Finally, there are the "hired guns"—all-transactional, "show-me-the-cash" relationships. Brokerage houses, real estate firms, and auto dealerships in the United States fit this category.

While labeling these companies is fun, and even convenient for describing different deals, it may be misleading. For example, the CEO of the Starbucks "family" states that he pays more than his competitors and offers health insurance and "bean stock" to Star-buck partners-employees as part of the total relationship. In spite of this, Starbucks' turnover rate is about 60 percent. Most "partners" do not stay in the family very long. So whether or not a deal is successful may depend on your criteria. Perhaps employees are joining Starbucks with different expectations of the implicit contract offered. As Ahmad Fawzi, commenting on U.S. support of Afghanistan, noted, "Reassurances are good. Cash is better." And perhaps both cash *and* reassurances are best. Compensation is an important part, albeit not the only part, of the employment relationship.

[26]Steve Balmer, speech quoted in *Wall Street Journal* Interactive Edition, May 11, 1999, *www.wsj.com;* D. McKenna and J. McHenry, *Microsoft's Maniacal Work Ethic* (Redmond, WA: Microsoft, 1996).
[27]R. Thomkins, "Touchy-Feely Coffee Company," *Financial Times,* October 9, 1997, p. 14.

EXHIBIT 1.5 **The Pay Model**

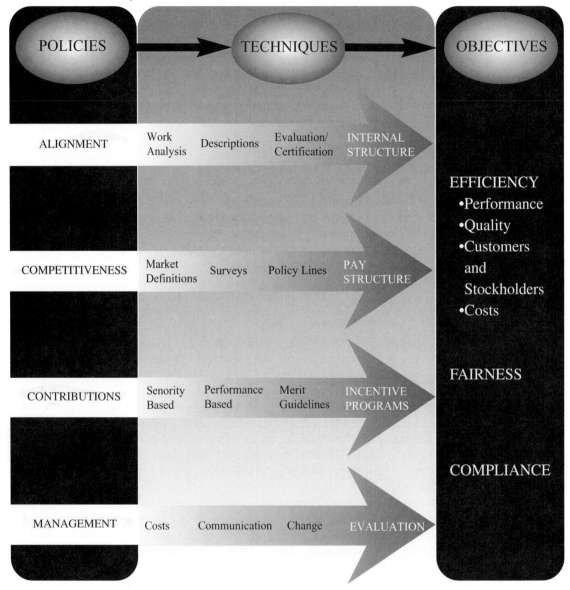

A PAY MODEL

The pay model shown in Exhibit 1.5 serves as both a framework for examining current pay systems and a guide for most of this book. It contains three basic building blocks: (1) the compensation objectives, (2) the policies that form the foundation of the compensation system, and (3) the techniques that make up the compensation system.

EXHIBIT 1.6
Comparisons of Pay System Objectives

Pay Objectives at Medtronic and AES	
Medtronic	**AES**
• Support objectives and increased complexity of business • Minimize increases in fixed costs • Emphasize performance through variable pay and stock • Competitiveness aligned with financial performance: 50th percentile performance paid at 50th percentile of market, 75th percentile performance paid at 75th percentile of market	Our guiding principles are to act with integrity, treat people fairly, have fun, and be involved in projects that provide social benefits. This means we will • Help AES attract self-motivated, dependable people who want to keep learning new things • Hire people who really like the place and believe in the AES system • Pay what others are paid both inside and outside AES, but hire people who are willing to take less to join AES • Use teams of employees and managers to manage the compensation system • Make all employees stockholders

Compensation Objectives

Pay systems translate the strategy into practice in order to achieve certain objectives. The basic objectives, shown at the right side of the model, include efficiency, fairness, and compliance with laws and regulations. *Efficiency* can be stated more specifically: (1) improving performance, increasing quality, delighting customers and stockholders, and (2) controlling labor costs. Compensation objectives at Medtronic and AES are contrasted in Exhibit 1.6. Medtronic is a medical technology company that pioneered cardiac pacemakers. Its compensation objectives emphasize performance, business success, and salaries that are competitive with other companies whose financial performance matches Medtronic's. AES generates and markets electricity around the world. Its goal is to "provide electricity worldwide in a socially responsible way." The notion of social responsibility pervades the company.

Fairness is a fundamental objective of pay systems. In Medtronic's objectives, fairness means "ensure fair treatment" and "be open and understandable." AES's mission statement acknowledges, "Defining what is fair is often difficult, but we believe it is helpful to routinely question the relative fairness of alternative courses of action. It does not mean that everyone gets treated equally, but instead treated fairly or with justice given the appropriate situation."[28]

Thus, the fairness objective calls for fair treatment for all employees by recognizing both employee contributions (e.g., higher pay for greater performance, experience, or training) and employee needs (e.g., a fair wage as well as fair procedures). *Procedural*

[28]Further information on each company's philosophy and way of doing business can be deduced from their websites: *www.medtronic.com* and *www.aesc.com*. Readers of earlier editions of this book will note that "fairness" is substituted for "equity". The word "equity" has taken on several meanings in compensation, e.g., stock ownership and pay discrimination. We decided that "fairness" better conveyed our meaning in this book.

fairness refers to the process used to make pay decisions.[29] It suggests that the way a pay decision is made may be as important to employees as the results of the decision.

Compliance as a pay objective means conforming to federal and state compensation laws and regulations. If they change, pay systems may need to be adjusted to ensure continued compliance.

There are probably as many statements of pay objectives as there are employers. In fact, highly diversified firms such as General Electric and Eaton, which operate in multiple lines of businesses, may have different pay objectives for different business units. Objectives at Medtronic and AES emphasize the increased complexity of the business and the importance of integrity, competitiveness, ability to attract and retain quality people, and having fun.

Objectives serve several purposes. First, they guide the design of the pay system. If an objective is to increase customer satisfaction, then incentive programs and merit pay (techniques) might be used to pay for performance (policy). Another employer's objective may be to develop new products, to innovate. Job design, training, and team building may be used to reach this objective. The pay system aligned with this employer's objective may have a policy of paying salaries that at least equal those of competitors (external competitiveness) and that go up with increased skills or knowledge (internal alignment). This pay system could be very different from our first example, where the focus is on increasing customer satisfaction.

So, objectives guide the design of pay systems. They also serve as the standards for judging the success of the pay system. If the objective is to attract and retain the best and the brightest, yet skilled employees are leaving to take higher-paying jobs with other employers, the system may not be performing effectively. Although there may be many non-pay reasons for turnover, objectives provide standards for evaluating the effectiveness of a pay system.

Four Policies

Every employer must address the policy decisions shown on the left side of the pay model: (1) internal alignment, (2) external competitiveness, (3) employee contributions, and (4) management of the pay system. These policies are the foundation on which pay systems are built. They also serve as guidelines for managing pay in ways that accomplish the system's objectives.

---

[29]J. Brockner, Y. Chen, K. Leung, and D. Skarlick, "Culture and Procedural Fairness: When the Effects of What You Do Depend on How You Do It," *Administrative Science Quarterly* 45 (2000), pp. 138–159; Marcia P. Miceli and P. Mulvey, "Consequences of Satisfaction with Pay Systems: Two Field Studies," *Industrial Relations* 39 (2000), pp. 62–87; S. Masterson, K. Lewis, B. M. Goldman, and M. S. Taylor, "Integrating Justice and Social Exchange: The Differing Effects of Fair Procedures and Treatment on Work Relationships," *Academy of Management Journal,* 43, 2000, pp. 738–748; Frederick P. Morgeson, Michael A. Campion, and Carl P. Maertz, "Understanding Pay Satisfaction: The Limits of a Compensation System Implementation," *Journal of Business and Psychology* 16(1) (Fall 2001), pp. 133–149; Mary Konovsky, "Understanding Procedural Justice and Its Impact on Business Organizations," *Journal of Management* 26(3) (2000), pp. 489–511; Joel Brockner, "Making Sense of Procedural Fairness: How High Procedural Fairness Can Reduce or Heighten the Influence of Outcome Favorability," *Academy of Management Review* 27(1) (2002), pp. 58–76; Charlie O. Trevor and David L. Wazeter, "Reactions to Interdependence among Pay Dispersion, Pay Relative to Internal and External Referents, and Procedural Fairness: Toward a General Compensatory Effect," working paper, University of Wisconsin–Madison, May 2003.

Internal Alignment

Internal alignment refers to comparisons among jobs or skill levels inside a single organization. Jobs and people's skills are compared in terms of their relative contributions to the organization's business objectives. How, for example, does the work of the programmer compare with the work of the systems analyst, the software engineer, and the software architect? Does one contribute to providing solutions for customers and satisfying shareholders more than another? Think back to our friend from *Cats* and the variety of work required in a touring company to put on the show. Does one actor's role require more knowledge or experience than another's? Internal alignment pertains to the pay rates both for employees doing equal work and for those doing dissimilar work. In fact, determining what is an appropriate difference in pay for people performing different work is one of the key challenges facing managers.

Pay relationships within the organization affect all three compensation objectives. They affect employee decisions to stay with the organization, to become more flexible by investing in additional training, or to seek greater responsibility. By motivating employees to choose increased training and greater responsibility in dealing with customers, internal pay relationships indirectly affect the capabilities of the workforce and hence the efficiency of the entire organization. Fairness is affected through employees' comparisons of their pay to the pay of others in the organization. Compliance is affected by the basis for making internal comparisons. Paying on the basis of race, gender, age, or national origin is forbidden in the United States.

External Competitiveness

External competitiveness refers to compensation relationships external to the organization: comparison with competitors. How should an employer position its pay relative to what competitors are paying? *How much* do we wish to pay accountants in comparison to what other employers would pay them? *What mix* of pay forms—base, incentives, stock, benefits—will help achieve the compensation objectives? Recall that Medtronic's policy is to pay competitively in its market on the basis of its financial performance versus the financial performance of its competitors, while AES's policy is to expect people to be willing to take less to join the company.

Increasingly, organizations claim their pay systems are market-driven, that is, based almost exclusively on what competitors pay. However, "market driven" gets translated into practice in different ways. Some employers may set their pay levels higher than their competition, hoping to attract the best applicants. Of course, this assumes that someone is able to identify and hire the "best" from the pool of applicants.

What mix of pay forms a company uses is also part of its external competitive policy. Medtronic sets its base pay to match its competitors but ties incentives to performance. Plus it offers stock options to all its employees to promote a culture of ownership. The big assumption is that owners will pay closer attention to the business.[30] Further, Medtronic believes that its benefits, particularly its emphasis on programs that balance work and life, make it a highly attractive place to work. It believes that *how* its pay is positioned and *what forms* it uses create

[30]Mary Graham et al., "In the Land of Milk and Money: One Dairy Farm's Strategic Compensation System," *Journal of Agribusiness* 15(2) (1997), 171–188.

an advantage over competitors. A Medtronic competitor, say, Boston Scientific, may offer lower base pay but greater opportunity to work overtime or fatter bonuses.

External competitiveness decisions—both how much and what forms—have a twofold effect on objectives: (1) to ensure that the pay is sufficient to attract and retain employees— if employees do not perceive their pay as competitive in comparison to what other organizations are offering for similar work, they may be more likely to leave—and (2) to control labor costs so that the organization's prices of products or services can remain competitive. So external competitiveness directly affects both efficiency and fairness. And it must do so in a way that complies with relevant legislation.

Employee Contributions

How much emphasis should there be on paying for performance? Should one programmer be paid differently from another if one has better performance and/or greater seniority? Or should there be a flat rate for programmers? Should the company share any profits with employees? With all employees?

The emphasis to place on employee contributions is an important policy decision since it directly affects employees' attitudes and work behaviors. Eaton and Motorola use pay to support other "high-performance" practices in their workplaces.[31] Both use team-based pay and corporate profit-sharing plans. Starbucks emphasizes stock options and sharing the success of corporate performance with the employees. General Electric uses different performance-based pay programs at the individual, division, and companywide level. Performance-based pay also affects fairness in that employees need to understand the basis for judging performance in order to believe that their pay is fair.

Management

Policy regarding management of the pay system is the last building block in our model. It means ensuring that the right people get the right pay for achieving objectives in the right way. The greatest system design in the world is useless without competent management. While it is possible to design a system that is based on internal alignment, external competitiveness, and employee contributions, the system will not achieve its objectives unless it is properly managed.

Management means understanding and communicating how the pay system works and doing so in ethical and fair ways. Questions to answer include, Are we able to attract skilled workers? Can we keep them? Do our employees believe our pay system is fair? Do they understand what is expected of them? Do they understand how their pay is determined? How do the better-performing firms, with better financial returns and a larger share of the market, pay their employees? Are the systems used by these firms different from those used by less successful firms? How do our labor costs compare to those of our

[31]B. E. Becker and Mark Huselid, "High Performance Work Systems and Firm Performance: A Synthesis of Research and Management Implications," in *Research in Personnel and Human Resources,* ed. G. Ferris (Greenwich, CT: JAI Press, 1998); Rosemary Batt, "Managing Customer Services: Human Resource Practices, Quit Rates, and Sales Growth," *Academy of Management Journal* 45(3) (2002), pp. 587–597; A. Colvin, R. Batt, and H. Katz, "How High Performance HR Practices and Workforce Unionization Affect Managerial Pay," *Personnel Psychology* 4 (2001), pp. 903–934; Benjamin Schneider, Paul J. Hanges, D. Brent Smith, and Amy N. Salvaggio, "Which Comes First: Employee Attitudes or Organizational, Financial, and Market Performance?" *Journal of Applied Psychology,* October 2003, 88(5), pp. 836–851.

competitors? Answers to these questions are necessary to tune or redesign the system, to adjust to changes, and to highlight potential areas for further investigation. *Ethical behavior* means the organization cares about how the results are achieved.[32]

Pay Techniques

The remaining portion of the pay model in Exhibit 1.5 shows the techniques that make up the pay system. The exhibit provides only an overview since techniques are discussed throughout the rest of the book. Techniques tie the four basic policies to the pay objectives. Internal alignment is typically established through a sequence of techniques that starts with analysis of the work done and the people needed to do it. Information about the person and/or the job is collected, organized, and evaluated. Based on these evaluations, a structure of the work is designed.

> **Cybercomp**
> WorldatWork (*www.worldatwork.org*) provides information on its compensation-related journals and special publications, as well as short courses aimed at practitioners. The Society of Human Resource Managers (*www.shrm.org*) also offers compensation-related information as well as more general human resource management (HRM) information. The society's student services section offers guidance on finding jobs in the field of human resources. Both sites are good sources of information for people interested in careers in HRM. Information on pay trends in Europe is available from the European Industrial Relations Observatory (*www.eiro.eurofound.ie*). The Employee Benefits Research Institute (EBRI) includes links to other benefits sources on its website (*www.ebri.org*). The appendix to Chapter 18 describes many additional compensation websites. Every chapter also mentions interesting websites. Use them as a starting point to search out others.

This structure depicts relationships among jobs and skills or competencies inside an organization. It is based on the relative importance of the work in achieving the organization's objectives. The goal is to establish a structure that is aligned with and supports the organization's objectives. In turn, fairness of the pay system affects employee attitudes and behaviors as well as the organization's regulatory compliance.

External competitiveness is established by setting the organization's pay level in comparison with how much competitors pay for similar work and what pay forms they use. The sequence of techniques is to define the relevant labor markets in which the employer competes, conduct surveys of other employers' pay, and use that information in conjunction with the organization's policy decisions to generate a pay structure. The pay structure influences how efficiently the organization is able to attract and retain a competent workforce and control its labor costs.

The relative emphasis on employee contributions is established through performance and/or seniority-based pay increases, incentive plans, and stock options and other performance-based approaches. Increasingly, organizations in the United States and around the globe are using some form of incentive plan to share their success with employees.[33] In

[32]Robert Prentice, "An Ethics Lesson for Business Schools," *New York Times,* August 20, 2002, p. A21; Thomas Catan and Joshua Chaffin, "Bribery Has Long Been Used to Land International Contracts. New Laws Will Make That Tougher," *Financial Times,* May 8, 2003, p. 11; Charles Elson, "Worry about the Details," *Across the Board,* September/October 2002, pp. 37–48.

[33]Towers Perrin and Economist Intelligence Unit, *High Performance in the New Economy* (London: Towers Perrin, 2000).

addition to managing costs, these practices are all intended to affect employee attitudes and behaviors, in particular the decisions to join the organization, to stay, and to perform effectively.

Uncounted variations in pay techniques exist; many are examined in this book. Surveys report differences in compensation policies and techniques among firms. Indeed, most consultant firms have web pages in which they report their survey results. You can obtain updated information on various practices by simply surfing the web.

BOOK PLAN

Compensation is such a broad and compelling topic that several books could be devoted to it. The focus of this book is on the design and management of compensation systems. To aid in understanding how and why pay systems work, our pay model provides the structure for much of the book.

Chapter 2 discusses how to formulate and execute a compensation strategy. We analyze what it means to be strategic about how people are paid and how compensation can help achieve and sustain an organization's competitive advantage.

The pay model plays a central role in formulating and implementing an organization's pay strategy. The model identifies four basic policy decisions that are the core of the pay strategy. After we discuss strategy, the next sections of the book examine each of these decisions in detail. Part 1, on *internal alignment* (Chapters 3 through 6) examines pay relationships within a single organization. Part 2 (Chapters 7 and 8) examines *external competitiveness*—the pay relationships among competing organizations—and analyzes the influence of market-driven forces.

Once the compensation rates and structures are established, other issues emerge. How much should we pay each individual employee? How much and how often should a person's pay be increased and on what basis—experience, seniority, or performance? Should pay increases be contingent on the organization's and/or the employee's performance? How should the organization share its success (or failure) with employees? These are questions of *employee contributions,* the third building block in the model, covered in Part 3 (Chapters 9 through 11). In Part 4, we cover employee services and benefits (Chapters 12 and 13). Next, in Part 5, we cover systems tailored for special groups—sales representatives, executives, contract workers, unions (Chapters 14 and 15) as well as provide more detail on global compensation systems (Chapter 16). We conclude, in Part 6, with information essential for *managing the compensation system.* The government's role in compensation is examined in Chapter 17. Chapter 18 includes understanding, communicating, budgeting, and evaluating the results obtained.

Even though the book is divided into sections that reflect the pay model, pay decisions are not discrete. All of them are interrelated. Together, they influence employee behaviors and organization performance and can create a pay system that can be a source of competitive advantage.

Throughout the book our intention is to examine alternative approaches. We believe that rarely is there a single correct approach; rather, alternative approaches exist or can be designed. The one most likely to be effective depends on the circumstances. We hope that this book will help you become better informed about these options and how to design new ones. Whether as an employee, a manager, or an interested member of society, you should be able to assess the effectiveness and fairness of pay systems.

CAVEAT EMPTOR—BE AN INFORMED CONSUMER

Most managers do not read research. They don't subscribe to research journals; they find them too full of jargon and esoterica, and they see them as impractical and irrelevant.[34] However, a recent study of 5,000 HR managers concluded that "not knowing this research can be costly to organizations." A team of researchers at the University of Iowa asked the managers if they agreed or disagreed with a number of statements. The results for compensation-related items are presented in Exhibit 1.7. The first column shows the statement; the second, whether the statement is true or false based on research, as well as the percentage who agreed with the statement. The researchers have concluded, "Organizations seeking the latest motivational technique may not realize that . . . monetary incentives produce the largest, most reliable increases in job performance, almost twice as large as the effects of goal setting and job enrichment. Money is the crucial incentive . . . no other incentive or motivational technique even comes close." [35]

So it pays to read the research. There is no question that some studies are irrelevant and poorly performed. But if you are not a reader of research literature, you become prey for the latest business self-help fad. Belief, even enthusiasm, is a poor substitute for informed judgment. Therefore, we end the chapter with a consumer's guide that includes three questions to help make you a critical reader.

[handwritten margin note: Know 3 Questions to Ask when assessing the worth of a study related to compensation theory]

1. Does the Research Measure Anything Useful?

How useful are the variables in the study? How well are they measured? For example, many studies purport to measure organization performance. However, performance may be accounting measures such as return on assets or cash flow, financial measures such as earnings per share or total shareholder return, operational measures such as scrap rates or defect indicators, or qualitative measures such as customer satisfaction. It may even be the opinions of compensation managers, as in, "How effective is your gain-sharing plan?" (Answer choices are "highly effective," "effective," "somewhat," "disappointing," "not very effective." "Disastrous" is not usually one of the choices. If I am the designer of the plan, how do you think I will answer?) The informed consumer must ask, Does this research measure anything important?

2. Does the Study Separate Correlation from Causation?

Once we are confident that our variables are accurately defined and measured, we must be sure that they are actually related. Most often this is addressed through the use of statistical analysis. The *correlation coefficient* is a common measure of association and indicates how changes in one variable are related to changes in another. Many research studies use a statistical analysis known as *regression analysis*. One output from a regression analysis is the R^2. The R^2 is much like a correlation in that it tells us what percentage of

---

[34]Sara L. Rynes, Amy E. Colbert, and Kenneth G. Brown, "HR Professionals' Beliefs about Effective Human Resource Practices: Correspondence between Research and Practice," *Human Resource Management* 41(2) (Summer 2002), pp. 149–174; and Sara L. Rynes, Amy E. Colbert, and Kenneth G. Brown, "Seven Common Misconceptions about Human Resource Practices; Research Findings versus Practitioner Beliefs," *Academy of Management Executive* 16(3) (2002), pp. 92–102.

[35]Ibid.

EXHIBIT 1.7   Compensation: Managers' Beliefs versus Research Findings

Item	Answer % Correct (% Uncertain)	Research Evidence
When pay must be reduced or frozen, there is little a company can do or say to reduce employee dissatisfaction and dysfunctional behaviors.	False 72% (13%)	Both laboratory and organizational field research shows that providing procedurally just explanations of pay cuts can dramatically reduce the negative side effects (Greenberg, 1990, 1993).
Most employees prefer to be paid on the basis of individual performance rather than team or organizational performance.	True 81% (8%)	Multiple studies have demonstrated this result (e.g., BNA, 1988; Cable & Judge (1994) found that of seven organizational characteristics, the one that best predicted simulated organizational choice was pay for individual (versus team-based) productivity.
Merit pay systems cause so many problems that companies without them tend to have higher performance than companies with them.	False 66% (7%)	Positive relationships have been shown between merit systems and organization-level performance by Kopelman & Reinharth (1982) and Kopelman, Rovenpor, & Cayer (1991). Heneman (1992) reviewed five studies establishing a positive merit system–performance link. Even the major empirical study to raise "cautions" about merit pay (Pearce et al., 1985) found increases in performance after merit pay implementation; the increases simply failed to reach statistical significance (with a very small sample size).
There is a positive relationship between the proportion of managers receiving organizationally based pay incentives and company profitability.	True 62% (23%)	Gerhart & Milkovich (1990) found that companies with 80% managerial eligibility for stock options had 25% higher return on assets than companies where only 20% of managers were eligible. (See also Welbourne & Andrews, 1996.)
New companies have a better chance of surviving if all employees receive incentives based on organizationwide performance.	True 59% (17%)	New companies that placed a high value on their employees (as coded from prospectuses) and that included high levels of organizational-performance-based pay had dramatically higher five-year survival rates (92%) than those that were low on both dimensions (34%: Welbourne & Andrews, 1996).
Talking about salary issues during performance appraisals tends to hurt morale and future performance.	False 51% (10%)	In a field study of nine different sites, Prince & Lawler (1986) found that salary discussions had positive rather than negative effects on employee attitudes and subsequent performance improvement. In addition, the positive effects were strongest for those with lower initial performance and where initial perceptions of performance were most discrepant between supervisors and employees. For similar results based on employee surveys at General Electric, see Welch (2001).

Source: Sara L. Rynes, Amy E. Colbert, and Kenneth G. Brown, "HR Professionals' Beliefs about Effective Human Resource Practices: Correspondence between Research and Practice," *Human Resource Management* 41(2) (Summer 2002), pp. 149–174. Full citations for the articles listed can be found in the appendix to the Rynes et al. article.

EXHIBIT 1.7 *continued*

Item	Answer % Correct (% Uncertain)	Research Evidence
Most employees prefer variable pay systems (e.g., incentive schemes, gain sharing, stock options) to fixed pay systems.	False 40% (12%)	A national survey showed that 63% of workers surveyed prefer straight salary, followed by individual incentives (22%) and companywide incentives (12%; BNA, 1988). Cable & Judge, (1994) found a similar preference for fixed pay among job-seeking college students. Also, theories of risk and agency theory have as a core assumption that employees require a compensating risk differential in order to make variable pay acceptable to them (e.g., Jensen & Meckling, 1976).
Surveys that directly ask employees how important pay is to them are likely to overestimate pay's true importance in actual decisions.	False 35% (10%)	Probably due to social desirability and/or lack of self-insight, people tend to say pay is less important to them than the weights they actually place on pay in making choice decisions (Feldman & Arnold, 1978; Rynes et al., 1983). People also think that others who are "just like them" place a higher importance on pay than they themselves do (Jurgensen, 1978)—further evidence of possible lack of self-insight about motivations. These results are also consistent with broader findings from the decision sciences that people tend to underestimate the importance of the most important factors in their decisions (Slovic & Lichtenstein, 1971).

the variation is accounted for by the variables we are using to predict or explain. For example, one study includes a regression analysis of the change in CEO pay due to change in company performance. The resulting R^2 of between 0.8 percent and 4.5 percent indicates that only a very small amount of change in CEO pay is related to changes in company performance.

But even if there is a relationship, correlation does not ensure causation. For example, just because a manufacturing plant initiates a new incentive plan and the facility's performance improves, we cannot conclude that the incentive plan caused the improved performance. Perhaps new technology, reengineering, improved marketing, or the general expansion of the local economy underlies the results. The two changes are associated or related, but causation is a tough link to make.

Too often, case studies, benchmarking studies of best practices, or consultant surveys are presented as studies that reveal cause and effect. They are not. Case studies are descriptive accounts whose value and limitations must be recognized. Just because the best-performing companies are using a practice does not mean the practice is causing the performance.

IBM provides an example of the difficulty of deciding whether a change is a cause or an effect. For a long time IBM pursued a no-layoff policy. Clearly, that policy did not cause the value of IBM stock to increase or improve IBM's profitability. Arguably, it was IBM's profitability that enabled its full-employment policy. However, compensation research often attempts to answer questions of causality. Does the use of performance-based pay lead to greater customer satisfaction, improved quality, and better company performance? Causality is one of the most difficult questions to answer and continues to be an important and sometimes perplexing problem for researchers.

3. Are There Alternative Explanations?

Consider a hypothetical study that attempts to assess the impact of a performance-based pay initiative. The researchers measure performance by assessing quality, productivity, customer satisfaction, employee satisfaction, and the facility's performance. The final step is to see whether future periods' performance improves over this period's. If it does, can we safely assume that it was the incentive pay that caused performance? Or is it equally likely that the improved performance has alternative explanations, such as the fluctuation in the value of currency or perhaps a change in executive leadership in the facility? In this case, causality evidence seems weak.

If the researchers had measured the performance indicators several years prior to and after installing the plan, then the evidence of causality is only a bit stronger. Further, if the researchers repeated this process in other facilities and the results are similar, then the preponderance of evidence is stronger. Clearly, the organization is doing something right, and incentive pay may be part of it.

The best way to establish causation is to account for competing explanations, either statistically or through control groups. The point is that alternative explanations often exist. And if they do, they need to be accounted for to establish causality. It is very difficult to disentangle the effects of pay plans to clearly establish causality. However, it is possible to look at the overall pattern of evidence to make judgments about the effects of pay.

So we encourage you to become a critical reader of all management literature, including this book. As Hogwarts' famous Professor Alaster Moody cautions, be on "constant vigilance for sloppy analysis masquerading as research."[36]

---

[36]J. K. Rowling, *Harry Potter and the Goblet of Fire* (London: Scholastic, 2000).

Your Turn   Glamorous Internships? Or House Elves?

Harry Potter readers will recall the house elves who work in the kitchen at Hogwarts. They would never think of asking to be paid. Hermione finds this outrageous. "This is slavery!" she contends. Of course, Harry Potter is fantasy. Or is it?

Greg Petouvis, a junior at Cornell University, worked for the Equal Employment Opportunity Commission in Washington, DC, during a recent summer. The job included performing site compliance visits at several companies, interviewing people who filed discrimination complaints, determining whether complaints had merit, and settling disputes. The work was very similar to that done by full-time EEOC field analysts. In fact, the agency manager reported that Greg was one of the top field analysts. But Greg received no pay. Not even a housing allowance for living in Washington, DC, during two and one-half summer months.

Trent Mayberry, from the University of Minnesota, worked for the City of Saint Paul on its "Peanuts on Parade" promotion. (Saint Paul is the birthplace of Charles Schulz, the creator of the *Peanuts* cartoon strip.) Trent was paid $9 per hour. Krista Lehmkuhl from Notre Dame helped design the cover for this textbook while an intern at McGraw-Hill. McGraw pays their interns about $12 an hour.

Hope Wagner, from the University of Nebraska, worked in media relations for a professional sports team one summer. She drafted news releases, filed clippings, and worked on a 75-page media guide. She took home plenty of team souvenirs—coffee mugs, key chains, T-shirts—but not one cent.

The giant chip maker Intel pays undergraduate interns between $450 and $750 a week and tosses in a free rental car during the summer.* General Motors doesn't provide the car, but it does pay $450 to $600 a week and provide paid vacation days, round-trip travel, plus health insurance. The *Late Show with David Letterman* pays nothing, yet claims to receive over 800 applications for 30 unpaid summer intern positions.

So are house elves alive and well?

1. What do employers receive from summer interns? What returns do students get from the opportunities?

2. Should summer interns be paid? If so, how much? How would you recommend that an employer decide the answers to both these questions?

3. What added information would you like to have before you make your recommendations? How would you use this information?

Sources: *America's Top Internships* and *The Internship Bible*, both part of the Princeton Review series published by Random House.

Summary

The model presented in this chapter provides a structure for understanding compensation systems. The three main components of the model are the compensation objectives, the policy decisions that guide how the objectives are going to be achieved, and the techniques that make up the pay system. The following sections of the book examine each of the four policy decisions—internal alignment, external competitiveness, employee performance, and management—as well as the techniques, new directions, and related research.

Two questions should constantly be in the minds of managers and readers of this text. First, why do it this way? There is rarely one correct way to design a system or pay an individual. Organizations, people, and circumstances are too varied. But a well-trained manager can select or design a suitable approach.

Second, so what? What does this technique do for us? How does it help achieve our goals? If good answers to the "so-what" question are not apparent, there is no point to the technique. Adapting the pay system to meet the needs of the employees and help achieve the goals of the organization is what this book is all about.

The basic premise of this book is that compensation systems do have a profound impact. Yet, too often, traditional pay systems seem to have been designed in response to some historical but long-forgotten problem. The practices continue, but the logic underlying them is not always clear or even relevant.

Review Questions

1. How do differing perspectives affect our views of compensation?
2. What is your definition of compensation? Which meaning of compensation seems most appropriate from an employee's view: return, reward, or entitlement? Compare your ideas with someone with more experience, someone from another country, someone from another field of study.
3. What is the deal between your instructor and the college? Is it similar to the hired-gun, commodity, family, or cultlike relationship? Discuss whether it would make any difference in teaching effectiveness if the deal were changed. What would you recommend and why?
4. What are the four policy issues in the pay model? How does the pay model help organize one's thinking about compensation?
5. List all the forms of pay you receive from work. Compare your list to someone else's list. Explain any differences.
6. Answer the three questions in *caveat emptor* for any study or business article that tells you how to pay people.

Chapter Two

Strategic Perspectives

Chapter Outline

You probably think you can skip this chapter. After all, what can be so challenging about a compensation strategy? How about this for a strategy: We'll let the market decide what we need to pay people!

Unfortunately, a dose of reality quickly reveals that employers cannot behave so simply. Companies compete very differently for very similar talent. We have already compared compensation objectives in Chapter 1. In Exhibit 2.1, we compare compensation strategies at Firepond, Microsoft, and Bristol-Myers Squibb (BMS). The three companies approach the five dimensions of compensation strategy in very different ways. However, each company's compensation strategy supports its business strategy. Firepond is a small start-up that offers "software solutions" to traditional firms trying to grow the e-sales part of their business. All three of the companies in the exhibit emphasize employee performance and commitment, but each company does it very differently. In spite of the dramatic decline of the stock market in the early 2000s, Firepond continues to offer its employees the chance to hit it big by emphasizing stock options and deemphasizing cash (base and bonus) compared to its competitors.[1] This strategy remains common among

---

[1] John L. Nesheim, *High Tech Start Up* (Saratoga, CA: John L. Nesheim, 1997); Michael Wanderer, "Dot-Comp: A 'Traditional' Pay Plan with a Cutting Edge," *WorldatWork Journal*, Fourth Quarter 2000, pp. 15–24.

EXHIBIT 2.1 **Strategic Perspectives toward Total Compensation**

	Microsoft	Bristol-Myers Squibb	Firepond
Objectives	• Support the business objectives • Support recruiting, motivation, and retention of MS-caliber talent • Preserve MS core values	• Support business mission and goals • Develop global leaders at every level • Reinforce team-based culture • Reduce costs, increase productivity	• Demonstrate respect for individual talent and the limitless potential of a highly motivated team • Encourage high standards of excellence, original thinking, a passion for the process of discovery, and a willingness to take risks • Reward fresh ideas, hard work, and a commitment to excellence • Value diverse perspectives as a key to discovery
Internal Alignment	• Integral part of MS culture • Support MS performance-driven culture • Business/technology-based organization design structure	• Reflect responsibilities, required competencies, and business impact • Flexibility for development and growth	• Pay differences that foster a collegial atmosphere • Reinforce high expectations

start-up companies because it conserves cash for operating expenses (e.g., Friday beer and pizza, and paying the rent on the garage) and funding growth.

In its earlier years, Microsoft followed this same strategy explicitly. It asked its employees to "put some skin in the game," or accept less base pay to join a company whose stock options were increasing in worth exponentially.[2] But things changed. Confronted with pressure from current employees dissatisfied with their pay and nonperforming

---

[2] R. Herbolt, "Inside Microsoft," *Harvard Business Review,* January 2002; Richard Waters and Scott Morrison, "Microsoft Ends Employee Stock Options," *Financial Times* July 9, 2003; Holman W. Jenkins Jr., "Stock Options are Dead, Long Live Stock Options," *Wall Street Journal* July 16, 2003, p. A15; Sarah Kershaw, "For Newer Microsoft Employees, A Sense of Redress," *New York Times* July 10, 2003. An *option* is the opportunity to buy stock at a set price. If the value of shares increases, then the option has value (market price minus the set option price). Awards grant employees stock whose value is its market price. Later chapters discuss stock options and awards in detail.

EXHIBIT 2.1   *continued*

	Microsoft	**Bristol-Myers Squibb**	**Firepond**
Externally Competitive	• Lead in *total* compensation • Meet base pay and bonuses • Lead with stock awards	• Compare favorably to higher-performing competitors • Cash between the 50th and 75th percentile	• "Pay what others are paying"
Employee Contributions	• Bonuses and stock awards based on individual performance	• Support high performance, leadership culture • Team-based increases • Options align employee and shareholder interest • Tailor to business and team results	• Bonus pool based on Firepond financial performance; individual share of pool based on individual performance • Push stock ownership deep into company
Management	• Open, transparent communications • Centralized administration • Software supported	• Performance and leadership feedback—everyone is a leader • Administrative ease	• Goal-focused, team-oriented, and self-managed

stock, Microsoft first shifted its strategy to increase its base and bonus to the 65th percentile from the 45th percentile, of competitors' pay, while retaining its strong emphasis on options. More recently, Microsoft replaced eye-popping stock options with stock awards based on individual performance. Beyond this, it added a level to its internal structure, a new title of "Distinguished Engineer" for jobs critical to Microsoft's success. A former Microsoft executive calls the company "the new Boeing—a solid place to work in Seattle for a good salary." Microsoft has shifted from a "workaholic, high risk–maybe get rich quick" to a "work hard–get a great return" philosophy. It has not only changed *how much* (total compensation) but also *what mix of pay forms* it offers (relative importance of base, bonus, stock, and benefits).

The approach at BMS, a global pharmaceutical, differs. BMS's mission is "to extend and enhance human life." While it, too, uses options and bonuses tied to performance, the amounts are much smaller than those at Firepond and Microsoft. BMS's strategy emphasizes greater balance among cash compensation (base and bonus), options, and a generous package of work/life balance programs. BMS uses its compensation to reinforce teamwork; it does not offer individual incentives except for a few extraordinary contributors. It also focuses on developing skills and leadership at all levels in the organization.

SAS Institute, the world's largest privately owned software company, provides yet another compensation strategy. It emphasizes its work/life programs over cash compensation and gives only limited bonuses and no options. SAS headquarters in Cary, North Carolina, includes free onsite child care centers, subsidized private schools for children of employees, two doctors on site for free medical care, plus recreation facilities.[3] Working more than 35 hours per week is discouraged. By removing as many of the frustrations and distractions of day-to-day life as possible, SAS believes people will focus on work when they are at work. In contrast, Microsoft built part of its mystique on stories of engineers sleeping under their desks and competing to be first in, last out of the company parking lot. These companies have very different strategic perspectives on total compensation.

The importance of a strategic perspective is backed up by research, too. Recent studies make it clear that a simple, "let the market decide our compensation" strategy does not work when the focus is on improving performance. How much and what mix of forms you pay (base and incentives) combined with other HR practices (e.g., selective hiring, training, and performance management) enable employees to improve performance. Practices that link employees' behaviors to each company's specifics—knowledge of the specific work required, of specific products offered, and of specific customers served—are required for success.[4]

A simple, "let the market decide our compensation" strategy doesn't work internationally either. In many nations, markets do not operate as in the United States or may not even exist. People either do not, or in some cases, cannot easily change employers. In China, central Asia, and some eastern European countries, markets for labor are just emerging. Even in some countries with more developed economies, such as Germany and Sweden, the labor market is highly regulated. Consequently, there is less movement of people among companies than is common in the United States, Canada, or even Korea and Singapore.[5]

---

[3]"SAS Institute," Stanford Business School case; Also, "SAS: The Royal Treatment," *60 Minutes,* October 13, 2002.

[4]Rosemary Batt, "Managing Customer Services: Human Resource Practices, Quit Rates, and Sales Growth," *Academy of Management Journal* 45(3) (2002), pp. 587–597; Casey Ichniowski, Thomas A. Kochan, David Levine, Craig Olson, and George Strauss, "What Works at Work: Overview and Assessment," *Industrial Relations* 35(3) (July 1996), pp. 299–333; A.Colvin, R. Batt, and H. Katz, "How High Performance HR Practices and Workforce Unionization Affect Managerial Pay," *Personnel Psychology* 54 (2001), pp. 903–934; Watson Wyatt Worldwide, "Human Capital Index: Human Capital as a Lead Indicator of Shareholder Value", research report, *www.watsonwyatt.com,* 2001; Jason D. Shaw, Nina Gupta, and John Delery, "Congruence between Technology and Compensation Systems: Implications for Strategy Implementation," *Strategic Management Journal* 22 (2001), pp. 379–386; Jason D. Shaw, Nina Gupta, and John Delery, "Pay Dispersion and Workforce Performance: Moderating Effects of Incentives and Interdependence," *Strategic Management Journal* 23 (2002), pp. 491–512.

[5]D. Vaughan Whitehead, "Wage Reform in Central and Eastern Europe," in *Paying the Price,* ed. Vaughn-Whitehead (New York: St. Martin's Press, 2000); Marshall Meyer, Yuan Lu, Hailin Lan, and Xiaohui Lu, "Decentralized Enterprise Reform: Notes on the Transformation of State-Owned Enterprises," in *The Management of Enterprises in the People's Republic of China,* eds. Anne S. Tsui and Chung-Ming Lau (Boston: Kluwer Academic, 2002) pp. 241–274.

Understanding the differences in compensation strategies becomes important during acquisitions and mergers as well. Autoworkers at the Volvo plant (now owned by Ford) in Gothenburg, Sweden, can enjoy a gym, Olympic-size swimming pool, tennis, track and tanning beds, along with a hot-water pool and physical therapy sessions after a hard day (30 hours per week) on the assembly line. Autoworkers at Ford's pickup truck assembly plant in St. Paul, Minnesota, enjoy no such comparable facilities. Will Ford be able to continue such divergent compensation strategies at its Volvo plants in Sweden and Ford plants in the United States? It is possible for different business units within the same company to adopt different compensation strategies. But if Volvo and Ford begin to share common parts and distribution channels and form global teams to design new cars, then these differences may become obstacles to achieving the needed cooperation and integration.

The point is that a strategic perspective on compensation is more complex than it first appears. So we suggest that you continue to read this chapter.

STRATEGIC PERSPECTIVE

Because pay matters so much to most of us, it is sometimes too easy to become fixated on techniques: Debating so-called "best practices" becomes the end in itself. Questions such as "What does this technique do for (to) us?" or "How does it help achieve our objectives?" are not asked. So before proceeding to the particulars, we need to think about how pay might help achieve organization success. After completing this chapter, you should know how to develop a compensation strategy. More importantly, you should also know why you would bother doing so. If you train yourself to ask the "so-what" question as you read this book you will be prepared when your employer asks if your proposal makes sense.

SUPPORT BUSINESS STRATEGY

A currently popular theory found in almost every book and consultant's report tells managers to tailor their pay systems to align with the organization's business strategy. The rationale is based on contingency notions. That is, differences in a firm's strategy should be supported by corresponding differences in its human resource strategy, including compensation. The underlying premise is that the greater the alignment, or fit, between the organization and the compensation system, the more effective the organization.[6]

Strategy refers to the fundamental directions that an organization has chosen. An organization defines its strategy through the tradeoffs it makes in choosing what (and what not) to do. Exhibit 2.2 relates these strategic choices to the quest for competitive advantage. At the corporate level, the fundamental strategic choice is, *What business should we be in?* At

[6]Henry Mintzberg, "Five Tips for Strategy," in *The Strategy Process: Concepts and Contexts,* eds. Henry Mintzberg and James Brian Quinn (Englewood Cliffs, NJ: Prentice-Hall, 1992); J. E. Delery and D. H. Doty, "Models of Theorizing in Strategic Human Resource Management," *Academy of Management Journal* 39(4), pp. 802–835; L. R. Gomez-Mejia and D. B. Balkin, *Compensation, Organization Strategy, and Firm Performance* (Cincinnati: Southwestern, 1992); P. K. Zingheim and R. Schuster, *Pay People Right!* (San Francisco: Jossey-Bass, 2000); Edilberto F. Montemayor, "Congruence between Pay Policy and Competitive Strategy in High-Performing Firms," *Journal of Management* 22(6) (1996), pp. 889–908

EXHIBIT 2.2   Strategic Choices

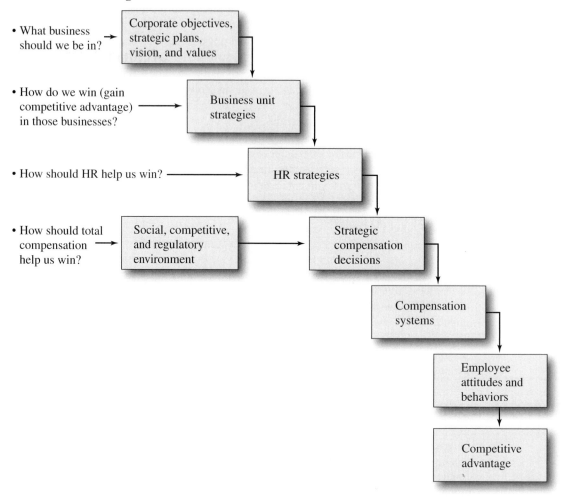

• What business
  should we be in? →   Corporate objectives,
                       strategic plans,
                       vision, and values

• How do we win (gain
  competitive advantage)
  in those businesses?   →   Business unit
                             strategies

• How should HR help us win? ──────→   HR strategies

• How should total
  compensation   →   Social, competitive,
  help us win?   and regulatory
                      environment   →   Strategic
                                                compensation
                                                decisions

                                          Compensation
                                          systems

                                          Employee
                                          attitudes and
                                          behaviors

                                          Competitive
                                          advantage

the business unit level, the choice shifts to, *How do we gain and sustain competitive advantage? How do we win in those businesses?* At the function level the strategic choice is, *How should total compensation help gain and sustain competitive advantage?* The ultimate purpose—the "so what?"—is to gain and sustain competitive advantage.[7]

It then follows from the exhibit that when business strategies change, pay systems should change, too. A classic example is IBM's strategic and cultural transformation in

[7]B. Gerhart, "Pay Strategy and Firm Performance," in *Compensation in Organizations: Current Research and Practice,* eds. S. L. Rynes and B. Gerhart (San Francisco; Jossey-Bass, 2000); Barry Gerhart and Sara Rynes, *Compensation: Theory, Evidence, and Strategic Implications* (Thousand Oaks, CA: Sage, 2003).

**EXHIBIT 2.3
IBM's
Strategic
Principles
and Priorities**

Source: Adapted
from IBM. ©
2002 IBM
Corporation.

Principles	Priorities
1. The marketplace is the driving force behind everything 2. At our core, we are a technology company with an overriding commitment to quality. 3. Our primary measures of success are customer satisfaction and shareholder value. 4. We operate as an entrepreneurial organization with a minimum of bureaucracy and a never-ending focus on productivity. 5. We never lose sight of our strategic vision. 6. We think and act with a sense of urgency. 7. Outstanding, dedicated people make it happen, particularly when they work together as a team. 8. We are sensitive to the needs of all employees and to the communities in which we operate.	1. Delivering business value 2. Offering world-class open infrastructure 3. Developing innovative leadership technology 4. Exploiting new profitable growth opportunities 5. Creating brand leadership and a superior customer experience 6. Attracting, motivating and retaining the best talent in our industry

the 1990s. IBM's emphasis on internal alignment (well-developed job evaluation plan, clear hierarchy for decision making, work/life balance benefits, policy of no layoffs) had served well during the last century when the company dominated the market for high-profit mainframe computers. But it did not provide flexibility to adapt to competitive changes in the new century. A redesigned IBM is a "solutions-led business offering diversified information technology capabilities." Exhibit 2.3 depicts the "new blue's" strategic business principles and priorities. A new business strategy requires a new compensation strategy. At IBM, this meant creating a high-performance work culture (incentive pay), increasing employee and organization flexibility (work design), winning in the marketplace (attract/retain talent), and constantly containing costs. IBM changed its pay strategy and system to support its changed business strategy. And it changed from a doomed dinosaur to the "t-Rex of the technology industry." [8]

If the basic premise of a strategic perspective is to align the compensation system to the business strategy, then different business strategies will translate into different compensation approaches. Exhibit 2.4 gives an example of how compensation systems might be tailored to three different business strategies.[9] The *innovator* stresses new products and short response time to market trends. A supporting compensation approach places

[8]A. Richter, "Paying the People in Black at Big Blue," *Compensation and Benefits Review,* May/June 1998, pp. 51–59; Thomas Fleming, *Compensating a Global Workforce,* presentation at Cornell University, February 21, 2003.

[9]M. Porter, "What Is Strategy?" *Harvard Business Review,* November–December 1996, pp. 61–78; J. Jackson, "Why Being Different Pays," *Financial Times,* June 23, 1997, p. B1; M. Treacy and F. Wiersma, *The Discipline of Market Leaders* (Reading, MA: Addison-Wesley, 1997).

EXHIBIT 2.4 **Tailor the Compensation System to the Strategy**

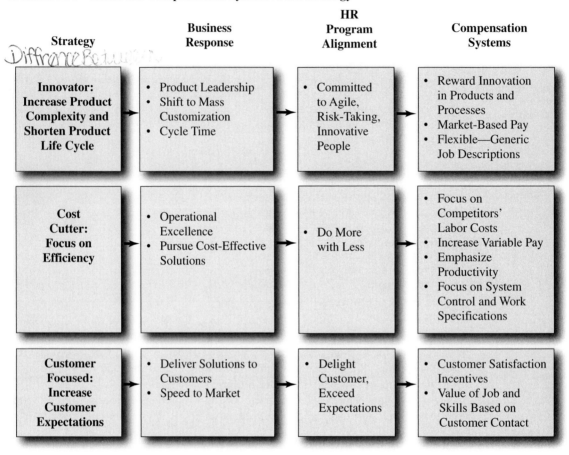

Strategy	Business Response	HR Program Alignment	Compensation Systems
Innovator: Increase Product Complexity and Shorten Product Life Cycle	• Product Leadership • Shift to Mass Customization • Cycle Time	• Committed to Agile, Risk-Taking, Innovative People	• Reward Innovation in Products and Processes • Market-Based Pay • Flexible—Generic Job Descriptions
Cost Cutter: Focus on Efficiency	• Operational Excellence • Pursue Cost-Effective Solutions	• Do More with Less	• Focus on Competitors' Labor Costs • Increase Variable Pay • Emphasize Productivity • Focus on System Control and Work Specifications
Customer Focused: Increase Customer Expectations	• Deliver Solutions to Customers • Speed to Market	• Delight Customer, Exceed Expectations	• Customer Satisfaction Incentives • Value of Job and Skills Based on Customer Contact

less emphasis on evaluating skills and jobs and more emphasis on incentives designed to encourage innovations. The *cost cutter's* efficiency-focused strategy stresses doing more with less by minimizing costs, encouraging productivity increases, and specifying in greater detail exactly how jobs should be performed. The *customer-focused* business strategy stresses delighting customers and bases employee pay on how well they do this. Different business strategies require different compensation approaches. One size does not fit all.[10]

[10]L. R. Gomez-Mejia, "Structure and Process of Diversification, Compensation Strategy, and Firm Performance," *Strategic Management Journal,* October 1992, pp. 44–56; Edilberto F. Montemayor. "Congruence between Pay Policy and Competitive Strategy in High-Performing Firms," *Journal of Management* 22 (1996), pp. 889–908; Jason D. Shaw, Nina Gupta, and John Delery, "Congruence between Technology and Compensation Systems: Implications for Strategy Implementation," *Strategic Management Journal* 22 (2001), pp. 379–386.

WHICH PAY DECISIONS ARE STRATEGIC?

It is possible that different units within the same corporation face very different competitive conditions, adopt different business strategies, and thus fit different compensation strategies. Large conglomerates such as United Technologies, whose business units include Otis Elevator, Sikorski Aircraft, and Carrier (air conditioning), and the Korean company SK Group, whose business units include a gasoline retailer, a cellular phone manufacturer, and SK Construction, will have different compensation strategies aligned to each of their very different businesses.

A *strategic perspective* focuses on those compensation choices that help the organization gain and sustain competitive advantage.

The competitive advantage of Starbucks is apparent with the first sip of its specialty drink, mocha valencia. What started out as a Seattle seller of coffee beans has, through strategic decisions, grown to a familiar chain of coffeehouses stretching around the globe.[11] Along the way, Starbucks managers have designed a total compensation system to support this change in fundamental direction (from coffee bean importer to trendy coffeehouses) and growth (phenomenal, global).

Using our pay model, the strategic compensation decisions facing Starbucks managers can be considered in terms of the objectives and the four basic policies:

1. *Objectives:* How should compensation support the business strategy and be adaptive to the cultural and regulatory pressures in a global environment? (Starbucks' objectives: Grow by making employees feel valued. Recognize that every dollar earned passes through employees' hands. Use pay, benefits, and opportunities for personal development to help gain employee loyalty and become difficult to imitate.)

2. *Alignment:* How differently should the different types and levels of skills and work be paid within the organization? (Starbucks: Deemphasize differences. Use egalitarian structures, cross-train employees to handle many jobs, and call employees "partners.")

3. *Competitiveness:* How should total compensation be positioned against competitors? (Starbucks: Pay just slightly above other fast-food businesses [a low-wage industry].) What forms of compensation should be used? (Starbucks: Provide health insurance and stock options [called "bean stocks"] for all employees including part-timers [even though most are relatively young and healthy and few stay long enough to earn stock options], and give everyone a free pound of coffee every week.)

4. *Contributions:* Should pay increases be based on individual and/or team performance, on experience and/or continuous learning, on improved skills, on changes in cost of living, on personal needs (housing, transportation, health services), and/or on each

---

[11]Howard Schultz and Dori Jones Yang, *How Starbucks Built a Company One Cup at a Time* (New York: Hyperion, 1997); J. Lee-Young, "Starbucks Expansion in China," *Wall Street Journal,* March 12, 2000, p. B6; Stanley Holmes, Irene M. Kunii, and Jack Ewing, "For Starbucks, There's No Place Like Home," *Business Week,* June 9, 2003.

business unit's performance? (Starbucks: Emphasize team performance and share-holder returns [options]. For new managers in Beijing and Prague, provide training opportunities in the United States.)

5. *Management:* How open and transparent should the pay decisions be to all employees? Who should be involved in designing and managing the system? (Starbucks: As members of the Starbucks "family," our employees realize what is best for them. Partners can and do get involved.)

The decisions underlying these five issues, taken together, form a pattern that becomes an organization's compensation strategy.

Stated versus Unstated Strategies

All organizations that pay people have a compensation strategy. Some may have written, or stated, compensation strategies for all to see and understand. Others may not even realize they have a compensation strategy. Ask a manager at one of these organizations about its compensation strategy and you may get a pragmatic response: "We do whatever it takes." Its compensation strategy emerges from the pay decisions it has made. Unstated compensation strategy is inferred from compensation practices.[12] Managers in all organizations make the five strategic decisions discussed earlier. Some do it in a rational, deliberate way, while others do it more chaotically—as ad hoc responses to pressures from the economic, sociopolitical, and regulatory context in which the organization operates. But in any organization that pays people, there is a compensation strategy at work.

DEVELOPING A TOTAL COMPENSATION STRATEGY

Developing a compensation strategy involves four simple steps, shown in Exhibit 2.5. While the steps are simple, executing them is complex. Trial and error, experience, and insight play major roles.

Step 1: Assess Total Compensation Implications

Think about any organization's past, present, and, most vitally, future. What factors in its business environment have contributed to the company's success? Which of these factors are likely to become more (or less) important as the company looks ahead? Exhibit 2.5 classifies the factors as competitive dynamics, culture/values, social and political context, employee/union needs, and other HR systems.

Competitive Dynamics

This first step includes an understanding of the industry in which the organization operates and how it plans to compete. To cope with the turbulent competitive dynamics, focus on what factors in the business environment (i.e., changing customer needs, competitors' actions, changing labor market conditions, changing regulations, globalization) are im-

[12]H. Mintzberg, "Crafting Strategy," *Harvard Business Review,* July–August 1970, pp. 66–75.

EXHIBIT 2.5   **Key Steps in Formulating a Total Compensation Strategy**

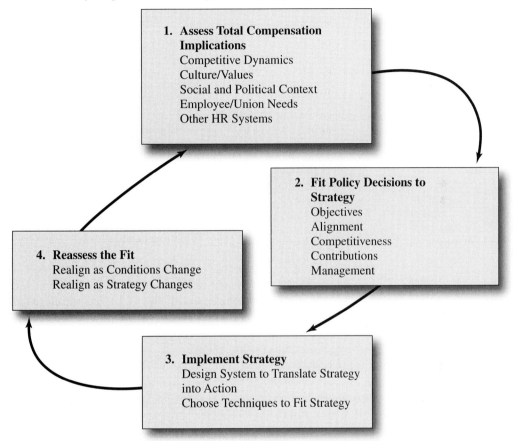

1. **Assess Total Compensation Implications**
   Competitive Dynamics
   Culture/Values
   Social and Political Context
   Employee/Union Needs
   Other HR Systems

2. **Fit Policy Decisions to Strategy**
   Objectives
   Alignment
   Competitiveness
   Contributions
   Management

3. **Implement Strategy**
   Design System to Translate Strategy into Action
   Choose Techniques to Fit Strategy

4. **Reassess the Fit**
   Realign as Conditions Change
   Realign as Strategy Changes

portant today. What will be important in the future? Start with the basics. What is your business strategy? How do you compete to win? How should the compensation system change to support that strategy? Learn to gauge the underlying dynamics in your business (or build relationships with those who can). We have already discussed fitting different compensation strategies with different business strategies using the examples of cost cutter, customer centered, and innovator (Exhibit 2.4). But be cautious: Reality is more complex and chaotic. Organizations are not necessarily innovators or cost cutters or customer-centered. Instead, they are some of each, and more. So the rational and orderly image conveyed in Exhibit 2.5 does not adequately capture the turbulent competitive dynamics underlying this process.[13]

[13]Peter F. Drucker, "They're Not Employees, They're People," *Harvard Business Review,* February 2002, pp. 70–77; Jessica Collison and Cassandra Frangos, "Aligning HR with Organization Strategy" Survey, SHRM/Balanced Scorecard Collaborative, Alexandria, VA, November 2002.

EXHIBIT 2.6
Toshiba's
Managerial
Compensation
Plan, Annual
Amount (in
Yen)

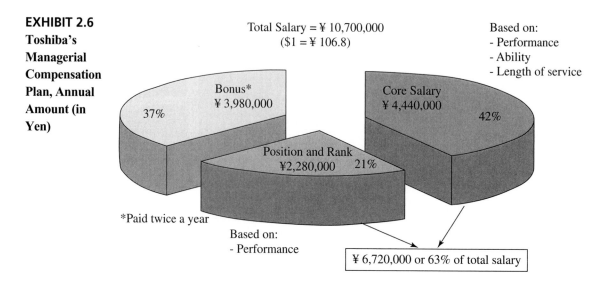

Total Salary = ¥ 10,700,000
($1 = ¥ 106.8)

Based on:
- Performance
- Ability
- Length of service

Bonus*
¥ 3,980,000
37%

Core Salary
¥ 4,440,000
42%

Position and Rank
¥2,280,000   21%

*Paid twice a year

Based on:
- Performance

¥ 6,720,000 or 63% of total salary

Competitive dynamics can be assessed globally.[14] However, comparing pay among countries is complex. In Chapter 1, we noted differences in hourly labor costs and productivity (output per dollar of wages) among countries. But as we shall see in Chapter 16, countries also differ on the average length of the workweek, the average number of paid holidays, the kinds of national health care and retirement programs, and even how pay is determined.[15] Nevertheless, managers must become knowledgeable about the pay systems of their global competitors. Exhibit 2.6 describes Toshiba's total cash compensation for its managers. Bonuses constitute 37 percent of a Toshiba manager's pay, compared to about 10 percent for a typical U.S. manager. Because these bonuses are paid twice a year rather than in a biweekly paycheck, they give Toshiba a cash flow advantage. While bonuses are not added into the employee's base pay, they are "guaranteed," or expected. Japan levies payroll taxes on base wages only (in the exhibit, "core salary"), not on bonuses or allowances. Hence, the mix of forms at Toshiba (and most Japanese employers) emphasizes bonuses and allowances. A common misperception is that Japanese pay systems are based solely on seniority, but Toshiba's managers' pay depends on educa-

[14]Watson Wyatt Worldwide, "Strategic Rewards: Managing through Uncertain Times," survey report, 2001/2002; G. T. Milkovich and M. Bloom, "Rethinking International Compensation: From National Cultures to Markets and Strategic Flexibility," *Compensation and Benefits Review,* January 1998, pp. 1–10; Atul Mitra, Matt Bloom, and George Milkovich, "Crossing a Raging River: Seeking Far-Reaching Solutions to Global Pay Challenges," *WorldatWork Journal* 22(2) (Second Quarter 2002); M. Bloom and G. Milkovich, "Strategic Perspectives on International Compensation and Reward Systems," in *Research and Theory in Strategic HRM: An Agenda for the Twenty-First Century,* eds. Pat Wright et al. (Greenwich, CT: JAI Press, 1999); M. Bloom, G. Milkovich, & A. Mitra, "International Compensation: Learning from How Managers Respond to Variations in Local Host Contexts." *International Journal of Human Resource Management* special issue, 2003; Allen D. Engle, Sr., and Mark Mendenhall, "Transnational Roles and Transnational Rewards: Global Integration in Executive Compensation," presentation at International HR conference, Limerick, Ireland, June 2003; Paul Evans, Vlado Pucik, and Jean-Louis Barsoux, *The Global Challenge* (New York: McGraw-Hill, 2002).

[15]See the Bureau of Labor Statistics website for the most current figures on international wage comparisons: *www.bls.gov.*

EXHIBIT 2.7   Strategic Differences in Pay Forms at Daimler and Chrysler

Managerial Total Pay at Chrysler
"As Little as 25% in Base Pay"

Managerial Total Pay at Daimler
"Up to 60% in Base Pay"

□ Base
□ Bonus + Options

□ Base
□ Bonus

tional level (ability), experience (i.e., seniority), and performance. Toshiba's use of performance-based pay is not unique in Japan. Toyota, Mitsubishi, and other traditional Japanese firms are also increasing their performance-based plans.[16]

The importance of competitive dynamics globally is highlighted in Daimler-Benz's acquisition of Chrysler. At the time, the pay of the top 10 Daimler executives amounted to $10.7 million, compared to over $11 million paid to Chrysler's CEO alone. Such differences were not confined to the top executives. They rippled throughout the newly merged company. Exhibit 2.7 shows that at Chrysler, as little as 25 percent of managers' pay is base salary. Performance-based bonuses and stock options made up the rest. At Daimler, up to 60 percent of managers' pay was in the form of base salary. Because of German tax codes at the time of the merger (since changed), stock options were used sparingly. So what difference does this make? If DaimlerChrysler is to win in the worldwide automobile market with a new global business strategy, it must consider the implications of how it compensates its company leadership worldwide rather than just nationwide.

Culture/Values

A pay system reflects the values that guide an employer's behaviors and underlie its treatment of its employees. The pay system mirrors the company's image and reputation. Exhibit 2.8 shows the value statements for Medtronic and Microsoft, companies also mentioned in Chapter 1. Medtronic's value 5 recognizes employees' worth by fostering "personal satisfaction in work accomplished, security, advancement opportunity, and means to share in the company's success." Its compensation strategy reflects this value by including work/life balance programs for security, incentives, and stock options to share the company's success. Microsoft gives its mission and values statement—"to enable people and businesses throughout the world to realize their full potential"—a prominent place on the company's website. Preserving its core values is one of the objectives of its compensation system (Exhibit 2.1).

But there are some skeptics out there. Dilbert's "Mission Statement Generator" (*www. unitedmedia.com/comics/dilbert/games*) reflects a cynical view of value statements. One study described them as "an assemblage of trite phrases which impressed no one." In contrast, Johnson and Johnson considers its statement "the glue that holds our corporation together."[17]

---

[16]A. Harney, "Toyota Plans Pay Based on Merit," *Financial Times,* July 8, 1999, p. 20; Yoshio Yanadori and George Milkovich, "Minimizing Wage Competition? Entry-level Compensation in Japanese Firms," working paper, Center for Advanced HR Studies, Ithaca, NY, 2003.

[17]S. Greenhouse, "Mission Statements: Words That Can't Be Set to Music," *New York Times,* June 21, 2000, p. C1.

EXHIBIT 2.8   Comparison of Medtronic and Microsoft Mission and Values

Medtronic Values

Medtronic's mission imparts stability and provides a firm foundation for the company's growth. Written more than 30 years ago, our mission statement gives purpose to our work, describes the values we live by, and is the motivation behind every action we take.

1. To contribute to human welfare by application of biomedical engineering in the research, design, manufacture,and sale of instruments or appliances that alleviate pain, restore health, and extend life.
2. To direct our growth in the areas of biomedical engineering where we display maximum strength and ability; to gather people and facilities that tend to augment these areas; to continuously build on these areas through education and knowledge assimilation; to avoid participation in areas where we cannot make unique and worthy contributions.
3. To strive without reserve for the greatest possible reliability and quality in our products; to be the unsurpassed standard of comparison and to be recognized as a company of dedication, honesty, integrity, and service.
4. To make a fair profit on current operations to meet our obligations, sustain our growth, and reach our goals.
5. To recognize the personal worth of employees by providing an employment framework that allows personal satisfaction in work accomplished, security, advancement opportunity, and means to share in the company's success.
6. To maintain good citizenship as a company.

Microsoft Values

There are two key aspects to Microsoft's past and future success: our vision of technology and the values that we live by every day as a company. To reflect our role as an industry leader and to focus our efforts on the opportunities ahead, we have embraced a new corporate mission:

To enable people and businesses throughout the world to realize their full potential

Delivering on this mission requires a clearly defined set of values and tenets. Our company values are not new, but have recently been articulated to reinforce our new mission.

Achieving our mission requires great people who are bright, creative, and energetic, and who share the following values:

• Integrity and honesty.
• Passion for customers, partners, and technology.
• Open and respectful with others and dedicated to making them better.
• Willingness to take on big challenges and see them through.
• Self-critical, questioning, and committed to personal excellence and self-improvement
• Accountable for commitments, results, and quality to customers, shareholders, partners, and employees.

Source: Both companies publish their values statement on their company websites: *www.microsoft.com* and *www.medtronic.com.* Medtronic publishes theirs in six languages.

Social and Political Context

Context refers to a wide range of factors, including legal and regulatory requirements, cultural differences, changing workforce demographics, expectations, and the like. These also affect compensation choices. In the case of Starbucks, business is very people-intensive. Consequently, Starbucks managers expect that an increasingly diverse workforce and increasingly diverse forms of pay (child care, chemical dependency counseling, educational reimbursements, employee assistance programs) may add value and be difficult for competitors (fast-food outlets and other coffee shops) to imitate.

As Starbucks continues to open more shops in Beijing, Tokyo, Paris, and Prague, it is finding that workforce diversity takes on a whole new meaning.[18] Cultural norms about minorities' and women's work roles and pay may be at odds with Starbucks' values and compensation strategy. Operating in different regions of the world requires more flexible approaches to pay.

Because governments are major stakeholders in determining compensation, lobbying to influence laws and regulations may also be part of compensation strategies. In the United States, employers will not sit by while Congress considers taxing employee benefits. Similarly, the European Union's "social contract" is a matter of interest for the Starbucks leadership. And in China, Starbucks has undoubtedly discovered that building relationships with government officials is essential. So, from a strategic perspective, managers of compensation may try to shape the sociopolitical environment as well as be shaped by it.

Employee Needs

The simple fact that employees differ is too easily overlooked in formulating a compensation strategy. Individual employees join the organization, make investment decisions, interact with customers, design new products, assemble components, and so on. Individual employees receive the pay. A major limitation of contemporary pay systems is the degree to which individual needs and preferences are ignored. Older, highly paid workers may wish to defer taxes by putting their pay into retirement funds, while younger employees may have high cash needs to buy a house, support a family, or finance an education. Dual-career couples who are overinsured medically may prefer to use more of their combined pay for child care, automobile insurance, financial counseling, or other benefits such as flexible schedules. Employees who have young children or dependent parents may desire dependent care coverage.[19]

Watson Wyatt, a major compensation consulting firm, asked different groups of employees about their pay preferences. Exhibit 2.9 shows the results.[20] Low-income employees rank flexible work schedules, paid time off, and benefits as their top three preferences; for those over 50, above-average total cash (base plus bonus) ranks highest. The under-30 crowd rank opportunities for advancement, skill development, and flexible schedules the highest. These differences are consistent with the idea of customizing pay to meet individual needs and preferences. However, preferences are notoriously unstable and change with economic and personal conditions that people face. (People under 30 inevitably turn 30.)

---

[18]*Competing in a Global Economy* (Bethesda, MD: Watson Wyatt Worldwide, 1998); Dan Cable and Tim Judge, "Pay Preferences and Job Search Decisions: A Person-Organization Fit Perspective," *Personnel Psychology,* Summer 1994, pp. 317–348; Timothy A. Judge, Carl J. Thoresen, Joyce E. Bono, and Gregory K. Patton, "The Job Satisfaction–Job Performance Relationship: A Qualitative and Quantitative Review," *Psychological Bulletin* 127(3) (2001), pp. 376–407; Rosemary Batt, Alexander J. S. Colvin, and Jeffrey Keefe, "Employee Voice, Human Resource Practices, and Quit Rates: Evidence from the Telecommunications Industry," *Industrial and Labor Relations Review* 55(4) (July 2002), pp. 573–594; Watson Wyatt Worldwide, "Strategic Rewards: Charting the Course Forward: Maximizing the Value of Reward Programs," survey report, 2002/2003; J. Stewart Black, "Time to Get Back to the Basics," in "Mastering People Management" *Financial Times,* November 19, 2001, pp. 2–3.

[19]R. Winslow and C. Gentry, "Give Workers Money and Let Them Buy a Plan," *Wall Street Journal,* February 8, 2000, p. A1.

[20]Watson Wyatt Worldwide, "Strategic Rewards: Managing through Uncertain Times," survey report, 2001/2002.

EXHIBIT 2.9   **Watson Wyatt Survey of Pay Preferences**

Male	Female	Professional/ Technical	Secretarial/ Production	Under $35K
Above-average total cash	Flexible work schedules	Above-average total cash	Paid time off ·	Flexible work schedules
Above-average base pay	Skill development	Flexible work schedules	Group benefits	Paid time off
Skill development	Above-average base pay	Skill development	Above-average base pay	Group benefits
Advancement opportunities	Above-average total cash	Above-average base pay	Flexible work schedules	Skill development
Group benefits	Advancement opportunities	Cash-based long-term incentives	Skill development	Cash-based long-term incentives

$95K+	Age 50+	Under Age 30	1-Year Tenure or Less	10-Year Tenure or More
Above-average total cash	Above-average total cash	Advancement opportunities	Above-average total cash	Above-average base pay
Above-average base pay	Above-average base pay	Skill development	Cash-based long-term incentives	Above-average total cash
Skill development	Stock grants	Flexible work schedules	Above-average base pay	Stock grants
Advancement opportunities	Group benefits	Above-average total cash	Advancement opportunities	Skill development
Group incentives	Retention/stay bonus	Career development	Skill development	Retirement plan

Source: Watson Wyatt Worldwide, "Strategic Rewards: Managing through Uncertain Times," 2001/2002.

Customization and Flexibility

Perhaps it is time to consider letting employees choose their pay forms. Putting people in the driver's seat is not going to happen overnight. Unlimited choice would meet with disapproval from the U.S. Internal Revenue Service and would be a challenge to design and manage. (Health benefits are not viewed by the IRS as income.) Offering greater choice to employees in different nations would open a bewildering maze of codes and regulations. Nevertheless, pay systems in the United States are increasingly being designed to encourage some employee choices. Flexible benefits and customized health care and retirement plans are examples.[21] General Mills even allows many employees to swap several weeks' salary for stock options. The company believes that allowing employees their

[21]Melissa Barringer and George Milkovich, "Employee Health Insurance Decisions in a Flexible Benefit Environment," *Human Resource Management* 35 (1996), pp. 293–315; M. P. Patterson, "Health Benefit Evolutions for the 21st Century: Vouchers and Other Innovations?" *Compensation and Benefits Review* 32(4) (July/August 2000), pp. 6–14.

choice adds value and is difficult for other companies to imitate—it is a source of competitive advantage for General Mills. Whether or not this belief is correct remains to be studied.

Unions

Pay strategies also need to be adapted to the nature of the union-management relationship.[22] Strategies for dealing with unions vary widely. The Denver School Board and the teachers union (American Federation of Teachers) agreed to experiment with performance-based pay for teachers. Conversely, the teachers union in a Philadelphia suburb walked off the job when the local school board attempted to install performance-based pay.

Even though union membership among private-sector workers in the United States is now just under 10 percent of the workforce, union influence on pay decisions remains significant. Union preferences for different forms of pay (e.g., retirement, improved health care plans) and their concern with job security affect pay strategy. A recent study found that when union workers were included in a performance-based pay plan, managers also received greater pay and the differences in pay between managers and union workers were reduced.[23]

Internationally, the role of unions in pay determination varies greatly. In some European nations (Germany, Sweden, Belgium, Spain), unions are major players in all strategic pay decisions. Union interests are part of pressures that help shape compensation strategies.

Prominence of Pay in Overall HR Strategy: Supporting Player or Catalyst for Change?

The pay strategy is also influenced by how it fits with other HR systems in the organization. If an organization is decentralized and emphasizes flexibility, then a centralized and confidential pay system controlled by a few people in a corporate unit will not work.

The importance of fit between pay and other HR systems is illustrated in the "high-performance" approaches created at IBM, Eaton, and Motorola.[24] High-performance systems generally include three features: (1) high skill/knowledge requirements (selective hiring), (2) work designed so that employees have discretion and opportunities to collaborate with others (teams) and continue to learn (training and development), and (3) performance-based pay systems. Whatever the overall HR strategy, a decision about the prominence of pay in that HR strategy is required. Pay can be a supporting player, as in the high-performance approach, or it can take the lead and be a catalyst for change. Whatever the role, compensation is embedded in the total HR approach.

---

[22]Morris M. Kleiner, Jonathan S. Leonard, and Adam M. Pilarski, "How Industrial Relations Affects Plant Performance: The Case of Commercial Aircraft Manufacturing," *Industrial and Labor Relations Review* 55(2) (January 2002), pp. 195–218.

[23]Rosemary Batt, Alexander J. S. Colvin, and Jeffrey Keefe, "Employee Voice, Human Resource Practices, and Quit Rates: Evidence from the Telecommunications Industry," *Industrial and Labor Relations Review* 55(4) (July 2002), pp. 573–594; ; A. Colvin, R. Batt, and H. Katz, "How High Performance HR Practices and Workforce Unionization Affect Managerial Pay," *Personnel Psychology* 54 (2001) pp. 903–934.

[24]Eileen Butensky, "Eaton Corporation Compensation Summary," presentation at Cornell University, March 7, 2003.

In sum, assessing the compensation implications of all the above factors, including the organization's business strategy, the global competitive dynamics, the organization's culture and values, the sociopolitical context, employee needs, unions, and how pay fits with other HR systems, is necessary to formulate a compensation strategy.

Step 2: Map a Total Compensation Strategy

The compensation strategy is made up of the five choices outlined in the pay model: objectives, alignment, competitiveness, contributions, and management. Mapping these decisions is step 2 in developing a compensation strategy. The aim is to make the right compensation choices based on how the organization competes.

Strategic maps offer a picture of a company's compensation strategy. Mapping is often used in marketing to clarify and communicate a product's identity. It can also clarify the message that the company is trying to deliver with its compensation system.

Exhibit 2.10 maps the compensation strategies of Microsoft and Bristol-Myers Squibb. The five strategy dimensions are subdivided into a number of descriptors rated on impor-

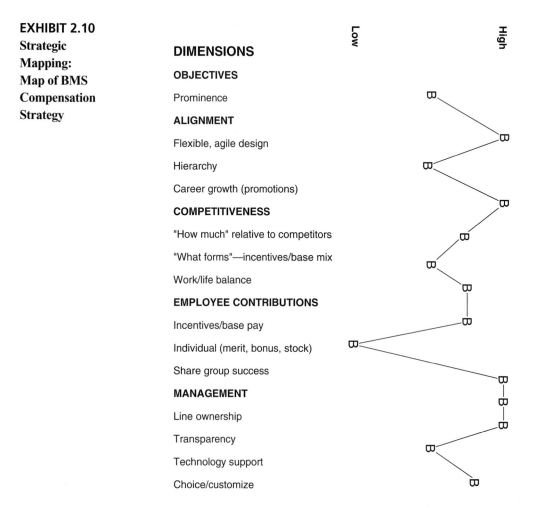

EXHIBIT 2.10
Strategic Mapping: Map of BMS Compensation Strategy

tance. These ratings are from your fearless (read "tenured") authors. They are not ratings assigned by managers in the companies. The descriptors used under each of the strategy dimensions can be modified as a company sees fit. In the illustration:

Objectives: Prominence—how important is total compensation in the overall HR strategy? Is it a catalyst, playing a lead role? Or is it less important, playing a more supporting character to other HR programs? At Microsoft, compensation is rated highly prominent, whereas at BMS it is more supportive.

Alignment: This is described in terms of flexibility, the degree of internal hierarchy, and how well compensation supports career growth. Both BMS and Microsoft use pay to support flexible work design and promotions, but Microsoft is more individual-oriented compared to BMS, whose focus is on teams and philosophy is "everyone is a leader."

Competitiveness: This is described as the total pay relative to what competitors offer (how much?) and the importance of incentives relative to base pay (what forms?). The

EXHIBIT 2.10
continued
Map of Microsoft Compensation Strategy

importance of work/life balance achieved via benefits and services is also included. According to the strategy map, Microsoft's competitive position is critical to its pay strategy, whereas BMS competes on factors other than total pay.

Contributions: These two companies take a very different approach to performance-based pay. BMS emphasizes team- and group-based success sharing (no individual-based performance pay). This is consistent with its overall approach. Microsoft is a heavy user of pay based on individual performance.

Management: This is described in terms of ownership (non-HR managers' role in managing pay), transparency (openness and communication about pay), technology (software support to administer pay), and the degree of employee choices and customization. As one might expect, Microsoft is rated high on the use of technology to manage the pay system but rates lower than BMS on the importance placed on communications and employee choice.

The profile on the strategy map reflects the main message or "pay brand" for each company:

Microsoft: Total compensation is prominent, with a strong emphasis on market competitiveness and performance-based strategy.

BMS: Total compensation plays a vital support role in the success-sharing strategy. Competitive market position, flexibility, work/life balance, and open communications are the hallmarks.

In contrast to the verbal description in Exhibit 2.1, strategic maps provide a visual reference. They are useful in creating a compensation strategy that is focused and clearly understood by employees and managers.[25] Maps do *not* tell what strategy is "best." Rather, they provide a framework and guidance. They can be used to achieve consensus on what the strategy should be. Just like a road map, they can show where you are going.[26]

The rest of the book discusses these compensation decisions in detail. It is important to realize, however, that the decisions on the five dimensions work in concert. It is the totality of the decisions that forms the compensation strategy.

Steps 3 and 4: Implement and Reassess

Step 3 is to implement the strategy through the design and execution of the compensation system. The compensation system translates strategy into practice—and into people's bank accounts. Step 4, reassess and realign, closes the loop. This step recognizes that the compensation strategy must change to fit changing conditions. Thus, periodic reassessment is needed.

Managing the links between the compensation strategy (those grand policy decisions) and the pay system (those techniques used to pay people) and people's perceptions and behaviors (those behaviors that either make money for the company or don't) is vital to implementing a pay strategy.

[25]W. Chan Kim and Renee Mauborgne, "Pursuing the Holy Grail of Clear Vision," *Financial Times,* August 6, 2002, p. 8; Robert S. Kaplan and David P. Norton, "Having Trouble with Your Strategy? Then Map It," *Harvard Business Review,* September–October 2000, pp. 167–176.

[26]George Milkovich and Carolyn Milkovich, *Cases in Compensation,* 9th ed. (Santa Monica, CA: Milkovich, 2004), p. 8.

SOURCE OF COMPETITIVE ADVANTAGE: THREE TESTS

Designing and implementing a pay strategy that is a source of sustained competitive advantage is easier said than done. Not all compensation decisions are strategic or a source of competitive advantage. Three tests determine whether a pay strategy is a source of advantage: (1) Is it aligned? (2) Does it differentiate? (3) Does it add value?[27]

Align

Alignment of the pay strategy includes three aspects, as we have already discussed: (1) align with the business strategy, (2) align externally with the economic and sociopolitical conditions, and (3) align internally within the overall HR system. Alignment is probably the easiest test to pass.

Differentiate

Some believe that the only thing that really matters about a strategy is how it is different from everyone else's.[28] If the pay system is relatively simple for any competitor to copy, then how can it possibly be a source of competitive advantage? The answer, according to the advocates of the strategic approach, is that sustained advantage comes from how the pay system is managed. This rhetoric is appealing, but the evidence to support it is slim.

The map profiles in Exhibit 2.10 show how the two companies' strategies differ. One uses pay as a strong signal; the other uses pay to support its "everyone is a leader" HR strategy. Both organizations claim to have performance cultures; their strategies differ. Are they difficult to imitate? Probably, since each strategy is woven into the fabric of the company's overall HR strategy. Copying one or another strategy means ripping apart the overall approach and patching in a new one. So, in a sense, the alignment test (weaving the fabric) helps ensure passing the differentiation test. Microsoft's use of stock awards for all employees, often worth considerably more than people's base pay, is difficult for its competitors to copy. The Medtronic and SAS work-family-balance and total-presence-at-the-workplace strategies are difficult to copy. It may be relatively easy to copy any individual thing a competitor does (i.e., grant stock options to more employees or offer more choice in their medical insurance). But the strategic perspective implies that it is the *way* programs fit together and fit the organization that is hard to copy. Simply copying others, blindly benchmarking and following so-called best practices, amounts to trying to stay in the race—not win it.

[27]J. Barney, "Firm Resources and Sustained Competitive Advantage," *Journal of Management* 17 (1997), pp. 99–120; P. M. Wright, B. Dunford, and S. Snell, "HR and the Resource-Based View of the Firm," *Journal of Management* 27 (2001), pp. 701–721.
[28]Simon London, "The Growing Pains of Business," *Financial Times,* May 8, 2003, p. B1; Preston McAffee, *Competitive Solutions: The Strategist's Toolkit* (Princeton, NJ: Princeton University Press).

Cybercomp: Compensation Consultants

Compensation consultants are major players, and practically every organization uses at least one for data and advice. So learning more about the services these consultants offer is useful. Go to the website of at least two of them. You can choose from the consulting firms listed below or find others.

Fred Cook	*www.fredericwcook.com*
Wyatt Watson Worldwide	*www.watsonwyatt.com*
Hay	*haygroup.com*
Mercer	*www.mercer.com*
Link Group	*www.linkg.co.uk*
Towers Perrin	*www.towersperrin.com*
Clark Consulting	*www.clarkconsulting.com*

1. Compare consultants. From their websites, construct a chart comparing their stated values and culture and their business strategies, and highlight the services offered.
2. Critically assess whether their strategies and services are unique and/or difficult to imitate. Which one would you select (based on the web information) to help you formulate a company's total compensation strategy?
3. Based on the web information, which one would you prefer to work for? Why?
4. Be prepared to share this information with others in class.

Result: If everyone does a great job on this Cybercomp, you will all have useful information on consultants.

For more background, see Lewis Pinault, *Consulting Demons: Inside the Unscrupulous World of Global Corporate Consulting* (New York: Harpers Business, 2000), and Fred Cook, "A Personal Perspective of the Consulting Profession," *ACA News,* October 1999, pp. 35–43.

Add Value

Organizations today continue to look for the return they are getting from their incentives, benefits, and even base pay. Compensation is often a company's largest controllable expense. Since consultants and a few researchers treat different forms of pay as investments, the task is to come up with ways to calculate the return on those investments (ROI). But this is a difficult proposition. As one writer put it, "It is easier to count the bottles than describe the wine."[29] Costs are easy to fit into a spreadsheet, but any value created as a result of those costs is difficult to specify, much less measure.[30]

Trying to measure an ROI for any compensation strategy implies that people are "human capital," similar to other factors of production. Many people find this view dehu-

---

[29]Thomas Stewart, *Intellectual Capital: The New Wealth of Organizations* (New York: Currency, 1997).

[30]John Boudreau and Peter M. Ramstad, "Measuring Intellectual Capital: Learning from Financial History," *Human Resource Management* 36(3) (Fall 1997), pp. 343–356; Watson Wyatt Worldwide, "Human Capital Index: Human Capital as a Lead Indicator of Shareholder Value," *www.watsonwyatt.com,* 2001; Brian Becker, Mark Huselid, and Dave Ulrich, *The HR Scorecard: Linking People, Strategy, and Performance* (Boston: Harvard Business School Press, 2001).

manizing. They argue that viewing pay as an investment with measurable returns diminishes the importance of treating employees fairly.[31] No doubt about it, of the three tests of strategy—align, differentiate, add value—the last is the most difficult.

It is possible to align and differentiate and still fail to add value. The incentive plan at consumer electronics retailer Circuit City paid off big for experienced, high-performing salespeople: At its retail stores, salespeople who moved more than $1 million a year could earn over $50,000 in salary and sales bonuses. One successful salesperson knew the products and kept up to date so well that customers would seek him out for advice before they made a purchase. Circuit City's compensation strategy aligned with its business by rewarding such experienced top performers.

The strategy also differentiated Circuit City from archrival Best Buy. Best Buy featured self-service stores with huge inventories. It hired young, less-experienced people and offered lower wages and smaller bonuses. But, in today's economy, Best Buy's sales and total shareholder returns soared past those of Circuit City. The compensation strategy at both companies aligned with their business strategies; they also differentiated. But Circuit City's compensation strategy no longer added value when compared to Best Buy's. Recently Circuit City laid off 3,900 top-earning salespeople and replaced them with 2,100 less-experienced people who receive lower wages and smaller bonuses. Circuit City says it can no longer afford to pay big commissions to its sales staff while its rivals pay less.[32]

Are there advantages to an innovative compensation strategy? We do know that in products and services, first movers (innovators) have well-recognized advantages that can offset the risks involved—high margins, market share, and mindshare (brand recognition).[33] But we do not know whether such advantages accrue to innovators in total compensation. A recent Ford innovation was giving computers to its 360,000 employees around the world. Toyota and Honda responded by saying they did not see the value added by such a move, and General Motors and DaimlerChrysler claimed to be "studying" it.

[31]Jeffrey Pfeffer, "Pitfalls on the Road to Measurement: The Dangerous Liaison of Human Resources with the Ideas of Accounting and Finance," *Human Resource Management* 36(3) (Fall 1997), pp. 357–365; J. Pfeffer, "When It Comes to 'Best Practices,' Why Do Smart Organizations Occasionally Do Dumb Things?" *Organizational Dynamics* 25 (1997), pp. 33–44; J. Pfeffer, *The Human Equation: Building Profits by Putting People First* (Boston: Harvard Business School Press, 1998); P. Wright, L. Dyer, and M. Takla, "Execution: The Critical 'What's Next' in Strategic HRM," CAHRS Working Paper 99–11, Ithaca, NY, 1999; D. Koys, "Describing the Elements of Business and HR Strategy Statements," *Journal of Business and Psychology* 15 (Winter 2000); Richard Donkin, "Challenge to 'Human Capital' Assumption," *Financial Times,* October 4, 2002, p. VI; Richard Donkin, "Measuring the Worth of Human Capital," *Financial Times,* November 7, 2002; Peter F. Drucker, "They're Not Employees, They're People," *Harvard Business Review,* February 2002, pp. 70–77; Stephen Gates, *Value at Work: The Risks and Opportunities of Human Capital Measurement and Reporting* (New York: Conference Board, 2002); Jakub Sovina and Christopher Collins, "The Effects of Organizational Brand Equity on Employment Brand Equity and Recruitment Outcomes," presentation at Academy of Management annual meetings, Seattle, 2003.

[32]Carlos Tejada and Gary McWilliams, "New Recipe for Cost Savings: Replace Expensive Workers," *Wall Street Journal,* June 11, 2002, pp. 1, A12.

[33]Connie Willis, *Bellwether* (London: Bantam Books, 1996); M. Gladwell, *The Tipping Point: The Next Big Thing* (Boston: Little, Brown, 2000); Patrick M. Wright, Benjamin B. Dunford, and Scott A. Snell, "Human Resources and the Resource Based View of the Firm," *Journal of Management* 27 (2001), pp. 701–721.

What, if any, benefits accrued to Microsoft, one of the first to offer very large stock options to all employees, once many competitors did the same thing? What about TRW or American Can Company (since acquired by another company), among the first to offer flexible benefit programs? Does a compensation innovator attract more and better people? Induce people to stay and contribute? Are there cost advantages? Studies are needed to find the answers.

"BEST FIT" VERSUS "BEST PRACTICES"

The premise of any strategic perspective is that if managers align pay decisions with the organization's strategy and values, are responsive to employees and union relations, and are globally competitive, then the organization is more likely to achieve competitive advantage.[34] The challenge is to design the "fit" with the environment, business strategy, and pay plan. The better the fit, the greater the competitive advantage.

But not everyone agrees. In contrast to the notion of strategic fit, some believe that (1) a set of best-pay practices exists and (2) these practices can be applied universally across situations.[35] Rather than having a better fit between business strategy and compensation plans that yields better performance, they say that using best practices results in better performance with almost any business strategy.

The premise in this perspective is that adopting best-pay practices will allow the employer to gain preferential access to superior employees. These superior people will in turn influence the strategy the organization adopts and be the source of its competitive advantage.

If best practices do exist, what are they? It depends on whom you ask. Exhibit 2.11 summarizes two different views. One view is called the "new pay." Employee pay is based primarily on market rates; pay increases depend on performance (not cost of living or seniority increases); and the employment relationship is a partnership in which success (and risk) is shared.

A competing set of best practices, "high commitment," prescribes having high base pay, sharing performance success only (not risk), guaranteeing employment security, promoting from within, and the like. These practices are believed to attract and retain a highly committed workforce, which will become the source of competitive advantage.

[34]J. Purcell, "Best Practices and Best Fit: Chimera or Cul-de-Sac?" *Human Resources Management Journal* 9(3), pp. 26–41; Andrew S. Grove, *Only the Paranoid Survive* (New York: Doubleday, 1996).

[35]J. R. Schuster, and Patricia Zingheim *The New Pay* (San Francisco: Jossey-Bass, 1996); E. Lawler, *Rewarding Excellence* (San Francisco: Jossey-Bass, 2000); T. Kochan and P. Osterman, *The Mutual Gains Enterprise* (Boston: Harvard Business School Press, 1994); P. K. Zingheim and J. R. Schuster, *Pay People Right!* (San Francisco: Jossey-Bass, 2000);. J. Pfeffer, "Seven Practices of Successful Organizations," *California Management Review* 49(2) (1998), pp. 96–124.

EXHIBIT 2.11
Best-Practices Options

The New Pay	High Commitment
• External market-sensitive-based pay, not internal alignment	• High wages: You get what you pay for
• Variable performance-based pay, not annual increases	• Guarantee employment security
• Risk-sharing partnership, not entitlement	• Apply incentives; share gains, not risks
• Flexible opportunities to contribute, not jobs	• Employee ownership
• Lateral promotions, not career path	• Participation and empowerment
• Employability, not job security	• Teams, not individuals, are base units
• Teams, not individual contributors	• Smaller pay differences
	• Promotion from within
	• Selective recruiting
	• Enterprisewide information sharing
	• Training, cross-training, and skill development are crucial
	• Symbolic egalitarianism adds value
	• Long-term perspective matters
	• Measurement matters

Source: for the left column: J. R. Schuster, *The New Pay;* E. Lawler, *Rewarding Excellence;* for the right column: J. Pfeffer, "Seven Advantages of Successful Organizations." (See footnote 35.)

SO WHAT MATTERS MOST—BEST PRACTICES OR BEST FIT?

It would be nice to be able to say which compensation strategy best fits each situation or which list of best practices truly represents the best. Unfortunately, little research has directly examined the competing views. However, there is an increasing amount of research that gets us beyond the rhetoric.[36]

One study examined eight years of data from 180 U.S. companies.[37] The authors reported that while pay levels differed among these companies, these differences were not related to

[36]B. Gerhart, "Pay Strategy and Firm Performance," in *Compensation in Organizations: Current Research and Practice,* eds. S. Rynes and B. Gerhart (San Francisco: Jossey-Bass, 2000); B. Gerhart and G. Milkovich, "Employee Compensation" in *Handbook of Industrial and Organization Psychology 3,* eds. M. Dunnette and L. Hough (Palo Alto, CA: Consulting Psychologists Press, 1992); B. Gerhart, C. Trevor, and M. E. Graham, "New Directions in Compensation Research," in *Research in Personnel and Human Resource Management,* ed. G. R. Ferris (Greenwich, CT: JAI Press, 1996); M. Bloom, "The Performance Effects of Pay Dispersion on Individuals and Organizations," *Academy of Management Journal* 42(1) (1999), pp. 7–24; H. Tosi, S. Werner, J. Katz, and L. Gomez-Mejia, "How Much Does Performance Matter? A Meta-Analysis of CEO Pay Studies," *Journal of Management* 26(2) (2000), pp. 301–339; E. Montemayer, "Congruence, Behavior, Pay Policy, and Competitive Strategy in High Performance Firms," *Journal of Management* 22 (1996), pp. 884–908.

[37]B. Gerhart and G. Milkovich, "Organization Differences in Managerial Compensation and Financial Performance," *Academy of Management Journal* 33 (1990), pp. 663–691; K. Murphy and M. Jensen, "It's Not How Much, but How You Pay," *Harvard Business Review* January–February 1993, pp. 32–45.

their subsequent financial performance. However, differences in the size of bonuses and the number of people eligible for stock options were related to future financial success of the organizations. This study concluded that it is not *how much* you pay but *how* you pay that matters; thus, bonuses and broadly based stock options are examples of best practices.

Another study not only found similar results but also reported that the effect of the compensation strategy equaled the impact of all other aspects of the HR system (high involvement, teams, training programs, etc.) combined.[38] These findings are near and dear to the hearts of many of our compensation cronies. Again, performance-based bonuses and broadly based options appear to be best practices. Money matters.

Virtuous and Vicious Circles

A group of studies suggests that emphasizing performance-based pay affects firm performance only when the organization is already doing well.[39] This phenomenon is like a circle: When there is success to share, success-sharing plans work best. As depicted in Exhibit 2.12a, an organization whose profits or market share are increasing pays out larger bonuses and stock options based on that improving oganization performance. And

EXHIBIT 2.12   Virtuous and Vicious Circles

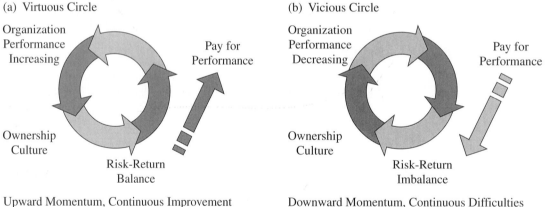

(a) Virtuous Circle

Organization Performance Increasing

Pay for Performance

Ownership Culture

Risk-Return Balance

Upward Momentum, Continuous Improvement

(b) Vicious Circle

Organization Performance Decreasing

Pay for Performance

Ownership Culture

Risk-Return Imbalance

Downward Momentum, Continuous Difficulties

[38]Brian Becker and Mark Huselid, "High Performance Work Systems and Firm Performance: A Synthesis of Research and Managerial Implications," in *Research in Personnel and Human Resource Management,* ed. G. R. Ferris (Greenwich, CT: JAI Press, 1997).

[39]B. Gerhart, "Pay Strategy and Firm Performance," in *Compensation and Organizations: Progress and Prospects,* eds. S. Rynes and B. Gerhart (San Francisco: New Lexington Press, 2000); J. Abowd, "Does Performance Based Managerial Compensation Affect Corporate Performance?" *Industrial and Labor Relations Review* 435 (1990), pp. 52S–73S; B. Gerhart and G. Milkovich, "Organization Differences in Managerial Compensation and Financial Performance," *Academy of Management Journal* 90(33), pp. 663–691; B. Becker and M. Huselid, "High Performance Work Systems and Firm Performance: A Synthesis of Research and Managerial Implications," *Research in Personnel and Human Resources,* ed. G. Ferris (Greenwich, CT: JAI Press, 1997); S. Werner and H. Tosi, "Other People's Money: The Effects of Ownership on Compensation Strategy," *Academy of Management Journal* 38(6), pp. 1672–1691; B. Hall and J. Liebman, "Are CEOs Really Paid Like Bureaucrats?" *Quarterly Journal of Economics,* August 1998, pp. 653–691.

offering these incentives boosts employee performance. Improved employee performance results in improved organization performance, and so on. The circle gains upward momentum.[40]

It cannot have escaped your attention that circles can also gain momentum going downward. As shown in Exhibit 2.12b, when organization performance declines, performance-based pay plans do not pay off; there are no bonuses, and the value of stock options declines—with potentially negative effects on organization performance.[41]

Declining organization performance increases the risks facing employees—risks of still smaller bonuses, demotions, wage cuts, and even layoffs. The increased risks, unless they are offset by larger returns, create a risk-return imbalance that reinforces the downward spiral. Unfortunately, we do not yet know what compensation strategy can be used to shift an organization caught in a downward spiral into an upward one.

Caution and more evidence are required to interpret and apply many of these studies. Nevertheless, they do seem to indicate that performance-based pay may be a best practice, under the right circumstances. Could performance-based pay sometimes be a "worst practice"?

What about evidence supporting the notion of best fit? An increasing number of studies tend to confirm that compensation strategies affect employee behaviors (e.g., turnover) and organization performance.[42] These studies focus on specific U.S. industries—auto, steel, and telecommunications—and report that high-performance work systems (which, as noted earlier, include incentives and competitive pay levels plus selective hiring, training, and work design that offers employees discretion) all acting together are more effective than any single pay program.[43]

Further supporting the perspective that HR systems are interconnected, two researchers found relationships between compensation system design and employment security.[44] They report fewer layoffs and less downsizing in companies that have more

[40]M. Bloom and G. Milkovich, "Relationships among Risk, Incentive Pay, and Organization Performance," *Academy of Management Journal* 41(3) (1998), pp. 283–297.

[41]Ibid.; J. Abowd, "Does Performance Based Managerial Compensation Affect Corporate Performance?" *Industrial and Labor Relations Review* 435 (1990), pp. 52S–73S.

[42]S. A. Snell and J. W. Dean, Jr., "Strategic Compensation for Integrated Manufacturing: The Moderating Effects of Job and Organizational Inertia," *Academy of Management Journal* 37 (1994), pp. 1109–1114.

[43]J. P. MacDuffie, "Human Resource Bundles and Manufacturing Performance: Organizational Logic and Flexible Production Systems in the World Auto Industry," *Industrial and Labor Relations Review* 48 (1995), pp. 197–221; J. B. Arthur, "Effects of Human Resource Systems on Manufacturing Performance and Turnover," *Academy of Management Journal* 37 (1994), pp. 670–687; C. Ichniowski, K. Shaw, and G. Prennush, "The Effects of HRM Practices on Productivity: A Study of Steel Finishing Lines,"*American Economic Review* 87(3) (1998), pp. 291–313; Rosemary Batt, Alexander J. S. Colvin, and Jeffrey Keefe, "Employee Voice, Human Resource Practices, and Quit Rates: Evidence from the Telecommunications Industry," *Industrial and Labor Relations Review* 55(4) (July 2002), pp. 573–594; Casey Ichniowski, Thomas A. Kochan, David Levine, Craig Olson, and George Strauss, "What Works at Work: Overview and Assessment," *Industrial Relations* 35(3) (July 1996), pp. 299–333.

[44]B. Gerhart and C. O. Trevor, "Employment Variability under Different Managerial Compensation Systems," *Academy of Management Journal* 39(6) (1996), pp. 1692–1712. Also see R. Gibbons and M. Waldman, "Careers in Organizations: Theory and Evidence," in *Handbook of Labor Economics 3,* eds. O. Ashenfelder and D. Card (Burlington, MA: Elsevier Science & Technology, 1999).

performance-based pay strategies. Managers in these companies are less likely to lay employees off in bad times because labor costs are controlled through lower pay (fewer performance incentives) rather than lower head count.

So the research to date supports the use of bonuses and stock tied to performance. What remains an open question is whether best fit matters. Do compensation systems that are aligned with the business, strategic, and environmental context and other HR systems have greater effects? Much of the research suggests that best-practice compensation strategies do have an impact; a few seem to support a best-fit model.[45]

Additionally, we do not have much information about how people perceive various pay strategies. Do all managers "see" the total compensation strategy at Firepond or BMS the same way? Some evidence suggests that if you ask 10 managers about their company's HR strategy, you get 10 different answers. If the link between the strategy and people's perceptions is not clear, then maybe we are building on unstable ground.

Your Turn   Mapping Compensation Strategies

Take any organization that you know—your current employer, your business school, the place you interned one summer, maybe even a friend's or parent's employer. Look again at Exhibit 2.10, "Strategic Mapping." Try mapping your organization's compensation strategy. Then compare it to that of Microsoft and Bristol-Myers Squibb.

1. Summarize the key points of your company's strategy.
2. What are the key differences compared to the strategies of Microsoft and Bristol-Myers Squibb?

Alternatively, ask several managers in the *same* organization to map that organization's compensation strategy. You will probably need to assist them in completing the map. Then compare the managers' maps.

1. Summarize the key similarities and differences.
2. Why do these similarities and differences occur?
3. How can maps be used to clarify and communicate compensation strategies to leaders? To employees?

[45]Edilberto F. Montemayor, "Congruence between Pay Policy and Competitive Strategy in High-Performing Firms," *Journal of Management* 22(6) (1996), pp. 889–908; L. R. Gomez-Mejia and D. B. Balkin, *Compensation, Organization Strategy, and Firm Performance* (Cincinnati: Southwestern, 1992).

Still Your Turn   Difficult to Copy?

Consider the Microsoft, Bristol-Myers Squibb, and Firepond compensation strategies depicted in Exhibit 2.1. Do they meet the tests of align, differentiate, and add value? On the face of it, these strategies seem easy to copy (or at least to articulate). But determining which one best fits an organization's business strategy and culture and the external pressures it faces may make the strategy more difficult to truly imitate. It is alignment, the fit, or the way a pay system works with other aspects of the organization that makes it difficult to imitate and adds value. It is not the techniques themselves but their interconnections that make a strategic perspective successful.

Spend some time looking at the websites of each of these three companies.[46] Look at their annual reports. What can you infer about each company's business strategy and its organization culture? Consider the industry in which each company operates. What are the external pressures each company is facing?

After you have a sense of what each company is like, decide whether you think each company's compensation strategy aligns with its business strategy, organization culture, and external pressures. How would you change it?

Summary   A strategic perspective on compensation takes the position that how employees are compensated can be a source of sustainable competitive advantage. Two alternative approaches are highlighted: a "best-fit"/contingent business strategy/environmental context approach and a "best-practices" approach. The best-fit approach presumes that one size does not fit all. Managing compensation strategically means fitting the compensation system to the business and environmental conditions. In contrast, the best-practices approach assumes that there exists a universal best way. So the focus is a question not so much of what the best strategy is but of how best to implement the system. And agreement on what are the best practices does not exist, either.

Because the best-fit approach is the most commonly used, we spent more time discussing it. The four-step process includes (1) assessing conditions, (2) deciding on the best strategic choices following the pay model (objectives, alignment, competitiveness, contributions, and management), (3) implementing the strategy through the design of the pay system, and (4) reassessing the fit.

Recent studies have begun to research what aspect of the compensation relationship really does matter, but the answer is still fuzzy. While more research is required before an answer emerges, the notion of virtuous and vicious circles has some appeal.

[46]Jaguar Technology has offered to purchase Firepond. Jaguar's website is *www.jaguartech.com.*

Review Questions

1. Select a company with which you are familiar. Or analyze the approach your college uses to pay teaching assistants and/or faculty. Infer its compensation strategy using the five issues (objectives, alignment, competitiveness, employee considerations, and management). How does your company compare to Microsoft? To Starbucks? What business strategy does it seem to "fit" (i.e., cost cutter, customer centered, innovator, or something else)?

2. Contrast the essential differences between the best-fit (strategic business-based) and best-practices perspectives.

3. Reread the culture/values statements in Exhibit 2.8. Discuss how, if at all, those values might be reflected in a compensation system. Are these values consistent with "let the market decide"?

4. Three tests for any source of competitive advantage are align, differentiate, and add value. Discuss whether these tests are difficult to pass. Can compensation really be a source of competitive advantage?

5. Set up a debate over the following proposition: The best-practices approach is superior to the "best-fit" approach when designing a compensation system.

Internal Alignment: Determining the Structure

"After struggling all morning to come up with a plot for the television season's final episode of *Everwood*, the seven writers hit their stride. Ideas for dialogue and story-lines flowed. Colin, Amy, and Bright, characters in the hit series, spend a 'perfect day' together before Colin undergoes brain surgery."[1] Okay, so maybe perfect days and brain surgery aren't everyday events. But there is not much that is everyday in the process of creating the TV series, either. Greg Berlanti, the creator and executive pro-ducer of the program, manages an unusual work process that involves over 100 peo-ple performing a wide variety of jobs. Berlanti leads the team of creative writers and manages the cast, support crew, and production crew. In addition to the writers, jobs on the series include director of photography, editor, story editor, executive story edi-tor, and gaffers, among others. Berlanti's job also includes coordinating and negotiat-ing with the network executives of Warner Brothers Television. They approve script outlines and any plot changes that require extra money, such as guest stars or new sets. Together, all these people churn out 22 episodes of *Everwood* each season.

What determines the pay for all the different types of work involved in creating *Everwood*? It seems likely that the executive story editor, Blake Neely, gets paid more than the story editor, David Schulner. How much more? Does it matter? Can a story editor be promoted to the executive-story-editor position for this or some other series? Is the story editor paid more than the accountant or the gaffer? And what's a gaffer, anyway?

What criteria are used to set pay—the content of the work itself, the value of what is contributed to each episode, the person's skill/experience/reputation? Per-haps the ratings for the show? How do pay differences between jobs in the organi-zation affect behavior? Do they support the organization's business strategy? Do they help attract and retain employees? Do they motivate employees to do their best work? Or are the pay procedures bureaucratic burdens that drive away creative talent?

So many questions! Two of them lie at the core of compensation management: (1) How is pay determined for the wide variety of work performed in organizations? And (2) how do the pay differences affect employees' attitudes and work behavior?

---

[1]Emily Nelson, "Think You've Got a Tricky Staff? Try Herding Writers," *Wall Street Journal*, May 16, 2003, pp. A1, A6.

These questions are examined within the framework of the pay model introduced in Chapter 1 and shown again in Exhibit I.1. This part of the book examines internal alignment. The focus is within the organization. What is internal alignment, what affects it, and what is affected by it are considered in Chapter 3. Chapter 4 discusses how to assess the similarities and differences in work content. Chapters 5 and 6 scrutinize job-based, skill-based, and competency-based approaches for valuing those similarities and differences and using them to determine internal pay structures.

EXHIBIT I.1 The Pay Model

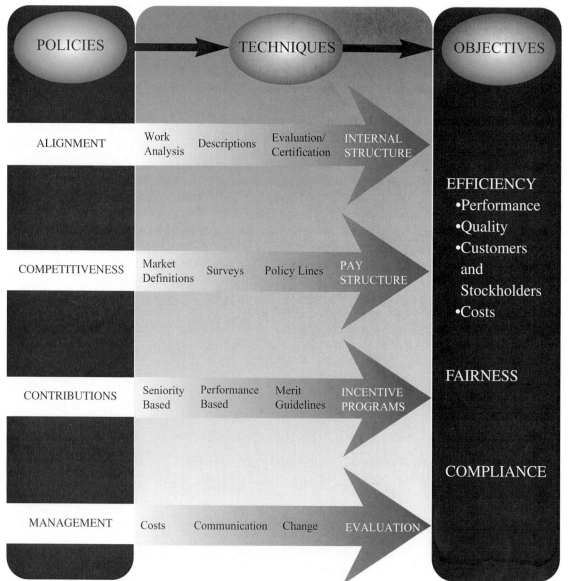

Defining Internal Alignment

Chapter Outline

For the kingdom of heaven is like a householder who went out early in the morning to hire laborers for his vineyard. And having agreed with the laborers for a denarius a day, he sent them into his vineyard. And about the third hour, he went out and saw others standing . . . idle; and he said to them, "Go you also into the vineyard, and I will give you whatever is just." And again he went out about the ninth hour, and did as before . . . But about the eleventh hour he went out and found others . . . and he said to them, "Go you also into the vineyard." When evening came, the owner said to his steward, "Call the laborers, and pay them their wages, beginning from the last even to the first." When the first in their turn came . . . they also received each his denarius. . . . They began to murmur against the householder, saying, "These last have worked a single hour, and thou hast put them on a level with us, who have borne the burden of the day's heat." But answering them, he said, "Friend, I do thee no injustice; take what is thine and go."[1]

Matthew's parable raises age-old questions about internal alignment and pay structures within a single organization.[2] The laborers felt that those "who have borne the burden of the day's heat" should be paid more. But perhaps the householder was using a different criterion: an individual's needs without regard to time worked or tasks performed.[3] Matthew doesn't tell us how the work in the vineyard was organized. Perhaps laborers worked in teams, with some trimming and others tying the vines. Does trimming require more judgment than tying?

Today's pay structures are typically designed by assessing the content of the work, the skills and knowledge required to perform it, and its relative value for achieving the organization's objectives. The procedures to do this must be acceptable to the parties involved. If not, today's managers and employees murmur, too. That murmuring translates into turnover, unwillingness to try new technologies, and even an indifference to the quality of the grapes or the customer's satisfaction with them. This chapter examines internal alignment and its consequences.

COMPENSATION STRATEGY: INTERNAL ALIGNMENT

Setting objectives was our first issue in a strategic approach. Our second, internal alignment, addresses relationships *inside* the organization. How do the responsibilities and pay of a trimmer versus tyer relate to each other? How do they relate to the responsibilities and pay of the householder's cook or the steward? Internal alignment addresses the logic underlying these relationships.

> **Internal alignment,** often called *internal equity,* refers to the pay relationships among different jobs/skills/competencies within a single organization.[4] The relationships form a pay structure that should *support the organization strategy, support the work flow, be fair to employees,* and *motivate behavior* toward organization objectives.

Exhibit 3.1 shows a structure for the engineering work at a division of Lockheed Martin, the world's largest defense contractor. Lockheed also builds rockets, shuttles, and rovers for NASA. The six levels in Lockheed's structure range from entry to consultant. You can see the relationships in the descriptions of each level of work. Decisions on how much to pay the six levels create a pay structure.

---

[1]Matthew 20: 1–16.

[2]For a history of the different standards for pay, see Thomas Mahoney, *Compensation and Reward Perspectives* (Burr Ridge, IL: Irwin, 1979); G. Milkovich and J. Stevens, "From Pay to Rewards: 100 Years of Change," *ACA Journal* 9(1) (2000), pp. 6–18; D. F. Schloss, *Methods in Industrial Remuneration* (New York: Putnam's, 1892).

[3]Several Japanese firms still base a small portion of a worker's pay on the number of dependents. In the early 1900s, workers who were "family men" received a pay supplement in some U.S. firms as well. The "iron rice bowl," which until recently prevailed in China's state enterprises, provided entire families with cradle-to-grave welfare.

[4]"Equity" could refer to stock, to some perceived balance of effort and rewards, and/or pay discrimination (gender equity). We believe "internal alignment" better reflects the meaning and importance underlying pay structures.

**EXHIBIT 3.1
Engineering
Structure at
Lockheed
Martin**

Entry Level

Engineer
Limited use of basic principles and concepts. Develops solutions to limited problems. Closely supervised.

Senior Engineer
Full use of standard principles and concepts. Provides solutions to a variety of problems. Under general supervision.

Systems Engineer
Wide applications of principles and concepts, plus working knowledge of other related disciplines. Provides solutions to a wide variety of difficult problems. Solutions are imaginative, thorough, and practicable. Works under only very general direction.

Lead Engineer
Applies extensive expertise as a generalist or specialist. Develops solutions to complex problems that require the regular use of ingenuity and creativity. Work is performed without appreciable direction. Exercises considerable latitude in determining technical objectives of assignment.

Advisor Engineer
Applies advanced principles, theories, and concepts. Contributes to the development of new principles and concepts. Works on unusually complex problems and provides solutions that are highly innovative and ingenious. Works under consultative direction toward predetermined long-range goals. Assignments are often self-initiated.

Consultant Engineer
Exhibits an exceptional degree of ingenuity, creativity, and resourcefulness. Applies and/or develops highly advanced technologies, scientific principles, theories, and concepts. Develops information that extends the existing boundaries of knowledge in a given field. Often acts independently to uncover and resolve problems associated with the development and implementation of operational programs.

**Recognized
Authority**

Pay structure refers to the array of pay rates for different work or skills within a single organization. The *number of levels,* the *differentials* in pay between the levels, and the *criteria* used to determine those differences describe the structure:

Supports Organization Strategy

Fundamentally, organizations exist for a purpose (profits, not-for-profits, government agencies, and so on). The organization's strategy tells us how it plans to achieve its purpose. Internal structures that are aligned with a strategy help achieve it. Lockheed decided that six levels of engineering work would support the research, design, and development of advanced technology systems to achieve the company's objectives. The householder's internal pay structure may have been aligned with his business strategy, but the employee dissatisfaction raises concerns about its fairness to employees.

Supports Work Flow

Work flow refers to the process by which goods and services are delivered to the customer. The pay structure ought to support the efficient flow of that work and the design of the organization.[5] For example, drug companies traditionally base the size of their sales forces on the number of physicians to be called on per day and the number of working days per year. The U.S. drug manufacturer Merck decided to take a nontraditional approach to organizing sales and marketing. Merck created teams of account executives, client representatives, and medical information scientists to serve a broader clientele of health maintenance organizations, insurance companies, and physicians. A cross-functional team responsible for a distinct geographic area (rather than a list of physician-clients) provides a relationship-building approach to selling products. Rather than hawking a specific drug and giving out free samples, the Merck teams are a source of knowledge for the physicians and the health organizations. The teams keep clients apprised of regulations and cover drugs for a wider range of medical conditions. One team even translated brochures that explain a course of treatment into Chinese, Russian, and Spanish for a physician whose patients included non-English-speaking immigrants. Such a response would have been beyond the resources of a single sales representative under Merck's old approach. (Of course, the brochure recommended treatment with Merck products.)

To support these work teams, Merck designed a new compensation structure. The pay differences between account executives, customer representatives, and medical information scientists who served on the same teams were a major issue—just as they are for Lockheed engineers and just as they likely are for the cast of *Everwood*.

Think globally. Ford Motor does. Ford acquired Volvo (Sweden), Jaguar and Land Rover (Britain), and most of Mazda (Japan). To leverage its new engineering and manufacturing knowledge, Ford is creating global teams. This changes the work flow and organization design at Ford. Ford also needs to rethink pay structures to be sure they support the new global teams. Global pay structures create special challenges due to different wages and benefits paid for the same jobs in different parts of the world. Later chapters will discuss various ways companies manage this challenge.

Supports Fairness

An internally aligned pay structure is more likely to be judged fair if it is based on the work and the skills required to perform the work and if people have an opportunity to be involved in some way in determining the pay structure.[6]

---

[5]J. S. Shaw, N. Gupta, and J. E. Delery, "Pay Dispersion and Workforce Performance: Moderating Effects of Incentives and Interdependence," *Strategic Management* 23 (2002), pp. 491–512; R. A. Guzzo and M. W. Dickson, "Teams in Organizations: Recent Research in Performance and Effectiveness," *Annual Review of Psychology* 47 (1996), pp. 307–338.

[6]Marcia P. Miceli and Paul Mulvey, "Satisfaction with Pay Systems: Antecedents and Consequences," *Industrial Relations* (January 2000), 39(1); G. Hundley and J. Kim, "National Culture and the Factors Affecting Perception of Pay Fairness in Korea and the U.S.," *International Journal of Organization Analysis* 5, pp. 325–341; M. A. Konovsky, "Understanding Procedural Justice and Its Impact on Business Organizations," *Journal of Management* 26(3) (2000), pp. 489–511; Foard F. Jones, Vida Scarpello, and Thomas Bergmann, "Pay Procedures—What Makes Them Fair?" *Journal of Occupational and Organizational Psychology* 72 (1999), pp. 129–145.

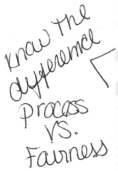

know the difference

Process vs. Fairness

Two sources of fairness are important: the *procedures* for determining the pay structure, called *procedural justice;* and the *results* of those procedures—the pay structure itself—called *distributive justice.*

Suppose you are given a ticket for speeding. Procedural justice refers to the process by which a decision is reached: the right to an attorney, the right to an impartial judge, and the right to receive a copy of the arresting officer's statement. Distributive justice refers to the fairness of the decision: guilty. Researchers report that employees' perceptions of procedural fairness significantly influence their acceptance of the results; employees and managers are more willing to accept low pay if they believe that the way this result was obtained was fair. This research also suggests that pay procedures are more likely to be perceived as fair (1) if they are consistently applied to all employees, (2) if employees participated in the process, (3) if appeals procedures are included, and (4) if the data used are accurate. Nevertheless, a newer study raises a question about the usefulness of employee participation.[7] In a low-wage company, there was no connection between employee participation and pay fairness. It may be that employees were paid so low that no amount of participation could overcome their dissatisfaction. So rather than tossing aside the idea of participation, it may be that in extreme cases (very low wages), a pay raise may trump participation.

Applied to internal structures, procedural justice addresses how design and administration decisions are made and whether procedures are applied in a consistent manner. Distributive justice addresses whether the actual internal pay differences among employees are reasonable.[8]

Motivates Behavior

Internal pay structures are part of the network of rewards discussed in Chapter 1: pay increases for promotions, bigger titles, more challenging work. The challenge is to design the structures so that they engage people to help achieve organization objectives. Merck marketing teams work together to share unique knowledge with each other and with their clients. Lockheed engineers do, too. And so do the writers, actors, and crew on *Everwood*. The structure ought to make clear the relationship between each job and the organization's objectives.[9] This is an example of "line-of-sight." The more employees can "see" or understand links between their work, the work of others, and the organization's objectives, the more likely they will be to achieve those objectives.

[7]Frederick P. Morgeson, Michael A. Campion, Carl P. Maertz, "Understanding Pay Satisfaction: The Limits of a Compensation System Implementation," *Journal of Business & Psychology* Fall 16(1) (2001), pp. 133–163.

[8]Edilberto F. Montemayor, "Decisional and Interactional Fairness: Supervisor Influence on Merit Pay Satisfaction," *Management Research: The Journal of the Iberoamerican Academy of Management* 1(2) (Spring 2003), pp. 145–160; Foard F. Jones, Vida Scarpello, and Thomas Bergmann, "Pay Procedures—What Makes Them Fair?" *Journal of Occupational and Organizational Psychology* 72 (1999), pp. 129–145.

[9]R. H. Thaler, "From Homo Economicus to Homo Sapiens," *Journal of Economic Perspectives* 14(1) (Winter 2000), pp. 133–141; Rosemary Batt, Alexander J. S. Colvin, and Jeffrey Keefe, "Employee Voice, Human Resource Practices, and Quit Rates: Evidence from the Telecommunications Industry," *Industrial and Labor Relations Review* 55(4) (July 2002), pp. 573–594; Casey Ichniowski, Kathryn Shaw, and Jon Grant, "Working Smarter by Working Together: Connective Capital in the Workplace," working paper, Columbia University, New York, 2002.

STRUCTURES VARY AMONG ORGANIZATIONS

An internal pay structure can be defined by (1) number of *levels* of work, (2) the pay *differentials* between the levels, and (3) the *criteria* used to determine those levels and differentials.

Levels

One feature of any pay structure is its hierarchical nature: the number of levels and reporting relationships. Some are more hierarchical, with multiple levels; others are compressed, with few levels.[10] GE Plastics engineers thermoplastic resin "solutions." (With so many companies offering "solutions," are we running short of problems?) In comparison to Lockheed's six levels for engineering alone (Exhibit 3.1), GE Plastics uses five broad levels, described in Exhibit 3.2, to cover engineering as well as all professional and executive work. GE Plastics would probably fit the Lockheed Martin structure into two or three levels.

Differentials

The pay differences among levels are referred to as *differentials*. If we assume that an organization has a compensation budget of a set amount to distribute among its employees, there are a number of ways it can do so. It can divide the budget by the number of employees to give everyone the same amount. The Moosewood Restaurant in Ithaca, New York, adopts this approach. But few organizations in the world are that egalitarian. In most, pay varies among employees.[11] Work that requires more knowledge or skills, is performed under unpleasant working conditions, and/or adds more value is usually paid

EXHIBIT 3.2
Managerial/
Professional
Levels at
General
Electric
Plastics
(GEP)

Level	Description
Executive	Provides vision, leadership, and innovation to major business segments or functions of GEP
Director	Directs a significant functional area or smaller business segment
Leadership	Individual contributors leading projects or programs with broad scope and impact, or managers leading functional components with broad scope and impact
Technical/managerial	Individual contributors managing projects or programs with defined scope and responsibility, or first-tier management of a specialty area
Professional	Supervisors and individual contributors working on tasks, activities, and/or less complex, shorter-duration projects

[10] Michael Gibbs, "Incentive Compensation in a Corporate Hierarchy," *Journal of Accounting and Economics* 19 (1995), pp. 247–277.

[11] Researchers use a statistic called the *gini coefficient* to describe the distribution of pay. A gini of zero means everyone is paid the identical wage. The higher the gini coefficient (maximum = 1), the greater the pay differentials among the levels.

more.[12] Exhibit 3.3 shows the differentials attached to Lockheed Martin's engineering structure. The intention of these differentials is to motivate people to strive for promotion to a higher-paying level.

Criteria

Content and Value

Content refers to the work performed in a job and how it gets done (tasks, behaviors, knowledge required, etc.) *Value* refers to the worth of the work: its relative contribution to the organization objectives. A structure based on content typically ranks jobs based on skills required, complexity of tasks, and/or responsibility. In contrast, a structure based on the value of the work focuses on the relative contribution of the skills, tasks, and responsibilities of a job to the organization's goals. While the resulting structures may be the same, there are some important differences. In addition to including relative contribution, value may also include external market pressures (i.e., what competitors pay for this level of contribution). Or it may include rates that have been agreed upon through collective bargaining, or even legislated rates (minimum wage). Job values across all organizations in Cuba are set by a government agency. Following the now-discarded approaches of the former Soviet Union and China, Cuba's government dictates a universal structure: 8 levels for industrial workers, 16 levels for technical and engineering work, and 26 levels for government employees.

Use Value and Exchange Value *Use value* reflects the value of goods or services an employee produces in a job. *Exchange value* is whatever wage the employer and employee agree on for a job. Think about IBM software engineers living in Bangalore, Kiev, and Purchase, New York. Now think about them working together on the same project—same company, same job content, same internal job value. Same use value. Yet they are in very different geographies and external markets. Wage rates in Bangalore and Kiev are a lot less than in Purchase. The exchange value varies.[13] For promotions, IBM treats these jobs as being at the same level in the structure. But the competitive practices and markets in India, the Ukraine, and the United States yield very different pay rates.[14]

The difference between exchange value and use value also surfaces when one firm acquires another. IBM's acquisition of PricewaterhouseCoopers (PWC), where consultants were the lifeblood of the company, is a case in point. PricewaterhouseCoopers consultants added more knowledge to IBM's marketing teams. But the use value of their knowledge within IBM

[12] Barry Gerhart and Sara Rynes, *Compensation: Theory, Evidence, and Strategic Implications* (Thousand Oaks, CA: Sage, 2003); Robert Gibbons and Michael Waldman, "A Theory of Wage and Promotion Dynamics inside Firms," *Quarterly Journal of Economics,* November 1999, pp. 1321–1358; George Baker, Michael Gibbs, and Bengt Holmstrom, "The Internal Economics of the Firm: Evidence from Personnel Data," *Quarterly Journal of Economics,* November 1994, pp. 881–919; M. Bloom and G. Milkovich, "Money, Managers, and Metamorphosis," in *Trends in Organizational Behavior,* 3d ed., eds. D. Rousseau and C. Cooper (New York: Wiley, 1996).

[13] David Kirkpatrick, "The Net Makes It All Easier—Including Exporting U.S. Jobs," *Fortune,* May 26, 2003, p. 146; Laurie Bienstock and Sandra McLellan, "Job Leveling in a Changing Environment: Does Your Organization Measure Up?" *WorldatWork Journal* 11(4) (Fourth Quarter 2002), *www.worldatwork.org.*

[14] Towers Perrin and other consulting firms offer extensive global surveys: *www.towers.com/towers/tpdata/.*

EXHIBIT 3.3 **Engineering Pay Structure at Lockheed Martin**

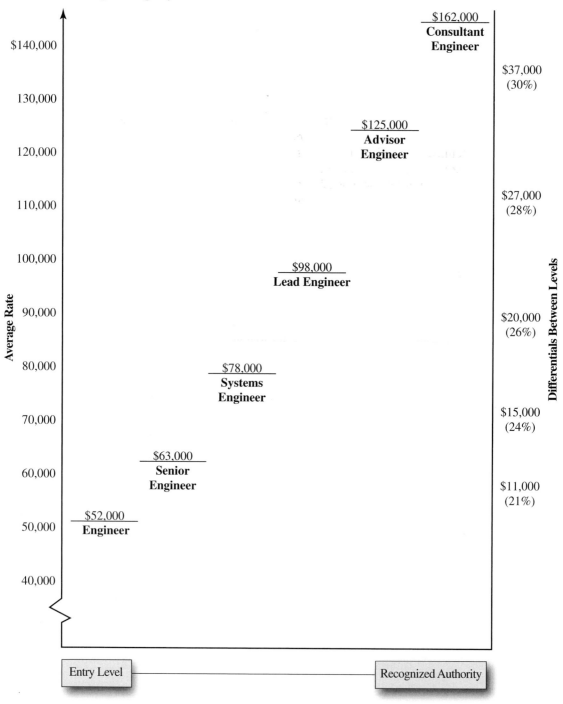

differs from that within PWC. So basically similar job content in two different companies may be valued differently based on how it contributes to organization objectives. Alternatively, the same work content in the same company (IBM's software engineers) may have different exchange values based on the different geographies.

Job- and Person-Based Structures

A *job-based structure* relies on the work content—tasks, behaviors, responsibilities. A *person-based structure* shifts the focus to the employee: the *skills, knowledge, or competencies* the employee possesses, whether or not they are used in the employee's particular job.[15] The engineering structure at Lockheed Martin (Exhibit 3.1) uses the work performed as the criterion. GE Plastics (Exhibit 3.2) uses the individual employees' competencies required at each level of work.

In the real world, it is often hard to describe a job without reference to the jobholder's knowledge and skills. Conversely, it is hard to define a person's job-related knowledge or competencies without referring to work content. So rather than a job- or person-based structure, reality includes both job *and* person.

WHAT SHAPES INTERNAL STRUCTURES?

The major factors that shape internal structures are shown in Exhibit 3.4. We categorize them as *external* and *organization* factors, even though they are connected and interacting. Exactly how they interact is not well understood. As we discuss the factors, we will also look at various theories.

Economic Pressures

Adam Smith was an early advocate of letting economic market forces influence pay structures. He was the first to ascribe both an exchange value and a use value to human resources. Smith faulted the new technologies associated with the Industrial Revolution for increasing the use value of labor without a corresponding increase in exchange value (i.e., higher wages for workers).

Karl Marx took this criticism even further.[16] He said that employers unfairly pocketed the surplus value created by the difference between use value and exchange value. He urged workers to overthrow capitalistic systems to become owners themselves and reap the full use value of their labor.

A countering theory put forth in the last half of the 19th century, *marginal productivity*, says that employers do in fact pay use value.[17] Unless an employee can produce a value equal to the value received in wages, it will not be worthwhile to hire that worker. Pay differences among the job levels reflect differences in use value associated with different

---

[15] E. E. Lawler III, "From Job-Based to Competency-Based Organizations," *Journal of Organization Behavior* 15 (1994), pp. 3–15.

[16] C. Tucker, ed., *The Marx-Engels Reader* (New York: Norton, 1978).

[17] Allan M. Cartter, *Theory of Wages and Employment* (Burr Ridge, IL: Irwin, 1959).

EXHIBIT 3.4 **What Shapes Internal Structures?**

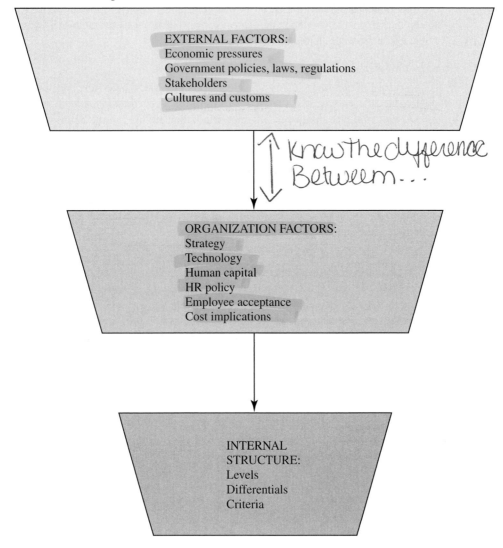

EXTERNAL FACTORS:
Economic pressures
Government policies, laws, regulations
Stakeholders
Cultures and customs

Know the difference Between...

ORGANIZATION FACTORS:
Strategy
Technology
Human capital
HR policy
Employee acceptance
Cost implications

INTERNAL STRUCTURE:
Levels
Differentials
Criteria

jobs. One job is paid more or less than another because of differences in relative productivity of the job and/or differences in how much a consumer values the output. Hence, differences in productivity provide a rationale for the internal pay structure.

In addition to supply and demand for labor, supply and demand for products and services also affect internal structures. Rapid, often turbulent changes, either in competitors' products/services (as in the rise of the Internet for making purchases) or in customers' tastes (as in the popularity of sport-utility or low-emission vehicles), force organizations to redesign work flow and force employees to continuously learn new skills. Turbulent, unpredictable external conditions require pay structures that support agile organizations and flexible people.[18]

Government Policies, Laws, and Regulations

In the United States, equal employment legislation forbids pay systems that discriminate on the basis of gender, race, religion, or national origin. The Equal Pay Act and the Civil Rights Act require "equal pay for equal work," with work considered equal if it requires equal skill, equal effort, and equal responsibility and if it is performed under equal working conditions. An internal structure may contain any number of levels, with differentials of any size, as long as the criteria for setting them are not gender, race, religion, or national origin.

Much pay-related legislation attempts to regulate economic forces to achieve social welfare objectives. The most obvious place to affect an internal structure is at the minimums (minimum-wage legislation) and maximums (special reporting requirements for executive pay). But legislation also aims at the differentials. A contemporary U.S. example is the "living wage."[19] A number of U.S. cities require minimum hourly wage rates well above what federal law requires. The anticipated outcome of such legislation is a flatter, more compressed structure of wage rates in society.

We have already described the mandated pay structures in Cuba. Cuba wasn't alone. Until recently, an entire government agency in the Slovak Republic in central Europe was devoted to maintaining a 15-level pay structure that was required in all Slovak companies (but not foreign ones). The detailed procedures manuals and job descriptions filled a number of shelves. People dissatisfied with the pay rate for their jobs could appeal to this agency. Not surprisingly, few did. Recent reforms offer greater freedom to companies and unions to negotiate pay structures.[20]

External Stakeholders

Unions, stockholders, and even political groups have a stake in how internal pay structures are determined. Unions are the most obvious case. Most unions seek smaller pay differences among jobs and seniority-based promotions as a way to promote solidarity among members. At the minimum, unions want the interests of their members represented. In the United States, the AFL-CIO uses information on the pay differences between top executives and employees to rally support for union membership (see *www.aflcio.org*).

---

[18]G. Milkovich and M. Bloom, "Rethinking International Compensation: From Expats and National Cultures to Strategic Flexibility," *Compensation & Benefits Review,* Issue 1, 1998; S. Brown and K. Eisenhardt, *Competing on the Edge: Strategy and Structured Chaos* (Boston: Harvard Business Press, 1998); George Baker, Michael Gibbs, and Bengt Holmstrom, "The Internal Economics of the Firm: Evidence from Personnel Data," *Quarterly Journal of Economics,* November 1994, pp. 881–919; Michael Gibbs, "Incentive Compensation in a Corporate Hierarchy," *Journal of Accounting and Economics* 19 (1995), pp. 247–277.

[19]Scott Adams and David Neumark, "Living Wage Effects: New and Improved Evidence," NBER working paper 9702, 2003.

[20]M. Bloom, G. Milkovich, and A. Mitra, "International Compensation: Learning from How Managers Respond to Variations in Local Host Contexts," *International Human Resource Management* (in press); M. Mendenhall and G. Oddou, *Readings and Cases in International HRM* (Cincinnati: Southwestern, 2000).

Stockholders pay attention to the gap between executive and employee pay. The $6 million cash compensation (plus stock options worth $197 million) for Disney CEO Michael Eisner stands in sharp contrast to that earned by Disney employees who perform as Mickey or Minnie Mouse. Mickey, Minnie, Pluto, Goofy, and even Snow White earn union rates of between $18 and $25 an hour. (Yes, Mickey and Minnie are Teamsters.) Shareholders of several companies ranging from General Electric to Glaxo Smith Kline are beginning to pressure companies to control or at least better justify executive pay. Research is beginning to determine the effects of these pay differentials on employees' behaviors and performance and, consequently, organization performance.[21]

Cultures and Customs

Garrison Keillor defines culture by what songs we know in common—camp songs, religious hymns, the big hits of the year we were 15. A more academic definition of culture is the mental programming for processing information that people share in common.[22] Shared mind-sets may judge what size pay differential is fair. In ancient Greece, Plato declared that societies are strongest when the richest earned a maximum of four times the lowest pay. Aristotle favored a five-times limit. In 1942 President Franklin Roosevelt proposed a maximum wage: a 100 percent tax on all income above 10 times the minimum wage.

Historians tell us that in 14th-century western Europe, the church endorsed a "just wage" doctrine, a structure of wages that supported the existing class structure. The doctrine was an effort to end the economic and social chaos resulting from the death of one-third of the population from plague. The shortage of workers that resulted gave common people power to demand higher wages, much to the dismay of church and state. Market forces such as skills shortages (higher exchange value) were explicitly denied as appropriate determinants of pay structures. Today, advocates of the living wage are trying to change societal judgments about what wage is just.

Even today cultural factors continue to shape pay structures. Many traditional Japanese employers place heavy emphasis on seniority in their internal pay structures. But pressures from global competitors plus an aging work force have made age-based pay

[21]Michael L. Bognanno, "Corporate Tournaments," *Journal of Labor Economics,* 19(2) (2001), pp. 290–315; Mason A. Carpenter and James B. Wade, "Microlevel Opportunity Structures as Determinants of Non-CEO Executive Pay," *Academy of Management Journal* 6 (2002), pp. 1085–1103.

[22]G. Hoefstede, *Culture's Consequences: International Differences in Work Relationships and Values* (Thousand Oaks, CA: Sage, 1980); R. Donkin, "The Pecking Order's Instinctive Appeal," *Financial Times,* August 23, 2002; A. Mitra, M. Bloom, and G. Milkovich, "Crossing a Raging River: Seeking Far-Reaching Solutions to Global Pay Challenges," *WorldatWork Journal,* 11(2) (Second Quarter 2002); F. Trompenaars, *Riding the Waves of Culture: Understanding Diversity in Global Business* (Burr Ridge, IL: Irwin,1995); J. Brockner, Y. Chen, K. Leung, and D. Skarlick, "Culture and Procedural Fairness: When the Effects of What You Do Depend on How You Do It," *Administrative Science Quarterly* 45 (2000), pp. 138–159; Thomas Li-Ping Tang, Vivenne Wai-Mei Luk, and Randy K. Chiu, "Pay Differentials in the People's Republic of China: An Examination of Internal Equity and External Competitiveness," *Compensation and Benefits Review* 32(3) (May/June 2000), pp. 43–49; Jing-Lih Farh, Chen-Bo Zhong, and Dennis W. Organ, "Organizational Citizenship Behavior in the People's Republic of China," in *Organization Science,* special issue: *Corporate Transformations in China* (in press).

structures very expensive. Consequently, some Japanese employers are emphasizing performance and downplaying seniority.[23] This change is particularly irksome; as we have grown older, the wisdom of basing pay on age has become more obvious to us.

Organization Strategy

You have already read how organization strategies influence internal pay structures. The basic belief of a strategic perspective is that pay structures that are not aligned with the organization strategy may become obstacles to the organization's success.

Organization's Human Capital

Human capital—the education, experience, knowledge, abilities, and skills that people possess—is a major influence on internal structures.[24] The stronger the link between the skills and experience a person possesses and an organization's objectives, the more pay those skills will command. Lockheed's structure pays consultant engineers more than lead or senior engineers because the human capital of consultant engineers brings a greater return to Lockheed. It is more crucial to Lockheed's success.

Organization Work Design

Technology used in producing goods and services influences the *organizational design,* the *work* to be performed, and the *skills/knowledge* required to perform the work.[25] The technology required to produce precision military hardware differs from that used to manufacture plastics. Defense contract work is more labor-intensive (more than 50 percent of operating expenses are labor costs) than is plastics (less than 20 percent); hence, different structures emerge. Apparently the engineering labor costs for Mars rovers and military weapons exceed those for engineering the coatings for such products as DVDs, automobile parts, building materials, and bullets. Lockheed uses six levels for engineering alone, whereas GE Plastics uses five levels for all managerial/professional/technical employees.

The design of organizations is undergoing profound changes. According to Drucker, "A staggering number of people who work in organizations are no longer traditional employees of these organizations."[26] These "nonemployees" are employed by someone—either a supplier of information technology services (e.g., IBM or Hewlett-Packard) or perhaps a

---

[23]Yoshio Yanadori and George Milkovich, "Minimizing Wage Competition? Entry-Level Compensation in Japanese Firms," working paper, Center for Advanced HR Studies, Ithaca, NY, 2003.

[24]D. Levine, D. Belman, G. Charness, E. Groshen, and K. C. O'Shaugnessy, *The New Employment Contract: How Little Wage Structures at U.S. Employers Have Changed* (Kalamazoo, MI: Upjohn, 2001).

[25]Rosemary Batt, Alexander J. S. Colvin, and Jeffrey Keefe, "Employee Voice, Human Resource Practices, and Quit Rates: Evidence from the Telecommunications Industry," *Industrial and Labor Relations Review* 55(4) (July 2002), pp. 573–594; P. Milgrom and J. Roberts, *Economics, Organization, and Management* (Englewood Cliffs, NJ: Prentice-Hall, 1992); J. S. Shaw, N. Gupta, and J. E. Delery, "Pay Dispersion and Workforce Performance: Moderating Effects of Incentives and Interdependence," *Strategic Management* 23 (2002), pp. 491–512.

[26]Peter F. Drucker, "They're Not Employees, They're People," *Harvard Business Review,* February 2002, pp. 70–77.

contractor or temporary work supplier (e.g., Accountemps, Manpower Services). The security guards, software engineers, accountants, and even entire company functions such as information technology services may be supplied by outsourcing specialists. Pay for these employees is based on the internal structure of their home employer (e.g., IBM or Accountemps) rather than of the workplace at which they are currently located.

Another major work design change is *delayering*. Entire levels of work are disappearing. Delayering can cut unnecessary, noncontributing work. It can also add work to other jobs, enlarging them. This changes the job's value and subsequently the job structure. Delayering is occurring at the top of the structure, where the number of firms with chief operating officers has decreased by 20 percent in the past decade.[27] Delayering is also occurring in operations. Through the use of self-managed work teams, entire levels of supervisory jobs are removed and the work is delegated to the teams.[28] All these changes influence the type of internal pay structures required to support them.

Overall HR Policies

The organization's other *human resource policies* also influence internal pay structures. Most organizations tie money to promotions to induce employees to apply for higher-level positions.[29] However, some organizations believe that offering a grander job title is a sufficient inducement and little or no pay differential is required.[30] Nevertheless, a theory to explain why people might want a bigger title without additional pay to go with it has yet to be worked out.

Internal Labor Markets: Combining External and Organization Factors

Internal labor markets combine both external and organizational factors. *Internal labor markets* refer to the rules and procedures that (1) determine the pay for the different jobs within a single organization and (2) allocate employees among those different jobs.[31] As

[27]Raghuram G. Rajan and Julie Wulf, "The Flattening Firm: Evidence from Panel Data on the Changing Nature of Corporate Hierarchies," working paper, Wharton, November 2002.

[28]Rosemary Batt, Alexander J. S. Colvin, and Jeffrey Keefe, "Employee Voice, Human Resource Practices, and Quit Rates: Evidence from the Telecommunications Industry," *Industrial and Labor Relations Review* 55(4) (July 2002), pp. 573–594; Casey Ichniowski, Kathryn Shaw, and Jon Grant, "Working Smarter by Working Together: Connective Capital in the Workplace," working paper, Columbia University, New York, 2002.

[29]Paul Schumann, Dennis Ahlburg, and Christine B. Mahoney, "The Effects of Human Capital and Job Characteristics on Pay," *Journal of Human Resources* 29(2), pp. 481–503.

[30]A. Kohn, *Punished by Rewards: The Trouble with Gold Stars, Incentive Plans, A's, Praise and Other Bribes* (Boston: Houghton Mifflin, 1993); Jerald Greenberg and Suzy N. Ornstein, "High Status Job Titles as Compensation for Underpayment: A Test of Equity Theory," *Journal of Applied Psychology* 68(2) (1983), pp. 285–297.

[31]Thomas A. Mahoney, "Organizational Hierarchy and Position Worth," *Academy of Management Journal,* December 1979, pp. 726–737; Barry Gerhart and Sara Rynes, *Compensation: Theory, Evidence, and Strategic Implications* (Thousand Oaks, CA: Sage, 2003).

EXHIBIT 3.5
**Illustration of
an Internal
Labor
Market**

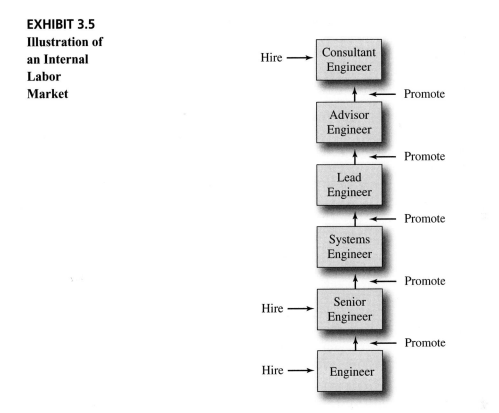

depicted in Exhibit 3.5, in many organizations individuals are recruited only for specific entry-level jobs (an engineer would be hired right out of college; a senior engineer would have a few years' experience) and are later promoted or transferred to other jobs. Because the employer competes in the external market for people to fill these entry jobs, their pay must be high enough to attract a pool of qualified applicants. In contrast, pay for jobs filled via transfer and promotions is buffered from external forces. External factors are dominant influences on pay for entry jobs, but the differences for nonentry jobs tend to reflect the organization's internal factors.[32]

[32]John Sutherland, "Wages In and Voluntary Quits from an Establishment Internal Labour Market," *Applied Economics* 34 (2002), pp. 395–400.; Philip Moss, "Earnings Inequality and the Quality of Jobs," in *Corporate Governance and Sustainable Prosperity,* eds. W. Lazonick and M. O'Sullivan (New York: Macmillan, 2001); Erica L. Groshen and David I. Levine, "The Rise and Decline (?) of U.S. Internal Labor Markets," Research Paper No. 9819, (New York Federal Reserve Bank, 1998); S. Bacharach and E. Lawler, "Political Alignments in Organizations" chap. 4 in *Research in the Sociology of Organizations,* Vol. IV, eds. Sam Bacharach and Stephen Mitchell (Greenwich, CT: JAI Press, 1998).

Ee's need to accept the D's in pay, etc

Employee Acceptance: A Key Factor

Employees judge the fairness of their pay through comparisons with the compensation paid others for work related in some fashion to their own.[33] Accordingly, an important factor influencing the internal pay structure is its *acceptability to the employees involved*.[34]

Pay structures change in response to changing external pressures such as skill shortages. Over time, the distorted pay differences became accepted as equitable and customary; efforts to change them are resisted. Thus, pay structures established for organizational and economic reasons at an earlier time may be maintained for cultural or other political reasons. It may take another economic jolt to overcome the cultural resistance. Then new norms for employee acceptance are formed around the new structure. This "change-and-congeal" process does not yet support the continuous changes occurring in today's economy. New norms for employee acceptance will probably need to include recognition that people must get used to constant change, even in internal pay relationships.

The pay for airport security screeners relative to other airport jobs illustrates the change and congeal process. Prior to 9/11, airport screeners were paid about $5.50 an hour with no benefits. Recent immigrants, some undocumented, and relatively unskilled people were hired to screen travelers and their luggage. After the 9/11 attacks, the Transportation Security Administration (TSA) took over airport security and screening. Wages are now comparable to police and fire protection jobs. Entry-level pay starts at around $20 an hour plus U.S. federal employee benefits. Employees in other jobs need to accept the changes in the security jobs—or they will be at the door asking for more pay.[35]

STRATEGIC CHOICES IN DESIGNING INTERNAL STRUCTURES

The basic premise underlying the strategic approach is that "fit" matters. Aligned pay structures support the way the work gets done, fit the organization's business strategy, and are fair to employees. Greater internal alignment—fit—is more likely to lead to success. Misaligned structures become obstacles. They may still motivate employee behavior, but it may be undesirable behavior. Jeff Goldblum's mathematician character may never have stolen the dinosaur egg in *Jurassic Park* if he had been given the pay raise he felt he deserved.

[33]E. Robert Livernash, "The Internal Wage Structure," in *New Concepts in Wage Determination,* eds. G. W. Taylor and F. C. Pierson (New York: McGraw-Hill, 1957), pp. 143–172.

[34]Charlie O. Trevor and David L. Wazeter, "Reactions to Interdependence among Pay Dispersion, Pay Relative to Internal and External Referents, and Procedural Fairness: Toward a General Compensatory Effect," working paper, University of Wisconsin–Madison, May 2003; T. Judge and H. G. Heneman III, "Pay Satisfaction," in *Compensation in Organizations: Current Research and Practice,* eds. S. Rynes and G. Gerhart (San Francisco: Jossey-Bass, 2000); Robert Folger and Mary Konovsky, "Effects of Procedural and Distributive Justice on Reactions to Pay Raise Decisions," *Academy of Management Journal,* March 1989, pp. 115–130; Kimberly D. Elsbach and Greg Elofson, "How the Packaging of Decision Explanations Affects Perceptions of Trustworthiness," *Academy of Management Journal* 43(1) (2000), pp. 80–89; Suzanne S. Masterson, Kyle Lewis, Barry M. Goldman, and M. Susan Taylor, "Integrating Justice and Social Exchange: The Differing Effects of Fair Procedures and Treatment on Work Relationships," *Academy of Management Journal* 43(4) (2000), pp. 738–748; Stefanie E. Naumann and Nathan Bennett, "A Case for Procedural Justice Climate: Development and Test of a Multilevel Model," *Academy of Management Journal* 43(5) (2000), pp. 881–889.

[35]"Federal Uniformed Police: Selected Data on Pay, Recruitment, and Retention at 13 Police Forces in the Washington, D.C. Metropolitan Area," GAO-03-658, June 13, 2003.

But what does it mean to fit or tailor the pay structure to be internally aligned? Two strategic choices are involved: (1) how tailored to organization design and work flow to make the structure, and (2) how to distribute pay throughout the levels in the structure.

Tailored versus Loosely Coupled

A low-cost, customer-focused business strategy such as that followed by McDonald's or Wal-Mart may be supported by a closely tailored structure. Jobs are well defined with detailed tasks or steps to follow. You can go into a McDonald's in Cleveland, Prague, or Shanghai and find they all are very similar. Their pay structures are, too. The customer representative and the food preparation jobs are very well defined in order to eliminate variance in how they are performed. The amount of ketchup that goes on the burger is premeasured; even the keys on the cash register are labeled with menu items rather than numbers. It is hard to make a mistake in these jobs. It is also hard to be the very best french fryer in the whole company. Differences in pay among jobs are relatively small.

In contrast to McDonald's, 3M's business strategy requires constant product innovation and short product-design-to-market cycle times. The 3M competitive environment is turbulent and unpredictable. 3M engineers may work on several teams developing several products at the same time. 3M's pay system needs to accommodate this flexibility. Hence, its pay structures are more loosely linked to the organization in order to facilitate constant change.

Egalitarian versus Hierarchical

Pay structures can range from egalitarian at one extreme to hierarchical at the other. Exhibit 3.6 clarifies the differences. Egalitarian structures have fewer levels and smaller differentials between adjacent levels and between the highest- and lowest-paid workers.

In Exhibit 3.7, Structure A has eight different levels, with relatively small differentials in comparison to structure B, which has only three levels. Structure A is hierarchical compared to the egalitarian structure of B; the multiple levels typically include detailed descriptions of work done at each level and delineate who is responsible for what. Hierarchical structures provide a lot more opportunities for promotion. Hierarchies send the message that the organization values the differences in work content, individual skills, and contributions to the organization.[36]

EXHIBIT 3.6
Strategic Choice: Hierarchical versus Egalitarian

	Hierarchical ◄──────► Egalitarian	
Levels	Many	Fewer
Differentials	Large	Small
Criteria	Person or job	Person or job
Supports:	Close fit	Loose fit
Work Organization	Individual performers	Teams
Fairness	Performance	Equal treatment
Behaviors	Opportunities for promotion	Cooperation

[36]Elliot Jaques, "In Praise of Hierarchies," *Harvard Business Review,* January–February 1990, pp. 32–40; Matthew C. Bloom, "The Performance Effects of Pay Structures on Individuals and Organizations," *Academy of Management Journal* 42(1) 1999, pp. 25–40.

EXHIBIT 3.7
Which Structure Has the Greatest Impact on Performance? on Fairness?

Structure A Layered	Structure B Delayered
Chief Engineer	Chief Engineer
Engineering Manager	
Consulting Engineer	
Senior Lead Engineer	
Lead Engineer	Consulting Engineer
Senior Engineer	
Engineer	
Engineer Trainee	Associate Engineer

Structure B can also be characterized as delayered or compressed. Several levels of work are removed so that all employees at all levels become responsible for a broader range of tasks but also have greater freedom to determine how best to accomplish what is expected of them. An egalitarian structure sends the message that all employees are valued equally. It implies that more equal treatment will improve employee satisfaction, support cooperation, and therefore affect workers' performance.[37]

Yet more egalitarian structures are not problem-free, either. For example, Ben and Jerry's Homemade, a purveyor of premium ice cream, tried to maintain a ratio of only 7 to 1 between its highest-paid and lowest-paid employees. (When the company started, the spread was 5 to 1.) The relatively narrow differential reflected the company's philosophy that the prosperity of its production workers and its management should be closely linked. The compressed structure also generated a great deal of favorable publicity. However, it eventually became a barrier to recruiting. Ben and Jerry's was forced to abandon this policy to hire an accounting manager and a new CEO. And only when the company was acquired by Unilever, a Dutch multinational, did the press publicize the fact that the value of Ben and Jerry's stock increased the total compensation for founders Ben Cohen and Jerry Greenfield to much more than the 7-to-1 ratio.

Still, it is hard to be against anything called "egalitarian." If we instead use the word "averagism," as Chinese workers do when describing the pay system under socialism's state-owned enterprises, where maximum differentials of 3 to 1 were mandated, some of the possible drawbacks of this approach become clear.[38] Equal treatment can mean that the more knowl-

---

[37]R. D. Bretz and S. L. Thomas, "Perceived Equity, Motivation, and Final-Offer Arbitration in Major League Baseball," *Journal of Applied Psychology* 77 (1992), pp. 280–287; M. Bloom and J. Michel, "The Relationships among Organizational Context, Pay Dispersion and Managerial Turnover," *Academy of Management Journal* (1) (2002), pp. 33–42.

[38]Daniel Z. Ding, Keith Goodall, and Malcolm Warner, "The End of the 'Iron Rice-Bowl': Whither Chinese Human Resource Management?" *International Journal of Human Resource Management* 11(2) (April 2000), pp. 217–236; Thomas Li-Ping Tang, Vivienne Wai-Mei Luk, and Randy K. Chiu, "Pay Differentials in the People's Republic of China: An Examination of Internal Equity and External Competitiveness," *Compensation and Benefits Review* 32(3) (May/June 2000), pp. 43–49; Li Hua Wang, "Pay Policies and Determination in China," working paper, Northwestern University, 2003; Chao Chen, Jaepil Dhoi, and Shu-Cheng Chi, "Making Justice Sense of Local-Expatriate Compensation Disparity: Mitigation by Local Referents, Ideological Explanations, and Interpersonal Sensitivity in China-Foreign Joint Ventures," *Academy of Management Journal* 43(4) (2002), pp. 807–817.

edgeable employees—the stars—feel underpaid. They may quit or simply tune out and refuse to do anything that is not specifically required of them. Their change in behavior will lower overall performance. So a case can be made for both egalitarian and hierarchical structures.

Keep in mind, though, that the choice is rarely either/or. Rather, the differences are a matter of degree: Levels can range from many to few, differentials can be large or small, and the criteria can be based on the job, the person, or some combination of the two.

Career Path Differentials

Reexamine the differentials for engineers shown in Exhibit 3.3. They range from $11,000 (21 percent differential between senior engineer and engineer) to $37,000 (30 percent differential between consulting engineer and advisor engineer). These represent pay differences available for promotion from one level in the structure to the next. Recall from Chapter 1 that promotion increases add into base pay, so their expected value compounds over the employee's entire career.

WHAT THE RESEARCH TELLS US

Before managers recommend a pay structure for their organizations, we hope they will not only look at organization strategy, work flow, fairness, and employee motivation but also look at the research. Both economists and psychologists have something to tell us about the effects of various structures.

Equity Theory

Employees judge the equity of their pay by comparing the work, qualifications, and pay for jobs similar to theirs.[39] However, very little research addresses the question of what specific factors influence employees' perceptions of the equity or fairness of the *pay structure,* as opposed to the equity or fairness of the *amount of pay.*[40] Consequently, equity theory could support both egalitarian and hierarchical structures.[41]

Tournament Theory

Economists have focused more directly on the motivational effects of structures. Their starting point is a golf tournament where the prizes total, say, $100,000. How that $100,000 is distributed affects the performance of all players in the tournament. Compare a 3-prize schedule of $60,000, $30,000 and $10,000 with a ten-prize schedule of $19,000,

[39]E. E. Lawler, *Pay and Organizational Effectiveness: A Psychological View* (New York: McGraw-Hill, 1971); E. E. Lawler, *Rewarding Excellence: Pay Strategies for the New Economy* (San Francisco: Jossey-Bass, 2000); T. A. Mahoney, *Compensation and Reward Perspectives* (Homewood, IL: Irwin, 1979).

[40]T. Judge and H. G. Heneman III, "Pay Satisfaction," in *Compensation in Organizations: Current Research and Practice,* eds. S. Rynes and G. Gerhart (San Francisco: Jossey-Bass, 2000); Foard F. Jones, Vida Scarpello, and Thomas Bergmann, "Pay Procedures—What Makes Them Fair?" *Journal of Occupational and Organizational Psychology* 72 (1999), pp. 129–145; Charlie O. Trevor and David L. Wazeter, "Reactions to Interdependence among Pay Dispersion, Pay Relative to Internal and External Referents, and Procedural Fairness: Toward a General Compensatory Effect," working paper, University of Wisconsin–Madison, May 2003.

[41]J. S. Shaw, N. Gupta, and J. E. Delery, "Pay Dispersion and Workforce Performance: Moderating Effects of Incentives and Interdependence," *Strategic Management* 23 (2002), pp. 491–512.

$17,000, $15,000, $13,000, and so on. According to tournament theory, *all* players will play better in the first tournament where the prize differentials are sizable.[42] Raising the total prize money by $100,000 in the Professional Golf Association tournament lowered each player's score, on average, by 1.1 strokes over 72 holes.[43] And the closer the players got to the top prize, the more their scores were lowered. (Note to nongolfers: A lower score is an improvement.)

Applying these results to organization structures, the greater the differential between your salary and your boss's, the harder you (and everyone else but the boss) will work. If Lockheed pays its advisor engineers $125,000, and its consultant engineers $162,000, the tournament model says that everyone (except the consultants) will work harder if the consultants are instead paid $200,000. Rather than resenting the big bucks paid to the consultants, engineers at all levels in the structure will be motivated by the greater differential to work harder to be a "winner," that is, get promoted to the next level on the way to being a consultant engineer. Within limits, the bigger the prize for getting to the next level of the structure, the greater the motivational impact the structure will have.

Several studies support tournament theory. One reported that giving larger raises with a promotion increases effort and reduces absenteeism.[44] Others find that performance improves with larger differentials at the top levels of the structure. The "winner-take-all" idea springs from these studies.[45] However, a study of the National Basketball Association revealed that once teams fail to get into the playoffs, where players would have made a lot more money, team performance drops precipitously. In fact, it can be called a "race for the bottom." Why? The poorest teams have first-draft choice for next year's new players. So, overnight, the reward is for worst record rather than best.[46]

But most work is not a round of golf or a good jump shot. Virtually all the research that supports hierarchical structures and tournament theory is on situations where individual performance matters most (auto racing, bowling, golf tournaments) or, at best, where the demand for cooperation among a small group of individuals is relatively low (professors, stockbrokers). In contrast, team sports provide a setting where both individual players' performance and the cooperative efforts of the entire team make a difference.[47] Using eight years of data on major league baseball, one study found that teams with egal-

[42]B. E. Becker and M. A. Huselid, "The Incentive Effects of Tournament Compensation Systems," *Administrative Science Quarterly* 37 (1992), pp. 336–350; E. Lazear and S. Rosen, "Rank-Order Tournaments as Optimum Labor Contracts," *Journal of Political Economy* 89 (1981), pp. 841–864; Matthew C. Bloom, "The Performance Effects of Pay Structures on Individuals and Organizations," *Academy of Management Journal* 42(1) (1999), pp. 25–40; Michael L. Bognanno, "Corporate Tournaments," *Journal of Labor Economics* 19(2) (2001), pp. 290–315.

[43]R. G. Ehrenberg and M. L. Bognanno, "The Incentive Effects of Tournaments Revisited: Evidence from the European PGA Tour," *Industrial and Labor Relations Review* 43 (1990), pp. 74S–88S; Tor Eriksson, "Executive Compensation and Tournament Theory: Empirical Tests on Danish Data," *Journal of Labor Economics,* April 1999, pp. 262–280.

[44]E. P. Lazear, *Personnel Economics* (Cambridge, MA: MIT Press, 1995).

[45]Robert H. Frank and Philip J. Cook, *The Winner-Take-All Society: Why the Few at the Top Get So Much More Than the Rest of Us* (New York: Penguin, 1996).

[46]Beck A. Taylor and Justin G. Trogdon, "Losing to Win: Tournament Incentives in the National Basketball Association," *Journal of Labor Economics* 20(1) (2002), pp. 23–41.

[47]Matthew C. Bloom, "The Performance Effects of Pay Structures on Individuals and Organizations," *Academy of Management Journal* 42(1) (1999), pp. 25–40.

itarian structures (practically identical player salaries) did better than those with hierarchical structures (very large differentials among players). In addition to affecting team performance (games won, gate receipts, franchise value, total income), egalitarian structures had a sizable effect on players' individual performance, too (batting averages, errors, runs batted in, etc.). A mediocre player improved more on a team with an egalitarian structure than on a team with a hierarchical structure. Of course, it may also be that the egalitarian pay structure reflects a more flexible, supportive organization culture in which a mediocre player is given the training and support needed to improve. The egalitarian structure would be aligned with an egalitarian corporate culture.

Cybercomp

Salaries for all the players on the major league baseball teams are listed at *www.canoe.ca/BaseballMoneyMatters/salaries_players.html*. Pick some of your favorite teams and compare the highest- and lowest-paid players on the team. Based on the differentials, which teams do the models and research discussed in this chapter predict will have the better record?

Click on the link for "Standings" and check it out. Suggestion: Don't bet your tuition on the relationship between player salary differentials on a team and the team's performance.

Tournament theory does not directly address turnover. However, a study of executive leadership teams in 460 organizations concluded that executives were twice as likely to leave if the companies had large pay differentials among the leaders.[48] In this study, hierarchy breeds turnover. For example, Biomet CEO Dane Miller would hardly notice if his pay envelope was switched with someone else's on the leadership team. There is only about a 15 percent pay difference among the top five executives at Biomet. In contrast, at Louisiana Pacific, CEO Mark Suwyn's salary and bonus totaled $1.37 million, about three times the total of other executives on his team. True to prediction, Louisiana Pacific had 13 changes in its five-person executive team over five years, compared to only 1 change on the Biomet team (a retirement). Conclusion: If executives need to operate like a baseball team, then an egalitarian structure is probably a better fit.

Institutional Model: Copy Others

Some organizations ignore the question of strategy altogether. Instead, they simply copy what others are doing. By extension, internal pay structures are sometimes adopted because they have been called a "best practice."[49] It is still common for managers to bring back "the answers" discovered at the latest conference. Recent examples of such behaviors include the rush to delayer, to emphasize teams, to deemphasize individual contributions, and to shift to a competency-based pay system, often with little regard to whether

---

[48]M. Bloom and J. Michel, "The Relationships among Organizational Context, Pay Dispersion and Managerial Turnover," *Academy of Management Journal* (1) (2002), pp. 33–42; W. Jurgens, "Look Out Below," *Wall Street Journal,* April 1, 2000, p. R3.

[49].P. S. Tolbert and L. G. Zucker, "Institutionalization of Institution Theory," in; *Handbook of Organization Studies,* pp. 175–199; eds. G. Glegg, C. Hardy, and W. Nord (London: Sage, 1996), M. Barringer and G. Milkovich, "A Theoretical Exploration of the Adoption and Design of Flexible Benefit Plans: A Case of HR Innovation," *Academy of Management Review* 23(2) (1998), pp. 305–324; Y. Yanadori, "Organization Variations in Stock Option Designs: Insights of Organization Theory," working Paper, CAHRS, Ithaca, NY, 2004.

EXHIBIT 3.8
Some Consequences of an Internally Aligned Structure

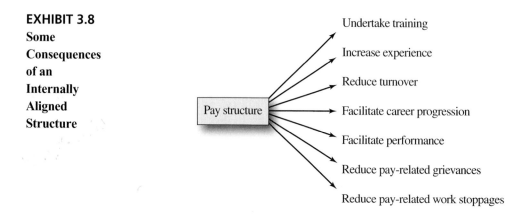

any of these practices make sense (fit) for the particular organization or its employees.[50] The institutional model predicts that very few firms are "first movers"; rather, they copy innovative practices after innovators learn whether the practices work. The copiers have little concern for best fit, opting instead for best practice.

Which Structure Fits Best?

Exhibit 3.8 summarizes the effects attributed to internally aligned structures:

- More hierarchical structures are related to greater performance when the work flow depends more on individual contributors (e.g., consulting and law practices, surgical units, stockbrokers, even university researchers).
- More egalitarian structures are related to greater performance when close collaboration and sharing of knowledge are required (e.g., firefighting and rescue squads, manufacturing teams, hotel customer service staffs, global software design teams). The competition fostered in the "winner-take-all" tournament hierarchies appears to have negative effects on performance when the work flow and organization design require teamwork.
- Structures that are not aligned with the work flow appear to be related to greater turnover.

Beyond these points, much remains to be studied. There is practically no research on the optimal size of the promotional increase or its effects on behaviors, satisfaction, or performance. Nor is much known about whether smaller, more frequent promotions are better (or worse) than fewer, larger, less frequent promotions. Perhaps informal expectations get developed at each workplace. ("You can expect to get promoted here after about three years, and a 10 percent hit usually goes with it.") In universities, promotion from assistant to associate professor tends to occur after six years, although there is no norm on promotion pay increases. In Japanese pay structures, promotion from associate to *kakaricho* occurs after five years in a company. Similar norms exist in the military. Little is known about how these rules of thumb develop and what their original logic was. But they do matter. Promotions sooner (or later) than expected, accompanied by a larger (or smaller) pay increase, send a powerful message.

---

[50]Harry Levinson, "Why the Behemoths Fell: Psychological Roots of Corporate Failure," *American Psychologist* 49(5) (1994), pp. 428–436.

So what size should the pay differentials be between the adjacent engineering levels within Lockheed? To answer this question, we would need to understand how differentials within the career path support Lockheed's business strategy and work flow, motivate engineers to contribute to Lockheed's success, and are considered fair by the engineers. The next several chapters discuss how to manage these internal structures.

CONSEQUENCES OF STRUCTURES

[handwritten: Know the key objectives used to evaluate the consequences of internal pay structure]

Let's turn again to that "so-what" question. Why worry about internal alignment at all? Why not simply pay employees whatever it takes to get them to take a job and to show up for work every day? Why not let external market forces or what competitors are paying determine internal wage differentials?

There are several very practical reasons for paying attention to internal structures. The first is unique jobs that reflect organization idiosyncrasies. For example, the National Aeronautics and Space Administration (NASA) employs a planet protection specialist whose job is to see that neither Mars nor Earth (nor any other planets) are inadvertently contaminated in the course of planetary exploration. No other employer in this world (or any other) has a planet protection specialist on the payroll. How does NASA determine the appropriate pay for this job? A friend suggested that NASA start with whatever it pays for "plant protection" (guards rather than sprayers of aphids) and add "a wee bit." Instead, NASA chose to compare the skills/knowledge/experience/responsibilities for the planet protection job with requirements for other NASA jobs. Its existing internal pay structure provides a basis for arriving at a rate for unique jobs.[51]

The second reason for paying attention to internal alignment is that, as we have already noted, different job structures must be harmonized during acquisitions and mergers. Increasingly, the most vivid illustration is from global companies paying people who are in different external markets. Yet many of these organizations say a common internal structure is required to support their global strategy.

Efficiency: Competitive Advantage

Why manage the internal pay structure? An aligned structure has the potential to lead to better organization performance. If the structure does not motivate employees to help achieve the organization's objectives, then it is a candidate for redesign.

Internal pay structures imply future rewards. The size of the differentials between the entry level in the structure and the highest level may induce employees to remain with the organization, increase their experience and training, cooperate with co-workers, and seek greater responsibility.[52]

Chapter 2 raised the strategy question, Do you want to be difficult to imitate? We already noted that the number of levels and titles in a career path may be rewarding beyond

---

[51]Previous editions of this textbook used an example of a unique job taken from Cornell University's School of Veterinary Medicine. Former students have expressed great affection for the "Cornell cows." However, in light of a changing environment, we are trying to move from the agrarian to the aquarian.

[52]Edward Lazear, "Labor Economics and Psychology of Organization," *Journal of Economic Perspectives* 5 (1991), pp. 89–110; David Wazeter, "Determinants and Consequences of Pay Structures," Ph.D. dissertation, Cornell University, 1991.

the pay attached to the titles. Microsoft added a "distinguished engineer" title to its structure. The consulting firm McKinsey and Company added an "associate partner." Their rationale was that more frequent steps in the career ladder offer employees more opportunities for rewards. These are new titles and levels that are not yet reflected in the external market.

Fairness

To employees

The early-20th-century U.S. labor leader George Meany is famous for his reaction to proposed pay innovations: "Tell me how much pay we will get, and I will tell you if I like it." Hierarchical structures evoke the same response. If I am at the top of the structure, I am probably persuaded that my high pay is an important signal to suppliers and customers that the company is doing well. If I am lower in the structure, I am probably less persuaded that the company ties its pay to employee contributions—at least, not *my* (undervalued) contributions.[53]

Several writers argue that employees' attitudes about the fairness of the pay structure affect their work behaviors.[54] Writers have long agreed that departures from an acceptable wage structure will occasion turnover, grievances, and diminished motivation.[55] But that is where the agreement ends. One group argues that if fair (i.e., sizable) differentials among jobs are not paid, individuals may harbor ill will toward the employer, resist change, change employment if possible, become depressed, and "lack that zest and enthusiasm which makes for high efficiency and personal satisfaction in work."[56] Others, including labor unions, argue for only small differentials, in the belief that more egalitarian structures support team cooperation, commitment to the organization, and improved performance.

Compliance

w/laws + regulations

As with any pay decision, the design and management of internal pay structures must comply with the regulations of the countries in which the organization operates.

While the research on internal alignment is very informative, there is still a lot we do not know. What about the appropriate number of levels, the size of the differentials, and the criteria for advancing employees through a structure? We believe the answers lie in understanding the factors discussed in this chapter: the organization's strategic intent, organization design and work flow, human capital, and the external conditions, regulations, and customs it faces. We also believe that aligning the pay structure to fit the organization and the surrounding conditions is more likely to lead to competitive advantage for the organization and a sense of fair treatment for employees. On the other hand, beliefs, experience, and common sense often mislead. Turns out there are no canals on Mars, and frogs don't cause warts. So there is general agreement that internal pay structures probably do motivate people. But exactly what behaviors result from this motivation needs to be better understood.[57]

[53]R. L. Heneman, *Merit Pay: Linking Pay Increases to Performance Ratings* (Reading, MA: Addison-Wesley, 1992); H. H. Meyer, "The Pay-for-Performance Dilemma," *Organization Science* 33 (1975), pp. 39–50.

[54]Foard F. Jones, Vida Scarpello, and Thomas Bergmann, "Pay Procedures—What Makes Them Fair?" *Journal of Occupational and Organizational Psychology* 72 (1999), pp. 129–145.

[55]E. Robert Livernash, "The Internal Wage Structure," in *New Concepts in Wage Determination,* eds. G. W. Taylor and F. C. Pierson (New York: McGraw-Hill, 1957), pp. 143–172.

[56]Elliot Jaques, "In Praise of Hierarchies," *Harvard Business Review,* January–February 1990, pp. 32–46.

[57]Richard Feynman, "Cargo Cult Science: Some Remarks on Science, Pseudoscience, and Learning How to Not Fool Yourself," in Feynman, *The Pleasure of Finding Things Out* (Cambridge: Perseus, 1999), pp. 205–216; Carl Sagan, *The Demon-Haunted World: Science as a Candle in the Dark* (New York: Ballantine, 1997).

Your Turn
So You Want to Lead the Orchestra!

Peter Drucker calls orchestras an example of an organization design that will become increasingly popular in the 21st century, in that they employ skilled and talented people, joined together as a team to create products and services. (Drucker may hear what he wants to hear. In spite of his confidence in orchestral teamwork, jokes like the following are common among orchestra members: *Q. Why do so many people take an instant dislike to the viola? A. It saves time.*)

Job descriptions for orchestras look simple: Play the music. *(Q. How is lightning like a keyboardist's fingers? A. Neither strikes the same place twice.)* Violins play violin parts; trumpets play trumpet parts. Yet one study reported that orchestra players' job satisfaction ranks below prison guards. However, they were more satisfied than operating room nurses and hockey players.

Exhibit 1 shows the pay structure for a regional chamber orchestra. *(Q. How can you make a clarinet sound like a French horn? A. Play all the wrong notes.)* The pay covers six full orchestra concerts, one Caroling by Candlelight event, three Sunday Chamber Series concerts, several Arts in Education elementary school concerts, two engagements for a flute quartet, and one Ring in the Holidays brass event as well as the regularly scheduled rehearsals. *(Q. How can you tell when a trombonist is playing out of tune? A. When the slide is moving.)* The figures do not include the 27-cents-per-mile travel pay provided to out-of-town musicians.

1. Describe the orchestra's pay structure in terms of levels, differentials, and job- or person-based approach.
2. Discuss what factors may explain the structure. Why does violinist I receive more than the oboist and trombonist? Why does the principal trumpet player earn more than the principal cellist and clarinetist but less than the principal viola and flute players? What explains these differences? Does the relative supply versus the demand for violinists compare to the supply versus the demand for trombonists? Is it that violins play more notes?
3. How well do equity and tournament models apply?

EXHIBIT 1   Orchestra Compensation Schedule

Instrument	Fee	Instrument	Fee
Violin, Concertmaster	$6,970	Violin I	$2,483
Principal Bass and Conductor	5,070	Violin I	2,483
		Violin I	2,483
Principal Viola	5,036	Violin II	2,483
Principal Flute	4,337	Violin II	2,483
Principal Trumpet	4,233	Viola	2,483
Principal Cello	4,181	Violin II	1,975
Principal Clarinet	4,146	Viola	2,212
Trumpet	3,638	Oboe	2,206
Principal Oboe	3,615	Trombone	2,137
Principal Violin II	3,488	Viola	2,033
Principal Horn	3,390	Violin II/Viola	1,784
Keyboard I	3,361	Cello	1,634
Cello	3,228	Clarinet	1,548
Principal Percussion	3,049	Horn	1,548
Violin I	2,899	Flute	1,455
Cello	2,882	Keyboard II	1,392
Principal Bassoon	2,824	Bassoon	1,265
Violin I	2,685	Violin II	1,178

Summary   This chapter discusses internal alignment and how it affects employees, managers, and employers. Internal alignment refers to the pay relationships among jobs/skills/competencies within a single organization. The potential consequences of internal pay structures are vital to organizations and individuals. Recent research plus experience offers guidance concerning the design and management of internal pay structures.

Pay structures—the array of pay rates for different jobs within an organization—are shaped by societal, economic, organizational, and other factors. Employees judge a structure to be equitable by comparing each job's pay with the qualifications required, the work performed, and the value of that work. Acceptance by employees of the pay differentials among jobs is a key test of an equitable pay structure. Such structures are part of the network of rewards offered by organizations.

Keep the goals of the entire compensation system in mind when thinking about internal pay structures. There is widespread experience and increasing research to support the belief that differences in internal pay structures, particularly employee career paths, influence people's attitudes and work behaviors and therefore the success of organizations.

Review Questions

1. Why is internal alignment an important policy in a strategic perspective of compensation?

2. Discuss the factors that influence internal pay structures. Based on your own experience, which ones do you think are the most important? Why?

3. Internal structures are part of the incentives offered in organizations. Look into any organization: your college, workplace, or the grocery store where you shop. Describe the flow of work. How is the job structure aligned with the organization's business, the work flow, and the organization's objectives. How do you believe it influences employee behaviors?

4. What is the "just-wage" doctrine? Can you think of any present-day applications?

5. Under what organization designs are more egalitarian versus more hierarchical structures likely to be effective?

✗ still need to answer

Job Analysis

Chapter Outline

Three people sit in front of their keyboards scanning their monitors. One is a sales representative in Ohio, checking the progress of an order for four dozen picture cell phones from a retailer in Texas, who just placed the four dozen into his shopping cart on the company's website. A second is an engineer logging in to the project design software for the next generation of these picture cell phones. Colleagues in China working on the same project last night (day in China) sent some suggestions for changes in the new design; the team in the United States will work on the project today and have their work waiting for their Chinese colleagues when they come to work in the morning. A third employee, in Ireland, is using the business software recently installed worldwide to analyze the latest sales reports. In today's workplace, people working for the same company need no longer be down the hallway from one another. They can be on-site and overseas. Networks and business software link them all. Yet all their jobs are part of the organization's internal structure.

If pay is to be based on work performed, some way is needed to discover and describe the differences and similarities among these jobs—observation alone is not enough. *Job analysis* is that systematic method.

STRUCTURES BASED ON JOBS, PEOPLE, OR BOTH

Exhibit 4.1 outlines the process for constructing a work-related internal structure. No matter the approach, the process begins by looking at people at work. Job-based structures look at the tasks the people are doing and the expected outcomes; skill- and competency-based structures look at the person. However, the underlying purpose of each phase of the process, called out in the left-hand column of the exhibit, remains the same for both job- and person-based structures: (1) collect and summarize information that identifies similarities and differences, (2) determine what is to be valued, (3) quantify the relative value, and (4) translate the relative value

**EXHIBIT 4.1
Many Ways
to Create
Internal
Structure**

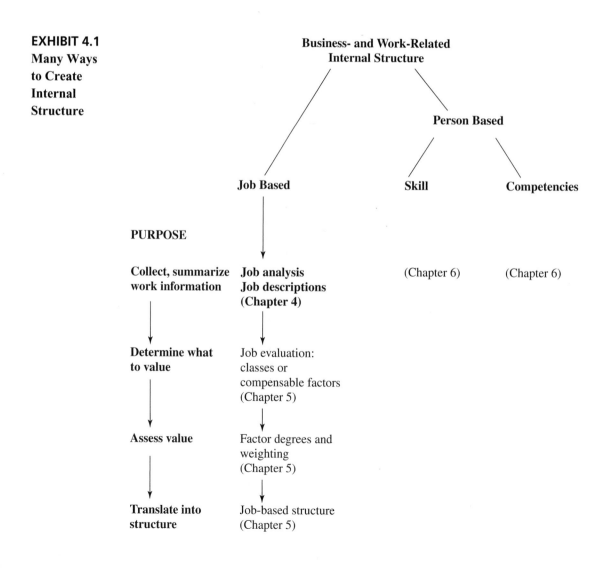

Business- and Work-Related
Internal Structure

Person Based

Job Based   Skill   Competencies

PURPOSE

	Job Based	Skill	Competencies
Collect, summarize work information	**Job analysis Job descriptions (Chapter 4)**	(Chapter 6)	(Chapter 6)
Determine what to value	Job evaluation: classes or compensable factors (Chapter 5)		
Assess value	Factor degrees and weighting (Chapter 5)		
Translate into structure	Job-based structure (Chapter 5)		

into an internal structure. (The blank boxes for the person-based structure will be filled in when we get to Chapter 6.) This chapter and the next focus on the job-based structure.[1]

Exhibit 4.2 is part of a job description for a registered nurse. The job summary section provides an overview of the job. The section on relationships to other jobs demonstrates where the job fits in the organization structure: which jobs are supervised by this jobholder, which job supervises this jobholder, and the nature of any internal and external relationships. The section on essential responsibilities elaborates on the summary: "Provides a written assessment of patient within one hour of admission and at least once a shift." Collecting information on these essential responsibilities is the heart of job analysis.

JOB-BASED APPROACH: MOST COMMON

Exhibit 4.3 shows how job analysis and the resulting job description fit into the process of creating an internal structure. Job analysis provides the underlying information. It identifies the content of the job. This content serves as input for describing and valuing work.

> **Job analysis** is the systematic process of collecting information that identifies similarities and differences in the work.

Exhibit 4.3 also lists the major decisions in designing a job analysis: (1) Why are we performing job analysis? (2) What information do we need? (3) How should we collect it? (4) Who should be involved? (5) How useful are the results?

Why Perform Job Analysis?

Potential uses for job analysis have been suggested for every major personnel function. Often the type of job analysis data needed varies by function. For example, identifying the skills and experience required to perform the work clarifies hiring and promotion standards and identifies training needs. In performance evaluation, both employees and supervisors look to the required behaviors and results expected in a job to help assess performance.

An internal structure based on job-related information provides both managers and employees a work-related rationale for pay differences. Employees who understand this rationale can see where their work fits into the bigger picture and can direct their behavior toward organization objectives. Job analysis data also help managers defend their decisions when challenged.

In compensation, job analysis has two critical uses: (1) It establishes similarities and differences in the work contents of the jobs, and (2) it helps establish an internally fair and aligned job structure. If jobs have equal content, then in all likelihood the pay established for them will be equal (unless they are in different geographies). If, on the other hand, the job content differs, then the differences, along with the market rates paid by competitors, are part of the rationale for paying jobs differently.

---

[1] Peter Cappelli, *The New Deal at Work: Managing the Market-Driven Workforce* (Boston: Harvard Business School Press, 1999); Jason D. Shaw, Nina Gupta, and John Delery, "Congruence between Technology and Compensation Systems: Implications for Strategy Implementation," *Strategic Management Journal* 22 (2001), pp. 379–386; P. K. Zingheim and J. R. Schuster, "Reassessing the Value of Skill-Based Pay," *WorldatWork Journal*, Third Quarter 2002, pp. 72–77.

EXHIBIT 4.2 **Contemporary Job Description for Registered Nurse**

Job Title
Registered Nurse

Job Summary

Accountable for the complete spectrum of patient care from admission through transfer or discharge through the nursing process of assessment, planning, implementation, and evaluation. Each R.N. has primary authority to fulfill responsibility of the nursing process on the assigned shift and for projecting future needs of the patient/family. Directs and guides patient teaching and activities for ancillary personnel while maintaining standard of professional nursing.

Relationships

Reports to: Head Nurse or Charge Nurse.
Supervises: Responsible for the care delivered by L.P.N.s, nursing assistants, orderlies, and transcribers.
Works with: Ancillary Care Departments.
External relationships: Physicians, patients, patients' families.

Qualifications

Education: Graduate of an accredited school of nursing.
Work experience: Critical care requires one year of recent medical/surgical experience (special care nursing preferred), medical/surgical experience (new graduates may be considered for noncharge positions).
License or registration requirements: Current R.N. license or permit in the State of Minnesota.
Physical requirements: A. Ability to bend, reach, or assist to transfer up to 50 pounds.
                              B. Ability to stand and/or walk 80 percent of 8-hour shift.
                              C. Visual and hearing acuity to perform job-related functions.

Essential Responsibilities

1. Assess physical, emotional, and psychosocial dimensions of patients.
   Standard: Provides a written assessment of patient within one hour of admission and at least once a shift. Communicates this assessment to other patient care providers in accordance with hospital policies.
2. Formulates a written plan of care for patients from admission through discharge.
   Standard: Develops short-and long-term goals within 24 hours of admission Reviews and updates care plans each shift based on ongoing assessment.
3. Implements plan of care.
   Standard: Demonstrates skill in performing common nursing procedures in accordance with but not limited to the established written R.N. skills inventory specific to assigned area. Completes patient care activities in an organized and timely fashion, reassessing priorities appropriately.

Note: Additional responsibilities omitted from exhibit.

The key issue for compensation decision makers is still to ensure that the data collected are useful and acceptable to the employees and managers involved. As the arrows in Exhibit 4.3 indicate, collecting job information is only an interim step, not an end in itself.

EXHIBIT 4.3   Determining the Internal Job Structure

Internal relationships within the organization →	Job analysis → The systematic process of collecting information that identifies similarities and differences in the work	Job descriptions → Summary reports that identify, define, and describe the job as it is actually performed	Job evaluation → Comparison of jobs within an organization	Job structure An ordering of jobs based on their content or relative value

Some Major Decisions in Job Analysis

- Why perform job analysis?
- What information is needed?
- How to collect information?
- Who should be involved?
- How useful are the results?

JOB ANALYSIS PROCEDURES

Exhibit 4.4 summarizes some job analysis terms and their relationship to each other. Job analysis usually collects information about specific tasks or behaviors. A group of tasks performed by one person makes up a *position*. Identical positions make a *job,* and broadly similar jobs combine into a *job family.*[2]

The U.S. federal government, one of the biggest users of job analysis data, has developed a step-by-step approach to conducting conventional job analysis.[3] The government's procedures, shown in Exhibit 4.5, include developing preliminary information, interviewing jobholders and supervisors, and then using the information to create and verify job descriptions. The picture that emerges from reading the steps in the exhibit is of a very stable workplace where the division from one job to the next is clear, with little overlap. In this workplace, jobs follow a steady progression in a hierarchy of increasing responsibility, and the relationship between jobs is clear. So is how to qualify for promotion into a higher-level job. While some argue that such a traditional, stable structure is a shrinking part of the workplace landscape, such structures nevertheless persist, in varying degrees,

[2]E. J. McCormick, "Job and Task Analysis," in *Handbook of Industrial and Organizational Psychology,* ed. M. D. Dunnette (Chicago: Rand McNally, 1976), pp. 651–696; Robert J. Harvey, "Job Analysis," in *Handbook of Industrial and Organizational Psychology,* Vol. 2, ed. M. D. Dunnette and L. Hough (Palo Alto, CA: Consulting Psychologists Press, 1991), pp. 72–157.

[3]Particularly valuable sources of information on job analysis definitions and methods are U.S. Department of Labor, Manpower Administration, *Revised Handbook for Analyzing Jobs* (Washington, DC: U.S. Government Printing Office, 1992); Robert J. Harvey, "Job Analysis," in *Handbook of Industrial and Organizational Psychology,* Vol. 2, ed. M. D. Dunnette and L. Hough (Palo Alto, CA: Consulting Psychologists Press, 1991), pp. 72–157; Sidney A. Fine and Steven F. Cronshaw, *Functional Job Analysis* (Mahwah, NJ: Lawrence Erlbaum, 1999).

EXHIBIT 4.4 Job Analysis Terminology

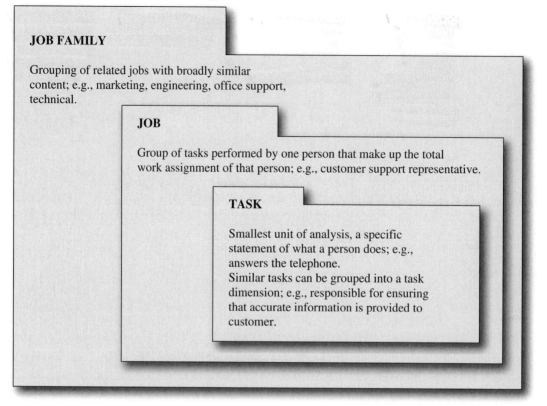

in many large organizations.[4] Thus, the federal Department of Labor's description of conventional job analysis provides a useful "how-to" guide.

WHAT INFORMATION SHOULD BE COLLECTED?

As Exhibit 4.5 suggests, a typical analysis starts with a review of information already collected in order to develop a framework for further analysis. Job titles, major duties, task dimensions, and work flow information may already exist. However, it may no longer be accurate. So the analyst must clarify existing information, too.

[4]Steven G. Allen, Robert L. Clark, and Sylvester J. Schieber, "Has Job Security Vanished in Large Corporations?" NBER Working Paper 6966 (1999); Janet Marler, Melissa Barringer, and George Milkovich, "Boundaryless and Traditional Contingent Employees: Worlds Apart," *Journal of Organizational Behavior* 23 (2002), pp. 425-453; Sanford M. Jacoby, "Are Career Jobs Headed for Extinction?" Kenneth M. Piper Memorial Lecture at Chicago–Kent Law School, April 1999.

EXHIBIT 4.5   General Procedures for Conventional Job Analysis

Step	Things to Remember or Do
1. Develop preliminary job information	a. Review existing documents in order to develop an initial "big-picture" familiarity with the job: its main mission, its major duties or functions, work flow patterns. b. Prepare a preliminary list of duties which will serve as a framework for conducting the interviews. c. Make a note of major items that are unclear or ambiguous or that need to be clarified during the data-gathering process.
2. Conduct initial tour of work site	a. The initial tour is designed to familiarize the job analyst with the work layout, the tools and equipment that are used, the general conditions of the workplace, and the mechanics associated with the end-to-end performance of major duties b. The initial tour is particularly helpful in those jobs where a firsthand view of a complicated or unfamiliar piece of equipment saves the interviewee the thousand words required to describe the unfamiliar or technical. c. For continuity, it is recommended that the first-level supervisor-interviewee be designated the guide for the job-site observations
3. Conduct interviews	a. It is recommended that the first interview be conducted with the first-level supervisor, who is considered to be in a better position than the jobholders to provide an overview of the job and how the major duties fit together. b. For scheduling purposes, it is recommended that no more than two interviews be conducted per day, each interview lasting no more than three hours.
Notes on selection of interviewees	a. The interviewees are considered subject-matter experts by virtue of the fact that they perform the job (in the case of job incumbents) or are responsible for getting the job done (in the case of first-level supervisors). b. The job incumbent to be interviewed should represent the *typical* employee who is knowledgeable about the job (*not* the trainee who is just learning the ropes *or* the outstanding member of the work unit). c. Whenever feasible, the interviewees should be selected with a view toward obtaining an appropriate race/sex mix.
4. Conduct second tour of work site	a. The second tour of the work site is designed to clarify, confirm, and otherwise refine the information developed in the interviews. b. As in the initial tour, it is recommended that the same first-level supervisor-interviewee conduct the second walk-through.
5. Consolidate job information	a. The consolidation phase of the job study involves piecing together into one coherent and comprehensive job description the data obtained from several sources: supervisor, jobholders, on-site tours, and written materials about the job. b. Past experience indicates that one minute of consolidation is required for every minute of interviewing. For planning purposes, at least five hours should be set aside for the consolidation phase. c. A subject-matter expert should be accessible as a resource person to the job analyst during the consolidation phase. The supervisor-interviewee fills this role. d. The job analyst should check the initial preliminary list of duties and questions—all must be answered or confirmed.
6. Verify job description	a. The verification phase involves bringing all the interviewees together for the purpose of determining if the consolidated job description is accurate and complete. b. The verification process is conducted in a group setting. Typed or legibly written copies of the job description (narrative description of the work setting *and* list of task statements) are distributed to the first-level supervisor and the job incumbent interviewees. c. Line by line, the job analyst goes through the entire job description and makes notes of any omissions, ambiguities, or needed clarifications. d. The job analyst collects all materials at the end of the verification meeting.

EXHIBIT 4.6
Typical Data
Collected for
Job Analysis

Data Related to Job	
Job Identification	**Job Content**
Title	Tasks
Department in which job is located	Activities
Number of people who hold job	Constraints on actions
	Performance criteria
	Critical incidents
	Conflicting demands
	Working conditions
	Roles (e.g., negotiator, monitor, leader)

Data Related to Employee		
Employee Characteristics	**Internal Relationships**	**External Relationships**
Professional/technical knowledge	Boss and other superiors	Suppliers
Manual skills	Peers	Customers
Verbal skills	Subordinates	Regulatory
Written skills		Professional industry
Quantitative skills		Community
Mechanical skills		Union/employee groups
Conceptual skills		
Managerial skills		
Leadership skills		
Interpersonal skills		

Generally, a good job analysis collects sufficient information to adequately identify, define, and describe a job. Exhibit 4.6 lists some of the information that is usually collected. The information is categorized as "related to the job" and "related to the employee."

Job Data: Identification

Job titles, departments, the number of people who hold the job, and whether it is exempt from the Fair Labor Standards Act are examples of information that identifies a job.

While a job title may seem pretty straightforward, it may not be. An observer of the U.S. banking system commented that "every employee over 25 seems to be a vice president." A Brookings Institute study accuses the U.S. government of creating more new job titles in a recent 6-year period than in the preceding 30 years.[5] Some of the newer positions include deputy to the deputy secretary, principal assistant deputy undersecretary, and associate principal deputy assistant secretary. Most of these titles were created at the highest levels of government service, often to attract a specific person with unique skills. On the other hand, your tax dollars are paying the wages of 484 deputy assistant secretaries, 148 associate assistant secretaries, 220 assistant assistant secretaries, and

[5]Paul C. Light, *The True Size of Government* (Washington, DC: Brookings Institute, 1999); Candice Prendergast, "The Role of Promotion in Inducing Specific Human Capital Acquisition," *Quarterly Journal of Economics,* May 1993, pp. 523–534.

82 deputy assistant assistant secretaries. But it is not only our government that is a well-spring of job titles. PepsiCo recently announced a new chief visionary officer. Many organizations are scrambling to hire visionaries of one sort or another. The Peabody Hotel in Orlando, Florida, recently advertised for a Duck Master to "join their flock."[6] A job title should be useful beyond providing fodder for the next *Dilbert* cartoon.

Job Data: Content

This is the heart of job analysis. Job content data involve the elemental tasks or units of work, with emphasis on the purpose of each task. An excerpt from a job analysis questionnaire that collects task data is shown in Exhibit 4.7. The inventory describes the job aspect of communication in terms of actual tasks, such as "read technical publications" and "consult with co-workers." The inventory takes eight items to cover "obtain technical information" and another seven for "exchange technical information." In fact, the task inventory from which the exhibit is excerpted contains 250 items and covers only systems and analyst jobs. New task-based questions need to be designed for each new set of jobs.

In addition to the emphasis on the task, the other distinguishing characteristic of the inventory in the exhibit is the emphasis on the objective of the task, for example, "read technical publications to keep current on industry" and "consult with co-workers to exchange ideas and techniques." Task data reveal the actual work performed and its purpose or outcome.

Employee Data

Once we have specified the tasks and outcomes, we can look at the kinds of behaviors that will result in the outcomes. Exhibit 4.6 categorizes employee data as employee characteristics, internal relationships, and external relationships. Exhibit 4.8 shows how communication can be described with verbs (e.g., negotiating, persuading). The verbs chosen are related to the employee characteristic being identified (e.g., bargaining skills, interpersonal skills). The rest of the statement helps identify whether the behavior involves an internal or external relationship. So both Exhibit 4.7 and Exhibit 4.8 focus on communication, but they come at it with different approaches.

The excerpt in Exhibit 4.8 is from the Position Analysis Questionnaire (PAQ), which groups work information into seven basic factors: information input, mental processes, work output, relationships with other persons, job context, other job characteristics, and general dimensions. Similarities and differences among jobs are described in terms of these seven factors, rather than in terms of specific aspects unique to each job.[7] The communication behavior in this exhibit is part of the relationships-with-other-persons factor.

[6]"If It's Easy, Don't Call It Duck Soup," *Wall Street Journal* September 3, 2002, p. B7. Who fits the bill? Someone who can feed, exercise, and train the ducks to march.

[7]Much of the developmental and early applications of the PAQ was done in the 1960s and 1970s. See, for example, E. J. McCormick, "Job and Task Analysis," in *Handbook of Industrial and Organizational Psychology*, ed. M. D. Dunnette (Chicago: Rand McNally, 1976), pp. 651–696; E. J. McCormick et al., "A Study of Job Characteristics and Job Dimensions as Based on the Position Analysis Questionnaire," Occupational Research Center, Purdue University, West Lafayette, IN, 1969. The PAQ is distributed by PAQ Services, *www.paq.com;* see PAQ's website and newsletters for recent discussions. For more recent information, see Robert J. Harvey, "Job Analysis," in *Handbook of Industrial and Organizational Psychology*, Vol. 2, ed. M. D. Dunnette and L. Hough (Palo Alto, CA: Consulting Psychologists Press, 1991).

EXHIBIT 4.7   Communication: Task-Based Data

1. Mark the circle in the "Do This" column for tasks that you currently perform.

   Time spent in current position

2. At the end of the task list, write in any unlisted tasks that you currently perform.

3. Rate each task that you perform for relative time spent by marking the appropriate circle in the "Time Spent" column.

   Please use a No. 2 pencil and fill all circles completely.

Do This / Very small amount / Much below average / Below average / Slightly below average / About average / Slightly above average / Above average / Much above average / Very large amount

PERFORM COMMUNICATION ACTIVITIES		
Obtain technical information		
421. Read technical publications about competitive products.	◯	①②③④⑤⑥⑦⑧⑨
422. Read technical publications to keep current on industry.	◯	①②③④⑤⑥⑦⑧⑨
423. Attend required, recommended, or job-related courses and/or seminars.	◯	①②③④⑤⑥⑦⑧⑨
424. Study existing operating systems/programs to gain/maintain familiarity with them.	◯	①②③④⑤⑥⑦⑧⑨
425. Perform literature searches necessary to the development of products.	◯	①②③④⑤⑥⑦⑧⑨
426. Communicate with system software group to see how their recent changes impact current projects.	◯	①②③④⑤⑥⑦⑧⑨
427. Study and evaluate state-of-the-art techniques to remain competitive and/or lead the field.	◯	①②③④⑤⑥⑦⑧⑨
428. Attend industry standards meetings.	◯	①②③④⑤⑥⑦⑧⑨
Exchange technical information		
429. Interface with coders to verify that the software design is being implemented as specified.	◯	①②③④⑤⑥⑦⑧⑨
430. Consult with co-workers to exchange ideas and techniques.	◯	①②③④⑤⑥⑦⑧⑨
431. Consult with members of other technical groups within the company to exchange new ideas and techniques.	◯	①②③④⑤⑥⑦⑧⑨
432. Interface with support consultants or organizations to clarify software design or courseware content.	◯	①②③④⑤⑥⑦⑧⑨

Source: Excerpted from Control Data Corporation's Quantitative Job Analysis. Used by permission.

EXHIBIT 4.8 **Communication: Behavioral-Based Data**

Section 4 Relationships with Others	*Code Importance to This Job (1)*
This section deals with different aspects of interaction between people involved in various kinds of work.	N Does not apply 1 Very minor 2 Low 3 Average 4 High 5 Extreme

4.1 Communication

Rate the following in terms of how important the activity is to the completion of the job. Some jobs may involve several or all of the items in this section.

4.1.1 Oral (communicating by speaking)

99 _____ Advising (dealing with individuals in order to counsel and/or guide them with regard to problems that may be resolved by legal, financial, scientific, technical, clinical, spiritual, and/or professional principles)

100 _____ Negotiating (dealing with others in order to reach an agreement on solution, for example, labor bargaining, diplomatic relations, etc.)

101 _____ Persuading (dealing with others in order to influence them toward some action or point of view, for example, selling, political campaigning, etc.)

102 _____ Instructing (the teaching of knowledge or skills, in either an informal or a formal manner, to others, for example, a public school teacher, a machinist teaching an apprentice, etc.)

103 _____ Interviewing (conducting interviews directed toward some specific objective, for example, interviewing job applicants, census taking, etc.)

104 _____ Routine information exchange job related (the giving and/or receiving of *job-related* information of a routine nature, for example, ticket agent, taxicab dispatcher, receptionist, etc.)

105 _____ Nonroutine information exchange (the giving and/or receiving of *job-related* information of a nonroutine or unusual nature, for example, professional committee meetings, engineers discussing new product design, etc.)

106 _____ Public speaking (making speeches or formal presentations before relatively large audiences, for example, political addresses, radio/TV broadcasting, delivering a sermon, etc.)

4.1.2 Written (communicating by written/printed material)

107 _____ Writing (for example, writing or dictating letters, reports, etc., writing copy for ads, writing newspaper articles, etc.; do *not* include transcribing activities described in item 4.3 but only activities in which the incumbent creates the written material)

Source: E. J. McConnick, P. R., Jeanneret, and R. C. Mecham, *Position Analysis Questionnaire,* copyright © 1969 by Purdue Research Foundation, West Lafayette, IN 47907. Reprinted with permission.

The entire PAQ consists of 194 items. Its developers claim that these items are sufficient to analyze any job. However, you can see by the exhibit that the reading level is quite high. A large proportion of employees need help to get through the whole thing.

However appealing it may be to rationalize job analysis as the foundation of all HR decisions, collecting all of this information for so many different purposes is very expensive. In addition, the resulting information may be too generalized for any single purpose, including compensation. If the information is to be used for multiple purposes, the analyst must be sure that the information collected is accurate and sufficient for each use. Trying to be all things to all people often results in being nothing to everyone.

Know what)

"Essential Elements" and the Americans with Disabilities Act

essental element of a job is / involves / examples

In addition to the job description having sections that identify, describe, and define the job, the Americans with Disabilities Act (ADA) requires that *essential elements* of a job—those that cannot be reassigned to other workers—must be specified for jobs covered by the legislation. If a job applicant can perform these essential elements, it is assumed that the applicant can perform the job. After that, reasonable accommodations must be made to enable an otherwise-qualified handicapped person to perform those elements.[8]

ADA regulations state that "essential functions refers to the fundamental job duties of the employment position the individual with a disability holds or desires." The difficulty of specifying essential elements varies with the discretion in the job and with the stability of the job. Technology changes tend to make some tasks easier for all people, including those with disabilities, by reducing the physical strength or mobility required to do them. Unfortunately, employment rates for people with disabilities are still low.

Settlements of complaints filed under the law seem to target blanket exclusions that ignore the individual in hiring and job assignments. For example, the metropolitan government of Nashville, Tennessee, settled a lawsuit by agreeing to hire an applicant for an emergency medical technician-paramedic position who was deaf in one ear. Even though the applicant had been working part-time as a paramedic in the state for over six years, Nashville applied an absolute medical/physical standard that automatically excluded him because of his hearing loss. His successful lawsuit forced the government to base hiring decisions on an individualized assessment of a candidate's physical condition.

While the law does not require any particular kind of analysis, many employers have modified the format of their job descriptions to specifically call out the essential elements. A lack of compliance places an organization at risk and ignores one of the objectives of the pay model.

Level of Analysis

The job analysis terms defined in Exhibit 4.4 are arranged in a hierarchy. The level at which an analysis begins influences whether the work is similar or dissimilar. The three jobs described in the beginning of the chapter—sales rep, engineer, account analyst—all involve use of computers, but a closer look showed that the jobs are very different. At the

---

[8]Adrienne Colella, "Co-worker Distributive Fairness Judgments of the Workplace Accommodation of Employees with Disabilities," *Academy of Management Review* 26(1) (January 2001), pp. 100–116; Edward H. Yelin and Laura Trupin, "Disability and the Characteristics of Employment," *Monthly Labor Review*, May 2003, pp. 20–31.

job-family level bookkeepers, tellers, and accounting clerks may be considered to be similar jobs, yet at the job level they are very different. An analogy might be looking at two grains of salt under a microscope versus looking at them as part of a serving of french fries. If job data suggest that jobs are similar, then the jobs must be paid equally; if jobs are different, they can be paid differently.

Cybercomp

Many companies post a sample of job openings on their websites. Compare the job postings from several companies. How complete are the job descriptions included with the postings? Are "essential elements" listed? Are job titles specific or generic? Can you get any sense of a company's culture from its job postings?

Links to fast-growing small private companies can be found via the Inc 500 link at *www.inc.com/500/about.html.* Are there any differences in job postings between large and small companies?

Does this mean that the microscopic approach is best? Not necessarily. Many employers find it difficult to justify the time and expense of collecting task-level information, particularly for flexible jobs with frequently changing tasks. They may collect just enough job-level data to make comparisons in the external market for setting wages. However, the ADA's essential-elements requirement for hiring and promotion decisions seems to require more detail than what is required for pay decisions. Designing career paths, staffing, and legal compliance may also require more detailed, finely grained information.

Using broad, generic descriptions that cover a large number of related tasks closer to the job-family level in Exhibit 4.4 is one way to increase flexibility. Two employees working in the same broadly defined jobs may be doing entirely different sets of related tasks. But for pay purposes, they may be doing work of equal value. Employees in these broadly defined jobs can switch to other tasks that fall within the same broad range without the bureaucratic burden of making job transfer requests and wage adjustments. Thus, employees can more easily be matched to changes in the work flow. Recruiter, compensation analyst, and training specialist could each be analyzed as a separate, distinct job, or could all be combined more broadly in the category "HR associate".

Still, a countervailing view deserves consideration. A promotion to a new job title is part of the organization's network of rewards. Reducing the number of titles may reduce the opportunities to reinforce positive employee behavior. E*Trade experienced an increase in turnover after it retitled jobs. It reduced its vice presidents and directors to 85, down from around 170 before the retitling.[9] Moving from the federal government job of assistant assistant secretary to that of associate assistant secretary (or reverse) may be far more meaningful than people outside Washington, DC, imagine. Reducing titles or labeling all employees as "associates," as Target, Wal-Mart, and others have done, may signal an egalitarian culture. But it also may sacrifice opportunities to reward employees with advancement.[10]

---

[9]Susanne Craig, "E*Trade Lowers Corporate Titles, in Move That Could Spur Departures," *Wall Street Journal,* September 6, 2001, pp. C1, C14.

[10]V. L. Huber and S. R. Crandall, "Job Measurement: A Social-Cognitive Decision Perspective," in *Research in Personnel and Human Resources Management,* Vol. 12, ed. Gerald R. Ferris (Greenwich, CT: JAI Press, 1994), pp. 223–269; Juan I. Sanchez, I. Prager, A. Wilson, and C. Viswesvaran, "Understanding Within-Job Title Variance in Job-Analytic Ratings", *Journal of Business and Psychology* 12 (1998), pp. 407–419.

EXHIBIT 4.9   3M's Structured Interview Questionnaire

I. Job Overview	

Job Summary	What is the main purpose of your job? (Why does it exist and what does the work contribute to 3M?)
	   Examples: To provide secretarial support in our department by performing office and administrative duties.
	        To purchase goods and services that meet specifications at the least cost.
	        To perform systems analysis involved in the development, installation, and maintenance of computer applications.
	
	Hint: It may help to list the duties first before answering this question.

		Percentage of Time Spent (Total may be less than but not more than 100%)
Duties and Respon-sibilities	What are your job's main duties and responsibilities? (These are the major work activities that usually take up a significant amount of your work time and occur regularly as you perform your work.) In the spaces below, list your job's five most important or most frequent duties. Then, in the boxes, estimate the percentage of the time you spend on each duty each day.	Percentage of Time Spent (Total may be less than but not more than 100%)
	1.	

II. Skills/Knowledge Applied	

Formal Training or Education	What is the level of formal training/education that is needed to start doing your job?
	   Example: High School, 2 Year Vo-Tech in Data Processing. Bachelor of Science in Chemistry.
	In some jobs, a combination of education and job-related experience can substitute for academic degrees.
	   Example: Bachelor's Degree in Accounting or completion of 2 years of general business plus 3–4 years' work experience in an accounting field.

HOW CAN THE INFORMATION BE COLLECTED?

Conventional Methods

The most common way to collect job information is to ask the people who are doing a job to fill out a questionnaire. Sometimes an analyst will interview the jobholders and their supervisors to be sure they understand the questions and the information is correct. Or the analyst may observe the person at work and take notes on what is being done. Exhibit 4.9 shows part of a job analysis questionnaire. Questions range from "Give an example of a particularly difficult problem that you face in your work. Why does it occur? How often does it occur? What special skills and/or resources are needed to solve this difficult problem?" to "What is the nature of any contact you have with individuals or companies in countries other than the United States?" These examples are drawn from the Complexity of Duties section of a job analysis questionnaire used by 3M. Other sections of the questionnaire are Skills/Knowledge Applied (19 to choose from), Impact This Job Has on 3M's Business, and Working Conditions. It concludes by asking respondents how well they feel the questionnaire has captured their particular job.

The advantage of conventional questionnaires and interviews is that the involvement of employees increases their understanding of the process. However, the results are only as good as the people involved. If important aspects of a job are omitted, or if the job-

EXHIBIT 4.9   *continued*

Experience	Months:		Years: None
	What important skills, competencies, or abilities are needed to do the work that you do? (Please give examples for each skill that you identify.)		
	A. Coordinating Skills (such as scheduling activities, organizing/maintaining records)		
Skills/ Compet- encies	Are coordinating skills required? ☐ Yes ☐ No If yes, give examples of specific skills needed		
	Example		
	B. Administrative Skills (such as monitoring		

III. Complexity of Duties

Structure and Variation of Work	How processes and tasks within your work are determined, and how you do them are important to understanding your work at 3M. Describe the work flow in your job. Think of the major focus of your job or think of the work activities on which you spend the most time.
	1. From whom/where (title, not person) do you receive work?
	2. What processes or tasks do you perform to complete
Problem Solving and Analysis	3.
	Give an example of a particularly difficult problem that you face in your work.
	Why does it occur?
	How often does it occur?
	What special skills and/or resources are needed to solve this difficult problem?

VI. General Comments

General Comments	What percentage of your job duties do you feel was captured in this questionnaire?
	☐ 0–25% ☐ 26–50% ☐ 51–75% ☐ 76–100%
	What aspect of your job was not covered adequately by this questionnaire?

holders themselves either do not realize or are unable to express the importance of certain aspects, the resulting job descriptions will be faulty. If you look at the number of jobs in an organization, you can see the difficulty in expecting a single analyst to understand all the different types of work and the importance of certain job aspects. Different people have different perceptions, which may result in differences in interpretation or emphasis. The whole process is open to bias and favoritism.[11]

As a result of this potential subjectivity, as well as the huge amount of time the process takes, conventional methods have given way to more quantitative (and systematic) data collection.

Quantitative Methods

Increasingly, employees are directed to a website where they complete a questionnaire online. Such an approach is characterized as *quantitative job analysis*, since statistical analysis of the results is possible. Exhibits 4.7 and 4.8 are excerpts from quantitative questionnaires. In addition to facilitating statistical analysis of the results, quantitative data collection allows more data to be collected faster.

[11]Richard Arvey, Emily M. Passino, and John W. Lounsbury, "Job Analysis Results as Influenced by Sex of Incumbent and Sex of Analyst," *Journal of Applied Psychology* 62(4) (1977), pp. 411–416; Richard Arvey, "Potential Problems in Job Evaluation Methods and Processes," in *Compensation*, ed. L. Gomez-Mejia and D. Balkin (Englewood Cliffs, NJ: Prentice-Hall, 1987). Juan I. Sanchez and Edward L. Levine, "Is Job Analysis Dead, Misunderstood, or Both? New Forms of Work Analysis and Design," in *Evolving Practices in Human Resource Management: Responses to a Changing World of Work*, eds. A. I. Kraut and A. K. Korman (San Francisco: Jossey-Bass, 1999), pp. 43–68.

A questionnaire typically asks jobholders to assess each item in terms of whether or not that particular item is part of their job. If it is, they are asked to rate how important it is and the amount of job time spent on it. The responses can be machine-scored, similar to the process for a multiple-choice test (only there are no wrong answers), and the results can be used to develop a profile of the job. Exhibit 4.10 shows part of an online job analysis questionnaire used by a U.K. consulting firm.[12] Questions are grouped around five compensable factors (discussed in Chapter 5): knowledge, accountability, reasoning, communication, and working conditions. Knowledge is further subcategorized as range of depth, qualifications, experience, occupational skills, management skills, and learning time. Assistance is given in the form of prompting questions and a list of jobs whose holders have answered each question in a similar way. Results can be used to prepare a job profile based on the compensable factors. If more than one person is doing a particular job, results of several people in the job can be compared or averaged to develop the profile. Profiles can be compared across jobholders in both the same and different jobs. Exhibit 4.11 is a job profile prepared from the results of the questionnaire used in Exhibit 4.10.

Some consulting firms have developed quantitative inventories that can be tailored to the needs of a specific organization or to a specific family of jobs, such as data/information processing jobs.[13] Many organizations find it practical and cost-effective to modify these

EXHIBIT 4.10 Online Job Analysis Questionnaire

Source: Link Group Consultants, Limited, *www.hrlink.co.uk.* Used by permission.

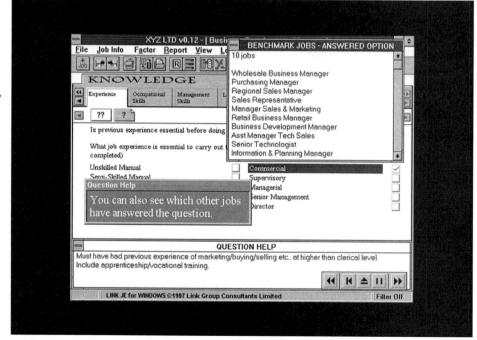

[12]Link Group Consultants, Limited, Chester, U.K., *www.linkg.co.uk.*

[13]Towers Perrin has done a lot of research on this issue. See its website at *www.towers.com;* "Joint Compensation Study: Technical Occupational Analysis Questionnaire," Control Data Business Advisors, Minneapolis, 1985.

existing inventories rather than to develop their own analysis from ground zero. But keep in mind that the results are only as good as the items in the questionnaire. If important aspects of a job are omitted or if the jobholders themselves do not realize the importance of certain aspects, the resulting job descriptions will be faulty. In one study, the responses of high-performing stockbrokers on amounts of time spent on some tasks differed from those of low performers. The implication seems to be that any analysis needs to include good performers to ensure that the work is usefully analyzed.[14]

Who Collects the Information?

Collecting job analysis information through one-on-one interviews can be a thankless task. No matter how good a job you do, some people will not be happy with the resulting job descriptions. In the past, organizations often assigned the task to a new employee, saying it would help the new employee become familiar with the jobs of the company. Today, if job analysis is performed at all, human resource generalists and supervisors do it. The analysis is best done by someone thoroughly familiar with the organization and its jobs and trained in how to do the analysis properly.[15]

**EXHIBIT 4.11
Online Job
Profile**

Source: Link
Group Consultants,
Limited,
www.hrlink.co.uk.
Used by
permission.

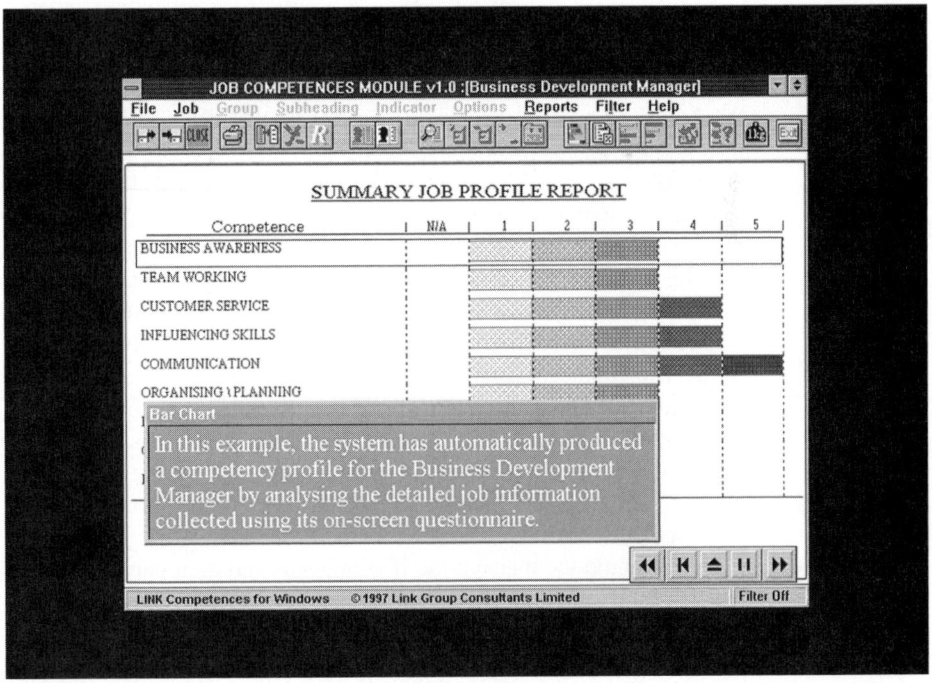

---

[14]W. C. Borman, D. Dorsey, and L. Ackerman, "Time-Spent Responses and Time Allocation Strategies: Relations with Sales Performance in a Stockbroker Sample," *Personnel Psychology* 45 (1992), pp. 763–777.

[15]Richard Arvey, Emily M. Passino, and John W. Lounsbury, "Job Analysis Results as Influenced by Sex of Incumbent and Sex of Analyst," *Journal of Applied Psychology* 62(4) (1977), pp. 411–416; Richard Arvey, "Potential Problems in Job Evaluation Methods and Processes," in *Compensation,* ed. L. Gomez-Mejia and D. Balkin (Englewood Cliffs, NJ: Prentice-Hall, 1987); Paul Sackett, E. Cornelius, and E. T. Carron, "A Comparison of Global Judgment versus Task-Oriented Approaches to Job Classification", *Personnel Psychology* 34 (1981), pp. 791–804.

Who Provides the Information?

The decision on the source of the data (jobholders, supervisors, and/or analysts) hinges on how to ensure consistent, accurate, useful, and acceptable data. Expertise about the work resides with the jobholders and the supervisors; hence, they are the principal sources. For key managerial/professional jobs, supervisors "two levels above" have also been suggested as valuable sources since they may have a more strategic view of how jobs fit in the overall organization. In other instances, subordinates and employees in other jobs that interface with the job under study are also involved.

The number of incumbents per job from which to collect data probably varies with the stability of the job, as well as the ease of collecting the information. An ill-defined or changing job will require either the involvement of more respondents or a more careful selection of respondents. Obviously, the more people involved, the more time-consuming and expensive the process, although computerization helps mitigate these drawbacks.

Whether through a conventional analysis or a quantitative approach, completing a questionnaire requires considerable involvement by employees and supervisors. Involvement can increase their understanding of the process, thereby increasing the likelihood that the results of the analysis will be acceptable.[16]

What about Discrepancies?

What happens if the supervisor and the employees present different pictures of the jobs? While supervisors, in theory, ought to know the jobs well, they may not, particularly if jobs are changing or ill-defined in the first place. People actually working in a job may change it. They may find ways to do things more efficiently, or they may not have realized that certain tasks were supposed to be part of their jobs. As in the previously mentioned case of the stockbrokers, employees with differences in performance or experience may have different views of the job. The crossfire from these differing views can make job analysis a dangerous assignment for a brand-new HR employee.

3M had an interesting problem when it collected job information from a group of engineers. The engineers listed a number of responsibilities that they viewed as part of their jobs; however, the manager realized that those responsibilities actually belonged to a higher level of work. The engineers had enlarged their jobs beyond what they were being paid to do. No one wanted to tell these highly productive employees to throttle back and slack off. Instead, 3M looked for additional ways to reward these engineers rather than bureaucratize them.

What should the manager do if employees and their supervisors do not agree on what is part of the job? Differences in job data may arise among the jobholders as well. Some may see the job one way, some another. The best answer is to collect more data. Enough data are required to ensure consistent, accurate, useful, and acceptable results. In general, the more unique the job, the more sources of data will be required. Holding a meeting of multiple jobholders and supervisors to discuss discrepancies and then asking both employees and supervisors to sign off on the proposed analysis helps ensure agreement on,

---

[16]V. L. Huber and S. R. Crandall, "Job Measurement: A Social-Cognitive Decision Perspective," in *Research in Personnel and Human Resources Management,* Vol. 12, ed. Gerald R. Ferris (Greenwich, CT: JAI Press, 1994), pp. 223–269.

or at least understanding of, the results. Discrepancies among employees may even reveal that more than one job has been lumped under the same job title.

Top Management Support Is Critical

In addition to involvement by analysts, jobholders, and their supervisors, support of top management is absolutely essential. They know (hopefully) what is strategically relevant. They must be alerted to the cost of a thorough job analysis, its time-consuming nature, and the fact that changes will be involved. For example, jobs may be combined; pay rates may be adjusted. If top management is not willing to seriously consider any changes suggested by job analysis, the process is probably not worth the bother and expense.

JOB DESCRIPTIONS SUMMARIZE THE DATA

So now the job information has been collected, maybe even organized. But it still must be summarized in a way that will be useful for HR decisions, including job evaluation (Chapter 5). That summary of the job is the *job description*. The job description provides a "word picture" of the job. Let us return to Exhibit 4.2, our job description for a registered nurse. It contains information on the tasks, people, and things included. Trace the connection between different parts of the description and the job analysis data collected. The job is identified by its title and its relationships to other jobs in the structure. A job summary provides an overview of the job. The section on essential responsibilities elaborates on the summary. It includes the tasks. Related tasks may be grouped into task dimensions. This particular job description also includes very specific standards for judging whether an essential responsibility has been met—for example, "Provides a written assessment of patient within one hour of admission and at least once a shift." A final section lists the qualifications necessary in order to be hired for the job. These are the *job specifications* that can be used as a basis for hiring—the knowledge, skills, and abilities required to adequately perform the tasks. But keep in mind that the summary needs to be relevant for pay decisions and thus must focus on similarities and differences in content.

Describing Managerial/Professional Jobs

Descriptions of managerial/professional jobs often include more detailed information on the nature of the job, its scope, and accountability. One challenge is that an individual manager will influence the job content.[17] Professional/managerial job descriptions must capture the relationship between the job, the person performing it, and the organization objectives—how the job fits into the organization, the results expected, and what the person performing it brings to the job. Someone with strong information systems and computer expertise performing the compensation manager's job will probably shape it differently, based on this expertise, than someone with strong negotiation and/or counseling expertise. This is a classic example of how job-based and person-based approaches blend together in practice, even though the distinctions are easy to make in a textbook.

[17]K. C. O'Shaughnessy, David Levine, and Peter Cappelli, "Changes in Management Pay Structures, 1986–1992, and Rising Returns to Skill," working paper, University of California–Berkeley, Institute of Industrial Relations, 1998.

EXHIBIT 4.12
Job
Description
for a Manager

Title: Nurse Manager

Department: ICU

Position Description:
Under the direction of the Vice President of Patient Care Services and Directors of Patient Care Services, the Nurse Manager assumes 24-hour accountability and responsibility for the operations of defined patient specialty services. The Nurse Manager is administratively responsible for the coordination, direction, implementation, evaluation, and management of personnel and services. The Nurse Manager provides leadership in a manner consistent with the corporate mission, values, and philosophy and adheres to policies and procedures established by Saint Joseph's Hospital and the Division of Patient Care Services. The Nurse Manager participates in strategic planning and defining future direction for the assigned areas of responsibility and the organization.

Qualification:
Education: Graduate of accredited school of nursing. A bachelor's degree in Nursing or related field required. Master's degree preferred. Current license in State of Wisconsin as a Registered Nurse, Experience: A minimum of three years' clinical nursing is required. Minimum of two years' management experience or equivalent preferred.

Exhibit 4.12 excerpts this scope and accountability information for a nurse manager. Rather than emphasizing the tasks to be done, this description focuses on the accountabilities (e.g., "responsible for the coordination, direction, implementation, evaluation, and management of personnel and services; provides leadership; participates in strategic planning and defining future direction").

Verify the Description

The final step in the job analysis process is to verify the accuracy of the resulting job descriptions (step 6 in Exhibit 4.5). Verification often involves the interviewees as well as their supervisors to determine whether the proposed job description is accurate and complete. The description is discussed, line by line, with the analyst, who makes notes of any omissions, ambiguities, or needed clarifications (an often excruciating and thankless task). It would have been interesting to hear the discussion between our nurse from 100 years ago, whose job is described in Exhibit 4.13, and her supervisor. The job description paints a vivid picture of expectations at that time, although we suspect the nurse probably did not have much opportunity for input regarding the accuracy of the job description.

JOB ANALYSIS: BEDROCK OR BUREAUCRACY?

HRNet, an Internet discussion group related to HR issues, provoked one of its largest number of responses ever with the query, "What good is job analysis?" Some felt that managers have no basis for making defensible, work-related decisions without it. Others called the process a bureaucratic boondoggle. Yet job analysts are an endangered species. Many employers, as part of their drive to contain expenses, no longer have job analysts. If the job information is needed to manage compensation, the compensation specialist or

**EXHIBIT 4.13
Job
Description
for Nurse 100
Years Ago**

In addition to caring for your 50 patients each nurse will follow these regulations:

1. Daily sweep and mop the floors of your ward, dust the patient's furniture and window sills.
2. Maintain an even temperature in your ward by bringing in a scuttle of coal for the day's business.
3. Light is important to observe the patient's condition. Therefore, each day, fill kerosene lamps, clean chimneys, and trim wicks. Wash the windows once a week.
4. The nurse's notes are important in aiding the physician's work. Make your pens carefully, you may whittle nibs to your individual taste.
5. Each nurse on the day duty will report every day at 7 A.M. and leave at 8 P.M. except on the Sabbath on which day you will be off from 12:00 noon to 2:00 P.M.
6. Graduate nurses in good standing with the director of nurses will be given an evening off each week for courting purposes, or two evenings a week if you go regularly to church.
7. Each nurse should lay aside from each pay day a goodly sum of her earnings for her benefit during her declining years, so that she will not become a burden. For example, if you earn $30 a month you should set aside $15.
8. Any nurse who smokes, uses liquor in any form, gets her hair done at a beauty shop, or frequents dance halls will give the director good reason to suspect her worth, intentions, and integrity.
9. The nurse who performs her labors and serves her patients and doctors faithfully and without fault for a period of five years will be given an increase by the hospital administration of five cents a day, provided there are no hospital debts that are outstanding.

HR generalist collects it. In many cases, the job analysis is simply no longer performed. The costs involved are too difficult to justify.

One expert writes, "Whenever I visit a human resources department, I ask whether they have any [job analysis]. I have not had a positive answer in several years, except in government organizations."[18] Yet if job analysis is the cornerstone of human resource decisions, what are such decisions based on if work information is no longer rigorously collected?

A large part of the disagreement centers on the issue of flexibility. Many organizations today are using fewer employees to do a wider variety of tasks as part of a cost reduction strategy. Streamlining job analysis and reducing the number of different jobs can reduce costs by making work assignments more fluid.[19]

Generic descriptions that cover a larger number of related tasks (e.g., "associate") can provide flexibility in moving people among tasks without adjusting pay. Employees may be more easily matched to changes in the work flow; the importance of flexibility in behavior is made clear to employees.

Traditional job analysis that makes fine distinctions among levels of jobs has been accused of reinforcing rigidity in the organization. Employees may refuse to do certain tasks that are not specifically called out in their job descriptions. It should be noted, however,

---

[18]"The Future of Salary Management," *Compensation* and *Benefits Review*, July/August 2001, p. 10.

[19]Lee Dyer and Richard A. Shafer, "From HR Strategy to Organizational Effectiveness," in *Strategic Human Resources Management in the Twenty-First Century,* Suppl. 4, eds. Patrick M. Wright, Lee D. Dyer, John W. Boudreau, and George T. Milkovich (Stamford, CT: JAI Press, 1999).

that this problem mainly arises where employee relations are already poor. In unionized settings, union members may "work to the rules" (i.e., not do anything that is not specifically listed in their job descriptions) as a technique for putting pressure on management. Where work relationships are poor, both managers and employees may use detailed job descriptions as a "weapon."[20]

On the other hand, the hierarchies and distinctions among jobs also represent rewards—career paths and promotion opportunities. Changing jobs often means a promotion and/or recognition of performance, not to mention a fatter paycheck. Reducing the number of jobs reduces these opportunities for recognition and advancement. Some people value a title change from "engineer" to "senior engineer" rather than the more generic "engineer associate", which includes the work of both. Johnson & Johnson (J&J) in China sought to cut turnover from around 25 percent a year by relayering. J&J went from 7 levels in its structure to 28, thereby responding to employees' desires for a greater sense of progress and promotion.

JUDGING JOB ANALYSIS

Beyond beliefs about its usefulness, or lack thereof, for satisfying both employees and employers, there are several ways to judge job analysis.

know the factors 2 consider regarding the usefulness of a job analysis

Reliability

If you measure something tomorrow and get the same results you got today, or if I measure and get the same result you did, the measurement is considered to be reliable. This doesn't mean it is right—only that repeated measures give the same result. *Reliability* is a measure of the consistency of results among various analysts, various methods, various sources of data, or over time.

Research on employee and supervisor agreement on the reliability of job analysis information is mixed.[21] For instance, experience may change an employee's perceptions about a job since the employee may have found new ways to do it or added new tasks to the job. The supervisor may not realize the extent of change. In such cases, the job the employee is actually doing may not be the same as the job originally assigned by the supervisor. Differences in performance seem to influence reliability. To date, no studies have found that gender and race differences affect reliability.[22]

Obviously, the way to increase reliability in a job analysis is to reduce sources of difference. Quantitative job analysis helps do this. But we need to be sure that we do not

[20]S. G. Cohen and D. E. Bailey, "What Makes Teams Work: Group Effectiveness Research from the Shop Floor to Executive Suite," *Journal of Management* 23 (1997), pp. 239–291.

[21]Juan I. Sanchez and E. L. Levine, "The Impact of Raters' Cognition on Judgment Accuracy: An Extension to the Job Analysis Domain," *Journal of Business and Psychology* 9 (1994), pp. 47–57; Juan I. Sanchez and Edward L. Levine, "Accuracy or Consequential Validity: Which Is the Better Standard for Job Analysis Data?" *Journal of Organizational Behavior* 21 (2000), pp. 809–818; Frederick P. Morgeson and Michael A. Campion, "Accuracy in Job Analysis: Toward an Inference-Based Model," *Journal of Organizational Behavior* 21(2000) pp. 819–827.

[22]Richard Arvey, Emily M. Passino, and John W. Lounsbury, "Job Analysis Results as Influenced by Sex of Incumbent and Sex of Analyst," *Journal of Applied Psychology* 62(4) (1977), pp. 411–416; Sara L. Rynes, Caroline L. Weber, and George T. Milkovich, "Effects of Market Survey Rates, Job Evaluation, and Job Gender on Job Pay," *Journal of Applied Psychology* 74(1) (1989), pp. 114–123.

eliminate the richness of responses while eliminating the differences. Sometimes there really may be more than one job.

Validity

Does the analysis create an accurate portrait of the work? There is almost no way of showing statistically the extent to which an analysis is accurate, particularly for complex jobs. No gold standard exists; how can we know? Consequently, *validity* examines the convergence of results among sources of data and methods. If several job incumbents, supervisors, and peers respond in similar ways to questionnaires, then it is more likely that the information is valid. However, a sign-off on the results does not guarantee the information's validity.[23] It may mean only that all involved were sick to death of the process and wanted to get rid of the analyst so they could get back to work.

Acceptability

If jobholders and managers are dissatisfied with the initial data collected and the process, they are not likely to buy into the resulting job structure or the pay rates attached to that structure. An analyst collecting information through one-on-one interviews or observation is not always accepted because of the potential for subjectivity and favoritism. One writer says, "We all know the classic procedures. One [worker] watched and noted the actions of another . . . at work on [the] job. The actions of both are biased and the resulting information varied with the wind, especially the political wind."[24] However, quantitative computer-assisted approaches may also run into difficulty, especially if they give in to the temptation to collect too much information for too many purposes. After four years in development, one application ran into such severe problems due to its unwieldy size and incomprehensible questions that managers simply refused to use it.

Usefulness

Usefulness refers to the practicality of the information collected. For pay purposes, job analysis provides work-related information to help determine how much to pay for a job—it helps determine whether the job is similar to or different from other jobs. If job analysis does this in a reliable, valid, and acceptable way and can be used to make pay decisions, then it is useful.[25]

As we have noted, some see job analysis information as useful for multiple purposes, such as hiring and training. But multiple purposes may require more information than is required for pay decisions. The practicality of all-encompassing quantitative job analysis plans, with their relatively complex procedures and analysis, remains in doubt. Some advocates get

[23]Juan I. Sanchez and E. L. Levine, "The Impact of Raters' Cognition on Judgment Accuracy: An Extension to the Job Analysis Domain," *Journal of Business and Psychology* 9 (1994), pp. 47–57; Juan I. Sanchez and Edward L. Levine, "Accuracy or Consequential Validity: Which Is the Better Standard for Job Analysis Data?" *Journal of Organizational Behavior* 21 (2000), pp. 809–818; Frederick P. Morgeson and Michael A. Campion, "Accuracy in Job Analysis: Toward an Inference-Based Model," *Journal of Organizational Behavior* 21 (2000), pp. 819–827.

[24]E. M. Ramras, "Discussion," in *Proceedings of Division of Military Psychology Symposium: Collecting, Analyzing, and Reporting Information Describing Jobs and Occupations,* 77th Annual Convention of the American Psychological Association, Lackland Air Force Base, TX, September 1969, pp. 75–76.

[25]Edward L. Levine, Ronald A. Ash, Hardy Hall, and Frank Sistrunk, "Evaluation of Job Analysis Methods by Experienced Job Analysts," *Academy of Management* Journal 26(2) (1983), pp. 339–348.

so taken with their statistics and computers that they ignore the role that judgment must continue to play in job analysis. Dunnette's point, made 25 years ago, still holds true today: "I wish to emphasize the central role played in all these procedures by human judgment. I know of no methodology, statistical technique or objective measurements that can negate the importance of, nor supplement, rational judgment."[26]

A Judgment Call

In the face of all the difficulties, time, expense, and dissatisfaction, why on earth would you as a manager bother with job analysis? Because work-related information is needed to determine pay, and differences in work determine pay differences. There is no satisfactory substitute that can ensure the resulting pay structure will be work-related or will provide reliable, accurate data for making and explaining pay decisions.

If work information is required, then the real issue should be, How much detail is needed to make these pay decisions? The answer is, Enough to help set individual employees' pay, encourage continuous learning, increase the experience and skill of the work force, and minimize the risk of pay-related grievances. Omitting this detail and contributing to an incorrect and costly decision by uninformed managers can lead to dissatisfied employees who drive away customers with their poor service, file lawsuits, or complain about management's inability to justify their decisions. The response to inadequate analysis ought not to be to dump the analysis; rather, the response should be to obtain a more useful analysis.

Your Turn   The Customer-Service Agent

Read the accompanying article on a day in the work life of Bill Ryan. Then write a job description for the job of customer service agent. Use the exhibits in this chapter to guide you in deciding what information in the story is relevant for job analysis.

1. Does the day diary include sufficient information?
2. Identify the specific information in the article that you found useful.
3. What additional information do you require? How would that information help you?

Pick a teammate (or the instructor will assign one) and exchange job descriptions with your teammate.

1. How similar/different are the two descriptions? You and your teammate started with exactly the same information. What might explain any differences?
2. What process would you go through to understand and minimize the differences?
3. What are some of the relational returns of the job?

(Editor: article is on separate pages. It is a photocopy of a newspaper article.)

[26]M. D. Dunnette, L. M. Hough, and R. L. Rosse, "Task and Job Taxonomies as a Basis for Identifying Labor Supply Sources and Evaluating Employment Qualifications," in *Affirmative Action Planning,* eds. George T. Milkovich and Lee Dyer (New York: Human Resource Planning Society, 1979), pp. 37–51.

The Customer-Service Agent

When you're the public face of e-commerce, you have the power to make or break a business

Bill Ryan often deals with difficult people. It's what he gets paid for.

He's one of 30 customer-service agents at Half.com, an online marketplace owned by eBay Inc., the Internet auction company. Like eBay, Half.com attempts to match buyers and sellers in a vast flea market featuring millions of products ranging from trading cards to camcorders. But unlike eBay, there's no bidding. Half.com lists items only at fixed prices. If you see something you like, pay the price and it's yours.

The other big difference with eBay is that for most of the products listed on Half.com, there's no way for buyers and sellers to interact directly. Usually there's no need to. To make a purchase, buyers use their credit cards or checking accounts to pay Half.com, which then automatically credits the amount to the seller's card or account—minus a transaction fee. Once the payment is made, the seller ships the product.

Despite a well-oiled system, however, questions arise. Things can go wrong. A purchased item doesn't arrive, or isn't in the condition the buyer expected. Or maybe an interesting product is listed but its description isn't clear.

And that's where Mr. Ryan and his colleagues come in, handling the buckets of e-mail and intermittent phone calls from curious, addled and upset users. They pass information between buyers and sellers, answer questions and resolve the occasional dispute. Half.com says that fewer than 1% of the site's transactions require customer service's involvement. But with more than 15 million items for sale—well, you do the math.

In fact, the customer-service department receives about 1,500 to 2,000 e-mails a day, of which nearly a third are complaints about transactions. The rest are mostly questions about the goods and how the site works. Mr. Ryan himself on a typical day fields between 60 and 100 e-mails and half a dozen phone calls. The calls are the most stressful. "People panic and they want answers," Mr. Ryan says. "If they are calling, they are not happy."

For Half.com—as well as most other e-commerce companies—customer-service agents like Mr. Ryan are the crucial link between the faceless Web site and the consumer. And how they deal with the public can make or break a business. As George Leimer, Half.com's vice president for operations, says, "It costs too much to get a new customer only to fumble the relationship away."

Mr. Leimer says there has been virtually no turnover in customer service since the company began a year and a half ago. Half.com wouldn't discuss salaries. But Mr. Ryan and his colleagues, who are split into two shifts covering 8 a.m. to midnight, seven days a week, say they're satisfied with their wages, which include quarterly bonuses.

What he likes about the work, Mr. Ryan says, is the kind of customer problem that requires research and deep digging to find the resolution. What he sometimes doesn't like about his work are the routine questions that generate stock responses.

Here's a day in Mr. Ryan's work life:

The Answer Man

8 AM Mr. Ryan strolls into the Half.com office in Plymouth Meeting, Pa., a short drive from his home. The company's single-story gray building is a former tire factory in this colonial-era industrial town on the outskirts of Philadelphia. The office has an open feel with tall ceilings. Mr. Ryan works in a low-slung, black cubicle toward the back of the office, his space sparsely decorated save for photos of his parents, his wife, Melissa, their two-year-old beagle, Max, and an 8 1/2-by-11 inch picture of Dikembe Mutombo, the Philadelphia 76ers' star defensive center.

The atmosphere at Half.com is decidedly young and casual. Jeans are the uniform. Mr. Ryan certainly fits in, though at 32 he's a few years older than most of his cubicle mates. He wears a well-groomed goatee and small round glasses, and sits up straight at his desk. He started with Half.com last August, which makes him something of an old-timer, since the department has doubled in size since then.

He started doing strictly customer service, answering customer e-mails. Now he also does what the company calls "trust and safety work": investigating fraud and looking for things on the site that are "funky." For instance, when Half.com receives a complaint from a buyer about a seller, it's Mr. Ryan's job to contact both parties and make sure there is no fraud occurring.

This day, because the site has received a high volume of e-mails, he's on regular customer-service duty. After checking the few internal e-mail messages he receives each day, he gets right to work.

Mr. Ryan downloads his first batch of 10 e-mails for the day. He says it usually takes him about an hour to get through 10 messages.

8:10 AM The first e-mail is from a woman interested in buying an audio book on CD that she saw listed on the site. She wants to know whether the CD will work on her DVD player. But since she doesn't specify the exact listing, Mr. Ryan is stuck. He can't search for it among all the listings or contact the seller. The best he can do is suggest that she send him an item number so he can contact the seller with her question.

8:15 AM The next e-mail comes from a user who sold the Diana Krall CD "When I Look in Your Eyes," but lost the buyer's shipping information. The seller is concerned that a delay in her shipment will give the buyer reason to give her a negative rating on the site. After each purchase is made, the buyer gets a chance to rate the seller's performance on a scale from 1 to 5—"poor" to "excellent." Every rating sellers collect is dis-

played along with their user name next to subsequent items they list. Just one negative rating can ruin a seller's reputation, depending on how many sales he or she has made overall.

Mr. Ryan tracks down the details on this particular transaction in the Half.com user database. He identifies the buyer and writes an e-mail to explain that the seller lost the shipping address and "wants to let you know they are sorry for the inconvenience." He then e-mails the buyer's shipping address to the seller.

Mr. Ryan says he doesn't find the e-mails tedious. "There is such a variety of topics to respond to," he says. "I never get 50 of the same questions in a row". But, a few e-mails later, he shrugs with disapproval. The user's question could easily have been answered by going to the help section of the Web site: "Do I include shipping in the sale price or is it added later?"

Says Mr. Ryan, "It's a general question. Nothing specific. Nothing major. I like the detailed research questions." Mr. Ryan pastes in an answer from a database of stock responses the customer-service team has put together. He then tacks onto the end of the e-mail a salutation that he draws from a list of suggested message closers provided by Half.com. The list, the company says, makes it easier for the agents to write so many e-mails. For this message, Mr. Ryan chooses, "It was my pleasure to assist you."

Got Juice

9:30 AM After answering a few more messages, it's time for a coffee break. Mr. Ryan says he drinks two cups of coffee a day, a habit he picked up since starting at Half.com.

"A year ago I wouldn't have touched the stuff," he says. He heads to the kitchen, which is just down the hall from his desk. The well-lit room is stocked with free cappuccino, juice, soda, fruit, cereal, cookies and other munchies. The cafeteria also doubles as a lounge with a satellite television playing ESPN, a Foosball table and a ping-pong table. This early in the morning, however, most people are interested in the coffee.

9:48 AM An e-mail arrives from a Half.com colleague in charge of the stock-answer database. He writes that a response Mr. Ryan submitted on how users can sign up for direct deposit—linking their Half.com transactions with their checking accounts—would be included in the database.

"There are so many things we don't have responses to," Mr. Ryan says. "It makes everyone's life easier to have the [database]."

9:50 AM The first 10 e-mails are done. Mr. Ryan downloads 10 more. One is from a father who several days earlier ordered a Sony PlayStation 2 for his son's birthday and is concerned because it hasn't arrived yet. Half.com's policy is that if a buyer hasn't received an item within 30 days of the purchase, he or she can lodge an official complaint. The PlayStation 2 seller is thus a long way from the delivery deadline. Nevertheless, as a courtesy, Mr. Ryan sends the seller an e-mail asking whether he can provide a shipping date and tracking number that Mr. Ryan can pass on to the restless father.

Half.com believes that help like this—beyond the requirements of its own rules—separates its customer-service approach from that of other companies. When the company was starting out, says Training Supervisor Ed Miller, customer service tried to respond to as many messages as it could, as fast as possible. What the company learned, however, is that "customers don't mind if you take a little more time to answer their specific question." Instead of just firing off e-mails, Half.com now sees it as important to personalize each message. Even with the personalization, Half.com says it responds to most messages within 24 hours.

Chris Finnin, the company's community liaison, is charged with ensuring that communications with customers have a consistent and pleasant tone. E-mail messages should conform to the "grandmother rule," says Mr. Finnin. Each message should "make sense to my grandmother." If it doesn't, "then we are not heading in the right direction."

10:10 AM Bathroom break.

10:15 AM "All right," Mr. Ryan says eagerly, returning to his desk. He cracks his knuckles and starts typing.

A buyer who purchased the video game "Twisted Metal II" two months ago but never received it writes to thank Half.com for "hounding" the seller to send him the item. But he wants a refund. Mr. Ryan verifies the buyer's version of events in Half.com's records, then refunds the buyer's money and charges the seller's account for the amount of the sale. Mr. Ryan sends e-mails to both parties informing them of his action. Half.com's rules say that when an official complaint has been lodged the other party has five days in which to respond. In this case, the seller didn't respond, so the buyer won the dispute by default.

10:25 AM Snack time. Mr. Ryan breaks into a high-energy Balance bar—a little nourishment to get him ready for what comes next.

Wrecking Crew

10:30 AM Time to knock down some walls. Lively human-resources worker Alicia DiCiacco invites Mr. Ryan and his colleagues to pick up sledgehammers and knock through a wall at the end of the office. Half.com's staff has doubled in the past year, and the company is expanding into adjacent space in the old tire factory.

Everyone in the office takes turns whacking at the wall. Some of the younger males dish out screams of "I'm not going to take it any more!" and "Where's the Pink Floyd?!"—a reference to the 1970s rock album "The Wall" by Pink Floyd.

Mr. Ryan eats up the office energy. "It's exciting to work here," he says. "We're growing.

We had the second launch of the site. [Half.com expanded its product line in April]. We're doing construction. It's good to come to work when the company is doing well."

11:15 AM Finished with another batch of 10 e-mails, he downloads 10 more.

Mr. Ryan's wife, Melissa, a corporate recruiter for a dot-com in a nearby town, calls to ask who is walking their dog today. Mr. Ryan quickly informs her that it's her sister's turn. She lives nearby.

No chit-chat. He gets straight back to work answering e-mails, including two separate queries from customers who can't redeem special introductory coupons Half.com offers to new users.

11:47 AM Mr. Ryan gets an e-mail from a seller responding to a message from Half.com. A potential buyer has asked Half.com whether the seller's 75-cent copy of Carolyn Davidson's Harlequin romance "The Midwife" is a paperback or hardcover. Half.com forwarded the question to the seller, who now is writing back to say it's a paperback.

Mr. Ryan sends two e-mails: one to the buyer, answering his question, and one to the seller, thanking him for the information.

12:10 PM Lunch. Mr. Ryan usually packs his lunch, but today he drives over to the local supermarket for takeout. He eats his turkey wrap in the company cafeteria with some colleagues and heads back to his desk by 1 p.m.

1:06 PM E-mail from a user who can't find the new Stephen King novel, "Dreamcatcher," on Half.com. The site is supposed to list all new books from major publishers, even if no one is selling them. That way, if a user is interested, he or she can put it on a wish list and the site will automatically e-mail him or her when a copy has been posted for sale.

Mr. Ryan searches for the book meticulously, checking by title, author and publisher's ISBN number. Once he's sure the book isn't listed, he e-mails Matt Walsh, who is in charge of fixing catalog errors. Mr. Ryan then e-mails the user and instructs him to check back at the site soon.

1:21 PM First phone call of the day. Because Half.com prefers to conduct customer service on e-mail, to keep its costs down, it doesn't display its phone number on its Web site. Still, persistent users get the number through directory assistance or other sources.

This caller, an agitated buyer of the video "Valley Girl," a 1983 comedy starring Nicolas Cage, says she received a damaged tape. She has lodged an official complaint against the seller on the Web site, but the seller hasn't responded. Mr. Ryan tells her that the five days the seller has to respond aren't up yet. He assures her that if the seller doesn't respond within the allotted time, he will refund her money and charge the seller's account. Until then, there's nothing Mr. Ryan can do except comfort the caller with apologies and explanations.

In the event that the seller disputes the buyer's claim about the tape, Half.com is still likely to grant a refund, especially on such an inexpensive item. Half.com makes it clear, however, that its customer-service team keeps a close watch on users' complaints, looking out for fraudulent refund requests. If Half.com suspects foul play, it doesn't grant refunds so easily.

2:02 PM A seller of the video "I Know What You Did Last Summer" got the package returned, marked address unknown. Mr. Ryan looks up the buyer's information in the user database and e-mails him, asking for an updated address to forward to the seller. He then e-mails the seller, telling him the address should be on its way shortly.

2:21 PM He downloads 10 more e-mails.

Home Stretch

2:30 PM The day is starting to get long, at least to an observer. But Mr. Ryan says sitting still all day doesn't cramp his style. "Sometimes it's tough to work at a desk, but it doesn't really bother me," he says. "I work out after work, and that really loosens thing up."

3 PM Bathroom break.

3:15 PM With the clock ticking toward quitting time, Mr. Ryan hunkers down to finish his last batch of e-mails. It's more of the same: a user unsure how Half.com works; a seller who wants to list a 1976 edition of "The Grapes of Wrath" but can't figure out where to put it on the site; a buyer who wants a book shipped second-day air, even though the order was already placed.

3:30 PM A call from a buyer interrupts Mr. Ryan's streak of dispensing e-mails. The buyer felt the quality of a book she bought was not up to snuff. The book, a $2 copy of Danielle Steel's "Secrets," apparently had a torn cover.

The buyer is upset, but Mr. Ryan remains calm, calling on skills he learned in a one-day seminar called "Dealing With Difficult People."

In the class, which he took before coming to Half.com, he learned to paraphrase what the customer is saying to make sure he understands the complaint. Mr. Ryan also takes care to speak clearly with a strong sense of empathy. At one point he says, "I understand your frustration." When he explains that the buyer will have to wait some time for a final resolution of the matter, he makes sure to preface it with a heartfelt "I'm sorry to let you know . . ." An observer listening to Mr. Ryan gets the sense that he is not acting.

"If you don't understand what they are saying, then you have a problem," he says. Though he can't satisfy this customer then and there, he promises to talk to his supervisor and to call her back tomorrow with more information.

4 PM The day is done. Mr. Ryan finishes his last e-mail, closes up his desk and shoves on home.

A new shift of workers picks up where Mr. Ryan left off, toiling from 4 p.m. to 12 a.m. When they finish, the customer-service staff in eBay's facility in Salt Lake City will take over.

Tomorrow, Mr. Ryan will be back on duty at 8 a.m., downloading his first 10 e-mails.

Source: Alex Frangos, *Wall Street Journal,* July 16, 2001.

Summary

Encouraging employee behaviors that help achieve an organization's objectives and fostering a sense of fairness among employees are two hallmarks of a useful internal pay structure. One of the first strategic pay decisions is how much to align a pay structure internally compared to aligning it to external market forces. Do not be misled. The issue is *not* achieving internal alignment *versus* alignment with external market forces. Rather, the strategic decision focuses on sustaining the optimal balance of internally aligned and externally responsive pay structures that helps the organization achieve its mission. *Both are required.* This part of the book focuses on one of the first decisions managers face in designing pay systems: how much to emphasize pay structures that are internally aligned with the work performed, the organization's structure, and its strategies. Whatever the choice, the decision needs to support (and be supported by) the organization's overall human resource strategy.

Next, managers must decide whether job and/or individual employee characteristics will be the basic unit of analysis supporting the pay structure. This is followed by deciding what data will be collected, what method(s) will be used to collect the information, and who should be involved in the process.

A key test of an effective and fair pay structure is acceptance of results by managers and employees. The best way to ensure acceptance of job analysis results is to involve employees as well as supervisors in the process. At the minimum, all employees should be informed of the purpose and progress of the activity.

If almost everyone agrees about the importance of job analysis, does that mean everyone does it? Of course not. Unfortunately, job analysis can be tedious and time-consuming. Often the job is given to newly hired compensation analysts, ostensibly to help them learn the organization, but perhaps there's also a hint of "rites of passage" in such assignments.

Alternatives to job-based structures such as skill-based or competency-based systems are being experimented with in many firms. The premise is that basing structures on these other criteria will encourage employees to become more flexible, and thus fewer workers will be required for the same level of output. This may be the argument, but as experience increases with the alternatives, managers are discovering that they can be as time-consuming and bureaucratic as job analysis. Bear in mind, job content remains the conventional criterion for structures.

Review Questions

1. Job analysis has been considered the cornerstone of human resource management. Precisely how does it support managers making pay decisions?
2. What does job analysis have to do with internal alignment?
3. Describe the major decisions involved in job analysis.
4. Distinguish between task data and behavioral data.
5. What is the critical advantage of quantitative approaches over conventional approaches to job analysis?
6. How would you decide whether to use job-based or person-based structures?
7. Why do many managers say that job analysis is a colossal waste of their time and the time of their employees? Are they right?

Chapter Five

Evaluating Work: Job Evaluation

Chapter Outline

As soon as my daughter turned 14, she absolutely refused to go shopping with me. At first I thought it was because I like to hum along with the mall music. But she says it is because I embarrass her when I interrogate assistant store managers about how they are paid—more precisely, how their pay compares to that of the stock clerks, managers, and regional managers in the same company. My daughter claims I do this everywhere I go. *Compensationitis,* she calls it. And I know it's contagious, because a colleague grills his seatmates on airplanes. He's learned the pay rates for American Airlines captains who pilot Boeing 737s versus those who pilot the A330 Airbus.

How does any organization go about valuing work? The next time you go to the supermarket, check out the different types of work there: store manager, produce manager, front-end manager, deli workers, butchers, stock clerks, checkout people, bakers—the list is long, and the work surprisingly diverse. If you managed a supermarket, how would you value work? But be careful—*compensationitis* is contagious, and it can embarrass your friends.

This chapter and the next one discuss techniques used to value work. Both chapters focus on "how to"—the specific steps involved. Job evaluation techniques are discussed in this chapter. Person-based techniques, both skill-based and competency-based, are discussed in Chapter 6. All these techniques are used to design pay structures that will influence employee behavior and help the organization sustain its competitive advantage.

JOB-BASED STRUCTURES: JOB EVALUATION

Exhibit 5.1 is variation on Exhibit 4.1 in the previous chapter. It orients us to the process used to build a job-based internal structure. Our job analysis and job descriptions (Chapter 4) collected and summarized work information. In this chapter, the focus is on what to value in the jobs, how to assess that value, and how to translate it into a job-based structure. Job evaluation is a process for determining relative value.

EXHIBIT 5.1
Many Ways to Create Internal Structure

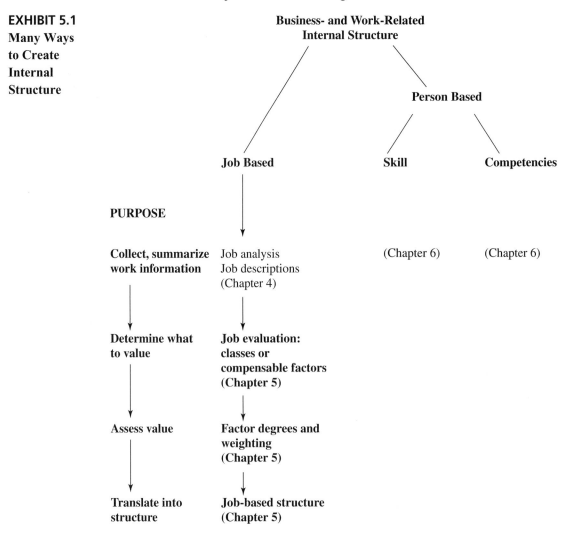

Job evaluation is the process of systematically determining the relative worth of jobs to create a job structure for the organization. The evaluation is based on a combination of job content, skills required, value to the organization, organizational culture, and the external market. This potential to blend organizational forces and external market forces is both a strength and a challenge of job evaluation.

DEFINING JOB EVALUATION: CONTENT, VALUE, AND EXTERNAL MARKET LINKS

Content and Value

We noted in Chapter 3 that *content* refers to what work is performed and how it gets done. Perspectives differ on whether job evaluation is based on job content or job value. Internal alignment based on content orders jobs on the basis of the skills required for the jobs and the duties and responsibilities associated with the jobs. A structure based on job value orders jobs on the basis of the relative contribution of the skills, duties, and responsibilities of each job to the organization's goals. But can this structure translate directly into pay rates, without regard to the external market, government regulations, or any individual negotiation process? Most people think not. Recall that internal alignment is just one of the building blocks of the pay model. Job content matters, but it is not the only basis for pay. Job value may also include the job's value in the external market (*exchange value*). Plus, pay rates may be influenced by collective bargaining or other negotiations.

In addition, the value added by the same work may be more (or less) in one organization than in another. We observed in Chapter 3 that the value added by consultants in Pricewaterhouse, whose earnings were generated by consultants, may differ from the value added by the same consultants now merged into IBM, whose revenues come through a wide variety of services. At Pricewaterhouse, consultants were critical to organization objectives. At IBM, they are less so. As a result, those who remain with IBM are earning less than before. So while we talk about internal job value based on contributions to organization objectives, external market value may differ. There is not necessarily a one-to-one correspondence between internal job value and pay rates.

Linking Content with the External Market

Some see job evaluation as a process for linking job content and internal value with external market rates. Aspects of job content (e.g., skills required and customer contacts) take on value based on their relationship to market wages. Because higher skill levels or willingness to work more closely with customers usually commands higher wages in the labor market, then skill level and nature of customer contacts become useful criteria for establishing differences among jobs. If some aspect of job content, such as stressful working conditions, is not related to wages paid in the external labor market, then that aspect may be excluded in the job evaluation. In this perspective, the value of job content is based on what it can command in the external market; it has no intrinsic value.[1]

[1]Donald P. Schwab, "Job Evaluation and Pay Setting: Concepts and Practices," in *Comparable Worth: Issues and Alternatives,* ed. E. Robert Livernash (Washington, DC: Equal Employment Advisory Council, 1980), pp. 49–77.

But not everyone agrees. A developer of the Hay job evaluation plan (probably still the plan most widely used by large corporations) claims that job evaluation establishes the relative value of jobs based on their content, independent of a link to the market.

"Measure for Measure" versus "Much Ado about Nothing"

Researchers, too, have their own perspective on job evaluation. Some say that if job evaluation takes on the trappings of measurement (objective, numerical, generalizable, documented, and reliable), then it can be judged according to technical standards. Just as with employment tests, the reliability, validity, and usefulness of job evaluation plans can be compared.

As you might expect, those actually making pay decisions hold different views. They see job evaluation as a process that helps gain acceptance of pay differences among jobs—an administrative procedure through which the parties become involved and committed. Its statistical validity is not an issue. Its usefulness is that it provides a framework for give-and-take—an exchange of views. Employees, union representatives, and managers haggle over "the rules of the game" for determining the relative value of work. If all participants agree that skills, effort, responsibilities, and working conditions are important, then work is evaluated based on these factors. As in sports and games, we are more willing to accept the results if we accept the rules and believe they are applied fairly.[2]

This interpretation is consistent with the history of job evaluation, which began as a way to bring labor peace and order to an often-chaotic and dispute-riven wage-setting process.[3]

Exhibit 5.2 summarizes the assumptions that underlie the perspectives on job evaluation. Some say the content of jobs has intrinsic value that the evaluation will uncover; others say the only fair measure of job value is found in the external market. Some say contemporary job evaluation practices are just and fair; others say they are just fair. "Beneath the superficial orderliness of job evaluation techniques and findings, there is much that smacks of chaos."[4] We try to capture all these perspectives in this chapter.

"HOW TO": MAJOR DECISIONS

Exhibit 5.3 shows job evaluation's role in determining the internal structure. You already know that the process begins with job analysis, in which the information on jobs is collected, and that job descriptions summarize the information and serve as input for the evaluation. The exhibit calls out some of the major decisions in the job evaluation

[2] M. A. Konovsky, "Understanding Procedural Justice and Its Impact on Business Organizations," *Journal of Management* 26(3) (2000), pp. 489–511; R. Crepanzano, *Justice in the Workplace:* Vol. 2. *From Theory to Practice.* (Mahwah, NJ: Lawrence Erlbaum, 2000); R. Folger and R. Crepanzano, *Organizational Justice and Human Resource Management* (Thousand Oaks, CA: Sage, 1998); R. B. Foreman and J. Rogers, *What Workers Want* (Ithaca, NY: ILR/Cornell University Press, 1999); B. H. Sheppard, R. J. Lewicki, and J. W. Minton, *Organizational Justice: The Search for Fairness in the Workplace* (New York: Macmillan, 1992); Frederick P. Morgeson, Michael A. Campion, and Carl P. Maertz, "Understanding Pay Satisfaction: The Limits of a Compensation System Implementation," *Journal of Business and Psychology* 16(1), (Fall 2001).

[3] E. Robert Livernash, "Internal Wage Structure," in *New Concepts in Wage Determination,* ed. George W. Taylor and Frank C. Pierson (New York: McGraw-Hill, 1957).

[4] M. S. Viteles, "A Psychologist Looks at Job Evaluation," *Personnel* 17 (1941), pp. 165–76.

EXHIBIT 5.2
Assumptions Underlying Different Views of Job Evaluation

Aspect of Job Evaluation	Assumption
Assessment of job content	Content has intrinsic value outside external market.
Assessment of relative value	Stakeholders can reach consensus on value.
External market link	Value cannot be determined without external market.
Measurement	Honing instruments will provide objective measures.
Negotiation	Negotiating brings rationality to a social/political process; establishes rules of the game and invites participation.

EXHIBIT 5.3   Determining an Internally Aligned Job Structure

Internal alignment: Work relationships within the organization → Job analysis → Job description → Job evaluation → Job structure

Some Major Decisions in Job Evaluation
- Establish purpose of evaluation.
- Decide whether to use single or multiple plans.
- Choose among alternative approaches.
- Obtain involvement of relevant stakeholders.
- Evaluate plan's usefulness.

[handwritten note: know the 5 major decisions to make in a job evaluation]

process. They are (1) establish the purpose(s), (2) decide on single versus multiple plans, (3) choose among alternative methods, (4) obtain involvement of relevant stakeholders, and (5) evaluate the usefulness of the results.

Establish the Purpose

Job evaluation is part of the process for establishing an internally aligned pay structure. Recall from Chapter 2 that a structure is aligned if it supports the organization strategy, fits the work flow, is fair to employees, and motivates their behavior toward organization objectives.

- *Supports organization strategy:* Job evaluation aligns with the organization's strategy by including what it is about work that adds value—that contributes to pursuing the organization's strategy and achieving its objectives. Job evaluation helps answer, How does this job add value?[5]
- *Supports work flow:* Job evaluation supports work flow in two ways. It integrates each job's pay with its relative contributions to the organization, and it helps set pay for new, unique, or changing jobs.

[5]Robert L. Heneman, and Peter V. LeBlanc, "Developing a More Relevant and Competitive Approach for Valuing Knowledge Work," *Compensation and Benefits Review*, July/August 2002, pp. 43–47; Robert L. Heneman, and Peter V. LeBlanc, "Work Valuation Addresses Shortcomings of Both Job Evaluation and Market Pricing," *Compensation and Benefits Review*, January/February 2003, pp. 7–11.

- *Is fair to employees:* Job evaluation can reduce disputes and grievances over pay differences among jobs by establishing a workable, agreed-upon structure that reduces the role of chance, favoritism, and bias in setting pay.
- *Motivates behavior toward organization objectives:* Job evaluation calls out to employees what it is about their work that the organization values, what supports the organization's strategy and its success. It can also help employees adapt to organization changes by improving their understanding of what is valued in their new assignments and why that value may have changed. Thus, job evaluation helps create the network of rewards (promotions, challenging work) that motivates employees.

If the purpose of the evaluation is not called out, it becomes too easy to get lost in complex procedures, negotiations, and bureaucracy. The job evaluation process becomes the end in itself instead of a way to achieve an objective. Establishing its purpose can help ensure that the evaluation actually is a useful systematic process.

Single versus Multiple Plans

Rarely do employers evaluate all jobs in the organization at one time. More typically, a related group of jobs, for example, production, engineering, or marketing, will be the focus. Many employers design different evaluation plans for different types of work. They do so because they believe that the work content is too diverse to be usefully evaluated by one plan. For example, production jobs may vary in terms of manipulative skills, knowledge of statistical quality control, and working conditions. But these tasks and skills may not be relevant to engineering and finance jobs. Rather, the nature of the contacts with customers may be relevant. Consequently, a single, universal plan may not be acceptable to employees or useful to managers if the work covered is highly diverse. Even so, there are some plans that have been successfully applied across a wide breadth and depth of work. The most prominent examples include the Hay plan (more on this later) and the Position Analysis Questionnaire (discussed in Chapter 4).

Benchmark Jobs

To be sure that all relevant aspects of work are included in the evaluation, an organization may start with a sample of benchmark jobs. In Exhibit 5.4, benchmark jobs would be identified for as many of the levels in the structure and groups of related jobs (office, production, engineering) as possible. The heavy shading in the exhibit marks the benchmark jobs.

A *benchmark job* has the following characteristics:

- Its contents are well known and relatively stable over time.
- The job is common across a number of different employers. It is not unique to a particular employer.
- A sizable proportion of the work force is employed in this job.

A representative sample of benchmark jobs will include the entire domain of work being evaluated—office, production, engineering, and so on—and capture the diversity of the work within that domain.

Diversity in the work can be thought of in terms of depth (vertically) and breadth (horizontally). The *depth of work* in most organizations probably ranges from strategic lead-

EXHIBIT 5.4   Benchmark Jobs

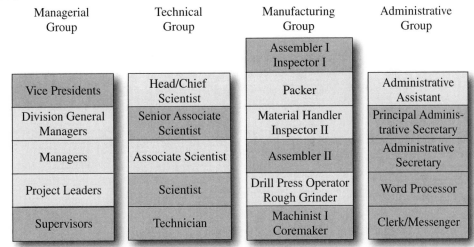

More heavily shaded jobs have been selected as benchmarks.

ership jobs (CEOs, general directors) to the filing and mail distribution tasks in entry-level office jobs. Horizontally, the *breadth of work* depends on the nature of business. Relatively similar work can be found in specialty consulting firms (e.g., compensation or executive search firms). The breadth of work performed in some multinational conglomerates such as General Electric mirrors the occupations in the entire nation. GE includes jobs in businesses spanning financial services, entertainment (NBC), aircraft engines, medical instruments, power systems, and home appliances.

Selecting a benchmark job from each level ensures coverage of the entire work domain, thus helping to ensure the accuracy of the decisions based on the job evaluation. Typically, a job evaluation plan is developed using benchmark jobs, and then the plan is applied to the remaining nonbenchmark jobs.

The number of job evaluation plans used hinges on how detailed an evaluation is required to make pay decisions and how much it will cost. There is no ready answer to the question of "one plan versus many." Current practice (not always the best answer for the future, since practice is based on the past) is to use separate plans for major domains of work: top-executive/leadership jobs, managerial/professional jobs, operational/technical jobs, and office/administrative jobs. Open the door on some organizations and you will find additional plans for sales, legal, engineers/scientists, and skilled trades.

The costs associated with all these plans (including time) give impetus to the push to simplify job structures (reduce titles and levels). Some employers, notably Hewlett-Packard, simplify by using a single plan with a core set of common factors for all jobs and additional factors specific to particular occupational or functional areas (finance, manufacturing, software and systems, sales).

**EXHIBIT 5.5
Comparison
of Job
Evaluation
Methods**

	Advantage	**Disadvantage**
Ranking	Fast, simple, easy to explain.	Cumbersome as number of jobs increases. Basis for comparisons is not called out.
Classification	Can group a wide range of work together in one system.	Descriptions may leave too much room for manipulation.
Point	Compensable factors call out basis for comparisons. Compensable factors communicate what is valued.	Can become bureaucratic and rule-bound.

Choose among Methods

Ranking, classification, and point method are the most common job evaluation methods, though uncounted variations exist. Research over 40 years consistently finds that different job evaluation plans generate different pay structures. So the method you choose matters.[6]

Exhibit 5.5 compares the methods. They all begin by assuming that a useful job analysis has been translated into job descriptions.

RANKING

Ranking simply orders the job descriptions from highest to lowest based on a global definition of relative value or contribution to the organization's success. Ranking is simple, fast, and easy to understand and explain to employees; it is also the least expensive method, at least initially. However, it can create problems that require difficult and potentially expensive solutions because it doesn't tell employees and managers what it is about their jobs that is important.

Two ways of ranking are common: alternation ranking and paired comparison. *Alternation ranking* orders job descriptions alternately at each extreme. Agreement is reached among evaluators on which jobs are the most and least valuable (i.e., which is a 10, which is a 1), then the next most and least valued (i.e., which is a 9, which is a 2), and so on, until all the jobs have been ordered. The *paired comparison* method uses a matrix to compare all possible pairs of jobs. Exhibit 5.6 shows that the higher-ranked job is entered in the cell of the matrix. When all comparisons have been completed, the job most frequently judged "more valuable" becomes the highest-ranked job, and so on.

[6]Robert M. Madigan and David J. Hoover, "Effects of Alternative Job Evaluation Methods on Decisions Involving Pay Equity" *Academy of Management Journal* 29 (1986), pp. 84–100; Tjarda Van Sliedregt, Olga F. Voskuijl, and Henk Thierry, "Job Evaluation Systems and Pay Grade Structures: Do They Match?" *International Journal of Human Resource Management* 12(8) (December 2001), pp. 1313–1324; E. Jane Arnault et al., "An Experimental Study of Job Evaluation and Comparable Worth," *Industrial and Labor Relations Review* 54(4) (July 2001), pp. 806–815; Judith M. Collins and Paul M. Muchinsky, "An Assessment of the Construct Validity of Three Job Evaluation Methods: A Field Experiment," *Academy of Management Journal* 36(4) (1993), pp. 895–904.

EXHIBIT 5.6
Paired
Comparison
Ranking

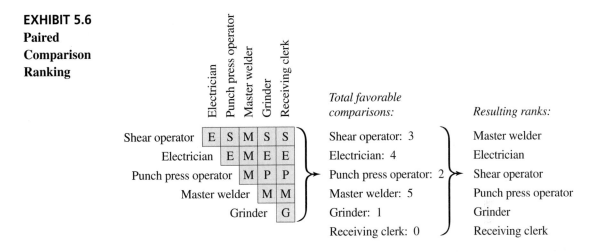

	Electrician	Punch press operator	Master welder	Grinder	Receiving clerk
Shear operator	E	S	M	S	S
Electrician		E	M	E	E
Punch press operator			M	P	P
Master welder				M	M
Grinder					G

Total favorable comparisons:

Shear operator: 3
Electrician: 4
Punch press operator: 2
Master welder: 5
Grinder: 1
Receiving clerk: 0

Resulting ranks:

Master welder
Electrician
Shear operator
Punch press operator
Grinder
Receiving clerk

Alternation-ranking and paired-comparison methods may be more reliable (produce similar results consistently) than simple ranking. Nevertheless, ranking has drawbacks. The criteria on which the jobs are ranked are usually so poorly defined, if they are specified at all, that the evaluations become subjective opinions that are impossible to justify in strategic and work-related terms. Further, evaluators using this method must be knowledgeable about every single job under study. The numbers alone turn what should be a simple task into a formidable one—50 jobs require 1,225 comparisons—and as organizations change, it is difficult to remain knowledgeable about all jobs. Some organizations try to overcome this difficulty by ranking jobs within single departments and merging the results. However, even though the ranking appears simple, fast, and inexpensive, in the long run the results are difficult to defend and costly solutions may be required to overcome the problems created.

CLASSIFICATION

Picture a bookcase with many shelves. Each shelf is labeled with a paragraph describing the kinds of books on that shelf and, perhaps, one or two representative titles. This same approach describes the *classification system* of job evaluation. A series of classes covers the range of jobs. Class descriptions are the labels. A job description is compared to the class descriptions to decide which class is the best fit for that job. Each class is described in such a way that the "label" captures sufficient work detail yet is general enough to cause little difficulty in slotting a job description onto its appropriate "shelf" or class. The classes may be described further by including titles of benchmark jobs that fall into each class.

Determining the number of classes and writing class descriptions to define the boundaries between each class (e.g., how many book shelves and what distinguishes each from the other—fiction, nonfiction; or mysteries, biographies, etc.) are something of an art form. One way to begin is to find the natural breaks or changes in the work content. At Lockheed, the engineering work discussed in previous chapters has obvious natural breaks between engineers (individual contributors) and lead engineers (responsible for overall projects). But how many classes within each of these make sense? Exhibit 5.7

EXHIBIT 5.7   Classifications for Engineering Work Used by Clark Consulting

Engineer 1	Engineer 2	Engineer 3	Engineer 4	Engineer 5	Eng Mgr 1	Eng Mgr 2	Eng Mgr 3
Participates in development, testing, and documentation of software programs. Performs design and analysis tasks as a project team member. Typical minimum requirements are a bachelor's degree in a scientific or technical field or the equivalent and up to two years of experience.	Develops, tests, and documents software programs of a more difficult nature. Assists in the development of assignments and schedules. Typical minimum requirements are a bachelor's degree in a scientific or technical field and two years to four years of experience or a master's degree and up to two years of experience.	Develops project plans, functional specifications, and schedules. Designs and performs analysis on complex programs and systems. Assists in determining product needs and enhancements. Typical minimum requirements are a bachelor's degree in engineering, computer science, or related technical field and four to six years of experience or a master's degree and two to four years of experience.	Acts as project engineer for complex programs in design, development, and analysis. Proposes new ideas and products and guides their implementation. Provides technical direction in area of specialty on major products. Typical minimum requirements are a bachelor's degree in engineering, computer science, or a related technical field and six or more years of experience or a master's degree and four to six years of experience.	Provides technical direction and advice to management in long-range planning for new areas of technological research. Designs, researches, and develops new systems while providing guidance to support staff. Typical minimum requirements are a bachelor's degree in engineering, computer science, or a related technical field and ten or more years of experience or a master's degree and six years or more of experience.	Supervises the design and development of software products or systems and related schedules and costs. Participates in developing management policies for software group. Typically manages up to 10 employees performing similar tasks. First level of management with human resource responsibilities.	Establishes work environment for development or implementation of complete products and programs. Develops long-range plans, schedules, and cost objectives. Typically manages 10 to 25 employees, including first-level managers. (May be from multiple disciplines.)	Develops long-range strategy for a product family including positioning, marketing, and pricing. Manages engineering product group to ensure timely delivery of high-quality products. Typically manages over 25 employees from multiple disciplines.

Source: Clark Consulting. Used by permission.

EXHIBIT 5.8 Federal Government's Job Classification Method, General Schedule Descriptions

Grade-General Schedule 1 includes all classes of positions the duties of which are to be performed, under immediate supervision, with little or no latitude for the exercise of independent judgment (1) the simplest routine work in office, business, or fiscal operations, or (2) elementary work of a subordinate technical character in a professional, scientific, or technical field.

Grade-General Schedule 9 includes all classes of positions the duties of which are (1) to perform, under general supervision, very difficult and responsible work along lines requiring special technical, supervisory, or administrative experience which has (A) demonstrated capacity for sound independent work, (B) thorough and fundamental knowledge of a special and complex subject matter, or of the profession, art, or science involved, and (C) considerable latitude for the exercise of independent judgment; (2) with considerable latitude for the exercise of independent judgment, to perform moderately difficult and responsible work, requiring (A) professional, scientific, or technical training equivalent to that represented by graduation from a college or university of recognized standing, and (B) considerable additional professional, scientific, or technical training or experience which has demonstrated capacity for sound independent work; or (3) to perform other work of equal importance, difficulty, and responsibility, and requiring comparable qualifications.

Grade-General Schedule 13 includes all classes of positions the duties of which are (1) to perform, under administrative direction, with wide latitude for the exercise of independent judgment work of unusual difficulty and responsibility along special technical, supervisory, or administrative lines, requiring extended specialized, supervisory, or administrative training and experience which has demonstrated leadership and marked attainments; (2) to serve as assistant head of a major organization involving work of comparable level within a bureau; (3) to perform, under administrative direction, with wide latitude for the exercise of independent judgment, work of unusual difficulty and responsibility requiring extended professional, scientific, or technical training and experience which has demonstrated leadership and marked attainments in professional, scientific, or technical research, practice, or administration; or (4) to perform other work of equal importance, difficulty, and responsibility, and requiring comparable qualification.

Source: Office of Personnel Management (*www.opm.gov*).

shows classifications used by Clark Consulting to conduct salary surveys of engineering salaries at many different employers. Managerial work includes three classes; individual contributors, five classes. Information to guide the writing of class descriptions can come from managers, job incumbents, job descriptions, and career progression considerations.

Writing class descriptions can be troublesome when jobs from several job families are covered by a single plan. Although greater specificity of the class definition improves the reliability of evaluation, it also limits the variety of jobs that can easily be classified. For example, class definitions written with sales jobs in mind may make it difficult to slot office or administrative jobs and vice versa. Exhibit 5.8 gives some of the class definitions from the U S. federal government's 18-class evaluation system. These 18 classes correspond to 18 levels in the government's internal structure. The vagueness of the descriptions seems to leave a lot of room for "judgment."[7] Including titles of benchmark jobs for each class helps make the descriptions more concrete.

In practice, with a classification method, the job descriptions not only are compared to the class descriptions and benchmark jobs but also can be compared to each other to be sure that jobs within each class are more similar to each other than to jobs in adjacent classes.

The end result is a job structure made up of a series of classes with a number of jobs in each. All these comparisons are used to ensure that this structure is based on the organization strategy and work flow, is fair, and focuses behaviors on desired results. The jobs within each class are considered to be equal (similar) work and will be paid equally. Jobs in different classes should be dissimilar and may have different pay rates.

The *Wall Street Journal* once compiled a list of the 10 most unusual U.S. government jobs. It included Smokey Bear's manager, a Supreme Court seamstress (job responsibility: keeping the Supremes in stitches), a gold stacker, condom tester, currency reconstructor, and Air Force art curator. Most government jobs are in 15 grades. The top three have been combined into a "supergrade" covering senior executives. Employees in the supergrade are eligible for special bonuses and allowances. The Office of Personnel Management publishes the complete system on its website (*www.opm.gov*). Visit the site to discover the level of detail in the government's approach. Contrast that with "Big Blue" (IBM), which puts its complete classification plan on a single page.

POINT METHOD *Know the 3 characteristics of the Point Method*

Point methods have three common characteristics: (1) compensable factors, with (2) factor degrees numerically scaled, and (3) weights reflecting the relative importance of each factor.[8] Each job's relative value, and hence its location in the pay structure, is determined by the total points assigned to it.

Point plans are the most commonly used job evaluation approach in the United States and Europe. They represent a significant change from ranking and classification methods in that they make explicit the criteria for evaluating jobs: *compensable factors.*

Compensable factors are based on the strategic direction of the business and how the work contributes to these objectives and strategy. The factors are scaled to reflect the degree to which they are present in each job and weighted to reflect their overall importance to the organization. Points are then attached to each factor weight. The total points for each job determine its position in the job structure.

---

[7]Howard Risher and Charles Fay, *New Strategies for Public Pay* (Saratoga Springs, NY: AMACOM, 2000). The Office of Personnel Management (OPM) has done a series of Special Studies on the Federal Civil Service. They are on the OPM's website at *www.opm.gov/studies/index.htm*. The OPM says, "We study human resource management issues and policies that have a critical effect on the Federal civil service. These studies are prompted by analyses of personnel trends, the findings from oversight reviews of agencies, and by such stakeholders as the Congress and other interested parties."

[8]Factor comparison, another method of job evaluation, bears some similarities to the point method in that compensable factors are clearly defined and the external market is linked to the job evaluation results. However, factor comparison is used by less than 10 percent of employers that use job evaluation. The method's complexity makes it difficult to explain to employees and managers, thus limiting its usefulness.

There are six steps in the design of a point plan.

1. Conduct job analysis.
2. Determine compensable factors.
3. Scale the factors.
4. Weight the factors according to importance.
5. Communicate the plan and train users; prepare manual.
6. Apply to nonbenchmark jobs.

1. Conduct Job Analysis

Just as with ranking and classification, point plans begin with job analysis. Typically a representative sample of jobs, that is, benchmark jobs, is drawn for analysis. The content of these jobs is the basis for defining, scaling, and weighting the compensable factors.

2. Determine Compensable Factors

Compensable factors play a pivotal role in the point plan. These factors reflect how work adds value to the organization. They flow from the work itself and the strategic direction of the business.

> **Compensable factors** are those characteristics in the work that the organization values, that help it pursue its strategy and achieve its objectives.

To select compensable factors, an organization asks itself, What is it about the work that adds value? One company chose decision making as a compensable factor. As shown in Exhibit 5.9, the definition of *decision making* is three-dimensional: (1) the risk and complexity (hence the availability of guidelines to assist in making the decisions), (2) the impact of the decisions, and (3) the time that must pass before the impact is evident.

In effect, this firm determined that its competitive advantage depends on decisions employees make in their work. And the relative value of the decisions depends on their risk, their complexity, and their impact on the company. Hence, this firm is signaling to all employees that jobs will be valued based on the nature of the decisions required by employees in those jobs. Jobs that require riskier decisions with greater impact have a higher relative worth than jobs that require fewer decisions with less consequence.

To be useful, compensable factors should be

- Based on the strategy and values of the organization.
- Based on the work performed.
- Acceptable to the stakeholders affected by the resulting pay structure.

Based on the Strategy and Values of the Organization

The leadership of any organization is the best source of information on where the business should be going and how it is going to get there. Clearly, the leaders' input into factor selection is crucial. If the business strategy involves providing innovative, high-quality products and services designed in collaboration with customers and suppliers, then jobs with greater responsibilities for product innovation and customer contacts should be valued higher. Or if the business strategy is more Wal-Mart-like, "providing goods and services to

EXHIBIT 5.9 Compensable Factor Definition: Decision Making

Compensable Factor Definition:	Evaluates the extent of required decision making and the beneficial or detrimental effect such decisions would have on the profitability of the organization.

Consideration is given to the:
- *Risk and complexity* of required decision making
- *Impact* such action would have on the company

What type of guidelines are available for making decisions?

____ 1. Few decisions are required; work is performed according to standard procedures and/or detailed instructions.

____ 2. Decisions are made within an established framework of clearly defined procedures. Incumbent is only required to recognize and follow the prescribed course of action.

____ 3. Guidelines are available in the form of clearly defined procedures and standard practices. Incumbent must exercise some judgment in selecting the appropriate procedure.

____ 4. Guidelines are available in the form of some standard practices, well-established precedent, and reference materials and company policy. Decisions require a moderate level of judgment and analysis of the appropriate course of action.

____ 5. Some guidelines are available in the form of broad precedent, related practices, and general methods of the field. Decisions require a high level of judgment and/or modification of a standard course of action to address the issue at hand.

____ 6. Few guidelines are available. The incumbent may consult with technical experts and review relevant professional publications. Decisions require innovation and creativity. The only limitation on course of action is company strategy and policy.

What is the impact of decisions made by the position?

____ 1. Inappropriate decisions, recommendations, or errors would normally cause minor delays and cost increments. Deficiencies will not affect the completion of programs or projects important to the organization.

____ 2. Inappropriate decisions, recommendations, or errors will normally cause moderate delays and additional allocation of funds and resources within the immediate work unit. Deficiencies will not affect the attainment of the organization's objectives.

____ 3. Inappropriate decisions, recommendations, or errors would normally cause considerable delays and reallocation of funds and resources. Deficiencies will affect scheduling and project completion in other work units and, unless adjustments are made, could affect attainment of objectives of a major business segment of the company.

____ 4. Inappropriate decisions, recommendations, or errors would normally affect critical programs or attainment of short-term goals for a major business segment of the company.

____ 5. Inappropriate decisions, recommendations, or errors would affect attainment of objectives for the company and would normally affect long-term growth and public image.

The effectiveness of the majority of the position's decisions can be measured within:

____ 1. One day.
____ 2. One week.
____ 3. One month.

____ 4. Six months.
____ 5. One year.
____ 6. More than a year.

Source: Jill Kanin-Lovers, "The Role of Computers in Job Evaluations: A Case in Point," *Journal of Compensation and Benefits* (New York: Warren Gorham and Lamont, 1985).

EXHIBIT 5.10   Compensable Factor Definition: Multinational Responsibilities

This factor concerns the multinational scope of the job. Multinational responsibilities are defined as line or functional managerial activities in one or several countries.

1. **The multinational responsibilities of the job can best be described as:**
   A. Approving major policy and strategic plans.
   B. Formulating, proposing, and monitoring implementation of policy and plans.
   C. Acting as a consultant in project design and implementation phases.
   D. Not applicable.

2. **Indicate the percentage of time spent on multinational issues:**
   A. >50%
   B. 25–49%
   C. 10–24%
   D. <10%

3. **The number of countries (other than your unit location) for which the position currently has operational or functional responsibility:**
   A. More than 10 countries
   B. 5 to 10 countries
   C. 1 to 4 countries
   D. Not applicable

Source: 3M. Used by permission.

delight customers at the lowest cost and greatest convenience possible," then compensable factors might include impact on cost containment, customer relations, and so on.

Compensable factors reinforce the organization's culture and values as well as its business direction and the nature of the work. If the direction changes, then the compensable factors may also change. For example, strategic plans at many companies call for increased globalization. Gillette and 3M include a "multinational responsibilities" factor similar to the one in Exhibit 5.10 in their managerial job evaluation plan. In this example, multinational responsibilities are defined in terms of the type of responsibility, the percent of time devoted to international issues, and the number of countries covered. Do you suppose that managers at 3M or Gillette got raises when Czechoslovakia, Yugoslavia, and the Soviet Union rearranged themselves into a greater number of smaller, independent countries?

Factors may also be eliminated if they no longer support the business strategy. The railway company Burlington Northern revised its job evaluation plan to omit the factor "number of subordinates supervised." It decided that a factor that values increases to staff runs counter to the organization's objective of reducing bureaucracy and increasing efficiency. Major shifts in the business strategy are not daily occurrences, but when they do occur, compensable factors should be reexamined to ensure they are consistent with the new directions.[9]

[9]Robert L. Heneman, "Job and Work Evaluation: A Literature Review," *Public Personnel Management* (in press); Robert L. Heneman and Peter V. LeBlanc, "Work Valuation Addresses Shortcomings of Both Job Evaluation and Market Pricing," *Compensation and Benefits Review*, January/February 2003, pp. 7–11.

Based on the Work Itself

Employees and supervisors are experts in the work actually done in any organization. Hence, it is important to seek their answers to what should be valued in the work itself. Some form of documentation (i.e., job descriptions, job analysis, employee and/or supervisory focus groups) must support the choice of factors. Work-related documentation helps gain acceptance by employees and managers, is easier to understand, and can withstand a variety of challenges to the pay structure. For example, managers may argue that the salaries of their employees are too low in comparison to those of other employees or that the salary offered a job candidate is too low. Union leaders may wonder why one job is paid differently from another. Allegations of pay discrimination may be raised. Employees, line managers, union leaders, and compensation managers must understand and be able to explain why work is paid differently or the same. Differences in factors that are obviously based on the work itself provide that rationale or even diminish the likelihood of the challenges arising.

Acceptable to the Stakeholders

Acceptance of the compensable factors used to slot jobs into the pay structure may depend, at least in part, on tradition. For example, people who work in hospitals, nursing homes, and child care centers make the point that responsibility for people is used less often as a compensable factor, and valued lower, than responsibility for property.[10] This omission may be a carryover from the days when nursing and child care service were provided by family members, usually women, without reimbursement. People now doing these jobs for pay say that properly valuing a factor for people responsibility would raise their wages. So the question is, acceptable to whom? The answer ought to be, to the stakeholders.

Adapting Factors from Existing Plans

Although a wide variety of factors are used in standard existing plans, the factors tend to fall into four generic groups: skills required, effort required, responsibility, and working conditions. These four were used more than 60 years ago in the National Electrical Manufacturers Association (NEMA) plan and are also included in the Equal Pay Act (1963) to define equal work. Many of these early point plans, such as those of the National Metal Trades Association (NMTA) and NEMA, and the Steel Plan, were developed for manufacturing and/or office jobs. Since then, point plans have also been applied to managerial and professional jobs. The *Hay Guide Chart*—Profile Method of Position, used by 5,000 employers worldwide (including 130 of the 500 largest U.S. corporations), is perhaps the most widely used. The three Hay factors—know-how, problem solving, and accountability—use guide charts to quantify the factors in more detail. Exhibit 5.11 summarizes the basic definitions of the three Hay factors. A fourth factor, working conditions, is used when applied to nonmanagerial

know the 4 Compencable factors used

---

[10]M. K. Mount and R. A. Ellis, "Investigation of Bias in Job Evaluation Ratings of Comparable Worth Study Participants," *Personnel Psychology* 40 (1987), pp. 85–96; H. Remick, "Strategies for Creating Sound, Bias-Free Job Evaluation Plans," paper presented at the I.R.C. Colloquium, Atlanta, GA, September 1978.

EXHIBIT 5.11
Factors in
Hay Plan

Know-how—the sum total of what a person must have the capability to do to be effective
• Technical, specialized depth and breadth
• Managerial requirements to plan, organize, staff, direct, and control resources for results
• Human relations skills to influence, motivate, change behavior, and build relationships

Problem solving—the requirement for and ability to use know-how effectively to develop solutions that improve effectiveness
• Environment—the context of the job and its focus
• Challenge—the availability of guides and complexity of analyses required

Accountability—the requirement for and ability to achieve desired results
• Freedom to act—focus on decision-making authority vested in the position to achieve results
• Scope—focus on the magnitude of the results expected relative to the enterprise
• Impact—focus on the impact the position has on the relevant scope measure for the position

work. In Exhibit 5.12, the Hay factor know-how is first measured on two dimensions: scope (practical procedures, specialized techniques, or scientific disciplines); and depth (minimal, related, diverse, or broad). After that, the degree of human relations skills required (basic, important, or critical) is judged. The cell that corresponds to the right level of all three dimensions for the job being evaluated is located in the guide chart. The cell gives the points for this factor. In the exhibit, the supervisor position gets 152 points for know-how.[11]

How Many Factors?

A remaining issue to consider is how many factors should be included in the plan. Some factors may have overlapping definitions or may fail to account for anything unique in the criterion chosen. In fact, the NEMA plan explicitly states that the compensable factor experience should be correlated with education. One writer calls this the "illusion of validity"—we want to believe that the factors are capturing divergent aspects of the job and that both are important.[12] It has long been recognized that factors overlap or are highly correlated, raising the concern about double counting the value of a factor. Indeed, in the Hay plan, problem solving is defined as a percentage of know-how. So by definition, they overlap.

Another challenge is called "small numbers."[13] If even one job in our benchmark sample has a certain characteristic, we tend to use that factor for the entire work domain. Unpleasant working conditions are a common example. If even one job is performed in unpleasant working conditions, it is tempting to make those conditions a compensable factor and apply it to all jobs. Once a factor is part of the system, other workers are likely to say their jobs have it, too. For example, office staff may feel that ringing telephones or leaky toner cartridges constitute stressful or hazardous conditions.

[11]Howard Risher and Charles Fay, *New Strategies for Public Pay* (Saratoga Springs, NY: AMACOM, 2000).
[12]D. F. Harding, J. M. Madden, and K. Colson, "Analysis of a Job Evaluation System," *Journal of Applied Psychology* 44 (1960), pp. 354–357.
[13]R. Nisbett, D. Krantz, C. Jepson, and A. Kunda, "The Use of Statistical Heuristics in Everyday Intuition," *Psychological Review* 90 (1983), pp. 339–363.

EXHIBIT 5.12 Hay Guide Chart—Profile Method of Job Evaluation

KNOW-HOW DEFINITIONS

DEFINITION: Know-How is the sum total to every kind of skill however acquired, required for acceptable job performance. This sum total which comprises the overall savvy has 3 dimensions–the requirements for:

1 Practical procedures, specialized techniques, and scientific disciplines.

2 Know-How of integrating and harmonizing the diversified functions involved in managerial situations occurring in operating, supporting, and administrative fields. This Know-How may be exercised consultatively (about management) as well as executively and involves in some combination the areas of organizing, planning, executing, controlling and evaluating.

3 Active, practicing, face-to-face skills in the area of human relationships (as defined at right).

MEASURING KNOW-HOW: Know-How has both scope (variety) and depth (thoroughness). Thus, a job may require some knowledge about a lot of things, or a lot of knowledge about a few things. The total Know-How is the combination of scope and depth. This concept makes practical the comparison and weighing of the total Know-How content of different jobs in terms of: "How much knowledge about how many things."

2 HUMAN RELATIONS SKILLS

1. **BASIC:** Ordinary courtesy and effectiveness in dealing with others.

2. **IMPORTANT:** Understanding, influencing, and/or serving people are important, but not critical considerations.

3. **CRITICAL:** Alternative or combined skills in understanding, selecting, developing and motivating people are important in the highest degree.

KNOW-HOW 1↓	3→ 2→	MANAGERIAL KNOW-HOW											
		I. MINIMAL			II. RELATED			III. DIVERSE			IV. BROAD		
		1	2	3	1	2	3	1	2	3	1	2	3
A. PRIMARY		50	57	66	66	76	87	87	100	115	115	132	152
		57	66	76	76	87	100	100	115	132	132	152	175
		66	76	87	87	100	115	115	132	152	152	175	200
B. ELEMENTARY VOCATIONAL		66	76	87	87	100	115	115	132	152	152	175	200
		76	87	100	100	115	132	132	152	175	175	200	230
		87	100	115	115	132	152	152	175	200	200	230	264
C. VOCATIONAL		87	100	115	115	132	152	152	175	200	200	230	264
		100	115	132	132	152	175	175	200	230	230	264	304
		115	132	152	152	175	200	200	230	264	264	304	350
D. ADVANCED VOCATIONAL		115	132	(152)	152	175	200	200	230	264	264	304	350
		132	152	175	175	200	230	230	264	304	304	350	400
		152	175	200	200	230	264	264	304	350	350	400	460
E. BASIC TECHNICAL-SPECIALIZED		152	175	200	200	230	264	264	304	350	350	400	460
		175	200	230	230	264	304	304	350	400	400	460	528
		200	230	264	264	304	350	350	400	460	460	528	608
F. SEASONED TECHNICAL-SPECIALIZED		200	230	264	264	304	350	350	400	460	460	528	608
		230	264	304	304	350	400	400	460	528	528	608	700
		264	304	350	350	400	460	460	528	608	608	700	800
G. TECHNICAL-SPECIALIZED MASTERY		264	304	350	350	400	460	460	528	(608)	608	700	800
		(304)	350	400	400	460	528	528	608	(700)	700	800	920
		350	400	460	460	528	608	608	700	800	800	920	1056
H. PROFESSIONAL MASTERY		350	400	460	460	528	608	608	700	800	800	920	1056
		400	460	528	528	608	700	700	800	920	920	1056	1216
		460	528	608	608	700	800	800	920	1056	1056	1216	1400

KH	PS	AC	TOTAL
152			

SUPERVISOR

KH	PS	AC	TOTAL
304			

ACTUARIAL SPECIALIST RESEARCH ASSOCIATE

KH	PS	AC	TOTAL
700			

AREA MANAGER

In one plan, a senior manager refused to accept a job evaluation plan unless the factor working conditions was included. The plan's designer, a recent college graduate, showed through statistical analysis that working conditions did not vary enough among 90 percent of the jobs to have a meaningful effect on the resulting pay structure. Nevertheless, the manager pointed out that the recent grad had never worked in the plant's foundry, where working conditions were extremely meaningful. In order to get the plan accepted by the foundry workers, the working-conditions factor was included.

This situation is not unusual. In one study, a 21-factor plan produced the same rank order of jobs that could be generated using only 7 of the factors. Further, the jobs could be correctly slotted into pay classes using only 3 factors. Yet the company decided to keep the 21-factor plan because it was "accepted and doing the job." Research as far back as the 1940s demonstrates that the skills dimension explains 90 percent or more of the variance in job evaluation results; three factors generally account for 98 to 99 percent of the variance.[14]

3. Scale the Factors

Once the factors are determined, scales reflecting the different degrees within each factor are constructed. Each degree may also be anchored by the typical skills, tasks, and behaviors taken from the benchmark jobs that illustrate each factor degree. Exhibit 5.13 shows NMTA's scaling for the factor of knowledge.

Most factor scales consist of four to eight degrees. In practice, many evaluators use extra, undefined degrees such as plus and minus around a scale number. So what starts as a 5-degree scale—1, 2, 3, 4, 5—ends up as a 15-degree scale, with –1, 1, 1+, –2, 2, 2+, and so on.

The reason for adding plus/minus is that users of the plan believe more degrees are required to adequately differentiate among jobs. If we are trying to design 15 levels into the job structure but the factors use only three or five degrees, such users may be right.[15]

Another major issue in determining degrees is whether to make each degree equidistant from the adjacent degrees (*interval scaling*). For example, the difference between the first and second degrees in Exhibit 5.13 should approximate the difference between the fourth and fifth degrees, since the differences in points will be the same. In contrast, the intervals in the U.S. government plan range from 150 to 200 points.

The following criteria for scaling factors have been suggested: (1) Ensure that the number of degrees is necessary to distinguish among jobs, (2) use understandable terminology, (3) anchor degree definitions with benchmark-job titles, and (4) make it apparent how the degree applies to the job.

[14]See a series of studies conducted by C. H. Lawshe and his colleagues published in the *Journal of Applied Psychology* from 1944 to 1947. For example, C. H. Lawshe, "Studies in Job Evaluation: II. The Adequacy of Abbreviated Point Ratings for Hourly Paid Jobs in Three Industrial Plans," *Journal of Applied Psychology* 29 (1945), pp. 177–184. Also see Theresa M. Welbourne and Charlie O. Trevor, "The Roles of Departmental and Position Power in Job Evaluation," *Academy of Management Journal* 43 (2000), pp. 761–771.

[15]Tjarda Van Sliedregt, Olga F. Voskuijl, and Henk Thierry, "Job Evaluation Systems and Pay Grade Structures: Do They Match?" *International Journal of Human Resource Management* 12(8), (December 2001), pp. 1313–1324.

EXHIBIT 5.13
**Factor
Scaling—
National
Metal Trades
Association**

1. Knowledge
This factor measures the knowledge or equivalent training required to perform the position duties.

1st Degree

Use of reading and writing, adding and subtracting of whole numbers; following of instructions; use of fixed gauges, direct reading instruments, and similar devices; where interpretation is not required.

2nd Degree

Use of addition, subtraction, multiplication, and division of numbers including decimals and fractions; simple use of formulas, charts, tables, drawings, specifications, schedules, wiring diagrams; use of adjustable measuring instruments; checking of reports, forms, records, and comparable data; where interpretation is required.

3rd Degree

Use of mathematics together with the use of complicated drawings, specifications, charts, tables; various types of precision measuring instruments. Equivalent to 1 to 3 years' applied trades training in a particular or specialized occupation.

4th Degree

Use of advanced trades mathematics, together with the use of complicated drawings, specifications, charts, tables, handbook formulas; all varieties of precision measuring instruments. Equivalent to complete accredited apprenticeship in a recognized trade, craft, or occupation; or equivalent to a 2-year technical college education.

5th Degree

Use of higher mathematics involved in the application of engineering principles and the performance of related practical operations, together with a comprehensive knowledge of the theories and practices of mechanical, electrical, chemical, civil, or like engineering field. Equivalent to completing 4 years of technical college or university education.

4. Weight the Factors According to Importance

Once the degrees have been assigned, the factor weights can be determined. Different weights reflect differences in importance attached to each factor by the employer. For example, the National Electrical Manufacturers Association plan weights education at 17.5 percent; another employer's association weights it at 10.6 percent; a consultant's plan recommends 15.0 percent; and a trade association weights education at 10.1 percent.

Weights are often determined through an advisory committee that allocates 100 percent of the value among the factors.[16] In the illustration in Exhibit 5.14, a committee allocated 40 percent of the value to skill, 30 percent to effort, 20 percent to responsibility, and 10 percent to working conditions. Each factor has two subfactors, with five degrees each. In the example for the bookstore manager, the subfactor mental skill gets half the

[16]Charles Fay and Paul Hempel, "Whose Values? A Comparison of Incumbent, Supervisor, Incumbent-Supervisor Consensus and Committee Job Evaluation Ratings," working paper, Rutgers University, 1991; John Doyle, Rodney Green, and Paul Bo Homley, "Judging Relative Importance: Direct Rating and Point Allocation Are Not Equivalent," *Organization Behavior and Human Decision Processes,* April 1997, pp. 65–72.

EXHIBIT 5.14
Job
Evaluation
Form

Compensable Factors	Degree	x	Weight	=	Total

Job _bookstore manager_
Check one: ☒ Administrative
　　　　　　☐ Technical

Skill: (40%)

Degree scale: 1 2 3 4 5

Compensable Factor	Degree (X position)	Weight	Total
Mental	X (degree 4)	20%	80
Experience	X (degree 3)	20%	60
Effort: (30%)			
Physical	X (degree 2)	15%	30
Mental	X (degree 4)	15%	60
Responsibility: (20%)			
Effect of Error	X (degree 4)	10%	40
Inventiveness/ Innovation	X (degree 3)	10%	30
Working Conditions: (10%)			
Environment	X (degree 1)	5%	5
Hazards	X (degree 1)	5%	5
			(310)

40 percent given to skill and the subfactor experience gets the other half: 4 degrees of mental skill times 20 equals 80 points, and 3 degrees of experience times 20 equals another 60 points.

Criterion Pay Structure

A supplement to committee judgment for determining weights is the use of a statistical analysis.[17] In this approach, the committee members choose the *criterion pay structure,* that is, a pay structure they wish to duplicate with the point plan. The criterion structure may be the current rates paid for benchmark jobs, market rates for benchmark jobs, rates for predominantly male jobs (in an attempt to eliminate gender bias), or union-negotiated rates.[18] Once a criterion structure is agreed on, statistical modeling techniques are used to determine what weight for each factor will reproduce, as closely as possible, the chosen structure. The statistical approach is often labeled *policy capturing* to differentiate it from the *committee a priori judgment* approach. Not only do the weights reflect the relative

[17]Paul M. Edwards, "Statistical Methods in Job Evaluation," *Advanced Management* (December 1948), pp. 158–163.

[18]Donald J. Treiman, "Effect of Choice of Factors and Factor Weights in Job Evaluation," in *Comparable Worth and Wage Discrimination*, ed. H. Remick (Philadelphia: Temple University Press, 1984), pp. 79–89.

importance of each factor, but research clearly demonstrates that the weights influence the resulting pay structure.[19]

Perhaps the clearest illustration can be found in municipalities. Rather than using market rates for firefighters, some unions have successfully negotiated a link between firefighters pay and police rates. So the criterion structure for firefighters becomes some percentage of whatever wage structure is used for police.

5. Communicate the Plan and Train Users

Once the job evaluation plan is designed, a manual is prepared so that other people can apply the plan. The manual describes the method, defines the compensable factors, and provides enough information to permit users to distinguish varying degrees of each factor. The point of the manual is to allow users who were not involved in the plan's development to apply the plan as its developers intended. Users will also require training on how to apply the plan and background information on how the plan fits into the organization's total pay system. An appeals process may also be included so that employees who feel their jobs are unfairly evaluated have some recourse. Employee acceptance of the process is crucial if the organization is to have any hope that employees will accept the resulting pay as fair. In order to build this acceptance, communication to all employees whose jobs are part of the process used to build the structure is required. This communication may be done through informational meetings, websites, or other methods.

6. Apply to Nonbenchmark Jobs

Recall that the compensable factors and weights were derived using a sample of benchmark jobs. The final step is to apply the plan to the remaining jobs. This can be done by people who were not necessarily involved in the design process but have been given adequate training in applying the plan. Trained evaluators will also be asked to evaluate new positions that may be created or to reevaluate jobs whose work content has changed. They may also be part of panels that hear appeals from murmuring employees.

WHO SHOULD BE INVOLVED?

If the internal structure's purpose is to aid managers and if ensuring high involvement and commitment from employees is important, those managers and employees with a stake in the results should be involved in the process of designing it. A common approach is to use committees, task forces, or teams that include representatives from key operating functions, including nonmanagerial employees. In some cases, the group's role is only

---

[19]M. K. Mount and R. A. Ellis, "Investigation of Bias in Job Evaluation Ratings of Comparable Worth Study Participants," *Personnel Psychology* 40 (1987); Tjarda Van Sliedregt, Olga F. Voskuijl, and Henk Thierry, "Job Evaluation Systems and Pay Grade Structures: Do They Match?" *International Journal of Human Resource Management* 12(8), (December 2001), pp. 1313–1324; Judith M. Collins and Paul M. Muchinsky, "An Assessment of the Construct Validity of Three Job Evaluation Methods: A Field Experiment," *Academy of Management Journal* 36(4) (1993), pp. 895–904; Robert M. Madigan and David J. Hoover, "Effects of Alternative Job Evaluation Methods on Decisions Involving Pay Equity," *Academy of Management Journal* 29 (1986), pp. 84–100.

advisory; in others, the group designs the evaluation approach, chooses compensable factors, and approves all major changes. Organizations with unions often find that including union representatives helps gain acceptance of the results. Union-management task forces participated in the design of a new evaluation system for the federal government. However, other union leaders believe that philosophical differences prevent their active participation. They take the position that collective bargaining yields more equitable results. So the extent of union participation varies. No single perspective exists on the value of active participation in the process, just as no single management perspective exists.

Cybercomp

O*Net, the Occupational Information Network, is the U.S. Department of Labor's database that identifies and describes occupations; worker knowledge, skills, and abilities; and workplace requirements for jobs across the country in all sectors of the economy. For more information, visit O*Net's website: *www.onetcenter.org.*

How can public sector agencies use this information? Go to an occupation that is of interest to you. Compare the information offered by the Department of Labor to the job-opening descriptions you looked at for specific companies (Chapter 4's Cybercomp).

Why are they different? What purpose does each serve?

The Design Process Matters

Research suggests that attending to the fairness of the design process and the approach chosen (job evaluation, skill/competency-based plan, and market pricing), rather than focusing solely on the results (the internal pay structure), is likely to achieve employee and management commitment, trust, and acceptance of the results.[20] The absence of participation may make it easier for employees and managers to imagine ways the structure might have been rearranged to their personal liking. Two researchers note, "If people do not participate in decisions, there is little to prevent them from assuming that things would have been better, 'if I'd been in charge.'"[21]

Additional research is needed to ascertain whether the payoffs from increased participation offset potential costs (time involved to reach consensus, potential problems caused by disrupting current perceptions, etc.). We noted earlier that no amount of participation overcomes low wages. In multinational organizations the involvement of both corporate compensation and country managers raises the potential for conflict due to their differing

---

[20]One of the key findings of a National Academy of Science report that examined virtually all research on pay was that the process used to design pay plans is vital to achieving high commitment. George Milkovich and Alexandra Wigdor, eds., *Pay and Performance* (Washington, DC: National Academy Press, 1991). Also see Carl F. Frost, John W. Wakely, and Robert A. Ruh, *The Scanlon Plan for Organization Development: Identity, Participation, and Equity* (East Lansing: Michigan State Press, 1974); E. A. Locke and D. M. Schweiger, "Participation in Decision Making: One More Look," *Research in Organization Behavior* (Greenwich, CT: JAI Press, 1979); G. J. Jenkins, Jr., and E. E. Lawler III, "Impact of Employee Participation in Pay Plan Development," *Organizational Behavior and Human Performance* 28 (1981), pp. 111–128; Frederick P. Morgeson, Michael A. Campion, and Carl P. Maertz, "Understanding Pay Satisfaction: The Limits of a Compensation System Implementation," *Journal of Business and Psychology* 16(1), (Fall 2001).

[21]R. Crepanzano, *Justice in the Workplace:* Vol. 2. *From Theory to Practice.* (Mahwah, NJ: Lawrence Erlbaum Associates, 2000); R. Folger and R. Crepanzano, *Organizational Justice and Human Resource Management* (Thousand Oaks, CA: Sage, 1998).

perspectives. Country managers may wish to focus on the particular business needs in their markets, whereas corporate managers may want a system that operates equally well (or poorly) across all countries. The country manager has operating objectives, does not want to lose key individuals, and views compensation as a mechanism to help accomplish these goals; corporate adopts a worldwide perspective and focuses on ensuring that decisions are consistent with the overall global strategy.

Appeals/Review Procedures

No matter what the technique, no job evaluation plan anticipates all situations. It is inevitable that some jobs will be incorrectly evaluated—or at least employees and managers may suspect that they were. Consequently, review procedures for handling such cases and helping to ensure procedural fairness are required. Often the compensation manager handles reviews, but increasingly teams of peers are used. Sometimes these reviews take on the trappings of formal grievance procedures (e.g., documented complaints and responses and levels of approval). Problems may also be handled by managers and the employee relations generalists through informal discussions.[22]

When the evaluations are completed, approval by higher levels of management is usually required. An approval process helps ensure that any changes that result from evaluating work are consistent with the organization's operations and directions.

"I Know I Speak for All of Us When I Say I Speak for All of Us."

A recent study found that more powerful departments in a university (as indicated by number of faculty members and size of budget) were more successful in using the appeals process to get jobs paid more or reclassified (higher) than were weaker departments. The study's authors concluded that in addition to assessing the worth of a job, the entire job evaluation process reflects the political and social context within the organization.[23] This result is consistent with other research that showed that a powerful member of a job evaluation committee could sway the results.[24] Using students as subjects, a "senior evaluator" alternately recommended valuing the shorthand typist over the cost clerk and then the cost clerk over the shorthand typist with a different group of students. The students generally went along with whichever suggestion was made. Consequently, procedures should be judged for their susceptibility to political influences. "It is the decision-making process, rather than the instrument itself, that seems to have the greatest influence on pay outcomes," writes one researcher.[25]

---

[22]B. Carver and A. A. Vondra, "Alternative Dispute Resolution: Why It Doesn't Work and Why It Does," *Harvard Business Review,* May–June 1994, pp. 120–129.

[23]Theresa M. Welbourne and Charlie O. Trevor, "The Roles of Departmental and Position Power in Job Evaluation," *Academy of Management Journal* 43 (2000), pp. 761–771.

[24]A. G. P. Elliott, *Staff Grading* (London: British Institute of Management, 1960); N. Gupta and G. D. Jenkins, Jr., "The Politics of Pay," paper presented at the annual meeting of the Society for Industrial and Organizational Psychology, Montreal, 1992.

[25]Vandra Huber and S. Crandall, "Job Measurement: A Social-Cognitive Decision Perspective," in *Research in Personnel and Human Resources Management,* Vol. 12, ed. Gerald R. Ferris (Greenwich, CT: JAI Press, 1994).

EXHIBIT 5.15 Resulting Internal Structures— Job, Skill, and Competency Based

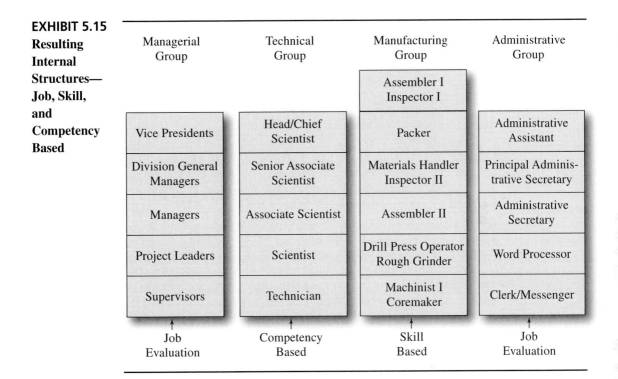

Managerial Group	Technical Group	Manufacturing Group	Administrative Group
		Assembler I Inspector I	
Vice Presidents	Head/Chief Scientist	Packer	Administrative Assistant
Division General Managers	Senior Associate Scientist	Materials Handler Inspector II	Principal Adminis-trative Secretary
Managers	Associate Scientist	Assembler II	Administrative Secretary
Project Leaders	Scientist	Drill Press Operator Rough Grinder	Word Processor
Supervisors	Technician	Machinist I Coremaker	Clerk/Messenger
Job Evaluation	Competency Based	Skill Based	Job Evaluation

THE FINAL RESULT: STRUCTURE

know they

The final result of the job analysis–job description–job evaluation process is a *structure, a hierarchy of work.* This hierarchy translates the employer's internal alignment policy into practice. Exhibit 5.15 shows four hypothetical job structures within a single organization. These structures were obtained via different approaches to evaluating work. The jobs are arrayed within four basic functions: managerial, technical, manufacturing, and administrative. The managerial and administrative structures were obtained via a point job evaluation plan; the technical and manufacturing structures, via two different person-based plans (Chapter 6). The manufacturing plan was negotiated with the union. The exhibit illustrates the results of evaluating work: structures that support a policy of internal alignment.

Organizations commonly have multiple structures derived through multiple approaches that apply to different functional groups or units. Although some employees in one structure may wish to compare the procedures used in another structure with their own, the underlying premise in practice is that internal alignment is most influenced by fair and equitable treatment of employees doing similar work in the same skill group.

BALANCING CHAOS AND CONTROL

Looking back at the material we have covered in the past three chapters (determining internal alignment, job analysis, job evaluation), you may be thinking that we have spent a lot of time and a lot of our organization's money to develop some admirable techniques. But we have yet to pay a single employee a single dollar. Why bother with all this? Why not just pay whatever it takes and get on with it?

Prior to the widespread use of job evaluation, employers in the 1930s and 1940s had irrational pay structures—the legacy of decentralized and uncoordinated wage-setting practices. Pay differences were a major source of unrest among workers. American Steel and Wire, for example, had more than 100,000 pay rates. Employment and wage records were rarely kept; only the foreman knew with any accuracy how many workers were employed in his department and the rates they received. Foremen were thus "free to manage," but they used wage information to vary the day rate for favored workers or assign them to jobs where piece rates were loose.

Job evaluation, with its specified procedures and documented results, helped change that. The technique provided work-related and business-related order and logic. However, over time, complex procedures and creeping bureaucracy can cause users to lose sight of the objectives, focusing instead on carefully prescribed and described activities. Too often we become so enamored with our techniques that we slip into knowing more and more about less and less.

At the same time, the world of work is changing. The work of many people now requires that they figure out what to do in a given situation instead of simply invoking a canned routine. They must identify problems and opportunities, make decisions, plan courses of action, marshal support, and, in general, design their own work methods, techniques, and tools. The challenge is to ensure that job evaluation plans afford flexibility to adapt to changing conditions.

Generic factors and vague descriptions such as "associates" or "technicians" may be very attractive to managers coping with increased competitive pressures and the need to restructure work and reduce costs. This flexibility avoids bureaucracy and leaves managers "free to manage"—just like the American Steel and Wire foremen. But it also reduces control and guidelines, and this in turn may make it harder to ensure that people are treated fairly. Some balance between chaos and control is required. History suggests that when flexibility without guidelines exists, chaotic and irrational pay rates too frequently result. Removing inefficient bureaucracy is important, but balanced guidelines are necessary to ensure that employees are treated fairly and that pay decisions help the organization achieve its objectives.

Your Turn

Job Evaluation for the State

Your state is enjoying economic growth. Tax revenues are up, but so is the workload for government employees. Recently there have been increasing complaints about pay. Some employees believe that their salaries are out of line in comparison to the amounts received by other employees. As a first step, the state personnel director hired you to perform job analysis and write job descriptions. The results are shown below. Now a job structure is needed.

1. Divide into teams of four to six students each. Each team should evaluate the eight jobs and prepare a job structure based on its evaluation. Assign titles to each job, and list your structure by title and job letter.
2. Each team should describe the process the group went through to arrive at that job structure. The job evaluation techniques and compensable factors used should be described, and the reasons for selecting them should be stated.
3. Each team should give each job a title and put its job structure on the board. Comparisons can then be made among job structures of the various teams. Does the job evaluation method used appear to affect the results? Do the compensable factors chosen affect the results? Does the process affect the results?
4. Evaluate the job descriptions. What parts of them were most useful? How could they be improved?

Job A

Kind of Work

Directs a large and complex fiscal management program in a large state department, agency, or institution. Provides technical and supervisory financial support to carry out policies and programs established by the department head. Serves as the chief liaison to activity managers to ensure coordination of their activities in planning with the accounting division. Maintains a close working relationship with the finance agency controller to ensure compliance with budgetary and financial planning requirements of the Department of Finance. Considerable latitude is granted employee in this class for developing, implementing, and administering financial methods and procedures. Typically reports to a high-level department manager with work reviewed through periodic conferences and reports.

Essential Responsibilities

- Directs all accounting functions of the department, agency, or institution so that adequate financial records and fiscal controls are maintained.
- Provides supervisory and high professional skills for the financial operations of the department consistent with the appropriate state and federal laws and regulations so that state and federal funds are utilized in the most efficient and effective manner.
- Provides coordination with other state and federal agencies relating to financial matters so that the department head and agency controller are informed as to matters pertaining to policies, procedures, and programs that may have an effect on the financial operation of the department.
- Develops authorized department budgets and financial plans, goals, and objectives for review

and approval by the agency controller and the department head so that maximum use will be made of financial resources.

- Consults with and advises the department head, managers, supervisors, and the agency controller on financial policies and procedures, organizational changes, and interpretation of financial data and reports to ensure efficient and effective fiscal management.

Job B

Kind of Work

Keeps financial records where the accounts are relatively complex or assists higher-level accountants and accounting technicians when the accounts are complex and extensive.

Receives direction from higher-level accounting personnel in the form of a review of work for accuracy and completeness. In some cases, may provide lead-work direction to account clerks or clerical personnel engaged in the bookkeeping operation. Prepares relatively simple reports, makes preliminary analyses of financial conditions for use by other employees, and implements minor procedural and transactional changes in the fiscal operation. Emphasis is on bookkeeping procedures and the smooth transition of fiscal operations.

Essential Responsibilities

- Maintains the financial records of a moderate-size department according to established procedures and makes adjustments to the records as directed.
- Prepares special analytical data for use by others in preparing budget requests or other reports.
- Approves and processes travel, account, invoice, and claim documents for payment.
- Codes and records all receipts and disbursement of funds.

- Reviews encumbrance or liquidation documents for accuracy and conformity with procedures and expedites financial transactions.
- Accesses or inputs information to the statewide accounting system.
- Investigates errors or problems in the processing of fiscal transactions and recommends changes in procedures.
- Issues purchase orders.
- Provides lead-work direction to other bookkeeping and clerical employees.
- Performs related work as required.

Job C

Kind of Work

Serves as section chief or top assistant to an accounting director or other high-level fiscal management officer in a moderate- or large-size state department. Directs the activities of an accounting or fiscal management section consisting of several subsections or assists the supervisor with the supervision of a very large and complex accounting operation. Works closely with the chief fiscal officer in formulating fiscal policies and independently establishes new accounts in payroll procedures to accomplish the department's program. Considerable independence of action is granted the employee, with work reviewed through reports and conferences.

Essential Responsibilities

- Prepares and administers the department budget, confers with operating officials on projected needs, and devises methods of adjusting budgets so that agency programs may be carried on efficiently and effectively.
- Provides technical accounting assistance and guidance to operational accounting units within a large- or medium-size agency so that operating procedures and staff skills will be

upgraded on a continuing basis with resultant improvement in quality and reduction in cost.

- Produces special accounting plans, reports, and analyses involving complex accounting methods and principles as a basis for decision making by the chief fiscal officer and the department head.
- Constructs and maintains the department's accounting structure and cost accounting capabilities so that the department can conform to legislative intent and meet state and federal regulatory requirements.
- Assists in the coordination and ongoing analysis and control of fiscal matters relevant to satellite institutions under departmental supervision.

Job D

Kind of Work

Performs professional accounting work as the fiscal officer of a small department, institution, or major division or as an assistant to a higher-level accountant in a large fiscal operation. Work involves providing a wide range of accounting services to professional and managerial employees. Assists in the development and maintenance of broad fiscal programs. Regularly performs complex fiscal analysis, prepares fiscal reports for management, and recommends alternative solutions to accounting problems. May supervise account clerks, accounting technicians, or clerical employees engaged in the fiscal operation. Receives supervision from a higher-level accountant, business manager, or other administrative employee.

Essential Responsibilities

- Helps administrative employees develop budgets to ensure that sufficient funds are available for operating needs.

- Monitors cash flow to ensure minimum adequate operating balance.
- Produces reports so that management has proper fiscal information.
- Submits reports to federal and state agencies to ensure that financial reporting requirements are met.
- Analyzes and interprets fiscal reports so that information is available in useful form.
- Instructs technicians and clerks in proper procedures to ensure smooth operation of accounting functions.
- Investigates fiscal accounting problems so that adequate solutions may be developed.
- Recommends and implements new procedures to ensure the efficient operation of the accounting section.
- Interprets state laws and department policies to ensure the legality of fiscal transactions.

Job E

Kind of Work

Performs semiprofessional accounting work within an established accounting system. Responsible for maintaining accounting records on a major set of accounts, preauditing transactions in a major activity, or handling cash receipts in a major facility and for classifying transactions, substantiating source documents, balancing accounts, and preparing reports as prescribed. Responsible for recognizing errors or problems in the fiscal transactions of an agency and recommending alternative solutions for consideration by other staff. Must regularly exercise initiative and independent judgment and may provide lead-work direction to account clerks or clerical employees engaged in the fiscal operation. Receives supervision from other accounting personnel.

Essential Responsibilities

- Controls expenditures so that they do not exceed budget totals and prepares allotment requests in the agency's budgetary accounts.
- Processes encumbrance changes of expenditures authorization and adjusts budget as necessary and desired.
- Reconciles department accounting records with the statewide accounting system and records documents so that funds may be appropriated, allotted, encumbered, and transferred.
- Authorizes reimbursement for goods and services received by a major department.
- Develops and maintains a system of accounts receivable, including issuance of guidelines for participants and preparation of state and federal reports.
- Provides daily accounting on loans receivable or financial aids for a major college.
- Audits cost vendor statements for conformity within departmental guidelines.
- Supervises cash accounting unit and prepares reports on receipts and deposits.
- Performs related work as required.

Job F

Kind of Work

Keeps financial records when the accounts are relatively simple, or assists others in assigned work of greater difficulty where accounting operations are more complex and extensive. The work involves a combination of clerical and bookkeeping responsibilities requiring specialized training or experience. Receives direction from higher-level accounting personnel in the form of detailed instructions and close review for accuracy and conformance with law, rules, or policy. Once oriented to the work, employee may exercise independent judgment in assigned duties.

Essential Responsibilities

- Maintains complete bookkeeping records independently when scope, volume, or complexity is limited or maintains a difficult part of an extensive bookkeeping operation.
- Codes and records all receipts and disbursement of funds.
- Prepares travel, account, invoice, and claim documents for payment.
- Reviews encumbrance or liquidation documents for accuracy and conformity with procedures and expedites financial transactions.
- Prepares financial information of reports and audits, invoices, and expenditure reports.
- Keeps general, control, or subsidiary books of accounts such as cash book appropriation and disbursement ledgers and encumbrance records.
- Accesses or inputs information to the statewide accounting system as directed.
- Performs related tasks as required.

Job G

Kind of Work

Performs varied and difficult semiprofessional accounting work within an established accounting system. Maintains a complex set of accounts and works with higher management outside the accounting unit in planning and controlling expenditures. Works with higher-level employees in providing technical fiscal advice and service to functional activities. Receives supervision from higher-level management or accounting personnel. May provide lead work direction to lower-level accounting, bookkeeping, or clerical personnel.

Essential Responsibilities

- Assists the chief accounting officer in the preparation of all budgets to ensure continuity in financial operations.

- Prepares and assembles the biennial budget and coordinates all accounting functions for a small department according to overall plan of department head and needs expressed by activity managers.
- Maintains cost coding and allocation system for a major department to serve as a basis for reimbursement.
- Provides accounting and budgetary controls for federal, state, and private grants, including reconciling bank statements and preparing reports on the status of the budget and accounts.
- Evaluates the spending progress of budget activities, ensures that budgetary limits are not exceeded, and recommends or effects changes in spending plans.
- Provides technical services to divisions of an agency in the supervision of deposits, accounts payable, procurement, and other business management areas.
- Performs related work as required.

Job H

Kind of Work

Maintains a large and complex system of accounts. Serves as a section chief in the finance division of a very large department, maintains large state-federal or state-county accounts, and oversees a major statewide accounting function in the Department of Finance. Responsible for coordinating and supervising the various phases of the accounting function. Responsibility extends to the development of procedure and policies for the work involved. Supervises a staff of accounting personnel.

Essential Responsibilities

- Provides regular budget review so that program managers have adequate funds to be effective.

- Conducts financial analysis for economical and equitable distribution or redistribution of agency resource.
- Prepares long- and short-range program recommendations for fiscal action so that agency policies are consistent.
- Plans and directs the computerization of systems applied to fiscal services to ensure efficient operation.
- Develops and defines accounting office procedures to ensure the efficient delivery of fiscal services.
- Reviews and analyzes cost accounting computer output to ensure proper documentation of projected cost as required by federal policy and procedures.
- Prepares and supervises the preparation of federal budgets and grant requests, financial plans, and expenditure reports so that they accurately reflect needs and intent of the agency.
- Develops accounting and documentation procedures for county welfare departments so that state and federal auditing and reporting requirements are met.
- Establishes and maintains a financial reporting system for all federal and other nonstate funding sources so that all fiscal reporting requirements are adhered to on a timely and accurate basis.
- Assists grantee agencies in proper reporting procedures under federal grant programs so that requirements for reimbursement may be made on a timely basis.
- Determines the statewide indirect costs so that all state agencies are allocated their proportionate share of indirect costs.
- Supervises the review and processing of all encumbrance documents submitted to the Department of Finance so that necessary accounting information is recorded accurately and promptly in the accounting system.

Summary

The differences in the rates paid for different jobs and skills affect the ability of managers to achieve their business objectives. Differences in pay matter. They matter to employees, because their willingness to take on more responsibility and training, to focus on adding value for customers and improving quality of products, and to be flexible enough to adapt to change all depend at least in part on how pay is structured for different levels of work. Differences in the rates paid for different jobs and skills also influence how fairly employees believe they are being treated. Unfair treatment is ultimately counterproductive.

So far, we have examined the most common approach to designing pay differences for different work: job evaluation. In the next chapter, we will examine several alternative approaches. However, any approach needs to be evaluated for how useful it is.

Job evaluation has evolved into many different forms and methods. Consequently, wide variations exist in its use and how it is perceived. This chapter discussed some of the many perceptions of the role of job evaluation and reviewed the criticisms leveled at it. No matter how job evaluation is designed, its ultimate use is to help design and manage a work-related, business-focused, and agreed-upon pay structure.

Review Questions

1. How does job evaluation translate internal alignment policies (loosely coupled versus tight fitting) into practice? What does (a) organization strategy and objectives, (b) flow of work, (c) fairness, and (d) motivating people's behaviors toward organization objectives have to do with job evaluation?

2. Why are there different approaches to job evaluation? Think of several employers in your area (the college, hospital, retailer, 7-Eleven, etc.). What approach would you expect them to use? Why?

3. What are the advantages and disadvantages of using more than one job evaluation plan in any single organization?

4. Why bother with job evaluation? Why not simply market-price? How can job evaluation link internal alignment and external market pressures?

5. Consider your college or school. What are the compensable factors required for your college to evaluate jobs? How would you go about identifying these factors? Should the school's educational mission be reflected in your factors? Or are the more generic factors used in the Hay plan okay? Discuss.

6. You are the manager of 10 people in a large organization. All of them become very suspicious and upset when they receive a memo from the HR department saying their jobs are going to be evaluated. How do you try to reassure them?

Person-Based Structures

Chapter Outline

History buffs tell us that some form of job evaluation was in use when the pharaohs built the pyramids. Chinese emperors managed the Great Wall construction with the assistance of job evaluation. In the United States, job evaluation in the public sector came into use in the 1880s, when Chicago reformers were trying to put an end to patronage in government hiring and pay practices. To set pay based not on whom you voted for or whom you could boast of for family connections but instead on the work you did was a revolutionary old idea.

The logic underlying job-based pay structures flows from scientific management, championed by Taylor in the 1930s. Work was broken into a series of steps and analyzed so that the "one best way," the most efficient way to perform every element of the job (right down to how to shovel coal), could be specified. Strategically, Taylor's approach fit with mass-production technologies that were beginning to revolutionize the way work was done.

Taylorism pervades our lives. Not only are jobs analyzed and evaluated in terms of the "best way," but cookbooks and software manuals specify the methods for baking a cake or using a program as a series of simple, basic steps. Golf is analyzed as a series of basic tasks that can be combined successfully to lower one's handicap. At work, at play, in all daily life, "Taylor's thinking so permeates the soil of modern life we no longer realize it is there."[1]

But in today's "new work culture," employees are told they must go beyond the tasks specified in their job descriptions. They must know more, think more on the job, and take personal responsibility for their results. Pay systems that support continuous learning and improvement, flexibility, participation, and partnership are claimed to be essential for achieving competitive advantage today. Person-based structures hold out that promise. The logic supporting person-based approaches is that the structures based on differences in people's skills or competencies will be more flexible and thus encourage agility.

Person-based approaches are the topic of this chapter. At the end of this chapter, we shall discuss the usefulness of the various approaches—job- and person-based—for determining internal structures.

Exhibit 6.1 points out the similarities in the logic underlying job-based versus people-based approaches. No matter the basis for the structure, a way is needed to (1) collect and summarize information about the work, (2) determine what is of value to the organization, (3) quantify that value, and then (4) translate that value into internal structure. The last two chapters discussed the process for job-based structures (job analysis and job evaluation). This chapter discusses the process for person-based structures. You will not be surprised to discover that similarities abound.

PERSON-BASED STRUCTURES: SKILL PLANS

The majority of applications of skill-based pay have been in manufacturing and assembly work, where the work can be specified and defined. The advantage of a skill-based plan is that people can be deployed in a way that better matches the flow of work, thus avoiding bottlenecks as well as idle hands.[2]

Skill-based structures link pay to the depth or breadth of the skills, abilities, and knowledge a person acquires that are relevant to the work. Structures based on skill pay individuals for all the skills for which they have been certified regardless of whether the work they are doing requires all or just a few of those particular skills. In contrast, a job-based plan pays employees for the job to which they are assigned, regardless of the skills they possess.

Types of Skill Plans

Skill plans can focus on *depth* (specialists in corporate law, finance, or welding and hydraulic maintenance) and/or *breadth* (generalists with knowledge in all phases of operations including marketing, manufacturing, finance, and human resources).

[1]Robert Kanigel, *The One Best Way* (New York: Viking, 1997).

[2]N. Gupta, and J. D. Shaw, "Successful Skill-Based Pay Plans," in *The Executive Handbook of Compensation: Linking Strategic Rewards to Business,* ed. C. Fay, D. Knight, and M. A. Thompson (New York: Free Press, 2001); Laurie Bienstock and Sandra McLellan, "Job Leveling in a Changing Environment," *WorldatWork Journal,* Fourth Quarter 2002, pp. 37–44.

EXHIBIT 6.1
Many Ways to Create Internal Structure

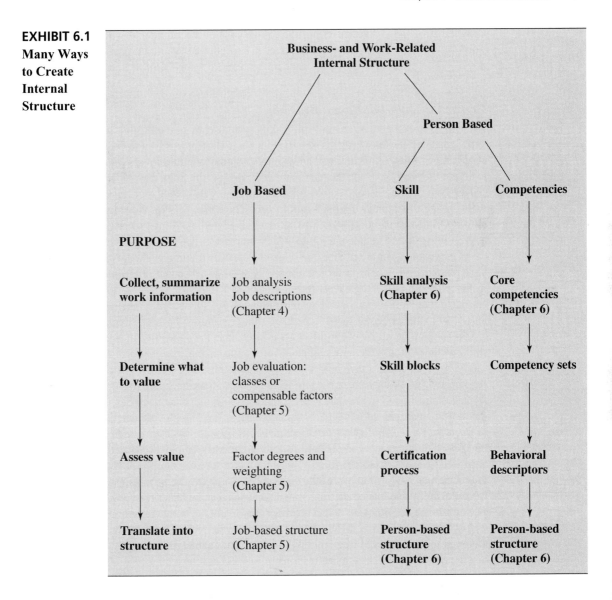

Business- and Work-Related Internal Structure

Person Based

Job Based

Skill

Competencies

PURPOSE			
Collect, summarize work information	Job analysis Job descriptions (Chapter 4)	Skill analysis (Chapter 6)	Core competencies (Chapter 6)
Determine what to value	Job evaluation: classes or compensable factors (Chapter 5)	Skill blocks	Competency sets
Assess value	Factor degrees and weighting (Chapter 5)	Certification process	Behavioral descriptors
Translate into structure	Job-based structure (Chapter 5)	Person-based structure (Chapter 6)	Person-based structure (Chapter 6)

Specialist: Depth

The pay structures for your elementary or high school teachers were likely based on their knowledge as measured by education level. A typical teacher's contract specifies a series of steps, with each step corresponding to a level of education. A bachelor's degree in education is step 1 and is the minimum required for hiring. To advance a step to higher pay requires additional education. For example, the salary schedule included in the Your Turn exercise at the end of this chapter requires 15 additional credits beyond the bachelor's degree to move to a higher step. Each year of seniority also is associated with a pay increase. The result can be that two teachers may receive different pay rates for doing essentially the same job—teaching English to high school juniors. The pay is based on the knowledge of the individual doing the job (measured by number of college credits and years of teaching experience) rather than on job content or output (performance of students).[3] The presumption is that teachers with more knowledge are more effective and more flexible—able to teach seniors, too.

Generalist/Multiskill Based: Breadth

As with teachers, employees in a multiskill system earn pay increases by acquiring new knowledge, but the knowledge is specific to a range of related jobs. Pay increases come with certification of new skills, rather than with job assignments. Employees can then be assigned to any of the jobs for which they are certified, based on the flow of work.[4] An example from Balzer Tool Coating makes the point. This company coats cutting tools by bombarding them with, among other things, titanium nitrate ions. The coating makes the sharp edge last much longer. Originally, eight different jobs were involved in the coating process. Everyone started at the same rate, no matter the job to which the person was assigned. Employees received cross-training in a variety of jobs, but without a specific training path or level. Different locations started new people in different jobs. In order to put some order into its system and make better use of its employees, Balzer moved to a skill-based plan for all its hourly workers, including administrative and sales employees. Its new structure includes four different levels, from fundamental to advanced. Exhibit 6.2 shows the new structure and the skill blocks in each level. New employees are hired into the fundamental level. Fundamental skills include familiarity with company forms and procedures, basic product knowledge, safety, basic computer usage, and so on. Once they have been certified in all the skills at the fundamental level, they receive a pay increase of $.50 an hour and move to the basic skill level. Certification in each of the four skill blocks (blasting, cleaning, stripping, and degas) in this level is worth an additional $.50 an hour. Basic-level employees can be assigned to any of the tasks for which they are certified; they will be paid whatever is their highest certification rate. The same approach is used to train and certify employees at the intermediate and advanced levels. A person certified at the very top of the structure, earning at least $10.50 an hour, could be assigned to any of the tasks in the structure. The advantage to Balzer is workforce flexibility and, hence, staffing assignments that can be better matched to the work flow. The advantage to employees is that the more they learn, the more they earn.

The system at Balzer differs from the system for teachers in that the responsibilities assigned to an employee in a multiskill system can change drastically over a short period of time, whereas teachers' basic responsibilities do not vary on a day-to-day basis. Additionally, Balzer's system is designed to ensure that all the skills are clearly work-related. Training improves skills that the company values. In contrast, a school district has no guarantee that courses taken improve teaching skills.

[3]Diana Southall and Jerry Newman, *Skill-Based Pay Development* (Buffalo, NY: HR Foundations, 2000). The Consortium for Public Research in Education at the University of Wisconsin (*www.wcer.wisc.edu/cpre/tcomp/research*) publishes research on teachers' pay and analysis of emerging issues; see A. Milanowski, "The Varieties of Knowledge and Skill-based Pay Design: A Comparison of Seven New Pay Systems for K-12 Teachers," Working Paper TC-01-2, University of Wisconsin, Wisconsin Center for Education Research, Consortium for Policy Research in Education, Madison, 2001; *Stand by Me: What Teachers Really Think About Unions, Merit Pay, and other Professional Matters* (New York: Public Agenda) 2003.

[4]G. Douglas Jenkins, Jr., Gerald E. Ledford, Jr., Nina Gupta, and D. Harold Doty, *Skill-Based Pay* (Scottsdale, AZ: American Compensation Association, 1992).

EXHIBIT 6.2
Skill Ladder
at Balzer
Tool Coating

Grade	Administration	Sales	Tool	Machine
Advanced ($10.50–$13.50)	Office administration	Inside sales	Incoming inspection	Service Arc technology
Intermediate ($9.50–$12.50)	Blueprint Expediting	Customer service Pricing–B	Outgoing inspection Shipping	Evaporation technology Coating
Basic ($7.50–$11.50)	Software Pricing File/route General office	Van driver Licensing Packing Courier	Receiving Racking Packing Fixturing	Degas Stripping Cleaning Blasting
Fundamental ($7.00–$7.50)	Fundamental	Fundamental	Fundamental	Fundamental

Purpose of the Skill-Based Structure

To evaluate the usefulness of skill-based structures, we shall use the objectives already specified for an internally aligned structure: supports the organization strategy, supports work flow, is fair to employees, and directs their behavior toward organization objectives. How well do skill-based structures do?

Supports the Strategy and Objectives

The skills on which to base a structure need to be directly related to the organization's objectives and strategy. In practice, however, the "line of sight" between changes in the specific work skills (fundamental to advanced) required to operate the titanium nitrate ion coaters and increased shareholder returns is difficult to make clear. In some cosmic sense, we know that these operating skills matter, but the link to the plant's performance is clearer than the link to corporate goals.

Supports Work Flow

The link here is more clear. One of the main advantages of a skill-based plan is that it facilitates matching people to a changing work flow.[5] For example, one national hotel chain moves many of its people to the hotel's front desk between 4 P.M. and 7 P.M., when the majority of guests check in. After 7 P.M., these same employees move to the food and beverage service area to match the demand for room service and dining room service. By ensuring that guests will not have to wait long to check in or to eat, the hotel believes it can provide a high level of service with fewer staff. (Yes, the same thought occurred to us on the tastiness of food prepared by the checkin staff—which makes the point that skill-based systems focus on inputs, not results.)

[5]Gerald E. Ledford, Jr., "Three Case Studies of Skill-Based Pay: An Overview," *Compensation and Benefits Review,* March/April 1991, pp. 11–23.

Is Fair to Employees

Employees like the potential of higher pay that comes with learning. And by encouraging employees to take charge of their own development, skill-based plans may give them more control over their work lives.

However, favoritism and bias may play a role in determining who gets first crack at the training necessary to become certified at higher-paying skill levels. Employees complain that they are forced to pick up the slack for those who are out for training. Additionally, the courts have not yet been asked to rule on the legality of having two people do the same task but for different (skill-based) pay.

Motivates Behavior toward Organization Objectives

Person-based plans have the potential to clarify new standards and behavioral expectations. The fluid work assignments that skill-based plans permit encourage employees to take responsibility for the complete work process and its results, with less direction from supervisors.[6]

"HOW TO": SKILL ANALYSIS

Exhibit 6.3 depicts the process for determining a skill-based structure. It begins with an analysis of skills, which is similar to the task statements in a job analysis. Related skills can be grouped into a skill block; skill blocks can be arranged by levels into a skill structure. To build the structure, a process is needed to describe, certify, and value the skills.

> **Skill analysis** is a systematic process of identifying and collecting information about skills required to perform work in an organization.

Exhibit 6.3 also identifies the major skill analysis decisions: (1) What is the objective of the plan? (2) What information should be collected? (3) What methods should be used? (4) Who should be involved? (5) How useful are the results for pay purposes? These are exactly the same decisions as in job analysis.

EXHIBIT 6.3   Determining the Internal Skill-Based Structure

Internal alignment: Work relationships within the organization	→	Skill analysis	→	Skill blocks	→	Skill certification	→	Skill-based structure

Basic Decisions
- What is the objective of the plan?
- What information should be collected?
- What methods should be used to determine and certify skills?
- Who should be involved?
- How useful are the results for pay purposes?

[6]B. Murray and B. Gerhart, "An Empirical Analysis of a Skill-Based Pay Program and Plant Performance Outcomes," *Academy of Management Journal* 41 (1998), pp. 68–78.

What Information to Collect?

There is far less uniformity in the use of terms in person-based plans than there is in job-based plans. For example, food products manufacturer General Mills uses four skill categories corresponding to the steps in the production process: materials handling, mixing, filling, and packaging.[7] Each skill category has three blocks: (1) entry level, (2) accomplished, and (3) advanced. Exhibit 6.4 is a schematic of the plan. It shows that a new employee can start at entry level in materials handling and, after being certified on all skills included in skill block A1, can begin training for skills in either B1 or A2.

FMC does not group skills into blocks. Instead, it assigns points and groups skills as foundation, core electives, and optional electives. Its plan for technicians is more fully developed in Exhibit 6.5.

- *Foundation skills* include a quality seminar, videos on materials handling and hazardous materials, a three-day safety workshop, and a half-day orientation. All foundation skills are mandatory and must be certified to reach the Technician I rate ($11).

EXHIBIT 6.4
General Mills' Skill-Based Structure

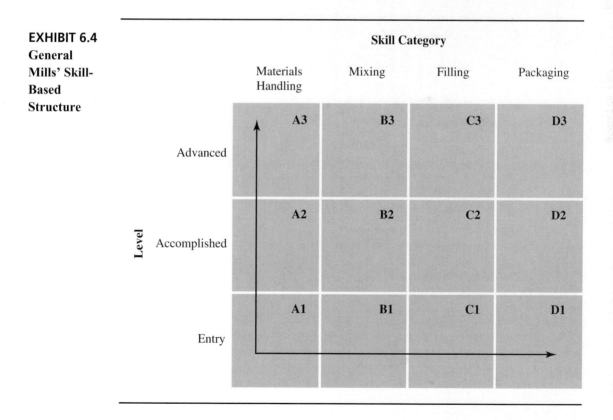

[7]Gerald E. Ledford, Jr., "Three Case Studies of Skill-Based Pay: An Overview," *Compensation and Benefits Review,* March/April 1991, pp. 11–23. Pages 23–77 of this issue contain case studies of applications at General Mills, Northern Telecom, and Honeywell.

EXHIBIT 6.5 **FMC's Technician Skill-Based Structure**

	Entry	Tech I	Tech II	Tech III	Tech IV
$17.00					5 Optional electives
$14.50				3 Optional electives	365 Core electives
13.00			Optional elective	240 Core electives	
12.00		40 Core electives	140 Core electives	Foundation	Foundation
11.00		Foundation all mandatory	Foundation		
10.50					

Foundations

Quality course
Shop floor control
Materials handling
Hazardous materials video
Safety workshop
Orientation workshop

Core Electives

Points	Skills		Skills	Points
10	Longeron Fabrication		Leak Check/Patch Weld	5
15	Panel Fabrication		Final Acceptance Test	10
15	Shell Fabrication		Welding Inspection	15
20	End Casting Welding		Flame Spraying	15
20	Finishing—Paint		Assembly Inspection	5
20	Finishing—Ablative/Autoclave		Safe % Arm Assembly	15
10	Finishing—Surface Prep		MK 13 Machining	25
15	MK 13 Assembly		MK 14 Machining	25
15	MK 14 Assembly		Tool Setup	10
15	Finishing Inspection		NC1 Inspection	30
5	Machining Inspection		Degrease	10
20	Pad Welding		Guide Rail Assembly	5
			Receiving Inspection	5

Optional Electives

Maintenance	Career Development
Logistics—JIT	Group Decision Making
Plant First Aid	Public Relations
Geometric Tolerancing	Group Facilitator
Computer—Lotus	Training
Computer—dBASE III	Group Problem Solving
Computer—Word Processing	Administration
Assessment Center	Plant Security
Consensus Building	

- *Core electives* are necessary to the facility's operations (e.g., fabrication, welding, painting, finishing, assembly, inspection). Each skill is assigned a point value.
- *Optional electives* are additional specialized competencies ranging from computer applications to team leadership and consensus building.

To reach Technician I ($12 per hour), 40 core elective points (of 370) must be certified, in addition to the foundation competencies. To reach Technician II, an additional 100 points of core electives must be certified, plus one optional elective.

A fully qualified Technician IV (certified in the foundations, 365 points of core electives, and 5 optional electives) is able to perform all work in any cell at the facility. Technician IVs earn $17.00 per hour no matter what task they are doing. FMC's approach should look familiar to any college student: required courses, required credits chosen among specific categories, and optional electives. There is a minor difference, of course—FMC employees get paid for passing these courses, whereas college students pay to take courses!

The General Mills and FMC plans illustrate the kind of information that underpins skill-based plans: very specific information on every aspect of the production process. This makes the plans particularly suited for continuous-flow technologies where employees work in teams.

Whom to Involve?

Employee involvement is almost built into skill-based plans. Employees and managers are the source of information on defining the skills, arranging them into a hierarchy, bundling them into skill blocks, and certifying whether a person actually possesses the skills. At Balzer and FMC, a committee consisting of managers from several sites developed the skill listing and certification process for each of the four skill ladders, with input from employees.

Establish Certification Methods

Practices for certifying that employees possess the skills and are able to apply them vary widely. Some organizations use peer review, on-the-job demonstrations, and tests for certification, similar to the traditional apprentice/journeyman/master path. Northern Telecom uses a preassessment meeting between supervisor and employee for discussion of skill accomplishments and training needs. Honeywell evaluates employees during the six months after they have learned the skills. Again, leaders and peers are used in the certification process. Still other companies require successful completion of formal courses. However, we do not need to point out to students that sitting in the classroom doesn't guarantee that anything is learned. School districts address this issue in a variety of ways. Some are more restrictive than others on what courses will increase teachers' pay. Some will certify for any courses; others only for courses in the teacher's subject area. However, no districts require evidence that the course makes any difference on results.

Newer skill-based applications appear to be moving away from an on-demand review and toward scheduling fixed review points in the year. Scheduling makes it easier to budget and control payroll increases. Other changes include ongoing recertification, which replaces the traditional one-time certification process and helps ensure skills are kept fresh, and removal of certification (and accompanying pay) when a particular skill is deemed obsolete.[8] However, it can be difficult to change certification procedures once a system is in place. TRW Automotive faced this problem in regard to using formal classes for its Mesa, Arizona, airbag facility. TRW felt that some employees were only putting in "seat time." Yet no one was willing to take the responsibility for refusing to certify, since an extra sign-off beyond classroom attendance had not been part of the original system design.

Many plans require that employees be recertified, since the skills may get rusty if they are not used frequently. Airplane pilots, for example, must go through an emergency-landing simulation every 12 months. The airlines want to ensure that the skills involved are *not* actually demonstrated on the job with any frequency. Similarly, the introduction of new skill requirements and the obsolescence of previous skills require recertification. At its Ome facility in Tokyo, where Toshiba manufactures laptops, all team members are required to recertify their skills every 24 months. Those who fail have the opportunity to retrain and attempt to recertify before their pay rate is reduced. However, the pressure to keep up to date and avoid obsolescence is intense.

Skill-based plans become increasingly expensive as the majority of employees become certified at the highest pay levels. As a result, the employer may have an average wage higher than competitors who are not using skill-based plans. Unless the increased flexibility permits leaner staffing, the employer may also experience higher labor costs. Some employers are combating this by requiring that employees stay at a rate a certain amount of time before they can take the training to move to a higher rate. Motorola abandoned its skill-based plan because at the end of three years, everyone had topped out (by accumulating the necessary skill blocks). TRW, too, found that after a few years, people at two manufacturing plants on skill-based systems had all topped out. They were flexible and well trained. So now what? What happens in the next years? Does everybody automatically receive a pay increase? In a firm with labor-intensive products, the increased labor costs under skill-based plans may also become a source of competitive disadvantage.

Research on Skill-Based Plans

Skill-based plans are generally well accepted by employees because it is easy to see the connection between the plan, the work, and the size of the paycheck.[9] Consequently, the plans provide strong motivation for individuals to increase their skills. "Learn to earn" is a popular slogan used with these plans. One study connected the ease of communication and understanding of skill-based plans to employees' general perceptions of being treated fairly by the employer.[10] The design of the certification process is crucial in this perception of fairness. Two studies related use of a skills system to productivity. One found positive results; the other did not.[11] Another study found that younger, more educated employ-

---

[8]N. Fredric Crandall and Marc J. Wallace, Jr., "Paying Employees to Develop New Skills," in *Aligning Pay and Results,* ed. Howard Risher (New York: American Management Association, 1999).

[9]E. E. Lawler III, S. A. Mohrman, and G. E. Ledford, Jr., *Strategies for High Performance Organizations* (San Francisco: Jossey-Bass, 1998).

[10]Cynthia Lee, Kenneth S. Law, and Philip Bobko, "The Importance of Justice Perceptions on Pay Effectiveness: A Two-Year Study of a Skill-Based Pay Plan," *Journal of Management* 25(6) (1999), pp. 851–873.

[11]K. Parrent and C. Weber, "Case Study: Does Paying for Knowledge Pay Off?" *Compensation and Benefits Review,* September–October 1994, pp. 44–50; B. Murray and B. Gerhart, "An Empirical Analysis of a Skill-Based Pay Program and Plant Performance Outcomes," *Academy of Management Journal* 41 (1998), pp. 68–78.

ees with strong growth needs, organizational commitment, and a positive attitude toward workplace innovations were more successful in acquiring new skills.[12] Nevertheless, for reasons not made clear, the study's authors recommend allocating training opportunities by seniority (i.e., to those who have a lower likelihood of benefiting from such training!).

So what kind of workplace seems best suited for a skill-based plan? Some of the early researchers on skill-based plans recently published the results of their survey on factors related to the longevity of skill-based plans. Sixty-one percent of the companies in their original sample were still using skill-based plans seven years later. One of the key factors that determined a plan's success was how well it was aligned with the organization's strategy. Plans were more viable in organizations following a defender strategy.[13] Recall from Chapter 2 that organizations that follow a cost-cutter strategy focus on operational efficiency, doing more with less. These characteristics favor the use of a skill-based plan. Although skill-based plans encourage learning additional skills (with higher pay), the resulting employee flexibility reduces the number of employees required and the overall costs.

A final question is whether a multiskilled "jack-of-all-trades" might really be the master of none. Some research suggests that the greatest impact on results occurs immediately after just a small amount of increased flexibility.[14] Greater increments in flexibility achieve fewer improvements. So more skills may not necessarily improve productivity. There may be an optimal number of skills for any individual to possess. Beyond that number, productivity returns are less than the pay increases. Additionally, some employees may not be interested in giving up the job they are doing. Such a "camper" creates a bottleneck for rotating other employees into that position to acquire those skills. Organizations should decide in advance whether they are willing to design a plan to work around campers or whether they will force campers into the system. Does the camper possess unique skills that cannot easily be learned by others? If so, perhaps that job should be carved out of the multiskill system. Either approach carries a price.[15]

The bottom line is that skill-based approaches may be only short-term initiatives for specific settings. They may refocus employees on learning new skills and adapting to a radically different work environment. They may also change how employees think about their work. However, as with any other pay technique, they do not appear suitable for all situations. The usefulness may vary, depending on how long the plan has been in place and on whether employees and managers continue to accept the plan.

[12]Kenneth Mericle and Dong-One Kim, "Determinants of Skill Acquisition and Pay Satisfaction under Pay-for-Knowledge Systems," Working Paper Series, Institute of Industrial Relations, University of California, Berkeley, *www.iir.berkeley.edu/ncwl*, 1996; Stand by Me: What Teachers Really Think about Unions, Merit Pay, and Other Professional Matters (New York: Public Agenda) 2003. *www.publicagenda.org.*

[13]Jason D. Shaw, Nina Gupta, Gerald E. Ledford, Jr., and Atul Mitra, "Survival of Skill-Based Pay Plans," paper presented at the annual meetings of the Academy of Management, Toronto, 2000.

[14]E. E. Lawler, III, S. A. Mohrman, and G. E. Ledford, Jr., *Strategies for High Performance Organizations* (San Francisco: Jossey-Bass, 1998); B. Gerhart, C. O. Trevor, and M. E. Graham, "New Directions in Compensation Research: Synergies, Risk, and Survival," *Research in Personnel and Human Resources Management* 14 (1996), pp. 143–203.

[15]N. Fredric Crandall and Marc J. Wallace, Jr., "Paying Employees to Develop New Skills," in *Aligning Pay and Results,* ed. Howard Risher (New York: American Management Association, 1999).

PERSON-BASED STRUCTURES: COMPETENCIES

There is confusion over what competencies are and what they are supposed to accomplish. As with job evaluation, perspectives proliferate. Are competencies a skill that can be learned and developed, or, are they a trait that is more difficult to learn and includes attitudes and motives? Do competencies focus on the minimum requirements that the organization needs to stay in business, or do they focus on outstanding performance? Are they characteristics of the organization or of the employee? Unfortunately, the answer to all of these questions is "yes."[16] A lack of consensus means that competencies can be a number of things; consequently, they stand in danger of becoming nothing.

By now you should be able to draw the next exhibit (Exhibit 6.6) yourself. The top part shows the process of using competencies to address the need for internal alignment by creating a competency-based structure. All approaches to creating a structure begin by looking at the work performed in the organization. While skill- and job-based systems hone in on information about specific tasks, competencies take the opposite approach. They look at the organization and try to abstract the underlying, broadly applicable knowledge, skills, and behaviors that form the foundation for successful work performance at any level or job in the organization. These are the *core competencies*. Core competencies are often linked to mission statements that express an organization's philosophy, values, business strategies, and plans.

Competency sets begin to translate each core competency into action. For the core competency of *business awareness*, for example, competency sets might be related to organizational understanding, cost management, third-party relationships, and ability to identify business opportunities.

EXHIBIT 6.6 **Determining the Internal Competency-Based Structure**

Internal alignment: Work relationships within the organization	→	Core competencies	→	Competency sets	→	Behavioral descriptors	→	Competency-based structure

Basic Decisions
- What is objective of plan?
- What information to collect?
- Methods used to determine and certify competencies?
- Who is involved?
- How useful for pay purposes?

[16]Patricia Zingheim, Gerald E. Ledford, Jr., and Jay R. Schuster, "Competencies and Competency Models: Does One Size Fit All?" *ACA Journal*, Spring 1996, pp. 56–65.

Competency indicators are the observable behaviors that indicate the level of competency within each set. These indicators may be used for staffing and evaluation as well as for pay purposes.

TRW's competency model for its human resource management department, shown in Exhibit 6.7, includes the four core competencies considered critical to the success of the business. All TRW HR employees are expected to demonstrate varying degrees of these competencies. However, not all individuals would be expected to reach the highest level in all competencies. Rather, the HR function would want to be sure it possessed all levels of mastery of all the core competencies within its HRM group, and individual employees would use the model as a guide to what TRW values and what capacities it wants people to develop.

The *competency indicators* anchor the degree of a competency required at each level of complexity of the work. Exhibit 6.8 shows five levels of competency indicators for the

**EXHIBIT 6.7
TRW Human
Resources
Competencies**

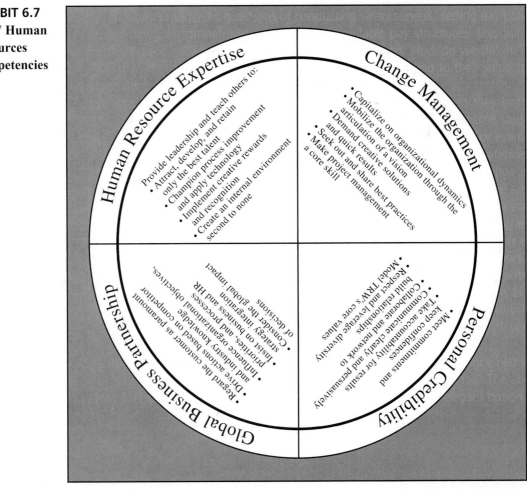

EXHIBIT 6.8
Sample Behavioral Competency Indicators

Source: Reprinted from *Raising the Bar: Using Competencies to Enhance Employee Performance* with permission from the American Compensation Association (ACA), 14040 N. Northsight Blvd., Scottsdale, AZ USA 85260; telephone (602) 483-8352. © ACA.

Impact and Influence: The intention to persuade, convince, or influence to have a specific impact. It includes the ability to anticipate and respond to the needs and concerns of others.
"Impact and Influence" is one of the competencies considered "most critical."

Level	Behaviors
0: Not shown	• Lets things happen • Quotes policy and issues instruction
1: Direct persuasion	• Uses direct persuasion in a discussion or presentation • Appeals to reason; uses data or concrete examples • Does not adapt presentation to the interest and level of the audience • Reiterates the same points when confronted with opposition
2: Multiple attempts to persuade	• Tries different tactics when attempting to persuade without necessarily making an effort to adapt to the level or interest of an audience (e.g., making two or more different arguments or points in a discussion)
3: Builds trust and fosters win-win mentality (expected performance level)	• Tailors presentations or discussions to appeal to the interest and level of others • Looks for the "win-win" opportunities • Demonstrates sensitivity and understanding of others in detecting underlying concerns, interests, or emotions, and uses that understanding to develop effective responses to objections
4: Multiple actions to influence	• Takes more than one action to influence, with each action adapted to the specific audience (e.g., a group meeting to present the situation, followed by individual meetings) • May include taking a well-thought-out unusual action to have a specific impact
5: Influences through others	• Uses experts or other third parties to influence • Develops and maintains a planned network of relationships with customers, internal peers, and industry colleagues • When required, assembles "behind the scenes" support for ideas regarding opportunities and/or solving problems

competency *impact and influence.* These behavioral anchors make the competency more concrete. The levels range from "uses direct persuasion" at level 1 to "uses experts or other third parties to influence" at level 5. Sometimes the behavioral anchors might include scales of the intensity of action, the degree of impact of the action, its complexity, and/or the amount of effort expended. Scaled competency indicators are similar to job analysis questionnaires and degrees of compensable factors, discussed in previous chapters.[17]

Defining Competencies

Because competencies are trying to get at what underlies work behaviors, there is a lot of fuzziness in defining them. Early conceptions of competencies focused on five areas:[18]

Skills (demonstration of expertise)

Knowledge (accumulated information)

Self-concepts (attitudes, values, self-image)

Traits (general disposition to behave in a certain way)

Motives (recurrent thoughts that drive behaviors)

The first two areas—skills and knowledge—were considered the *essential characteristics that everyone needs to be effective in a job.* Examples might include effective listening or team problem solving. Such competencies are observable and measurable and can be acquired through training and development.

The other three competency categories—self-concepts, traits, and motives—are not directly measurable; rather, they must be inferred from actions. And it is these inferred characteristics that were judged to be the *differentiating competencies—critical factors that distinguish superior performance from average performance.*[19] In team settings, differentiating characteristics might include a strong identification with the team (self-concept), personal flexibility (trait), and the drive to produce results (motive). As experience with competencies has grown, organizations seem to be moving away from the vagueness of self-concepts, traits, and motives, placing a greater emphasis on business-related descriptions of behaviors "that excellent performers exhibit much more consistently than average performers" and less on underlying inferences. Competencies are becoming "a collection of observable behaviors (not a single behavior) that require no inference, assumption or interpretation."[20]

---

[17]Vandra Huber and S. Crandall, "Job Measurement: A Social-Cognitive Decision Perspective," in *Research in Personnel and Human Resources Management,* Vol. 12, ed. Gerald R. Ferris (Greenwich, CT: JAI Press, 1994).

[18]Lyle M. Spencer, Jr., and Signe M. Spencer, *Competence at Work* (New York: Wiley, 1993).

[19]Patricia Zingheim, Gerald E. Ledford, Jr., and Jay R. Schuster, "Competencies and Competency Models: Does One Size Fit All?" *ACA Journal,* Spring 1996, pp. 56–65; Patricia K. Zingheim and Jay R. Schuster, "Reassessing the Value of Skill-Based Pay: Getting the Runaway Train Back on Track," *WorldatWork Journal* 11(3) (Third Quarter 2002).

[20]*Competencies, Performance and Pay* (New York: William M. Mercer, 1995).

Purpose of the Competency-Based Structure

Do competencies help support an internally aligned structure? Using our by-now familiar yardstick, how well do competencies support the organization strategy and work flow, treat employees fairly, and motivate their behavior toward organization objectives?

Organization Strategy

Frito-Lay, which has used competency-based structures for over 10 years, lists four competencies for managerial work, shown in Exhibit 6.9. Frito believes four are required in managerial work: leading for results, building work-force effectiveness, leveraging technical and business systems, and doing it the right way. The top of the exhibit shows the levels. At the first level, exhibiting the competency affects the team. At the next level, it has an impact across teams. And at the highest level, it has an impact on the entire location.

Work Flow

As you can judge from reading the previous exhibits, competencies are chosen to ensure that all the critical needs of the organization are met. For example, it is common practice to note: "These skills are considered important for all HR professionals but the weighting of importance and the level of proficiency varies for different positions, organizations, and business conditions."[21] So rather than having the skills to smoothly perform today's

EXHIBIT 6.9   **Frito-Lay Managerial Competencies**

Competency Dimension	Behaviors
Leading for results	Using initiative and influence with others to drive results and promote continuous improvement.
Building workforce effectiveness	Coaching individual development and building capability of operational, project, or cross-functional teams to achieve business results.
Leveraging technical and business systems	Acquiring and applying a depth and/or breadth of knowledge, skills, and experience to achieve functional excellence.
Doing it the right way	Modeling, teaching, and coaching company values.

Source: Nancy Jagmin, "Assessing and Rewarding Competencies: The Ten-Year Tune-up at Frito-Lay," Presentation for Center for Organization Effectiveness, April 2003, Marina del Rey, California.

[21]TRW, *Corporate Competency Manual.*

work, the emphasis is on competence that will transcend work flow. This abstract quality is both a strength and a weakness.

Fair to Employees

Advocates of competencies say they can empower employees to take charge of their own development. By focusing on optimum performance rather than average performance, competencies can help employees maintain their marketability.[22] However, critics of competencies worry that the field is going back to the 1950s and 1960s, when basing pay on personal characteristics was standard practice.[23] Basing pay on race or sex seems appalling today, yet it was standard practice at one time. Basing pay on someone's judgment of another person's integrity raises a similar flag. Trying to justify pay differences based on inferred competencies creates risks that need to be managed.

Cybercomp

Look again at the Your Turn at the end of Chapter 5. How much do you think Bill Evans, the customer service representative, is making? Go to *www.salary.com* and search on the Salary Wizard—Basic Report for some information. How does your job description for Mr. Evans's job compare to those on salary.com? Does it matter?

Motivate Behavior toward Organization Objectives

The main appeal of competencies is the direct link to the organization's strategy. Rather than having platoons of employees on committees defining tasks, the process of identifying competencies starts with the company leadership deciding what will spell success for the company. So the process resembles identifying compensable factors as part of job evaluation.

The potential for refocusing and redirecting toward core issues is the biggest selling point for a competency approach. Competencies can be the basis for a shared vision of the direction of the organization and the purpose of that direction. Competencies in effect provide guidelines for behavior and keep people focused. They can also provide a common basis for communicating and working together. This latter possibility has become increasingly important as organizations go global, and as employees with widely differing viewpoints and experiences fill leadership positions in these global organizations.

"HOW TO": COMPETENCY ANALYSIS

The bottom part of Exhibit 6.6 shows the basic decisions in creating a competency-based structure. The first decision, and by far the most important, is to clarify the objective of the plan.

---

[22]James T. Kochanski and Howard Risher, "Paying for Competencies: Rewarding Knowledge, Skills, and Behaviors," in *Aligning Pay and Results,* ed. Howard Risher (New York: American Management Association, 1999).

[23]C. A. Bartlett and Sumantra Ghoshal, "The Myth of the Generic Manager: New Personal Competencies for New Management Roles," *California Management Review* 40(1) (1997), pp. 92–105.

Objective

We have already pointed out that one of the pitfalls of competency systems is trying to do too many things with ill-suited systems. Competencies may have value for personal development and communicating organization direction. However, the vagueness and subjectivity (what exactly *are* this person's motives?) continue to make competencies a "risky foundation for a pay system."[24] The competency structure may exist on paper by virtue of the competency sets and scaled behavioral indicators but bear little connection to the work employees do. In contrast, companies like Frito-Lay have been using theirs for over 10 years. Perhaps paying for competencies is the only way to get people to pay attention to them. So the first issue is to clarify the purpose of the competency system.

What Information to Collect?

A number of schemes for classifying competencies have been proposed.[25] One of them uses three groups:

1. *Personal characteristics:* These have the aura of the Boy Scouts about them: trustworthy, loyal, courteous. In business settings, the relevant characteristics might be personal integrity, maturity of judgment, flexibility, and respect for others. Employees are expected to come in the door with these characteristics and then develop and demonstrate them in increasingly complex and ambiguous job situations.

2. *Visionary:* These are the highest-level competencies. They might be expressed as possessing a global perspective, taking the initiative in moving the organization in new directions, and able to articulate the implications for the organization of trends in the marketplace, in world events, in the local community.

3. *Organization specific:* Between the above two groups are the competencies that are tied specifically to the particular organization and to the particular function where they are being applied. They generally include leadership, customer orientation, functional expertise (e.g., able to leap tall buildings and explain the difference between competencies and compensable factors), and developing others—whatever reflects the company values, culture, and strategic intent.

Exhibit 6.10 shows the leadership competencies that 3M developed internally for its global executives.[26] Behavioral anchors are used to rate an executive on each of these competencies. Exhibit 6.11 shows the behavioral anchors for the global-perspective competency. Executives' ratings on these competencies are used to assess and develop executives worldwide. Because 3M relies heavily on promotion from within, competency ratings help develop executive talent for succession planning. Again, the link to development is clear; the link to pay is less clear.

[24]Edward E. Lawler III, "From Job-Based to Competency-Based Organizations," *Journal of Organizational Behavior* 15 (1994), pp. 3–15.

[25]R. H. Dorr and Thomas Gresch, *Human Resources Concept: Europe* (Wiesbaden, Germany: General Motors Acceptance Corporation, 1996); Graham L. O'Neill and David Doig, "Definition and Use of Competencies by Australian Organizations: A Survey of HR Practitioners," *ACA Journal,* Winter 1997, pp. 45–56.

[26]Margaret E. Allredge and Kevin J. Nilan, "3M's Leadership Competency Model: An Internally Developed Solution," *Human Resource Management* 39 (Summer/Fall 2000), pp. 133–45.

EXHIBIT 6.10 3M Leadership Competencies

Fundamental

- **Ethics and Integrity**
  Exhibits uncompromising integrity and commitment to 3M's corporate values, human resource principles, and business conduct policies. Builds trust and instills self-confidence through mutually respectful, ongoing communication.
- **Intellectual Capacity**
  Assimilates and synthesizes information rapidly, recognizes the complexity in issues, challenges assumptions, and faces up to reality. Capable of handling multiple, complex, and paradoxical situations. Communicates clearly, concisely, and with appropriate simplicity.
- **Maturity and Judgment**
  Demonstrates resiliency and sound judgment in dealing with business and corporate challenges. Recognizes when a decision must be made and acts in a considered and timely manner. Deals effectively with ambiguity and learns from success and failure.

Essential

- **Customer Orientation**
  Works constantly to provide superior value to the 3M customer, making each interaction a positive one.
- **Developing People**
  Selects and retains an excellent work force within an environment that values diversity and respects individuality. Promotes continuous learning and the development of self and others to achieve maximum potential. Gives and seeks open and authentic feedback.
- **Inspiring Others**
  Positively affects the behavior of others, motivating them to achieve personal satisfaction and high performance through a sense of purpose and spirit of cooperation. Leads by example.
- **Business Health and Results**
  Identifies and successfully generates product, market, and geographic growth opportunities, while consistently delivering positive short-term business results. Continually searches for ways to add value and position the organization for future success.

Visionary

- **Global Perspective**
  Operates from an awareness of 3M's global markets, capabilities, and resources. Exerts global leadership and works respectfully in multicultural environments to 3M's advantage.
- **Vision and Strategy**
  Creates and communicates a customer-focused vision, corporately aligned and engaging all employees in pursuit of a common goal.
- **Nurturing Innovation**
  Creates and sustains an environment that supports experimentation, rewards risk taking, reinforces curiosity, and challenges the status quo through freedom and openness without judgment. Influences the future to 3M's advantage.
- **Building Alliances**
  Builds and leverages mutually beneficial relationships and networks, both internal and external, which generate multiple opportunities for 3M.
- **Organizational Agility**
  Knows, respects, and leverages 3M culture and assets. Leads integrated change within a business unit to achieve sustainable competitive advantage. Utilizes teams intentionally and appropriately.

Source: Margaret E. Allredge and Kevin J. Nilan, "3M's Leadership Competency Model: An Internally Developed Solution," *Human Resource Management* 39 (Summer/Fall 2000), pp.133–15. Reprinted by permission of John Wiley & Sons, Inc.

EXHIBIT 6.11 **Behavioral Anchors for Global-Perspective Competency**

Global Perspective: Behaviors
• Respects, values, and leverages other customs, cultures, and values. Uses a global management team to better understand and grow the total business. Able to leverage the benefits from working in multicultural environments.
• Optimizes and integrates resources on a global basis, including manufacturing, research, and businesses across countries, and functions to increase 3M's growth and profitability.
• Satisfies global customers and markets from anywhere in the world.
• Actively stays current on world economies, trade issues, international market trends and opportunities.

Source: Margaret E. Allredge and Kevin J. Nilan, "3M's Leadership Competency Model: An Internally Developed Solution," *Human Resource Management* 39 (Summer/Fall 2000), pp. 133–45. Reprinted by permission of John Wiley & Sons, Inc.

Because they stem from each organization's mission statement or its strategy to achieve competitive advantage, you might conclude that the core competencies would be unique for each company. In fact, they are not. One analysis showed that most organizations appear to choose from the same list of 20 core competencies.[27] (See Exhibit 6.12.) So if the competencies do not differ, how can they be a source of competitive advantage? What does appear to differ among organizations is how they operationalize competencies. This parallels an issue we discussed in the strategy chapter: There may be only slight differences in the words, but the actions differ.[28]

Whom to Involve?

Like compensable factors, competencies are derived from the executive leadership's beliefs about the organization and its strategic intent. However, anecdotal evidence indicates that not all employees understand that connection. Employees at one bank insisted that processing student tuition loans was a different competency from processing auto loans. The law department at Polaroid generated a list of over 1,000 competencies it felt were unique to the law department and that created value for the organization.

Exhibit 6.13 shows part of the competencies used by a major toy company. This is one of eight competencies for the marketing department. Other departments have separate competencies. Notice the mind-numbing level of detail. While this approach may be useful for career development, it is doubtful that all this information is useful, much less necessary, for compensation purposes. The initial promise of simplicity and flexibility in person-based systems remains unfulfilled.

Establish Certification Methods

The heart of the person-based plan is that employees get paid for the relevant skills or competencies they possess whether or not those skills are used. Skill-based plans assume that possessing these skills will make it easier to match work flow with

---

[27]Patricia Zingheim, Gerald E. Ledford, Jr., and Jay R. Schuster, "Competencies and Competency Models," in *Raising the Bar: Using Competencies to Enhance Employee Performance* (Scottsdale, AZ: American Compensation Association, 1996).

[28]S. Ghoshal and C. A. Bartlett, *The Individualized Corporation* (New York: Harper Business, 1997).

EXHIBIT 6.12
The Top 20
Competencies

Achievement orientation
Concern of quality
Initiative
Interpersonal understanding
Customer service orientation
Influence and impact
Organization awareness
Networking
Directiveness
Teamwork and cooperation
Developing others
Team leadership
Technical expertise
Information seeking
Analytical thinking
Conceptual thinking
Self-control
Self-confidence
Business orientation
Flexibility

staffing levels, so whether or not an individual is *using* a particular skill on a particular day is not an issue. Competency-based plans assume—what? That all competencies are used all the time? The assumptions are not clear. What is clear, however, is the requirement that if people are to be paid based on their competencies, then there must be some way to demonstrate or certify to all concerned that a person possesses that level of competency.

However, advocates of competencies are relatively silent on the topic of certification. While consultants discuss competencies as compatible with 360-degree feedback and personal development, they are silent on objectively certifying whether a person possesses a competency. Competency indicators can also become obsolete as strategies shift.[29] However, the same sense of urgency to avoid obsolescence that pervades skill-based systems does not affect competency systems since competencies are less specific to particular work.

Resulting Structure

Recall that internal structures are described in terms of number of levels, pay differentials, and criterion on which the job structure is based. In practice, competency-based structures generally are designed with relatively few levels—four to six—and relatively

[29]Odd Nordhaug, "Competence Specificities in Organizations," *International Studies of Management and Organization* 28(1) (Spring 1998), pp. 8–29.

EXHIBIT 6.13 Product Development Competency for Marketing Department at a Toy Company

Manages the product development process by:

- Analyzing and evaluating marketplace to identify niches/opportunities
- Evaluating product/concepts
- Developing marketing strategies
- Coordinating and evaluating research/testing
- Generating product recommendations and obtaining management support
- Driving product schedules/activities

Phase I: Baseline Expectation	Phase II: Competent/Proficient	Phase III: Advanced/Coach	Phase IV: Expert/Mentor
• Analyzes market/competitive data (e.g., TRST, NPD) and provides top-line trend analysis, with supervision	• Monitors and analyzes market/competitive data (e.g., TRST, NPD) with minimal supervision, and provides recommendations for product development opportunities	• Independently monitors and analyzes market/competitive data (e.g., TRST, NPD), provides recommendations for product development opportunities, and coaches others to do so	• Reviews/approves recommendations for product development opportunities
• Evaluates products/concepts (see Toy Viability competency)	• Makes substantial contributions in product brainstorming sessions	• Leads and facilitates formal product brainstorming sessions	• Provides short- and long-term vision and goals for developing the corporate product portfolio across categories or brands
• Contributes to product brainstorming sessions	• Analyzes market research results and makes appropriate product recommendations	• Coaches others in analyzing market research results and making product recommendations	• Reviews/approves marketing strategy, and proactively adjusts strategy in response to internal/external changes
• Oversees market research activities and ensures timely completion	• Partners with Account Management group to obtain their buy-in to the product development effort	• Develops innovative marketing plans (e.g., new channels of distribution, niche markets)	• Approves cost reduction recommendations
• Obtains Account Management input to the product development effort	• Develops and implements marketing strategy, with minimal supervision.	• Independently develops and implements marketing strategy, and coaches others to do so	• Anticipates critical issues that may impact product schedules and develops alternate plans
• Develops and implements marketing strategy, with supervision: product, positioning, pricing/financial, promotion, packaging, merchandising, and advertising	• Drives cost reductions to achieve price/profit goals	• Identifies/evaluates cost reduction opportunities, and coaches others to do so	• Ensures on-strategy delivery
• Facilitates cost reductions to achieve price/profit goals; ensures execution of cost meeting next steps	• Drives product schedules and resolves product scheduling issues (late delivery, late debug)	• Identifies and implements product schedule improvement tactics	
• Ensures adherence to product schedules	• Negotiates with licensors to obtain product approvals	• Coaches others to manage product schedules	
• Coordinates licensor approval of product concept/models		• Coaches others in managing licensor relationships	
		• Shares product ideas/strategies with other teams/categories	

EXHIBIT 6.14
Toy Company's Structure Based on Competencies

Level	Phase	Title
4	Expert	Visionary; Champion; Executive
3	Advanced	Coach; Leader
2	Resource	Contributor; Professional
1	Proficient	Associate

wide differentials for increased flexibility. Exhibit 6.14 depicts the toy company's structures based on the four phases (levels) shown in Exhibit 6.13. Such a generic structure could be applied to almost any professional work, even the work of a university faculty. Consequently internal alignment using competencies appears loosely linked to the organization strategy.

Research on Competencies

While the notion of competencies may have value in identifying what distinguishes typical from truly outstanding performance, there is debate on whether competencies can be translated into a measurable, objective basis for pay. Much of the writing on competencies describes applications and the processes for arriving at the competencies; given the abstract nature of the topic, it is not surprising that little empirical research exists.

According to advocates, competencies are enhanced by the extent to which people throughout the organization are business-driven, focused, adaptive, and values-driven.[30] The key is to ensure that all employees share a common vision, have a clear understanding of the business dynamics, and know how and why their contributions make a difference.

An area of research with potential application to competencies deals with intellectual capital and knowledge management.[31] Viewing the competencies of an organization's employees as a portfolio similar to a diversified investment portfolio highlights the fact that not all competencies are unique or equally valuable strategically. The focus then changes to managing existing competencies and developing new ones in ways that maximize the overall success of the organization. As organizations globalize, they may rebalance their values and perspectives to allow a global strategy to function.[32] They seek the

[30]Lee Dyer and Richard A. Shafer, "From HR Strategy to Organizational Effectiveness," in *Strategic Human Resources Management in the Twenty-First Century,* suppl. 4, eds. Patrick M. Wright, Lee D. Dyer, John W. Boudreau, and George T. Milkovich (Stamford, CT: JAI Press, 1999).

[31]Scott A. Snell, David P. Lepak, and Mark A. Youndt, "Managing the Architecture of Intellectual Capital," in *Strategic Human Resources Management in the Twenty-First Century,* suppl. 4, eds. Patrick M. Wright, Lee D. Dyer, John W. Boudreau, and George T. Milkovich (Stamford, CT: JAI Press, 1999).

[32] Robert L. Heneman and Peter V. Leblanc, "Developing a More Relevant and Competitive Approach for Valuing Knowledge Work," *Compensation and Benefits Review,* July/August 2002, pp. 43–47; James R. Bowers, "Valuing Work—An Integrated Approach," chap. 16 in *The Executive Handbook on Compensation—Linking Strategic Rewards to Business Performance,* eds. Charles H. Fay, Michael A. Thompson, and Damien Knight (New York: Free Press, 2001).

right balance among the range and depth of cultural, functional, and product competencies in the global organization.[33]

The basic question remains, Is it appropriate to pay you for what I believe you would *like to do* or are *capable of doing* versus what you are doing? Isn't it "likely to be more effective, for *pay purposes,* to focus on what is easily measurable and directly related to organizational effectiveness" (i.e., knowledge and skills that are task/performance related)?

ONE MORE TIME: INTERNAL ALIGNMENT REFLECTED IN STRUCTURES

Now that we have spent three chapters examining all the trees, let's look again at the forest. The purpose of job- and person-based procedures is really very simple—to design and manage an internal pay structure that helps achieve the organization's objectives.

As with job-based evaluation, the final result of the person-based plan is an internal structure of work in the organization. This structure should reflect the organization's internal alignment policy (loosely versus tightly linked, egalitarian versus hierarchical) and support its business operations. Further, managers must ensure that the structure *remains* internally aligned by reassessing work/skills/competencies when necessary. Failure to do so risks structures that lack strategic, work- and performance-related logic and opens the door to bias and misdirected behaviors.

ADMINISTERING THE PLAN

Whatever plan is designed, a crucial issue is the fairness of its administration. Just as with job evaluation, details of the plan should be described in a manual that includes information necessary to apply the plan, such as definitions of compensable factors, degrees, or details of skill blocks, competencies, and certification methods. The manual will help ensure that the plan is administered as its designers intended.

We have mentioned the issue of employee acceptance throughout our discussion of job analysis and job evaluation. Communication and employee involvement are crucial for acceptance of the resulting pay structures. See Chapter 18 for more discussion of pay communication.

RESULTS: HOW USEFUL?

The usefulness of different approaches to designing pay structures, whether job- or person-based, depends on how well they achieve their objectives. While there is vast research literature on job evaluation, most of it focuses on the procedures used rather than the resulting structure's usefulness in motivating employee behaviors or achieving organization objectives. Job-based evaluation is treated as a measurement device and the re-

[33]Allen D. Engle, Sr., and Mark E. Mendenhall "Spinning the Global Competency Cube: Toward a Timely Transnational Human Resource Decision Support System," working paper, Eastern Kentucky University, Richmond, 2000.

search considers its reliability, validity, the costs involved in its design and implementation, and its compliance with laws and regulations. Any value added by job evaluation (e.g., reducing pay dissatisfaction, improving employees' understanding of how their pay is determined) has been ignored. In contrast, research on person-based structures tends to focus on their effects on behaviors and organization objectives and virtually ignores the procedures' reliability and validity.

Reliability of Job Evaluation Techniques

A reliable evaluation would be one where different evaluators produce the same results. Most studies report relatively high agreement in rank order of jobs—correlations between .85 and .96—although none of these studies included the plus and minus degrees that we discussed earlier.[34] All this matters because organizations need several people to be able to evaluate jobs and do not want the results to depend on which individual conducted the evaluation. Reliability can be improved by using evaluators who are familiar with the work and trained. Many organizations use group consensus to increase reliability. Each evaluator makes a preliminary independent evaluation. Then, meeting as a committee, evaluators discuss their results until consensus emerges. However, some studies report that results obtained through group consensus were not significantly different from those obtained by independent evaluators or by averaging individual evaluators' results. Nevertheless, the process may matter in terms of acceptability of results. Others report that a forceful or experienced person on the committee can sway the results, as can knowledge about the job's salary level.[35]

Validity

Validity refers to the degree to which the evaluation assesses what it is supposed to, the relative worth of jobs to the organization. Validity of job evaluation has been measured in two ways: (1) by agreement—the degree of agreement between rankings that resulted from the job evaluation compared to an agreed-upon rank of benchmarks used as the criterion, and (2) by "hit rates"—the degree to which the job evaluation plan matches (hits) an agreed-upon pay structure for benchmark jobs. In both cases, the predetermined, agreed-upon ranking or pay structure is for benchmark jobs. It can be established by organization leadership or be based on external market data, negotiations with unions, or the market rates for benchmarks held predominantly by men (to try to eliminate any gender discrimination reflected in the market), or some combination of these.

Many studies report that when different job evaluation plans are compared to each other, they generate very similar rankings of jobs but very low hit rates—they disagree on how much to pay the jobs.[36]

[34]Tjarda van Sliedregt, Olga F. Voskuijl, and Henk Thierry, "Job Evaluation Systems and Pay Grade Structures: Do They Match?" *International Journal of Human Resource Management* 12(8) (December 2001), pp. 1313–1324.

[35]Vandra Huber and S. Crandall, "Job Measurement: A Social-Cognitive Decision Perspective," in *Research in Personnel and Human Resources Management,* Vol. 12, ed. Gerald R. Ferris (Greenwich, CT: JAI Press, 1994), pp. 223–269; Sheila M. Rutt and Dennis Doverspike, "Salary and Organizational Level Effects on Job Evaluation Ratings," *Journal of Business and Psychology,* Spring 1999, pp. 379–385.

[36]R. M. Madigan and D. J. Hoover, "Effects of Alternative Job Evaluation Methods on Decisions Involving Pay Equity," *Academy of Management Journal,* March 1986, pp. 84–100.

Studies of the degree to which different job evaluation plans produce the same results start with the assumption that if different approaches produce the same results, then those results must be "correct," valid.

One study that looked at three different job evaluation plans applied to the same set of jobs reported similar rank order among evaluators using each plan but substantial differences in the resulting pay.[37] Some studies have found pay differences of up to $427 per month ($750/per month in today's dollars, or $9,000 a year) depending on the method used. So it is clear that the definition of validity needs to be broadened to include impact on pay decisions. How the results are judged depends on the standards used. For managing compensation the correct standard is the pay structure rather than simply the jobs' rank order.

In another study, three plans all gave the same result (they were reliable) but all three ranked a police officer higher than a detective (not valid).[38] TV fans of *Law and Order* know that in U.S. police departments, the detectives outrank the uniforms. What accounts for the reliability of invalid plans? Either the compensable factors did not pick up something deemed important in the detectives' jobs or the detectives have more power to negotiate higher wages. So while these three plans gave the same results, it is clear that they would have little employee acceptance, at least among detectives.

You may wonder, Why should any manager or employee even care about such mind-numbing details? Is this so much compensation balderdash? Not if your organization is facing challenges by dissatisfied employees or their lawyers. To miss this point is to place your organization at risk.

Acceptability

Several methods are used to assess and improve employee acceptability. An obvious one is to include a *formal appeals process*. Employees who believe their jobs are evaluated incorrectly should be able to request reanalysis and/or skills reevaluation. Most firms respond to such requests from managers, but few extend the process to all employees unless those employees are represented by unions who have negotiated a grievance process.[39] *Employee attitude surveys* can assess perceptions of how useful evaluation is as a management tool. Employees can say how well their pay is related to their jobs and how well they understand what is expected in their jobs.[40] A third method is to *audit* how the plan is being used. Exhibit 6.15 lists examples of audit measures used by various employers. They range from the percentage of employees who understand the reasons for evaluation to the percentage of jobs with current descriptions and the rate of requests for revaluation.

[37]D. Doverspike and G. Barrett, "An Internal Bias Analysis of a Job Evaluation Instrument," *Journal of Applied Psychology* 69 (1984), pp. 648–662; Kermit Davis, Jr., and William Sauser, Jr., "Effects of Alternative Weighting Methods in a Policy-Capturing Approach to Job Evaluation: A Review and Empirical Investigation," *Personnel Psychology* 44 (1991), pp. 85–127.

[38]Judith Collins and Paul M. Muchinsky, "An Assessment of the Construct Validity of Three Job Evaluation Methods: A Field Experiment," *Academy of Management Journal* 36(4) (1993), pp. 895–904; Todd J. Maurer and Stuart A. Tross, "SME Committee vs. Field Job Analysis Ratings: Convergence, Cautions, and a Call," *Journal of Business and Psychology* 14(3), (Spring 2000), pp. 489–499.

[39]D. Lipsky and R. Seeber, "In Search of Control: The Corporate Embrace of Alternative Dispute Resolution," *Journal of Labor and Employment Law* 1(1) (Spring 1998), pp. 133–157.

[40]"Mercer 2002 People at Work Survey," *www.mercer.com.*

EXHIBIT 6.15
Illustrations
of Audit
Indexes

A. Overall indicators
   1. Ratio of number of current descriptions to numbers of employees
   2. Number of job descriptions evaluated last year and previous year
   3. Number of jobs evaluated per unit
      (a) Newly created jobs
      (b) Reevaluation of existing jobs
B. Timeliness of job descriptions and evaluations
   1. Percentage of total jobs with current descriptions
   2. Percentage of evaluation requests returned within 7 working days, within 14 working days
   3. Percentage of reevaluation requests returned with changed (unchanged) evaluations
C. Workability and acceptability of job evaluation
   1. Percentage of employees (managers) surveyed who know the purposes of job evaluation
   2. The number of employees who appeal their job's evaluation rating
   3. The number of employees who receive explanations of the results of their reevaluation requests

BIAS IN INTERNAL STRUCTURES

The continuing differences in jobs held by men, women, and people of color, and the accompanying pay differences, have focused attention on internal structures as a possible source of discrimination. Much of this attention has been directed at job evaluation as both a potential source of bias against women and a mechanism to reduce bias.[41] It has been widely speculated that job evaluation is susceptible to gender bias, that is, whether jobs held predominantly by women are undervalued relative to jobs held predominantly by men simply because of the jobholder's gender. But evidence does not support the proposition that the gender of an individual *jobholder* influences the evaluation of the job.[42] Additionally, there is no evidence that the job *evaluator's* gender affects the results.

However, a study found that compensable factors related to job content (such as contact with others and judgment) did reflect bias but those pertaining to employee requirements (such as education and experience) did not.[43]

[41]D. J. Treiman and H. I. Hartmann, eds., *Women, Work and Wages: Equal Pay for Jobs of Equal Value* (Washington, DC: National Academy of Sciences, 1981); H. Remick, *Comparable Worth and Wage Discrimination* (Philadelphia: Temple University Press, 1984); Morley Gunderson, "The Evolution and Mechanics of Pay Equity in Ontario," *Canadian Public Policy* 28(1) (2002), pp. S117–S126; Deborah M. Figart, "Equal Pay for Equal Work: The Role of Job Evaluation in an Evolving Social Norm," *Journal of Economic Issues,* March 2000, pp. 1–19.

[42]D. Schwab and R. Grams, "Sex-Related Errors in Job Evaluation: A `Real-World' Test," *Journal of Applied Psychology* 70(3) (1985), pp. 533–559; Richard D. Arvey, Emily M. Passino, and John W. Lounsbury, "Job Analysis Results as Influenced by Sex of Incumbent and Sex of Analyst," *Journal of Applied Psychology* 62(4) (1977), pp. 411–416.

[43]Michael K. Mount and Rebecca A. Ellis, "Investigation of Bias in Job Evaluation Ratings of Comparable Worth Study Participants," *Personnel Psychology,* Spring 1987, pp. 85–96.

Wages Criteria Bias

The second potential source of bias affects job evaluation indirectly, through the current wages paid for jobs. In this case, job evaluation results may be biased if the jobs held predominantly by women are incorrectly underpaid. If this is the case and if job evaluation is based on the current wages paid, then the job evaluation results simply mirror any bias in the current pay rates. Considering that many job evaluation plans are purposely structured to mirror the existing pay structure, it should not be surprising that the current wages for jobs influence the results of job evaluation. One study of 400 compensation specialists revealed that market data had a substantially larger effect on pay decisions than did job evaluations or current pay data.[44]

This study is a unique look at several factors that may affect pay structures. If market rates and current pay already reflect gender bias, then these biased pay rates could work indirectly through the job evaluation process to deflate the evaluation of jobs held primarily by women.[45] Clearly, the standard (the predetermined, agreed-upon structure for benchmark jobs) used in the design of evaluation plans must be directly related to the organization's strategy and to the work.

Several recommendations seek to ensure that job evaluation plans are bias-free. The recommendations include the following:

1. Define the compensable factors and scales to include the content of jobs held predominantly by women. For example, working conditions may include the noise and stress of office machines and the repetitive movements associated with the use of computers.
2. Ensure that factor weights are not consistently biased against jobs held predominantly by women. Are factors usually associated with these jobs always given less weight?
3. Apply the plan in as bias-free a manner as feasible. Ensure that the job descriptions are bias-free, exclude incumbent names from the job evaluation process, and train diverse evaluators.

At the risk of pointing out the obvious, all issues concerning job evaluation also apply to skill-based and competency-based plans. For example, the acceptability of the results of skill-based plans can be studied from the perspective of measurement (reliability and validity) and administration (costs, simplicity). The various points in skill certification at which errors and biases may enter into judgment (e.g., different views of skill-block definitions, potential favoritism toward team members, defining and assessing skill obsolescence) and whether skill-block points and evaluators make a difference all need to be studied. In light of the detailed bureaucracy that has grown up around job evaluation, we confidently predict a growth of bureaucratic procedures around person-based plans, too. In addition to bureaucracy to manage costs, the whole approach to certification may be fraught with potential legal vulnerabilities if employees who fail to be certified challenge the process. Unfortunately, no studies of gender effects in skill-based or competency-based plans exist. Little attention has been paid to assessor training or validating the certification process. Just as employment tests used for hiring and promotion decisions must be demonstrably free of illegal bias, it seems logical that certification procedures used to determine pay structures would face the same requirement.

[44]S. Rynes, C. Weber, and G. Milkovich, "The Effects of Market Survey Rates, Job Evaluation, and Job Gender on Job Pay," *Journal of Applied Psychology* 74 (1989), pp. 114–123.

[45]D. Schwab and R. Grams, "Sex-Related Errors in Job Evaluation: A 'Real-World' Test," *Journal of Applied Psychology* 70(3) (1985), pp. 533–559.

EXHIBIT 6.16 **Contrasting Approaches**

	Job Based	Skill Based	Competency Based
What is valued **Quantify the value**	• Compensable factors • Factor degree weights	• Skill blocks • Skill levels	• Competencies • Competency levels
Mechanisms to translate into pay	• Assign points that reflect criterion pay structure	• Certification and price skills in external market	• Certification and price competencies in external market
Pay structure	• Based on job performed/market	• Based on skills certified/market	• Based on competency developed/market
Pay increases	• Promotion	• Skill acquisition	• Competency development
Managers' focus	• Link employees to work • Promotion and placement • Cost control via pay for job and budget increase	• Utilize skills efficiently • Provide training • Control costs via training, certification, and work assignments	• Be sure competencies add value • Provide competency-developing opportunities • Control costs via certification and assignments
Employee focus	• Seek promotions to earn more pay	• Seek skills	• Seek competencies
Procedures	• Job analysis • Job evaluation	• Skill analysis • Skill certification	• Competency analysis • Competency certification
Advantages	• Clear expectations • Sense of progress • Pay based on value of work performed	• Continuous learning • Flexibility • Reduced work force	• Continuous learning • Flexibility • Lateral movement
Limitations	• Potential bureaucracy • Potential inflexibility	• Potential bureaucracy • Requires costs controls	• Potential bureaucracy • Requires cost controls

THE PERFECT STRUCTURE

Exhibit 6.16 contrasts job-, skill-, and competency-based approaches. Pay increases are gained via promotions to more responsible jobs under job-based structures or via the acquisition of more valued skills/competencies under the person-based structures. Logically, employees will focus on how to get promoted (experience, performance) or on how to acquire the required skills or competencies (training, learning).

Managers whose employers use job-based plans focus on placing the right people in the right job. A switch to skill-/competency-based plans reverses this procedure. Now, managers must assign the right work to the right people, that is, those with the right skills and competencies. A job-based approach controls costs by paying only as much as the work performed is worth, regardless of any greater skills the employee may possess. So, as Exhibit 6.16 suggests, costs are controlled via job rates or work assignments and budgets.

In contrast, skill-/competency-based plans pay employees for the highest level of skill/competency they have achieved *regardless of the work they perform.* This maximizes flexibility. But it also encourages all employees to become certified at top rates. Unless an employer can either control the rate at which employees can certify skill/competency mastery or employ fewer people, the organization may experience higher labor costs than do competitors using job-based approaches. The key is to offset the higher rates with greater productivity. One consulting firm claims that an average company switching to a skill-based system experiences a 15 to 20 percent increase in wage rates, a 20 to 25 percent increase in training and development costs, and initial *increases* in head count to allow people to cross-train and move around.[46] But one study found costs were no higher.[47]

In addition to having potentially higher rates and higher training costs, skill/competency plans may become as complex and burdensome as job-based plans. Additionally, questions still remain about a skill/competency system's compliance with the Equal Pay Act. If a member of a protected group has a lower skill-mastery level and lower pay than a white male who is doing the same work, does this violate the equal-pay/equal-work standard specified in the legislation?

So where does all this come out? What is the best approach to pay structures, and how will we know it when we see it? The answer is, it depends. The best approach may be to provide sufficient ambiguity (loosely linked internal alignment) to afford flexibility to adapt to changing conditions. Too generic an approach may not provide sufficient detail to make a clear link between pay, work, and results; too detailed an approach may become rigid.

On the one hand, bases for pay that are too strictly defined may miss changes in work that are inevitable in a changing economy; on the other hand, bases for pay that are too vaguely defined will have no credibility with employees, will fail to signal what is really important for success, and may lead to suspicions of favoritism and bias.

This chapter concludes our section on internal alignment. Before we move on to external considerations, let's once again address the issue of, So what? Why bother with a pay structure? The answer should be, because it supports improved organization performance. An internally aligned pay structure, whether strategically loosely linked or tightly fitting, can be designed to (1) help determine pay for the wide variety of work in the organization, and (2) ensure that pay influences peoples' attitudes and work behaviors and directs them toward organization objectives.

[46]N. Fredric Crandall and Marc J. Wallace, Jr., "Paying Employees to Develop New Skills," in *Aligning Pay and Results,* ed. Howard Risher (New York: American Management Association, 1999); B. Murray and B. Gerhart, "An Empirical Analysis of a Skill-Based Pay Program and Plant Performance Outcomes," *Academy of Management Journal* 41 (1998), pp. 68–78.
[47]Howard Risher, ed., *Aligning Pay and Results* (New York: American Management Association, 1999).

Your Turn

Targeting Teachers' Pay

Of the 14,568 school districts in the United States, each one creates its own plan for paying teachers. The pay schedule shown in Exhibit 1 is typical of many plans; it contains steps by which a teacher's salary increases with each year of experience as well as with additional college credits beyond a bachelor's degree.

EXHIBIT 1   Teacher Salary Schedule

This Year

	BA	BA + 15	BA + 30	MA	MA + 15	MA + 30	MA + 45	MA + 60/PhD
1	28,393	29,817	31,242	31,795	34,090	35,514	36,939	38,363
2	29,118	30,625	32,131	33,639	35,146	36,653	38,160	39,667
3	29,842	31,433	33,022	34,613	36,203	37,793	39,383	40,972
4	30,567	32,241	33,914	35,587	37,259	38,931	40,605	42,278
5	31,292	33,048	34,804	36,560	38,314	40,070	41,826	43,582
6	32,017	33,857	35,695	37,534	39,372	41,210	43,051	44,889
7	32,742	34,664	36,586	38,507	40,429	42,349	44,272	46,194
8	33,468	35,472	37,476	39,480	41,485	43,489	45,493	47,497
9	34,193	36,280	38,367	40,455	42,541	44,628	46,716	48,803
10	34,918	37,088	39,257	41,427	43,597	45,767	47,937	50,107
11	35,643	37,895	40,148	42,402	44,654	46,907	49,159	51,414
12	36,368	38,703	41,038	43,374	45,711	48,046	50,383	52,717
13	37,092	39,511	41,930	44,349	46,767	49,185	51,604	54,022
14	37,817	40,318	42,821	45,322	47,824	50,325	52,827	55,329
15	38,542	41,127	43,710	47,745	48,880	51,464	54,049	56,633

Next Year   (2% increase)

	BA	BA + 15	BA + 30	MA	MA + 15	MA + 30	MA + 45	MA + 60/PhD
1	28,961	30,413	31,867	32,431	34,771	36,224	37,677	39,130
2	29,700	31,237	32,774	34,312	35,849	37,386	38,923	40,460
3	30,439	32,062	33,683	35,305	36,927	38,548	40,171	41,792
4	31,179	32,886	34,592	36,299	38,004	39,710	41,417	43,123
5	31,918	33,709	35,500	37,291	39,081	40,872	42,663	44,454
6	32,657	34,534	36,409	38,285	40,160	42,035	43,912	45,786
7	33,396	35,357	37,318	39,277	41,238	43,196	45,157	47,118
8	34,138	36,181	38,225	40,270	42,314	44,359	46,403	48,447
9	34,877	37,006	39,134	41,264	43,392	45,521	47,650	49,779
10	35,616	37,830	40,042	42,256	44,469	46,682	48,896	51,109
11	36,356	38,653	40,951	43,250	45,547	47,845	50,142	52,442
12	37,095	39,477	41,859	44,241	46,625	49,007	51,390	53,771
13	37,834	40,301	42,768	45,235	47,703	50,169	52,636	55,103
14	38,573	41,124	43,677	46,228	48,780	51,331	53,883	56,435
15	39,313	41,950	44,584	48,700	49,857	52,493	55,130	57,766

Source: Tom Dial, researcher with the National Education Association, and David Wazeter, director of research for Pennsylvania State Education Association.

Say that Jane begins teaching in September of the current year. She has a bachelor's degree and no experience. She will earn $28,393 during the current school year. During the year, her union negotiates a 2 percent increase to the entire schedule. The new amounts are shown in the bottom of the exhibit. Additionally, Jane is taking classes. If she earns fewer than 15 college credits over the course of the year, she will move up one step in the new schedule and earn $29,700 next school year, a raise of $1,307, or 4.6 percent. If she earns 15 or more credits but fewer than 30 credits this year, she will earn $31,237, a raise of $2,844, or 10 percent.

Once she has accumulated an additional 15 credits, she will "move over" to the next column, BA + 30 credits. Otherwise, she will stay in the BA + 15 column and advance one step each year until she reaches step 15, when she "tops out." Note that she will receive the step increase as well as any entire schedule increases that the school board gives each year. So the 2 percent increase to the entire schedule translates into a larger increase for those teachers currently being paid according to the schedule.

1. While the stepped salary schedule has many features of a knowledge-based pay system, not everyone agrees. Is this a knowledge-based pay system? How might you change it to make it more like the person-based plans discussed in this chapter? What features would you add/drop?

2. In the pay scale in the exhibit, notice that the column differentials increase with years of experience. What message do these increasing differentials send to teachers? What pay theories address this issue? How would these differentials affect teacher behaviors? How would they affect school district costs?

3. Calculate the size of the pay differential for increased seniority versus increased college credits. What behaviors do you believe these differentials will motivate; in other words, which pays more, growing older or taking courses?

4. Many metropolitan areas are facing a shortage of certified teachers. Some are trying a program whereby people with at least a bachelor's degree plus work experience are being given an intense six-week course in teaching methods and then are hired as regular teachers. Former engineers, social workers, and lawyers have gone through this program. One "new" teacher holds a PhD. Should these new teachers be paid according to the traditional stepped salary schedule? Why or why not? How would you anticipate that other teachers would react to paying these "pilot teachers" either the same or differently? How should the postdegree college credits (PhDs) be valued for the pilot teachers? Would it matter if they accumulated these credits before they switched to teaching?

5. Pay for performance for teachers is a hot topic in many school districts. How might the salary schedule be made compatible with a performance-based pay approach? Evaluate your ideas again after you have completed Part 3 of this book, which discusses employee contributions.

Summary
This section of the book started by examining pay structures within an organization. The premise underlying internal alignment is that internal pay structures need to be aligned with the organization's business strategy and objectives, the design of the work flow, a concern for the fair treatment of employees, and the intent of motivating employees. The work relationships within a single organization are an important part of internal alignment. The structures are part of the web of incentives within organizations. They affect satisfaction with pay, the willingness to seek and accept promotions to more responsible jobs, the effort to keep learning and undertake additional training, and the propensity to remain with the employer. They also reduce the incidence of pay-related grievances.

The techniques for establishing internally aligned structures include job analysis, job evaluation, and person-based approaches for skill-/competency-based plans. But, in practice, aspects of both jobs and people are used. Although viewed by some as bureaucratic burdens, these techniques can aid in achieving the objectives of the pay system when they are properly designed and managed. Without them, our pay objectives of improving competitiveness and fairness are more difficult to achieve.

We have now finished the first part of the book. We have discussed strategic perspectives on compensation, the key strategic issues in compensation management, and the total pay model that provides a framework for the book. Managing compensation requires creating the pay system to support the organization strategies, its culture and values, and the needs of individual employees. We examined the internal alignment of the pay structure. We discussed the techniques used to establish alignment as well as its effects on compensation objectives. The next part of the book focuses on the next strategic issue in our pay model: external competitiveness.

Review Questions

1. What are the pros and cons of having employees involved in compensation decisions? What forms can employee involvement take?

2. Why does the process used in the design of the internal pay structure matter? Distinguish between the processes used to design and administer a person-based and a job-based approach.

3. If you were managing employee compensation, how would you recommend that your company evaluate the usefulness of its job evaluation or person-based plans?

4. Based on the research on job evaluation, what are the sources of possible gender bias in skill-/competency-based plans?

5. How can a manager ensure that job evaluation or skill-/competency-based plans support a customer-centered strategy?

6. How would you decide whether to use job-based or person-based structures?

External Competitiveness: Determining the Pay Level

Tiger Woods's golfing prowess is legendary. So are his earnings. In a single year, he won over $9 million for playing (playing!) 76 rounds of golf. It took Mr. Woods 5,152 strokes to win this money, or $1,783 per stroke. One of the fascinations of golf is that the more strokes you take, the less you earn. The number-two person in the PGA ranking, Phil Mickelson, managed to earn $4.8 million, but he got only $856 per stroke. Other comparisons are equally fascinating. While a Los Angeles life-guard earns only $800 per week, an actor who plays a lifeguard on television gets $100,000 per episode. David Letterman appears on television a few hours a week, and for this CBS pays him $31.5 million a year. Compensation managers don't earn that much, no matter how well their decisions fit the organization's strategy.

The recent earnings for Mr. Woods and a host of others are shown in Exhibit II.2. For some people, these examples confirm what they have always suspected: that pay is determined without apparent reason or justice. Nevertheless, there is logic. Mr. Letterman is able to command $31.5 million a year because (1) other networks are also interested in his services and (2) they believe that his ability to attract young, hip (read "free-spending") viewers will create a stream of earnings for them that will be much greater than his pay.

The next two chapters discuss how employers set their pay level and decide forms of pay to use in comparison to their competitors. Exhibit II.1 shows that exter-nal competitiveness is the next strategic decision in the total pay model.

Two aspects of pay translate external competitiveness into practice: (1) how much to pay relative to competitors—whether to pay more than competitors, to match what they pay, or to pay less—and (2) what mix of base, bonus, stock op-tions, end benefits to pay relative to the pay mix of competitors. In a sense, "what forms" to pay (base, bonus, benefits) are the pieces of the pie. "How much" is the size of the pie. External competitiveness includes both questions.

As we shall see in the next two chapters, a variety of answers exist. Chapter 7 dis-cusses choosing the external competitiveness policy, the impact of that choice, and related theories and research. Chapter 8 has two parts: First, it discusses how to translate competitiveness policy into pay level and forms. Second, it discusses how to integrate information on pay level and forms with the internal structure from Part 1.

EXHIBIT II.1 **The Pay Model**

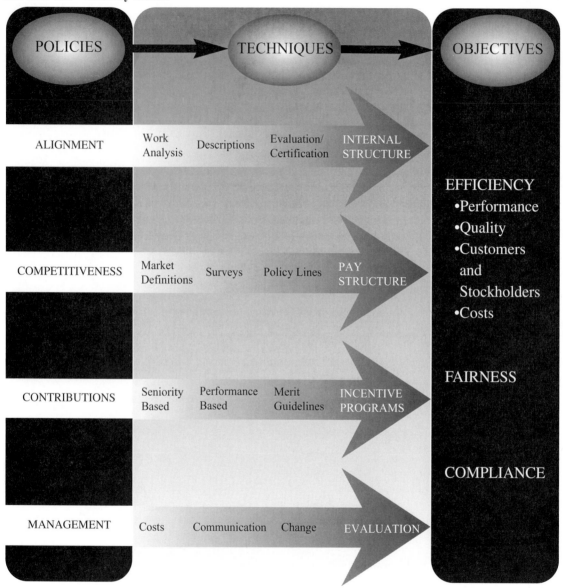

EXHIBIT II.2   Who Makes How Much?

Kathy Bauman	Service representative, Rosenbluth, Fargo, ND	$30,305
Sally Ibach	Service representative, Rosenbluth, New York City	$54,340
Ronald McDonald	Clown	$40,000
Lindsay Owens-Jones	CEO, L'Oreal, France	$7.3 million
Steve Ballmer	CEO, Microsoft	$758,810 (plus stock valued at $12.9 billion)
George W. Bush	President of the United States	$400,000
Junichiro Koizumi	Prime minister of Japan	20,880,000 yen ($174,000)
Nancy Pelosi	Democratic leader, U.S. House of Representatives	$171,900
Lew Gibbons	Longshoreman, Port of Los Angeles	$91,000
Jack Johnson	Senior pilot, Reno Air	$60,000
George Olsen	Captain, American Air	$195,000
Jay Leno	Talk-show host	$17 million
Lester Adams	Candy-cane maker	$50,000
Major-General Bryan Dutton	Last head of British military troops in Hong Kong	57,439 British pounds ($94,700)
Major-General Zhou Borong (Dutton's replacement)	Head of People's Liberation Army in Hong Kong	14,337 yuan ($1,730)
Spiros Mastoras	New York City hot dog and pretzel vendor	$21,000
Starr Figura	Assistant curator, Metropolitan Museum of Art	$39,000
Michael McCarney	Assembler of Ford Expeditions (includes overtime)	$100,000
Jesus Salvano	Front desk clerk, Brownsville, TX	$14,740
Al Smith	NYPD officer	$58,200
Pheng Kue	Firefighter, Detroit	$50,000
Elvis Presley	Recording legend (deceased)	$37 million
Melissa Ross	Schoolteacher	$43,000
Jeb Barsh	Zookeeper	$40,000
Quang Ngoc Do	Senior tool designer, Newington, CT	$62,000
Rhonda Principali	Piecework at home in Grand Junction, CO	$20,000
Judith Rodin	President, University of Pennsylvania	$808,021
Charles Futterer	Elementary school principal, Grand Marais, MN	$73,989
Sandra Feldman	President, American Federation of Teachers	$354,000
Jay Mazor	President, Union of Needle Trades	$498,554
Adam Bartkowski	Software engineer, Krakow, Poland	115,113 zlotys ($39,800)
Cindy Johnson	Software engineer, Minnetonka, MN	$93,000
Qiu Chao	Software engineer, Shanghai	57,600 yuan ($7,088)
Sandhya Bhatia	Technical project manager, New Delhi	1,200,000 rupees ($25,940)
Monica Jain	Technical team leader, New Delhi	850,000 rupees ($18,375)
Wang Yang Linda	HR supervisor for Hong Kong–based company in Shanghai	48,000 yuan ($5,806)
Wang Ying	Accountant for Korean company in Shanghai	30,000 yuan ($3,629)
Zhi Jiang	Analyst and PR for a security company in Shanghai	72,000 yuan ($8,709)
Hirobumi Katsui	Chief manager, HR ("Shunin" rank) Tokyo Electric Power	8,300,000 yen ($68,000)

Defining Competitiveness

Chapter Outline

January is always a good month for travel agents in Ithaca, New York. In addition to the permanent population eager to flee Ithaca's leaden skies (our computer has a screen saver whose color is titled "Ithaca"; it consists of 256 shades of gray), graduating students from Ithaca's two colleges are traveling to job interviews with employers across the country—at company expense, full fare, no Saturday-night stayovers required. When they return from these trips, students compare notes and find that even for people receiving the same degree in the same field from the same college, the offers vary from company to company. What explains the differences? Location has an effect: Firms in San Francisco and

New York City make higher offers. The work also has an effect: Jobs in employment pay a little less than jobs in compensation and employee relations. (Now aren't you glad you didn't drop this course?) And the industry to which the different firms belong has an effect: Pharmaceuticals, brokerage houses, and petroleum firms tend to offer more than consumer products, insurance, and heavy-manufacturing firms.[1]

Students would like to attribute these differences to themselves: differences in grades, courses taken, interviewing skills, and so on. But the same company makes the identical offer to most of its candidates at the school.

So it is hard to make the case that an individual's qualifications totally explain the offers. Why would companies extend identical offers to most candidates? And why would different companies extend different offers? This chapter discusses these choices and what difference they make for the organization.

The sheer number of economic theories related to compensation can make this chapter heavy going. Another difficulty is that the reality of pay decisions doesn't necessarily match the theories. The key to this chapter is to always ask, So what? How will this information help me? So grab the box of Krispy Kremes and let's find out.

COMPENSATION STRATEGY: EXTERNAL COMPETITIVENESS

In Part 1, we looked at comparisons *inside* the organization. In external competitiveness, our second pay policy, we look at comparisons *outside* the organization—comparisons with other employers that hire the same kinds of employees. A major decision when designing a compensation strategy is whether to mirror what competitors are doing with pay. Or is there an advantage in being different? Competitiveness includes choosing the mix of pay forms (i.e., bonuses, stock options, flexible benefits) that is right for the business strategy.

External competitiveness is expressed in practice by (1) setting a pay level that is above, below, or equal to that of competitors, and (2) determining the mix of pay forms relative to those of competitors.

External competitiveness refers to the pay relationships among organizations—the organization's pay relative to its competitors.

Pay level refers to the *average* of the array of rates paid by an employer:

(base + bonuses + benefits + options) number of employees

Pay forms are the various types of payments, or pay mix, that make up total compensation.

Both pay level and pay mix focus on two objectives: (1) Control costs, and (2) attract and retain employees.[2]

[1]Erica Groshen, "Five Reasons Why Wages Vary among Employers," *Industrial Relations* 30 (1991), pp. 350–381; J. Abowd and I. Kramarz, "Interindustry and Firm Size Wage Differentials: New Evidence," working paper, ILR-Cornell Institute of Labor Market Policies, July 2000.

[2]S. L. Rynes and B. Gerhart, eds., *Compensation in Organizations: Current Research and Practice* (San Francisco: Jossey-Bass, 2000).

Control Costs

Pay-level decisions have a significant impact on expenses. Other things being equal, the higher the pay level, the higher the labor costs:

$$\text{Labor costs} = \text{pay level} \times \text{number of employees}$$

Furthermore, the higher the pay level relative to what competitors pay, the greater the relative costs to provide similar products or services. So you might think that all organizations would pay the same job the same rate. However, they do not. A national survey of over 1,200 entry-level software engineers employed by high-tech companies found an average base salary of $50,675. The range of salaries for the same job ran from $34,600 to $86,900. Some entry-level software engineers make 2½ times what other entry-level software engineers make. The same work is paid differently. Why would Microsoft pay more (or less) than IBM? What could justify a pay level above whatever minimum amount is required to attract and retain engineers?

Attract and Retain Employees

One company may pay more because it believes its higher-paid engineers are more productive than those at other companies. They may be better trained; maybe they are more innovative in dreaming up new applications. Maybe they are less likely to quit, thus saving the company recruiting and training costs. Another company may pay less because it tries to differentiate itself on nonfinancial, more relational returns—more challenging and interesting projects, possibility of international assignments, superior rotational training program, more rapid promotions, or even greater job security. Arguably, such companies believe it is cheaper to compete on returns other than cash. Different employers set different pay levels; that is, they deliberately choose to pay above or below what others are paying for the same work. That is why there is no single "going rate" in the labor market for a specific job.[3]

Not only do the rates paid for similar jobs vary among employers, but a single company may set a different pay level for different job families.[4] The company in Exhibit 7.1 illustrates the point. The top chart shows that this particular company pays about 2 percent above the market for its entry-level engineer. (Market is set at zero in the exhibit.) However, it pays 13 percent above the market for most of its marketing jobs and over 25 percent above the market for marketing managers. Office personnel and technicians are paid below the market. So this company uses very different pay levels for different job families.

These data are based on comparisons of *base* wage. When we look at *total compensation* in the bottom of the exhibit, a different pattern emerges. The company still has a different pay level for different job families. But when bonuses, stock options, and benefits are included, only marketing managers remain above the market. Every other job family

---

[3]The National Association of Colleges and Employers, Bethlehem, PA, publishes a quarterly survey of starting-salary offers to college graduates; data are reported by curriculum, by functional area, and by degree at *www.naceweb.org*. It is one of several sources employers may use to establish the offers they extend to new graduates.

[4]Adapted from our analysis of CHiPS data set, by arrangement with Clark Consulting, Boston.

EXHIBIT 7.1
One
Company's
Market
Comparison:
Base versus
Total
Compensation

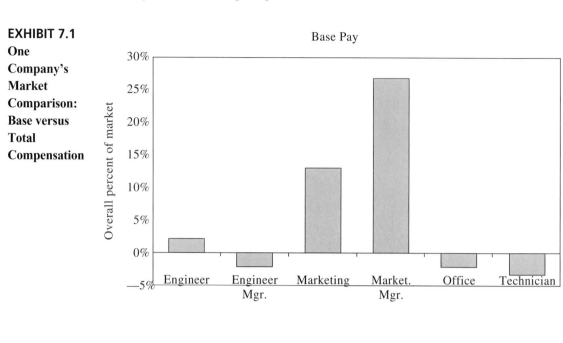

Base Pay

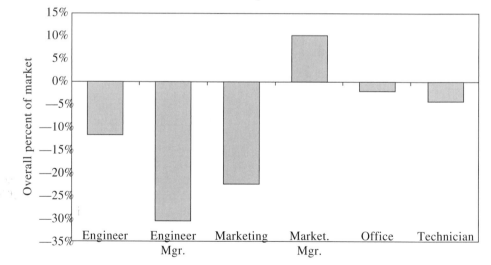

Total Compensation

is now substantially below the market. Engineering managers take the deepest plunge, from only 2 percent below the market to over 30 percent below.

The exhibit, based on actual company data, makes two points. First, companies often set different pay-level policies for different job families. Second, how a company looks in comparison to the market depends on the companies it is compared to and the pay forms included in the comparison. It is not clear whether this company deliberately chose to emphasize marketing managers and deemphasize engineering in its pay plan or if it is paying the price for not hiring one of you readers to design its plan.[5] Either way, the point is that even though people love to talk about "market rates," there is no single "going rate" in the marketplace.

There is no single "going mix" of pay forms, either. Exhibit 7.2 compares the mix of pay forms for the same job (software marketing manager) at two companies in the same geographic area. Both companies offer about the same total compensation. Yet the percentages allocated to base, bonuses, benefits, and options are very different.

WHAT SHAPES EXTERNAL COMPETITIVENESS?

Exhibit 7.3 shows the factors that affect a company's decision on pay level and mix. The factors include (1) competition in the *labor market* for people with various skills; (2) competition in the *product and service markets,* which affects the financial condition of the organization; and (3) characteristics unique to each organization and its employees, such as its business strategy, technology, and the productivity and experience of its work force. These factors act in concert to influence pay-level and pay-mix decisions.

LABOR MARKET FACTORS

Economists describe two basic types of markets: the quoted price and the bourse. Stores that label each item's price or ads that list a job opening's starting wage are examples of *quoted-price* markets. You cannot name your own price when you order from Amazon, but Priceline says you can. However, Priceline does not guarantee that your price will be accepted, whereas an Amazon order arrives in a matter of days. In contrast with Amazon's quoted price, eBay allows haggling over the terms and conditions until an agreement is reached; eBay is a *bourse*. Graduating students usually find themselves in a quoted-labor market, though minor haggling may occur.[6] In both the bourse and the quoted market, employers are the buyers and the potential employees are the sellers. If the inducements (total compensation) offered by the employer and the skills offered by the employee are mutually acceptable, a deal is struck. It may be formal contracts negotiated by unions, professional athletes, and executives, or it may be a brief letter or maybe only the implied understanding of a handshake. All this activity makes up the labor market; the result is that people and jobs match up at specified pay rates.

---

[5]Barry Gerhart and George Milkovich, "Employee Compensation: Research and Practice," in *Handbook of Industrial and Organizational Psychology,* 2d ed., eds. M. D. Dunnette and L. M. Hough (Palo Alto, CA: Consulting Psychologists Press, 1992).

[6]Barry Gerhart and Sara Rynes, "Determinants and Consequences of Salary Negotiations by Male and Female MBA Graduates," *Journal of Applied Psychology* 76(2) (1991), pp. 256–262. Also see S. L. Rynes and B. Gerhart, eds., *Compensation in Organizations: Current Research and Practice* (San Francisco: Jossey-Bass, 2000).

EXHIBIT 7.2
**Two
Companies:
Same Total
Compensation,
Different
Mixes**

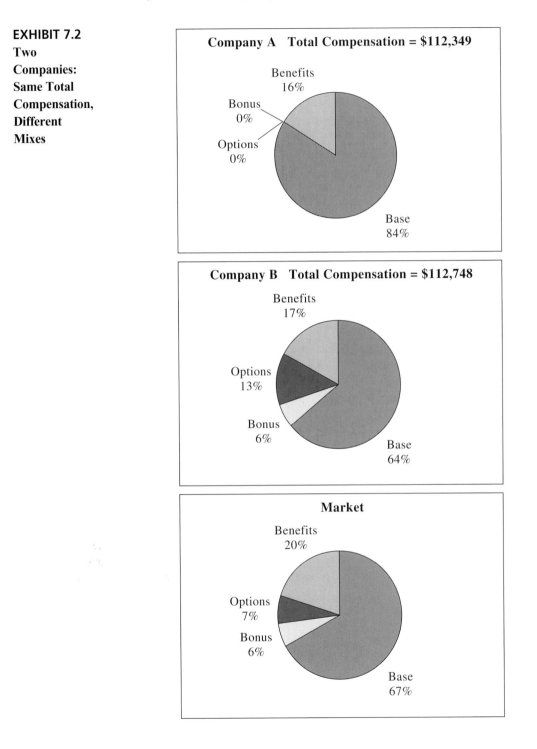

EXHIBIT 7.3
What Shapes
External
Competitiveness?

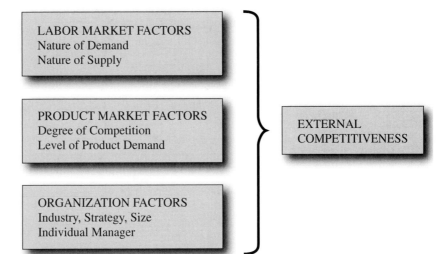

LABOR MARKET FACTORS
Nature of Demand
Nature of Supply

PRODUCT MARKET FACTORS
Degree of Competition
Level of Product Demand

ORGANIZATION FACTORS
Industry, Strategy, Size
Individual Manager

EXTERNAL
COMPETITIVENESS

How Labor Markets Work

Theories of labor markets usually begin with four basic assumptions:

1. Employers always seek to maximize profits.
2. People are homogeneous and therefore interchangeable; a business school graduate is a business school graduate is a business school graduate.
3. The pay rates reflect all costs associated with employment (e.g., base wage, bonuses, holidays, benefits, even training).
4. The markets faced by employers are competitive, so there is no advantage for a single employer to pay above or below the market rate.

Although these assumptions oversimplify reality, they provide a framework for understanding labor markets. As we shall see later, as reality forces us to change our assumptions, our theories change too.

Compensation managers often claim to be "market-driven"; that is, they pay competitively with the market or even are market leaders. Understanding how markets work requires analysis of the demand and supply of labor. The demand side focuses on the actions of the employers: how many employees they seek and what they are able and willing to pay those employees. The supply side looks at potential employees: their qualifications and the pay they are willing to accept in exchange for their services.

Exhibit 7.4 shows a simple illustration of demand and supply for business school graduates. The vertical axis represents pay rates from $25,000 to $100,000 a year. The horizontal axis depicts the number of business school graduates in the market, ranging from 100 to 1,000. The line labeled "Demand" is the sum of *all* employers' hiring preferences for business graduates at various pay levels. At $100,000, only 100 business graduates will be hired because only a few firms are able to afford them. At $25,000, companies can afford to hire 1,000 business graduates. However, as we look at the line labeled "Supply," we see that there aren't 1,000 business graduates willing to be hired at $25,000. In

EXHIBIT 7.4
Supply and
Demand for
Business
School
Graduates in
the Short
Run

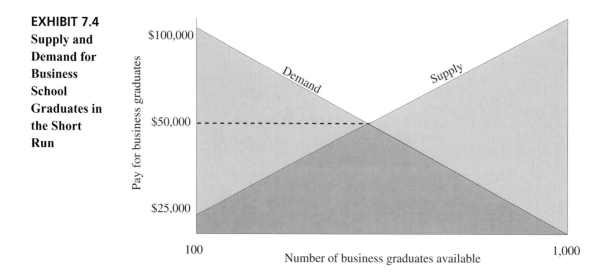

fact, only 100 are willing to work for $25,000. As pay rates rise, more graduates become interested in working, so the labor supply line slopes upward. The point where the lines for labor demand and labor supply cross determines the market rate. In this illustration, the interaction among all employers and all business graduates determines the $50,000 market rate. Because any single employer can hire all the business graduates it wants at $50,000 and all business graduates are of equal quality (assumption 2), there is no reason for any wage other than $50,000 to be paid.

Labor Demand

If $50,000 is the market-determined rate for business graduates, how many business graduates will a specific employer hire? The answer requires an analysis of labor demand. In the short term, an employer cannot change any other factor of production (i.e., technology, capital, or natural resources). Thus, its level of production can change only if it changes the level of human resources. Under such conditions, a single employer's demand for labor coincides with the marginal product of labor.

> The **marginal product of labor** is the additional output associated with the employment of one additional human resource unit, with other production factors held constant.
>
> The **marginal revenue of labor** is the additional revenue generated when the firm employs one additional unit of human resources, with other production factors held constant.

Marginal Product

Assume that two business graduates form a consulting firm that provides services to 10 clients. The firm hires a third person, who brings in five more clients. The marginal product (the change in output associated with the additional unit of labor) of employing the third business graduate is five. But adding a fourth business graduate generates only four new clients. This diminishing marginal productivity results from the fact that each

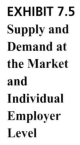

EXHIBIT 7.5
Supply and Demand at the Market and Individual Employer Level

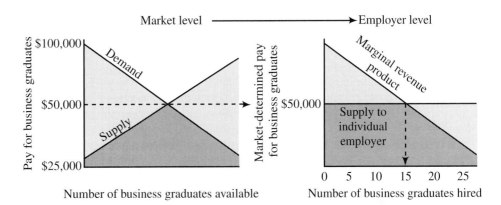

additional graduate has a progressively smaller share of the other factors of production with which to work. In the short term, other factors of production (e.g., office space, number of computers, telephone lines) are fixed. As more business graduates are brought into the firm without changing other production factors, the marginal productivity must eventually decline.

Marginal Revenue

Now let's look at marginal revenue. Marginal revenue is the money generated by the sale of the marginal product, the additional output from the employment of one additional person. In the case of the consulting firm, it's the revenues generated by each additional business graduate. If the graduate's marginal revenue exceeds $50,000, profits are increased by the additional hiring. Conversely, if marginal revenue is less than $50,000, the employer would lose money on the last hire. Recall that our first labor market theory assumption is that employers seek to maximize profits. Therefore, the employer will continue to hire graduates until the marginal revenue generated by the last hire is equal to the costs associated with employing that graduate. Because other potential costs will not change in the short run, the level of demand that maximizes profits is that level at which the marginal revenue of the last hire is equal to the wage rate for that hire.

Exhibit 7.5 shows the connection between the labor market model and the conditions facing a single employer. On the left is the supply and demand model from Exhibit 7.4, showing that pay level ($50,000) is determined by the interaction of all employers' demands for business graduates. The right side of the exhibit shows supply and demand for an individual employer. At the market-determined rate ($50,000), the individual employer can hire as many business graduates as it wants. Therefore, supply is now an unlimited horizontal line. However, the demand line still slopes downward. The two lines intersect at 15. So for this employer the marginal revenue of the 15th graduate is $50,000. The marginal revenue of the 16th graduate is less than $50,000 and so will not add enough revenue to cover costs. The point on the graph at which the incremental income from hiring the graduate—the *marginal revenue product*—equals the wage rate for that graduate is 15.[7]

[7]Robert Pindyck and Daniel Rubinfeld, *Microeconomics,* 5th ed. (Upper Saddle River, NJ: Prentice-Hall, 2001).

A manager using the marginal revenue product model must do only two things: (1) Determine the pay level set by market forces, and (2) determine the marginal revenue generated by each new hire. This will tell the manager how many people to hire. Simple? Of course not.

The model provides a valuable analytical framework, but it oversimplifies the real world. In most organizations, it is almost impossible to quantify the goods or services produced by an individual employee, since most production is through joint efforts of employees with a variety of skills. Even in settings that use piece rates (i.e., 50 cents for each soccer ball sewn), it is hard to separate the contributions of labor from those of other resources (capital and raw materials).

So neither the marginal product nor the marginal revenue is directly measurable. However, managers do need some measure that reflects value. In the last two chapters, we discussed compensable factors, skill blocks, and competencies. If compensable factors define what organizations value, then job evaluation reflects the job's contribution and may be viewed as a proxy for marginal revenue product. However, compensable factors are usually defined as input (skills required, problem solving required, responsibilities), rather than value of output. This same logic applies to skills and competencies.

Labor Supply

Now let us look more closely at the assumptions about the behavior of potential employees. This model assumes that many people are seeking jobs, that they possess accurate information about all job openings, and that no barriers to mobility (discrimination, licensing provisions, or union membership requirements) among jobs exist.

Just as with the analysis of labor demand, these assumptions greatly simplify the real world. As the assumptions change, so does the supply. For example, the upward-sloping supply assumes that as pay increases, more people are willing to take a job. But if unemployment rates are low, offers of higher pay may not increase supply—everyone who wants to work is already working. If competitors quickly match a higher offer, the employer may face a higher pay level but no increase in supply. For example, when Giant Foods raised its hourly pay $1 above the minimum wage in the Chicago area, Wendy's and Burger King quickly followed suit. The result was that the supermarket was paying more for the employees it already had but was still shorthanded. Although some firms find lowering the job requirements and hiring less-skilled workers a better choice than raising wages, this choice incurs increased training costs (which were included in assumption 3).

MODIFICATIONS TO THE DEMAND SIDE

The story is told of the economics professor and the student who were strolling through campus. "Look," the student cried, "there's a $100 bill on the path!"

"No, that cannot be," the wiser head replied. "If there were a $100 bill, someone would have picked it up."

The point of the story is that economic theories must frequently be revised to account for reality. When we change our focus from *all* the employers in an economy to a *particular* employer, models must be modified to help us understand what actually occurs.

**EXHIBIT 7.6
Labor
Demand
Theories and
Implications**

Theory	Prediction	So What?
Compensating differentials	Work with negative characteristics requires higher pay to attract workers.	Job evaluation and compensable factors must capture these negative characteristics.
Efficiency wage	Above-market wages will improve efficiency by attracting workers who will perform better and be less willing to leave.	Staffing programs must have the capability of selecting the best employees; work must be structured to take advantage of employees' greater efforts.
Signaling	Pay policies signal the kinds of behavior the employer seeks.	Pay practices must recognize desired behaviors with more pay, larger bonuses, and other forms of compensation.

A particularly troublesome issue for economists is why an employer would pay more than what theory states is the market-determined rate. Exhibit 7.6 looks at three modifications to the model that address this phenomenon: compensating differentials, efficiency wage, and signaling.

Compensating Differentials

More than 200 years ago, Adam Smith argued that individuals consider the "whole of the advantages and disadvantages of different employments" and make decisions based on the alternative with the greatest "net advantage."[8] If a job has negative characteristics—that is, if the necessary training is very expensive (medical school), job security is tenuous (stockbrokers), working conditions are disagreeable (highway construction), or chances of success are low (professional sports)—then employers must offer higher wages to compensate for these negative features.

Such compensating differentials explain the presence of various pay rates in the market. Although the notion is appealing, it is hard to document, due to the difficulties in measuring and controlling all the factors that go into a net-advantage calculation.

Efficiency Wage

According to efficiency-wage theory, high wages may increase efficiency and actually lower labor costs if they:

1. Attract higher-quality applicants.
2. Lower turnover.
3. Increase worker effort.
4. Reduce "shirking" (what economists say when they mean "screwing around").
5. Reduce the need to supervise employees (academics say "monitoring").

[8]Thomas A. Mahoney, *Compensation and Reward Perspective* (Burr Ridge, IL: Irwin, 1979), p. 123.

So, basically, efficiency increases by hiring better employees or motivating present employees to work smarter or harder. The underlying assumption is that pay level determines effort—again, an appealing notion that is difficult to document.

There is some research on efficiency-wage theory.[9] One study looked at shirking behavior by examining employee discipline and wages in several auto plants. Higher wages were associated with lower shirking, measured as the number of disciplinary layoffs. Shirking was also lower where high unemployment made it more difficult for fired or disciplined employees to find another job. So while the higher wages cut shirking, the authors of the study were unable to say whether it was cut enough to offset the higher wage bill.[10]

Do higher wages actually attract more qualified applicants? Research says yes.[11] But higher wages also attract more unqualified applicants. Few companies evaluate their recruiting programs well enough to show whether they do in fact choose only superior applicants from the larger pool. So an above-market wage does not guarantee a more productive work force.

Does an above-market wage allow an organization to operate with fewer supervisors? Some research evidence says yes. For example, a study of hospitals found that those that paid high wages to staff nurses employed fewer nurse supervisors.[12] The researchers did not speculate on whether the higher wages attracted better nurses or caused average nurses to work harder or whether the hospital was able to reduce its overall nursing costs.

Notice that the discussion so far has dealt with pay level only. What forms to pay—the mix question—is virtually ignored in these theories. The simplifying assumption is that the pay level includes the value of different forms. Abstracted away is the distinct possibility that some people find more performance-based bonus pay or better health insurance more attractive. Signaling theory is more useful in understanding what pay mix influences.

Signaling

Signaling theory holds that employers deliberately design pay levels and mix as part of a strategy that signals to both prospective and current employees the kinds of behaviors that are sought.[13] A policy of paying below the market for base pay yet offering generous bonuses or training opportunities sends a different signal, and presumably attracts different people, than does a policy of matching the market wage and offering no performance-based

[9]David Levine, Dale Belman, Gary Charness, Erica Groshen, and K. C. O'Shaughnessy, *Changes in Careers and Wage Structures at Large American Employers* (Kalamazoo, MI: Upjohn Institute, 2001); David I. Levine, D. Belman, G. Charness, E. Groshen, and K. C. O'Shaughnessy, *The New Employment Contract: Evidence about How Little Wage Structures Have Changed* (Kalamazoo, MI: Upjohn Institute, 2001); C. Murphy, "Inequality," *Fortune,* September 4, 2000, pp. 253–257; Edward P. Lazear, *Personnel Economics* (New York: Wiley, 1998); Carl M. Campbell III, "Do Firms Pay Efficiency Wages? Evidence with Data at the Firm Level," *Journal of Labor Economics* 11(3) (1993), pp. 442–469.
[10]Peter Cappelli and Keith Chauvin, "An Interplant Test of the Efficiency Wage Hypothesis," *Quarterly Journal of Economics,* August 1991, pp. 769–787.
[11]L. Rynes and J. W. Boudreau, "College Recruiting in Large Organizations: Practice, Evaluation, and Research Implications," *Personnel Psychology* 39 (1986), pp. 729–757.
[12]E. Groshen and A. B. Krueger, "The Structure of Supervision and Pay in Hospitals," *Industrial and Labor Relations Review,* February 1990, pp. 134S–146S.
[13]Allison Barber, "Pay as a Signal in Job Choice," working paper, Graduate School of Business Administration, Michigan State University; A. VanVinnen, "Person-Organization Fit: The Match between Newcomers' and Recruiters' Preferences for Organization Cultures," *Personnel Psychology* 53 (2000), pp. 115–125.

pay. An employer that combines lower base with high bonuses may be signaling that it wants employees who are risk takers. Its pay policy helps communicate expectations. Check out Exhibit 7.2 again. It shows a breakdown of forms of pay for two competitors, as well as their relationship to the market. The pay mix at company A emphasizes base (84 percent) more than does the mix at company B (64 percent) or the market average (67 percent). Company A pays no bonuses, no stock options, and somewhat lighter benefits. Company B's mix is closer to the market average. What is the message that A's pay mix is communicating? Which message appeals to you, A's or B's? The astute reader will note that at A, you can earn the $112,349 with very little apparent link to performance. Looks secure. Maybe just showing up is enough. At B, earning the $112,748 requires performance bonuses and options as well. Riskier? Why would anyone work at B without extra returns for the riskier pay? Without a premium, it is surprising that B is able to attract and retain employees. Maybe B has interesting projects, flexible schedules, or more opportunity for promotions.

A study of college students approaching graduation found that both pay level and mix affected their job decisions.[14] Students wanted jobs that offered high pay, but they also showed a preference for individual-based (rather than team-based) pay, fixed (rather than variable) pay, job-based (rather than skill-based) pay, and flexible benefits. Job seekers were rated on various personal dimensions—materialism, confidence in their abilities, and risk aversion— that were related to pay preferences. Pay level was most important to materialists and less important to those who were risk-averse. So applicants appear to select among job opportunities based on the perceived match between their personal dispositions and the nature of the organization, as signaled by the pay system. Both pay level and pay mix send a signal.

Signaling works on the supply side of the model, too, as suppliers of labor signal to potential employers. People who are better trained, have higher grades in relevant courses, and/or have related work experience signal to prospective employers that they are likely to be better performers. (Presumably they signal with the same degree of accuracy as employers.) So both characteristics of the applicants (degrees, grades, experience) and organization decisions about pay level (lead, match, lag) and mix (higher bonuses, benefit choices) act as signals that help communicate.

MODIFICATIONS TO THE SUPPLY SIDE

Two theories shown in Exhibit 7.7—reservation wage and human capital—focus on understanding employee behavior rather than employers—the supply side of the model.

Reservation Wage

Economists are renowned for their great sense of humor. So it is not surprising that they describe pay as "noncompensatory."[15] What they mean is that job seekers have a reservation-wage level below which they will not accept a job offer, no matter how attractive the other job attributes. If pay level does not meet their minimum standard, no other job attributes can make up (i.e., compensate) for this inadequacy. Other theorists go a step further and

---

[14]Daniel M. Cable and Timothy A. Judge, "Pay Preferences and Job Search Decisions: A Person-Organization Fit Perspective," *Personnel Psychology,* Summer 1994, pp. 317–348.

[15]C. Brown, "Firms' Choice of Method of Pay," *Industrial and Labor Relations Review,* February 1990, pp. S165–S182.

EXHIBIT 7.7
Supply Side
Theories and
Implications

Theory	Prediction	So What?
Reservation wage	Job seekers will not accept jobs whose pay is below a certain wage, no matter how attractive other job aspects.	Pay level will affect ability to recruit.
Human capital	The value of an individual's skills and abilities is a function of the time and expense required to acquire them.	Higher pay is required to induce people to train for more difficult jobs.

say that some job seekers—satisfiers—take the first job offer they get where the pay meets their reservation wage. A reservation wage may be above or below the market wage. The theory seeks to explain differences in workers' responses to offers.

Human Capital

The theory of human capital, perhaps the most influential economic theory for explaining pay-level differences, is based on the premise that higher earnings flow to those who improve their potential productivity by investing in themselves (by acquiring additional education, training, and experience).[16] The theory assumes that people are in fact paid at the value of their marginal product. Improving productive abilities by investing in training or even in one's physical health will increase one's marginal product. The value of an individual's skills and abilities is a function of the time, expense, and resources expended to acquire them. Consequently, jobs that require long and expensive training (engineering, physicians) should receive higher pay levels than jobs that require less investment (clerical work, elementary school teaching). As pay level increases, the number of people willing to overcome these barriers increases, thereby creating an upward-sloping supply.

So brain beats brawn. But there is a limit: A Stanford University professor recently challenged the value of a Stanford (or any other) MBA. Researchers also find that different types of education get different levels of pay. In the United Kingdom, new graduates with a degree in math, law, or economics will earn around 25 percent more than job seekers their age who do not have a college degree. However, job seekers with degrees in education, languages, and the arts will earn the same as or even less than what they would have earned if they had not gotten their degrees but had gained work experience instead.[17]

[16]Gary S. Becker, *Human Capital* (Chicago: University of Chicago Press, 1975); Barry Gerhart, "Gender Differences in Current and Starting Salaries: The Role of Performance, College Major, and Job Title," *Industrial and Labor Relations Review* 43 (1990), pp. 418–433; Robert Bretz, C. Quinn Trank, and S. L. Rynes, "Attracting Applicants in the War for Talent: Differences in Work Preferences among High Achievers," *Journal of Business and Psychology* 16 (2002), pp. 331–345.

[17]"Money Back: University Education May Be a Waste of Time and Money for Many," *The Economist,* June 21, 2003, p. 46; Jeffrey Pfeffer and Christina Fong, "The End of Business Schools? Less Success Than Meets the Eye," *Academy of Management Learning and Education,* Fall 2002; George F. Dreher and Taylor H. Cox, Jr., "Labor Market Mobility and Cash Compensation: The Moderating Effects of Race and Gender," *Academy of Management Journal* 43(5) (2000), pp. 890–900. U.S. differentials are available at *www.census.gov/population/socdemo/fld-of-trn.html.*

A number of additional factors affect the supply of labor. Geographic barriers to mobility among jobs, union requirements, lack of information about job openings, the degree of risk involved, and the degree of unemployment also influence labor markets.

PRODUCT MARKET FACTORS AND ABILITY TO PAY

The supply and demand for labor are major determinants of an employer's pay level. However, any organization must, over time, generate enough revenue to cover expenses, including compensation. It follows that an employer's pay level is constrained by its ability to compete in the product/service market. So product market conditions to a large extent determine what the organization can afford to pay.

Product demand and the degree of competition are the two key product market factors. Both affect the ability of the organization to change what it charges for its products and services. If prices cannot be changed without decreasing sales, then the ability of the employer to set a higher pay level is constrained.

Product Demand   Although labor market conditions (and legal requirements) put a floor on the pay level required to attract sufficient employees, the product market puts a lid on the maximum pay level that an employer can set. If the employer pays above the maximum, it must either pass on to consumers the higher pay level through price increases or hold prices fixed and allocate a greater share of total revenues to cover labor costs.

Degree of Competition   Employers in highly competitive markets, such as manufacturers of automobiles or generic drugs, are less able to raise prices without loss of revenues. At the other extreme, single sellers of a Lamborghini or the allergy drug Allegra are able to set whatever price they choose. However, too high a price often invites the eye of political candidates and government regulators.

Other factors besides product market conditions affect pay level. Some of these have already been discussed. The productivity of labor, the technology employed, the level of production relative to plant capacity available—all affect compensation decisions. These factors vary more across than within industries. The technologies employed and consumer preferences may vary among auto manufacturers, but the differences are relatively small compared to the differences between the technologies and product demands of auto manufacturers and those of the oil or financial industry.

A Dose of Reality: What Managers Say

Discussions with managers provide insight into how all of these economic factors translate into actual pay decisions. In one study, a number of scenarios were presented in which unemployment, profitability, and labor market conditions varied.[18] The managers were asked to make wage adjustment recommendations for several positions. Level of

[18]David I. Levine, "Fairness, Markets, and Ability to Pay: Evidence from Compensation Executives," *American Economic Review,* December 1993, pp. 1241–1259; B. Klaas, "Containing Compensation Costs: Why Firms Differ in Their Willingness to Reduce Pay," *Journal of Management* 25(6) (1999), pp. 829–850.

unemployment made almost no difference. One manager was incredulous at the suggestion: "You mean take advantage of the fact that there are a lot of people out of work?" The company's profitability was considered a factor for higher management in setting the overall pay budget but not something managers consider for individual pay adjustments. What it boiled down to was "whatever the chief financial officer says we can afford!" They thought it shortsighted to pay less, even though market conditions would have permitted lower pay. In direct contradiction to efficiency-wage theory, managers believed that problems attracting and keeping people were the result of poor management rather than inadequate compensation. They offered the opinion that, "supervisors try to solve with money their difficulties with managing people."[19]

But asking people what they might do in hypothetical scenarios is not quite reality. Faced with severe economic pressures, a number of employers around the world have cut people's pay.[20] Significant declines in demand for goods and services made such actions necessary financially and even more palatable politically.

More Reality: Splintering Supply of Labor

Observing managers' actual responses to shifting economic pressures also gives insights into how economic pressures translate into actual pay decisions. Some organizations change their sources of people; they "splinter" their labor supply.

People Flow to the Work

St. Luke's, a 100-bed hospital in the Phoenix, Arizona, area, staffs between 15 and 20 registered nurses each shift, depending on patient loads. The nurse manager staffs from four different sources:

- Regular nurses (St. Luke's full-time employees paid for 35 hours per week).
- Pool nurses (not St. Luke full-time regulars).
- "Registry" nurses (employees of temporary-help agencies specializing in nursing—on call for any hospital in the Phoenix area).
- "Travelers" (nurses from outside the Phoenix area, employed by agencies that send them to hospitals around the country for extended periods (e.g., six months).

St. Luke's faces a *splintered labor supply.* This means it uses multiple sources of nurses, from multiple locations, with multiple employment relationships. The level and mix of cash and benefits paid each nurse depends on the source. Regulars earn about $20 per hour plus benefits. Pools earn about $27 per hour but no benefits. Registries get $30 plus benefits, paid to them by the agency. Travelers get $30 plus benefits and expenses, including rent, paid by the contracting agencies. St. Luke's pays a fee to the registry and traveler agencies in addition to the nurses' compensation. The splintered supply results in nurses working the same jobs side by side on the same shift but earning significantly different pay.

This is a case of people flowing to the work. St. Luke's cannot send its nursing tasks off-site to other cities or offshore to other nations.

---

[19]David I. Levine, "Fairness, Markets, and Ability to Pay: Evidence from Compensation Executives," *American Economic Review,* December 1993, p. 1250.

[20]"National Wages Council Recommends the Restructuring of Wage System for Competitiveness—Ministers and Top Civil Servants to Lead with Wage Cuts," *Singapore Straits,* May 22, 2003.

Work Flows to the People—On-site, Off-site, Offshore

Apriso, a Long Beach, California, company, designs and installs computer-assisted man-ufacturing software that makes factories around the world more efficient. When Apriso competes for a project, it has many ways to design the project and structure the bid. The bid is structured in part on the compensation paid to people in different locations. Apriso can staff the project with employees who are on-site (in Long Beach), off-site (contract employees from throughout the United States), or offshore. Design engineers in Long Beach earn about $80,000 to $100,000; those in Krakow, Poland, get about $40,000 to $50,000. Apriso can "mix and match" its people from different sources. Which source Apriso includes in its bid depends on many factors: customer preferences, time schedules, the nature of the project. To put together its bids, Apriso managers need to know pay lev-els and mixes of forms not only in the market in Long Beach but also in other locations, including Krakow, Shanghai, Vancouver, and Bangalore.

Work flowing to lower-wage locations, presuming similar levels of output and quality, is not new. Historically, clothing (needle trades) and furniture jobs flowed from New England to southern states. Work flows across national borders, too. First, it was low-skill, low-wage jobs (T-shirts and sneakers) to China and Central America; then it was higher-paid blue-collar jobs (electronics, appliances, cars); now it is service and professional jobs (accounting, engineer-ing). Vastly improved communication and software connectivity has accelerated these dy-namics. Studies estimate that over the next 10 to 15 years more than 3.3 million service jobs (accounting, information technology) will flow out of the United States to India, China, and eastern Europe.[21] In its Bangalore, India, offices Ernst & Young employs over 200 CPA-qualified accountants paid about 40 percent of its U.S. CPAs' wages to work on processing taxes and conducting financial analyses for its clients.[22] The next time you call a service center, ask where the person is located. Don't be surprised if the perfect English is coming from India.

There are three points ("so whats") to take with you from this discussion.

1. Reality is complex; theory abstracts. It is not that our theories are useless. They simply abstract away the detail, clarifying the underlying factors that help us understand how reality works. Theories of market dynamics, the interaction of supply and demand, form a useful foundation.

2. The splintering of labor supplies means that determining pay levels and mix increas-ingly requires understanding market conditions in different locations, even worldwide locations.

3. Managers also need to know the jobs required to do the work, the tasks to be per-formed, and the knowledge and behaviors required to perform them (sound like job analysis?) so that they can bundle the various tasks to send to different locations.[23]

[21]Chris Gentle, "The Cusp of a Revolution: How Offshoring Will Transform the Financial Services Industry," Deloitte Consulting, *www.dc.com/insights/research/financial/offshoring.asp*, June 2003; Nelson D. Schwartz, "Down and Out in White-Collar America," *Fortune,* June 23, 2003, pp. 79–86; Peter Drucker, "They're Not Employees, They're People," *Harvard Business Review,* February 2002, pp. 70–77.

[22]Rafiq Dossani and Martin Kenney, "Went for Cost, Stayed for Quality? Moving the Back Office to India," working paper, Asia/Pacific Research Center, Stanford University, 2003.

[23]Vivek Agrawal, James M. Manyika, and John E. Richards,"Matching People and Jobs," *The McKinsey Quarterly,* no. 2, 2003, pp. 1–7; Steven Greenhouse, "IBM Explores Shift of White-Collar Jobs Overseas," *New York Times,* July 22, 2003.

ORGANIZATION FACTORS

Although product and labor market conditions create a range of possibilities within which managers create a policy on external competitiveness, organizational factors influence pay level and mix decisions, too.[24]

Industry

The industry in which an organization competes influences the technologies used. Labor-intensive industries such as education and health care tend to pay lower than technology-intensive industries such as petroleum or pharmaceuticals, whereas professional services such as consulting firms pay high. In addition to differences in technology across industries affecting compensation, the introduction of new technology *within an industry* influences pay levels. The next time you are waiting in line at the supermarket, instead of catching up on the gossip in the *Enquirer,* think about the pay the checkout person gets. The use of universal product codes, scanners, scales built into the counter, even do-it-yourself checkout has reduced the skills required of checkers. As a result, the average pay level for checkers has declined by over 8 percent since 1984.[25]

Qualifications and experience tailored to particular technologies is important in the analysis of labor markets. Machinists and millwrights who build General Electric diesel locomotives in Erie, Pennsylvania, have very different qualifications from machinists and millwrights who build Boeing airplanes in Seattle.[26]

Employer Size

There is consistent evidence that large organizations tend to pay more than small ones. A study of manufacturing firms found that firms with 100 to 500 workers paid 6 percent higher wages than did smaller firms; firms of more than 500 workers paid 12 percent more than did the smallest firms.[27] This relationship between organization size, ability to pay, and pay level is consistent with economic theory. It says that talented individuals have a higher marginal value in a larger organization because they can influence more people and decisions, thereby leading to more profits. Compare the advertising revenue that David Letterman can bring to CBS versus the potential revenue to station WBNS if his late-night show was only seen in Athens, Ohio. No matter how cool he is in Athens, WBNS could

[24]Erica L. Groshen and David Levine, *The Rise and Decline (?) of Employer Wage Structures* (New York: Federal Reserve Bank, 2000); John Haltowanger, *The Creation and Analysis of Employer-Employee Matched Data* (Amsterdam: North Holland, 1999).

[25]John W. Budd and Brian P. McCall, "The Grocery Stores Wage Distribution: A Semi-Parametric Analysis of the Role of Retailing and Labor Market Institutions," *Industrial and Labor Relations Review* 54(2A)(2001), pp. 484–501.

[26]D. M. Raff, "The Puzzling Profusion of Compensation Systems in the Interwar Automobile Industry," working paper, NBER, 1998. Raff attributes the fantastic diversity of compensation programs for blue-collar employees (firm-based, piece rate, companywide, team-based) to differences in technology employed among competitors.

[27]J. Abowd and I. Kramarz, "Interindustry and Firm Size Wage Differentials: New Evidence," working paper, ILR-Cornell Institute of Labor Market Policies, July 2000; Walter Oi and Todd L. Idson, "Firm Size and Wages," in *Handbook of Labor Economics,* eds., O. Ashenfelter and D. Card (Amsterdam: North Holland, 1999), pp. 2165–2214.

not generate enough revenue to be able to afford to pay Mr. Letterman his multimillion-dollar salary; CBS can. However, theories are less useful in explaining why practically everyone at bigger companies such as CBS, including janitors and compensation managers, is paid more. It seems unlikely that everyone has Letterman's impact on revenues.

People's Preferences

What pay forms (health insurance, eye care, bonuses, pensions) do employees really value? What forms should be changed (or instituted) to improve (or provide) their value to employees? Better understanding of employee preferences is increasingly important in determining external competitiveness. Markets, after all, involve both employers' and employees' choices.[28] However, there are substantial difficulties in reliably measuring preferences. In response to the survey question "What do you value most in your work?" who among us would be so crass as to (publicly) rank money over cordial co-workers or challenging assignments? The Iowa researchers cited in Exhibit 1.7 pointed out that people place more importance on pay than they are willing to admit.[29]

Organization Strategy

A variety of pay-level and mix strategies exist. Some employers adopt a low-wage, no-services strategy; they compete by producing goods and services with the lowest total compensation possible. Nike and Reebok reportedly do this. Others select a low-wage, high-services strategy. Marriott offers its low-wage room cleaners a hotline to social workers who assist with child care and transportation crises. English and citizenship courses are available for recent immigrants. Seminars cover how to manage one's paycheck and one's life. Still other employers use a high-wage, high-services approach. Medtronic's "fully present at work" approach, discussed in Chapter 2, is an example of high wage, high services. Obviously, these are extremes on a continuum of possibilities.

RELEVANT MARKETS

Economists take "the market" for granted—as in "The market determines wages." This strikes compensation managers as bizarrely abstract. Managers at St. Luke's and Apriso realize that defining the relevant markets is a big part of figuring out how much to pay and what mix of pay forms to offer.

[28]H. Heneman and T. Judge, "Pay and Employee Satisfaction," in *Compensation in Organizations: Current Research and Practice,* eds. S. L. Rynes and B. Gerhart, (San Francisco: Jossey-Bass, 2000); T. R. Mitchell and A. E. Mickel, "The Meaning of Money: An Individual Differences Perspective," *Academy of Management Review* 24 (1999), pp. 568–578; *Playing to Win: Strategic Rewards in the War for Talent* (New York: Watson Wyatt, 2001); Gerry Ledford, Paul Mulvey, and Peter LeBlanc, *The Rewards of Work: What Employees Value* (Scottsdale, AZ: World at Work, 2000).

[29]Sara L. Rynes, Amy E. Colbert, and Kenneth G. Brown, "HR Professionals' Beliefs about Effective Human Resource Practices: Correspondence between Research and Practice," *Human Resource Management* 41(2) (Summer 2002), pp. 149–174; Sara L. Rynes, Amy E. Colbert, and Kenneth G. Brown, "Seven Common Misconceptions about Human Resource Practices: Research Findings versus Practitioner Beliefs," *Academy of Management Executive* 16(3) 2002, pp. 92–102.

Although the notion of a single homogeneous labor market may be a useful analytical device, each organization operates in many labor markets, each with unique demand and supply. Some, as in the case of hospitals, face splintered supplies for the same skills in the same market. Others, such as Apriso must think creatively and more broadly about which markets they will select their people from. They seek to answer, What is the right pay to get the right people to do the right things.

Consequently, managers must define the markets that are relevant for pay purposes and establish the appropriate competitive positions in these markets. The three factors usually used to determine the relevant labor markets are the occupation (skill/knowledge required), geography (willingness to relocate, commute, or become virtual employees), and competitors (other employers in the same product/service and labor markets).

Defining the Relevant Market

How do employers choose their relevant markets? Surprisingly little research has been done on this issue. But if the markets are incorrectly defined, the estimates of competitors' pay rates will be incorrect and the pay level and mix inappropriately established.

> **Cybercomp**
>
> These two sites provide an online tutorial for researching companies on the web:
>
> *home.sprintmail.com/~debflanagan/index.html*
>
> *home.sprintmail.com/~debflanagan/business.html*
>
> Select several companies that you believe might be labor market competitors (e.g., Microsoft, Oracle, IBM; or Johnson & Johnson, Merck, Pfizer). Compare their job postings. Do any of the companies list salaries for their jobs? Do they quote a single salary? Do they allow room for haggling?

Two studies do shed some light on this issue.[30] They conclude that managers look at both *competitors*—their products, location, and size—and the *jobs*—the skills and knowledge required and their importance to the organization's success (e.g., lawyers in law firms, software engineers at Microsoft). So depending on its location and size, a company may be deemed a relevant comparison even if it is not a product market competitor.

The data from product market competitors (as opposed to labor market competitors) are likely to receive greater weight when:

1. Employee skills are specific to the product market (recall the differences in Boeing millwrights versus GE Locomotive millwrights).
2. Labor costs are a large share of total costs.

[30]Charlie Trevor and M. E. Graham, "Deriving the Market Wage: Three Decision Areas in the Compensation Survey Process," *WorldatWork Journal* 9(4)(2000), pp. 69–77; Chockalingham Viswesvaran and Murray Barrick, "Decision Making Effects on Compensation Surveys: Implications for Market Wages," *Journal of Applied Psychology* 77(5)(1992), pp. 588–597.

3. Product demand is responsive to price changes. That is, people won't pay $4 for a bottle of Leinenkugel; instead, they'll go to Trader Joe's for a bottle of Charles Shaw wine, a.k.a. "two-buck Chuck."[31]

4. The supply of labor is not responsive to changes in pay (recall the earlier low-wage, low-skill example).

Compensation theories offer some help in understanding the variations in *pay levels* we observe among employers. They are less helpful in understanding differences in the *mix of pay forms.* Relevant markets are shaped by pressures from the labor and product markets and the organization. But so what? How, in fact, do managers set pay-level and pay-mix policy, and what difference does it make? In the remainder of this chapter, we will discuss those two issues.

COMPETITIVE PAY POLICY ALTERNATIVES

Recall that pay level is the average of the array of rates inside an organization. There are three conventional pay-level policies: to lead, to meet, or to follow competition. Newer policies emphasize flexibility: among policies for different employee groups, among pay forms for individual employees, and among elements of the employee relationship that the company wishes to emphasize in its external competitiveness policy.

What Difference Does the Pay-Level Policy Make? The basic premise is that the competitiveness of pay will affect the organization's ability to achieve its compensation objectives, and this in turn will affect the organization's performance.[32] The probable effects of alternative policies are shown in Exhibit 7.8 and discussed in more detail below. The problem with much pay-level research is that it focuses on base pay and ignores bonuses, incentives, options, employment security, benefits, or other forms of pay. Yet the exhibits and discussion in this chapter should have convinced you that base pay represents only a portion of compensation. Comparisons on base alone can

EXHIBIT 7.8 **Probable Relationships between External Pay Policies and Objectives**

Policy	Compensation Objectives				
	Ability to Attract	Ability to Retain	Contain Labor Costs	Reduce Pay Dissatisfaction	Increase Productivity
Pay above market (lead)	+	+	?	+	?
Pay with market (match)	=	=	=	=	?
Pay below market (lag)	−	?	+	−	?
Hybrid policy	?	?	+	?	+
Employer of choice	+	+	+	−	?

[31]*www.traderjoes.com/new/chuckshaw.asp.*

[32]David I. Levine, "Fairness, Markets, and Ability to Pay: Evidence from Compensation Executives," *American Economic Review,* December 1993, pp. 1241–1259.

mislead. In fact, many managers believe they get more bang for the buck by allocating dollars away from base pay and into variable forms that more effectively shape employee behavior.[33]

Pay with Competition (Match)

Given the choice to match, lead, or lag, the most common policy is to match rates paid by competitors.[34] Managers historically justify this policy by saying that failure to match competitors' rates would cause murmuring among present employees and limit the organization's ability to recruit. Many nonunionized companies tend to match or even lead competition to head off unions.[35] A pay-with-competition policy tries to ensure that an organization's wage costs are approximately equal to those of its product competitors and that its ability to attract applicants will be approximately equal to its labor market competitors. While this policy avoids placing an employer at a disadvantage in pricing products, it may not provide an employer with a competitive advantage in its labor markets. Classical economic models predict that employers meet competitive wages.

Lead Policy

A lead policy maximizes the ability to attract and retain quality employees and minimizes employee dissatisfaction with pay. It may also offset less attractive features of the work, à la Adam Smith's "net advantage." Combat pay premiums paid to military personnel offset some of the risk of being fired upon. The higher pay offered by brokerage firms offsets the risk of being fired when the market tanks.

As noted earlier, sometimes an entire industry can pass high pay rates on to consumers if pay is a relatively low proportion of total operating expenses or if the industry is highly regulated. But what about specific firms within a high-pay industry? For example, Merck adheres to a pay leadership position for researchers and salespeople *in its industry*. Do any advantages actually accrue to Merck? If all firms *in the industry* have similar technologies and operating expenses, then the lead policy must provide some competitive advantage to Merck that offsets the higher costs.

A number of researchers have linked high wages to ease of attraction, reduced vacancy rates and training time, and better-quality employees.[36] Research also suggests that high pay levels reduce turnover and absenteeism.[37] Several studies found that the use of

[33]See, for example, any of the surveys conducted by leading consulting firms: Hewitt, *www.hewitt.com;* Wyatt Watson, *www.watsonwyatt.com;* Hay, *www.haygroup.com;* Mercer, *www.mercer.com;* Towers Perrin, *www.towersperrin.com;* Executive Alliance, *www.executivealliance.com.*

[34]Brian S. Klaas and John A. McClendon, "To Lead, Lag, or Match: Estimating the Financial Impact of Pay Level Policies," *Personnel Psychology* 49 (1996), pp. 121–140.

[35]R. B. Freeman and J. Rogers, *What Workers Want* (Ithaca, NY: Cornell University Press, 1999).

[36]M. B. Tannen, "Is the Army College Fund Meeting Its Objectives?" *Industrial and Labor Relations Review* 41 (1987), pp. 50–62; Hyder Lakhani, "Effects of Pay and Retention Bonuses on Quit Rates in the U.S. Army," *Industrial and Labor Relations Review* 41 (1988), pp. 430–438.

[37]Robert Bretz, J. W. Boudreau, W. R. Boswell, and T. A. Judge, "Personality and Cognitive Ability as Predictors of Job Search among Employed Managers," *Personnel Psychology* 54, (2001), pp. 25–50; Charlie Trevor, Barry Gerhart, and John Boudreau, "Voluntary Turnover and Job Performance: Curvilinearity and the Moderating Influences of Salary Growth and Promotions," *Journal of Applied Psychology* 82 (1997), pp. 44–61.

variable pay (bonuses and long-term incentives) is related to an organization's improved financial performance but that pay level is not.[38]

A lead policy can also have negative effects. It may force the employer to increase wages of current employees, too, to avoid internal misalignment and murmuring. Additionally, a lead policy may mask negative job attributes that contribute to high turnover later on (e.g., lack of challenging assignments or presence of hostile colleagues). Remember the managers' view that high turnover was likely to be a managerial problem rather than a compensation problem.[39]

Lag Policy

A policy of paying below market rates may hinder a firm's ability to attract potential employees. But if a lagged pay level is coupled with the promise of higher future returns (e.g., stock ownership in a high-tech start-up firm), this combination may increase employee commitment and foster teamwork, which may increase productivity. But how long this promise works, in the face of flat or declining stock markets, is unknown. Unmet expectations probably have negative effects. Additionally, it is possible to lag competition on pay level but to lead on other returns from work (e.g., hot assignments, desirable location, outstanding colleagues, cool tools, work/life balance).

Flexible Policies

In practice, many employers go beyond a single choice among the three policy options. They may vary the policy for different occupational families, as did the company in Exhibit 7.1. They may vary the policy for different forms of pay, as did the companies back in Exhibit 7.2. They may also adopt different policies for different business units that face very different competitive conditions. Praxair offers a bonus of up to 40 days' pay if operating profits exceed certain targets. However, Praxair repositioned its base pay to 5 percent below its previous "match" policy. In effect, Praxair lags the market but pays a bonus in good years that yields a slight lead position. Praxair's hybrid policy is intended to focus attention on the firm's financial performance and motivate productivity improvements. It also signals that Praxair wants people who are willing to perform and able to tolerate some risk. In the meantime, the 5 percent lag helps control labor costs.

Limited attention has been devoted to pay-mix policies. Some obvious alternatives include *performance driven, market match, work/life balance,* and *security.* Exhibit 7.9 illustrates these four alternatives. Compared to the other three, incentives and stock options

---

[38]B. Gerhart and G. Milkovich, "Organizational Differences in Managerial Compensation and Financial Performance," *Academy of Management Journal* 33 (1990), pp. 663–691; M. Bloom and J. Michel, "The Relationships among Organization Context, Pay, and Managerial Theories," working paper, University of Notre Dame, Department of Management, 2000; M. Bloom and G. Milkovich, "Relationships among Risk, Incentive Pay, and Organization Performance," *Academy of Management Journal* 41(3) (1998), pp. 283–297; B. Hall and J. Liebman, "Are CEOs Really Paid Like Bureaucrats?" *Quarterly Journal of Economics,* August 1998, pp. 653–691. Variable pay is discussed in Chapters 9 through 11. "Variable" indicates that the pay increase (bonus) is not added to base pay; hence, it is not part of fixed costs but is variable, since the amount may vary next year.

[39]David I. Levine, "Fairness, Markets, and Ability to Pay: Evidence from Compensation Executives," *American Economic Review,* December 1993, pp. 1241–1259.

EXHIBIT 7.9 **Pay-Mix Policy Alternatives**

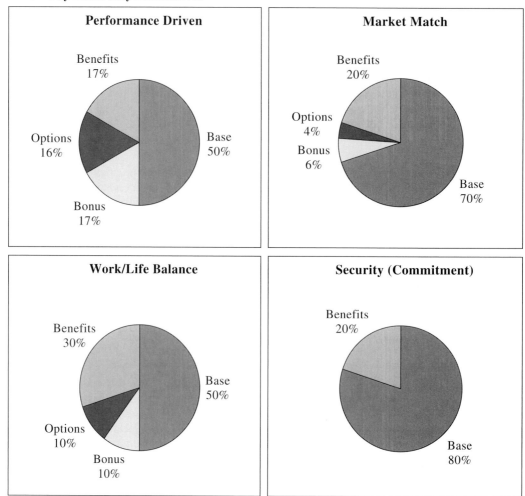

make up a greater percent of total compensation in *performance-driven* policies. The *market match* simply mimics the pay mix competitors are paying. How managers actually make these mix decisions is a ripe issue for more research.

How managers position their organization's pay against competitors is changing. Some alternatives that are emerging focus on total returns from work (beyond financial returns) and offering people choices among these returns. Rather than "flexible", perhaps a better term would be "fuzzy" policies.

Employer of Choice/Shared Choice

Some companies compete based on their overall reputation as a place to work, beyond pay level and mix. For example, IBM compares within the information technology marketplace and positions its pay "among the best" in this group. Further, it claims to "strongly differentiate based on business and individual results." It leads the market with its strong emphasis on performance. IBM also offers extensive training opportunities, challenging work assignments, and the like. In a sense, "employer of choice" corresponds to the brand or image the company projects as an employer.

Shared choice begins with the traditional alternatives of lead, meet, or lag. But it then adds a second part, which is to *offer employees choices* (within limits) in the pay mix. This "employee-as-customer" perspective is not all that revolutionary, at least in the United States. Many employers offer choices on health insurance (individual versus dependent coverage), retirement investments (growth or value), and so on.[40] (See flexible benefits in Chapter 13.) More advanced software is making the employee-as-customer approach more feasible. Mass customization—being able to select among a variety of features—is routine when purchasing a new laptop or auto. It is now possible with total compensation, too. Does offering people choices matter? One risk is that employees will make "wrong" choices that will jeopardize their financial well-being (e.g., inadequate health insurance). Another is the "24 jars of jam" dilemma. Supermarket studies report that offering consumers a taste of just a few different jams increases sales. But offering a taste of 24 different jams decreases sales. Consumers feel overwhelmed by too many choices and simply walk away. Perhaps offering employees too many choices of different kinds of pay will lead to confusion, mistakes, and dissatisfaction.[41]

Pitfalls of Pies

The pie charts in Exhibit 7.9 contrast various pay mix policies. However, thinking about the mix of pay forms as pieces in a pie chart has limitations. These are particularly clear when the value of options is volatile. The pie charts in Exhibit 7.10 show a well-known software company's mix before and after a major stock market decline (stock prices plummeted 50 percent within a month). Note the effects on the composition of the pay forms. Base pay went from 47 to 55 percent of total compensation, whereas the value of stock options fell from 28 to 16 percent. (The reverse has happened in this company, too.) But wait, it can get worse. One technology company was forced to disclose that three-quarters of all its stock options were "under water," that is, exercisable at prices higher than the market price. Due to stock market volatility, the options had become worthless to employees. So what is the message to employees? To competitors? Has the compensation strategy changed? The company's intended strategy has not changed, but in reality the mix has changed. So the possible volatility in the value of different pay forms needs to be anticipated.

Some companies prefer to report the mix of pay forms using a "dashboard," as depicted in Exhibit 7.11. The dashboard changes the focus from emphasizing the relative importance

[40]L. Gaughan and J. Kasparek, "Employees as Customers: Using Market Research to Manage Compensation and Benefits," *Workspan* (9) (2000), pp. 31–38; M. Sturman, G. Milkovich, and J. Hannon, "Expert Systems' Effect on Employee Decisions and Satisfaction," *Personnel Psychology* (1997), pp. 21–34; J. Shaw and S. Schaubrock, "The Role of Spending Behavior Patterns in Monetary Rewards," working paper, University of Kentucky, 2001.

[41]Stephen J. Dubner, "Calculating the Irrational in Economics," *New York Times,* June 28, 2003.

EXHIBIT 7.10
Volatility of Stock Value Changes Total Pay Mix

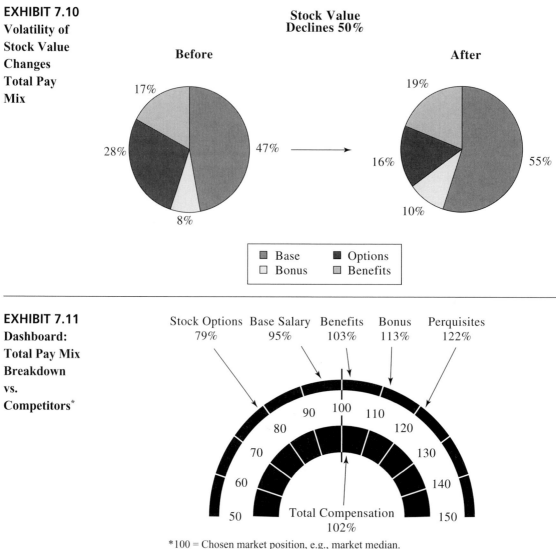

Stock Value Declines 50%

Before

17%
28%
47%
8%

After

19%
16%
10%
55%

■ Base   ■ Options
□ Bonus   ▨ Benefits

EXHIBIT 7.11
Dashboard: Total Pay Mix Breakdown vs. Competitors*

Stock Options   Base Salary   Benefits   Bonus   Perquisites
79%   95%   103%   113%   122%

90   100   110
80   120
70   130
60   140
50   150

Total Compensation
102%

*100 = Chosen market position, e.g., market median.

of each form within a single company to comparing each form by itself to the market (many companies). In the example, the value of stock options is 79 percent of competitors' median, base pay is at 95 percent of competitors' median, and overall total compensation is 102 percent of (or 2 percent above) the market median. Pies, dashboards—different focus, both recognizing the importance of the mix of pay forms.

Another limitation is that it can be misleading to focus solely on the mix for the entire organization. Like pay levels, the mix employees receive differs at different levels in the internal job structure. Exhibit 7.12 shows the different mix of base, cash incentives, and stock options Merrill Lynch pays at different organization levels. Executive leadership positions receive less than 10 percent in base, about 20 percent in stock, and the rest in annual incentives. This compares to 50 percent in base, 40 percent in annual incentives, and 10 percent in stock for midlevel manager/professional positions, and 80 percent base,

EXHIBIT 7.12
Pay Mix
Varies within
the Structure

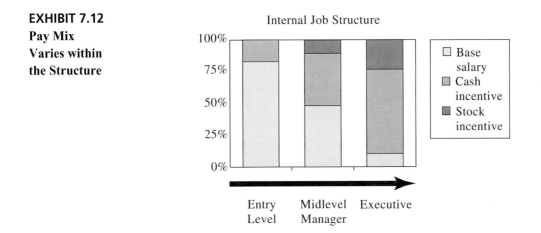

Internal Job Structure

20 percent incentives, and no stock for entry- and lower-level jobs. While the percentages vary among organizations, greater emphasis on performance (through incentives and stock) at higher levels is common practice. This is based on the belief that jobs at higher levels in the organization have greater opportunity to influence organization performance.

CONSEQUENCES OF PAY-LEVEL AND MIX DECISIONS

Earlier we noted that external competitiveness has two major consequences: It affects (1) operating expenses and (2) employee attitudes and work behaviors. Exhibit 7.13 summarizes these consequences, which have been discussed throughout this chapter. The competitiveness policy directly affects the compensation objectives of efficiency, fairness, and compliance.

Efficiency

Compensation represents an expense, so any decisions that affect its level and mix are important. A variety of theories make assumptions about the effects of relative pay levels on an organization's effectiveness. Some recommend lead policies to diminish shirking and permit hiring better-qualified applicants. Others—such as marginal productivity theory—recommend matching. A utility model even supports a lag policy.[42] Virtually no research suggests under what circumstances managers should choose which pay-mix alternative.

Which Policy Achieves Competitive Advantage?

Research on the effect of pay-level policies is difficult because companies' stated policies often do not correspond to reality. For example, HR managers at 124 companies were asked to define their firm's target pay level. All 124 of them reported that their companies paid above the median![43]

[42]Brian Klaas and John A. McClendon, "To Lead, Lag, or Match: Estimating the Financial Impact of Pay Level Policies," *Personnel Psychology* 49 (1996), pp. 121–140.

[43]Barry Gerhart and George Milkovich, "Employee Compensation: Research and Practice," in *Handbook of Industrial and Organizational Psychology,* 2d ed., eds. M. D. Dunnette and L. M. Hough (Palo Alto, CA: Consulting Psychologists Press, 1992).

EXHIBIT 7.13

Some Consequences of Pay Levels

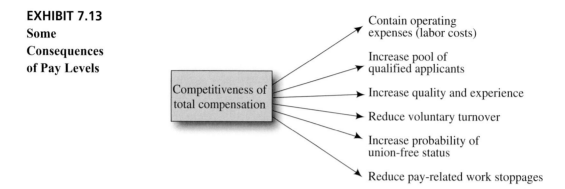

Beyond opinions, there is little evidence of the consequences of different policy alternatives. We do know that pay level affects costs; we do not know whether any effects it might have on productivity or attracting and retaining employees are sufficient to offset costs. Nor is it known how much of a pay-level variation makes a difference to employees; will 5 percent, 10 percent, or 15 percent be a noticeable difference? Although lagging competitive pay could have a noticeable reduction in short-term labor costs, it is not known whether this savings is accompanied by a reduction in the quality and performance of the work force. It may be that an employer's pay level will not gain any competitive *advantage;* however, the wrong pay level may put the organization at a serious *disadvantage.* Similarly, we simply do not know the effects of the different pay-mix alternatives or the financial results of shifting the responsibility for choosing the mix to employees. Perhaps it is the message communicated by pay mix and levels that is the key to achieving competitive advantage. That is our belief, anyway.

So where does this leave the manager? In the absence of convincing evidence, the least-risk approach may be to set both pay level and pay mix to match competition. An organization may adopt a lead policy for skills that are critical to its success, a match policy for less critical skills, and a lag policy for jobs that are easily filled in the local labor market. An obvious concern with flexible policies is to achieve some degree of business alignment and fair treatment for employees among the choices.

Fairness

Satisfaction with pay is directly related to the pay level: More is better.[44] But employees' sense of fairness is also related to how others are paid. A friend at Stanford claims that if all but one of the faculty in their business school got $1,000,000 and one person received $1,000,001, the others would all be lined up at the dean's office demanding an explanation.

Compliance

It's not enough to say that an employer must pay at or above the legal minimum wage. Provisions of prevailing wage laws and equal rights legislation must also be met. In fact, we will return to the subject of market wages again when we discuss pay discrimination

[44]H. Heneman and T. Judge, "Pay and Employee Satisfaction," in *Compensation in Organizations: Current Research and Practice,* eds. S. L. Rynes & B. Gerhart, (San Francisco: Jossey-Bass, 2000).

and the emerging concept of "living wage." In addition to pay level, various pay forms are also regulated. Pensions and health care are considered part of every citizen's economic security and are regulated to some degree in most countries. This is discussed again when we look at international practices and benefits.

No matter the competitive pay policy, it needs to be translated into practice. The starting point is measuring the market through use of a salary survey. For this, we turn to the next chapter.

Your Turn — Sled Dog Software

Software engineers directly affect the success of many start-up companies. Suppose you are facing a clean slate: A group of investors is about to invest in a new start-up, a specialty software company based in Laramie, Wyoming. These investors have hired you to help them determine the marketing manager's pay. What would you advise? Consider the information in Exhibits 7.1, 7.2 and 7.12 in making your recommendation.

1. What policy regarding external competitiveness would you advise? List the options and the pros and cons of each policy option. Offer the rationale for your recommendation.
2. What forms of pay and in what percentages would you recommend? Again, offer your rationales.
3. Consider the theories and research presented in this chapter. Which ones did you use to support your recommendation?
4. List three pieces of additional information you would like to have to refine your recommendation. Explain how this information would help you.

Your Turn — Managing a Low-Wage, Low-Skill Work Force

Take another look at the section about practices of the low-wage, low-skill employers like Marriott or McDonald's. Then look again at the alternative mix of pay forms policies.

1. Which pay-mix policy would you recommend these employers adopt?
2. What results do you anticipate? Don't forget efficiency, including costs, fairness, and compliance.
3. How, if at all, do the theories discussed help you understand what the anticipated results will be?

Summary   One reviewer of this book told us that "there are three important contributions of this chapter: (1) that there is no 'going rate' and so managers make conscious pay level and mix decisions influenced by several factors; (2) that there are both product market and labor market competitors that impact the pay level and mix decisions; and (3) that alternative pay level and mix decisions have different consequences." That is a great summary of the key points.

The pay model used throughout this book emphasizes strategic policy issues: objectives, alignment, competitiveness, contributions, and management. Policies need to be designed to achieve specific pay objectives. This part of the book is concerned with external competitiveness, or pay comparisons among organizations. Does Apple Computer pay its accountants the same wage that Florida Power pays its accountants? Probably not. Different companies pay different rates; the average of the overall array of rates in an organization constitutes the pay level. Different companies also use different forms of pay. To achieve the objectives stipulated for the pay system, both the pay level and the pay mix must be properly positioned relative to competitors. Each integrated job structure or career path within the organization may have its own competitive position in the market. The next chapter considers the decisions involved and the variety of techniques available to implement those decisions.

Before we proceed, let us reemphasize that the major reason we are interested in the external competitiveness policy—pay level and mix of pay forms—is that it has profound consequences on the organization's objectives. Theories and practical experience support this belief. But as we have also noted, more research is needed to guide us in making decisions. We have clearly established that differences among organizations' competitive policies and their pay levels and forms exist. We have examined the factors that determine these differences. What remains to be better understood is the potential effects of various policies.

Review Questions

1. Distinguish policies on external competitiveness from policies on internal alignment. Why is external competitiveness so important?
2. What factors shape an organization's external competitiveness?
3. What does marginal revenue product have to do with pay?
4. What pay level does the efficiency wage predict? Does the theory accurately predict organization behavior? Why or why not?
5. What is a relevant market? What difference does it make when determining people's pay?
6. Can you think of any companies that follow a lag and/or lead policy? Why do they believe it pays to pay differently? Can you think of any companies that follow performance-driven and/or work/life balance policies?

Designing Pay Levels, Mix, and Pay Structures

Chapter Outline

Average pay of benchmark jobs set to average pay of similar jobs in comparable companies.—3M

Pay among the leaders. Base pay will be fully comparable (50th percentile of competitors). Total compensation, including benefits and performance incentives, will bring our compensation to the 75th percentile of competitors.—Colgate

Our competitive strategy will deliver rewards at the market competitive median for median performance, at the 75th percentile for 75th percentile performance, and so on. We emphasize work-life balance; our benefits insure that every person is fully present and focused when they are at work.—Medtronic[1]

These are statements of different organizations' external competitiveness policies—comparisons of the compensation offered by an employer relative to its competitors. In the last chapter, we discussed the market and organization factors that influence these policies. Now we examine how managers use these factors to design pay levels, mix of forms, and structures.

MAJOR DECISIONS

The major decisions in setting externally competitive pay and designing the corresponding pay structures are shown in Exhibit 8.1. They include (1) specify the employer's competitive pay policy, (2) define the purpose of the survey, (3) select relevant market competitors, (4) design the survey, (5) interpret survey results and construct the market line, (6) construct a pay policy line that reflects external pay policy, and (7) balance competitiveness with internal alignment through the use of ranges, flat rates, and/or bands. This is a lengthy list. Think of Exhibit 8.1 as a road map through this chapter. The guideposts are the major decisions you face in designing a pay structure. Don't forget to end with, So what? "So what" means understanding how pay structures support business success and ensure fair treatment for employees.

SPECIFY COMPETITIVE PAY POLICY

The first decision, specifying the external competitive pay policy, was covered in the previous chapter. Translating any external pay policy into practice requires information on the external market. Surveys provide the data for translating that policy into pay levels, pay mix, and structures.

> A **survey** is the systematic process of collecting and making judgments about the compensation paid by other employers.

THE PURPOSE OF A SURVEY

An employer conducts or participates in a survey for a number of reasons: (1) to adjust the pay level in response to changing rates paid by competitors, (2) to set the mix of pay forms relative to that paid by competitors, (3) to establish or price its pay structure, (4) to analyze pay-related problems, or (5) to estimate the labor costs of product/service market competitors.

---

[1]Adapted from each company's compensation strategy statements.

EXHIBIT 8.1 **Determining Externally Competitive Pay Levels and Structures**

| External competitiveness: Pay relationships among organizations | → | Specify policy | → | Select market | → | Design survey | → | Draw policy lines | → | Merge internal & external pressures | → | Competitive pay levels, mix, and structures |

Some Major Decisions in Pay-Level Determination
- Specify pay-level policy.
- Define purpose of survey.
- Specify relevant market.
- Design and conduct survey.
- Interpret and apply result.
- Design grades and ranges or bands.

Adjust Pay Level—How Much to Pay?

Most organizations make adjustments to employees' pay on a regular basis. Such adjustments can be based on the overall movement of pay rates caused by the competition for people in the market. Adjustments may also be based on performance, ability to pay, or terms specified in a contract.

Adjust Pay Mix—What Forms?

Adjustments to the different forms of pay competitors use (base, bonus, stock, benefits) and the relative importance they place on each form occur less frequently than adjustments to overall pay level. It is not clear (without good research) why changes to the pay mix occur less frequently than changes in the pay level. Perhaps organizations wish to signal to the market that what is valued is fairly stable. Perhaps the high costs of redesigning a different mix create a barrier. Perhaps it is due to bureaucratic inertia. More likely, insufficient attention has been devoted to mix decisions. That is, the mix organizations use may have been based on external pressures such as health care costs, stock values, government regulations, union demands, and what others did. Yet some pay forms may affect employee behavior more than others. So collecting accurate information on total compensation, the mix of pay competitors use, and costs of various forms is increasingly important.

Adjust Pay Structure?

Many employers use market surveys to validate their own job evaluation results. For example, job evaluation may place purchasing assistant jobs at the same level in the job structure as some secretarial jobs. But if the market shows vastly different pay rates for the two types of work, most employers will recheck their evaluation process to see whether the jobs have been properly evaluated. Some may even establish a separate structure for different types of work. IBM sets pay according to market conditions for each separate occupation (finance, engineering, law). Thus, the job structure that results from internal job evaluation may not match competitors' pay structures in the external market. Reconciling these two pay structures is a major issue.

Rather than integrating an internal and external structure, some employers go straight to market surveys to establish their internal structures. Such "market pricing" mimics competitors' pay structures. More on this later in the chapter. As organizations move to more generic work descriptions (associate, leader) that focus on the person more than the job, the need for accurate market data increases. Former relationships between job evaluation points and dollars may no longer hold. Informed judgment and accurate information are vital for making all these decisions.

Study Special Situations

Information from specialized surveys sheds light on specific pay-related problems. Many special studies focus on targeted groups, such as patent attorneys, retail sales managers, secretaries, or software engineers. Unusual increases in an employer's turnover in specific jobs may require focused market surveys to find out if market changes are occurring.[2]

Estimate Competitors' Labor Costs

Employers continuously search for ways to squeeze out more costs and become more productive. They may use salary survey data to benchmark against competitors' product pricing and manufacturing practices. Industrywide labor cost estimates are reported in the Employment Cost Index (ECI), one of four types of salary surveys published regularly by the Department of Labor on its website at *www.bls.gov/ncs/*.[3] The ECI measures quarterly changes in employer costs for compensation. The index allows a firm to compare changes in its average costs to an all-industry or specific-industry average. However, this comparison may have limited value because industry averages may not reflect relevant competitors.[4]

SELECT RELEVANT MARKET COMPETITORS

We are up to the third of our major decisions shown in Exhibit 8.1: Specify relevant markets. To make decisions about pay level, mix, and structures, a relevant labor market must be defined that includes employers who compete in one or more of the following areas:

1. The same occupations or skills
2. Employees within the same geographic area
3. The same products and services.[5]

---

[2]Consulting firms' websites list their specialized surveys. See, for example, Clark Consulting's Total Compensation Survey of the computer and semiconductor industries, *www.clarkconsulting.com;* Towers Perrin, *www.towers.com/towers/services_products/TowersPerrin/online.htm;* Hay *www.haypaynet.com;* Radford's "Total Compensation Survey and Overall Practices Report," *www.radford.com/rbss/index.html;* Hewitt, *www.hewitt.com;* Wyatt Watson *www.watsonwyatt.com;* and Mercer, *www.mercer.com.*

[3]Office of Personnel Management, "A Fresh Start for Federal Pay: A Case for Modernization," April 2002.

[4]A NASA website contains a link to an "employment cost index" inflation calculator for adjusting costs from one year to another: *www.jsc.nasa.gov/bu2/inflation/eci/inflateECI.html.* The information is based on data from the U.S. Department of Labor's Bureau of Labor Statistics. (Another NASA link lets you model costs for expendable launch vehicles and spacecraft, but that's probably a different textbook.)

[5]Charlie Trevor and Mary E. Graham, "Deriving the Market Wage Derivatives: Three Decision Areas in the Compensation Survey Process," *WorldatWork Journal* 9(4) (2000), pp. 69–77; Brian Klaas and John A. McClendon, "To Lead, Lag, or Match: Estimating the Financial Impact of Pay Level Policies," *Personnel Psychology* 49 (1996), pp. 121–140.

Exhibit 8.2 shows how qualifications interact with geography to define the scope of relevant labor markets. As the importance and the complexity of the qualifications increase, the geographic limits also increase. Competition tends to be national or international for managerial and professional skills but local or regional for clerical and production skills.

However, these generalizations do not always hold true. In areas with high concentrations of scientists, engineers, and managers (e.g., Boston, Austin, or Palo Alto), the primary market comparison may be regional, with national data used only secondarily. As Exhibit 8.3 shows, pay differentials vary among localities. A job that averages $80,000 nationally can range from $85,520 in Boston to $76,960 in Cleveland. However, some larger firms ignore local market conditions.[6] Rather, they emphasize internal alignment across geographic areas to facilitate the use of virtual teams. But it turns out that team members in different locations compare their pay. What a surprise.

Some writers argue that if the skills are tied to a particular industry, as underwriters, actuaries, and claims representatives are to insurance, it makes sense to define the market on an industry basis, and some research agrees.[7] If accounting, sales, or clerical skills are not limited to one particular industry, then industry considerations are less important. From the perspective of cost control and ability to pay, including competitors in the product/service market is crucial.[8] The pay rates of product/service competitors will affect both costs of operations and financial condition (e.g., ability to pay). However, this becomes a problem when the major competitors are based in countries with far lower pay rates, such as China or Mexico. As our discussion of splintered labor supplies showed, multiple country comparisons have also become important.[9] This creates additional complexities because legal regulations and tax policies, as well as customs, vary among countries. For example, because of tax laws, managers in Korea and Spain receive company credit cards to use for personal expenses (groceries, clothing). In the United States, these purchases count as taxable income, but they do not in Korea and Spain.

While the quantity of data available for international comparisons is improving, using the data to adjust pay still requires a lot of judgment. Labor markets are just emerging in some regions (China, Russia). Historically, state agencies set nationwide wage rates, so there was no need for surveys.[10] Japanese companies share information among themselves but not with outsiders, so no surveys were available.[11]

[6]Andrew Klein, David G. Blanchflower, and Lisa M. Ruggiero, "Pay Differentials Hit Employees Where They Live," *Workspan,* June 2002, pp. 36–40.

[7]Charlie Trevor and Mary E. Graham, "Deriving the Market Wage Derivatives: Three Decision Areas in the Compensation Survey Process," *WorldatWork Journal* 9(4) (2000), pp. 69–77.

[8]Barry Gerhart and George Milkovich, "Employee Compensation," in *Handbook of Industrial and Organizational Psychology,* 2d ed., eds. M. D. Dunnette and L. M. Hough (Palo Alto, CA: Consulting Psychologists Press, 1992).

[9]Beyond the US consultants, international organizations also do surveys. See Income Data Services' website (*www.incomesdata.co.uk*) and publication "Employment Europe Pay Objectives 2000"; or Link Group Consultants, Ltd., Chester, UK (*www.linkg.co.uk*). Also see William M. Mercer's "International Compensation Guidelines 2000" (information on 61 nations); Towers Perrin's "Global Surveys," and Organization Resource Counselors online survey for positions in countries ranging from Azerbaijan to Yugoslavia (*www.orcinc.com*). The Mercer and Towers Perrin website addresses are provided in footnote 2.

[10]M. Bloom, G. Milkovich, and A. Mitra, "International Compensation: Learning from How Managers Respond to Variations in Local-Host Conditions," *International Journal of Human Resource Management* (in press).

[11]Yoshio Yanadori and George Milkovich, "Minimizing Wage Competition? Entry-Level Compensation in Japanese Firms," working paper, Center for Advanced HR Studies, Ithaca, NY, 2003.

EXHIBIT 8.2   Relevant Labor Markets by Geographic and Employee Groups

Geographic Scope	Production	Office and Clerical	Technicians	Scientists and Engineers	Managerial Professional	Executive
Local: Within relatively small areas such as cities or Metropolitan Statistical Areas (e.g., Dallas metropolitan area)	Most likely	Most likely	Most likely			
Regional: Within a particular area of the state or several states (e.g., oil-producing region of southwestern United States)	Only if in short supply or critical	Only if in short supply or critical	Most likely	Likely	Most Likely	
National: Across the country				Most likely	Most likely	Most likely
International: Across several countries				Only for critical skills or those in very short supply	Only for critical skills or those in very short supply	Sometimes

EXHIBIT 8.3
Pay
Differences
by Location

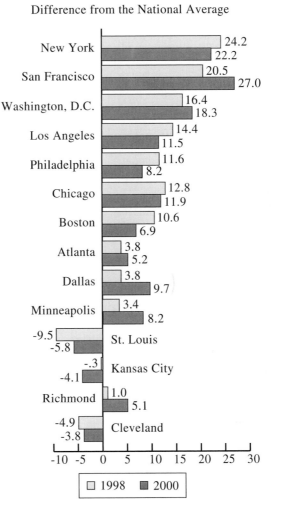

Difference from the National Average

Legend: □ 1998   ■ 2000

Location	1998	2000
New York	24.2	22.2
San Francisco	20.5	27.0
Washington, D.C.	16.4	18.3
Los Angeles	14.4	11.5
Philadelphia	11.6	8.2
Chicago	12.8	11.9
Boston	10.6	6.9
Atlanta	3.8	5.2
Dallas	3.8	9.7
Minneapolis	3.4	8.2
St. Louis	-9.5	-5.8
Kansas City	-.3	-4.1
Richmond	1.0	5.1
Cleveland	-4.9	-3.8

Cybercomp 1
For a demonstration of online surveys, go to *www.haypaynet.com* or *www.salary.com* or *www.radford.com/general.welcome.html*. How do the sites compare? Do they give information on which employers are included and which ones are not? Where do their data come from? Do the sites tell you?

But even if an employer possesses good international survey data, careful judgment is still required. For example, while salaries at international companies in developing economies are low by U.S., western European, and Japanese standards, they are often very high compared to salaries at domestic companies in those countries. Pay practices of foreign companies can disrupt emerging local markets in developing economies.[12] Software engineers working for IBM in India told us that while they are paid very well by Indian standards, they feel underpaid compared to IBM engineers in the United States with whom they work on virtual-project teams.[13]

Fuzzy Markets

Walk through a bay of cubicles (plastered with *Dilbert* cartoons) at Yahoo and you are likely to find former kindergarten teachers, software engineers, and former sales representatives all collaborating on a single team. Yahoo combines technology, media, and commerce into one company. What is the relevant labor market? Which firms should be included in Yahoo's surveys?

Even within traditional companies, unique talent is required for unique jobs. West Publishing, the leading provider of legal information to law firms, recently designed the position of Senior Director of Future Vision Services. The holder of this mouthful title is responsible for ensuring that West's customers (litigious lawyers) increase their purchases over the web plus increase their satisfaction with West's services. The job was filled by a software engineer with e-commerce, marketing, and theater experience. Try finding that job in the market. These new organizations and jobs fuse together diverse knowledge and experience, so "relevant" markets appear more like "fuzzy" markets.[14] Organizations with unique jobs and structures face the double bind of finding it hard to get comparable market data at the same time they are placing more emphasis on external market data.

DESIGN THE SURVEY

Consulting firms offer a wide choice of ongoing surveys covering almost every job family and industry group imaginable. Their surveys are getting better and better.[15] While we would like to attribute this to the fact that our textbook has improved the sophistication of compensation education (the first edition of our book was published in 1985, and at least some of those early readers ought to be in power positions by now), it is more likely that the improvement is the result of technological advances. Increasingly, consultants offer clients the option of electronically accessing the consultants' survey databases. Clients then do whatever special analysis they need. General Electric conducts most of its market analysis in this manner. Hay PayNet permits organizations to tie into Hay's vast survey data 24/7.[16]

---

[12]Daniel Vaughn-Whitehead, *Paying the Price: The Wage Crisis in Central and Eastern Europe* (Handmill Hampshire, UK: McMillin Press Ltd., 1998); Sheila M. Puffer and Stanislav V. Shekshnia, "Compensating Local Employees in Post-Communist Russia: In Search of Talent or Just Looking for a Bargain?" *Compensation and Benefits Review,* September–October 1994, pp. 35–43.

[13]M. Bloom, G. Milkovich, and A. Mitra, "International Compensation: Learning from How Managers Respond to Variations in Local-Host Conditions," *International Journal of Human Resource Management* (in press).

[14]Michael Wanderer, "Dot-Comp: A `Traditional' Pay Plan with a Cutting Edge," *WorldatWork Journal,* Fourth Quarter 2000, pp. 15–24.

[15]For consultancies' websites, see the Appendix at the end of this book as well as footnotes 2 and 9 in this chapter. Also see WorldatWork's *2003–04 Survey Handbook and Directory* (Scottsdale, AZ: WorldatWork, 2002).

[16]Hay PayNet is at *www.haypaynet.com.*

Designing a survey requires answering the following questions: (1) Who should be involved in the survey design? (2) How many employers should be included? (3) Which jobs should be included? and (4) What information should be collected?

Who Should Be Involved?

In most organizations, the responsibility for managing the survey lies with the compensation manager. But since compensation expenses have a powerful effect on profitability, including managers and employees on task forces makes sense.

Outside consulting firms are typically used as third-party protection from possible "price-fixing" lawsuits. Suits have been filed alleging that the exchange of survey data violates Section 1 of the Sherman Act, which outlaws conspiracies in restraint of trade. Survey participants may be guilty of price fixing if the overall effect of the information exchange is to *interfere with competitive prices* and *artificially hold down wages.* Identifying participants' data by company name is considered price fixing.[17] In response to a lawsuit, the Boston Survey Group agreed to publish only aggregated (rather than individual employee) information and not categorize information by industry.

Eight hospitals in Utah made the mistake of exchanging information on their *intentions* to increase starting pay offers.[18] They were charged with keeping entry-level wages for registered nurses in the Salt Lake City area artificially low. As part of the legal settlement, no health care facility in Utah can design, develop, or conduct a wage survey. They can respond in writing (only) to a written request for information for wage survey purposes from a third party, but only after the third party provides written assurance that the survey will be conducted with particular safeguards.

Such "arms-length guidelines" may buy legal protection, but they also give up control over the decisions that determine the quality and usefulness of the data. Prohibiting exchange of industry data eliminates the ability to make industry or product market comparisons. This might not be important in nursing or clerical jobs, but industry groups are important when making comparisons of wages for other skills/competencies and jobs.[19]

How Many Employers?

There are no firm rules on how many employers to include in a survey.[20] Large firms with a lead policy may exchange data with only a few (6 to 10) top-paying competitors. Recall IBM's policy to pay "the best of the best IT companies." A small organization in an area dominated by two or three employers may decide to survey only smaller competitors. National surveys conducted by consulting firms often include more than 100 employers. Clients of these consultants often stipulate special analyses that report pay rates by selected industry groups, geographic region, and/or pay levels (e.g., top 10 percent).

[17]Michael B. Shea, "Antitrust Implications in the Salary Survey Process," in *2003–04 Survey Handbook and Directory* (Scottsdale, AZ: WorldatWork; 2002).

[18]*District of Utah U.S. District Court v. Utah Society for Healthcare Human Resources Administration, et al.,* 59 Fed. Reg. 14,203 (March 25, 1994).

[19]Brian Klaas and John A. McClendon, "To Lead, Lag, or Match: Estimating the Financial Impact of Pay Level Policies," *Personnel Psychology* 49 (1996), p. 121.

[20]Chockalingam Viswesvaran and Murray Barrick, "Decision-Making Effects on Compensation Surveys: Implications for Market Wages," *Journal of Applied Psychology* 77(5) (1992), pp. 588–597.

Publicly Available Data

In the United States, the Bureau of Labor Statistics (BLS) is the major source of publicly available compensation (cash, bonus, and benefits but not stock ownership) data. The BLS publishes extensive information on various occupations (very broadly defined—e.g., professional, executive, sales, and administrative support are the categories for white-collar occupations) in different geographic areas. According to the BLS, a person in administrative support in the Los Angeles area averages $14.29 an hour in the private sector and $15.56 in government. In Bloomington, Indiana, the comparable rates are $11.49 and $12.05.

Public sector employers use BLS data more often than do private sector employers. While some private firms may track the rate of change in BLS data as a cross-check on other surveys, the data are not specific enough to be used alone. Their job descriptions are very generic and so may cover too wide a range of tasks for direct comparisons.

"Word of Mouse"

Once upon a time (about 10 years ago) individual employees had a hard time comparing their salaries to others. Confidentiality was the policy of the land. Information was gathered haphazardly, via word of mouth. Today, a click of the mouse makes a wealth of data available to everyone. Employees are comparing their compensation to data from the BLS or Salary.com.[21] This ease of access means that managers must be able to explain (defend?) the salaries paid to employees compared to those a mouse click away. Unfortunately, the quality of much salary data on the web is highly suspect. Few of the sites (except the BLS, of course) offer any information on how the data were collected, what pay forms are included, and so on. Some popular websites even misuse the cost-of-living index when making geographic salary comparisons.[22] On the other hand, *www.salary.com* includes seven pages of a compensation glossary, identifies where the site's information comes from, and explains what the statistics mean. Exhibit 8.4 shows the level of detail salary.com provides.

Where Are the Standards?

Opinions about the value of consultant surveys are rampant; research is not. Do Hay, Mercer, Towers Perrin, Radford, or Clark Consulting surveys yield significantly different results? Many firms select one survey as their primary source and use others to cross-check or "validate" the results. Some employers routinely combine the results of several surveys and weight each survey in this composite according to somebody's judgment of the quality of the data reported.[23] No systematic study of the effects of differences in market definition, participating firms, types of data collected, quality of data, analysis

---

[21]"The Value of Pay Data on the Web," *Workspan,* September 2000, pp. 25–28.

[22]Some websites treat the federal government's Consumer Price Index as a measure of the cost of living in an area. It is not. The Consumer Price Index measures the rate of *change* in the cost of living in an area. So it can be used to compare how quickly prices are rising in one area versus another, but it cannot be used to compare living costs between two different areas.

[23]L. S. Hartenian and N. B. Johnson, "Establishing the Reliability and Validity of Wage Surveys," *Public Personnel Management* 20(3) (1991), pp. 367–383; Sara L. Rynes and G. T. Milkovich, "Wage Surveys: Dispelling Some Myths about the 'Market Wage,'" *Personnel Psychology,* Spring 1986, pp. 71–90; Frederic Cook, "Compensation Surveys Are Biased," *Compensation and Benefits Review,* September–October 1994, pp. 19–22.

EXHIBIT 8.4
Salary Data
on the Web

Salary Wizard

The median expected salary for a typical Compensation Manager in **Minneapolis - St. Paul, MN**, is **$80,043**. This basic market pricing report was prepared using our Certified Compensation Professionals' analysis of survery data collected from thousands of HR departments at employers of all sizes, industries and geographies.

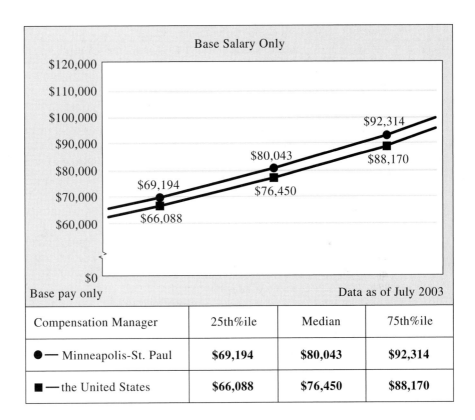

Compensation Manager	25th%ile	Median	75th%ile
● — Minneapolis-St. Paul	**$69,194**	**$80,043**	**$92,314**
■ — the United States	**$66,088**	**$76,450**	**$88,170**

Job Description
Designs, plans, and implements compensation programs, policies, and procedures. Responsible for achieving organization's desired position in market and compensation goals, and conducting or participating in surveys. Ensures the compensation program enhances the organization's ability to recruit and retain employees. Requires a bachelor's degree in a related area and at least 7 years of experience in the field. Generally manages a group of compensation analysts. Relies on experience and judgment to plan and accomplish goals. Typically reports to an executive.

performed, and/or results is available. Issues of sample design and statistical inference are seldom considered. For other HR responsibilities such as staffing decisions, employment test designers report the test's performance against a set of standards (reliability, validity, etc.). The reliability and validity of job evaluation has been studied. Yet for market surveys and analysis, similar indices and standards do not exist.[24]

Which Jobs to Include?

A general guideline is to select as few employers and jobs as necessary to accomplish the purpose. The more complex the survey, the less likely other employers will participate. There are several approaches to selecting jobs for inclusion.

Benchmark-Job Approach

In Chapter 5 we noted that benchmark jobs have stable job content, are common across different employers, and include sizable numbers of employees. If the purpose of the survey is to price the entire structure, then benchmark jobs can be selected to include the entire job structure—all key functions and all levels, just as in job evaluation. In Exhibit 8.5, the more heavily shaded jobs in the structures are benchmark jobs. Benchmark jobs are chosen from as many levels in each of these structures as can be matched with the descriptions of the benchmark jobs that are included in the survey.

The degree of match between the survey's benchmark jobs and each company's benchmark jobs is assessed by various means. The Hay Group, for example, has installed the same job evaluation plan in many companies that participate in its surveys. Consequently, jobs in different organizations can be compared on their job evaluation points and the distribution of points among the compensable factors. Other surveys simply ask participants to judge the degree of match, using a scale similar to the following one.

**EXHIBIT 8.5
Benchmarks**

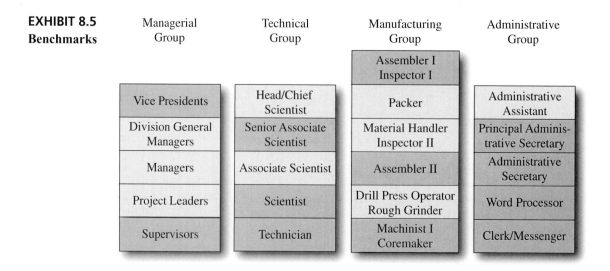

Managerial Group	Technical Group	Manufacturing Group	Administrative Group
		Assembler I / Inspector I	
Vice Presidents	Head/Chief Scientist	Packer	Administrative Assistant
Division General Managers	Senior Associate Scientist	Material Handler / Inspector II	Principal Administrative Secretary
Managers	Associate Scientist	Assembler II	Administrative Secretary
Project Leaders	Scientist	Drill Press Operator / Rough Grinder	Word Processor
Supervisors	Technician	Machinist I / Coremaker	Clerk/Messenger

[24]*2003–04 Survey Handbook and Directory* (Scottsdale, AZ: WorldatWork, 2002).

Please check ( ) degree to which your job matches the benchmark job described in the survey:

My company's job is

Of moderately less value	( )
Of slightly less value	( )
Of equal value	( )
Of slightly more value	( )
Of moderately more value	( )

A good survey will include this information in its results. A consultant friend insists that when the compensation manager of a company changes, the job matches change, too.

Low-High Approach

If an organization is using skill-competency-based structures or generic job descriptions, it may not have benchmark jobs to match with jobs at competitors that use a traditional job-based approach. Market data must be converted to fit the skill or competency structure. The simplest approach is to identify the lowest- and highest-paid benchmark jobs for the relevant skills in the relevant market and to use the wages for these jobs as anchors for the skill-based structures. Work at various levels within the structure can then be slotted between the anchors. For example, if the entry market rate for operator A in a skill-based structure is $12 per hour and the rate for a team leader is $42 per hour, then the rate for operator B can be somewhere between $12 and $42 per hour.[25]

The usefulness of this approach depends on how well the extreme benchmark jobs match the organization's work and whether they really do tap the entire range of skills. Hanging a pay system on two pieces of market data raises the stakes on the accuracy of those data.

Benchmark Conversion Approach

An alternative approach to job-matching difficulties is to apply the plan used to create internal alignment to the descriptions of survey jobs. If an organization uses job evaluation, then its job evaluation system can be applied to the survey jobs. The magnitude of difference between job evaluation points for internal jobs and survey jobs provides guidance for adjusting the market data. Again, a judgment.

What Information to Collect?

Three basic types of data typically are requested: ① information about the nature of the organization, ② information about the total compensation system, and ③ specific pay data on each incumbent in the jobs under study. Exhibit 8.6 lists the basic data elements and the logic for including them. No survey includes all the data that will be discussed. Rather, the data collected depend on the purpose of the survey and the jobs and skills included.

[25]Years-since-degree (YSD) or maturity curves, commonly used for scientists, are discussed in Chapter 14, "Special Groups."

EXHIBIT 8.6   Possible Survey Data Elements and Rationale

Basic Elements	Examples	Rationale
Nature of Organization		
Identification	Company, name, address, contact person	Further contacts
Financial performance	Assets, sales, profits, cash flow	Indicates nature of product/service markets, ability to pay, size, and financials.
Size	Profit centers, product lines Total number of employees	Importance of specific job groups Impact on labor market
Structure	Organizational charts	Indicates how business is organized
Nature of Total Compensation System		
Cash forms used	Base pay, pay-increase schedules, long- and short-term incentives, bonuses, cost-of-living adjustments, overtime and shift differentials	Indicate the mix of compensation offered; used to establish a comparable base
Noncash forms used	Benefits and services, particularly coverage and contributions to medical and health insurance and pensions	
Incumbent and Job		
Date	Date survey data in effect	Update to current date
Job	Match generic job description	Indicates degree of similarity with survey's key jobs
	Reporting levels	Scope of responsibilities
Individual	Years since degree, education, date of hire	Indicates training tenure
Pay	Actual rates paid to each individual, total earnings, last increase, bonuses, incentives	
HR Outcomes		
Productivity	Revenues/employee Revenues/labor costs	Reflect organization performance and efficiency
Total labor costs	Number of employees × (averages wages + benefits)	Major expense
Attraction	Yield ratio: Number accepting offers/Number of job offers	Reveals recruiting success, a compensation objective
Retention	Turnover rate: Number of high or low performers who leave/ number of employees	Reveals outflow of people, which is related to a compensation objective
Employee views	Total pay satisfaction	Reveals what employees think about their pay

Organization Data

This information reflects the similarities and differences among survey users. Surveys for executive and upper-level positions include more detailed financial and reporting relationships data, since compensation for these jobs is more directly related to the organization's financial performance. More often than not, the financial data are simply used to group firms by size, expressed in terms of sales or revenues, rather than considering the performance of competitors. Some surveys such as Clark and Radford collect turnover data. Other outcomes such as participating companies' earnings per share, market share, employee satisfaction with compensation, and recruiting yield ratios are not included. So organization data are useful for determining pay levels and mix but not for assessing the value added by a company's pay system.[26] You need to go to other sources for information on outcomes.

Total Compensation Data

All the basic types of pay forms are required to assess the total pay package and competitors' practices.[27] The list shown in Exhibit 8.6 reveals the range of forms that could be included in each company's definition of total compensation. As a practical matter, it can be hard to include *all* the pay forms. Too much detail on benefits, such as medical coverage deductibles and flexible schedules, can make a survey too cumbersome to be useful. Alternatives range from including a brief description of a benchmark benefit package to including only the most expensive and variable benefits or asking for an estimate of total benefit expenses as a percentage of total labor costs. Three alternatives—base pay, total cash (base, profit sharing, bonuses), and total compensation (total cash plus benefits and perquisites)—are the most commonly used. Exhibit 8.7 draws the distinction between these three alternatives and highlights the usefulness and limitations of each. Exhibit 8.8 shows some results of survey analysis using these three measures on a sample of engineers. The "going market rate" varies, depending on the measure.

> A: *Base pay.* This is the amount of *cash* the competitors decided *each job and incumbent* is worth. A company might use this information for its initial observations of how "good" the data appear to fit a range of jobs. The market line A is based on base pay.
>
> B: *Total cash.* This is base plus bonus—line B in the exhibit. Total cash measures reveal competitors' use of performance-based cash payments.
>
> C: *Total compensation.* This includes total cash plus stock options and benefits. Total compensation reflects the total overall value of the employee (performance, experience, skills, etc.) plus the value of the work itself.

It is no surprise that for all seven jobs, total compensation is higher than base pay alone or base plus bonus. However, the variability and magnitude of the difference may be a surprise: from $7,842 (34 percent) for the job of technician A, to $244,103.38 (182 percent)

[26] J. Fitz-ens, *The ROI of Human Capital* (New York: American Management Association), 2000; and J. Fitz-ens, *How to Measure HRM* (Burr Ridge, IL: McGraw-Hill), 2002. Also see the website of the Saratoga Institute: *www.pwcservices.com/saratoga-institute/default.htm.*

[27] Joseph R. Rich and Carol Caretta Phalen, "A Framework for the Design of Total Compensation Surveys," *ACA Journal,* Winter 1992–93, pp. 18–29.

EXHIBIT 8.7   **Advantages and Disadvantages of Measures of Compensation**

Base pay	Tells how competitors are valuing the work in similar jobs	Fails to include performance incentives and other forms, so will not give true picture if competitors offer low base but high incentives.
Total cash (base + bonus)	Tells how competitors are valuing work; also tells the cash pay for performance opportunity in the job	All employees may not receive incentives, so it may overstate the competitors' pay; plus, it does not include long-term incentives.
Total compensation (base + bonus + stock options + benefits)	Tells the total value competitors place on this work	All employees may not receive all the forms. Be careful: Don't set base equal to competitors' total compensation. Risks high fixed costs.

EXHIBIT 8.8
Salary Graphs Using Different Measures of Compensation

ACTUAL SALARIES

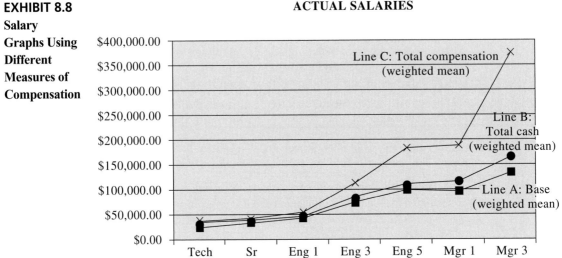

JOBS

	A: Base, Wtd Mean	B: Cash, Wtd Mean	C: Total Comp, Wtd Mean
Tech A	$22,989.17	$24,554.61	$30,831.04
Sr Tech	$37,748.74	$42,510.23	$51,482.48
Eng 1	$46,085.21	$48,289.66	$56,917.08
Eng 3	$73,134.74	$81,285.93	$112,805.98
Eng 5	$102,415.07	$112,587.43	$179,449.81
Mgr 1	$95,260.05	$115,304.66	$188,509.84
Mgr 3	$134,173.33	$171,030.50	$378,276.71

for the job of manager 3. Base pay is, on average, only 35 percent of total compensation for the manager 3s in this survey. So the measure of compensation is an important decision. Misinterpreting competitors' pay practices can lead to costly mispricing of pay levels and structures.

INTERPRET SURVEY RESULTS AND CONSTRUCT A MARKET LINE

Survey data today are typically exchanged online. Technology has made processing data and spitting out reports easy. The greatest challenge of total compensation surveys is to understand how to evaluate the information. A well-designed total compensation database allows each participating firm to determine the models, financial assumptions, and demographic profiles that best reflect its view of the world. In the best total compensation projects, each firm sees the survey as a customizable database project where they can specify the characteristics of the employers and jobs to analyze.

After the survey data are all collected, the next step is to analyze the results and use statistics to construct a market line. Twenty years ago, Belcher interviewed compensation professionals to discover how survey data are actually analyzed. He reported:

> Every organization uses its own methods of distilling information from the survey; uses different surveys for different purposes; and uses different methods for company surveys. I could find no commonality in these methods of analysis by industry, by firm size, or by union presence. For example, some did nothing except read the entire survey, some emphasized industry data, others geographic competitors (commuting distances), some made comparisons with less than five competitors, some emphasized only large firms, others threw out the data from large firms.[28]

His conclusion still holds today. We hope this diversity reflects the flexibility in dealing with a variety of circumstances. We worry that it reflects expediency and a lack of business- and work-related logic.

Verify Data

A common first step is to check the *accuracy* of the job matches, and then check for anomalies (i.e., an employer whose data are substantially out of line from data of others), age of data, and the nature of the organizations (e.g., industry, size—State Farm Insurance versus Yahoo). Exhibit 8.9 is an excerpt from the survey used to prepare Exhibit 8.8. The survey was conducted at the behest of FastCat, a small start-up familiar to many readers.[29] While there were a number of jobs included in the survey, we use information for just one job—engineer 1—to illustrate. As you can see, surveys do not make light reading. However, they contain a wealth of information. To extract that information, step through the portal . . . to being the FastCat analyst.

---

[28]Letter from D. W. Belcher to G. T. Milkovich, in reference to D. W. Belcher, N. Bruce Ferris, and John O'Neill, "How Wage Surveys Are Being Used," *Compensation and Benefits Review,* September–October 1985, pp. 34–51.

[29]Users of Milkovich and Milkovich's *Cases in Compensation,* 9th ed. (Santa Monica, CA: Milkovich 2004) will recognize the software company FastCat. The casebook offers the opportunity for hands-on experience. For more information, contact the authors at *gtm1@cornell.edu.*

EXHIBIT 8.9 Survey Data (in Dollars, Except as Noted)

A. Job Description: Engineer 1

Participates in development, testing, and documentation of software programs. Performs design and analysis tasks as a project team member. Typical minimum requirements are a bachelor's degree in a scientific or technical field or the equivalent and up to two year of experience.

B. Individual Salary Data (partial data; for illustration only)

Job	Base	Bonus	Total Cash	Stock Option	Benefits	Total Comp
Engineer 1					JE Points:	50
					Number of Incumbents:	585
Company 1						
Engineer 1	79,000	500	79,500	0	8,251	87,751
Engineer 1	65,500	2,500	68,000	0	8,251	76,251
Engineer 1	65,000	0	65,000	0	8,251	73,251
Engineer 1	58,000	4,000	62,000	0	8,251	70,251
Engineer 1	57,930	3,000	60,930	0	8,251	69,181
Engineer 1	57,200	2,000	59,200	0	8,251	67,451
Engineer 1	56,000	1,100	57,100	0	8,251	65,351
Engineer 1	54,000	0	54,000	0	8,251	62,251
Engineer 1	52,500	0	52,500	0	8,251	60,751
Engineer 1	51,500	1,500	53,000	0	8,251	61,251
Engineer 1	49,000	3,300	52,300	0	8,251	60,551
Engineer 1	48,500	0	48,500	0	8,251	56,751
Engineer 1	36,500	0	36,500	0	8,251	44,751
Company 2						
Engineer 1	57,598	0	57,598	28,889	8,518	95,004
Engineer 1	57,000	0	57,000	31,815	8,518	97,332
Engineer 1	55,000	0	55,000	20,110	8,518	83,628

EXHIBIT 8.9 *(Continued)*

C. Company Data (partial data; for illustration only)

No.of Incumbents		Base	Short Term	Total Cash	LTI	Benefits	Total Comp
Company 1							
13	*Avg.*	56,202.31	1,376.92	57,579.23	0.00	8,250.89	65,830.12
	Min.	36,500.00	0.00	36,500.00	0.00	8,250.89	44,750.89
	Max.	79,000.00	4,000.00	79,500.00	0.00	8,250.89	87,750.89
Company 2							
13	*Avg.*	52,764.80	1,473.56	54,238.36	21,068.91	8,517.56	83,824.83
	Min.	47,376.20	0.00	50,038.33	4,878.98	8,517.56	65,416.54
	Max.	57,598.21	3,716.89	58,494.01	31,814.83	8,517.56	97,332.39
Company 4							
2		56,004.00	0.00	56,004.00	0.00	9,692.56	65,696.56
		55,016.00	0.00	55,016.00	0.00	9,692.56	64,708.56
	Avg.	55,510.00	0.00	55,510.00	0.00	9,692.56	65,202.56
Company 8							
14	*Avg.*	54,246.00	4,247.21	58,493.21	0.00	7,204.50	65,697.71
	Min.	45,000.00	860.00	48,448.00	0.00	7,204.50	55,363.50
	Max.	62,000.00	8,394.00	68,200.00	0.00	7,204.50	75,404.50
Company 12							
35	*Avg.*	50,459.34	1,123.26	51,582.60	1,760.05	7,693.11	61,035.76
	Min.	42,000.00	0.00	43,092.00	0.00	7,693.11	52,606.26
	Max.	64,265.00	1,670.89	65,935.89	9,076.52	7,693.11	73,629.00
Company 13							
5	*Avg.*	48,700.80	400.00	49,100.80	2,050.00	8,001.00	59,152.20
	Min.	45,456.00	0.00	45,456.00	0.00	8,001.00	53,458.00
	Max.	54,912.00	2,000.00	54,912.00	8,506.00	8,001.00	66,507.00
Company 14							
10	*Avg.*	44,462.40	863.43	45,325.83	0.00	7,337.00	52,662.83
	Min.	37,440.00	372.95	37,812.95	0.00	7,337.00	45,149.95
	Max.	47,832.00	1,197.12	49,029.12	0.00	7,337.00	56,366.12

EXHIBIT 8.9   (*Continued*)

		Base Salary	Bonuses	Total Cash		Stock Options	Total Compensation
Company 15	**71**						
	Avg.	49,685.92	8,253.61	57,939.52	1,762.97	8,404.00	68,106.48
	Min.	44,900.00	0.00	49,022.00	0.00	8,404.00	57,426.00
	Max.	57,300.00	14,132.00	68,357.00	63,639.00	8,404.00	125,471.00
Company 51	**4**						
	Avg.	46,193.88	1,399.75	47,593.63	41,954.39	7,640.89	97,188.90
	Min.	42,375.06	0.00	44,988.75	20,518.14	7,640.89	75,159.23
	Max.	48,400.04	2,985.31	51,385.35	74,453.00	7,640.89	133,479.24
Company 57	**226**						
	Avg.	44,091.57	1,262.43	45,354.00	0.00	6,812.00	52,166.00
	Min.	38,064.00	0.00	39,372.00	0.00	6,812.00	46,184.00
	Max.	60,476.00	2,179.00	62,655.00	0.00	6,812.00	69,467.00
Company 58	**107**						
	Avg.	44,107.18	1,367.04	45,474.21	0.00	6,770.00	52,244.21
	Min.	36,156.00	0.00	37,569.00	0.00	6,770.00	44,339.00
	Max.	57,600.00	2,147.00	58,913.00	0.00	6,770.00	65,683.00
Company 59	**71**						
	Avg.	44,913.63	1,152.85	46,066.48	0.00	6,812.00	52,878.48
	Min.	39,156.00	407.00	40,473.00	0.00	6,812.00	47,285.00
	Max.	57,000.00	1,639.00	57,407.00	0.00	6,812.00	64,219.00

D. Summary Data for Engineer 1

	Base Salary	Total Cash	Total Compensation
Wtd Mean:	46,085.21	48,289.66	56,917.08
Mean:	49,092.71	50,940.53	65,524.22
50th:	45,000.00	46,422.00	53,271.00
25th:	42,600.00	43,769.00	50,593.11
75th:	48,500.00	51,854.04	60,750.89

Bonuses
Avg: 2,370.59
As %. of Base: 5.18%
% Who Receive: 92.99%

Stock Options
Avg: 16,920.18
As % of Base: 33.96%
% Who Receive 8.38%

Accuracy of Match

Part A of the survey contains the description of the survey job. If the company job is similar but not identical, some companies use *survey leveling;* that is, they multiply the survey data by some factor that the analyst judges to be the difference between the company job and the survey job.[30] Leveling is another example of judgment entering survey analysis. It clearly leaves the objectivity of the decisions open to challenge.

Anomalies

Part B of the survey gives real salaries received by actual engineer 1s. Perusal of actual salary data gives the analyst a sense of the quality of the data and helps identify any areas for additional consideration. For example, Part B of Exhibit 8.9 shows that no engineer 1s at company 1 receive stock options, and five of them receive no bonuses. The bonuses range from $500 to $4,000. (Because there are 585 engineer 1s in this survey, we have not included all their salary information.) Individual-level data provide a wealth of information about specific practices. Understanding minimums, maximums, and what percent actually receive bonuses and/or options is essential. Unfortunately, many surveys provide only summary information such as company averages.

Part C of Exhibit 8.9 provides company data. Again, the first step is to look for anomalies:

1. *Does any one company dominate?* For example, company 57 employs 226 engineer 1s, whereas four companies report only one engineer 1. A separate analysis of the largest company's data will isolate that employer's pay practices and clarify the nature of its influence.

2. *Do all employers show similar patterns?* Probably not. In our survey, base pay at company 1 ranges from $36,500 to $79,000 for a single job. This raises the possibility that this company might use broad bands (discussed later in this chapter) or simply let managers "run free" with pay decisions. While seven of the companies have a bonus-to-base-pay ratio of around 2 to 3 percent, company 15 pays an average bonus of $8,254 for a bonus-to-base ratio of over 6 percent.

3. *Outliers?* Company 51 gives one of its engineers options valued at $74,453 on top of base pay. The FastCat analyst may consider dropping a company with such an atypical pay practice. The question is, What difference will it make if companies 15 and 51 are dropped? What difference will it make if they are included?

One way to answer questions on anomalies is to do an analysis of them alone. They may have deliberately differentiated themselves with pay as part of their strategy. Other firms may simply match. Learning more about competitors that differentiate can offer valuable insights. Part D at the bottom of Exhibit 8.9 contains summary data: five different measures of base pay, cash, and total compensation, as well as the percent of engineers who receive bonuses and options. The data suggest that most of FastCat's competitors use bonuses but are less likely to use options for this particular job. Summary data help abstract the survey information into a smaller number of measures for further statistical analysis. Statistics help FastCat get from pages of raw data (Exhibit 8.9) to graphs of actual salaries (Exhibit 8.8) and from there to a market line that reflects its competitive pay policy.

[30]Margaret A. Coil, "Salary Surveys in a Blended-Role World," in *2003–04 Survey Handbook and Directory* (Scottsdale, AZ: WorldatWork, 2002), pp. 57–64.

Statistical Analysis

While the statistics necessary to analyze survey data, including regression, are covered in basic statistics classes, a number of websites are probably more fun. Our favorite lets us click anywhere we want on a graph to see how adding that new data point (the mouse click) changes a regression line.[31] A useful first step in our analysis is to look at a frequency distribution of the pay rates.

Frequency Distribution

Exhibit 8.10 shows two frequency distributions created from the data in the Exhibit 8.9 survey. The top one shows the distribution of the base wages for the 585 engineer 1s in increments of $1,000. The second one shows the *total compensation* for 719 engineer 5s in increments of $10,000. (The wide range of dollars—from under $90,000 to over $900,000—is the reason that many surveys switch to logs of dollars for higher-level positions.) Frequency distributions help the user visualize information and may highlight anomalies. For example, the base wage above $79,000 may be considered an outlier. Is this a unique person? Or an error in reporting the data? A phone call (or e-mail) to the survey provider may answer the question.

Shapes of frequency distributions can vary. Unusual shapes may reflect problems with job matches, widely dispersed pay rates, or employers with widely divergent pay policies. If the data look reasonable at this point, one wag has suggested that it is probably the result of two large, offsetting errors.

Central Tendency

A measure of central tendency reduces a large amount of data into a single number. Exhibit 8.11 defines commonly used measures. The distinction between "mean" and "weighted mean" is important. If only company averages are reported in the survey, a *mean* may be calculated by adding each company's base wage and dividing by the number of companies. While use of the mean is common, it may not accurately reflect actual labor market conditions, since the base wage of the largest employer is given the same weight as that of the smallest employer. *Weighted mean* is calculated by adding the base wages for all 585 engineers in the survey and then dividing by 585 ($46,085). A weighted mean gives equal weight to *each individual employee's* wage.

Variation

The distribution of rates around a measure of central tendency is called *variation.* The two frequency distributions in Exhibit 8.10 show very different patterns of variation. Information about variation tells us about how spread out the rates in the market are. *Standard deviation* is probably the most common statistical measure of variation, although its use in salary surveys is rare.

Quartiles and *percentiles* are more common measures of variation in salary survey analysis. Recall from the chapter introduction that someone's policy was "to be in the 75th percentile nationally." The 75th percentile means that 75 percent of all pay rates are

[31]For an online tutorial in statistics, go to *www.robertniles.com;* for reading on the bus, try Larry Gonick and Woollcott Smith, *Cartoon Guide to Statistics* (New York: Harper Perennial, 1993); for the fun stuff, see the Cybercomp on page 241.

EXHIBIT 8.10
Frequency
Distributions

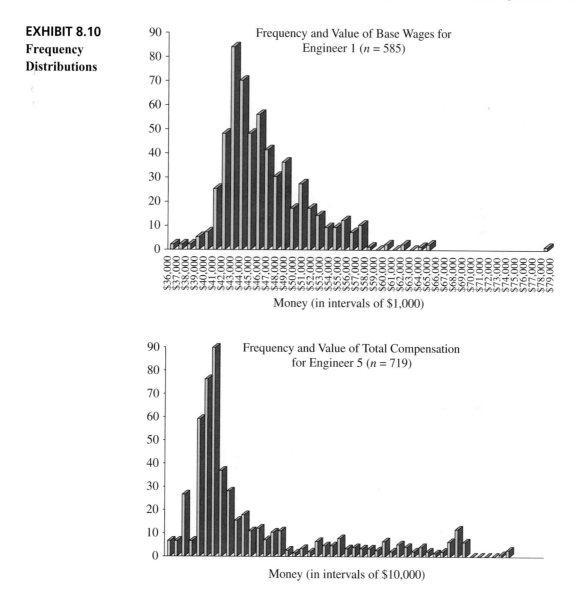

at or below that point and 25 percent are above. Quartiles (25th and 75th percentiles) are commonly used to set pay ranges. More on pay ranges later.

Update the Survey Data

Because they reflect decisions of employers, employees, unions, and government agencies, wages paid by competitors are constantly changing. And competitors adjust their wages at different times. Universities typically adjust to match the academic year. Unionized employers adjust on dates negotiated in labor agreements. Many employers adjust each employee's pay on the anniversary of the employee's date of hire. Even though

EXHIBIT 8.11   **Statistical Measures for Analyzing Survey Data**

Measure	What Does It Tell Us?	Advantage/Disadvantage
Central Tendency Mode	Most commonly occurring rate.	Must draw frequency distribution to calculate it.
Mean	Sum all rates and divide by number of rates. If have only company (rather than individual) data, wage of largest employer given same weight as smallest employer.	Commonly understood (also called the "average"). However, if have only company data, will not accurately reflect actual labor market conditions.
Median	Order all data points from highest to lowest; the one in the middle is the median.	Minimizes distortion caused by outliers.
Weighted mean	If have only companywide measures (rather than individual measures), the rate for each company is multiplied by the number of employees in that company. Total of all rates is divided by total number of employees.	Gives equal weight to each individual's wage. Captures size of supply and demand in market.
Variation Standard deviation	How tightly all the rates are clustered around the mean. A small SD means rates are tightly bunched at the center; a large SD means rates are more spread out.	Tells how similar or dissimilar the market rates are from each other.
Quartiles and percentiles	Order all data points from lowest to highest, then convert to percentages. 75th percentile means 75% of data points are below that point	Common in salary surveys; frequently used to set pay ranges or zones.

these changes do not occur smoothly and uniformly throughout the year, as a practical matter we assume that they do. Therefore, a survey that requires three months to collect, code, and analyze is probably outdated before it is available. The pay data are usually updated (a process often called *aging* or *trending*) to forecast the competitive rates for the future date when the pay decisions will be implemented.

The amount to update is based on several factors, including historical trends in the labor market, prospects for the economy in which the employer operates, and the manager's judgment, among others. Some recommend using the Consumer Price Index (CPI). We do not. CPI measures the rate of change in prices for goods and services in the product market, not wage changes in labor markets. Chapter 18 has more information on this distinction.

EXHIBIT 8.12 **Choices for Updating Survey Data Reflect Pay Policy**

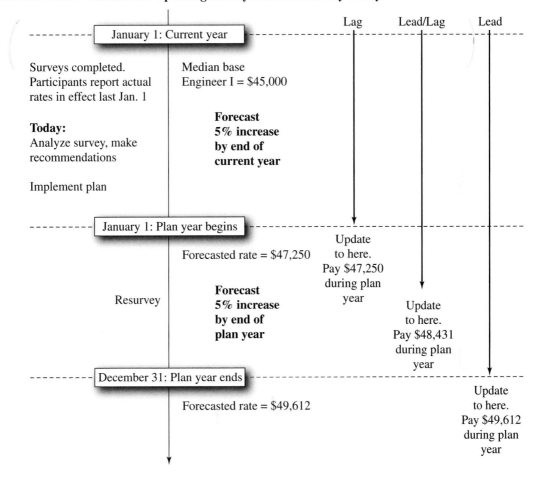

Exhibit 8.12 illustrates updating. In the example, the base pay rate of $45,000 collected in the survey was in effect at January 1 of the *current year*—already in the past. The compensation manager will use this information for pay decisions that go into effect on January 1 of the *plan year*. So if base pay has been increasing by approximately 5 percent annually, and we assume that the future will be like the past, the rate is multiplied by 105 percent to account for the change expected by the end of the *current year* (to $47,250) and then by an additional percentage to estimate pay rates for the *plan* year.

Construct a Market Pay Line

Look again at Exhibit 8.8. It shows the results of the FastCat analyst's decisions on which benchmark jobs to include (seven jobs on the *x* [horizontal] axis), which companies to include, and which measures of pay to use. For each of the compensation metrics, a line has been drawn connecting the pay for the seven jobs. Jobs are ordered on the horizontal axis according to their position in the internal structure. Thus, the line trends upward to create a market line.

> A **market line** links a company's benchmark jobs on the horizontal axis (internal structure) with market rates paid by competitors (market survey) on the vertical axis. It summarizes the distribution of going rates paid by competitors in the market.

A market line may be drawn freehand by connecting the data points, as was done in Exhibit 8.8. Or statistical techniques such as regression analysis may be used. Regression generates a straight line that best fits the data by minimizing the variance around the line. Exhibit 8.13 shows the regression lines that used the same data as those in Exhibit 8.8. Compare the data tables in Exhibits 8.8 and 8.13. Exhibit 8.8 shows the market rates for survey jobs. Exhibit 8.13 shows the job evaluation points for the FastCat jobs that match these survey jobs plus the regression's statistical "prediction" of the salary of each job. The actual base wage for the survey job technician A is $22,989 (Exhibit 8.8); the "predicted" base for the matching FastCat job is $23,058 (Exhibit 8.13).

EXHIBIT 8.13 From Regression Results to a Market Line

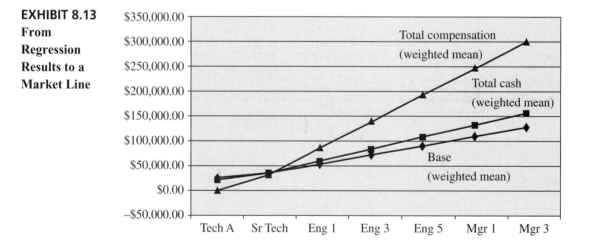

Job	JEPts	Predicted Base, Wtd Mean	Predicted Cash, Wtd Mean	Predicted Total Comp
Tech A	10	$23,057.96	$20,543.71	−$1,330.36
Sr Tech	25	$34,361.06	$35,116.51	$31,172.24
Eng 1	50	$53,199.56	$59,404.51	$85,343.24
Eng 3	75	$72,038.06	$83,692.51	$139,514.24
Eng 5	100	$90,876.56	$107,980.51	$193,685.24
Mgr 1	125	$109,715.06	$132,268.51	$247,856.24
Mgr 3	150	$128,553.56	$156,556.51	$302,027.24

Cybercomp 2

Calculating a Market Line Using Regression Analysis

Regression analysis uses the mathematical formula for a straight line, $y = a + bx$, where

y = dollars
x = job evaluation points
a = the y value (in dollars) at which $x = 0$ (i.e., the straight line crosses the y axis)
b = the slope of the line

If $b = 0$, the line is parallel to the x axis and all jobs are paid the same, regardless of job evaluation points. Using the dollars from the market survey data and the job evaluation points from the internal structure, solve this equation to construct a line based on the relationship between internal job structure and market rates. An upward-sloping line means that more job evaluation points are associated with higher dollars.

The market line can be written as

Pay for job A = $a + (b \times$ job evaluation points for job A)
Pay for job B = $a + (b \times$ job evaluation points for job B)

and so on.

Regression estimates the values of a and b in an efficient manner, so errors of prediction are minimized.

For a demonstration of regression that is a lot of fun, go to *www.math.csusb.edu/faculty/stanton/m262/regress/regress.html*. Click on points and the program immediately draws the new regression line. A site that does the regression and also shows the correlation coefficient is *www.stat.uiuc.edu/~stat100/java/guess/PPApplet.html*. Play around with both these sites until you have an understanding of what a regression line tells you. Then use the sites to analyze data. You might even study the relationship between the height of your classmates and what they expect to be earning when they graduate.

In Exhibit 8.14, the diamonds are the actual results of the survey and the solid line is the regression result. As the exhibit shows, regression "smoothes" large amounts of data while minimizing variations. As the number of jobs in the survey increases, the advantage of the straight line that regression provides becomes clear.

Before we leave survey data analysis, we must emphasize that not all survey results look like our examples and that not all companies use these statistical and analytical techniques. There is no one "right way" to analyze survey data. It has been our intent to provide some insight into the kinds of calculations that are useful and the assumptions that underlie salary surveys.

We are now beyond the halfway point of this long chapter. May we suggest that it might be a good time to consider resorting to the Puking Pastilles, one of the Weasleys' Wizarding Wheezes described in the fifth Harry Potter book? The Puking Pastilles make you just ill enough to convince your professor to give you an extension on an assignment before you magically recover to enjoy your illicit time off.[32]

---

[32] J. K. Rowling, *Harry Potter and the Order of the Phoenix* (New York: Scholastic, 2003).

EXHIBIT 8.14 **Understanding Regression**

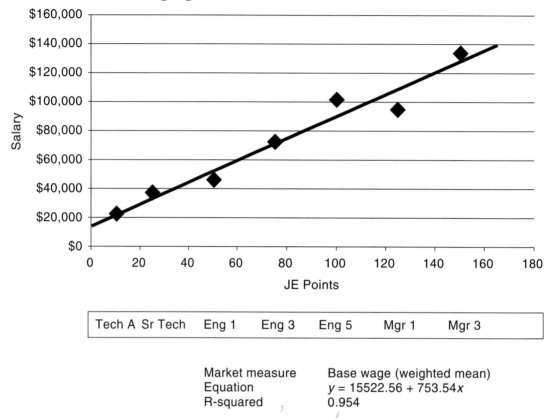

| Tech A | Sr Tech | Eng 1 | Eng 3 | Eng 5 | Mgr 1 | Mgr 3 |

Market measure	Base wage (weighted mean)
Equation	$y = 15522.56 + 753.54x$
R-squared	0.954

Combine Internal Structure and External Market Rates

At this point, two parts of the total pay model have merged. Their relationship to each other can be seen in Exhibit 8.15.[33]

- The *internally aligned structure* developed in Part 1 is shown on the horizontal (x) axis. For this illustration, our structure consists of jobs A through P, with P being engineering manager 3, the most complex job in this structure. Jobs B, F, G, H, J, M, and P are the seven benchmark jobs that have been matched in the survey. Job F is our engineer 1.
- The salaries paid by relevant competitors for those benchmark jobs, as measured by the survey—*the external competitive data*—are shown on the vertical (y) axis.

These two components—internal alignment and external competitiveness—come together in the pay structure. The pay structure has two aspects: the *pay-policy line* and *pay ranges.*

[33]Brian Hinchcliffe, "Juggling Act: Internal Equity and Market Pricing," *Workspan,* February 2003, pp. 42–45.

EXHIBIT 8.15
Develop Pay
Grades

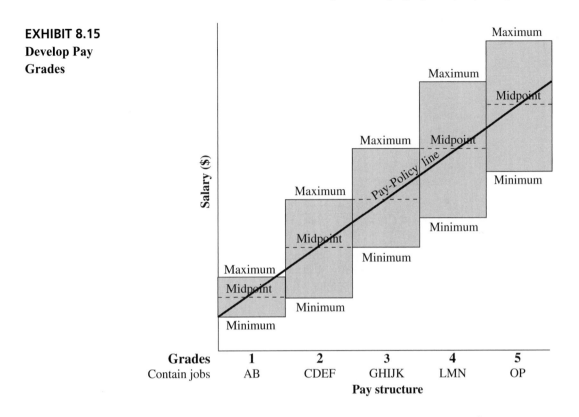

Grades	1	2	3	4	5
Contain jobs	AB	CDEF	GHIJK	LMN	OP

Pay structure

FROM POLICY TO PRACTICE: THE PAY-POLICY LINE

The next major decision is to construct a pay-policy line that puts into effect FastCat's external competitive policy. There are several ways to translate external competitive policy into practice. You have already made some of the choices that help you do this.

Choice of Measure   If Colgate practices what it claims at the beginning of the chapter, then we would expect Colgate to use the 50th percentile for base pay and the 75th percentile for total compensation as compensation measures in its regression.

Updating   Look again at Exhibit 8.12. The arrows on the right side of the exhibit show how updating survey data reflects policy. If the company chooses a "match" policy but then updates survey data to the end of the current year/start of the plan year and keeps this rate in effect throughout the plan year, the company will actually be lagging the market. It will match its desired market pay level only at the beginning of the plan year. The market rates continue to rise throughout the year; the company's rates do not.

Aging the market data to a point halfway through the plan year (middle arrow in Exhibit 8.12) is called *lead/lag*. The original survey rates are updated to the end of the current year plus half the projected amount for the plan year ($48,431). An employer that wants to lead the market may age data to the *end* of the plan year ($49,612) and pay at this rate throughout the plan year.

Policy Line as Percent of Market Line

Another way to translate pay-level policy into practice is to simply *specify a percent* above or below the regression line (market line) that an employer intends to match and then draw a new line at this higher (or lower) level. This would carry out a policy statement of, "We lead the market by 10 percent." Other possibilities exist. An employer might lead by including only a few top-paying competitors in the analysis and then matching them ("pay among the leaders") or lead for some job families and lag for others. The point is that there are alternatives among competitive pay policies, and there are alternative ways to translate policy into practice. If the practice does not match the policy (e.g., we say one thing but do another), then employees receive the wrong message.

FROM POLICY TO PRACTICE: GRADES AND RANGES

The next step is to design pay grades and ranges. These analyses are usually done with base pay data, since base pay reflects the basic value of the work rather than performance levels of employees (see Exhibit 8.7 for a comparison of metrics).

Why Bother with Grades and Ranges?

Grades and ranges offer flexibility to deal with pressures from external markets and differences among organizations. These include:

1. *Differences in quality (skills, abilities, experience) among individuals applying for work* (e.g., Microsoft may have stricter hiring requirements for engineers than does FastCat, even though job descriptions appear identical).
2. *Differences in the productivity or value of these quality variations* (e.g., the value of the results from a software engineer at Microsoft probably differs from that of the results of a software engineer at Best Buy).
3. *Differences in the mix of pay forms competitors use* (e.g., Oracle uses more stock options and lower base compared to IBM).

In addition to offering flexibility to deal with these external differences, an organization may use differences in rates paid to employees on the same job. *A pay range exists whenever two or more rates are paid to employees in the same job.* Hence, ranges provide managers the opportunity to:

1. Recognize individual performance differences with pay.
2. Meet employees' expectations that their pay will increase over time, even while holding the same job.
3. Encourage employees to remain with the organization.

From an internal alignment perspective, the range reflects the differences in performance or experience that an employer wishes to recognize with pay. From an external competitiveness perspective, the range is a control device. A range maximum sets the lid on what the employer is willing to pay for that work; the range minimum sets the floor.

Not all employers use ranges. Skill-based plans establish single *flat rates* for each skill level regardless of performance or seniority. And many collective bargaining contracts establish single flat rates for each job (i.e., all senior machinists II receive $17.50 per hour regardless of performance or seniority). This flat rate often corresponds to some midpoint on a survey of that job. And increasingly, *broad bands* (think "really fat ranges") are being adopted for even greater flexibility. Banding is discussed below.

Develop Grades

The first step in building flexibility into the pay structure is to group different jobs that are considered substantially equal for pay purposes into a grade. Grades enhance an organization's ability to move people among jobs within a grade with no change in pay. In Exhibit 8.15 the jobs are grouped into five grades on the horizontal axis.

The question of which jobs are substantially equal and therefore slotted into one grade requires that the analyst reconsider the original job evaluation results. Each grade will have its own pay range, and *all the jobs within a single grade will have the same pay range.* Jobs in different grades (e.g., jobs C, D, E, and F in grade 2) should be dissimilar to those in other grades (grade 1 jobs A and B) and will have a different pay range.

Although grades permit flexibility, they are challenging to design. The objective is for all jobs that are similar for pay purposes to be placed within the same grade. If jobs with relatively close job evaluation point totals fall on either side of grade boundaries, the magnitude of difference in the salary treatment may be out of proportion to the magnitude of difference in the value of the job content. Resolving such dilemmas requires an understanding of the specific jobs, career paths, and work flow in the organization, as well as considerable judgment.

Establish Range Midpoints, Minimums, and Maximums

Grades group job evaluation data on the horizontal axis; ranges group salary data on the vertical axis. Ranges set upper and lower pay limits for all jobs in each grade. A range has three salient features: a midpoint, a minimum, and a maximum. Exhibit 8.16 is an enlargement of grade 2 in Exhibit 8.15, which contains the engineer 1 job. The midpoint is $54,896. This is the point where the pay-policy line crosses the center of the grade. The range for this grade has been set at 20 percent above and 20 percent below the midpoint. Thus, all FastCat engineer 1s are supposed to receive a salary higher than $43,917 but lower than $65,875.[34]

What Size Should the Range Be?

The size of the range is based on some judgment about how the ranges support career paths, promotions, and other organization systems. Top-level management positions commonly have ranges of 30 to 60 percent above and below the midpoint; entry to midlevel professional and managerial positions, between 15 and 30 percent; office and production work, 5 to 15 percent. Larger ranges in the managerial jobs reflect the greater opportunity for individual discretion and performance variations in the work.

---

[34]An alternative formula for calculating minimum is midpoint / [100%+(1/2 range)] and for calculating maximum is minimum + (range × minimum). This approach gives a different result than does adding 20 percent above and below the midpoint. The important points are to be consistent in whatever approach you choose and to be sure other users of the survey are apprised of how range minimums and maximums are calculated.

EXHIBIT 8.16
Range
Midpoint,
Minimum,
and
Maximum

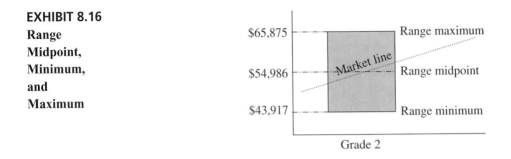

Some compensation managers use the actual survey rates, particularly the 75th and 25th percentiles, as their range maximums and minimums. Others ensure that the proposed range includes at least 75 percent of the rates in the survey data. Still others establish the minimum and maximum separately, with the amount between the minimum and the midpoint a function of how long it takes a new employee to become fully competent. Short training time may translate to minimums much closer to the midpoints. The maximum becomes the amount above the midpoint that the company is willing to pay for sustained performance on the job. In the end, the size of the range is based on judgment that weighs all these factors.

Overlap

Exhibit 8.17 shows two extremes in overlap between adjacent grades. The high degree of overlap and low midpoint differentials in Exhibit 8.17(a) indicate small differences in the value of jobs in the adjoining grades. Being promoted from one grade to another may include a title change but not much change in pay. The smaller ranges in Exhibit 8.17(b) create less overlap, which permits the manager to reinforce a promotion into a new grade with a larger pay increase. The downside is that there may be fewer opportunities for promotion.

Promotion Increases Matter

The size of differentials between grades should support career movement through the structure. A managerial job would typically be at least one grade higher than the jobs it supervises. Although a 15 percent pay differential between manager and employee has been offered as a rule of thumb, large overlap and possible overtime in some jobs but not in managerial jobs can make it difficult to maintain manager-employee differentials. We are cautious about such rules of thumb. They are often ways to avoid thinking about what makes sense.

What is the optimal overlap between grades? It ought to be large enough to induce employees to seek promotion into a higher grade. However, there is virtually no research to indicate how much of a differential is necessary to influence employees to do so. Tracing how an employee might move through a career path in the structure (e.g., from engineer 1 to engineer 2 . . . to manager 3) and what size pay increases will accompany that movement will help answer that question.

EXHIBIT 8.17
Range
Overlap

EXHIBIT 8.18
From Grades
to Bands

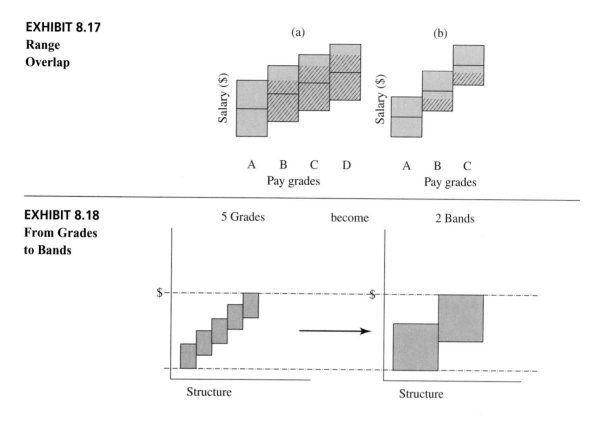

FROM POLICY TO PRACTICE: BROAD BANDING

Exhibit 8.18 collapses salary grades into only a few broad bands, each with a sizable range. This technique, known as *broad banding,* consolidates as many as four or five traditional grades into a single band with one minimum and one maximum. Because the band encompasses so many jobs of differing values, a range midpoint is usually not used.[35]

Contrasts between ranges and broad bands are highlighted in Exhibit 8.19. Supporters of broad bands list several advantages over traditional approaches. First, broad bands provide flexibility to define job responsibilities more broadly. They support redesigned, downsized, or boundaryless organizations that have eliminated layers of managerial jobs. They foster cross-functional growth and development in these new organizations. Employees can move laterally across functions within a band in order to gain depth of experience. Companies with global operations such as 3M and TRW use bands to move managers among worldwide assignments. The emphasis on lateral movement with no pay adjustments helps manage the reality of fewer promotion opportunities in flattened organization structures. The flexibility of banding eases mergers and acquisitions since there

---

[35]Kenan S. Abosch and Beverly L. Hmurovic, "A Traveler's Guide to Global Broadbanding," *ACA Journal,* Summer 1998, pp. 38–47.

EXHIBIT 8.19
Contrasts between Ranges and Bands

Ranges Support:	Bands Support:
Some flexibility within controls	Emphasis on flexibility within guidelines
Relatively stable organization design	Global organizations
Recognition via titles or career progression	Cross-functional experience and lateral progression
Midpoint controls, comparatives	Reference market rates, shadow ranges
Controls designed into system	Controls in budget, few in system
Giving managers "freedom with guidelines"	Giving managers "freedom to manage" pay
Up to 150 percent range spread	100 to 400 percent spreads

are not a lot of levels to argue over.[36] Broad bands are often combined with more traditional salary administration practices by using midpoints, "zones," or other control points within bands.[37] Perhaps the most important difference between the grades-and-ranges and broad-banding approaches is the location of the controls. The grade-and-range approach has guidelines and controls designed right into the pay system. Range minimums, maximums, and midpoints ensure consistency across managers. Managers using bands have only a total salary budget limiting them. But as experience with bands has advanced, guidelines and structure are increasingly designed into them (e.g., reference market rates or shadow ranges).

Bands may add flexibility: Less time will be spent judging fine distinctions among jobs. But perhaps the time avoided judging jobs will now be spent judging individuals, a prospect managers already try to avoid. How will an organization avoid the appearance of salary treatment based on personality and politics rather than objective criteria? Ideally, with a well-thought-out performance management system.

Banding takes two steps:

1. *Set the number of bands.* Merck uses six bands for its entire pay structure. Band titles range from "contributor" to "executive." A unit of General Electric replaced 24 levels of work with 5 bands. Usually bands are established at the major "breaks," or differences, in work or skill/competency requirements. Titles used to label each band reflect these major breaks, such as "associates" (entry-level individual contributor), "professional" (experienced, knowledgeable team member), "leader" (project or group supervisor), "director" or "coach," or even "visionary."

   The challenge is how much to actually pay people who are in the same band but in different functions performing different work.

2. *Price the bands: reference market rates.* The four bands in Exhibit 8.20 (associates, professionals, lead professionals, senior professionals) include multiple job families within each band, e.g., finance, purchasing, engineering, marketing, and so on. It is

---

[36]Life with Broadbands," ACA Research Project, 1998; "Broad Banding Case Study: General Electric," *WorldatWork Journal,* Third Quarter 2000, p. 43.

[37]Kenan S. Abosch and Janice S. Hand, *Broadbanding Models* (Scottsdale, AZ: American Compensation Association, 1994).

EXHIBIT 8.20   References Rates within Bands

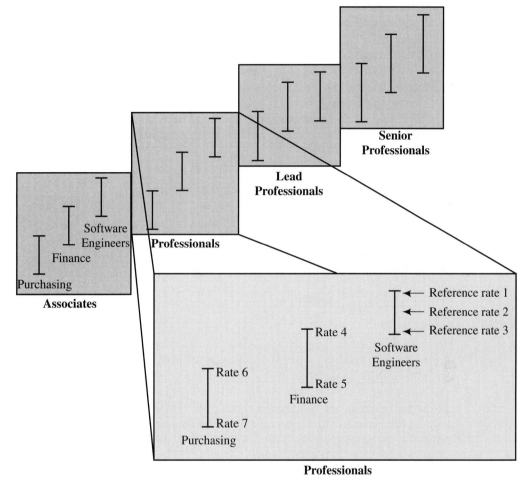

unlikely that General Electric pays associates and professionals with business degrees the same as associates and professionals with engineering degrees. Usually external market differences exist, so the different functions or groups within bands are priced differently. As the pop-out in Exhibit 8.20 depicts, the three job families (purchasing, finance, and engineering) in the professionals band have different *reference rates,* drawn from survey data.

You might say that this is beginning to look a lot like grades and ranges within each band. You would be correct. The difference is that ranges traditionally serve as controls, whereas reference rates act as guides. Today's guides grow to tomorrow's bureaucracy.

Flexibility-Control Broad banding encourages employees to move cross-functionally (e.g., from purchasing to finance) to increase cross-fertilization of ideas. Hence, career moves within bands are more common than between bands. According to supporters, the principal payoff of broad banding is this flexibility. But flexibility is one side of the coin; chaos and favoritism is the other. Banding presumes that managers will manage employee pay to accomplish the organization's objectives (and not their own) and treat employees fairly. Historically, this is not the first time managers have sought greater flexibility. Indeed, the rationale for using grades and ranges was to reduce inconsistencies and favoritism in previous generations.[38] The challenge today is to take advantage of flexibility without increasing labor costs or leaving the organization vulnerable to charges of inconsistent or illegal practices.

BALANCING INTERNAL AND EXTERNAL PRESSURES: ADJUSTING THE PAY STRUCTURE

Up until now, we have made a distinction between the job structure and the pay structure. A *job structure* orders jobs on the basis of internal organizational factors (reflected in job evaluation or skill certification). The *pay structure,* on the other hand, is anchored by the organization's external competitive position and reflected in its pay-policy line.

Reconciling Differences

The problem with using two standards (internal and external) to create a structure is that they are likely to result in two different structures. The orders in which jobs are ranked on internal and external factors probably will not completely agree. Differences between market structures and rates and job evaluation rankings warrant a review of the basic decisions in evaluating and pricing a particular job. This may entail a review of the job analysis, the evaluation of the job, or the market data for the job in question. Often this reanalysis solves the problem. Sometimes, however, discrepancies persist; survey data may be discarded; benchmark-job matches may be changed.

One study of how differences are actually reconciled found that managers weigh external market data more heavily than internal job evaluation data. In light of all the judgments that go into internal evaluation, market data are often considered to be more objective.[39] Yet this chapter and research show that market data are also based on judgments.

Sometimes differences arise because a shortage of a particular skill has driven up the market rate. But reclassifying a market-sensitive job (one in which a supply and demand imbalance exists) into a higher salary grade, where it will remain long after the imbalance has been corrected, creates additional problems. Creating a special range that is clearly designated as *market responsive* may be a better approach. However, decisions made on the basis of expediency may undermine the integrity of the pay decisions.

---

[38]Robert Kanigel, *The One Best Way* (New York: Viking, 1997).

[39]S. Rynes, C. Weber, and G. Milkovich, "Effects of Market Survey Rates on Job Evaluation, and Job Gender on Job Pay," *Journal of Applied Psychology* 74 (1989), pp. 114–123.

MARKET PRICING

Many organizations in the United States have adopted pay strategies that emphasize external competitiveness and deemphasize internal alignment. Called *market pricing,* this approach sets pay structures almost exclusively on external market rates.[40] Market pricers match a large percentage of their jobs with market data and collect as much market data as possible. The competitive rates for jobs for which external market data are available are calculated; then the remaining (nonbenchmark) jobs are blended into the pay hierarchy created by the external rates ("rank to market"). Pfizer, for example, begins with job analysis and job descriptions. This is immediately followed by market analysis and pricing for as many jobs as possible. After that, the few remaining jobs are blended in and the internal job relationships are reviewed to be sure they are *"reasonable in light of organization work flow and other uniqueness."* The final step is pricing the nonbenchmark jobs. This is done by comparing the value of these jobs to the Pfizer jobs already priced in the market.

Market pricing goes beyond the use of benchmark jobs and then slotting nonbenchmarks. The objective of market pricing is to base most, if not all, of the internal pay structure on external rates, breaking down the boundaries between the internal organization and the external market forces. Some companies even match all forms of pay for each job to its competitors in the market. For example, if the average rate for a controller job is $150,000, then the company pays $150,000. If 60 percent of the $150,000 is base pay, 20 percent is annual bonus, 5 percent is stock options, and 15 percent is benefits, the company matches not only the amount but also this mix of pay forms. Another $150,000 job, say, director of marketing, may have a different pattern among market competitors, which is also matched.

Pure market pricing carried to this extreme deemphasizes internal alignment completely. Gone is any attempt to align internal pay structures with the business strategy and the work performed. Rather, the internal pay structure is aligned with competitors' decisions as reflected in the market. In a very real sense, the decisions of its competitors determine an organization's pay structure.

This approach raises several issues. Among them: Just how valid are market data?[41] Does the information really lend itself to such decisions? Why should competitors' pay decisions be the sole or even primary determinant of another company's pay structure? If they are, then *how much or what mix of forms* a company pays is no longer a potential source of competitive advantage. It is not unique, nor is it difficult to imitate. The premise is that little value is added through internal alignment.

Any unique or difficult-to-imitate aspects of the organization's pay structure, which may have been based on its unique technology or the way work is organized, are deemphasized by market pricers. Fairness is presumed to be reflected by market rates; employee behavior is presumed to be reinforced by totally market-priced structures, which are the very same as those of competitors.

---

[40]*Market Pricing: Methods to the Madness* (Scottsdale, AZ: WorldatWork, 2002).

[41]Frederic W. Cook, "Compensation Surveys Are Biased," *Compensation and Benefits Review,* September–October 1994, pp. 19–22.

In sum, the process of balancing internal and external pressures is a matter of judgment, made with an eye on the pay system objectives. De-emphasizing internal alignment may lead to unfair treatment among employees and inconsistency with the fundamental culture of the organization. Neglecting external competitive pay practices, however, will affect both the ability to attract applicants and the ability to hire applicants who match the organization's needs. External pay relationships also impact labor costs and hence the ability to compete in the product/service market.

REVIEW

The end of Part Two of the textbook is a logical spot for a midterm exam. Exhibit 8.21 has been designed to help you review.

EXHIBIT 8.21 **Open-Book Midterm Exam**

Answer true or false to the following questions:

You know you are spending too much time working on compensation when you

- Use "pay mix" and "external competitiveness" when you e-mail home for money.
- Think that paying for lunch requires a strategic approach.
- Ask your date to specify his or her competencies.
- Think that copying your classmate's answers on this exam is benchmarking.
- Can explain the difference between traditional pay grades and ranges and new broad bands with shadow ranges.
- Believe your answer to the above.
- Would cross the street to listen to economists and psychologists discuss the "likely effects of alternative external competitiveness policies."
- Consider your Phase II assignment a wonderful opportunity to increase your human capital.
- Think adding points to your project grade creates a "balanced scorecard."
- Are willing to pay your instructor to teach any other course.
- Are surprised to learn that some people think a COLA is a soft drink.
- Turn your head to listen rather than roll your eyes when someone talks about being "incentivized" with pay.
- Believe that instead of your mom, "the market" knows best.

How did you do? Good. Now let's move on to the next chapters.

Your Turn

Word of Mouse: Dot-Com Compensation Comparisons

More compensation information is available than ever before. Click on the website *www.salary.com.* This site provides pay data on hundreds of jobs in cities all over the United States in many different industries. Identify several jobs of interest to you, such as accountant, financial analyst, product manager, or stockbroker. Select specific cities or use the U.S. national average. Obtain the median, the low and high base wage, and total cash compensation rates for each job. Then consider the following questions:

1. Which jobs are paid more or less? Is this what you would have expected? Why or why not? What factors could explain the differences in the salaries?
2. Do the jobs have different bonuses as a percentage of their base salaries? What could explain these differences?
3. Do the data include the value of stock options? What are the implications of this?
4. Read the job descriptions. Are they accurate descriptions for jobs that you would be applying for? Why or why not? Are there jobs for which you cannot find an appropriate match? Why do you think this is the case?
5. Check out pay levels for these types of jobs in your school's career office. How does the pay for jobs advertised in your career office differ from the pay levels on salary.com? Why do you think these differences exist?
6. How could you use this information while negotiating your salary in your job after graduation? What data would you provide to support your "asking price"? What factors will influence whether or not you get what you ask for?
7. What is the relevant labor market for these jobs? How big are the differences between salaries in different locations?
8. For each job, compare the median salary to the low and high averages. How much variation exists? What factors might explain this variation in pay rates for the same job?
9. Look for a description of how these salary data are developed. Do you think it provides enough information? Why or why not? Discuss some of the factors that might impair the accuracy of these data. What are the implications of using inaccurate salary data for individuals or companies?
10. With this information available for free, why would you bother with consultants' surveys?
11. If you were a manager, how would you justify paying one of your employees either higher or lower than the results shown on this website?

Summary   This chapter has detailed the decisions and techniques in setting pay levels and mix and designing pay structures. Most organizations survey other employers' pay practices to determine the rates competitors pay. An employer using the survey results considers how it wishes to position its total compensation in the market: to lead, to match, or to follow competition. This policy decision may be different for different business units and even for different job groups within a single organization. The policy on competitive position is translated into practice by setting pay-policy lines; they serve as reference points around which pay grades and ranges or bands are designed.

The use of grades and ranges or bands recognizes both external and internal pressures on pay decisions. No single "going rate" for a job exists in the market; instead, an array of rates exists. This array results from conditions of demand and supply, variations in the quality of employees, and differences in employer policies and practices. It also reflects the fact that employers differ in the values they attach to the jobs and people. And, very importantly, it reflects differences in the mix of pay forms different companies emphasize.

Internally, the use of ranges is consistent with variations in the discretion in jobs. Some employees will perform better than others; some employees are more experienced than others. Pay ranges permit employers to recognize these differences with pay.

Managers are increasingly interested in broad banding, which offers even greater flexibility than grades and ranges to deal with the continuously changing work assignments required in many successful organizations. Broad banding offers freedom to adapt to changes without requiring approvals but risks self-serving and potentially inequitable decisions on the part of the manager. Recently, the trend has been toward approaches with greater flexibility to adapt to changing conditions. Such flexibility also makes mergers and acquisitions easier and global alignment possible.

Let us step back for a moment to review what has been discussed and preview what is coming. We have examined two strategic components of the total pay model. A concern for internal alignment means that analysis and perhaps descriptions and evaluation are important for achieving a competitive advantage and fair treatment. A concern for external competitiveness requires competitive positioning, survey design and analysis, setting the pay policy line (how much and what forms), and designing grades and ranges or broad bands. The next part of the book is concerned with employee contributions—paying the people who perform the work. This is perhaps the most important part of the book. All that has gone before is a prelude, setting up the pay levels, mix, and structures by which people are to be paid. It is now time to pay the people.

Review Questions

1. Which competitive pay policy would you recommend to an employer? Why? Does it depend on circumstances faced by the employer? Which ones?

2. How would you design a survey for setting pay for welders? How would you design a survey for setting pay for financial managers? Do the issues differ? Will the techniques used and the data collected differ? Why or why not?

3. What factors determine the relevant market for a survey? Why is the definition of the relevant market so important?

4. What do surveys have to do with pay discrimination?

5. Contrast pay ranges and grades with bands. Why would you use either? Does their use assist or hinder the achievement of internal alignment? External competitiveness?

Employee Contributions: Determining Individual Pay

The first two sections of the pay model outlined in Exhibit 1.3 essentially deal with fairness. Alignment, covered in Part 1, is all about internal fairness: describing jobs and determining their worth relative to each other based on content of the jobs and impact on the organization's objectives. Part 2 extended fairness to the external market. It's not enough that jobs within a company are treated fairly in comparison to each other; we also need to look at external competitiveness with similar jobs in other companies. This raises questions of conducting salary surveys, setting pay policies, and arriving at competitive pay levels and equitable pay structures. This third part of the book finally brings people into the pay equation. How do we design a pay system so that individual contributors are rewarded according to their value to the organization?

How much should one employee be paid relative to another when they both hold the same jobs in the same organization? If this question is not answered satisfactorily, all prior efforts to evaluate and price jobs may have been in vain. For example, the compensation manager determines that all customer service representatives (CSRs) should be paid between $28,000 and $43,000. But where in that range is each individual paid? Should a good CSR be paid more than a poor one? If the answer is yes, how should performance be measured and what should be the differential reward? Similarly, should the CSR with more years of experience (i.e., higher seniority) be paid more than one with less time on the job? Again, if the answer is yes, what is the tradeoff between seniority and performance in assigning pay raises? Should Brian, the compensation manager's son-in-law, be paid more simply because he is family? What is a legitimate factor to consider in the reward equation? As Exhibit III.1 suggests, all of these questions involve the concept of employee contribution. For the next three chapters we will be discussing different facets of employee contribution.

Chapter 9 asks whether companies should invest in pay-for-performance plans. In other words, does paying for performance result in higher performance? The answer may seem obvious, but there are many ways to complicate this elegant notion.

Chapter 10 looks at actual pay-for-performance plans. The compensation arena is full of programs that promise to link pay and performance. We identify these plans and discuss their relative advantages and disadvantages.

Chapter 11 acknowledges that performance can't always be measured objectively. What do we do to ensure that subjective appraisal procedures are as free from error as possible? Much progress has been made here, and we provide a tour of the different strategies for measuring performance.

EXHIBIT III.1   The Pay Model

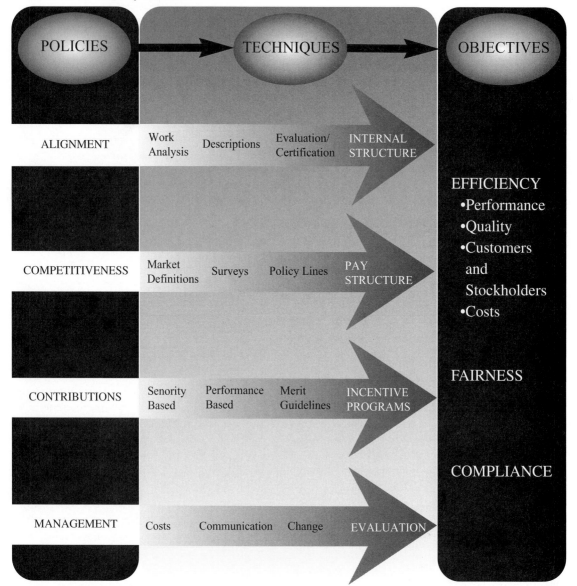

Chapter Nine

Pay for Performance: The Evidence

Chapter Outline

What Behaviors Do Employers Care About? Linking Organization Strategy to Compensation and Performance Management

What Does It Take to Get These Behaviors? What Theory and Research Say

What Does It Take to Get These Behaviors? What Compensation People Say

Total Reward System: Besides Money, Other Rewards Influence Behavior!

Does Compensation Motivate Behavior? General Comments

Does Compensation Motivate Behavior? Specific Comments
  Do People Join a Firm because of Pay?
  Do People Stay in a Firm (or Leave) because of Pay?
  Do Employees More Readily Agree to Develop Job Skills because of Pay?
  Do Employees Perform Better on Their Jobs because of Pay?

Designing a Pay-for-Performance Plan
  Efficiency
  Equity/Fairness
  Compliance

Your Turn: Clinton Pharmaceutical

The primary focus of the last part was on determining the worth of jobs, independent of who performed those jobs. Job analysis, job evaluation, and job pricing all have a common theme. They are techniques to identify the value a firm places on its jobs. Now we introduce people into the equation. Now we declare that different people performing the same job may add different value to the organization. Brian is a better programmer than Kelly. Erinn knows more programming languages than Ian. Who should get what?

Entering people into the compensation equation greatly complicates the compensation process. People don't behave like robots. We can't simply tighten a bolt here, oil a joint there (do robots have joints? Do they need oil?), and walk away secure in the knowledge that people will behave in ways that support organizational objectives. Indeed, there is growing evidence that the way we design HR practices, like performance management, strongly affects the way employees perceive the company. The simple (or not so simple, as we will discuss) process of implementing a performance appraisal system that employees find acceptable goes a long way toward increasing trust for top management.[1] So as we discuss pay and performance in Chapters 9 to 11, remember that there are other important outcomes that also depend on building good performance measurement tools.

In Chapter 1 we talked about compensation objectives complementing overall human resource objectives and both of these helping an organization achieve its overall strategic objectives. But this begs the question, "How does an organization achieve its overall strategic objectives?" In this part of the book we argue that organizational success ultimately depends on human behavior. Our compensation decisions and practices should be designed to increase the likelihood that employees will behave in ways that help the organization achieve its strategic objectives. This chapter is organized around employee behaviors. First, we identify the four kinds of behaviors organizations are interested in. Then we note what theories say about our ability to motivate these behaviors. And, finally, we talk about our success, and sometimes lack thereof, in designing compensation systems to elicit these behaviors.

WHAT BEHAVIORS DO EMPLOYERS CARE ABOUT? LINKING ORGANIZATION STRATEGY TO COMPENSATION AND PERFORMANCE MANAGEMENT

The simple answer is that employers want employees to perform in ways that lead to better organizational performance. Our focus in this chapter, then, is on employee performance. There is growing evidence that employee performance depends on three general factors:[2]

$$\text{Employee performance} = f\,(SKM)$$

where

S = skill and ability to perform task

K = knowledge of facts, rules, principles, and procedures

M = motivation to perform

Let's use an example from baseball to illustrate what this equation says. When Barry Bonds attempts to hit a pitched ball, his performance depends on three things: (1) his physical ability (including vision) to master the coordination and strength requirements of hitting a pitch coming at approximately 90 mph, (2) his knowledge of the necessary mechanics, and, (3) his motivation. Wanting to succeed isn't enough. Having the ability without the desire to train also isn't enough. The same thing is true in more traditional jobs. For an organization to succeed, it needs employees who perform well. As we noted in Chapter 2, this involves not only good compensation strategy and practice but also

[1]Bonnie G. Mani, "Performance Appraisal Systems, Productivity, and Motivation: A Case Study," *Public Personnel Management* 31(2) (2000) pp.141–159; R. Mayer & J. Davis, "The Effect of the Performance Appraisal System on Trust for Management," *Journal of Applied Psychology* 84(1) (1999), pp. 123–136.
[2]Rodney A. McCloy, John P. Campbell and Robert Cuedeck, "A Confirmatory Test of a Model of Performance Determinants," *Journal of Applied Psychology* 79(4) (1994), pp. 493–505.

other well-developed HR practices.[3] We need to hire people with skill and ability (*S*). We need to make sure the good employees (high *S*) stay with the company. If we can succeed at these first two things, we can then concentrate on building further knowledge and skills (*K* and *S*). And, finally, we need to find ways to motivate (*M*) employees to perform well on their jobs—to take their knowledge and abilities and apply them in ways that contribute to organizational performance.

The oil that lubricates this HR engine (e-mail the authors if you agree this is a horrible metaphor) is performance measurement and performance management. We need to accurately measure performance to tell if our HR efforts are working. We can't tell if we select good employees if we don't know how to measure what constitutes *good.* We can't tell if employees are building the kinds of knowledge base they need if we can't measure knowledge accumulation. We can't reward performance if we can't measure it! As a simple example, think about companies where piece-rate systems are used to pay people. Why do many sales jobs use commissions (a form of piece rate) as the primary compensation vehicle? Conventional wisdom has always been that it is are relatively easy to measure performance in sales jobs—just measure the dollar sales generated by salespeople if you want to know how well each of them is doing. There is little ambiguity in the measure of performance, and this makes it easy to create a strong link between units of performance and amount of compensation. One of the biggest recent advances in compensation strategy has been to document and extend this link between ease of measuring performance and the type of compensation system that works best.

Let's take a minute to talk about each of the cells in Exhibit 9.1: They help explain why incentives work in some situations and not in others.[4] The columns in Exhibit 9.1 divide companies into those with widely variable performance from year to year and those with much more stable performance across time. What might cause wide swings in corporate performance? Often this occurs when something in the corporation's external environment fluctuates widely too (e.g., exchange rates with a major foreign customer, raw material costs). It probably wouldn't be fair, and employees would certainly object, if a large part of pay were incentive-based in this kind of environment. Things the employees don't control (in the external environment) would be dictating a big part of pay. Lack of employee control translates into perceptions of unfair treatment. Cells B and D both suggest that a low-incentive component is appropriate in organizations with highly variable annual performance. Conversely, as cells A and C indicate, larger-incentive components are appropriate in companies with stable annual performance.

The rows in Exhibit 9.1 note that individual employee performance also can vary. Some jobs are fairly stable, with expectations fairly consistent across time. What I do

[3]Sara L Rynes, Kenneth G Brown, and Amy E. Colbert, "Seven Common Misconceptions about Human Resource Practices: Research Findings versus Practitioner Beliefs,".*Academy of Management Executive* 16(3) (2002), pp. 92–102; Brian Becker and Barry Gerhart, "The Impact of Human Resource Management on Organizational Performance: Progress and Propsects," *Academy of Management Journal* 39(4) (1996), pp. 779–801.

[4]This table extrapolates the findings from two studies: Matthew C. Bloom & George T. Milkovich, "The Relationship among Risk, Incentive Pay, and Organizational Performance," *Academy of Management Journal* 14(3) (1998), pp. 283–297; Anne Tsui, Jone L. Pearce, Lyman W. Porter, and Angela M. Tripoli, "Alternative Approaches to the Employee-Organization Relationship: Does Investment in Employees Pay Off?" *Academy of Management Journal* 40(5) (1997), pp. 1089–1121.

EXHIBIT 9.1 **Performance Measurement Relates to Compensation Strategy**

		Variability in Organizational Performance	
		Low variability: Few swings in overall corporate performance	*High variability: Regular and large swings in overall Corporate Performance*
Variability/ease of measurement in individual performance	*Unstable, unclear, and changing objectives*	Cell A—provide wide range of rewards beyond just money. Include significant incentive component.	Cell B—provide wide range of rewards beyond just money. Emphasize base pay with low-incentive portion.
	Stable and easily measured	Cell C—emphasize monetary rewards with large-incentive component.	Cell D—emphasize monetary rewards: large base pay with low-incentive portion.

today is basically the same thing I did yesterday. And tomorrow looks like a repeat too! In other jobs, though, there might be high fluctuation in the kinds of things expected of employees, and employees willing to be flexible and adjust to changing demand are much in demand for these jobs. Here using incentive pay exclusively might not work. Incentive systems are notorious for getting people to do exactly what is being incentivized. Pay me big money to sell suits, and that's just what I'm going to do. You want me to handle customer returns too? No way, not unless the compensation system rewards a broader array of duties. Evidence suggests that companies are best able to get employees to adjust, be flexible, and show commitment when a broader array of rewards, rather than just money, is part of the compensation package.[5] For example, why does Lincoln Electric out-produce other companies in the same industry year after year? Normally we think it's because the company has a well-designed incentive system that links to level of production. Certainly this is a big factor! But when you talk to people at Lincoln Electric, they suggest that part of the success comes from other forms of reward, including the strong commitment to job security—downsizing simply isn't part of the vocabulary there—that reinforces a willingness to try new technologies and new work processes. Cell A describes the kind of reward package that fits the job and organizational performance characteristics.

When we distill all of this, what can we conclude? We think the response depends on how we answer the following four questions:

1. How do we get good employment prospects to *join* our company?
2. How do we *retain* these good employees once they join?
3. How do we get employees to *develop skills* for current and future jobs?
4. How do we get employees to *perform well* while they are here?

[5]Anne Tsui, Jone L. Pearce, Lyman W. Porter, and Angela M. Tripoli, "Alternative Approaches to the Employee-Organization Relationship: Does Investment in Employees Pay Off?" *Academy of Management Journal* 40(5) (1997), pp. 1089–1121.

First, how do we get good people to join our company? How did Nike get Tiger Woods to serve as a corporate spokesperson? Part of the answer is rumored to be cold hard cash, estimated to be in excess of $100 million today. Even when the decision doesn't involve millions of dollars, the long-run success of any company depends on getting good people to accept employment. And the compensation challenge is to figure out what components of our compensation package are likely to influence this decision to join.

Second, the obvious complement to the decision to join is the decision to stay. How do we retain employees? It doesn't do much good to attract exceptional employees to our company only to lose them a short time later. Once our compensation practices get a good employee in the door, we need to figure out ways to ensure it's not a revolving door.

Third, we also must recognize, that what we need employees to do today may change, literally, overnight. A fast-changing world requires employees who can adjust more quickly. How do we get employees, traditionally resistant to change, to willingly develop skills today that may not be vital on the current job but are forecast to be critical as the company's strategic plan adjusts to change? Another compensation challenge!

Finally, we want employees to do well on their current jobs. This means performing, and performing well, tasks that support our strategic objectives. What motivates employees to succeed? The compensation challenge is to design rewards that enhance job performance.

WHAT DOES IT TAKE TO GET THESE BEHAVIORS? WHAT THEORY AND RESEARCH SAY

Another way of phrasing these same questions is to ask, "What motivates employees?" If you know the right answer, you're way ahead of the so-called experts. In the simplest sense, *motivation* involves three elements: (1) what's important to a person, and (2) offering it in exchange for some (3) desired behavior. As to the first element, what's important to employees, data suggest employees prefer pay systems that are influenced by individual performance, changes in cost of living, seniority, and the market rate, to name the most important factors.[6] To narrow down specific employee preferences, though, there has been some exciting new work on what's important to employees. The new idea is called *cafeteria-style* or *flexible compensation*—a takeoff on cafeteria-style benefits, to be described further when we talk about employee benefits in Chapters 12 and 13. Cafeteria-style compensation is based on the idea that only the individual employee knows what package of rewards would best suit personal needs. Employees who hate risk could opt for more base pay and less incentive pay. Tradeoffs between pay and benefits could also be selected. The key ingredient in this new concept is careful cost analysis to make sure the dollar cost of the package an employee selects meets employer budgetary limits.[7]

In Exhibit 9.2 we briefly summarize some of the important motivation theories. Pay particular attention to the "So What?" column, in which we talk about the implications for employee behavior.

[6]A. Mamman, M. Sulaiman, and A. Fadel, "Attitude to Pay Systems: An Exploratory Study within and across Cultures," *International Journal of Human Resource Management* 7(1) (February 1996), pp. 101–121.

[7]IOMA, "Are You Ready to Serve Cafeteria Style Comp?" *Pay for Performance Report,* June 2000, pp. 1, 13.

EXHIBIT 9.2 Motivation Theories

Theory	Essential Features	Predictions about Performance-Based Pay	So What?
Maslow's need hierarchy	People are motivated by inner needs. Needs form a hierarchy from most basic (food and shelter) to higher-order (e.g., self-esteem, love, self-actualization). Needs are never fully met; they operate cyclically. Higher-order needs become motivating after lower-order needs have been met. When needs are not met, they become frustrating.	1. Base pay must be set high enough to provide individuals with the economic means to meet their basic living needs. 2. An at-risk program will not be motivating since it restricts employees' ability to meet lower-order needs. 3. Success-sharing plans may be motivating to the extent they help employees pursue higher-order needs.	A. Performance-based pay may be demotivating if it impinges upon employees' capacity to meet daily living needs. B. Incentive pay is motivating to the extent it is attached to achievement, recognition, or approval.
Herzberg's two-factor theory	Employees are motivated by two types of motivators: hygiene factors and satisfiers. Hygiene, or maintenance, factors in their absence prevent behaviors, but in their presence cannot motivate performance. They are related to basic living needs, security, and fair treatment. Satisfiers, such as recognition, promotion, and achievement, motivate performance.	1. Base pay must be set high enough to provide individuals with the economic means to meet hygiene needs, but it cannot motivate performance. 2. Performance is obtained through rewards—payments in excess of that required to meet basic needs. 3. Performance-based pay is motivating to the extent it is connected with meeting employees' needs for recognition, pleasure attainment, achievement, and the like. 4. Other factors such as interpersonal atmosphere, responsibility, type of work, and working conditions influence the efficacy of performance-based pay.	A. Pay level is important—must meet minimum requirements before performance-based pay can operate as motivator. B. Security plans will induce minimum, but not extra, performance. Success-sharing plans will be motivating. At-risk plans will be demotivating. C. Other conditions in the working relationship influence the effectiveness of performance-based pay.

Theory	Essential Features	Predictions about Performance-Based Pay	So What?
Expectancy	Motivation is the product of three perceptions: expectancy, instrumentality, and valence. Expectancy is employees' assessment of their ability to perform required job tasks. Instrumentality is employees' beliefs that requisite job performance will be rewarded by the organization. Valence is the value employees attach to the organization rewards offered for satisfactory job performance.	1. Job tasks and responsibilities should be clearly defined. 2. The pay-performance link is critical. 3. Performance-based pay returns must be large enough to be seen as rewards. 4. People choose the behavior that leads to the greatest reward.	A. Larger incentive payments are better than smaller ones. B. Line of sight is critical—employees must believe they can influence performance targets. C. Employee assessments of their own ability are important—organizations should be aware of training and resource needs required to perform at target levels.
Equity	Employees are motivated when perceived outputs (i.e., pay) are equal to perceived inputs (e.g., effort, work behaviors). A disequilibrium in the output-to-input balance causes discomfort. If employees perceive that others are paid more for the same effort, they will react negatively (e.g., shirk) to correct the output-to-input balance.	1. The pay-performance link is critical; increases in performance must be matched by commensurate increases in pay. 2. Performance inputs and expected outputs must be clearly defined and identified. 3. Employees evaluate the adequacy of their pay via comparisons with other employees.	A. Performance measures must be clearly defined, and employee must be able to affect them through work behaviors. B. If payouts do not match expectations, employees will react negatively. C. Fairness and consistency of performance-based pay across employees in an organization is important. D. Since employees evaluate their pay-effort balance in comparison to other employees, relative pay matters.
Reinforcement	Rewards reinforce (i.e., motivate and sustain) performance. Rewards must follow directly after behaviors to be reinforcing. Behaviors that are not rewarded will be discontinued.	1. Performance-based payments must follow closely behind performance. 2. Rewards must be tightly coupled to desired performance objectives. 3. Withholding payouts can be a way to discourage unwanted behaviors.	A. Timing of payouts is very important.

EXHIBIT 9.2 (*Continued*)

Theory	Essential Features	Predictions about Performance-Based Pay	So What?
Goal setting	Challenging performance goals influence greater intensity and duration in employee performance. Goals serve as feedback standards to which employees can compare their performance. Individuals are motivated to the extent that goal achievement is combined with receiving valued rewards.	1. Performance-based pay must be contingent upon achievement of important performance goals. 2. Performance goals should be challenging and specific. 3. The amount of the incentive reward should match the goal difficulty.	A. Line of-sight is important; employees must believe they can influence performance targets. B. Performance targets should be communicated in terms of specific, difficult goals. C. Feedback about performance is important. D. Performance-based payouts should be contingent upon goal achievement.
Agency	Pay directs and motivates employee performance. Employees prefer static wages (e.g., a salary) to performance-based pay. If performance can be accurately monitored, payments should be based upon satisfactory completion of work duties. If performance cannot be monitored, pay should be aligned with achieving organizational objectives.	1. Performance-based pay must be tightly linked to organizational objectives. 2. Employees dislike risky pay and will demand a wage premium (e.g., higher total pay) in exchange for accepting performance-based pay. 3. Performance-based pay can be used to direct and induce employee performance.	A. Performance-based pay is the optimal compensation choice for more complex jobs where monitoring employees' work is difficult. B. Performance targets should be tied to organizational goals. C. Use of performance-based pay will require higher total pay opportunity.

Some of the theories in Exhibit 9.2 focus on content—identifying what is important to people. Those of Maslow and Herzberg, for example, both fall in this category. People have certain needs, such as physiological, security, and self-esteem, that influence behavior. Although neither theory is clear on how these needs influence behavior, presumably if we offer rewards that satisfy one or more needs, employees will behave in desired ways. These theories often drive compensation decisions about the breadth and depth of compensation offerings. Flexible compensation, with employees choosing from a menu of pay and benefit choices, clearly is driven by the issue of needs. Who best knows what satisfies needs? The employee! So let employees choose, within limits, what they want in their reward package.

A second set of theories, best exemplified by expectancy theory, equity theory, and agency theory, focus less on need states and more on the second element of motivation—the nature of the exchange between a company and its employees. Many of our compensation practices recognize the importance of a fair exchange. We evaluate jobs using a common set of compensable factors (Chapter 5) in part to let employees know that an explicit set of rules governs the evaluation process. We collect salary survey data (Chapter 8) because we want the exchange to be fair compared to external standards. We design incentive systems (Chapter 10) to align employee behavior with the needs of the organization. All of these pay decisions, and more, owe much to understanding how the employment exchange affects employee motivation.

Expectancy theory argues that people behave as if they cognitively evaluate what behaviors are possible (e.g., the probability that they can complete the task) in relation to the value of rewards offered in exchange. According to this theory, we choose behaviors that yield the most satisfactory exchange. Equity theory also focuses on what goes on inside an employee's head. Not surprisingly, equity theory argues that people are highly concerned about equity, or fairness of the exchange process. Employees look at the exchange as a ratio between what is expected and what is received. Some theorists say we judge transactions as fair when others around us don't have a more (or less) favorable balance between the give and get of an exchange.[8] Even greater focus on the exchange process occurs in the last of this second set of theories, agency theory.[9] Here, employees are depicted as agents who enter an exchange with principals—the owners or their designated managers. It is assumed that both sides to the exchange seek the most favorable exchange possible and will act opportunistically if given a chance (e.g., try to "get by" with doing as little as possible to satisfy the contract). Compensation is a major element in this theory, because it is used to keep employees in line: Employers identify important behaviors and important outcomes and pay specifically for achieving desired levels of each. Such incentive systems penalize employees who try to shirk their duties by giving proportionately lower rewards.

[8]J. S. Adams, "Toward an Understanding of Inequity," *Journal of Abnormal and Social Psychology* 67 (1963), pp. 422–436; J. S. Adams, "Injustice in Social Exchange," *Advances in Experimental Social Psychology,* Vol. 2, ed. L. Berkowitz (New York: Academic Press, 1965); R. Cosier and D. Dalton, "Equity Theory and Time: A Reformulation," *Academy of Management Review* 8(1983), pp. 311–319.

[9]B. Oviatt, "Agency and Transaction Cost Perspectives on the Manager-Shareholder Relationship: Incentives for Congruent Interests," *Academy of Management Review* 13 (1988), pp. 214–225.

Finally, at least one of the theories summarized in Exhibit 9.2 focuses on the third element of motivation: desired behavior. Identifying desired behaviors, and goals expected to flow from these behaviors, is the emphasis of a large body of goal-setting research. Most of this research says that how we set goals (the process of goal setting, the level and difficulty of goals, etc.) can influence the performance levels of employees.[10] For example, workers assigned "hard" goals consistently do better than workers told to "do your best."[11]

WHAT DOES IT TAKE TO GET THESE BEHAVIORS? WHAT COMPENSATION PEOPLE SAY

In the past, compensation people didn't ask this question very often. Employees learned what behaviors were important as part of the socialization process or as part of the performance management process.[12] If it was part of the culture to work long hours, you quickly learned this. If your performance appraisal at the end of the year stressed certain types of behaviors, or if your boss said certain things were important to her, then the signals were pretty clear: Do these things! Compensation might have rewarded people for meeting these expectations, but usually the compensation package wasn't designed to be one of the signals about expected performance. Not true today! Now compensation people talk about pay in terms of a neon arrow flashing "Do these things." Progressive companies ask, "What do we want our compensation package to do? How, for example, do we get our product engineers to take more risks?" Compensation is then designed to support this risk-taking behavior. In the next section we begin to talk about the different types of reward components, acknowledging that pay isn't the only reward that influences behavior. The remainder of the chapter looks at pay components and what we know about their effectiveness in motivating desired behaviors.

Cybercomp

The International Society for Performance Improvement has web information on performance journals, strategies for improving performance, and conferences covering the latest research on performance improvement techniques. Go to the Society's website, *www.ispi.org.*

[10]D. Knight, C. Durham, E. A. Locke, " The Relationship of Team Goals, Incentives, and Efficacy to Strategic Risk, Tactical Implementation, and Performance," *Academy of Management Journal* 44(2) (2001) pp 326–338.

[11]E. A. Locke, K. N. Shaw, L. M. Saari, and G. P. Latham, "Goal Setting and Task Performance: 1969–1980," *Psychological Bulletin* 90 (1981), pp. 125–52.

[12]M. R. Louis, B. Z. Posner, and G. N. Powell, "The Availability and Helpfulness of Socialization Practices," *Personnel Psychology* 36 (1983), pp. 857–866; E. H. Schein, "Organizational Socialization and the Profession of Management," *Industrial Management Review* 9 (1968), pp. 1–16.

TOTAL REWARD SYSTEM: BESIDES MONEY, OTHER REWARDS INFLUENCE BEHAVIOR!

Compensation is but one of many rewards that influence employee behavior. Sometimes this important point is missed by compensation experts. Going back at least to Henry Ford, we tend to look at money as the great equalizer. Job boring? No room for advancement? Throw money at the problem! Depending on the survey you consult, workers highly value such other job rewards as empowerment, recognition, and opportunities for advancement.[13] And there is growing sentiment for letting workers choose their own "blend" of rewards from the 13 we note in Exhibit 9.3. We may be overpaying in cash *and* missing the opportunity to let employees construct both a more satisfying and less expensive reward package. Known as cafeteria compensation, this idea is based on the notion of different rewards having different dollar costs associated with them. Armed with a fixed sum of money, employees move down the line, buying more or less of the 13 rewards as their needs dictate.[14] While widespread use of this type of system may be a long time in the future, the cafeteria approach still underscores the need for integration of rewards in compensation design.

If we don't think about the presence or absence of rewards other than money in an organization, we may find the compensation process producing unintended consequences.

EXHIBIT 9.3
Components of a Total Reward System

1. Compensation	Wages, commissions, and bonuses
2. Benefits	Vacations, health insurance
3. Social interaction	Friendly workplace
4. Security	Stable, consistent position and rewards
5. Status/recognition	Respect, prominence due to work
6. Work variety	Opportunity to experience different things
7. Workload	Right amount of work (not too much, not too little)
8. Work importance	Is work valued by society
9. Authority/control/autonomy	Ability to influence others; control own destiny
10. Advancement	Chance to get ahead
11. Feedback	Receive information helping to improve performance
12. Work conditions	Hazard free
13. Development opportunity	Formal and informal training to learn new knowledge skills/abilities

[13]IOMA, "Pay for Performance Report," *Pay for Performance Report,* January 1998, p. 8; P. Stang and B. Laird, "Working Women's Motivators," reported in *USA Today,* February 9, 1999, p.B1, for Nationwide Insurance/Working Women Magazine Survey.

[14]J. Tropman, *The Compensation Solution: How to Develop an Employee-Driven Rewards System* (Jossey-Bass: San Francisco, 2001).

Consider the following three examples, which show how compensation decisions have to be integrated with total reward system decisions:

1. This example transports us into a team-based work environment where the culture of the organization strongly supports empowerment of workers. Empowerment is a form of reward. In Exhibit 9.3 we identify the dimensions of empowerment (see item 9) as *authority* to make decisions, some *control* over factors that influence outcomes, and the *autonomy* to carry out decisions without overregulation by upper management. Some people find empowerment a very positive inducement, making coming to work each day a pleasure. Others may view empowerment as just added responsibility— legitimizing demands for more pay. In the first case, adding extra compensation may not be necessary. Some have even argued it can lessen motivation.[15] In the second case, extra compensation may be a necessity. Is it any wonder that companies are having trouble finding *one* right answer to the team compensation question.

2. This example comes from airline industry leader Southwest Airlines.[16] Southwest Airlines promotes a business culture of fun and encourages employees to find ways to make their jobs more interesting and relevant to them personally. All this is accomplished without using incentives as a major source of competitive advantage.

3. This example illustrates the relationship between the different forms of compensation and another of the general rewards listed in Exhibit 9.3: security. Normally, we think of security in terms of job security. Drastic reductions in middle-management layers during the downsizing decade of the 1980s increased employee concerns about job security and probably elevated the importance of this reward to employees today. For example, there is evidence that compensation at risk leaves employees less satisfied both with their pay level and with the process used to determine pay.[17] Security as an issue is creeping into the domain of compensation. It used to be fairly well established that employees would make more this year than they did last year, and employees counted on such *security* to plan their purchases and other economic decisions. The trend today is toward less stable and less secure compensation packages. The very design of compensation systems today contributes to instability and insecurity. Exhibit 9.4 outlines the different types of wage components.

Notice that Exhibit 9.4 generally orders compensation components from least risky to most risky for employees. We define risky in terms of stability of income, or the ability to accurately predict income level from year to year. Base pay is, at least as far as there are any guarantees, the guaranteed portion of income, as long as employees remain employed. There have been very few years since the Depression when base wages did not rise, or at least stay the same.[18] The next seven components are distinguished by increasing levels of uncertainty for employees. In fact, risk-sharing plans actually include a provision for cuts in base pay that are only recaptured in years when the organization meets performance objectives.

[15]E. L. Deci and R. M. Ryan, *Intrinsic Motivation and Self-Determination in Human Behavior* (New York: Plenum Press, 1985). Note, however, that the evidence is not very strong.

[16]N. Stein, "America's Most Admired Companies," *Fortune,* March. 3, 2003, pp. 81–87; J. Pfeffer, "Six Dangerous Myths about Pay" *Harvard Business Review,* May–June 1998, pp. 109–119.

[17]K. Brown and V. Huber, "Lowering Floors and Raising Ceilings: A Longitudinal Assessment of the Effects of an Earnings-at-Risk Plan on Pay Satisfaction," *Personnel Psychology* 45 (1992), pp. 279–311.

[18]Please note, though, most of the declines experienced in base pay have occurred since 1980.

EXHIBIT 9.4 Wage Components

Wage Component	Definition	Level of Risk to Employee
Base pay _least_	The guaranteed portion of an employee's wage package.	As long as employment continues, this is the secure portion of wages.
Across the board	Wage increase granted to all employees, regardless of performance. Size related to some subjective assessment of employer about ability to pay. Typically an add-on to base pay in subsequent years.	Some risk to employee since at discretion of employer. But not tied to performance differences, so risk lower in that respect.
Cost-of-living increase	Same as across-the-board increase, except magnitude based on change in cost of living (e.g., as measured by CPI).	Same as-across-the-board increases.
Merit pay	Wage increase granted to employee as function of some assessment of employee performance. Adds on to base pay in subsequent years.	Two types of risk faced by employees. Size of total merit pool at discretion of employer (risk element), and individual portion of pool depends on performance, which also is not totally predictable.
Lump-sum bonus	As with merit pay, granted for individual performance. Does not add into base pay, but is distributed as a one-time bonus.	Three types of risks faced here. Both types mentioned under merit pay, plus not added into base—requires annually "re-earning" the added pay.
Individual incentive	Sometimes this variable pay is an-add on to a fixed base pay. The incentive component ties increments in compensation directly to extra individual production (e.g., commission systems, piece rate). While measures of performance are typically subjective with merit and lump-sump components, this form of variable pay differs because measures of performance are objective (e.g., sales volume).	Most risk compensation component if sole element of pay, but often combined with a base pay. No or low fixed base pay means each year employee is dependent upon number of units of performance to determine pay.
Success-sharing plans	A generic category of pay add-on (variable pay) which is tied to some measure of group performance, not individual performance. Not added into base pay. Distinguished from risk-sharing plans, below, because employees share in any success—performance above standard—but are not penalized for performance below standard.	All success-sharing plans have risks noted in above pay components plus the risk associated with group performance measures. Now individual worker is also dependent upon the performance of others included in the group.

EXHIBIT 9.4 *(Continued)*

Wage Component	Definition	Level of Risk to Employee
• Gain sharing	Differs from profit sharing in that goal to exceed is not financial performance of organization but some cost index (e.g., labor cost is most common, might also include scrap costs, utility costs).	Less risk to individual than profit sharing because performance measure is more controllable.
• Profit sharing	Add-on linked to group performance (team, division, total company) relative to exceeding some financial goal.	Profit measures are influenced by factors beyond employee control (e.g., economic climate, accounting write-offs). Less control means more risk.
Risk Sharing Plans	Generic category of pay add-on (variable pay) that differs from success sharing in that employee not only shares in the successes but also is penalized during poor performance years. Penalty is in form of lower total compensation in poor corporate performance years. Reward, though, is typically higher than that for success-sharing programs in high performance years.	Greater risk than success-sharing plans. Typically, employees absorb a "temporary" cut in base pay. If performance targets are met, this cut is neutralized by one component of variable pay. Risk to employee is increased, though because even base pay is no longer totally predictable.

All of this discussion of risk is only an exercise in intellectual gymnastics unless we add one further observation: Over the last several decades, companies have been moving more toward compensation programs higher on the risk continuum. New forms of pay are less entitlement-oriented and more linked to the uncertainties of individual, group, and corporate performance.[19] Employees increasingly are expected to bear a share of the risks that businesses have solely born in the past. It's not entirely clear what impact this shifting of risk will have in the long run, but some authors are already voicing concerns that efforts to build employee loyalty and commitment may be an early casualty of these new pay systems.[20] Some research suggests that employees may need a risk premium (higher pay) to stay and perform in a company with pay at risk.[21] Even a premium might not work for employees who are particularly risk-averse. Security-driven employees actually might accept lower wages if they come in a package that is more stable.[22] To explore what impact these new forms of pay have, the remainder of this chapter summarizes what we know about the ability of different compensation components to motivate the four general behaviors we noted earlier.

[19]J. R. Schuster and P. K. Zingheim, *The New Pay: Linking Employee and Organizational Performance* (New York: Lexington Books, 1992).

[20]E. J. Conlon and J. M. Parks, "Effects of Monitoring and Tradition on Compensation Arrangements: An Experiment with Principal-Agent Dyads," *Academy of Management Journal* 33 (1990), pp. 603–622.

[21]Conlon and Parks, "Effects of Monitoring and Tradition."

[22]D. M. Cable, and T. A. Judge, "Pay Preferences and Job Search Decisions: A Person-Organization Fit Perspective," *Personnel Psychology* 47 (1994), pp. 317–348.

DOES COMPENSATION MOTIVATE BEHAVIOR? GENERAL COMMENTS

Although there are exceptions, a well-designed plan linking pay to behaviors of employees generally results in better individual and organizational performance.[23] One particularly good study looked at the HR practices of over 3,000 companies.[24] One set of questions asked, (1) Did the company have a formal appraisal process, (2) was the appraisal tied to the size of pay increases, and (3) did performance influence who would be promoted? Organizations significantly above the mean (by one standard deviation) on these and other "high-performance work practices" had annual sales that averaged $27,000 more per employee. So rewarding employees for performance pays off.

In a more comprehensive review, Heneman reports that 40 of 42 studies looking at merit pay claim performance increases when pay is tied to performance.[25] One study of 841 union and nonunion companies found gain-sharing and profit-sharing plans (both designed to link pay to performance) increased individual and team performance 18 to 20 percent.[26] How, though, does this translate into corporate performance? A review of 26 studies gives high marks to profit-sharing plans: Organizations with such plans had 3.5 to 5 percent higher annual performance.[27] Gerhart and Milkovich took the performance-based pay question one step further. Across 200 companies they found a 1.5 percent increase in return on assets for every 10 percent increase in the size of a bonus.[28] Further, they found that the variable portion of pay had a stronger impact on individual and corporate performance than did the level of base pay.

> **Cybercomp**
> IOMA is the Institute of Management and Administration. It specializes in finding studies from a wide variety of places that discuss different aspects of pay for performance. The index for IOMA's website is at *www.ioma.com/newsletters/pfp/index.shtml.*

[23]R. L. Heneman, *Strategic Reward Management: Design, Implementation, and Evaluation* (Greenwich, CT: Information Age Publishing, 2002); W. N. Cooke, "Employee Participation Programs, Group Based Incentives, and Company Performance," *Industrial and Labor Relations Review* 47 (1994), pp. 594–610; G. W. Florkowski, "The Organizational Impact of Profit Sharing," *Academy of Management Review* 12 (1987), pp. 622–636; R. Heneman, *Merit Pay: Linking Pay Increases to Performance Ratings* (Reading, MA: Addison-Wesley, 1992); J. L. McAdams and E. J. Hawk, *Organizational Performance and Rewards* (Phoenix, AZ: American Compensation Association, 1994); D. McDonaly and A. Smith, "A Proven Connection: Performance Management and Business Results," *Compensation and Benefits Review,* January–February 1995, pp. 59–64; G. T. Milkovich, "Does Performance-Based Pay Really Work? Conclusions Based on the Scientific Research," unpublished document for 3M, 1994; G. Milkovich and C. Milkovich, "Strengthening the Pay Performance Relationship: The Research," *Compensation and Benefits Review* May–June 1992, pp. 53–62.

[24]Mark A. Huselid, "The Impact of Human Resource Management Practices on Turnover, Productivity, and Corporate Financial Performance," *Academy of Management Journal,* 38(3) (1995), pp. 635–672.

[25]Heneman, *Merit Pay.*

[26]Cooke, "Employee Participation Programs."

[27]D. L. Kruse, *Profit Sharing: Does It Make a Difference?* (Kalamazoo, MI: Upjohn Institute, 1993).

[28]B. Gerhart and G. Milkovich, "Organizational Differences in Managerial Compensation and Financial Performance," *Academy of Management Journal* 33 (1990), pp. 663–690.

DOES COMPENSATION MOTIVATE BEHAVIOR? SPECIFIC COMMENTS

This section looks at the role of compensation in motivating the four types of behavior outlined earlier: the decision to join, to stay, to develop skills, and to perform well.

Do People Join a Firm because of Pay?

Level of pay and pay system characteristics influence a job candidate's decision to join a firm, but this shouldn't be too surprising.[29] Pay is one of the more visible rewards in the whole recruitment process. Job offers spell out the level of compensation and may even include discussions about the kind of pay such as bonuses and profit-sharing participation. Less common are statements such as "You'll get plenty of work variety," or "Don't worry about empowerment," or "The workload isn't too heavy." These other rewards are subjective and tend to require actual time on the job before we can decide if they are positive or negative features of the job. Not so for pay. Being perceived as more objective, it's more easily communicated in the employment offer.

Recent research suggests job candidates look for organizations with reward systems that fit their personalities.[30] Below we outline some of the ways that "fit" is important.

Person Characteristics	Preferred Reward Characteristics
Materialistic	Relatively more concerned about pay level[31]
Low self-esteem	Want large, decentralized organization with little pay for performance[32]
Risk takers	Want more pay based on performance[33]
Risk averse	Want less performance-based pay[34]
Individualists ("I control my destiny")	Want pay plans based on individual performance, not group performance[35]

[29]S. L. Rynes, K. G. Brown, & A. E. Colbert, "Seven Common Misconceptions about Human Resource Practices: Research Findings versus Practitioner Beliefs," *Academy of Management Executive,* 16(2) (2002), pp. 92–103; E. E. Lawler, *Pay and Organizational Effectiveness: A Psychological View* (New York: McGraw-Hill, 1971); E. E. Lawler and G. D. Jenkins, "Strategic Reward Systems" in *Handbook of Industrial and Organizational Psychology,* eds. M. D. Dunnette and L. M. Hough (Palo Alto, CA: Consulting Psychologist Press, 1992), pp. 1009–1055; W. Mobley, *Employee Turnover: Causes, Consequences and Control* (Reading, MA: Addison-Wesley, 1982).

[30]D. M. Cable and T. A. Judge, "Pay Preferences and Job Search Decisions: A Person-Organization Fit Perspective," *Personnel Psychology* 47 (1994), pp. 317–348.

[31]Ibid.

[32]D. B. Turban and T. L. Keon, "Organizational Attractiveness: An Interactionist Perspective," *Journal of Applied Psychology* 78 (1993), pp. 184–193.

[33]Cable and Judge, "Pay Preferences"; A. Kohn, *Punished by Rewards: The Trouble with Gold Stars, Incentive Plans, A's, Praise and Other Bribes* (Boston: Houghton-Mifflin, 1993).

[34]Cable & Judge, "Pay Preferences."

[35]Cable and Judge, "Pay Preferences."

None of these relationships is particularly surprising. People are attracted to organizations that fit their personalities. Evidence suggests talented employees are attracted to companies that have strong links between pay and performance.[36]

It's not a big jump, then, to suggest organizations should design their reward systems to attract people with desired personalities and values. For example, if we need risk takers, maybe we should design reward systems that have elements of risk built into them.

Do People Stay in a Firm (or Leave) because of Pay?

There is clear evidence that poor performers are more likely to leave an organization than are good performers.[37] How does pay affect this relationship? Much of the equity theory research in the 1970s documented that workers who feel unfairly treated in pay react by leaving the firm for greener pastures.[38] This is particularly true under incentive conditions. Turnover is much higher for poor performers when pay is based on individual performance (a good outcome!). Conversely, group incentive plans may lead to more turnover of better performers—clearly an undesirable outcome. When AT&T shifted from individual to team-based incentives a number of years ago, star performers either reduced their output or quit. Out of 208 above-average performers, only one continued to report performance increases under the group incentive plan. The rest felt cheated because the incentives for higher individual performance were now spread across all group members.[39]

Clearly, pay can be a factor in decisions to stay or leave. Data suggest dissatisfaction with pay can be a key factor in turnovers.[40] Too little pay triggers feelings of unfair treatment. Result? Turnover. Supporting this, pay that employees find reasonable can help reduce turnover.[41] Even the way we pay has an impact on turnover. Evidence suggests that some employees are uncomfortable with pay systems that put any substantial future earnings at risk or pay systems that link less to personal effort and more to group effort.[42] We need to make sure, as one critic has noted, that we don't let our design of new reward systems rupture our relationships with existing employees.[43] Recent efforts to use different

---

[36]T. R. Zenger, "Why Do Employers Only Reward Extreme Performance? Examining the Relationships among Performance Pay and Turnover," *Administrative Science Quarterly* 37 (1992), pp. 198–219.

[37]Chi-Sum Wong and Kenneth Law, 2002, "The Effects of Leader and Follower Emotional Intelligence on Performance and Attitude: An Exploratory Study," *Leadership Quarterly* 13(3) (2002), pp. 243–274; David A. Harrison, Meghna Virick, and Sonja William, "Working without a Net: Time, Performance, and Turnover under Maximally Contingent Rewards," *Journal of Applied Psychology* 81(4) (1996), pp. 331–345.

[38]M. R. Carrell and J. E. Dettrich, "Employee Perceptions of Fair Treatment," *Personnel Journal* 55 (1976), pp. 523–524.

[39]A. Weiss, "Incentives and Worker Behavior: Some Evidence" in *Incentives, Cooperation and Risk Sharing,* ed. H. R. Nalbantian (Totowa, NJ: Rowan & Littlefield, 1987), pp. 137–150.

[40]Susan Warren, "The Transient Workers," *Wall Street Journal,* October 28, 2002, R4; R Heneman and T. Judge, "Compensation Attitudes: A Review and Recommendations for Future Research," in *Compensation in Organizations: Progress and Prospects,* eds. S. L. Rynes and B. Gerhart (San Francisco: New Lexington Press, 1999).

[41]P. W. Hom and R. W. Griffeth, *Employee Turnover* (Cincinnati: Southwestern, 1995); M. Kim, "Where the Grass Is Greener: Voluntary Turnover and Wage Premiums," *Industrial Relations,* 38 (October 1999), p. 584.

[42]D. M. Cable and T. A. Judge, "Pay Preferences and Job Search Decisions: A Person-Organization Fit Perspective," *Personnel Psychology* 47 (1994), pp. 317–348.

[43]Kohn, *Punished by Rewards.*

types of compensation as a tool for retaining workers have focused on what is called *scarce talent*. For example, information technology employees have been scarce for much of the past decade, at least. One way to retain these workers is to develop a variable-pay component for each project. For example, reports of variable pay linked to individual length of stay on a project, to peer ratings, and to project results suggest that this pay-for-performance combination may appeal to scarce talent.[44]

The next time you go into an Applebee's restaurant, think about how the company uses compensation to reduce turnover. In an industry where manager turnover hovers around 50 percent, Applebee's allows general managers to earn as much as $30,000 above base salary for hitting sales, profitability, and customer satisfaction targets. To discourage turnover, this extra compensation is deferred for two years.[45]

Besides money, other rewards also influence the decision to stay (retention) in a firm. According to one recent study, the rewards that "work" to help retain employees in the tough economic times we face heading into the middle of this decade are as follows:[46]

Type of Reward	Percent Who Think It's Important in Retention
1. Work variety and challenge	50
2. Development opportunity	38
3. Social	40
4. Status recognition	23
5. Work importance	20
6. Benefits	22

In the early 2000s we are experiencing another form of turnover problem: key employees leaving companies because the firms appear financially troubled. The airline industry, in particular, has been hurt badly by 9/11, increased terrorism in general, and rising fuel prices. How does a company keep key personnel when the dangers of job loss are very real? One answer is to adopt "stay bonuses." These are generally lump-sum or installment bonuses designed specifically to retain key employees during and after a Chapter 11 restructuring. These bonuses can be as large as 50 to 75 percent of salary for CEOs, dropping down to 25 percent for middle-level managers and below.[47]

[44]P. Zingheim and J. R. Shuster, *Pay People Right* (San Francisco: Jossey-Bass, 2000); J. Boudreau, M. Sturman, C. Trevor, and B. Gerhart, "Is It Worth It to Win the Talent War? Using Turnover Research to Evaluate the Utility of Performance-Based Pay," Working Paper 99–06, Center for Advanced Human Resource Studies, Cornell University, 2000.

[45]Allison Perlik, "Payback Time," *Restaurants and Institutions,* Chicago, January 15, 2003, pp. 22–29.

[46]IOMA, "Top-Notch Retention Strategies for These Tight-Money Times," *Pay for Performance Report,* December 2002, p. 2.

[47]Claudia Z. Poster, "Retaining Key People in Troubled Companies," *Compensation and Benefits Review,* January–February 2002, pp. 7–11.

Do Employees More Readily Agree to Develop Job Skills because of Pay?

We don't know the answer to this question. Skill-based pay (Chapter 6) is intended, at least partially, to pay employees for learning new skills—skills that hopefully will help employees perform better on current jobs and adjust more rapidly to demands on future jobs. Whether this promise is fulfilled is unclear. Evidence is starting to accumulate that pay for skill may not increase productivity but does focus people on believing in the importance of quality and in turning out significantly higher quality products.[48]

Do Employees Perform Better on Their Jobs because of Pay?

Recent critics, led by Alfie Kohn, argue that incentives are both morally and practically wrong.[49] The moral argument suggests that incentives are flawed because they involve one person controlling another. The counterargument to this notes that employment is a reciprocal arrangement. In periods of low unemployment especially, workers can choose whether they want to work under compensation systems with strong pay-to-performance linkages (as in the case of incentive systems). Perhaps Kohn's greatest contribution is in magnifying a glaring research gap: We really don't have very good data about whether the presence of incentive systems affects people's interest in being recruited or, if already employed, willingness to stay under such incentive conditions. The controversy stirred by Kohn and others may direct studies in this area.

Kohn also suggests that incentive systems can actually harm productivity, a decidedly negative practical outcome. His rationale is based on cites of mostly laboratory studies where subjects work in isolation on a task for either pay or no pay. His conclusion, based heavily on the work of Deci and colleagues, is that rewarding a person for performing a task reduces interest in that task—extrinsic rewards (money) reduce intrinsic rewards (enjoyment of the task for its own sake).[50] Critics of this interpretation point out at least two important flaws in Kohn's conclusions.[51] First, the pragmatics of business demand that some jobs be performed—indeed, many jobs—that aren't the most intrinsically interesting. While Target may be a great store to shop at, spending day after day stocking shelves with towels and other nonbreakables falls far down the intrinsic-interest scale.[52] If it requires incentives to get real-world jobs to be completed and thus to create value for an organization and its consumers, so be it. This may simply be one of the costs of doing business. Second, Kohn's studies frequently looked at people in isolation. In the real world people interact with each other, know who is performing and who isn't, and react to this when rewards are allocated. Without any link to performance, the less motivated employees will eventually recognize that harder work isn't necessary. It quickly becomes evident

---

[48]IOMA, "Report on Salary Surveys," May 1997, p. 14; Kevin J. Parent and Caroline L. Weber, "Does Paying for Knowledge Pay Off?" *Compensation and Benefits Review,* September 1994, pp. 44–50.

[49]Kohn, *Punished by Rewards.*

[50]E. Deci, R. Ryan, and R. Koestner, *"A Meta-Analytic Review of Experiments Examining the Effects of Extrinsic Rewards on Intrinsic Motivation,"* Psychological Bulletin, 125(6), pp. 627–668.

[51]R. McKensie and D. Lee, *Managing through Incentives* New York: Oxford University Press, 1998); R. Eisenberger and J. Cameron, "Detrimental Effects of Rewards," *American Psychologist,* November 1996, pp. 1153–1156.

[52]The second author knows this all too well, based upon the daily whining of his daughter, a short-term Target employee.

that some workers are being paid the same for doing less. Think, for example, of the last time you completed a group project. Were you happy with the team member who did less but received the same grade? Did you think it fairer when you had a teacher who asked for evaluations of all group members' performance and used these data to assign individualized grades (rewards tied to performance). The same situation arises in industry and makes the case for rewards tied to performance at least worthy of examining further.

The first part of this examination perhaps should focus on an obvious but often overlooked question: Do employees think any link at all should be made between pay and performance. Substantial evidence exists that management and workers alike believe pay should be tied to performance. Dyer and colleagues asked 180 managers from 72 different companies to rate nine possible factors in terms of the importance they should receive in determining the size of salary increases.[53] This group believed the most important factor for salary increases should be job performance. Following close behind is a factor that presumably would be picked up in job evaluation (nature of job) and a motivational variable (amount of effort expended).

Other research supports these findings.[54] Both college students and a second group of managers ranked job performance as the most important variable in allocating pay raises. Once we move away from the managerial ranks, though, other groups express a different view of the pay-performance link. The role that performance levels should assume in determining pay increases is less clear-cut for blue-collar workers.[55] As an illustration, consider the frequent opposition to compensation plans that are based on performance (i.e., incentive piece-rate systems). Unionized workers prefer seniority rather than performance as a basis for pay increases.[56] Part of this preference may stem from a distrust of subjective performance measurement systems. Unions ask, "Can management be counted on to be fair?" In contrast, seniority is an objective index for calculating increases. Some evidence also suggests that women might prefer allocation methods not based on performance.[57]

It's probably a good thing that, in general, workers believe pay should be tied to performance, because it appears to help the bottom line (profits). Numerous studies indicate that tying pay to individual performance has a positive impact on employee performance.[58] Unfor-

[53]L. Dyer, D. P. Schwab, and R. D. Theriault, "Managerial Perceptions Regarding Salary Increase Criteria," *Personnel Psychology* 29 (1976), pp. 233–242.

[54]J. Fossum and M. Fitch, "The Effects of Individual and Contextual Attributes on the Sizes of Recommended Salary Increases," *Personnel Psychology* 38 (1985), pp. 587–603.

[55]L. V. Jones and T. E. Jeffrey, "A Quantitative Analysis of Expressed Preferences for Compensation Plans," *Journal of Applied Psychology* 48 (1963), pp. 201–210; Opinion Research Corporation, *Wage Incentives* (Princeton, NJ: Opinion Research Corporation, 1946); Opinion Research Corporation, *Productivity from the Worker's Standpoint* (Princeton, NJ: Opinion Research Corporation, 1949).

[56]D. Koys, T. Keaveny, and R. Allen, "Employment Demographics and Attitudes That Predict Preferences for Alternative Pay Increase Policies," *Journal of Business and Psychology* 4 (1989), pp. 27–47.

[57]B. Major, "Gender, Justice and the Psychology of Entitlement," *Review of Personality and Social Psychology* 7 (1988), pp. 124–148.

[58]IOMA, "Incentive Pay Programs and Results: An Overview," *IOMA,* May 1996, p. 11; G. Green, "Instrumentality Theory of Work Motivation," *Journal of Applied Psychology,* 53 (1965), pp. 1–25; R. D. Pritchard, D. W. Leonard, C. W. Von Bergen, Jr., and R. J. Kirk, "The Effects of Varying Schedules of Reinforcement on Human Task Performance," *Organizational Behavior and Human Performance* 16 (1976), pp. 205–230; D. P. Schwab and L. Dyer, "The Motivational Impact of a Compensation System on Employee Performance," *Organizational Behavior and Human Performance* 9 (1973), pp. 215–225; D. Schwab, "Impact of Alternative Compensation Systems on Pay Valence and Instrumentality Perceptions," *Journal of Applied Psychology* 58 (1973), pp. 308–312.

tunately, many of these studies are flawed. In one particularly thorough review of merit pay and performance, Heneman concluded that there are very few good scientific studies to help answer the question, "Can we increase performance of individuals by tying it to pay?"[59] Perhaps in answer to this challenge, one recent study of over 3,000 companies provided convincing evidence that linking pay to performance has a positive impact on the bottom line. Over a five-year period such practices can increase per-employee sales by as much as $100,000.[60]

When we move away from individuals and look at the impact of pay on group performance, the evidence is somewhat clearer. Pay matters! A number of recent studies provide strong evidence that pay for performance has a direct and, at times, substantial impact on firm performance. Those that pay for performance have stronger corporate earnings.[61] Companies like Corning, Nucor Steel and PepsiCo all strongly support variable pay based on group performance (usually the group is all employees in the organization, or some subset). Exhibit 9.5 describes elements of the variable-pay plans at these companies.

Most well-controlled studies on companies that Link part of pay to some measure of corporate or division performance report increases in performance of about 4 to 6 percent per year.[62] In one typical study a utility company placed one division on an experimental

EXHIBIT 9.5
Examples of Group Incentive Plans

Company	Pay Component
Corning	Competitive base pay. Group bonus based on meeting certain quality measures, customer satisfaction measures, and production targets.
Nucor	Plant manager base pay 25 percent below market. Five percent of excess over target goes to bonus. Bonus often equals base pay in amount.
PepsiCo	Competitive base pay. All employees get stock options equal to 10 percent of base pay. Employees share in corporate triumphs and failures as stock prices rise or fall.

[59]R. Bretz and G. Milkovich, "Performance Appraisal in Large Organizations: Practice and Research Implications," Working Paper 87–17, New York State School For Industrial And Labor Relations Research E. L. Deci, "The Effects of Contingent and Noncontingent Rewards and Controls on Intrinsic Motivation," *Organiational Behavior and Human Decision Processes* 8 (1972), pp. 217–229; Heneman, *Merit Pay;* F. S. Landy, J. L. Barnes and K. R. Murphy, "Correlates of Perceived Fairness and Accuracy of Performance Evaluations," *Journal of Applied Psychology* 63 (1978); pp. 751–754; J. B. Prince and E. E. Lawler, "Does Salary Discussion Hurt the Developmental Performance Appraisal," *Organizational Behavior and Human Decision Processes* 37 (1986), pp. 357–375; P. M. Wright, "Testing the Mediating Role of Goals in the Incentive-Performance Relationship," *Journal of Applied Psychology* 74 (1989), pp. 699–705.

[60]Mark A. Huselid, "The Impact of Human Resource Management Practices on Turnover, Productivity, and Corporate Financial Performance," *Academy of Management Journal,* 38(3), 1995, pp. 635–673.

[61]Mason Carpenter and W. M. Gerard Sanders, "Top Management Team Compensation: The Missing Link between CEO Pay and Firm Performance?" *Strategic Management Journal* 23(4), (April 2002) pp. 367–375; Barry Gerhart, "Pay Strategy and Firm Performance" in *Compensation in Organizations: Progress and Prospects.* eds. S. Rynes and B. Gerhart (San Francisco: New Lexington Press, 1999).

[62]Cooke, "Employee Participation Programs"; Kruse, *Profit Sharing;* G. T. Milkovich, "Does Performance-Based Pay"; M. M. Petty, B. Singleton, and D. W. Connell, "An Experimental Evaluation of an Organizational Incentive Plan in the Electric Utility Industry," *Journal of Applied Psychology* 77 (1992), pp. 427–436; J. R. Schuster, "The Scanlon Plan: A Longitudinal Analysis," *Journal of Applied Behavioral Science* 20 (1984), pp. 23–28.

EXHIBIT 9.6
Sears Makes
a Mistake

Strategic Goal	Supporting Compensation Component as Translated for Tire and Auto Centers	Unintended Consequence
Cut costs by $600 million, provide facelift to stores, cut prices, make every employee focus on profits.	Set high quotas for generating dollars from repairs and back up with commissions.	The California Consumer Affairs Division went undercover posing as customers. On 34 of 38 undercover runs Sears charged an average of $235 for unnecessary repairs.

group incentive plan and left the other division with no pay changes (the control group).[63] The goal in the experimental division was to lower the unit cost of electricity. The utility set performance goals for such things as operating expenses, maintenance expenses, and absenteeism. If these goals were exceeded, employees would receive a bonus that grew as the goals were exceeded by a larger amount. After the utility implemented this variable-pay plan (or group incentive plan), the experimental group's performance improved significantly over that of the control group on 11 of 12 objective performance measures. As an example, unit production costs fell 6 percent.

Compensation experts estimate that every dollar spent on any performance-based pay plan yields $2.34 more in organizational earnings.[64] Put differently, there is further documented evidence that every 10 percent increase in the bonus paid to employees yields a 1.5 percent increase in ROA (return on assets) to the firm.[65]

Before we rush out and develop a variable-pay component to the compensation package, though, we should recognize that such plans can, and do, fail. Sometimes the failure arises, ironically, because the incentive works too well, leading employees to exhibit rewarded behaviors to the exclusion of other desired behaviors. Exhibit 9.6 documents one such embarrassing incident that haunted Sears for much of the early '90s.[66]

Apparently the Sears example is no fluke. Other companies have found poorly implemented incentive pay plans can hurt rather than help. Green Giant, for example, used to pay a bonus based on insect parts screened in its pea-packing process. The goal, of course, was to cut the number of insect parts making their way into the final product (anyone planning on vegetables for dinner tonight?). Employees found a way to make this incentive system work for them. By bringing insect parts from home, inserting, and inspecting, their incentive dollars rose. Clearly, the program didn't work as intended. Experts contend this is evidence that the process wasn't managed well. What does this mean in terms of design?

---

[63]Petty et al., "An Experimental Evaluation."

[64]McAdams and Hawk, *Organizational Performance and Rewards.*

[65]Gerhart and Milkovich, "Organizational Differences."

[66]K. Kelly and E. Schine, "How Did Sears Blow This Gasket?" *Business Week,* June 29, 1992, p. 38.

EXHIBIT 9.7
Overall
Effectiveness
of Alternative
Reward Plans

Source: "May
2002 Pay for
Performance
Report," IOMA
(New York),
p. 13.

Type of Plan	Percent of Companies Reporting Effective for Achieving Corporate Goals
Long-term executive incentives	82
Annual bonus	79
Individual incentives	79
Employee stock ownership	79
Spot awards	74
Gain sharing	73
Lump-sum merit pay	67
Profit sharing	64
Suggestion box	43

DESIGNING A PAY-FOR-PERFORMANCE PLAN

A recent survey of HR professionals offers the following opinions about different reward systems and their effectiveness (see Exhibit 9.7). As the pay model suggests, this effectiveness is dependent on three things: efficiency, equity, and compliance in designing a pay system.

Efficiency

Efficiency involves three general areas of concern.

Strategy

Does the pay-for-performance plan support corporate objectives? For example, is the plan cost-effective, or are we making payouts that bear no relation to improved performance on the bottom line? Similarly, does the plan help us improve quality of service? Some pay-for-performance plans are so focused on quantity of performance as a measure that we forget about quality. Defect rates rise. Customers must search for someone to handle a merchandise return. A number of things happen that aren't consistent with the emphasis on quality that top organizations insist upon.

The plan also should link well with HR strategy and objectives. If other elements of our total HR plan are geared to select, reinforce, and nurture risk-taking behavior, we don't want a compensation component that rewards the status quo.

Finally, we address the most difficult question of all—how much of an increase makes a difference? What does it take to motivate an employee? Is 4 percent, the recent average of pay increases, really enough to motivate higher performance?[67] While there are few hard data on this question, most experts agree that employees don't begin to notice incentive payouts unless they are at least 10 percent, with 15 to 20 percent more likely to evoke the desired response.[68]

---

[67]Richard Metcalf, "A Modest Raise," *Albuquerque Tribune,* October 6, 2002, p. C1.

[68]IOMA, "When Are Bonuses High Enough to Improve Performance?" *IOMA,* November 1996, p. 12.

Structure

Is the structure of the organization sufficiently decentralized to allow different operating units to create flexible variations on a general pay-for-performance plan? For example, recent efforts by IBM to adapt performance reviews to the different needs of different units, and the managers in them, have resulted in a very flexible system. In this new system, midpoints for pay grades don't exist. Managers get a budget, some training on how to conduct reviews, and a philosophical mandate: Differentiate pay for stars relative to average performers, or risk losing stars. Managers are given a number of performance dimensions. Determining which dimensions to use for which employees is totally a personal decision. Indeed, managers who don't like reviews at all can input merit increases directly, anchored only by a brief explanation for the reason.[69] Different operating units may have different competencies and different competitive advantages. We don't want a rigid pay-for-performance system that detracts from these advantages, all in the name of consistency across divisions.

Standards

Operationally, the key to designing a pay-for-performance system rests on standards. Specifically, we need to be concerned about the following:

Objectives: Are they specific yet flexible? Can employees see that their behavior influences their ability to achieve objectives (called the "line-of-sight" issue in industry)?

Measures: Do employees know what measures (individual appraisals, peer reviews of team performance, corporate financial measures, etc.) will be used to assess whether performance is sufficiently good to merit a payout?

Eligibility: How far down the organization will the plan run? Companies like PepsiCo believe all employees should be included. Others think only top management can see how their decisions affect the bottom line.

Funding: Will you fund the program out of extra revenue generated above and beyond some preset standard? If so, what happens in a bad year? Many employees become disillusioned when they feel they have worked harder but economic conditions or poor management decisions conspire to cut or eliminate bonuses.

Equity/Fairness

Our second design objective is to ensure that the system is fair to employees. Two types of fairness are concerns for employees. The first type is fairness in the *amount* that is distributed to employees. Not surprisingly, this type of fairness is labeled *distributive justice.*[70] Does an employee view the amount of compensation received as fair? As we discussed earlier in the section on equity theory, perceptions of fairness here depend on the

---

[69]A. Richter, "Paying the People in Black at Big Blue," *Compensation and Benefits Review,* May/June 1998, pp. 51–59.

[70]John Thibaut and Laurens Walker, *Procedural Justice: A Psychological View* (Hillsdale, NJ: Wiley, 1975.

amount of compensation actually received relative to input (e.g., productivity) compared against some relevant standard. Notice that several of the components of this equity equation are frustratingly removed from the control of the typical supervisor or manager working with employees. A manager has little influence over the size of an employee's paycheck. It is influenced more by external market conditions, pay-policy decisions of the organization, and the occupational choice made by the employee. Indeed, recent research suggests that employees may look at the relative distribution of pay. For example, some major league ball teams have met with mixed success in trying to buy stars via the free-agent market. Some speculate that this creates feelings of inequity among other players. Some evidence suggests that narrower ranges for pay differences may actually have positive impacts on overall organizational performance.[71]

Managers have somewhat more control over the second type of equity. Employees are also concerned about the fairness of the *procedures* used to determine the amount of rewards they receive. Employees expect *procedural justice.*[72] Evidence suggests that organizations that use fair procedures and supervisors who are viewed as fair in the means they use to allocate rewards are perceived as more trustworthy and command higher levels of commitment.[73] Some research even suggests that employee satisfaction with pay may depend more on the procedures used to determine pay than on the actual level distributed.[74]

A key element in fairness is communications. Employees want to know in advance what is expected of them. They want the opportunity to provide input into the standards or expectations. And, if performance is judged lacking relative to these standards, they want a mechanism for appeals. In a union environment, this is the grievance procedure. Something similar needs to be set up in a nonunion environment.[75]

Compliance

Finally, our pay-for-performance system should comply with existing laws. We want a reward system that maintains and enhances the reputation of our firm. Think about the companies that visit a college campus. Some of them students naturally gravitate to—the interview schedule fills very quickly indeed. Why? Because of reputation.[76] We tend to undervalue the reward value of a good reputation. To guard this reputation, we need to make sure we comply with compensation laws.

---

[71]M. Bloom, "The Performance Effects of Pay Dispersion on Individuals and Organizations," *Academy of Management Journal,* 4(1) (1999), pp. 25–40.

[72]Joel Brockner, "Making Sense of Procedural Fairness: How High Procedural Fairness Can Reduce or Heighten the Influence of Outcome Favorability," *Academy of Management Review* 27(1) (2002), 58–76.

[73]Robert Folger and Mary Konovsky, "Effects of Procedural and Distributive Justice on Reactions to Pay Raise Decisions," *Academy of Management Journal* 32(1) (March 1989), pp. 155–130.

[74]S. Alexander and M. Ruderman, "The Role of Procedural and Distributive Justice in Organizational Behavior," *Social Justice Research* 1 (1987), pp. 177–198.

[75]G. S. Leventhal, J. Karuza, and W. R. Fry, "Beyond Fairness: A Theory of Allocation Preferences," in *Justice and Social Interaction,* ed. G. Mikula (New York: Springer Verlag, 1980), pp. 167–218.

[76]K. B. Stone, B. A. Backhaus, and K. Heiner, "Exploring the Relationship between Corporate Social Performance and Employer Attractiveness," *Business and Society,* September 2002, pp. 28–41.

Your Turn

Clinton Pharmaceutical

Clinton Pharmaceutical is a medium-size pharmaceutical company located in Sherwood, New Jersey. Most of Clinton's profits over the past 20 years have been generated by high-volume production of drugs that veterinarians use to care for domesticated animals. Since there is only a small markup in this market, Clinton must make its profit from high volume. The somewhat loose quality-control laws for drugs distributed to veterinarians have enabled Clinton to achieve unit production levels that are high for the pharmaceutical industry.

Unfortunately, in the past two years productivity has significantly deteriorated at Clinton. (Productivity for the past five years is shown in Exhibit 1.) In addition, turnover and absenteeism are up (Exhibits 2 and 3).

John Lancer, president of Clinton Pharmaceutical, is deeply concerned. The key to Clinton's success has always been its high productivity and resulting low unit production costs. For some reason profits have been down 18 percent during the past two years (1999 = –13%; 2000 = –23%). Lancer has an annual stockholders' meeting in two weeks, and he is determined to go in with some answers. Maybe the managers can't correct the decline in time for the meeting, but heads will roll if he doesn't get some answers. All department heads soon receive detailed letters outlining the profit picture and requesting explanations.

Ralph Simpson is the director of Human Resource Management. Lancer informed him three weeks ago that a marked drop in profits had occurred over the past year. Simpson offers the data in Exhibit 4 as a possible explanation for the profit decline.

1. Do Exhibits 1, 2, and 3 suggest any problems that might explain or be related to the profit declines?

2. Given the discussion of motivation theory in this chapter, do the data in Exhibit 4 suggest that productivity declines may be due to motivation problems? What other human resource management explanations are plausible?

EXHIBIT 1   Clinton Pharmaceutical Productivity Trends*

1999	2000	2001	2002	2003
127,000	123,000	122,786	104,281	100,222

*Gross revenue generated per employee in constant dollars.

EXHIBIT 2   Turnover Percentages, All Occupations

1999	2000	2001	2002	2003
14	12.5	19.0	26.8	29.3

EXHIBIT 3   **Absenteeism, Average Days per Employee**

1999	2000	2001	2002	2003
*	*	9.6	9.7	10.2

*Records not available.

EXHIBIT 4   **Attitude Survey toward Compensation: Level and Administration**

N = 1,427 (87 percent response rate)
Questions 1–15

Column A Scaling	**Column B Scaling**	**Column C Scaling**
1 = Very important to me	1 = Very satisfied	1 = Very dependent
2 = Important to me	2 = Satisfied	2 = Dependent
3 = Neither important nor unimportant	3 = Neutral	3 = Unsure
4 = Unimportant to me	4 = Dissatisfied	4 = Rarely dependent
5 = Very unimportant to me	5 = Very dissatisfied	5 = Never dependent

Indicate how important the following rewards available to Clinton employees are to you in column A.
Indicate how satisfied you are with the level Clinton delivers in column B.

How dependent are these rewards on your performance (column C)?

	A	B	C
1. A good salary	2	2	4
2. An annual raise equal to or greater than the cost of living	1	2	5
3. A profit-sharing plan	5	3	1
4. Paid sick days	5	3	5
5. Vacation	3	1	5
6. Life insurance	4	1	5
7. Pension	4	1	5
8. Medical plan	3	1	5
9. Opportunity for advancement	2	5	5
10. Job security	1	2	5
11. Good supervisors	2	2	5
12. Opportunity to develop new skills	2	5	5
13. Good co-workers	3	3	5
14. Steady hours	3	2	2
15. Feedback about performance	1	5	3

Summary

Why not admit it? We don't know what makes people tick! Reading this chapter should prove that we have more questions unanswered than we have supposed truths. We know that employee performance depends upon some blend of skill, knowledge, and motivation. If any of these three ingredients is missing, performance is likely to be suboptimal. This chapter concentrates on the motivation component of this performance triangle. Rewards must help organizations attract and retain employees; they must make high performance an attractive option for employees; they must encourage employees to build new skills and gradually foster commitment to the organization. A tall order, you say! The problem is especially big because we are just starting to realize all the different things that can serve as rewards (or punishments) for employees. This chapter outlines 13 rewards and makes a strong case that fair administration of these rewards can lead a company to higher performance levels.

Review Questions

1. A father decides to put his two sons to work washing cars. The business involves going to a customer's home and providing cleaning services (wash, wax, detail, or clean). Rather than paying a flat wage, the father decides to pay an incentive according to the following schedule:

	Incentive per Car	Time Required to Complete	Charge to Customer
Wash	$ 1	0.33 hr	$ 5
Wax	$ 2	0.5 hr	$10
Detail	$ 5	1.5 hrs	$35

These charges are less than local car washes charge, and there is the added convenience of having the car washed at your own home. Business is booming, but there is considerable fighting in the home. The boys drag their feet at waxing and detailing, and they fight over the chance to wash cars, if wash they must. Truth be told, both boys would rather work at the local McDonald's. Why the attitude from the sons, or are they right? What changes would you make to this incentive system? Justify your answer based on what you know about designing an incentive system from reading this chapter.

2. Lifton Wells Inc.(LWI) makes DVD players that are particularly well received on the international market. Because of currency fluctuation, the profits LWI generates vary widely from year to year. Beth Collins, who works for LWI, is in charge of a large product development group where the emphasis is on flexible performance, creativity, and "doing whatever it takes to get the job done." What kind of reward system would you recommend for this group of employees? In particular, should there be a large incentive component? Should rewards focus mostly on money, or should LWI work hard to incorporate the other 12 rewards noted in this chapter?

3. Raphael Bread Company is experiencing turnover in the range of 100 percent. Most of this occurs in the first 18 months of employment. What would you look at in both pay and other forms of rewards to identify ways of reducing turnover. Justify your choices based on your reading of this chapter.

4. How does procedural justice differ from distributive justice? Defend the position that supervisors have considerable control over procedural justice in their departments but little control over distributive justice? How might you use the principles of procedural justice to avoid having an employee quit because she believes her boss gave her an unfair evaluation?

Pay-for-Performance Plans

WHAT IS A PAY-FOR-PERFORMANCE PLAN?

What's in a name? The answer is . . . confusion, at least if we are talking about pay-for-performance plans. Listen long enough and you will hear about incentive plans, variable-pay plans, compensation at risk, earnings at risk, success sharing, and others. Sometimes these names are used interchangeably. They shouldn't be. The major thing all these names have in common is a shift in thinking about compensation. We used to think of pay as primarily an entitlement—if you went to work and did well enough to avoid being fired, you were entitled to the same-size check as everyone else. Pay-for-performance plans signal a movement away from entitlement—sometimes a very *slow* movement—toward pay that varies with some measure of individual or organizational performance. Of the pay components we discussed in Chapter 9, only base pay and across-the-board increases don't fit the pay-for-performance category. Curiously, though, many of the surveys on pay for performance tend to omit the grandfather of all these plans, merit pay.

EXHIBIT 10.1   Use of Different Variable-Pay-Plan-Types

Type of Plan	Percent of Companies with Plan				
	1996	**1997**	**1998**	**1999**	**2002**
Special-recognition plans	44	43	51	59	34
Stock option plans	21	25	46	43	40
Individual incentive plans	17	23	35	39	38
Cash profit sharing	22	20	22	23	18
Gainsharing plans	16	18	20	18	11
Team awards	13	13	17	15	8

Source: 2002 data are form IOMA, "Latest Data-What's Hot and Whats Not in PFP," *Pay for Performance Report,* May 2002, p. 11. And IOMA, "Variable Pay Popularity," *Pay For Performance Report,* January 2003, p. 8; 1996–1999, data are from IOMA, "The Goods and Evils of Variable-Based Pay," *Pay for Performance Report,* July 2000, 12.

Maybe the problem is that merit pay is out of favor right now.[1] One survey of 250 companies reports that 30 percent are thinking about eliminating merit pay and another 10 percent already have.[2] Despite this unrest, merit pay is still a pay-for-performance plan used for more than three-quarters of all exempt, clerical, and administrative employees.[3] While more innovative pay-for-performance plans may get more and better press, there is still no widespread evidence of their adoption, as Exhibit 10.1 suggests.

Exhibit 10.1 illustrates the wide variety of variable-pay plans in use today. What used to be primarily a compensation tool for top management is gradually becoming more prevalent for lower-level employees too. Exhibit 10.2 indicates that variable pay is commanding a larger share of total compensation for all employee groups.

The greater interest in variable pay probably can be traced to two trends. First, the increasing competition from foreign producers forces American firms to cut costs and/or increase productivity. Well-designed variable-pay plans have a proven track record in motivating better performance and helping cut costs. Second, today's fast-paced business environment means that workers must be willing to adjust what they do and how they do

EXHIBIT 10.2
Base versus
Variable Pay

Employee Group	Percent of Total Compensation			
	Today		Expected in 3 Years	
	Base	**Variable**	**Base**	**Variable**
Nonexempt	98	2	96	4
Exempt	92	8	87	13
Executive	76	24	71	29

[1] Adrienne Fox, "Is Merit Pay Dead?" *HR Magazine,* 48(1) (2003), pp. 12–18.

[2] American Management Association, "Survey of Merit Pay," *Compflash,* January 1994, p. 8.

[3] American Management Association, "Merit Raises Remain Popular among Fortune 1000," *Compflash,* December 1994, p.6.

it. There are new technologies, new work processes, new work relationships. All these require workers to adapt in new ways and with a speed that is unparalleled. Failure to move quickly means market share goes to competitors. If this happens, workers face possible layoffs and terminations. To avoid this scenario, compensation experts are focusing on ways to design reward systems so that workers will be able and willing to move quickly into new jobs and new ways of performing old jobs. The ability and incentive to do this come partially from reward systems that more closely link worker interests with the objectives of the company.[4]

DOES VARIABLE PAY IMPROVE PERFORMANCE RESULTS? THE GENERAL EVIDENCE

As the evidence pointed out in Chapter 9, pay-for-performance plans—those that introduce variability into the level of pay you receive—seem to have a positive impact on performance if designed well. Notice that we have qualified our statement that variable-pay plans can be effective—*if they are designed well.* In the next sections we talk about issues in design and the impacts they can have.

SPECIFIC PAY-FOR-PERFORMANCE PLANS: SHORT TERM

Merit Pay

A merit pay system links increases in base pay (called *merit increases*) to how highly employees are rated on a subjective performance evaluation. Chapter 11 covers performance evaluation, but as a simple illustration consider the following typical merit pay setup:

	Well Above Average	Above Average	Average	Below Average	Well Below Average
Performance rating	1	2	3	4	5
Merit pay increase	6%	5%	4%	3%	0%

At the end of a performance year, the employee is evaluated, usually by the direct supervisor. The performance rating, 1 to 5 in the above example, determines the size of the increase added into base pay. This last point is important. In effect, what you do this year in terms of performance is rewarded *every year* you remain with your employer. By building into base pay, the dollar amount, just like the Energizer bunny, keeps on going! With compounding, this can amount to tens of thousands of dollars over an employee's work career.[5]

[4]Jeffrey Arthur and Lynda Aiman-Smith, "Gainsharing and Organizational Learning: An Analysis of Employee Suggestions over Time," *Academy of Management Journal*, 44(4) (2001) pp. 737–754.

[5]Jerry M. Newman and Daniel J. Fisher, "Strategic Impact Merit Pay," *Compensation and Benefits Review*, July/August 1992, pp. 38–45.

Increasingly, merit pay is under attack. Not only is it expensive, but many argue it doesn't achieve the desired goal: improving employee and corporate performance.[6] In a thorough review of merit pay literature, though, Heneman concludes that merit pay does have a small, but significant, impact on performance.[7]

Interestingly, some of the most exciting experiments with merit pay are taking place in the public sector. The Office of Personnel Management (OPM), a huge federal bureaucracy, proposes to introduce pay for performance into the white-collar pay system.[8] While it will take a near miracle to change the culture and management processes needed to facilitate merit pay (e.g., a performance management system that is accepted as fair), the OPM seems intent on shaking up the system. Meanwhile, at the state level, public schools in Cincinnati, Denver, and Philadelphia are leading the way to merit pay for teachers. In Cincinnati, for example, teachers are held accountable for things they control: good professional practices. Teachers argue they should be held to standards similar to doctors: not a promise of a long healthy life but a promise that the highest professional standards will be followed. To assess teacher professional practices, in Cincinnati six evaluations are conducted over the school year, four by a trained teacher evaluator (essentially a trained teacher) and two by a building administrator. The size of pay increases is directly linked to performance during these observational reviews.[9]

If we want merit pay to live up to its potential, it needs to be managed better.[10] This requires a complete overhaul of the way we allocate raises: improving the accuracy of performance ratings, allocating enough merit money to truly reward performance, and making sure the size of the merit increase differentiates across performance levels. To illustrate the latter point, consider the employee who works hard all year, earns a 6 percent increase as our guidelines above indicate, and compares himself with the average performer who coasts to a 4 percent increase. First we take out taxes on that extra 2 percent. Then we spread the raise out over 52 paychecks. It's only a slight exaggeration to suggest that the extra money won't pay for a good cup of coffee. Unless we make the reward difference larger for every increment in performance, many employees are going to say "Why bother?"

Lump-Sum Bonuses

Lump-sum bonuses are an increasingly used substitute for merit pay. Based on employee or company performance, employees receive an end-of-year bonus that does not build into base pay. Because employees must earn this increase every year, it is viewed as less of an entitlement than merit pay. As Exhibit 10.3 indicates, lump-sum bonuses can be considerably less expensive than merit pay over the long run.

[6]Jonathan Day, Paul Mang, Ansgar Richter, and John Roberts, "Has Pay for Performance Had Its Day?" *McKinsey Quarterly,* 25(2), 2002, pp. 6–54.

[7]Robert Heneman, *Merit Pay: Linking Pay Increases to Performance Ratings* (Reading, MA: Addison-Wesley, 1992).

[8]Howard Risher, "Pay-for-Performance: The Keys to Making It Work," *Public Personnel Management,* 31(3) (2002), pp. 317–332.

[9]Cincinnati Federation of Teachers, "Teacher Quality Update," *www.cft-aft.org/prof/tqa_comp3.html,* (August 2000).

[10]D. Eskew and R. L. Heneman, "A Survey of Merit Pay Plan Effectiveness: End of the Line for Merit Pay or Hope for Improvement," in *Strategic Reward Management,* ed. R. L. Heneman (Greenwich, CT: Information Age Publishing, 2002).

EXHIBIT 10.3
Relative Cost
Comparisons

	Merit Pay		Lump-Sum Bonus
Base pay	$50,000		$50,000
Year 1 payout 5%	(2,500)	5%	(2,500)
New base pay	52,500		50,000
Extra cost total	2,500		2,500
Year 2 payout 5%	($2,625 = .05 × 52,500)	5%	(2,500 =.05 × 50,000)
New base pay	55,125 (52,500 + 2,625)		50,000
Extra cost total	5,125		5,000
After 5 years. . . .			
Year 5 payout	3,039		2,500
New base pay	63,814		50,000

Notice how quickly base pay rises under a merit pay plan. After just five years, base pay is almost $14,000 higher than it is under a lump-sum bonus plan. It should be no surprise that cost-conscious firms report switching to lump-sum pay. Twenty-six percent of companies report using lump-sum merit pay today.[11] It also should be no surprise that employees aren't particularly fond of lump-sum bonuses. After all, the intent of lump-sum bonuses is to cause shock waves in an entitlement culture. By giving lump-sum bonuses for several years, a company is essentially freezing base pay. Gradually this results in a repositioning relative to competitors. The message becomes loud and clear: "Don't expect to receive increases in base pay year after year—new rewards must be earned each year." Consider the bonus system developed by Prometric Thomson Learning call centers, which register candidates for computerized tests. The centers have very clear targets that yield specific employee bonuses, as shown in Exhibit 10.4.

Individual Spot Awards

Technically, spot awards should fall under pay-for-performance plans. About 34 percent of all companies use spot awards.[12] And an impressive 74 percent of companies in one recent survey reported that these awards were either highly or moderately effective.[13] Usually

EXHIBIT 10.4   Customer Service Bonus Scheme at Prometric Thomson Learning Call Centrers

Performance Measure	Minimum Performance	Bonus	Target Performance	Bonus	Superior Performance	Bonus
Average call wait	<32 min/day	0.5%	< 28min/day	1%	< 20min/day	1.75%
Average talk time	3 min50 sec	.5	< 3 min20 sec	1	3 min	1.75
Attendance	2 occurrences	.5	1 occurrence	1	0 occurrence	1.75
Quality	As monitored	.5	As monitored	1	As monitored	1.75
Total Bonus		2%		4%		7%

[11]IOMA, "2002 Incentive Pay Programs and Results," May 2002, p. 13.
[12]IOMA, "2002 Incentive Pay Programs and Results," May 2002, p. 13.
[13]IOMA, "2002 Incentive Pay Programs and Results," May 2002, p. 13.

these payouts are awarded for exceptional performance, often on special projects or for performance that so exceeds expectations as to be deserving of an add-on bonus. The mechanics are simple: After the fact, someone in the organization alerts top management to the exceptional performance. If the company is large, there may be a formal mechanism for this recognition, and perhaps some guidelines on the size of the spot award (so named because it is supposed to be awarded "on the spot"). Smaller companies may be more casual about recognition and more subjective about deciding the size of the award. One creative user of spot awards is Mary Kay Cosmetics. Top saleswomen get pink Cadillacs.[14]

Individual Incentive Plans: Types

These plans differ from the above because they offer a promise of pay for some objective, preestablished level of performance. For example, Cellular One pays its car phone installers on a very simple incentive system. Every customer complaint costs $10. Damage a car during installation-expect to lose $20. When this *reverse incentive plan* (penalty for poor performance rather than reward for good) was first implemented, vehicle damage dropped 70 percent.

All incentive plans have one common feature: an established standard against which worker performance is compared to determine the magnitude of the incentive pay. For individual incentive systems, this standard is compared against individual worker performance. From this basic foundation, a number of seemingly complex and divergent plans have evolved. Before discussing the more prevalent of these plans, however, it is important to note that each varies along two dimensions and can be classified into one of four cells, as illustrated in Exhibit 10.5.

The first dimension on which incentive systems vary is in the *method of rate determination.* Plans set up a rate based either on units of production per time period or on time period per unit of production. On the surface, this distinction may appear trivial, but, in fact, the deviations arise because tasks have different cycles of operation.[15] Short-cycle tasks, those that are completed in a relatively short period of time, typically have as a

EXHIBIT 10.5
**Individual
Incentive
Plans**

		Method of Rate Determination	
		Units of production per time period	*Time period per unit of production*
Relationship between Production Level and Pay	*Pay constant function of production level*	(1) Straight piecework plan	(2) Standard hour plan
	Pay varies as function of production level	(3) Taylor differential piece-rate system Merrick multiple piece-rate system	(4) Halsey 50-50 method Rowan plan Gantt plan

[14]*www.marykay.com/Joody,* visited 9/23/03.

[15]Thomas Patten, *Pay: Employee Compensation and Incentive Plans* (New York: Macmillan, 1977).

standard a designated number of units to be produced in a given time period. For long-cycle tasks, this would not be appropriate. It is entirely possible that only one task or some portion of it may be completed in a day. Consequently, for longer-cycle tasks, the standard is typically set in terms of time required to complete one unit of production. Individual incentives are based on whether or not workers complete the task in the designated time period.

The second dimension on which individual incentive systems vary is the *specified relationship between production level and wages*. The first alternative is to tie wages to output on a one-to-one basis, so that wages are some constant function of production. In contrast, some plans vary wages as a function of production level. For example, one common alternative is to provide higher dollar rates for production above the standard than for production below the standard.

Each of the plans discussed in this section has as a foundation a standard level of performance determined by some form of time study or job analysis completed by an industrial engineer or trained personnel administrator. (Exhibit 10.6 provides an illustration of

EXHIBIT 10.6 A Time Study

Task: Drilling Operation.
Elements:
  1. Move part from box to jig.
  2. Position part in jig.
  3. Drill hole in part.
  4. Remove jig and drop part in chute.

		Elements			
Notes and Remarks	**Observation Number**	**(1)**	**(2)**	**(3)**	**(4)**
	1	.17	.22	.26	.29
	2	.17	.22	.27	.34
	3	.16	.21	.28	.39
	4	.18	.21	.29	.29
	5	.19	.20	.30	.36
	6	.25	.21	.31	.31
	7	.17	.23	.29	.33
Observed time		.17 (mode)	.21 (mode)	.29 (median)	.33 (mean)
Effort rating	(130%)	1.30	1.30	1.30	1.30
Corrected time		.2210	.2730	.3370	.4290
Total corrected time					1.2600
Allowances:					
Fatigue	5%				
Personal needs	5%				
Contingencies	10%				
Total	20 % (of total corrected time of 1.2600)				.2520
Total allotted time for task					1.5120

Source: From Stephen J. Carroll and Craig E. Schneider, *Performance Appraisal and Review Systems* (Glenview, IL: Scott, Foresman, © 1982). Copyright 1982 by Scott, Foresman and Company. Reprinted by permission.

EXHIBIT 10.7
A Straight
Piece Rate
Plan

Piece rate standard (e.g., determined from time study): 10 units/hour
Guaranteed minimum wage (if standard is not met): $5/hour
Incentive rate (for each unit over 10 units): $.50/unit

Worker Output	Wage
10 units or less	$5.00/hour (as guaranteed)
20 units	20 × $.50 = $10/hour
30 units	30 × $.50 = $15/hour

a time study.) The variations in these plans occur in either the way the standard is set or the way wages are tied to output. As in Exhibit 10.5, there are four general categories of plans:

1. *Cell 1:* The most frequently implemented incentive system is a straight piecework system (Exhibit 10.7). Rate determination is based on units of production per time period, and wages vary directly as a function of production level.

   The major advantages of this type of system are that it is easily understood by workers and, perhaps consequently, is more readily accepted than some of the other incentive systems.

2. *Cell 2:* Two relatively common plans set standards based on time per unit and tie incentives directly to level of output: (1) standard hour plans and (2) Bedeaux plans. A standard hour plan is a generic term for plans setting the incentive rate based on completion of a task in some expected time period. A common example can be found in any neighborhood gasoline station or automobile repair shop. Let us assume that you need a new transmission. The estimate you receive for labor costs is based on the mechanic's hourly rate of pay, multiplied by a time estimate for job completion derived from a book listing average time estimates for a wide variety of jobs. If the mechanic receives $40 per hour and a transmission is listed as requiring four hours to be removed and replaced, the labor cost would be $160. All this is determined in advance of any actual work. Of course, if the mechanic is highly experienced and fast, the job may be completed in considerably less time than indicated in the book. However, the job is still charged as if it took the quoted time to complete. Standard hour plans are more practical than straight piecework plans for long-cycle operations and jobs that are nonrepetitive and require numerous skills for completion.[16]

   A *Bedeaux plan* provides a variation on straight piecework and standard hour plans. Instead of timing an entire task, a Bedeaux plan requires division of a task into simple actions and determination of the time required by an average skilled worker to complete each action. After the more detailed time analysis of tasks, the Bedeaux system functions similarly to a standard hour plan.

3. *Cell 3:* The two plans included in cell 3 provide for variable incentives as a function of units of production per time period. Both the Taylor plan and the Merrick plan provide

[16]Thomas Wilson, "Is It Time to Eliminate the Piece Rate Incentive System?" *Compensation and Benefits Review,* March–April 1992, pp. 43–49.

**EXHIBIT 10.8
The Taylor
and Merrick
Plans**

Piece rate standard: 10 units/hour
Standard wage: $5/hour
Piecework rate:

Output (Units/hour)	Taylor		Merrick	
	Rate per Unit	wage	Rate per Unit	Wage
7	$.50	$3.50	$.50	$3.50
8	$.50	$4.00	$.50	$4.00
9	$.50	$4.50	$.60	$5.40
10	$.50	$5.00	$.60	$6.00
11	$.70	$7.70	$.70	$7.70
12 +	Calculations at same rate as for 11 units.			

different piece rates, depending on the level of production relative to the standard. The Taylor plan establishes two piecework rates. One rate goes into effect when a worker exceeds the published standard for a given time period. This rate is set higher than the regular wage incentive level. A second rate is established for production below standard, and this rate is lower than the regular wage.

The Merrick system operates in the same way, except that three piecework rates are set: (1) high—for production exceeding 100 percent of standard; (2) medium—for production between 83 and 100 percent of standard; and (3) low—for production less than 83 percent of standard. Exhibit 10.8 compares these two plans.

4. *Cell 4:* The three plans included in cell 4 provide for variable incentives linked to a standard expressed as a time period per unit of production. The three plans include the Halsey 50–50 method, the Rowan plan, and the Gantt plan.

The *Halsey* 50–50 method derives its name from the shared split between worker and employer of any savings in direct cost. An allowed time for a task is determined via time study. The savings resulting from completion of a task in less than the standard time are allocated 50–50 (most frequent division) between the worker and the company.

The *Rowan plan* is similar to the Halsey plan in that an employer and employee both share in savings resulting from work completed in less than standard time. The major distinction in this plan, however, is that a worker's bonus increases as the time required to complete the task decreases. For example, if the standard time to complete a task is 10 hours and it is completed in 7 hours, the worker receives a 30 percent bonus. Completion of the same task in 6 hours would result in a 40 percent bonus above the hourly wage for each of the 6 hours.

The *Gantt plan* differs from both the Halsey and the Rowan plans in that the standard time for a task is purposely set at a level requiring high effort to complete. Any worker who fails to complete the task in the standard time is guaranteed a preestablished wage. However, for any task completed in standard time or less, earnings are pegged at 120 percent of the time saved. Consequently, workers' earnings increase faster than production whenever standard time is met or exceeded.

EXHIBIT 10.9 **Advantages and Disadvantages of Individualized Incentive Plans**

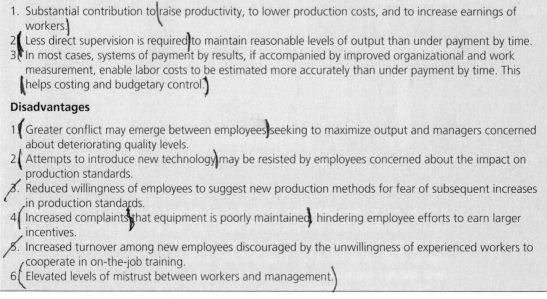

Advantages

1. Substantial contribution to raise productivity, to lower production costs, and to increase earnings of workers.
2. Less direct supervision is required to maintain reasonable levels of output than under payment by time.
3. In most cases, systems of payment by results, if accompanied by improved organizational and work measurement, enable labor costs to be estimated more accurately than under payment by time. This helps costing and budgetary control.

Disadvantages

1. Greater conflict may emerge between employees seeking to maximize output and managers concerned about deteriorating quality levels.
2. Attempts to introduce new technology may be resisted by employees concerned about the impact on production standards.
3. Reduced willingness of employees to suggest new production methods for fear of subsequent increases in production standards.
4. Increased complaints that equipment is poorly maintained, hindering employee efforts to earn larger incentives.
5. Increased turnover among new employees discouraged by the unwillingness of experienced workers to cooperate in on-the-job training.
6. Elevated levels of mistrust between workers and management.

Source: T. Wilson, "Is It Time to Eliminate the Piece Rate Incentive System?" Compensation and Benefits Review 24(2) (1992), pp. 43-49; Pinhas Schwinger, Wage Incentive Systems (New York: Halsted, 1975).

Individual Incentive Plans: Advantages and Disadvantages

We already mentioned that incentive plans can lead to unexpected, and undesired, behaviors. Certainly Sears, our example in Chapter 9, did not want mechanics to sell unnecessary repairs, but the incentive program encouraged that type of behavior. This is a common problem with incentive plans: Employees and managers end up in conflict because the incentive system often focuses only on one small part of what it takes for the company to be successful.[17] Employees, being rational, do more of what the incentive system pays for. Exhibit 10.9 outlines some of the other problems, as well as advantages, with individual incentive plans.

Individual Incentive Plans: Examples

Even though incentive systems are less popular than they used to be, there are still notable successes. Of course, most sales positions have some part of pay based on commissions, a form of individual incentive. Perhaps the longest-running success with individual incentives, going back to before World War I, belongs to a company called Lincoln Electric. In Exhibit 10.10, the compensation package for factory jobs at Lincoln Electric, no-

[17]Daniel Eisenberg, "Where People Are Never Let Go," *Time*, June 18, 2001, p.40; Kenneth Chilton, "Lincoln Electric's Incentive System: A Reservoir of Trust," *Compensation and Benefits Review* November–December 1994, pp. 29–34.

EXHIBIT 10.10   Lincoln Electric's Compensation System

Description of culture	Reservoir of trust. Long history of employment stability even during severe economic downturns. Employees with 3+ years seniority are guaranteed (on 1-year renewable basis) at least 75 percent full-time work for that year. In exchange, employees agree to flexible assignment across jobs.
Base wages	Market rate determined. Time study department sets piece rate so that average worker can earn market rate.
Bonus (short term)	Board of directors sets year-end bonus pool as function of company performance. Employee's share in pool is function of semiannual performance review (see below).
Incentive (long term)	Employees share in long-term company successes/failures in form of employee stock ownership plan (ESOP). Employees now own 28 percent of outstanding stock shares.
Performance review	Employees rated on four factors: (1) dependability, (2) quality, (3) output, (4) ideas and cooperation in comparison to others in department. To ensure against rating inflation, the average score in department cannot exceed 100.

tice how the different pieces fit together. This isn't a case of an incentive plan operating in a vacuum. All the pieces of the compensation and reward package fit together. Lincoln Electric's success is so striking that it's the subject of many case analyses.[18]

TEAM INCENTIVE PLANS: TYPES

When we move away from individual incentive systems and start focusing on people working together, we shift to group incentive plans. The group might be a work team. It might be a department. Or we might focus on a division or the whole company. The basic concept is still the same, though. A standard is established against which worker performance (that is, team performance) is compared to determine the magnitude of the incentive pay. With the focus on groups, now we are concerned about group performance in comparison against some standard, or level, of expected performance. The standard might be an expected level of operating income for a division. Or the measure might be more unusual, as at Litton industries. One division has a team variable-pay measure that is based on whether customers would be willing to act as a reference when Litton solicits other business. The more customers willing to do this, the larger the team's variable pay.[19] Another study, which tracked six retail stores, found team incentive plans improved customer satisfaction indices, raised sales performance, and lowered turnover rates.[20]

[18]Jon Katzenbach and Douglas Smith, *The Wisdom of Teams* (New York: HarperCollins, 1993).

[19]P. Zingheim and J.R. Shuster, *Pay People Right* (San Francisco: Jossey-Bass, 2000).

[20]K. Dow Scott, Jane Floyd, Philip G. Benson, and James W. Bishop, "The Impact of the Scanlon Plan on Retail Store Performance," 11(3) (2002), pp. 18–27.

EXHIBIT 10.11   A sampling of Performance Measures

Customer-Focused Measures	Financially Focused Measures
Time-to-Market Measures • On-time delivery • Cycle time • New product introductions	**Value Creation** • Revenue growth • Resource yields • Profit margins • Economic value added
Customer Satisfaction Measures • Market share • Customer satisfaction • Customer growth and retention • Account penetration	**Shareholder Return** • Return on invested capital • Return on sales/earnings • Earnings per share • Growth in profitability
Capability-Focused Measures	**Internal Process-Focused Measures**
Human Resource Capabilities • Employee satisfaction • Turnover rates • Total recruitment costs • Rate of progress on developmental plans • Promotability index • Staffing mix/head-count ratio	**Resource Utilization** • Budget-to-actual expenses • Cost-allocation ratios • Reliability/rework • Accuracy/error rates • Safety rates
Other Asset Capabilities • Patents/copyrights/regulations • Distribution systems • Technological capabilities	**Change Effectiveness** • Program implementation • Teamwork effectiveness • Service/quality index

As Exhibit 10.11 suggests, the range of performance measures for different types of corporate objectives is indeed impressive.[21]

Historically, financial measures have been the most widely used performance indicator for group incentive plans. Increasingly, though, top executives express concern that these measures do a better job of communicating performance to stock analysts than to managers trying to figure out how to improve operating effectiveness.[22] One of the refinements designed in part to address this concern is called *the balanced scorecard.*[23] Mobil Oil, for example, uses a constellation of measures that better indicate exactly where a company is succeeding and what needs to be improved. The process begins (just as we suggested, in Chapter 2, ought to be the case) with a careful analysis of strategic objectives for both the corporation and all of its divisions. Then leaders of all the strategic

[21]F. McKenzie and M. Shilling, "Ensuring Effective Incentive Design and Implementation," *Compensation and Benefits Review,* May–June 1998, pp. 57–65.

[22]Ibid.

[23]Gary H. Anthes, "Balanced Scorecard." *Computerworld,* February 17, 2003, pp. 34–47.

business units are challenged to identify measures that best reflect the directions being taken by the business. This leads to a constellation of measures that typically fall into four categories: financial results, process improvements, customer service, and innovation.[24] The balanced scorecard forces discussions about priorities among these different measures, and dissent is viewed positively. A picture begins to emerge about what is most important and what the necessary tradeoffs are to achieve the different objectives. What evolves is a series of objectives with different weights in terms of importance. These objectives send clear signals to managers, and then to their employees, about what is important. At places like Whirlpool, results on these scorecards become the subject of healthy discussion: What can we do to improve results on key dimensions, and how will this influence our progress on other objectives?[25] Practicing what they preach, even HR departments are starting to look at ways to create scorecards for their departments.[26]

Whatever our thinking is about appropriate performance measures, the central point is still that we are now concerned about group performance. This presents both problems and opportunities. As Exhibit 10.12 illustrates, we need to decide which type of group incentive plan best fits our objectives. Indeed, we should even ask if an incentive plan is appropriate. Recent evidence, for example, suggests that firms high on business risk, those with uncertain outcomes, are better off not having incentive plans at all—corporate performance is higher.[27]

Comparing Group and Individual Incentive Plans

In this era of heightened concern about productivity, we frequently are asked if setting up incentive plans really boosts performance. As we noted in Chapter 9, the answer is yes. We also are asked which is better, group or individual incentive plans. Often this is a misleading question. As we noted in Exhibit 10.8, things like the type of task, the organizational commitment to teams, and the type of work environment may preclude one or the other. Exhibit 10.13 provides a guide for when to choose group or individual plans. When forced to choose the type of plan with greater productivity "pep," experts agree that individual incentive plans have better potential for, and probably better track records in, delivering higher productivity. Group plans suffer from what is called the *free-rider problem*. See if this sounds familiar: You are a team member on a school project and at least one person doesn't carry his or her share of the load. Yet, when it comes time to divide the rewards, they are typically shared equally. Problems like this caused AT&T to phase out many of its team reward packages. Top-performing employees quickly grew disenchanted with having to carry free riders. End result—turnover of the very group that is most costly to lose.

---

[24]IOMA, "Balanced Scorecards Give Performance and Change Management a Very Timely Boost". *Pay for Performance Report*,. February 2003, p. 4.

[25]Miriam Erez and Anit Somech, "Is Group Productivity Loss the Rule or the Exception? Effects of Culture and Group-Based Motivation," *Academy of Management Journal* 39(6) (1996), pp. 1513–1537; Daniel G. Hansen, "Worker Performance and Group Incentives: A Case Study," *Industrial and Labor Relations Review* 51(1) (1997), pp. 37–49.

[26]Brian B. Becker, Mark A. Huselid, and Dave Ulrich, *The HR Scorecard: Linking People, Strategy, and Performance* (Cambridge, MA: Harvard Business School Press, 2001).

[27]M. Bloom and G. Milkovich, "Relationships among Risk, Incentive Pay, and Organizational Performance," *Academy of Management Journal,* 11 (3) (1998), pp. 283–297.

EXHIBIT 10.12   Typed of Variable-Pay Plans: Advantages and Disadvantages

Plan Type	What Is It?	Advantages	Disadvantages	Why?
Cash profit sharing	• Award based on organizational profitability • Shares a percentage of profits (typically above a target level of profitability) • Usually an annual payout • Can be cash or deferred 401(k)	• Simple, easily understood • Low administrative costs	• Profit influenced by many factors beyond employee control • May be viewed as an entitlement • Limited motivational impact	• To educate employees about business operations • To foster teamwork or "one-for-all" environment
Stock ownership or options	• Award of stock shares or options	• Option awards have minimal impact on the financial statements of the company at the time they are granted • If properly communicated, can have powerful impact on employee behavior • Tax deferral to employee	• Indirect pay/ performance link • Many factors outside individual's influence affect stock price • Employees may be required to put up money to exercise grants	• To recruit top-quality employees when organization has highly uncertain future (i.e., start-ups, high-tech, or biotech industries) • To address employee retention concerns
Balanced scorecard	• Awards that combine financial and operating measures for organization, business unit, and/or individual performance • Award pool based on achieving performance targets	• Communicates organizational priorities	• Performance criteria may be met, but if financial targets are not met, there may be a reduced payout or no payout at all • Can be complex	• To focus employees on need to increase shareholder value • To focus employees on organization, division, and/or individual goals • To link payouts to a specific financial and/or operational target

Plan Type	What Is It?	Advantages	Disadvantages	Why?
	• Multiple performance measures may include: 1. Nonfinancial/operating: quality improvements, productivity gains, customer service improvements 2. Financial: EPS, ROE, ROA, revenues			
Productivity/gain sharing	• Awards that share economic benefits of improved productivity, quality, or other measurable results • Focus on group, plant, department, or division results • Designed to capitalize on untapped knowledge of employees	• Clear performance–reward links • Productivity and quality improvements • Employee's knowledge of business increases • Fosters teamwork, cooperation	• Can be administratively complicated • Unintended effects, like drop-off in quality • Management must "open the books" • Payouts can occur even if company's financial performance is poor	• To support a major productivity/quality initiative (such as TQM or reengineering) • To foster teamwork environment • To reward employees for improvements in activities that they control
Team/group incentives	• Awards determined based on team/group performance goals or objectives • Payout can be more frequent than annual and can also extend beyond the life of the team • Payout may be uniform for team/group members	• Reinforces teamwork and team identity/results • Effective in stimulating ideas and problem-solving • Minimizes distinctions between team members • May better reflect how work is performed	• May be difficult to isolate impact of team • Not all employees can be placed on a team • Can be administratively complex • May create team competition • Difficult to set equitable targets for all teams	• To demonstrate an organizational commitment to teams • To reinforce the need for employees to work together to achieve results

Source: Kenan S. Abosch, "Variable Pay: Do We Have the Basics in Place?" *Compensation and Benefits Review*, 30(4) 1998, pp. 12–22.

EXHIBIT 10.13 **The Choice between Individual and Group Plans**

Characteristic	Choose an Individual Plan when. . . .	Choose a Group Plan when. . . .
Performance measurement	Good measures of individual performance exist. Task accomplishment not dependent on performance of others.	Output is group collaborative effort. Individual contributions to output cannot be assessed.
Organizational adaptability	Individual performance standards are stable. Production methods and labor mix relatively constant.	Performance standards for individuals change to meet environmental pressures on relatively constant organizational objectives. Production methods and labor mix must adapt to meet changing pressures.
Organizational commitment	Commitment strongest to individual's profession or superior. Supervisor viewed as unbiased and performance standards readily apparent.	High commitment to organization built upon sound communication of organizational objectives and performance standards.
Union status	Nonunion; unions promote equal treatment. Competition between individuals inhibits "fraternal" spirit.	Union or nonunion; Unions less opposed to plans that foster cohesiveness of bargaining unit and which distribute rewards evenly across group

Research on free riders suggests that the problem can be lessened through use of good performance measurement techniques. Specifically, free riders have a harder time loafing when there are clear performance standards. Rather than being given instructions to "do your best," poorer performers who were asked to deliver specific levels of performance at a specific time actually showed the most performance improvement.[28]

Team Compensation

Despite an explosion of interest in teams and team compensation, many of the reports from the front lines are not encouraging.[29] Companies report they generally are not satisfied with the way their team compensation systems work. Failures can be attributed to at least five causes.[30] First, one of the problems with team compensation is that teams come in many varieties. There are full-time teams (work group organized as a team). There are part-time teams that cut across functional departments (experts from different departments pulled together to improve customer relations). There are even full-time teams that are temporary (e.g., cross-functional teams pulled together to help ease the transition into a partnership or joint venture).

---

[28]American Management Association, "Team-Based Pay: Approaches Vary, but Produce No Magic Formulas," *Compflash*, April 1994, p. 4.

[29]Ibid.

[30]Conversation with Thomas Ruddy, manager of research, Xerox Corporation, 1997.

With so many varieties, of teams, it's hard to argue for one consistent type of compensation plan. Unfortunately, we still seem to be at the stage of trying to find the *one best way.* Maybe the answer is to look at different compensation approaches for different types of teams. Perhaps the best illustration of this differential approach for different teams comes from Xerox.

Xerox has a gain-sharing plan that pays off for teams defined at a very broad level—usually at the level of a strategic business unit. For smaller teams, primarily intact work teams (e.g., all people in a department or function), there are group rewards based on supervisory judgments of performance. Units that opt to have their performance judged as teams (it is also possible to declare that a unit wouldn't be fairly judged if team measures were used) have managers who judge the amount to be allocated to each team based on the team's specific performance results. For new teams, the manager might also decide how much of the total will go to each individual on the team. More mature teams do individual allocations on their own. In Xerox's experience, these teams start out allocating equal shares, but as they evolve the teams allocate based on each worker's performance. Out of about 2,000 work teams worldwide at Xerox, perhaps 100 have evolved to this level of sophistication. For problem-solving teams and other temporary teams, Xerox has a reward component called the Xerox Achievement Award. Teams must be nominated for exceptional performance. A committee decides which teams meet a set of predetermined absolute standards. Even contributors outside the core team can share in the award. If nominated by team members, extended members who provide crucial added value are given cash bonuses equal to those of team members.

A second problem with rewarding teams is called the "level problem." If we define teams at the very broad level-the whole organization being an extreme example-much of the motivational impact of incentives can be lost. As a member of a 1,000-person team, I'm unlikely to be at all convinced that my extra effort will significantly affect our team's overall performance. Why, then, should I try hard? Conversely, if we let teams get too small, other problems arise. TRW found that small work teams competing for a fixed piece of incentive awards tend to gravitate to behaviors that are clearly unhealthy for overall corporate success. Teams hoard star performers, refusing to allow transfers even for the greater good of the company. Teams are reluctant to take on new employees for fear that time lost to training will hurt the team-even when the added employees are essential to long-run success. Finally, bickering arises when awards are given. Because teams have different performance objectives, it is difficult to equalize for difficulty when assigning rewards. Inevitably, complaints arise.[31]

The last three major problems with team compensation involve the three Cs: complexity, control, and communications. Some plans are simply too complex. Xerox's Houston facility had a gain-sharing plan for teams that required understanding a three-dimensional performance matrix. Employees (and these authors!) threw their hands up in dismay when they tried to understand the "easy-to-follow directions." In contrast, Xerox's San Diego unit has had great success with a simple program called "bet the boss." Employees come to the boss with a performance-saving idea and bet their hard effort against the boss's incentive that they can deliver. Such plans have a simplicity that encourages employee buy-in.

[31]John G. Belcher, *Results Oriented Variable Pay System* (New York: AMACOM, 1996); Steven E. Gross, *Compensation for Teams* (New York: AMACOM, 1995).

The second C is control. Praxair, a worldwide provider of gases (including oxygen) extracted from the atmosphere, works hard to make sure all its team pay comes from performance measures under the control of the team. If mother nature ravages a construction site, causing delays and skyrocketing costs, workers aren't penalized with reduced team payouts. Such uncontrollable elements are factored into the process of setting performance standards. Indeed, experts assert that this ability to foretell sources of problems and adjust for them is a key element in building a team pay plan.[32] Key to the control issue is the whole question of fairness. Are the rewards fair given our ability to produce results? Recent research suggests that this perception of fairness is crucial. With it, employees feel it is appropriate to monitor all members of the group-slackers beware! Without fairness, employees seem to have less sense of responsibility for the team's outcomes.[33]

The final C is a familiar factor in compensation successes and failures: communication. Team-based pay plans simply are not well communicated. Employees asked to explain their plans often flounder because more effort has been devoted to designing the plan than to deciding how to explain it.

Although there is much pessimism about team-based compensation, many companies still seek ways to reward groups of employees for their interdependent work efforts. Companies that do use team incentives typically set team performance standards based on productivity improvements (38 percent of plans), customer satisfaction measures (37 percent), financial performance (34 percent), or quality of goods and services (28 percent).[34] For example, Kraft Foods uses a combination of financial measures (e.g., income from operations and cash flow) combined with measures designed to gauge success in developing managers, building diversity, and adding to market share.[35]

Gain-Sharing Plans

Our discussion of team-based compensation often mentioned gain-sharing plans as a common component. As the name suggests, employees share in the gains in these types of group incentive plans. With profit-sharing plans—surprise—the sharing involves some form of profits. Realistically, though, most employees feel as if little they can do will affect profits—that's something top-management decisions influence more. So gain sharing looks at cost components of the income ledger and identifies savings over which employees have more impact (e.g., reduced scrap, lower labor costs, reduced utility costs). It was just this type of thinking that led the United States Post Office to an annual cost avoidance of $497 million under its gain-sharing plan.[36]

[32]Theresa M. Welbourne, David B. Balkin, and Luis R. Gomez-Mejia, "Gainsharing and Mutual Monitoring: A Combined Agency-Organizational Justice Interpretation," *Academy of Management Journal* 38(3) (1995), pp. 881–899.

[33]American Management Association, "Team-Based Pay: Approaches Vary, but Produce No Magic Formulas," *Compflash,* April 1994, p. 4.

[34]Conversation with Sharon Knight, director of compensation, and Martha Kimber, manager of compensation, both at Kraft Foods, 1997.

[35]John G. Belcher, *Results Oriented Variable Pay System* (New York: AMACOM, 1996).

[36]G. K. Shives and K. D. Scott, "Gainsharing and EVA: The US Postal Experience," *WorldatWork Journal,* first Quarter, 2003 pp. 1–30.

The following issues are key elements in designing a gain-sharing plan:

1. *Strength of reinforcement:* What role should base pay assume relative to incentive pay? Incentive pay tends to encourage only those behaviors that are rewarded. For example, try returning an unwanted birthday present to a store that pays its sales force solely for new sales. Tasks carrying no rewards are only reluctantly performed (if at all).

2. *Productivity standards:* What standard will be used to calculate whether employees will receive an incentive payout? Almost all group incentive plans use a historical standard. A historical standard involves choice of a prior year's performance to use for comparison with current performance. But which baseline year should be used? If too good (or too bad) a comparison year is used, the standard will be too hard (or easy) to achieve, with obvious motivational and cost effects. One possible compromise is to use a moving average of several years (e.g., the average for the past five years, with the five-year block changing by one year on an annual basis).

   One of the major problems with historical standards is that changing environmental conditions can render a standard ineffective. For example, consider the company that sets a target of 6 percent return on investment based on historical standards. When this level is reached, it triggers an incentive for eligible employees. Yet, in a product market where the average for that year is 15 percent return on investment, it is apparent that no incentive is appropriate for our underachiever.[37] Such problems are particularly insidious during economic swings and for organizations facing volatile economic climates. Care must be taken to ensure that the link between performance and rewards is sustained. This means that environmental influences on performance, which are not controllable by plan participants, should be factored out when identifying incentive levels.

3. *Sharing the gains—split between management and workers:* Part of the plan must address the relative cuts between management and workers of any profit or savings generated. This also includes discussion of whether an emergency reserve (gains withheld from distribution in case of future emergencies) will be established in advance of any sharing of profits.

4. *Scope of the formula:* Formulas can vary in the scope of inclusions for both the labor inputs in the numerator and the productivity outcomes in the denominator.[38] Recent innovations in gain-sharing plans largely address broadening the types of productivity standards considered appropriate. Given that organizations are complex and require more complex measures, performance measures have expanded beyond traditional financial measures. For example, with the push for greater quality management, we could measure retention of customers or some other measure of customer satisfaction.

[37]Robert Masternak, "How to Make Gainsharing Successful: The Collective Experience of 17 Facilities," *Compensation and Benefits Review,* September/October 1997, pp. 43–52.

[38]John G. Belcher, "Gainsharing and Variable Pay: The State of the Art," *Compensation and Benefits Review,* May/June 1994, pp. 50–60.

Similarly, other measures include delivery performance, safety, absenteeism, turn-around time, and number of suggestions submitted. Four specific examples are:[39]

What Is Rewarded	Goal	Bonus per Month
Productivity	38,500 lb/month	$20
Cost	.009 lbs below standard	$40
Product damage	15 per 10,000 cases	$10
Customer complaints	14 per million lbs	$15

Great care must be exercised with such alternative measures, though, to ensure that the behaviors reinforced actually affect the desired bottom-line goal. Getting workers to expend more effort, for example, might not always be the desired behavior. Increased effort may bring unacceptable levels of accidents. It may be preferable to encourage cooperative planning behaviors that result in more efficient work.

5. *Perceived fairness of the formula:* One way to ensure the plan is perceived as fair is to let employees vote on whether implementation should go forward. This and union participation in program design are two elements in plan success.[40]

6. *Ease of administration:* Sophisticated plans with involved calculations of profits or costs can become too complex for existing company information systems. Increased complexities also require more effective communications and higher levels of trust among participants.

7. *Production variability:* One of the major sources of problems in group incentive plans is failure to set targets properly. At times the problem can be traced to volatility in sales. Large swings in sales and profits, not due to any actions by workers, can cause both elation (in good times) and anger (in bad times). As stated above a good plan ensures that environmental influences on performance, which are not controllable by plan participants, should be factored out when identifying incentive levels. One alternative would be to set standards that are relative to industry performance. To the extent data are available, a company could trigger gain sharing when performance exceeds some industry norm. The obvious advantage of this strategy is that economic and other external factors hit all firms in the industry equally hard. If our company performs better, relatively, it means we are doing something as employees to help achieve success.

Exhibit 10.14 illustrates three different formulas that can be used as the basis for gain-sharing plans. The numerator, or input factor, is always some labor cost variable, expressed in either dollars or actual hours worked; the denominator is some output measure such as net sales or value added. Each of the plans determines employees' incentives based on the difference between the current value of the ratio and the ratio in some agreed-upon base year. The more favorable the current ratio relative to the historical standard, the larger the incentive award.[41] The three primary types of gain-sharing plans, dif-

[39]John Belcher, "Design Options for Gain Sharing," unpublished paper, American Productivity Center, 1987.

[40]D. Kim, "Determinants of the Survival of Gainsharing Programs," *Industrial and Labor Relations Review,* 53(1) 1999, pp. 21–42.

[41]A. J. Geare, "Productivity from Scanlon Type Plans," *Academy of Management Review,* 1(3) (1976), pp. 99–108.

EXHIBIT 10.14   Three Gain-Sharing Formulas

	Scanlon Plan (Single Ratio Volume)	Rucker Plan	Improshare
Numerator of ratio (input factor)	Payroll costs	Labor cost	Actual hours worked
Denominator of ratio (output factor)	Net sales (plus or minus inventories)	Value added	Total standard value hours

Source: Adapted from M. Bazerman and B. Graham-Moore, "PG. Formulas: Developing a Reward Structure to Achieve Organizational Goals," in *Productivity Gainsharing,* ed. B. Graham-Moore and T. Ross (Englewood Cliffs, NJ: Prentice-Hall, 1983).

ferentiated by their focus on either cost savings (the numerator of the equation) or some measure of revenue (the denominator of the equation), are noted below.

Scanlon Plan

Scanlon plans are designed to lower labor costs without lowering the level of a firm's activity. Incentives are derived as a function of the ratio between labor costs and sales value of production (SVOP).[42] The SVOP includes sales revenue and the value of goods in inventory. To understand how these two figures are used to derive incentives under a Scanlon plan, see Exhibit 10.15.

In practice, the $50,000 bonus in Exhibit 10.15 is not all distributed to the work force. Rather, 25 percent is distributed to the company, 75 percent of the remainder is distributed as bonuses, and 25 percent of the remainder is withheld and placed in an emergency fund to reimburse the company for any future months when a "negative bonus" is earned (i.e., when the actual wage bill is greater than the allowable wage bill). The excess remaining in the emergency pool is distributed to workers at the end of the year. Appendix 10-A illustrates a variant of the Scanlon plan adopted at Dresser Rand's Painted Post facility.

EXHIBIT 10.15
Examples of a
Scanlon Plan

1997 Data (base year) for Alton, Ltd.

SVOP	=	$10,000,000
Total wage bill	=	4,000,000
$\dfrac{\text{Total wage bill}}{\text{SVOP}}$	=	$4,000,000 \div 10,000,000 = .40 = 40\%$

Operating Month, March 1998

SVOP	=	$950,000
Allowable wage bill	=	.40 ($950,000) = $380,000
Actual wage bill (August)	=	$330,000
Savings	=	$50,000

$50,000 available for distribution as a bonus.

[42]Ibid.

To look at the impact of Scanlon plans, consider the retail chain that adopted a Scanlon plan in six of its stores and compared results against six control stores chosen for their similarity.[43]

Presence of a Scanlon plan led to stores having higher customer satisfaction higher Sales and Lower turnover.

> **Cybercomp**
> HR Guide provides information about gainsharing plans, including critiques of plans and statistical studies. The website is at *www.hr-guide.com\data\G443.htm.*

Rucker Plan

The Rucker plan involves a somewhat more complex formula than a Scanlon plan for determining worker incentive bonuses. Essentially, a ratio is calculated that expresses the value of production required for each dollar of total wage bill. Consider the following illustration:[44]

1. Assume accounting records show that the company expended $.60 worth of electricity, materials, supplies, and so on, to produce $1.00 worth of product. The value added is $.40 for each $1.00 of sales value. Assume also that 45 percent of the value added was attributable to labor; a productivity ratio (PR) can be allocated from the formula in item 2.
2. *PR* (labor) $\times$ .40 $\times$ .45 = 1.00. Solving yields PR = 5.56.
3. If the wage bill equals $100,000, the *expected* production value is the wage bill ($100,000) $\times$ PR (5.56) = $555,556.
4. If *actual* production value equals $650,000, then the savings (actual production value minus expected production value) is $94,444.
5. Since the labor contribution to value added is 45 percent, the bonus to the work force should be .45 $\times$ $94,444 = $42,500.
6. The savings are distributed as an incentive bonus according to a formula similar to the Scanlon formula—75 percent of the bonus is distributed to workers immediately and 25 percent is kept as an emergency fund to cover poor months. Any excess in the emergency fund at the end of the year is then distributed to workers.

Implementation of the Scanlon/Rucker Plans

Two major components are vital to the implementation and success of a Rucker or Scanlon plan: (1) a productivity norm and (2) effective worker committees. Development of a productivity norm requires both effective measurement of base-year data and acceptance by workers and management of this standard for calculating bonus incentives. Effective measurement requires that an organization keep extensive records of historical cost relationships and make them available to workers or union representatives to verify cost accounting figures. Acceptance of these figures, assuming they are accurate, requires that the organization choose a base year that is neither a "boom" nor a "bust" year. The logic is apparent. A boom year would reduce opportunities for workers to collect bonus incen-

---

[43]K. D. Scott, J. Floyd, and P. Benson, "The Impact of the Scanlon Plan on Retail Store Performance," *WorldatWork Journal,* 11(3), 2002, pp 4–13.

[44]Patten, *Pay: Employee Compensation and Incentive Plans*; Schwinger, *Wage Incentive Systems.*

tives. A bust year would lead to excessive bonus costs for the firm. The base year chosen also should be fairly recent, allaying worker fears that changes in technology or other factors would make the base year unrepresentative of a given operational year.

The second ingredient of Scanlon/Rucker plans is a series of worker committees (also known as productivity committees or bonus committees). The primary function of these committees is to evaluate employee and management suggestions for ways to improve productivity and/or cut costs. Operating on a plantwide basis in smaller firms, or a departmental basis in larger firms, these committees have been highly successful in eliciting suggestions from employees. It is not uncommon for the suggestion rate to be above that found in companies with standard suggestion incentive plans.[45]

Scanlon/Rucker plans foster this type of climate, and that is perhaps the most vital element of their success. Numerous authorities have pointed out that these plans have the best chance for success in companies with competent supervision, cooperative union-management attitudes, strong top-management interest and participation in the development of the program, and management open to criticism and willing to discuss different operating strategies. It is beyond the scope of this discussion to outline specific strategies adopted by companies to achieve this climate, but the key element is a belief that workers should play a vital role in the decision-making process.

Similarities and Contrasts between Scanlon and Rucker Plans

Scanlon and Rucker plans differ from individual incentive plans in their primary focus. Individual incentive plans focus primarily on using wage incentives to motivate higher performance through increased effort. While this is certainly a goal of the Scanlon/Rucker plans, it is not the major focus of attention. Rather, given that increased output is a function of group effort, more attention is focused on organizational behavior variables. The key is to promote faster, more intelligent, and more acceptable decisions through participation. This participation is won by developing a group unity in achieving cost savings—a goal that is not stressed, and is often stymied, in individual incentive plans.

Even though Scanlon and Rucker plans share this common attention to groups and committees through participation as a linking pin, there are two important differences between the two plans. First, Rucker plans tie incentives to a wide variety of savings, not just the labor savings focused on in Scanlon plans.[46] Second, this greater flexibility may help explain why Rucker plans are more amenable to linkages with individual incentive plans.

Improshare

Improshare (Improved Productivity through Sharing) is a gain-sharing plan that has proved easy to administer and to communicate.[47] First, a standard is developed that identifies the expected hours required to produce an acceptable level of output. This standard comes either from time-and-motion studies conducted by industrial engineers or from a base-period

---

[45]B. Graham-Moore and T. Ross, *Productivity Gainsharing* (Englewood Cliffs, NJ: Prentice-Hall, 1983).

[46]J. Newman, "Selecting Incentive Plans to Complement Organizational Strategy," in *Current Trends in Compensation Research and Practice,* ed. L. Gomez-Mejia & D. Balkin (Englewood Cliffs, NJ: Prentice-Hall, 1987).

[47]Marhsall Fein, "Improshare: A Technique for Sharing Productivity Gains with Employees," *The Compensation Handbook,* ed. M. L. Rock and L. A. Berger(New York: McGraw-Hill, 1993), pp. 158–175

measurement of the performance factor. Any savings arising from production of the agreed-upon output in fewer than the expected hours is shared by the firm and by the worker's.[48] For example, if 100 workers can produce 50,000 units over 50 weeks, this translates into 200,000 hours (40 hours × 50 weeks) for 50,000 units, or 4 hours per unit. If we implement an Improshare plan, any gains resulting in less than 4 hours per unit are shared 50-50 between employees and management (wages times number of hours saved).[49]

One survey of 104 companies with an Improshare plan found a mean increase in productivity during the first year of 12.5 percent.[50] By the third year the productivity gain rose to 22 percent. A significant portion of this productivity gain was traced to reduced defect rates and downtime (e.g., repair time).

Profit-Sharing Plans

If you were to read most books or articles on variable-pay today, you would see less discussion of profit-sharing plans and much energy devoted to gain-sharing plans or related variants. An erroneous conclusion to draw from this is that profit sharing is dead. In reality, many variable-pay plans still require a designated profit target to be met before any payouts occur. Our experience with chief executive officers is that they have a hard time giving employees extra compensation if the company isn't also profiting. Thus, many variable-pay plans have some form of profit "trigger" linked to revenue growth or profit margins or some measure of shareholder return such as earnings per share or return on capital. Profit sharing continues to be popular because the focus is on the measure that matters most to the most people: a predetermined index of profitability. When payoffs are linked to such measures, employees spend more time learning about financial measures and the business factors that influence them.

On the downside, most employees don't feel their jobs have a direct impact on profits. A small cog in a big wheel is difficult to motivate very well. For example, Ford Motor recently announced its annual profit-sharing check to employees would average $160, compared to $940 for the same type of workers at General Motors.[51] You can bet the Ford employees believe they deserve more than one-sixth the payout. Complaints probably center on Ford's continuing sales problems. Further, even if workers are able to improve operating efficiency, there is no guarantee that profits will automatically increase. Strength of the market, global competition, even the way we enter accounting information into the balance sheet all can affect profits and serve to disenchant workers.

The trend in recent variable-pay design is to combine the best of gain-sharing and profit-sharing plans.[52] The company will specify a funding formula for any variable pay-

[48]R. Kaufman, "The Effects of Improshare on Productivity," *Industrial and Labor Relations Review*, 45(2) (1992), pp. 311–322

[49]Darlene O'Neill, "Blending the Best of Profit Sharing and Gainsharing," *HR Magazine*, March 1994, pp. 66–69.

[50]Darlene O'Neill, "Blending the Best of Profit Sharing and Gainsharing," *HR Magazine*, March 1994, pp. 66–69

[51]"Business Brief—Ford Motor Co.: Profit Sharing Is Planned for 95,000 Hourly Workers", *Wall Street Journal*, January 20, 2003, p. B3.

[52]K. Brown and V. Huber, "Lowering Floors and Raising Ceilings: A Longitudinal Assessment of the Effects of an Earnings-at-Risk Plan on Pay Satisfaction," *Personnel Psychology* 45 (1992), pp. 279–311.

out that is linked to some profit measure. As experts say, the plan must be self-funding. Dollars going to workers are generated by additional profits gained from operational efficiency. Along with having the financial incentive, employees feel they have a measure of control. For example, an airline might give an incentive for reductions in lost baggage, with the size of the payout dependent on hitting profit targets. Such a program combines the need for fiscal responsibility with the chance for workers to affect something they can control.

Earnings-at-Risk Plans

We probably shouldn't separate earnings-at-risk plans as a distinct category. In fact, any incentive plan could be an at-risk plan. Think of incentive plans as falling into one of two categories: success sharing or risk sharing. In success-sharing plans, employee base wages are constant and variable pay adds on during *successful years.* If the company does well, you receive a predetermined amount of variable pay. If the company does poorly, you simply forgo any variable pay—there is no reduction in your base pay, though. In a risk-sharing plan, base pay is reduced by some amount relative to the level that would be offered in a success-sharing plan. AmeriSteel's at-risk plan is typical of risk-sharing plans. Base pay was reduced 15 percent across the board in year 1. That 15 percent was replaced with a .5 percent increase in base pay for every 1 percent increase in productivity beyond 70 percent of the prior year's productivity. This figure would leave workers whole (no decline in base pay) if they only matched the prior-year productivity. Each additional percent improvement in productivity yielded a 1.5 percent increase in base wages. Everyone in AmeriSteel, from the CEO on down, is in this type of plan—and the result has been an 8 percent improvement in productivity.[53]

Clearly, at-risk plans shift part of the risk of doing business from the company to the employee. The company hedges against the devastating effects of a bad year by mortgaging part of the profits that would have accrued during a good year. Companies like DuPont and Saturn report mixed results. DuPont terminated its plan in the second year because of lackluster performance and the expectation of no payout. Much of the concern can be traced to employee dissatisfaction with the plan at DuPont. At-risk plans appear to be met with decreases in satisfaction with both pay in general and the process used to set pay.[54]

---

[53]S. E. Gross and D. Duncan, "Gainsharing Plan Spurs Record Productivity and Payouts at AmeriSteel," *Compensation and Benefits Review,* November–December 1998, pp. 46–50.

[54]These observations are drawn from a variety of sources, including K. Brown and V. Huber, "Lowering Floors and Raising Ceilings: A Longitudinal Assessment of the Effects of an Earnings-at-Risk Plan on Pay Satisfaction," *Personnel Psychology* 45 (1992), pp. 279–311; D. Collins, L. Hatcher, and T. Ross, "The Decision to Implement Gainsharing: The Role of Work Climate, Expected Outcomes and Union Status," *Personnel Psychology* 46 (1993), pp. 77–103; American Management Association, Team-Based Pay: Approaches Vary but Produce No Magic Formulas," *Compflash,* April 1994, p. 4; W. N. Cooke, "Employee Participation Programs, Group Based Incentives and Company Performance," *Industrial and Labor Relations Review* 47 (1994), pp. 594–610; G. W. Florowski, "The Organizational Impact of Profit Sharing," *Academy of Management Review* 12(4) (1987), pp. 622–636.

Group Incentive Plans: Advantages and Disadvantages

Clearly, group pay-for-performance plans are gaining popularity while individual plans are stable or declining in interest. Why? One explanation with intriguing implications suggests that group-based plans, particularly gain-sharing plans, cause organizations to evolve into learning organizations.[55] Apparently the suggestions employees are encouraged to make (how to do things better in the company) gradually evolve from first-order learning experiences of a more routine variety (maintenance of existing ways of doing things) into suggestions that exhibit second-order learning characteristics—suggestions that help the organization break out of existing patterns of behavior and explore different ways of thinking and behaving.[56]

Exhibit 10.16 outlines some of the general positive and negative features of group pay-for-performance plans.[57]

Group Incentive Plans: Examples

All incentive plans, as we noted earlier, can be described by common features: (1) the size of the group that participates in the plan, (2) the standard against which performance is compared, and (3) the payout schedule. Exhibit 10.17 illustrates some of the more interesting components of plans for leading companies.

EXHIBIT 10.16
Group Incentive Plans: Advantages and Disadvantages

Advantages

1. Positive impact on organization and individual performance of about 5 to 10 percent per year.
2. Easier to develop performance measures than it is for individual plans.
3. Signals that cooperation, both within and across groups, is a desired behavior.
4. Teamwork meets with enthusiastic support from most employees.
5. May increase participation of employees in decision-making process.

Disadvantages

1. Line of sight may be lessened, i.e., employees may find it more difficult to see how their individual performance affects their incentive payouts.
2. May lead to increased turnover among top individual performers who are discouraged because they must share with lesser contributors.
3. Increases compensation risk to employees because of lower income stability. May influence some applicants to apply for jobs in firms where base pay is a larger compensation component.

[55]P. M. Senge, *The Fifth Discipline: The Art and Practice of the Learning Organization* (New York: Doubleday, 1990).

[56]Jeffrey Arthur and Lynda Aiman-Smith, "Gainsharing and Organizational Learning: An Analysis of Employee Suggestions over Time," *Academy of Management Journal*, 44(4) (2001), pp. 737–754.

[57]T. H. Hammer and R. N. Stern, "Employee Ownership: Implications for the Organizational Distribution of Power," *Academy of Management Journal* 23 (1980), pp. 78–100.

EXPLOSIVE INTEREST IN LONG-TERM INCENTIVE PLANS

Exhibit 10.18 shows different types of long-term incentives and their definitions. These plans are also grouped by the level of risk faced by employees having these incentives, as well as the expected rewards that might come from them.

Long-term incentives (LTIs) focus on performance beyond the one-year time line used as the cutoff for short-term incentive plans. Recent explosive growth in long-term plans appears to be spurred in part by a desire to motivate longer-term value creation.[58] One recent analysis of over 200 empirical studies of the relation between stock ownership and financial performance casts a gloomy pallor indeed. There is very little empirical evidence that stock ownership by management leads to better corporate performance.[59] There is some evidence, though, that stock ownership is likely to increase internal growth, rather than more rapid external diversification.[60] Exhibit 10.19 illustrates the popularity of long-term incentive plans.

EXHIBIT 10.17 **Corporate** **Examples of** **Group** **Incentive** **Plans**		
	GE Information systems	A team-based incentive that also links to individual payouts. Team and individual performance goals are set. If the team hits its goals, the team members earn their incentive only if they also hit their individual goals. The team incentive is 12 to 15 percent of monthly base pay.
	Corning Glass	A gain-sharing program (goal sharing) where 75 percent of the payout is based on unit objectives such as quality measures, customer satisfaction measures, and production targets. The remainder is based on Corning's return on equity.
	3M	Operates with an earnings-at-risk plan. Base pay is fixed at 80 percent of market. Employees have a set of objectives to meet for pay to move to 100 percent of market. Additionally there is a modest profit-sharing component.
	Saturn	Earnings-at-risk plan where base pay is 93 percent of market. Employees meet individual objectives to capture at-risk component. All team members must meet objectives for any to get at-risk money. A profit-sharing component is based on corporate profits.
	DuPont Fibers	Earnings-at-risk plan where employees receive reduced pay increases over 5 years—resulting in 6 percent lower base pay. If department meets annual profit goal, employees collect all 6 percent. Variable payout ranges from 0 (reach less than 80 percent of goal) to 12 percent (150 percent of goal).

[58]B. J. Hall, "What You Need to Know about Stock Options," *Harvard Business Review*, March–April 2000, pp. 121–129

[59]D. R. Dalton, S. T. Certo, and R. Roengpitya, "Meta-Analyses of Financial Performance and Equity: Fusion or Confusion?" *Academy of Management Journal*, 46(1) (2003), pp. 13–26.

[60]Barry Gerhart, "Pay Strategy and Firm Performance" in *Compensation in Organizations: Progress and Prospects*, eds S. Rynes and B. Gerhart (San Francisco: New Lexington Press, 1999).

EXHIBIT 10.18

**Long-Term
Incentives and
Their
Risk/Reward
Tradeoffs**

Source: IOMA,
"PFP News
Brief," *Pay for
Performance
Report,* June
2000, p. 8.

Level One: Low Risk/Reward

1. *Time-based restricted stock:* An award of shares that actually are received only after the completion of a predefined service period. Employees who terminate employment before the restriction lapses must return their shares to the company.
2. *Performance-accelerated restricted stock:* Restricted stock granted only after attainment of specified performance objectives.
3. *Stock purchase plan:* Opportunity to buy shares of company stock either at prices below market price or with favorable financing.

Level Two: Medium Risk/Reward

4. *Time-vested stock option:* This is what most stock options are—the right to purchase stock at a specified price for a fixed time period.
5. *Performance-versed restricted stock:* This is a grant of stock to employees upon attainment of defined performance objective(s).
6. *Performance-accelerated stock option:* An option with a vesting schedule that can be shortened if specific performance criteria are met.

Level Three: High Risk/Reward

7. *Permium-priced stock option:* A stock option that has an exercise price about market value at the time of grant. This creates an incentive for employees to create value for the company, see the stock price rise, and thus be eligible to purchase the stock.
8. *Indexed stock option:* An option whose exercise price depends on what peer companies experiences are with stock prices. If industry stock prices are generally rising, it would be difficult to attribute any similar rise in a specific improvements beyond general industry improvement.
9. *Performance-vested stock option:* One that vests only upon the attainment of a predetermined performance objective.

EXHIBIT 10.19

**Stock Option
Plans (SOPs)**

Source: Ioma, *Pay
for Performance
Report,* July 2002,
p. 14.

	Percent with SOP
Public companies	80
Durable goods	100
Services	63
Financial Services	63
Private Companies	11

	Percent Eligible		
Employee Type	**2000**	**2001**	**2002**
Executive	99	98	98
Upper management	98	98	97
Middle management	84	85	86
Supervisors	61	63	63
IT staff	62	66	65
Other professional	62	65	65
Sales	64	67	67
Technical staff	58	59	60
Administrative staff	39	39	37
Part-time staff	28	29	28

Besides their perceived incentive value, stock options are also popular because, under current accounting rules, companies don't have to report them as an overhead cost. They are (wrongly) viewed as a free good.[61] Think about the executive issued 500,000 shares with a vesting period of five years (the shares can be bought in five years). After five years, the CEO can purchase the stock at the initial-offer price (if the market price is now lower than that, the stock option is said to be "underwater" and is not exercised).[62] If the executive buys the shares, they are typically issued from a pool of unissued shares. The money paid by the CEO is treated like money paid by any investor . . . found money? Not really. Options dilute the per-share earnings because they increase the denominator applied to net profits used to figure per-share earnings (ok, ok, we promise, no more accounting, ugh). While this hasn't put much of a damper on stock option popularity, recent very public stock scandals (e.g., Enron) have increased pressure to change accounting rules.[63] A recent poll indicates most companies think expensing will become mandatory within the next five years.[64] Estimates suggest this would lower earnings by 4 percent across the spectrum of companies with stock options.[65] In what may become a pattern, Microsoft just announced that it will no longer offer stock options, preferring instead to give outright stock grants. This change marks Microsoft's recognition that stock prices haven't moved much recently, making stock options less attractive.[66]

Employee Stock Ownership Plans (ESOPs)

Some companies believe that employees can be linked to the success or failure of a company in yet another way-through employee stock ownership plans.[67] At places like PepsiCo, Lincoln Electric, DuPont, Coca-Cola, and others the goal is to increase employee involvement in the organization, and hopefully this will influence performance. Toward this end, employees own 28 percent of the stock at Lincoln Electric. At Worthington Industries, an oft-praised performer in the steel industry, the typical employee owns $45,000 in stock.[68]

Despite these high-profile adoptions, ESOPs don't make sense as an incentive. First, the effects are generally long-term. How I perform today won't have much of an impact on the stock price at the time I exercise my option.[69] Nor does my working harder mean more for me. Indeed, we can't predict very well what makes stock prices rise—and this is the central ingredient in the reward component of ESOPs. So the performance measure is too complex to figure out how we can control our own destiny. Sounds like ESOPs do poorly on two of the three Cs we mentioned earlier as causing incentive plans to fail. Why

[61]T. McCoy, "Emerging Option to Stock Options," Pay for Performance Report,. June 2001, p. 2.

[62]T. Buyniski and B. Harsen, "The Cancel and Regrant: A Roadmap for Addressing Underwater Options," *Compensation and Benefits Review,* January–February 2002, pp. 28–32.

[63]W. Zellner, "An Insider's Tale of Enron's Toxic Culture," *Business Week,* March 31, 2003, pp. 16.

[64]PFP News Brief, "Expensing Stock Options Is Only a Matter of Time," *Pay for Performance Report,* November 2002, p. 8.

[65]McCoy, "Emerging Option to Stock Options."

[66]*USA Today,* July 9, 2003, p. B1.

[67]Chilton, "Lincoln Electric's Incentive System"; Howard Rudnitsky, "You Have to Trust the Workforce," *Forbes,* July 19, 1993, pp. 78–81.

[68]IOMA, *Pay for Performance Report,* May 1996, p. 3.

[69]IOMA "Another Pan of Stock Option Plans," *Pay for Performance Report,* January 1999, p. 11.

then do about 9,500 companies have ESOPs covering more than 10 million employees with holdings of over $150 billion in the stock's of their companies?[70] The answer may well be that ESOPs foster employee willingness to participate in the decision-making process.[71] And a company that takes advantage of that willingness can harness a considerable resource—the creative energy of its work force. Take, for example, the DuPont Shares Program. Initiated in 1991, the program was designed to share the benefits of success and the responsibility for achieving growth. In 1991 every DuPont employee around the world received an award of 100 stock options. These options had to be retained for a minimum of 1 year a before being exercised and could be held for a maximum of 10 years before being transferred into actual company stock. Distribution of these stock options is not an annual event, thus eliminating an "entitlement" perception by employees. Indeed, in recent years the granting of stock options has had performance objectives tied to exercise rights. One such provision awarded in 1997 expired in 2002. If the stock achieves a price of $75 for five days, individuals can exercise their options by paying a price (exercise price) of $52.50. The goal? To motivate employees to increase the value of DuPont.[72]

Beware of stock options in declining markets though. After Microsoft stock was battered by the company's antitrust battle in 2000, employee morale plummeted. Many of the options granted to employees had exercise prices higher than the current market value—in effect making the options all but worthless. In mid-2000 Microsoft issued 70 million shares of stock at $ 66.25, the then closing stock price. This price was considerably below that of many options issued in the past and was intended to motivate workers to help drive stock prices back up.[73]

Performance Plans (Performance Share and Performance Unit)

Performance plans typically feature corporate performance objectives for a time three years in the future. They are driven by financial earnings or return measures, and they pay out for meeting or exceeding specific goals.

Broad-Based Option Plans (BBOPs)

The latest trend in long-term incentives, and probably the component of compensation generating the most discussion in recent years, is broad-based option plans. BBOPs are stock grants: The company gives employees shares of stock over a designated time period. The strength of BBOPs is their versatility. Depending on the way they are distributed to employees, they can either reinforce a strong emphasis on performance (performance culture) or inspire greater commitment and retention (ownership culture) of employees.

Some of the best-known companies in the country offer stock grants to employees at all levels: Southwest Airlines, Chase Manhattan, DuPont, General Mills, Procter & Gamble, PepsiCo, Merck, Eli Lilly, Kimberly-Clark, Microsoft, and Amazon.com.[74] For ex-

---

[70]Ibid.

[71]Ibid.

[72]T. Wilson, *Rewards That Drive High Performance,* New York: AMACOM, (1999).

[73]R. Buckman, "Microsoft Uses Stock Options to Lift Morale," Wall Street Journal, April 26, 2000, p. A3.

[74]P. Singh, "Strategic Reward Systems at Southwest Airlines," *Compensation and Benefits Review,* March/April 2002, pp. 28–33; P. Zingheim and J. Schuster, *Pay People Right!* San Francisco: (Jossey-Bass, 2000).

ample, Starbucks has a stock grant program called Beanstock, and all employees who work at least 500 hours per year, up to the level of vice president, are eligible (broad-based participation). If company performance goals are reached, all employees receive equal stock grants worth somewhere between 10 and 14 percent of their earnings. The grants vest 20 percent each year, and the option expires 10 years after the grant date. This program exists to send the CEOs a clear signal that all employees, especially the two-thirds who are part-timers, are business partners. This effort to create a culture of owner-ship is viewed as the primary reason Starbucks has turnover that is only a fraction of the usually high turnover in the retail industry.

Microsoft's program shares one common feature with Starbucks. The stock grant pro-gram, again, is broad-based. By rewarding all employees, Microsoft hopes to send a strong signal to its employees that reinforces its culture: Take reasoned risks that have long-run potential for contributing to the company. Microsoft's BBOP is targeted at all permanent employees. Unlike Starbuck's plan, though, the size of the stock grant is linked to individual performance and estimated long-run contribution to the company. Starting 12 months after the stock grant date, 12.5 percent is vested every 6 months.

Kodak provides a third example. Only nonmanagement employees are eligible, and grants are given only to the small percentage of employees who are recognized for extraor-dinary accomplishments based on recommendations by an individual's or team's manager. Kodak prides itself on giving immediate grant options for outstanding contributions.

Finally, Paychex, a payroll processing firm, offers broad-based options both to create a sense of ownership and to attract and retain employees. The first grants were made in 1996. They vested 50 percent in 1999 and 100 percent in 2001. Grant amounts depend on pay grade level, with lower grades granted 100 shares and upper grades receiving 200 shares.[75]

Your Turn   Understanding Stock Options

Note: In order to successfully complete this exercise you do not need to have Internet access; the information required to do the exercise can be found online as well as on paper (e.g. *Wall Street Journal*). Just look up the company's stock symbol. The calculations can also be made by hand.

Information regarding calculations and data can be found online at *http://mgt.buffalo.edu/ departments/ohr/jmnewman/*. Especially links to sites displaying current share prices can be found there.

[75]S. Burzawa, "Broad Based Stock Options Are Used to Attract, Retain, and Motivate Employees," *Employee Benefit Plan Review,* July 1998, pp. 46–50.

Exercise 1

You have been working for Sun Microsystems (symbol SUNW) for about four years as a project manager and doing very well. Upon employment (10/1/2000) you were granted 4000 nonqualified stock options, which vested over 4 years, at 25% a year. The stock price at the date of grant was $4.02 (not adjusted for splits and dividends). How much did you gain? Experiment with different values for the stock price to see what would have happened if the stock increased or decreased dramatically. How would these numbers change, if all of your options had already vested?

Exercise 2

After graduation you and a friend both got great jobs, you with Dell (DELL) and your friend with Microsoft (MSFT). You and your friend started at the same salary and bonus and got 2000 nonqualified stock options each as a signing bonus (good negotiating!). You received 2000 stock options on July 28, 2000, and the grant price is $37.98. Your options vest over 4 years, 25 percent a year, and they expire in 10 years. Your friend's information is exactly the same, except the grant price is $22.45. Compare your friend's gain to yours. Whose stock options appreciated more? Did you earn money? If the stocks climbed up 40 percent, what would be the gain?

Exercise 3

You are a sales manager at American Express Company (AXP). Today you have been granted 8000 nonqualified stock options. The exercise price was chosen in such a way that the options will only be in the money if the stock price increases more than 10 percent in each of the following years. What will be the exercise price for each of the next five year's? At what stock price could you take home $1 million after taxes? What would be your gain if the stock price increased by 15 percent per year?

Hint: Assume for convenience that all shares vest today.

Exercise 4

You have been chosen to set up a stock option program at Southwest Airlines (LUV). The CEO and co-founder, Herb Kelleher, only holds 63 percent of the shares. He does not want to lose control over the company, so the number of options you can offer is limited. In order to retain control, Herb Kelleher needs 50 percent of the shares and one more share. (The total stock volume can be found on the Nasdaq homepage *www.nasdaq.com.*) Considering that the company will give out new shares to the option-holders and not buy back the stock in the market, how many stock options can be granted to employees? You would like the stock price to rise within the first 3 years at an average of 20 percent a year. Which grant price should you select to make sure that the employees will get rich only when the stock price outperforms the 20 percent offset?

You decide to give 5,000 nonqualified stock options to each of the 100 top employees. Imagine the share price rises to $60. How much does a grantee earn from exercising his or her options? What would have been the cost to the company if the money had been paid as a bonus after the third year?

Herb Kelleher earned $10 million (before taxes) from exercising stock options this year. How many options did he get if the exercise price was $1.

As in the last exercise assume all shares vest at once.

Financial Background: Stock Options

Making money with shares is pretty easy: One buys shares at a certain price and sells the shares at a different price. The win (or loss) can be calculated by multiplying the number of shares times the difference between the buying price and selling price. For example, buying 5000 shares at $20 and selling them for $15 will generate a loss of ($20–$15) × 5,000 = $25,000. The only problem is, that nobody knows what the share price will be in the future.

A stock option entitles the owner to buy (or sell, but that kind of options is of no relevance regarding the exercise) a share of a certain company at a certain price (the grant price). If you have an option to buy one share of a company for $10 and the stock price is at $20, you will make a gain of $10 exercising this option. You cannot lose any money with an option, as you don't need to exercise the option when the stock price is below the exercise price (this is why it is called *option*). Yet if the share price rises, the option will be worth more and more, as the gain exercising the option will increase even faster.

Example: Company X has a stock price of $500. You have an option to buy this stock at $480. Therefore the option is worth $500–$480 = $20. If the stock price rises by 10 percent, one share will be worth $550 . . . the option is now worth $550–$480 = $70, equivalent to a price increase of 350 percent. This effect is called the *leverage effect.*

Attention hobby-brokers: When buying stock options on the real market, you have to pay a certain amount for an option. If the stock price stays below the grant price, *this money will be lost.* While the risk of total loss is pretty slim when working with shares, it is clear and present when working with options.

The exercise of stock options is usually limited to a certain period of time (e.g., 10 years after issuance). It is therefore reasonable to exercise options before that date if they are "in the money."

Financial Background: Stock Options as Incentives

Stock options are a way to compensate employees while saving money. Doling them out virtually doesn't cost any money. In comparison to shares themselves, stock options have a tremendous advantage: Exercising the options grants only the course difference; the basic value of a share will not be part of the compensation.

A problem that occurs with this kind of compensation is dilution. Since every exercised stock option increases the number of shares (when not bought back from the market), the percentage of stock owned by the previous stockholders diminishes. This might lead to losing control over the company if the percentage of stock owned decreases beyond 50 percent.

In order to keep employees from exercising options and leaving the company as well as to keep them from conducting measures that, in the short run, lead to increasing stock prices but, in the long run, hurt the company (causing stocks to fall), it might prove helpful to permit the exercise of options only after a certain time. The time frame during which the exercise of the options is not allowed is called the *vesting period.* Typically stock options vest over 4 years, 25 percent after each year.

The differences between the different types of stock options used in compensation plans are described in Exhibit 14.6.

Summary

Pay-for-performance plans can work. But as this chapter demonstrates, the design and effective administration of these plans is key to their success. Having a good idea is not enough. The good idea must be followed up by sound practices that recognize rewards can, if used properly, shape employee behavior.

Review Questions

1. Every student at one time or another has been assigned group projects. How is a group project like a group incentive plan? Give an example of the free-rider problem in a group project at school. What other problems evident in group incentive plans are common to team projects at school?

2. As VP of HR at American Sales Company (a distribution center for a major food market) you are experiencing turnover problems with the employees who select items to be packed and shipped to different customers (food markets). Plant manager Sam Hartl has asked you to fix the problem. While your primary emphasis might be on having a competitive base pay, you need to decide if there is anything you can do in the incentive department. Before you can make this decisions, what information would you like about (a) pay (base + incentive) at major competitors, (b) the nature of the turnover, and (c) next year's labor budget.

3. How is an earnings-at-risk plan different from an ordinary gain-sharing or profit-sharing plan? How might earnings-at-risk plans affect attraction and retention of employees?

4. You own Higgins Tool Coating Company, a high-tech firm specializing in the coating of cutting tools (e.g., drill bits, cutting blades) to provide longer life before resharpening is needed. You are concerned that the competition continues to develop new coating methods and new applications of coating in different industries. You want to create a work environment where employees offer more new product ideas, and suggest new industries where these ideas might be applied. What type of compensation plan will you recommend? What are some of the problems you need to be aware of?

Appendix 10-A

Gain-Sharing at Dresser Rand

KEY FEATURES OF THE PAINTED POST FACILITIES (DRESSER RAND) GAIN-SHARING PLAN

1. A productivity, quality, and cost reduction formula to recognize employees for their efforts. Employees can earn a bonus by:

   - Increasing productivity
   - Improving quality
   - Saving on shop supplies

     This element of the plan gives employees a triple opportunity to be productive and, at the same time, be conscious of quality, material, and shop supplies.

2. An expansion of the Employee Involvement Teams (EITs) to provide employees with an opportunity to solve problems in a way that can increase productivity and quality while reducing the costs of material and shop supplies.
3. A Bonus Committee composed of four union and four management representatives responsible for the overall administration of the program.
4. The program recognizes Painted Post employees for performance efforts that exceed the plant's [base-line-year] levels.
5. Teamwork and employee participation are the key ingredients of the plan. Both require your support and commitment in order for the program to be successful.

The Employee Involvement Teams

The success of the Painted Post Gain-Sharing Plan will largely be determined by the extent to which all employees, hourly and salary, get involved in making Painted Post a successful business once again. The vehicle for doing this is an expanded and modified process of employee involvement. *all employees must get involved if we are to make this gain-sharing plan a success.*

You know more about your work operations than anyone else. You know best how they can be improved, what shortcuts can be taken, how materials can be saved and scrap minimized, and how work can be performed more efficiently.

The best suggestions are those which recognize the problem and propose a solution.

There will be Employee Involvement Teams (EITs) in each department of the plant, and where possible on the second shift as well. The primary purpose of the EITs should be in the areas of cost reduction, quality, and productivity. The teams will have the option of seeking their own projects. The Steering Committee will also form task forces, task teams, and project teams to work on specific projects, which, in the view of the Steering Committee, might contribute to reducing costs, increasing quality, or reducing production inefficiencies and bottlenecks. Based on results at other companies, expansion of the EITs will allow us to:

- Use our creative powers in our daily tasks to make suggestions which will improve productivity and quality and result in better earnings and bonuses.

- Communicate clearly with each other—management to employees and employees to management.
- Join fully and cooperatively in the common effort to increase productivity, quality, and earnings.
- Keep an open-minded attitude to change.

When an EIT team has developed a solution to a problem and the supervisor agrees with the solution, it may be implemented immediately if the cost of the solution is less than $200 and it does not impact on another department. The reason for this is that we want all employees to take greater responsibility for the success of the business.

If, after discussion and analysis, the employees feel the idea is still a good one and the supervisor or area manager does not, the employees may ask for a review by the EIT Steering Committee. The reason for this is that no one employee, hourly or salaried, can be permitted to stand in the way of a good idea being heard.

The only bad idea is one that is not suggested. You may think your suggestion is not important enough to bring up. Wrong. It may prove to be the catalyst needed by your fellow employees, to trigger another idea.

There will be an Employee Involvement Steering Committee which will coordinate all employee involvement activities. The EIT Steering Committee will have the following functions:

- Oversee the operation of the EIT teams.
- Encourage the teams to take on significant projects.
- Review ideas that have been rejected by supervisors or managers.
- Coordinate review of ideas that cut across more than one department.
- Provide regular communications on the activities of the EITs.
- Act as a mechanism that will create greater trust, confidence, and teamwork.

The Bonus Committee

The Bonus Committee is made up of four union and four company representatives. It is one of the most effective means of communication between employees and management. The committee meets once each quarter to review the bonus computation for the previous quarter and analyze why it was, or was not, favorable. Accurate minutes will be kept by the Bonus Committee.

The Gain-Sharing Bonus

The productivity bonus is paid to recognize employees for their efforts. The bonus is not a gift. It will be paid when it has been earned by exceeding [base-line-year] performance levels for labor costs, quality, and shop supplies.

The program utilizes three measurement points when calculating the bonus payout:

Productivity (as measured in labor costs)

Quality (as measured by spoilage, scrap, and reclamations)

Shop supplies

The Painted Post Gain-Sharing Plan permits gains in productivity to be enhanced by savings in scrap and reclamation expenses and shop supplies. Thus, a bonus is determined by the following formula:

$$\text{Gain-sharing bonus} = \text{productivity (labor costs)}$$
$$\pm\,\text{quality(spoilage, scrap, \& reclamation)} \pm \text{shop supplies}$$

However, if quality falls below the stated target, it will reduce the bonus earned from a productivity gain. Conversely, if productivity falls below the stated target, it will reduce a bonus that could have been earned from a quality improvement.

Thus, employees are required to focus on three very important indicators of plant performance. This measurement system ensures that productivity gains are not achieved at the expense of quality and prudent shop supply usage. At Painted Post, the dual importance of productivity and quality must be recognized by all employees.

The Role of Quality

Maintaining and increasing the quality of Painted Post products is achieved with this measurement formula in two ways:

First, only "good product" is to be recognized in accounting for sales.

Second, "bad product" will be scrapped and will adversely affect spoilage, scrap, and reclamation, as well as labor costs.

Thus, there is a double benefit for employees to produce good-quality products and a severe penalty for failure to do so.

Calculation of the Gain-Sharing Bonus

Employees will receive a bonus when they exceed their own levels of performance in [baseline-year]. Bonuses from the Painted Post Gain-Sharing Plan are not based upon management or employee opinion of how much work should be done and of what quality. Instead, the bonus is based upon improvements in how the work force actually performed in [baseline-year]. The following is an example of how the gain-sharing bonus will be calculated:

Painted Post Gain-Sharing Calculation Example	
Net sales	$9,000,000
Inventory change sales value	+ 1,000,000
Sales value of production	10,000,000
Labor Bonus pool	
Target labor and fringe (16.23%)	1,623,000
Actual labor and fringe	1,573,000
Labor/fringe savings bonus	50,000
Actual percent of sales value	15.73%
Waste Savings Bonus Pool	
Target spoiled and reclamation (3.34)	$ 334,000
Actual spoiled and reclamation	294,000
Waste savings bonus	40,000
Actual percent of sales value	2.94%

Operating Supplies Bonus Pool

Target operating supplies (4.00%)	$ 400,000
Actual operating supplies	370,000
Operating supplies savings bonus	30,000
Actual percent of sales value	3.70%

Distribution

Total all savings bonus pools	$ 120,000
Less: Current quarter reserve provision	40,000
Apply to prior quarter loss	-0-
Available for distribution	80,000
Employee share (65%)	52,000
Participating payroll	1,000,000
Employee share—percentage of participating payroll	5.20%
Reserve balance	$ 40,000

The reserve is established in order to safeguard the Company against any quarters with lower-than-normal output. At the end of each plan year, whatever is left in the reserve will be paid out with 65 percent going to the employees and 35 percent to the Company.

On the next several pages we examine the bonus formula in detail. Please read this information carefully. It is very important for every employee to understand how we arrive at a bonus.

QUESTIONS AND ANSWERS

Q: What should an employee do if he or she has a question about the plan or an idea that might increase the bonus?

A: Questions or ideas should be referred to the employee's supervisor, the EIT Steering Committee, the Plant Personnel office, or the Gain-Sharing Committee.

Q: Will being absent or tardy affect my bonus?

A: Employees will receive a bonus only for actual hours worked. The employee who has lost time will not be paid a bonus for that period of absences.

Q: What about other pay-for-time-not-worked benefits?

A: Bonuses will be excluded from all pay-for-time-not-worked benefits, such as vacations, holidays, death in family, jury duty, etc.

Q: What if there is ever a question as to the accuracy of the calculation of the bonus formula?

A: If there is ever a question as to the accuracy of the information, the Company has agreed to permit Price Waterhouse to conduct an audit.

Q: How long will the program last?

A: The Gain-Sharing Plan will exist for the life of the present collective bargaining agreement. Since the plan is an annual plan, each year the nature of the plan will be reviewed. The Union and the Company will have the right to meet to review the plan if either becomes dissatisfied with it.

Appendix **10-B**

Profit-Sharing at 3M

PROLOGUE

> ". . . In years of unusual company prosperity, incomes under a properly designed plan may go up, allowing the employee to participate in the company's prosperity; and during lean years, incomes automatically decrease. It seems to me that those in important positions should recognize that it is proper to expect their incomes to vary somewhat in relation to the prosperity of their division, subsidiary, and/or the prosperity of the company as a whole."
>
> William L. McKnight
> Chairman 1949–1966

3M's management compensation system is designed to reinforce the manager's responsibility to improve profitability. The formula is based on a simple philosophy: The individual manager's income should vary with the business unit's profitability. This booklet explains how "profit sharing" converts this philosophy into practice.

SALARY SURVEYS

Our management compensation system starts with a review of competitive pay rates in the marketplace. For 3M, the "marketplace" is not the average U.S. corporation but, rather, respected companies that are similar to us in management philosophies and human resource principles. In other words, the "peer" companies with which we compete for talent.

The survey process involves asking our peers for information about base salaries, discretionary bonuses, and any special incentive programs. These components are added together to provide the basis for 3M's salary range structure.

As you'll see, as a manager part of your total cash compensation is paid to you as base salary, and the remainder as profit sharing. The relationship of your total pay to the market rate determined by survey is illustrated by this diagram.

The diagram helps to illustrate a very important concept. Your profit sharing is not an "over and above" payment, nor is it a bonus. Rather, it is a variable portion of your total cash compensation that will fluctuate with the success of your business unit.

DEFINITIONS

Before explaining how a profit-sharing plan is developed, we must discuss two important terms.

As noted earlier, profit sharing is a variable part of your cash compensation. In order to calculate the variable payment, it is first necessary to assign a fixed number of profit sharing "shares." These shares are not owned, nor do they have a market value; they are a device to calculate profit sharing. Then, after the end of each quarter, the number of shares is multiplied by the profit sharing "rate." The rates vary with profitability; hence, your profit-sharing payment will increase or decrease, depending upon profitability.

The Rate Calculations section of this booklet describes how profit-sharing rates are determined.

YOUR INITIAL PLAN

When you are first appointed to management, 5 percent to 10 percent of your new total compensation is normally allocated to profit sharing. Let's go through an example to show how the initial plan is developed. The example assumes you work for an operating division; if you are a staff manager, you will normally receive company shares instead of the division shares referred to in the example.

Let's assume that when you are appointed, your total cash compensation is $45,600 per year, and you receive a promotional increase of approximately 15 percent. The computation works like this.

$45,600	Total compensation
× 1.15	15% promotional increase
$52,520	New total compensation
× 0.05	5% allocated to profit sharing
$ 2,600	Amount allocated to profit sharing

The next step is to determine your number of shares. To do this, your profit-sharing dollar allocation is divided by your division's four-quarter profit-sharing rate (the sum of the most recent four quarters' rates). In our example, the four-quarter rate is $0.17391. Accordingly,

$$\frac{\$2,600 \text{ allocation}}{\$0.17391 \text{ Division Rate}} = 14,950 \text{ division shares}$$

Your annualized profit-sharing compensation plan would then be

Base salary	$49,920	paid monthly
Division profit sharing		
14,950 shares @ $0.17391	2,600	paid quarterly
	$52,520	total compensation

Generally, your initial share assignment is division shares only, since, as a new manager, your most significant contributions will be at the division level. However, as your responsibilities increase, you may be assigned group and company shares. As a staff manager, you will receive company shares which will be increased as responsibilities increase.

Rate Calculations

The 3M profit-sharing system provides for profit sharing at the division, group, and company level. All three types of profit-sharing rates are described in this section.

All profit-sharing rates are calculated quarterly. Quarterly profit is determined as follows:

Year-to-date profit, current quarter
– Year-to-date profit, previous quarter
= Current quarter profit

Division Rates

A division's quarterly profit-sharing rate is determined by dividing the division's current-quarter profit by the number of 3M common shares outstanding at the end of the previous quarter. As an example, let's assume your division had a $5,000,000 profit and there were 115 million shares of 3M common stock outstanding:

$$\frac{\$5,000,000 \text{ quarterly profit}}{115,000,000 \text{ 3M common stock}} = \$0.04348 \text{ (division profit-sharing rate per share)}$$

Since the number of outstanding shares of 3M common stock remains relatively constant, the quarterly rate will increase if division profit increases. This creates the opportunity for you to earn more than your planned income; remember, your share allocation was based on the four-quarter rate at the time your shares were assigned. Conversely, if profit declines, the quarterly rate declines and you will be paid less than your planned income.

Group Rates

Group quarterly profit-sharing rates are calculated using the same formula as division rates. That is, group quarterly profit is divided by the number of 3M common shares outstanding. For example, if your group's quarterly income was $18,750,000, your group rate would be

$$\frac{\$18,750,000 \text{ group profit}}{115,000,000 \text{ 3M common stock}} = \$0.16304 \text{ (group profit-sharing rate per share)}$$

The assignment of group shares is determined using the most recent four-quarter group rate in the manner described for division share assignments.

Company Rates

The formula used to calculate company quarterly profit-sharing rates differs from the division/group formula.

The formula is: Current quarter 3M consolidated net income, minus 2.5 percent of the previous quarter's stockholders' equity (assets minus liabilities), divided by the previous quarter's number of 3M common shares outstanding. Using representative numbers, the quarterly calculation looks like this:

Reserve for return on stockholders' equity

Total Assets	$6,593,000,000
Less total liabilities	2,585,000,000
Stockholders' Equity	$4,008,000,000
	× 2 1/2%
Minimum Reserve	$ 100,200,000
Income Available for Profit Sharing	
Consolidated net income	$186,450,000
Less minimum reserve	100,200,000
Adjusted net income	$ 86,250,000
company share rate	

$$\frac{\$86,250,000 \text{ Profit-Sharing Income}}{115,000,000 \text{ 3M common stock}} = \$0.750 \text{ (company profit-sharing rate per share)}$$

By establishing the minimum reserve, this formula recognizes the fact that the shareholders own the company and are entitled to a reasonable return before profits are shared with management. And, the inclusion of assets and liabilities in the calculation provides an incentive for managers to use assets wisely in their efforts to increase profits.

The assignment of company shares uses the same four-quarter rate method described for division share assignments.

Another Example

Now that you understand rate calculations, let's go through another example that will build on the first.

Your initial plan was designed to pay you a total of $52,520, of which $2,600 was to be profit sharing. However, since that plan became effective, your division's four-quarter rate increased from $0.17391 to $0.20000. As a result, your plan is now paying at an annual rate of $52,910, as follows:

Base salary	$49,920 Paid monthly
Division profit-sharing	2,990 paid quarterly
14,950 shares @ $0.20000	$52,910 Total

Your manager has decided that:

- You have earned a 6 percent merit increase.
- You should have 10 percent of your total pay in profit sharing (up from 5 percent).
- You should receive some group and company shares.
- The value of the group/company profit sharing should be 10 percent of your profit sharing.

Assuming that the four-quarter group and company rates are $0.65216 and $3.000 respectively, your new plan would look like this:

Base salary	$50,460 paid monthly
Division profit sharing:	5,040 paid quarterly
25,200 shares @ $0.2000	
Group profit sharing:	277 paid quarterly
425 shares @ $0.65216	
Company profit sharing:	300 paid quarterly
100 shares @ $3.000	
	$56,077 total planned pay

It's important to note that your 6 percent increase was calculated at a value determined by the current four-quarter rate, and not from the rate used when your shares were originally assigned. In other words, $56,077 is 106 percent of $52,910.

The addition of group/company shares and a change in the percent allocated to profit sharing is most often timed to correspond with a merit or promotional increase. Other changes to your plan, called "conversions," are explained in the last section of this booklet.

You've noted that your profit-sharing allocation was not divided equally between division, group, and company profit sharing. The reasons are explained in the next section.

PROFIT-SHARING MIX

Our example illustrated an important feature of the 3M profit-sharing system. Because your most important contributions will always be at the division level (as long as you have a division job), division profit sharing will always be the most important. However, as your responsibility level increases, the value of the group/company portion may increase, to about 40 percent of the total profit-sharing allocation. When group shares are used, the value of group and company profit sharing will normally be kept approximately equal (up to 20 percent for each). The desired mix is achieved by adjusting the number of shares (without subtracting division shares), generally at the time of an increase.

Profit-Sharing/Base Salary Balance

It is also important to maintain a proper relationship between profit sharing and base salary. As you advance in management, more dollars are assigned to profit sharing, increasing your potential for an increase or decrease in earnings as a result of business unit profitability. For example, as a new or first-level manager, no more than 15 percent of your total planned compensation will be assigned to profit sharing, whereas senior managers may have up to 40 percent of their total planned compensation in profit sharing. At the time of compensation plan changes, increases are planned so as to retain the desired balance between base salary and profit sharing in your plan (without reducing base salary).

PARTICIPATION LIMITS

Profit sharing is intended to provide significant increases in total cash compensation during periods of improving profitability; however, profit growth rates vary by division, and sometimes dramatically. As a consequence, managers in divisions experiencing rapid or even explosive growth can significantly outearn their counterparts in divisions with lower profit growth or even declining profits. When profit growth is more related to the business/product cycle of the division than to relative managerial effectiveness, excessive earnings are not justified. To maintain internal equity while still permitting increased earnings through profit sharing, participation limits have been established.

Participation limits are calculated as a percent of your base salary, and they vary by salary grade. Participation limits are calculated on a year-to-date basis. It is important to emphasize that participation limits do not stop profit sharing; they only restrain the rate at which you participate in profit growth.

Suppose, using our last example, your division is extremely successful. The division, group, and company four-quarter profit-sharing rates have jumped to $0.75000,

$1.00000, and $3.500, respectively. At those rates, the annualized value of your profit-sharing has increased by approximately 350 percent:

Type	Planned	Now Paying
25,200 division shares	$5,020	$18,900
425 group shares	277	425
100 company shares	300	350
	$5,597	$19,675

However, at your salary grade, the participation limit is 35 percent. Here's how it works:

Base Salary	$50,420
	3 35%
100% participation up to	$17,647
50% participation in the next	$17,647
25% participation in the remainder	
So, in our example you would receive:	
100% participation	$17,647
50% participation in excess ($2,028)	1,014
Total	$18,661

Normally, after participation limits are reached, the plan will be revised to provide the desired balance between base salary and profit sharing without a loss in planned total compensation. The resulting new plan effectively captures the level of compensation attained and allows for full participation in future profit growth.

CONVERSIONS

Occasionally, events such as the sale or transfer of commodities, the acquisition or divestiture of a subsidiary or business, or the reorganization of a division will affect division profits, resulting in an increase or decrease in the profit-sharing rate that does not reflect operating results. If the event results in a net change of 3 percent in a division's rate or a 6 percent change in a group rate, the Compensation Department will automatically "convert" your plan.

Conversion is simply restating the number of shares you have in your plan, based on the four-quarter profit-sharing rates. For example, the number of division shares you are assigned will decrease if your division rate increased because of added profit, and they will increase if your division lost profit. The intent, of course, is to cancel the influence of the event and allow the profit-sharing rate to reflect normal changes in business operations.

SUMMARY

The 3M Management Profit-Sharing Compensation system has and continues to:

- Focus management attention on profits and the effective use of assets.
- Provide a measure of variable compensation.
- Allow managers to participate in the growth and decline of the profits of their division, group, and the company.

If there are any questions still unanswered, you should contact your manager, your Human Resource Manager, or the Compensation Department.

Performance Appraisals

Chapter Outline

Chapters 9 and 10 covered the merits of pay-for-performance plans. A key element of these plans is some measure of performance. Sometimes this measure is objective and quantifiable. Certainly, when we are measuring performance for a group incentive plan, objective financial measures may be readily available. As we move down to the level of the individual and the team, these "hard" measures are not as readily available. This chapter discusses in more detail the difficulties of measuring performance, particularly when we use subjective procedures.

THE ROLE OF PERFORMANCE APPRAISALS IN COMPENSATION DECISIONS

The first use of merit ratings apparently took place in a Scottish cotton mill around 1800. Wooden cubes, indicating different levels of performance, were hung above worker stations as a visible signal of who was doing well.[1] Some 200 years later, the Iraqi national soccer

---

[1]R. Heilbroner, *The Worldly Philosophers,* New York: Simon & Schuster, 1953.

team reports that bad performance reviews frequently led to torture of players during the Saddam Hussein reign. While performance reviews don't usually lead to such questionable outcomes, they are used for a wide variety of decisions in organizations—only one of which is to guide the allocation of merit increases. Unfortunately, as we will discover, the link between performance ratings and these outcomes is not always as strong as we would like. In fact, it's common to make a distinction between performance judgments and performance ratings.[2] Performance ratings—the things we enter into an employee's permanent record—are influenced by a host of factors besides the employee behaviors observed by raters. Such things as organization values (e.g., valuing technical skills or interpersonal skills more highly), competition among departments, differences in status between departments, economic conditions (labor shortages make for less willingness to terminate employees for poor performance)—all influence the way raters rate employees. Is it any wonder then that employees often voice frustration about the appraisal process. A recent survey of 2,600 employees nationwide yielded the following rather disheartening conclusions:

39 percent felt their performance goals weren't clearly defined.

39 percent felt they didn't know how their performance was evaluated.

45 percent didn't believe their last performance review guided them on how to improve.

45 percent didn't think the reviews could differentiate among good, average, and poor performers.

48 percent didn't think doing a good job was recognized.[3]

This dissatisfaction makes a difference. Employees unhappy with the appraisal process were less satisfied with their firms, less committed, and more likely to turn over.[4] Perhaps the biggest complaint of all from employees (and managers too) is that appraisals are too subjective. And lurking behind subjectivity, always, is the possibility of unfair treatment by a supervisor. Is it any surprise that most critics clamor for objective read "quantifiable" performance criteria.

At times, measurement of performance can be quantified. Indeed, some reliable estimates suggest that between 13 percent of the time (hourly workers) and 70 percent of the time (managerial employees), employee performance is tied to quantifiable measures.[5] Just because something is quantifiable, though, doesn't mean it is an objective measure of performance. As any accounting student knows, financial measures are arrived at through a process that involves some subjective decision making (can we spell "Enron"?). Which year we choose to take write-offs for plant closings, for example, affects the bottom line reported to the public. Such potential for subjectivity has led some experts to warn that so-called objective data can be deficient and may not tell the whole story.[6] Even with ex-

[2]K. Murphy & J. Cleveland, *Understanding Performance Appraisal* (Thousand Oaks, Ca.: Sage, 1995).

[3]*www.mercerhr.com,* visited on April 24, 2003.

[4]Ibid.

[5]Susan E. Jackson, Randall S. Schuler, and J. Carlos Rivero, "Organizational Characteristics as Predictors of Personnel Practices," Personnel Psychology 42 (1989), pp. 727–786.

[6]Robert L. Cardy and Gregory H. Dobbins, *Performance Appraisal: Alternative Perspectives* (Cincinnati: Southwestern, 1994).

EXHIBIT 11.1
Common
Errors in the
Appraisal
Process

Halo error	An appraiser giving favorable ratings to all job duties based on impressive performance in just one job function. For example, a rater who hates tardiness rates a prompt subordinate high across all performance dimensions exclusively because of this one characteristic.
Horn error	The opposite of a halo error. Downgrading an employee across all performance dimensions exclusively because of poor performance on one dimension.
First impression error	Developing a negative or positive opinion of an employee early in the review period and allowing that to negatively or positively influence all later perceptions of performance.
Recency error	The opposite of first impression error. Allowing performance, either good or bad, at the end of the review period to play too large a role in determining an employee's rating for the entire period.
Leniency error	Consistently rating someone higher than is deserved.
Severity error	The opposite of leniency error. Rating someone consistently lower than is deserved.
Central tendency error	Avoiding extremes in ratings across employees.
Clone error	Giving better ratings to individuals who are like the rater in behavior and/or personality.
Spillover error	Continuing to downgrade an employee for performance errors in prior rating periods.

ternal audits, supposedly solid financial performance indicators can be misrepresented for extended periods. Just ask the folks at HealthSouth, who overstated earnings for almost 15 years without being caught by their auditor, Ernst and Young.[7] Despite these concerns, most HR professionals probably would prefer to work with quantitative data. Sometimes, though, performance isn't easily quantified. Either job output is not readily quantifiable or the components that are quantifiable do not reflect important job dimensions. A secretarial job could be reduced to words per minute and errors per page of keyboarding. But many secretaries, and their supervisors, would argue this captures only a small portion of the job. Courtesy in greeting clients and in answering phones, initiative in solving problems without running to the boss, dependability under deadlines—all of these intangible qualities can make the difference between a good secretary and a poor one. Such subjective goals are less easily measured. The end result, all too often, is a performance appraisal process that is plagued by errors.

Perhaps the biggest attack against appraisals in general, and subjective appraisals in particular, comes from top names in the total-quality-management area. Edward Deming, the grandfather of the quality movement here and in Japan, launched an attack on appraisals because, he contended, the work situation (not the individual) is the major determinant of performance.[8] Variation in performance arises many times because employees

[7]J. Weil, "HealthSouth Becomes Subject of a Congressional Probe," *Wall Street Journal,* April 23, 2003, p. C1.
[8]W. E. Deming, *Out of the Crisis* (Cambridge, MA: MIT Press, 1986).

don't have the necessary information, technology, or control to adequately perform their jobs.[9] Further, Deming argued, individual work standards and performance ratings rob employees of pride and self-esteem.

Some experts argue that rather than throwing out the entire performance appraisal process, we should apply total-quality-management principles to improving the process.[10] A first step, of course, is recognition that part of performance is influenced more by the work environment and system than by employee behaviors. For example, sometimes when a student says "The dog ate my paper" (latest version: "The computer ate my disk"), it really happened. When we tell teachers, or other raters, that the system sometimes does affect performance, raters are more sympathetic and rate higher.[11]

A second way to improve performance appraisal, one that involves most of the remainder of this chapter, concerns identifying strategies for understanding and measuring job performance better. This may help us reduce the number and types of rating errors illustrated in Exhibit 11.1.

COMMON ERRORS IN APPRAISING PERFORMANCE

Suppose you supervise 1,000 employees. How many would you expect to rate at the highest level? How many would be average or below? If you're tempted to argue the distribution should look something like a normal curve, you might get an A in statistics but fail Reality 101. One of the authors (Hint: He's tired of Seinfeld jokes on his name) had a consulting project once with a county department of social services. Part of the project required collecting performance ratings for the prior 10 years. With over 10,000 performance reviews, guess how many times people were rated average or below average? Three times! Think that's just an aberration? Consider the following: One survey of 1,816 organizations reported that only 4.6 percent of the managers were rated below average see (Exhibit 11.2).

Now, we might argue that people who get to the managerial level do so because they are better-than-average performers.[12] So of course most of them rate average or better in

EXHIBIT 11.2
Ratings of Mangers

Rating	Percent of Managers Receiving Rating
Above average	46.4
Average	49.0
Below average	4.6

[9]David Waldman, "The Contributions of Total Quality Management to a Theory of Work Performance," *Academy of Management Review* 19 (1994), pp. 510–536.

[10]David Antonioni, "Improve the Performance Management Process before Discontinuing Performance Appraisals," *Compensation and Benefits Review*, May–June 1994, pp. 29–37.

[11]R. L. Cardy, C. L. Sutton, K. P. Carson, and G. H. Dobbins, "Degree of Responsibility: An Empirical Examination of Person and System Effects on Performance Ratings," paper presented at the national meeting of the Academy of Management, San Francisco, 1990.

[12]American Management Association, "Top performers? Most Managers Rated Average or Better," *Compflash*, September 1992, p. 3.

their jobs. But the truth is that as raters we tend to make mistakes. Our ratings differ from those that would occur if we could somehow, in a moment of clarity, divine (and report!) the truth. We make errors in ratings. Recognizing and understanding the errors, such as those noted in Exhibit 11.1, are the first steps to communicating and building a more effective appraisal process.

Not surprisingly, the potential for errors causes employees to lose faith in the performance appraisal process. Employees, quite naturally, will be reluctant to have pay systems tied to such error-ridden performance ratings. At the very least, charges that the evaluation process is political will abound.[13] There are several factors that lead raters to give inaccurate appraisals: (1) guilt, (2) embarrassment about giving praise, (3) taking things for granted, (4) not noticing, (5) the halo effect, (6) dislike of confrontation, and (7) spending too little time on preparation of the appraisal.[14] To counter such problems, companies and researchers alike have expended considerable time and money to identify ways job performance can be measured better.

STRATEGIES FOR BETTER UNDERSTANDING AND MEASURING JOB PERFORMANCE

Efforts to improve the performance rating process take several forms.[15] First, researchers and compensation people alike devote considerable energy to defining job performance—what exactly should be measured when we evaluate employees? Managers can be grouped into one of three categories, based on the types of employee behaviors they focus on. One group looks strictly at task performance, how the employees perform the responsibilities of their jobs. A second group looks primarily at counterproductive performance, evaluating based on the negative behaviors employees show. The final group looks at both these types of behavior.[16] Studies that examine more specific factors focus on such performance dimensions as planning and organizing, training, coaching, developing subordinates, and technical proficiency.[17]

A second direction for performance research notes that the definition of performance and its components is expanding. Jobs are becoming more dynamic, and the need for employees to adapt and grow is increasingly stressed. This focus on individual characteristics, or personal competencies, is consistent with the whole trend toward measuring job competency.[18]

---

[13]Clinton Longnecker, Henry Sims, and Dennis Gioia, "Behind the Mark: The Politics of Employee Appraisal," *Academy of Management Executive* 1(3) (1987), pp. 183–193.

[14]Timothy D. Schellhardt, "Annual Agony," *Wall Street Journal*, November 19, 1996, p. A1.

[15]R. Arvey and K. Murphy, "Performance Evaluation in Work Settings," *Annual Review of Psychology* 49 (1998), pp. 141–168.

[16]P. Gwynne, "How Consistent Are Performance Review Criteria," *MIT Sloan Management Review*, Summer 2002, pp. 15–22.

[17]W. Borman and D. Brush, "More Progress Towards a Taxonomy of Managerial Performance Requirements," *Human Performance,* 6(1) (1993), pp. 1–21.

[18]D. Coleman, *Working with Emotional Intelligence* (New York: Bantam Books 1998).

A third direction for improving the quality of performance ratings centers on identifying the best appraisal format. If only the ideal format could be found, so the argument goes, raters would use it to measure job performance better, that is, make more accurate ratings. Recent attention has focused less on the rating format and more on the raters themselves. This fourth direction identifies possible groups of raters (supervisor, peers, subordinates, customers, self) and examines whether a given group leads to more or less accurate ratings. The fifth direction attempts to identify how raters process information about job performance and translate it into performance ratings. Such information, including an understanding of the role irrelevant information plays in the evaluation of employees, may yield strategies for reducing the flaws in the total process. Finally, data also suggest that raters can be trained to increase the accuracy of their ratings. The following sections focus on these last four approaches to better understanding and measuring performance: improving the format, selecting the right raters, understanding the way raters process information, and training raters to improve rating skills.

Strategy 1: Improve Appraisal Formats

Types of Formats

Evaluation formats can be divided into two general categories: ranking and rating.[19] *Ranking formats* require that the rater compare employees against each other to determine the relative ordering of the group on some performance measure (usually some measure of overall performance). Exhibit 11.3 illustrates three different methods of ranking employees:

- The *straight ranking* procedure is just that: employees are ranked relative to each other.
- *Alternation ranking* recognizes that raters are better at ranking people at extreme ends of the distribution. Raters are asked to indicate the best employee and then the worst employee. Working at the two extremes permits a rater to get more practice prior to making the harder distinctions in the vast middle ground of employees.
- The *paired-comparison ranking* method simplifies the ranking process by forcing raters to make ranking judgments about discrete pairs of people. Each individual is compared separately with all others in the work group. The person who "wins" the most paired comparisons is ranked top in the group, and so on. Unfortunately, when the size of the work group goes above 10 to 15 employees, the number of paired comparisons becomes unmanageable.

The second category of appraisal formats, ratings, is generally more popular than ranking systems. The various *rating formats* have two elements in common. First, in contrast to ranking formats, rating formats require raters to evaluate employees on some absolute standard rather than relative to other employees. Second, each performance standard is measured on a scale whereby appraisers can check the point that best represents the employee's performance. In this way, performance variation is described along a continuum from good to bad. It is the types of descriptors used in anchoring this continuum that provide the major difference in rating scales.

[19]Daniel Ilgen and Jack Feldman, "Performance Appraisal: A Process Focus," *Research in Organizational Behavior* 5 (1983), pp. 141–197.

EXHIBIT 11.3
Three
Ranking
Formats

Straight Ranking Method

Rank	Employee's Name
Best	1. _____
Next Best	2. _____
Next Best	3. _____
Etc.	

Alternation Ranking*

Rank	Employee's Name
Best performer	1. _____
Next best	2. _____
Next best	3. _____
Etc.	4. _____
Next worst	3. _____
Next worst	2. _____
Worst performer	1. _____

Paired-Comparison Ranking Method+

	John	Pete	Sam	Tom	No. of Times Ranked Higher
Bill	X	X	X	X	4
John		X	X	X	3
Pete			X	X	2
Sam				X	1

*Alternate identifying best, then worst; next best, then next worst; etc.
+x indicates person in row ranked higher than person in column. Highest ranking goes to person with most "ranking wins."

These descriptors may be adjectives, behaviors, or outcomes. When adjectives are used as anchors, the format is called a *standard rating scale.* Exhibit 11.4 shows a typical rating scale with adjectives as anchors ("well above average" to "well below average").

Behaviorally anchored rating scales (BARS's) seem to be the most common format using behaviors as descriptors. By anchoring scales with concrete behaviors, firms adopting a BARS format hope to make evaluations less subjective. When raters try to decide on a rating, they have a common definition (in the form of a behavioral example) for each of the performance levels. Consider, as an example, the following behaviors as recorded on fictitious officer fitness reports for the British Royal Navy. They are easily identifiable and, hopefully, humorous:

"This Officer reminds me very much of a gyroscope—always spinning around at a frantic pace, but not really going anywhere."

"He would be out of his depth in a car park puddle."

"Works well when under constant supervision and cornered like a rat in a trap."

"This man is depriving a village somewhere of an idiot."

"Only occasionally wets himself under pressure."[20]

[20]Royal Navy and Marines fitness reports from S206.

EXHIBIT 11.4
Rating Scale
Using
Absolute
Standards

Standard Rating Scale with Adjective Anchors					
Communications skills	Written and oral ability to clearly and convincingly express thoughts, ideas, or facts in individual or group situations.				
Circle the number that best describes the level of employee performance	1 well above average	2 above average	3 average	4 below average	5 well below average

This rating format directly addresses a major criticism of standard rating scales: Different raters carry with them into the rating situation different definitions of the scale levels (e.g., different raters have different ideas about what "average work" is). Exhibit 11.5 illustrates a behaviorally anchored rating scale.

In both the standard rating scale and the BARS, overall performance is calculated as some weighted average (weighted by the importance the organization attaches to each dimension) of the ratings on all dimensions. The appendix to this chapter gives an example of the rating scale and total appraisal form used by Pfizer Pharmaceutical. As a brief illustration, though, consider Exhibit 11.6.

The employee evaluated in Exhibit 11.6 is rated slightly above average. An alternative method for obtaining the overall rating would be to allow the rater discretion not only in rating performance on the individual dimensions but also in assigning the overall evaluation. The weights (shown in the far-right column of Exhibit 11.6) would not be used, and the overall evaluation would be based on a subjective and internal assessment by the rater.

In addition to adjectives and behaviors, outcomes also are used as a standard. The most common form is *management by objectives (MBO)*.[21] Management by objectives is both a planning and an appraisal tool that has many different variations across firms.[22] As a first step, organization objectives are identified from the strategic plan of the company. Each successively lower level in the organizational hierarchy is charged with identifying work objectives that will support attainment of organizational goals. Exhibit 11.7 illustrates a common MBO objective. Notice that the emphasis is on outcomes achieved by employees. At the beginning of a performance review period, the employee and supervisor discuss performance objectives (column 1).[23] Months later, at the end of the review period, the two again meet to record results formally (of course, multiple informal discussions should have occurred before this time). Results are then compared against objectives, and a performance rating is determined based on how well the objectives were met.

Merck, the pharmaceutical giant, combines an MBO approach focusing on outcomes with a set of measures designed to assess how those outcomes were achieved—Merck calls this its multidimensional view of performance. The MBO portion of a performance review is regularly updated to ensure that individual objectives are aligned with corporate and department goals. At the end of the year, employees are reviewed both on goal performance and on five

[21]H. Levinson, "Management by Whose Objectives," *Harvard Business Review,* January 2003, pp. 1007–1016.

[22] Mark L. McConkie, "A Clarification of the Goal Setting and Appraisal Processes in MBO," *Academy of Management Review* 4(1) (1979), pp. 29–40.

[23]Mark L. McConkie, "A Clarification of the Goal Setting and Appraisal Processes in MBO," *Academy of Management Review* 4(1) (1979), pp. 29–40.

EXHIBIT 11.5   Standard Rating Scale with Behavioral Scale Anchors

Teamwork:	Ability to contribute to group performance, to draw out the best from others, to foster activities building group morale, even under high-pressure situations.	
Exceeds Standards	1	Seeks out or is regularly requested for group assignments. Groups this person works with inevitably have high performance and high morale. Employee makes strong personal contribution and is able to identify strengths of many different types of group members and foster their participation. Wards off personality conflicts by positive attitude and ability to mediate unhealthy conflicts, sometimes even before they arise. Will make special effort to ensure credit for group performance is shared by all.
	2	Seen as a positive contributor in group assignments. Works well with all types of people and personalities, occasionally elevating group performance of others. Good ability to resolve unhealthy group conflicts that flare up. Will make special effort to ensure strong performers receive credit due them.
Meets Standards	3	Seen as a positive personal contributor in group assignments. Works well with most types of people and personalities. Is never a source of unhealthy group conflict and will encourage the same behavior in others.
	4	When group mission requires skill this person is strong in, employee seen as strong contributor. On other occasions will not hinder performance of others. Works well with most types of people and personalities and will not be the initiator of unhealthy group conflict. Will not participate in such conflict unless provoked on multiple occasions.
	5	Depending on the match of personal skill and group mission, this person will be seen as a positive contributor. Will not be a hindrance to performance of others and avoids unhealthy conflict unless provoked.
Does Not Meet Standards	6	Unlikely to be chosen for assignments requiring teamwork except on occasions where personal expertise is vital to group mission. Not responsive to group goals, but can be enticed to help when personal appeals are made. May not get along with other members and either withdraw or generate unhealthy conflict. Seeks personal recognition for team performance and/or may downplay efforts of others.
	7	Has reputation for noncontribution and for creating conflicts in groups. Cares little about group goals and is very hard to motivate towards and goal completion unless personal rewards are guaranteed. May undermine group performance to further personal aims. Known to seek personal recognition and/or downplay efforts of others.
Rating:	Documentation of Rating (optional except for 6 and 7):	

EXHIBIT 11.6 An Example of Employee Appraisal

Employee: Kelsey T. Mahoney
Job Title: Supervisor, Shipping and Receiving

Performance Dimension	Dimension Rating					Dimension Weight
	Well Below Average 1	*Below Average* 2	*Average* 3	*Above Average* 4	*Well Above Average* 5	
Leadership Ability				X		0.2 (× 4) = 0.8
Job Knowledge					X	0.1 (× 5) = 0.5
Work Output				X		0.3 (× 4) = 1.2
Attendance			X			0.2 (× 3) = 0.6
Initiative			X			0.2 (× 3) = 0.6

Sum of Rating × weight = 3.7
Overall Rating = 3.7

EXHIBIT 11.7 Example of MBO Objective for Communications Skill

1. Performance objective	2. Results
By July 1 of this year Bill will complete a report summarizing employee reactions to the new performance appraisal system. An oral presentation will be prepared and delivered to all non-exempt employees in groups of 15-20. All oral presentations will be completed by August 31, and reactions of employees to this presentation will average at least 3.0 on a 5-point scale.	Written report completed by July 1. All but one oral presentation completed by August 31. Last report not completed until September 15 because of unavoidable conflicts in vacation schedules. Average rating of employees (reaction to oral presentation) was 3.4, exceeding minimum expectations.

other measures: quality of work, resource utilization, timeliness of completing objectives, innovation, and leadership. Ratings on these latter measures must be accompanied by examples of behaviors shown by employees that justify particular ratings.

A review of firms using MBO indicates generally positive improvements in performance both for individuals and for the organization. This performance increase is accompanied by managerial attitudes toward MBO that become more positive over time, particularly when the system is revised periodically to reflect feedback of participants. Managers are especially pleased with the way MBO provides direction to work units, improves the planning process, and increases superior/subordinate communication. On the negative side, MBO appears to require more paperwork and to increase both performance pressure and stress.[24] Exhibit 11.8 shows some of the common components of an MBO format and the percentage of experts who judge this component vital to a successful evaluation effort.

A final type of appraisal format does not easily fall into any of the categories yet discussed. In an *essay format*, supervisors answer open-ended questions, in essay form, de-

---

[24] J. S. Hodgson, "Management by Objectives: The Experiences of a Federal Government Department," *Canadian Public Administration* 16(4) (1973), pp. 422–431.

EXHIBIT 11.8   Components of a Successful MBO Program

	Total No. of Responses*	Percent of Authorities in Agreement
1. Goals and objectives should be specific.	37	97
2. Goals and objectives should be defined in terms of measurable results.	37	97
3. Individual goals should be linked to overall organization goals.	37	97
4. Objectives should be reviewed "periodically."	31	82
5. The time period for goal accomplishment should be specified.	27	71
6. Wherever possible, the indicator of the results should be quantifiable; otherwise, it should be at least verifiable.	26	68
7. Objectives should be flexible; changed as conditions warrant.	26	68
8. Objectives should include a plan of action for accomplishing the results.	21	55
9. Objectives should be assigned priorities of weights.	19	50

*In this table the total number of responses actually represents the total number of authorities responding; thus, percent also represent the percent of authorities in agreement with the statements made.
Source: Mark L. McConkie, "A Clarification of the Goal Setting and Appraisal Process in MBO," *Academy of Management Review* 4(1) (1979), pp. 29–40. © 1979, Academy of Management Review.

EXHIBIT 11.9   *Usage of Performance Evaluation Formats*

Type of System	Usage by Type of Employee (%)*	
	Nonexempt	Exempt
1. Standard Rating Scale	52	32
2. Essay	30	3
3. Management by objectives or other objective-based system	19	73
4. Behaviorally anchored scale	28	24
5. Other	33	32

*Usage columns total more than 100 percent because of multiple systems in different companies.
Source: Based on a survey of 256 firms, from a population of 1,300 large organizations, conducted by Drake, Beam and Morin, New York, 1983.

scribing employee performance. Since the descriptors used could range from comparisons with other employees to the use of adjectives describing performance, types of behaviors, and goal accomplishments, the essay format can take on characteristics of all the formats discussed previously.

Exhibit 11.9 illustrates the relative popularity of these formats in industry.

Evaluating Performance Appraisal Formats

Appraisal formats are generally evaluated against five criteria: (1) employee development potential (amount of feedback about performance that the format offers), (2) administrative ease, (3) personnel research potential, (4) cost, and (5) validity. Admittedly, different organizations will attach different weights to these dimensions. For example, a small organization in its formative years is likely to be very cost-conscious. A large organization with pressing affirmative action commitments might place relatively high weight on validity and nondiscrimination and show less concern about cost issues. A progressive firm concerned with employee development might demand a format allowing substantial employee feedback. For example, 10 years ago Dow Chemical Company did away with performance ratings but kept performance reviews; stress was placed on using reviews to help develop employee skills. The five main criteria are explained below:[25]

1. *Employee development criterion:* Does the method communicate the goals and objectives of the organization? Is feedback to employees a natural outgrowth of the evaluation format, so that employee developmental needs are identified and can be attended to readily? Keep in mind, though, that the desire for feedback doesn't extend across all cultures. Lucent Technologies found that certain cultures are very reluctant to give feedback, either positive or negative. In most Asian cultures feedback is viewed with great suspicion, and only the most reckless executive would jeopardize his reputation by giving feedback, particularly in public.

2. *Administrative criterion:* How easily can evaluation results be used for administrative decisions concerning wage increases, promotions, demotions, terminations, and transfers? Comparisons among individuals for personnel action require some common denominator. Typically this is a numerical rating of performance. Evaluation forms that do not produce numerical ratings cause administrative headaches.

3. *Personnel research criterion:* Does the instrument lend itself well to validating employment tests? Can applicants predicted to perform well be monitored through performance evaluation? Similarly, can the success of various employees and organizational development programs be traced to impacts on employee performance? As with the administrative criterion, evaluations typically need to be quantitative to permit the statistical tests so common in personnel research.

4. *Cost criterion:* Does the evaluation form initially require a long time to be developed? Is it time-consuming for supervisors to use in rating their employees? Is it expensive to use? All of these factors increase the format cost.

5. *Validity criterion:* By far the most research on formats in recent years has focused on reducing error and improving accuracy. Success in this pursuit would mean that decisions based on performance ratings (e.g., promotions, merit increases) could be made with increased confidence. In general, the search for the perfect format to eliminate rating errors and improve accuracy has been unsuccessful. The high acclaim, for example, accompanying the introduction of BARS has not been supported by research.[26]

Exhibit 11.10 provides a report card on the five most common rating formats relative to the criteria just discussed.

---

[25]Bruce McAfee and Blake Green, "Selecting a Performance Appraisal Method," *Personnel Administrator* 22(5) (1977), pp. 61–65.

[26]H. John Bernardin, "Behavioral Expectation Scales v. Summated Ratings: A Fairer Comparison," *Journal of Applied Psychology* 62 (1977), pp. 422–427; H. John Bernardin, Kim Alvares, and C. J. Cranny, "A Recomparison of Behavioral Expectation Scales to Summated Scales," *Journal of Applied Psychology* 61 (1976), pp. 284–291; C. A. Schriesheim and U. E. Gattiker, "A Study of the Abstract Desirability of Behavior-Based v. Trait-Oriented Performance Rating," *Proceedings of the Academy of Management* 43 (1982), pp. 307–311; F. S. Landy and J. L. Farr, "Performance Rating," *Psychological Bulletin* 87 (1980), pp. 72–107.

EXHIBT 11.10   An Evaluation of Performance Appraisal Formats

	Employee Development Criterion	Administration Criterion	Personnel Research Criterion	Economic Criterion	Validity Criterion
Ranking	Poor—ranks typically based on overall performance, with little thought given to feedback on specific performance dimensions.	Poor—comparisons of ranks across work units to determine merit raises are meaningless. Other administrative actions similarly hindered.	Average—validation studies can be completed with rankings of performance.	Good—inexpensive source of performance data. Easy to develop and use in small organizations and in small units.	Average—good reliability but poor on rating errors, especially halo.
Standard rating scales	Average—general problem areas identified. Some information on extent of developmental need is available, but no feedback on necessary behaviors/outcomes.	Average—ratings valuable for merit increase decisions and others. Not easily defended if contested.	Average—validation studies can be completed, but level of measurement contamination unknown.	Good—inexpensive to develop and easy to use.	Average—content validity is suspect. Rating errors and reliability are average.
Behaviorally anchored rating scales	Good—extent of problem and behavioral needs are identified.	Good—BARS good for making administrative decisions. Useful for legal defense because job-relevant.	Good—validation studies can be completed and measurement problems on BARS less than many other criterion measures.	Average—expensive to develop but easy to use.	Good—high content validity. Some evidence of interrater reliability and reduced rating errors.
Management by objectives	Excellent—extent of problem and outcome deficiencies are identified.	Poor—MBO not suited to merit income decisions. Level of completion and difficulty of objectives hard to compare across employees.	Poor—nonstandard objectives across employees and no overall measures of performance make validity studies difficult.	Poor—expensive to develop and time-consuming to use.	Excellent—high content validity. Low rating errors.
Essay	Unknown—depends on guidelines or inclusions in essay as developed by organization or supervisors.	Poor—essays not comparable across different employees considered for merit or other administrative actions.	Poor—no quantitative indices to compare performance against employee test scores in validation studies.	Average—easy to develop but time-consuming to use.	Unknown—unstructured format makes studies of essay method difficult.

Which of these appraisal formats is the best? Unfortunately, the answer is a murky "It depends." Keeley suggests that the choice of an appraisal format is dependent on the type of tasks being performed.[27] He argues that tasks can be ordered along a continuum from those that are very routine to those for which the appropriate behavior for goal accomplishment is very uncertain. In Keeley's view, different appraisal formats require assumptions about the extent to which correct behavior for task accomplishment can be specified. The choice of an appraisal format requires a matching of formats with tasks that meet the assumptions for that format. At one extreme of the continuum are behavior-based evaluation procedures that define specific performance expectations against which employee performance is evaluated. Keeley argues that behaviorally anchored rating scales fall into this category. The behavioral anchors specify performance expectations representing the different levels of performance possible by an employee. Only for highly routine, mechanistic tasks is it appropriate to specify behavioral expectations. For these routine tasks it is possible to identify the single sequence of appropriate behaviors for accomplishing a goal. Consequently, it is possible to identify behavioral anchors for a performance scale that illustrate varying levels of attainment of the proper sequence of activities.

However, when tasks are less routine, it is more difficult to specify a single sequence of procedures that must be followed to accomplish a goal. Rather, multiple strategies are both feasible and appropriate to reach a final goal. Under these circumstances, Keeley argues that the appraisal format should focus on evaluating the extent to which the final goal can be specified.[28] Thus, for less certain tasks an MBO strategy would be appropriate. As long as the final goal can be specified, performance can be evaluated in relation to that goal without specifying or evaluating the behavior used to reach that goal. The focus is exclusively on the degree of goal accomplishment.

At the other extreme of the continuum are tasks that are highly uncertain in nature. A relatively low consensus exists about the characteristics of successful performance. Moreover, the nature of the task is so uncertain that it may be difficult to specify expected goals. For this type of task, Keeley argues that judgment-based evaluation procedures—as exemplified by standard rating scales—may be the most appropriate. Raters make subjective estimates about the levels of employee performance on tasks for which neither the appropriate behavior nor the final goal is well specified. The extent of this uncertainty makes this type of appraisal very subjective and may well explain why trait rating scales are openly criticized for the number of errors that occur in performance evaluations.

Strategy 2: Select the Right Raters

A second way that firms have tried to improve the accuracy of performance ratings is by focusing on who might conduct the ratings and which of these sources is more likely to be accurate. For example, recent evidence indicates raters who are not particularly conscientious and raters who are too agreeable tend to give artificially high evaluations of employees.[29] To lessen the impact of one reviewer, and to increase participation in the process, a

---

[27]Michael Keeley, "A Contingency Framework for Performance Evaluation," *Academy of Management Review* 3 (July 1978), pp. 428–438.

[28]Ibid.

[29]H. J. Bernardin, K. Cooke, and P. Villanova, "Conscientiousness and Agreeableness as Predictors of Rating Leniency," *Journal of Applied Psychology* 85(2) (2000), pp 232–234.

method known as *360-degree feedback* has grown more popular in recent years. Generally, this system is used in conjunction with supervisory reviews.[30] The method assesses employee performance from five points of view: supervisor, peer, self, customer, and subordinate. The flexibility of the process makes it appealing to employees at all levels within an organization; most companies using the system report that their employees are satisfied with its results.[31] They feel that the 360-degree system has outperformed their old systems in improving employee understanding and self-awareness, promoting communication between supervisors and staff, and promoting better performance and results.[32] Hershey Foods, for example, uses a 360 process that identifies areas for leadership training, and employees have voiced support for continuation of the program.[33]

Regardless of the positive responses from those who have implemented the 360-degree feedback system, today most companies still use it only for evaluation of their top-level personnel and for employee development rather than for appraisal or pay decisions.[34] Some companies report frustration with the number of evaluation surveys each rater has to complete and the time necessary to complete the entire process.[35] Let's take a closer look at the role and benefit of each of the raters.

Supervisors as Raters

Who rates employees? Some estimates indicate that more than 80 percent of the input for performance ratings comes from supervisors.[36] There is good reason supervisors play such a dominant role. Supervisors assign (or jointly determine) what work employees are to perform. This makes a supervisor knowledgeable about the job and the dimensions to be rated. Also, supervisors frequently have considerable prior experience in rating employees, thus giving them some pretty firm ideas about what level of performance is required for any given level of performance rating.[37] Supervisor ratings also tend to be more reliable than those from other sources.[38] On the negative side, though, supervisors are particularly prone to halo and leniency errors.[39]

---

[30]Mark R. Edwards and Ann J. Ewen, *360 Degree Feedback: The Powerful New Model for Employee Assessment and Performance Improvement* (Toronto: American Management Association, 1996).

[31]Ibid.

[32]Ibid.

[33]IOMA, "Perils and Payoffs of Multi-Rater Feedback Programs," *Pay for Performance Report*, May 2003, p. 2.

[34]Mark R. Edwards and Ann J. Ewen, *360 Degree Feedback: The Powerful New Model for Employee Assessment and Performance Improvement* (Toronto: American Management Association, 1996).

[35]IOMA, "Perils and Payoffs of Multi-Rater Feedback Programs"; D. Waldman, L. Atwater, and D. Antonioni, "Has 360 Degree Feedback Gone Amok," *Academy of Management Executive* 12(2) (1998), pp. 86–94.

[36]Susan E. Jackson, Randall S. Schuller, and J. Carlos Rivero, "Organizational Characteristics as Predictors of Personnel Practices," *Personnel Psychology* 42 (1989), pp. 727–786.

[37]E. Pulakos and W. Borman, *Developing the Basic Criterion Scores for Army-wide and MOS-Specific Ratings.* (Alexandria, VA: U.S. Army Research Institute, 1983).

[38]Deniz S. Ones, Frank L. Schmidt, and Chockalingam Viswesvaran, "Comparative Analysis of the Reliability of Job Performance Ratings," *Journal of Applied Psychology* 81(5) (1996), pp. 557–574.

[39]F. S. Landy and J. L. Farr, "Performance Rating," *Psychological Bulletin* 87 (1980), pp. 72–107.

Peers as Raters

One of the major strengths of using peers as raters is that they work more closely with the ratee and probably have an undistorted perspective of typical performance, particularly in group assignments (as opposed to what a supervisor might observe in a casual stroll around the work area). Balanced against this positive are at least two powerful negatives. First, peers may have little or no experience in conducting appraisals, leading to rather mixed evidence about the reliability of this rating source. Second, in a situation where teamwork is promoted, placing the burden of rating peers on co-workers can either create group tensions (in the case of low evaluations) or yield ratings second only to self-ratings in level of leniency.[40] One exception to this leniency effect comes from top performers, who it seems give the most objective evaluations of peers.[41] However, Motorola, one of the leaders in the use of teams and in peer ratings, reports that peer ratings help team members exert pressure on co-workers to perform better.[42]

Self as Rater

Some organizations have experimented with self-ratings. Obviously self-ratings are done by someone who has the most complete knowledge about the ratee's performance. Unfortunately, though, self-ratings are generally more lenient and possibly more unreliable than ratings from other sources.[43] One compromise in the use of self-ratings is to use them for developmental rather than administrative purposes. Increasingly firms are asking employees to rate themselves as the first step in the appraisal process. Forcing employees to think about their performance in advance may lead to more realistic assessments, ones that are also more in tune with a supervisor's own perceptions.

Customer as Rater

This is the era of the customer. The drive for quality means more companies are recognizing the importance of customers. One logical outcome of this increased interest is ratings from customers. For example, Burger King surveys its customers, sets up 800 numbers to get feedback, and hires mystery customers to order food and report back on the service and treatment they receive. Increasingly we can expect the boundaries between organizations and the outside world to fade. While much of the customer rating movement is directed at performance of business units, we can expect some of this to distill down to individual workers.

Subordinate as Rater

Historically, upward feedback has been viewed as countercultural, but the culture within organizations has undergone a revolution in the past 10 years and views are ever-changing.[44] The notion of subordinates as raters is appealing since most employees want

[40]M. M. Harris and J. Schaubroeck, "A Meta Analysis of Self-Supervisor, Self-Peer and Peer-Supervisor ratings," *Personnel Psychology* 4 (1988), pp. 43–62.

[41]R. Saavedra and S. Kwun, "Peer Evaluation in Self Managing Work Groups," *Journal of Applied Psychology* 78(3) (1993), pp. 450–462.

[42]Conference on Performance Management, Center for Effective Organizations, April 23 2003.

[43]Harris and Schaubroeck, "A Meta Analysis of Self-Supervisor, Self-Peer and Peer-Supervisor Ratings."

[44]Mark R. Edwards and Ann J. Ewen, *360 Degree Feedback: The Powerful New Model for Employee Assessment and Performance Improvement* (Toronto: American Management Association, 1996).

to be successful with the people who report to them. Hearing how they are viewed by their subordinates gives them the chance to see both their strengths and their weaknesses as a leader and to modify their behavior.[45] The difficulty with this type of rating is in attaining candid reviews and also in counseling the ratee on how to deal with the feedback. Research shows that subordinates prefer, not surprisingly, to give their feedback to managers anonymously. If their identity is known, subordinates give artificially inflated ratings of their supervisors.[46]

> **Cybercomp**
> The American Compensation Association has an extensive website, including a bookstore. Go to *www.worldatwork.org/bookstore/* if you want information about other books on performance measurement, including books that talk about the advantages and disadvantages of using multiple raters.

Strategy 3: Understand How Raters Process Information

A third way to improve job performance ratings is to understand how raters think. When we observe and evaluate performance, what else influences ratings besides an employee's performance?[47] We know, for example, that feelings, attitudes, and moods influence raters. If your supervisor likes you, then regardless of how well you perform, you are likely to get better ratings.[48] Your boss's general mood also influences performance ratings. Hope for a rater who is generally cheerful rather than grumpy; it could influence how you are evaluated![49]

Researchers continue to explore how raters process information about the performance of the people they rate. In general, we think the following kinds of processes occur so:

1. The rater observes the behavior of a ratee.

2. The rater encodes this behavior as part of a total picture of the ratee (i.e., the rater forms stereotypes).

3. The rater stores this information in memory, which is subject to both short- and long-term decay. Simply put, raters forget things.

---

[45]William L. Bearly and John E. Jones, *360 Degree Feedback: Strategies, Tactics , and Techniques for Developing Leaders* (Amherst, MA: HRD Press, 1996).

[46]D. Antonioni, "The Effects of Feedback Accountability on Upward Appraisal Ratings," *Personnel Psychology* 47 (1994), pp. 349–356.

[47]J. Schaubroeck and S. Lam, "How Similarity to Peers and Supervisor Influences Organizational Advancement in Different Cultures," *Academy of Management Journal*, 45(6) (2002), pp. 1125–1136; K. Murphy and J. Cleveland, *Understanding Performance Appraisal.*

[48]J. Lefkowitz, "The Role of Interpersonal Affective Regard in Supervisory Performance Ratings: A Literature Review and Proposed Causal Model," *Journal of Occupational and Organizational Psychology* 73(1) (2000), pp. 61–85; R. L. Cardy and G. H. Dobbins, "Affect and Appraisal Accuracy: Liking as an Integral Dimension in Evaluating Performance," *Journal of Applied Psychology* 71 (1986), pp. 672–678; Robert C. Liden and Sandy J. Wayne, "Effect of Impression Management on Performance Ratings: A Longitudinal Study," *Academy of Management Journal* 38(1) (1995), pp. 232–260; Angelo S. Denisi, Lawrence H. Peters, and Arup Varma, "Interpersonal Affect and Performance Appraisal: A Field Study," *Personnel Psychology* 49 (1996), pp. 341–360.

[49]G. Alliger and K. J. Williams, "Affective Congruence and the Employment Interview," in *Advances in Information Processing in Organizations*, Vol. 4, ed. J. R. Meindl, R. L. Cardy, and S. M. Puffer (Greenwich, CT: JAI Press, 1986).

4. When it comes time to evaluate a ratee, the rater reviews the performance dimensions and retrieves stored observations/impressions to determine their relevance to the performance dimensions.

5. The information is reconsidered and integrated with other available information as the rater decides on the final ratings.[50]

Quite unintentionally, this process can produce errors, and they can occur at any stage.

Errors in the Rating Process

Ideally raters should notice only performance-related factors when they observe employee behavior. In fact, all of the processing stages should be guided by performance relevancy. Unless a behavior (or personality trait) affects performance, it should not influence performance ratings. Fortunately, studies show that performance actually does play an important role, perhaps the major role, in determining how a supervisor rates a subordinate.[51] Employees who are technically proficient and who do not create problems on the job tend to receive higher ratings than these who are weaker on these dimensions.[52] On the negative side, though, performance-irrelevant factors appear to influence ratings, and they can cause errors in the evaluation process.[53]

Errors in Observation (Attention)

Generally, researchers have varied three types of input information to see what raters pay attention to when they are collecting information for performance appraisals. First, it appears that raters are influenced by general appearance characteristics of the ratees. Males are rated higher than females (other things being equal). A female ratee is observed not as a ratee but as a female ratee. A rater may form impressions based on stereotypic beliefs about women rather than the reality of the work situation and quite apart from any performance information. Females are rated less accurately when the rater has a traditional

---

[50]Landy and Farr, "Performance Rating"; A. S. Denisi, T. P. Cafferty, and B. M. Meglino, "A Cognitive View of the Performance Appraisal Process: A Model and Research Propositions," *Organizational Behavior and Human Performance* 33 (1984), pp. 360–396; Jack M. Feldman, "Beyond Attribution Theory: Cognitive Processes in Performance Appraisal," *Journal of Applied Psychology* 66(2) (1981), pp. 127–148; W. H. Cooper, "Ubiquitous Halo," *Psychological Bulletin* 90 (1981), pp. 218–244.

[51]Angelo Denisi and George Stevens, "Profiles of Performance, Performance Evaluations, and Personnel Decisions," *Academy of Management* 24(3) (1981), pp. 592–602; Wayne Cascio and Enzo Valtenzi, "Relations among Criteria of Police Performance," *Journal of Applied Psychology* 63(1) (1978), pp. 22–28; William Bigoness, "Effects of Applicant's Sex, Race, and Performance on Employer Performance Ratings: Some Additional Findings," *Journal of Applied Psychology* 61(1) (1976), pp. 80–84; Dorothy P. Moore, "Evaluating In-Role and Out-of-Role Performers," *Academy of Management Journal* 27(3) (1984), pp. 603–618; W. Borman, L. White, E. Pulakos, and S. Oppler, "Models of Supervisory Job Performance Ratings," *Journal of Applied Psychology* 76(6) (1991), pp. 863–872.

[52]W. Borman, L. White, E. Pulakos, and S. Oppler, "Models of Supervisory Job Performance Ratings," *Journal of Applied Psychology* 76(6) (1991), pp. 863–872.

[53]H. J. Bernardin and Richard Beatty, *Performance Appraisal: Assessing Human Behavior at Work* (Boston: Kent, 1984).

view of women's "proper" role; raters without traditional stereotypes of women are not prone to such errors.[54] Race also matters in performance ratings. Both in layoff decisions and in performance ratings, blacks are more likely to do worse than whites.[55]

Researchers also look at change in performance over time to see if this influences performance ratings. Both the pattern of performance (performance gets better versus worse over time) and the variability of performance (consistent versus erratic) influence performance ratings, even when the overall level of performance is controlled.[56] Workers who start out high in performance and then get worse are rated lower than workers who remain consistently low.[57] Not surprisingly, workers whose performance improves over time are seen as more motivated, while those who are more variable in their performance are tagged as lower in motivation. All of us have seen examples of workers and students who intuitively recognize this type of error and use it to their advantage. The big surge of work at the end of an appraisal period is often designed to "color" a rater's perceptions.

3   ***Errors in Storage and Recall***

Research suggests that raters store information in the form of traits[58].More importantly, they tend to recall information in the form of trait categories. For example, a rater observes a specific behavior such as an employee resting during work hours. The rater stores this information not as the specific behavior but rather in the form of a trait, such as "That worker is lazy". Specific instructions to recall information about the ratee, as for a performance review, elicit the trait—lazy. Further, in the process of recalling information, a rater may remember events that didn't actually occur, simply because they are consistent with the trait category.[59] The entire rating process, then, may be heavily influenced by the trait categories that the rater adopts, regardless of their accuracy.

[54]G. Dobbins, R. Cardy, and D. Truxillo, "The Effects of Purpose of Appraisal and Individual Differences in Stereotypes of Women on Sex Differences in Performance Ratings: A Laboratory and Field Study," *Journal of Applied Psychology* 73(3) (1988), pp. 551–558.

[55]M. Elvira and C. Zatzick, "Who's Displaced First? The Role of Race in Layoff Decisions," *Industrial Relations.* 49(2) 2002, pp. 329–361.

[56]Denisi and Stevens, "Profiles of Performance, Performance Evaluations, and Personnel Decisions"; William Scott and Clay Hamner, "The Influence of Variations in Performance Profiles on the Performance Evaluation Process: An Examination of the Validity of the Criterion," *Organizational Behavior and Human Performance* 14 (1975), pp. 360–370; Edward Jones, Leslie Rock, Kelly Shaver, George Goethals, and Laurence Ward, "Pattern of Performance and Ability Attributions: An Unexpected Primacy Effect," *Journal of Personality and Social Psychology* 10(4) (1968), pp. 317–340.

[57]B. Gaugler and A. Rudolph, "The Influence of Assessee Performance Variation on Assessor's Judgments," *Personnel Psychology* 45 (1992), pp. 77–98.

[58]Landy and Farr, "Performance Rating,"; Barnardin and Beatty, *Performance Appraisal: Assessing Human Behavior at Work.*

[59]N. Cantor and W. Mischel, "Traits v. Prototypes: The Effects on Recognition and Memory," *Journal of Personality and Social Psychology* 35 (1977), pp. 38–48; R. J. Spiro, "Remembering Information from Text: The 'State of Schema' Approach," in *Schooling and the Acquisition of Knowledge*, eds. R. C. Anderson, R. J. Spiro, and W. E. Montague (Hillsdale, CA: Erlbaum, 1977); T. K. Srull and R. S. Wyer, "Category Accessibility and Social Perception: Some Implications for the Study of Person Memory and Interpersonal Judgments," *Journal of Personality and Social Psychology* 38 (1980), pp. 841–856.

Errors in storage and recall also appear to arise from memory decay. At least one study indicates that rating accuracy is a function of the delay between performance and subsequent rating. The longer the delay, the less accurate the ratings.[60] Some research suggests that memory decay can be avoided if raters keep a diary and record information about employee performance as it occurs. [61]

Errors in the Actual Evaluation

The context of the actual evaluation process also can influence evaluations.[62] Several researchers indicate that the purpose of an evaluation affects the rating process.[63] For example, performance appraisals sometimes serve a political end. Supervisors have been known to deflate performance to send a signal to an employee—"You're not wanted here".[64] Supervisors also tend to weigh negative attributes more heavily than positive attributes: You are more likely to receive a much lower score if you perform poorly than you are to receive a proportionally higher score if you perform well.[65]

If the purpose of evaluation is to divide up a fixed pot of merit increases, ratings also tend to be less accurate. Supervisors who know ratings will be used to determine merit increases are less likely to differentiate among subordinates than they are when the ratings will be used for other purposes.[66] Also being required to provide feedback to subordinates about their ratings yields less accuracy than a secrecy policy.[67] Presumably anticipation of an unpleasant confrontation with the angry ratee persuades the rater to avoid confrontation by giving a rating higher than is justified. However, when raters must justify their scoring of subordinates in writing, the rating is more accurate.[68]

---

[60]Robert Heneman and Kenneth Wexley, "The Effects of Time Delay in Rating and Amount of Information Observed on Performance Rating Accuracy," *Academy of Management Journal* 26(4) (1983), pp. 677–686.

[61]B. P. Maroney and R. M. Buckely, "Does Research in Performance Appraisal Influence the Practice of Performance Appraisal? Regretfully Not," *Public Personnel Management* 21 (1992), pp. 185–196.

[62]Robert Liden and Terence Mitchell, "The Effects of Group Interdependence on Supervisor Performance Evaluations," *Personnel Psychology* 36(2) (1983), pp. 289–299.

[63]See, for example, Dobbins, Cardy, and Truxillo, "The Effects of Purpose of Appraisal and Individual Differences in Stereotypes of Women on Sex Differences in Performance Ratings: A Laboratory and Field Study."

[64]G. R. Ferris and T. A. Judge, "Personnel/Human Resource Management: A Political Influence Persepctive," *Journal of Management* 17 (1991), pp. 1–42.

[65]Yoav Ganzach, "Negativity (and Positivity) in Performance Evaluation: Three Field Studies," *Journal of Applied Psychology* 80(4) (1995), pp. 491–499.

[66]Winstanley, "How Accurate Are Performance Appraisals?"; Landy and Farr, "Performance Rating"; and Heneman and Wexley, "The Effects of Time Delay in Rating and Amount of Information Observed on Performance Rating Accuracy."

[67]L. Cummings and D. Schwab, *Performance in Organization* (Glenview, IL., Scott Foresman, 1973).

[68]Neal P. Mero and Stephan J. Motowidlo, "Effects of Rater Accountability on the Accuracy and the Favorability of Performance Ratings," *Journal of Applied Psychology* 80(4) (1995), pp. 517–524.

Strategy 4: Training Raters to Rate More Accurately

Although there is some evidence that training is not effective[69] or is less important in reducing errors than are other factors,[70] most research indicates rater training is an effective method for reducing appraisal errors.[71] Rater training programs can be divided into three distinct categories:[72] (1) *Rater-error training,* in which the goal is to reduce psychometric errors (e.g., leniency, severity, central tendency, halo) by familiarizing raters with their existence; (2) *performance-dimension training,* which exposes supervisors to the performance dimensions to be used in rating (e.g., quality of work, job knowledge); and (3) *performance-standard training,* which provides raters with a standard of comparison or frame of reference for making appraisals (what constitutes good, average, and bad). Several generalizations about ways to improve rater training can be summarized from this research:

1. Straightforward lecturing to ratees (the kind we professors are notorious for) about ways to improve the quality of their ratings generally is ineffective.
2. Individualized or small-group discussion sections are more effective in conveying proper rating procedures.
3. When these sessions are combined with extensive practice and feedback sessions, rating accuracy significantly improves.
4. Longer training programs (more than two hours) generally are more successful than shorter programs.
5. Performance-dimension training and performance-standard training generally work better than rater-error training, particularly when they are combined.
6. The greatest success has come from efforts to reduce halo errors and improve accuracy.

Leniency errors are the most difficult form of error to eliminate. This shouldn't be surprising. Think about the consequences to a supervisor of giving inflated ratings versus those of giving accurate or even deflated ratings. The latter two courses are certain to result in more complaints and possibly reduced employee morale. The easy way out is to artificially inflate ratings.[73] Unfortunately, this positive outcome for supervisors may

[69]H. J. Bernardin and E. C. Pence, "Effects of Rater Training: Creating New Response Sets and Decreasing Accuracy, " *Journal of Applied Psychology* 6 (1980), pp. 60–66.

[70]Sheldon Zedeck and Wayne Cascio, "Performance Appraisal Decision as a Function of Rater Training and Purpose of the Appraisal," *Journal of Applied Psychology* 67(6) (1982), pp. 752–758.

[71]E. Rogers, C. Rogers, and W. Metlay, "Improving the Payoff from 360-Degree Feedback," *Human Resource Planning.* 25(3) 2002, pp. 44–54; H. J. Bernardin and M. R. Buckley, "Strategies in Rater Training," *Academy of Management Review* 6(2) (1981), pp. 205–212; D. Smith, "Training Programs for Performance Appraisal: A Review," *Academy of Management Review* 11(1) (1986), pp. 22–40; B. Davis and M. Mount, "Effectiveness of Performance Appraisal Training Using Computer Assisted Instruction and Behavioral Modeling," *Personnel Psychology* 3 (1984), pp. 439–452; H. J. Bernardin, "Effects of Rater Training on Leniency and Halo Errors in Student Ratings of Instructors," *Journal of Applied Psychology* 63(3) (1978), pp. 301–308; J. M. Ivancevich, "Longitudinal Study of the Effects of Rater Training on Psychometric Error in Ratings," *Journal of Applied Psychology* 64(5) (1979), pp. 502–508.

[72]Bernardin and Buckley, "Strategies in Rater Training."

[73]Longnecker, Sims, and Gioia, "Behind the Mask: The Politics of Employee Appraisal."

come back to haunt them: With everyone receiving relatively high ratings there is less distinction between truly good and poor performers. Obviously, it is also harder to pay for real performance differences.

PUTTING IT ALL TOGETHER: THE PERFORMANCE EVALUATION PROCESS

A good performance evaluation doesn't begin on the day of the performance interview. We outline here some of the key elements in the total process, from day one, that make for a good outcome in the appraisal process.[74] First, we need a sound basis for establishing the performance appraisal dimensions and the scales associated with each dimension. Performance dimensions should be relevant to the strategic plan of the company. If innovation of new products is key to success, we'd better have something in our performance dimensions that assesses that component of individual performance. Performance dimensions also should reflect what employees are expected to do in their jobs, that is, their job descriptions. If the job descriptions include nothing on quality (admittedly an unlikely event), the appraisal should not measure quality. Unclear job expectations are one of the most significant barriers to good performance. If employees don't know what you expect of them, how can they possibly please you?[75]

Second, we need to involve employees in every stage of developing performance dimensions and building scales to measure how well they perform on these dimensions. In cases where this occurs, employees have more positive reactions to ratings, regardless of how well they do. They are happier with the system's fairness and the appraisal accuracy. They give better evaluations of managers and indicate intentions to stay with their organization. Managers also respond well to this type of "due process" system. They feel they have a greater ability to resolve work problems. They have higher job satisfaction and less reason to distort appraisal results to further their own interests.[76] They also provide a unique perspective on what will or won't work. Consider the performance appraisal system developed by Lucent Technologies for its overseas operations. A performance dimension that worked well in Lucent's U.S. operations was translated in local cultures as "obsession with serving our customers." It turns out that the word "obsession" in Saudi Arabia, Thailand, the Caribbean, and Latin America has very, very erotic and negative connotations. The problem was discovered only when managers reported employees speaking with one voice: "I don't care how important the customer is—I'm not doing this!"[77]

---

[74]Robert Heneman, *Merit Pay: Linking Pay Increases to Performance Ratings* (Reading, MA: Addison-Wesley, 1992).

[75]Ann Podolske, "Creating a Review System That Works," *Pay for Performance Report*, March 1996, pp. 2–4.

[76]Stephen J. Carroll, J. Kline Harrison, Monika K. Renard, Kay B. Tracy, and M. Susan Taylor, "Due Process in Performance Appraisal: A Quasi-Experiment in Procedural Justice," *Administrative Science Quarterly* 40 (1995), pp. 495–523.

[77]IOMA, *Pay for Performance Report*, January 2002. p. 13.

   Third, we need to make sure raters are trained in use of the appraisal system and that all employees understand how the system operates and what it will be used for. Fourth, we need to make sure raters are motivated to rate accurately. One way to achieve this is to ensure that managers are rated on how well they utilize and develop human resources. A big part of this would be evaluation and feedback to employees. Less than one-half of managers report that they provide feedback, and of those who do give feedback, most admit they are unsure if their feedback is worthwhile.[78] Almost one-half of employees agreed with this assessment, feeling performance reviews did little to guide performance.[79] Regardless of the quality of feedback one receives, performance is not uniformly improved.[80]

   Fifth, raters should maintain a diary of employee performance, both as documentation and to jog the memory.[81] This will help ensure that supervisors are knowledgeable about subordinates' performance.[82] Sixth, raters should attempt a performance diagnosis to determine in advance if performance problems arise because of motivation, skill deficiency, or external environmental constraints;[83] this process in turn tells the supervisor whether the problem requires motivation building, training, or efforts to remove external constraints. Lastly, the actual appraisal process should follow the guidelines outlined in Exhibit 11.11.[84] At a minimum this performance measurement system should provide:

1. A clear sense of direction
2. An opportunity for employees to participate in setting the goals and standards for performance
3. Prompt, honest, and meaningful feedback
4. Immediate and sincere reinforcement
5. Coaching and suggestions for improving future performance
6. Fair and respectful treatment
7. An opportunity for employees to understand and influence decisions that affect them

---

[78]Ann Podolske, "Creating a Review System That Works," *Pay for Performance Report*, March 1996, pp. 2–4.

[79]*www.mercerhr.com,* visited on April 24, 2003.

[80]Avraham N. Kluger, and Angelo DeNisi, "The Effects of Feedback Interventions on Performance: A Historical Review, A Meta-Analysis, and a Preliminary Feedback Intervention Theory," *Psychological Bulletin* 119(2) (1996), pp. 254–284.

[81]A. DeNisi, T. Robbins, and T. Cafferty, "Organization of Information Used for Performance Appraisals: Role of Diary-Keeping," *Journal of Applied Psychology* 74(1) (1989), pp. 124–129.

[82]Angelo S. Denisi, Lawrence H. Peters, and Arup Varma, "Interpersonal Affect and Performance Appraisal: A Field Study," *Personnel Psychology* 49 (1996), pp. 341–360; F. J. Landy, J. L. Barnes, and K. R. Murphy, "Correlates of Perceived Fairness and Accuracy of Performance Evaluations," *Journal of Applied Psychology* 63 (1978), pp. 751–754.

[83]S. Snell and K. Wexley, "Performance Diagnosis: Identifying the Causes of Poor Performance," *Personnel Administrator*, April 1985, pp. 117–127.

[84]Ann Podolske, "Creating a Review System That Works," *Pay for Performance Report*, March 1996, pp. 2–4.

EXHIBIT 11.11 **Tips on Appraising Employee Performance**

Preparation for the Performance Interview

1. Keep a weekly log of individual's performance. Why?
   A. It makes the task of writing up the evaluation simpler. The rater does not have to strain to remember six months or a year ago.
   B. It reduces the chances of some rating errors (e.g., regency, halo).
   C. It gives support/backup to the rating.
2. Preparation for the interview should not begin a week or two before it takes place. There should be continual feedback to the employee on his or her performance so that (a) problems can be corrected before they get out of hand, (b) improvements can be made sooner, and (c) encouragement and support are ongoing.
3. Allow sufficient time to write up the evaluation. A well-thought-out evaluation will be more objective and equitable. Sufficient time includes (a) the actual time necessary to think out and write up the evaluation, (b) time away from the evaluation, and (c) time to review and possibly revise.
4. Have employees fill out an appraisal form prior to the interview. This prepares employees for what will take place in the interview and allows them to come prepared with future goal suggestions, areas they wish to pursue, and suggestions concerning their jobs or the company.
5. Set up an agreed-upon, convenient time to hold the interview (at least one week in advance). Be sure to pick a nonthreatening day.
6. Be prepared!
   A. Know what you are going to say. Prepare an outline (which includes the evaluation and future goal suggestions).
   B. Decide on developmental opportunities before the interview. Be sure you know of possible resources and contacts.
   C. Review performance interview steps.
7. Arrange the room in such a way as to encourage discussion.
   A. Do not have barriers between yourself and the employee (such as a large desk).
   B. Arrange with your secretary that there be no phone calls or interruptions.

Performance Appraisal Interview (Steps)

1. Set the subordinate at ease. Begin by stating the purpose of the discussion. Let the individual know that it will be a two-way process. Neither the superior nor the subordinate should dominate the discussion.
2. Give a general, overall impression of the evaluation.
3. Discuss each dimension separately. Ask the employee to give his or her impression on own performance first. Then explain your position. If there is a problem on some, dimensions; try together to determine the cause. When exploring causes, urge the subordinate to identify three or four causes. Then, jointly determine the most important ones. Identifying causes is important because it points out action plans which might be taken.
4. Together, develop action plans to correct problem areas. These plans will flow naturally from the consideration of the causes. Be specific about the who, what, and when. Be sure to provide for some kind of follow-up or report back.
5. Close the interview on an optimistic note.

EXHIBIT 11.11   (*Continued*)

Communication Technique Suggestions

1. Do not control the interview—make it two-way. Do this by asking open-ended questions rather than submitting your own solutions. For example, rather than saying, "Jim, I'd like you to do these reports over again," it would be better to say, "Jim, what sort of things might we do here?" Avoid questions that lead to one-word answers.
2. Stress behaviors and results rather than personal traits. Say, "I've noticed that your weekly report has been one to two days late in the last six weeks," rather than, "You tend to be a tardy, lazy person."
3. Show interest and concern. Instead of saying, "Too bad, but we all go through that," say, "I think I know what you're feeling. I remember a similar experience."
4. Allow the subordinate to finish a sentence or thought. This includes being receptive to the subordinate's own ideas and suggestions. For example, rather than saying, "You may have something there, but let's go back to the real problem," say, "I'm not certain I understand how that relates to this problem. Why don't you fill me in on it a bit more?"

These last four suggestions emphasize problem analysis rather than appraisal. Of course, appraisal of past performance is a part of the problem analysis, but these suggestions should lead to a more participative and less defensive subordinate role. These suggestions will also help improve creativity in problem solving. The subordinate will have a clearer understanding of why and how he or she needs to change work behavior. There should be a growth of a climate of cooperation, which increases motivation to achieve performance goals.

EQUAL EMPLOYMENT OPPORTUNITY AND PERFORMANCE EVALUATION

Equal employment opportunity (EEO) and affirmative action have influenced HR decision making for almost 30 years now. While there are certainly critics of these programs, at least one important trend can be traced to the civil rights vigil in the workplace. Specifically, EEO has forced organizations to document decisions and to ensure they are firmly tied to performance or expected performance. Nowhere is this more apparent than in the performance appraisal area. Just ask folks at the Social Security Administration, who recently settled an $8 million class action suit brought by blacks who successfully argued that the performance appraisal process, among other things, was biased.[85] Performance appraisals are subject to the same scrutiny as employment tests. Consider the use of performance ratings in making decisions about promotions. In this context, a performance appraisal takes on all the characteristics of a test used to make an initial employment decision. If employees pass the test—are rated highly in the performance evaluation process—they are predicted to do well at higher-level jobs. This interpretation of performance evaluation as a test, subject to validation requirements, was made in *Brito v. Zia Company*.[86] In this case, Zia Company used performance evaluations based on a rating

---

[85]LRP Publications, "Black SSA Employees Get 7.75 Million Settlement," *Federal Human Resources Week*, 8(39) (2002).

[86]*Brito v. Zia Company*, 478 F.2d 1200 (1973).

format to lay off employees. The layoffs resulted in a disproportionate number of minorities being discharged. The court held that:

> Zia, a government contractor, had failed to comply with the testing guidelines issued by the Secretary of Labor, and that Zia had not developed job-related criteria for evaluating employees' work performance to be used in determining employment promotion and discharges which is required to protect minority group applicants and employees from the discriminatory effects of such failure.[87]

Since the Brito case there has been growing evidence that the courts have very specific standards and requirements for performance appraisal.[88] The courts stress six issues in setting up a performance appraisal system.[89]

1. Courts are favorably disposed to appraisal systems that give specific written instructions on how to complete the appraisal. Presumably, more extensive training in other facets of evaluation would also be viewed favorably by the courts.

2. Organizations tend to be able to support their cases better when the appraisal system incorporates clear criteria for evaluating performance. Performance dimensions and scale levels that are written, objective, and clear tend to be viewed positively by courts in discrimination suits.[90] In part, this probably arises because behaviorally oriented appraisals have more potential to provide workers feedback about developmental needs.

3. As pointed out by every basic personnel book ever printed, and reinforced by this text, the presence of adequately developed job descriptions provides a rational foundation for personnel decisions. The courts reinforce this by ruling more consistently for defendants (companies) when their appraisal systems are based on sound job descriptions.

4. Courts also approve of appraisal systems that require supervisors to provide feedback about appraisal results to the employees affected. Absence of secrecy permits employees to identify weaknesses and to challenge undeserved appraisals.

5. The courts seem to like evaluation systems that incorporate a review of any performance rating by a higher-level supervisor.

6. Perhaps most importantly, the courts consistently suggest that the key to fair appraisals depends on consistent treatment across raters, regardless of race, color, religion, sex, or national origin.

---

[87]Ibid.

[88]G. L. Lubben, D. E. Thompson, and C. R. Klasson, "Performance Appraisal: The Legal Implications of Title VII," *Personnel* 57(3) (1980), pp. 11–21; H. Feild and W. Halley, "The Relationship of Performance Appraisal System Characsitics to Verdicts in Selected Employment Discrimination Cases," *Academy of Management Journal* 25(2) (1982), pp. 392–406; *Albermarle Paper Company v. Moody*, U.S. Supreme Court, no. 74-389 and 74-428, 10 FEP Cases 1181 (1975); *Moody v. Albermarle Paper Company*, 474 F.3d. 134.

[89]Feild and Hally, "The Relationship of Performance Appraisal System Characteristics to Verdicts in Selected Employment Discrimination Cases"; Gerald Barrett and Mary Kernan, "Performance Appraisal and Terminations: A Review of Court Decisions since *Brito v. Zia* with Implications for Personnel Practices," *Personnel Psychology* 40 (1987), pp. 489–503.

[90]D. Martin and K. Bartol, "The Legal Ramifications of Performance Appraisal: An Update," *Employee Relations* 17(2) (1991), pp. 286–293.

The focal question then becomes, Are similarly situated individuals treated similarly? This standard is particularly evident in a court case involving performance appraisal and merit pay.[91] A black male filed suit against General Motors, claiming race discrimination in both the timing and the amount of a merit increase. The court found this case without merit. General Motors was able to show that the same set of rules was applied equally to all individuals.

A word of caution, though, about the role of equal employment and performance appraisal: Experts note that firms approaching performance appraisal primarily as a way to defend against discrimination claims may actually create more claims. Documentation of performance to discourage such claims only causes poor employee relations, and it can lead to solid employees feeling like plaintiffs themselves.[92] A better strategy is to follow the guidelines we developed earlier. They permit both good performance reviews and a strong foundation in case legal issues arise.

TYING PAY TO SUBJECTIVELY APPRAISED PERFORMANCE

Think, for a moment, about what it really means to give employees merit increases. Bill Peterson makes $40,000 per year. He gets a merit increase of 3 percent, the approximate average increase over the past few years. Bill's take-home increase (adjusted for taxes) is a measly $16 per week more than he used to make. Before we console Bill, though, consider Jane Krefting, who is a better performer than Bill and receives a 6 percent merit increase. Should she be thrilled by this pay-for-performance differential and be motivated to continue as a high achiever? Probably not. After taxes, her paycheck (assuming a base salary similar to Bill's) is only $15 dollars per week more than Bill's check.

The central issue involving merit pay is, How do we get employees to view raises as a reward for performance? Chapter 9 illustrated this difficulty in theoretical terms. Now it is addressed from a pragmatic perspective. Very simply, organizations frequently grant increases that are not designed or communicated to be related to performance. Perhaps the central reason for this is the way merit pay is managed. Many companies view raises not as motivational tools to shape behavior but as budgetary line items to control costs.[93] Frequently this results in pay increase guidelines with little motivational impact. Three pay increase guidelines that particularly fit the low-motivation scenario will be discussed briefly below before we outline standard that attempts to link pay to performance.[94]

Two types of pay increase guidelines with low-motivation potential provide equal increases to all employees regardless of performance. The first type, a general increase, typically is found in unionized firms. A contract is negotiated that specifies an across-the-board, equal increase for each year of the contract. Similarly, in the second type, across-the-board increases often are linked to cost-of-living changes. When the CPI rises, some

[91]*Payne v. General Motors*, 53 FEP Cases 471 (D. C. Kan. 1990).

[92]C. Wood, "Measuring Progress, Avoiding Liability in Evaluating Employees," *Employment Law Weekly*, December 1999, pp. 1–9.

[93]Milkovich and Milkovich, "Strengthening the Pay-for-Performance Relationship."

[94]"Compensating Salaried Employees during Inflation: General vs. Merit Increases," Reported No. 796, New York: Conference Board, 1981.

companies adjust base pay for all employees to reflect the rising costs. This is discussed in more detail in Chapter 17).

The third form of guideline comes somewhat closer to tying pay to performance. Seniority increases tie pay increases to a preset progression pattern based on seniority. For example, a pay grade might be divided into 10 equal steps, with employees moving to higher steps based on seniority. To the extent that performance improves with time on the job, this method has the rudiments of paying for performance.

In practice, tying pay to performance requires three things. First, we need some definition of performance. One set of subjective measures, as we discussed in Chapter 6, involves the competencies that people possess or acquire. Increasingly companies assert that corporate performance depends on having employees who possess key competencies. Xerox identifies 17 core competencies. As a company with strong strategic objectives linked to customer satisfaction and quality, it's not surprising to find that Xerox values such competencies as quality orientation, customer care, dependability, and teamwork. Recent trends in compensation center on finding ways to build competencies in employees. Merit increases may be linked to employee ability and willingness to demonstrate key competencies. For example, showing more of the following behaviors might be tied to higher merit increases:

Competency: Customer Care

1. Follows through on commitments to customers in a timely manner
2. Defines and communicates customer requirements
3. Resolves customer issues in a timely manner
4. Demonstrates empathy for customer feelings
5. Presents a positive image to the customer
6. Displays a professional image at all times
7. Communicates a positive image of the company and individuals to customers

Whether we measure performance by behaviors, competencies, or traits, there must be agreement that higher levels of performance will have positive impacts on corporate strategic objectives. Second, we need some continuum that describes different levels from low to high on the performance measure. Third, we need to decide how much of a merit increase will be given for different levels of performance. Decisions about these three questions lead to some form of merit pay guide. In its simplest form a guideline specifies pay increases permissible for different levels of performance (see Exhibit 11.12).

A variant of the guideline in Exhibit 11.12 fosters managerial discretion by expressing increases as a range. Supervisors can choose any increase within that range to reward a particular employee. A twist on this guideline varies the time between increases. Better performers might receive increases every 8 months; the poorest performers might have to wait 15 months to 2 years for their next increase.

A more complex guideline ties pay not only to performance but also to position in the pay range. Exhibit 11.13 illustrates such a system for a food market firm. The percentages in the cells of Exhibit 11.13 are changed yearly to reflect changing economic conditions. Two patterns are evident in this merit guideline. First, as would be expected in a pay-for-performance system, lower performance is tied to lower pay increases. In fact, in

EXHIBIT 11.12   Performance-Based Guideline

	Performance Level				
	1	**2**	**3**	**4**	**5**
	Outstanding	**Very Satisfactory**	**Satisfactory**	**Marginally Unsatisfactory**	**Unsatisfactory**
Merit Increase	6-8 %	5-7 %	4-6%	2-4%	0 %

EXHIBIT 11.13   Performance Rating Salary Increase Matrix

Position in Range / Performance Rating	Unsatisfactory	Needs Improvement	Competent	Commendable	Superior
Fourth quartile	0%	0%	4%	5%	6%
Third quartile	0	0	5	6	7
Second quartile	0	0	6	7	8
First quartile	0	2	7	8	9
Below minimum of range	0	3	8	9	10

many organizations the poorest performers receive no merit increases. The second relationship is that pay increases at a decreasing rate as employees move through a pay range. For the same level of performance, employees low in the range receive higher percentage increases than employees who have progressed further through the range. In part this is designed to forestall the time when employees reach the salary maximum and have their salaries frozen. In part, though, it is also a cost-control mechanism tied to budgeting procedures, as discussed in Chapter 18.

Performance- and Position-Based Guidelines

Given a salary increase matrix, merit increases are relatively easy to determine. As Exhibit 11.13 indicates, an employee at the top of his or her pay grade who receives a "competent" rating would receive a 4 percent increase in base salary. A new trainee starting out below the minimum of a pay grade would receive a 10 percent increase for a "superior" performance rating.

Designing Merit Guidelines

Designing merit guidelines involves answering four questions. First, what should the poorest performer be paid as an increase? Notice that this figure is seldom negative. Base wages are, unfortunately, considered an entitlement. Wage cuts tied to poor performance are very rare. Most organizations, though, are willing to give no increases to very poor performers, perhaps as a prelude to termination if no improvements are shown.

The second question involves average performers: How much should they be paid as an increase? Most organizations try to ensure that average performers are kept whole (wages will still have the same purchasing power) relative to cost of living. This dictates that the midpoint of the merit guidelines equal the percentage change in the local or national consumer price index. Following this guideline, the 6 percent increase for an average performer in the second quartile of Exhibit 11.13 would reflect the change in CPI for that area. In a year with lower inflation, all the percentages in the matrix probably would be lower.

Third, how much should the top performers be paid? In part, budgetary considerations (Chapter 18) answer this question. But there is also growing evidence that employees do not agree on the size of increases that they consider meaningful (Chapter 8). Continuation of this research may help determine the approximate size of increases that is needed to make a difference in employee performance.

Finally, matrixes can differ in the size of the differential between different levels of performance. Exhibit 11.13 basically rewards successive levels of performance with 1 percent increases (at least in the portion of the matrix in which any increase is granted). A larger jump between levels would signal a stronger commitment to recognizing performance with higher pay increases. Most companies balance this, though, against cost considerations. Larger differentials cost more. When money is tight, this option is less attractive. Exhibit 11.14 shows how a merit grid is constructed when cost constraints (merit budget) are known.

PROMOTIONAL INCREASES AS A PAY-FOR-PERFORMANCE TOOL

Let's not forget that firms have methods of rewarding good performance other than by giving raises. One of the most effective is a promotion accompanied by a salary increase, generally reported as being in the 8 to 12 percent range. This method of linking pay to performance has at least two characteristics that distinguish it from traditional annual merit pay increases. First, the very size of the increment is approximately double a normal merit increase. A clearer message is sent to employees, in the forms of both money and promotion, that good performance is valued and tangibly rewarded. Second, promotion increases represent, in a sense, a reward to employees for commitment and exemplary performance over a sustained period of time. Promotions are not generally annual events. They complement annual merit rewards by showing employees that there are benefits to both single-year productivity and continuation of such desirable behavior.

EXHIBIT 11.14   Merit Grids

Merit grids combine three variables: level of performance, distribution of employees within their job's pay range, and merit increase percentages.

Example

1. Assume a performance rating scale of A through D: 30 percent of employees get A, 35 percent get B, 20 percent get C, and 15 percent get D. Change the percents to decimals.

A	B	C	D
.30	.35	.20	.15

2. Assume a range distribution as follows: 10 percent of all employees are in the top (fourth) quartile of the pay range for their job, 35 percent in the third quartile, 30 percent in second quartile, and 25 percent in the lowest quartile. Change the percents to decimals.

1	.10
2	.35
3	.30
4	.25

3. Multiply the performance distribution by the range distribution to obtain the percent of employees in each cell. Cell entries = performance × range.

	A	B	C	D
1	.30 ×.10 = .03	.35 ×.20 = .035	.30 ×.10 = .02	.15 ×.10 = .015
2	.30 ×.35 = .105	.35 ×.35 = .1225	.20 ×.35 = .07	.15 ×.35 = .0525
3	.30 ×.30 = .09	.35 ×.30 = .105	.20 ×.30 = .06	.15 ×.30 = .045
4	.30 ×.25 = .075	.35 ×.25 = .1225	.20 ×.25 = .05	.15 ×.25 = .0375

Cell entries tell us that 3 percent of employees are in the top quartile of pay range *and* received an A performance rating, 10.5 percent of employees are in the second quartile of pay range *and* received an A performance rating, etc.

4. Distribute increase percentage among cells, varying the percentages according to performance and range distribution, for example, 6 percent to those employees in cell A1, 5 percent to those employees in B1.
5. Multiply increase percentages by the employee distribution for each cell. The sum of all cells should equal the total merit increase percentage.

   Example: 6% × cell A1 = .06 × .03 = .0018
   5% × cell B1 = .05 × .035 = .00175
   Etc.   _____
   Targeted merit increase percentage = Sum
6. Adjust increase percentages among cells if needed in order to stay within budgeted increase.

Your Turn

Policy Implications of Merit Pay Guides

GEMCAR is a manufacturer of decals and hood ornaments for all varieties of American cars. During the past four years, profits have plummeted 43 percent. This decline is attributed to rising costs of production and is widely believed to have triggered the resignation of GEMCAR's long-time president, C. Milton Carol. The newly hired CEO is Winston McBeade, a former vice president of finance and of human resource management at Longtemp Enterprises, a producer of novelty watches. As his first policy statement in office, McBeade declared a war on high production costs. As his first official act, McBeade proposed implementing a new merit pay guide (see Exhibits 1 and 2 for former and revised pay guides). What can you deduce about McBeade's "philosophy" of cost control from both the prior and the newly revised merit guides? What implications does this new philosophy have for improving the link between pay and performance and, hence, productivity?

EXHIBIT 1   Merit Pay Guide for Last Year

Performance

Position in Salary Range		Well Below Average	Below Average	Average	Above Average	Well Above Average
Above Grade Maximum (red circle)		0	2	3	4	6
		0	0	10	5	15
	Q4	0	3	4	5	7
		0	0	5	10	15
	Q3	0	4	5	6	8
		0	0	10	25	10
	Q2	2	5	6	7	9
			2	9	9	10
	Q1	2	6	7	8	10
		0	3	6	5	9

Notes: 1. Cost of living rose 3 percent last year.
2. The number at the lower right corner of each cell represents the number of employees falling into that cell during the previous year.

EXHIBIT 2 Revised Pay Guide

		Performance				
		Well Below Average	*Below Average*	*Average*	*Above Average*	*Well Above Average*
	Above grade maximum (red circle)	0	0	0	0	0
	Q4	0	0	2	3	4
Position in Salary Range	Q3	0	0	3	4	5
	Q2	0	0	4	5	6
	Q1	0	0	5	6	7

Note: Cost of living is expected to rise 3 percent this year.

Summary

The process of appraising employee performance can be both time-consuming and stressful. These difficulties are compounded if the appraisal system is poorly developed or if a supervisor lacks the appropriate training to collect and evaluate performance data. Development of sound appraisal systems requires an understanding of organizational objectives balanced against the relative merits of each type of appraisal system. For example, despite its inherent weaknesses, an appraisal system based on ranking of employee performance may be appropriate in small organizations that, for a variety of reasons, choose not to tie pay to performance; a sophisticated MBO appraisal system may not be appropriate for such a company.

Training supervisors effectively to appraise performance requires an understanding of organizational objectives. We know relatively little about the ways raters process information and evaluate employee performance. However, a thorough understanding of organizational objectives combined with a knowledge of common errors in evaluation can make a significant difference in the quality of appraisals.

Review Questions

1. You own a nonunion company with 93 nonexempt employees. All of these employees pack books into boxes for shipment to customers throughout the United States. Because of wide differences in performance, you have decided to try performance appraisal, something never done before. Until now, you have given every worker the same-size increase. Now you want to measure performance and reward the best performers with bigger increases. Without any further information, which of the five types of appraisal formats do you think would be most appropriate? Justify your answer. Do you anticipate any complaints, or other comments, from employees after you implement your new system?

2. Think about the last group project you worked on. Describe that project and identify three performance criteria you think would be appropriate for evaluating the team members. Should every team member be able to rate one another on all these dimensions? Should the team member ratings be used for feedback only or for feedback and part of the overall grade (with teacher approval, of course). Should the teacher rate each team member on performance (all three criteria) in the group assignment? How are these questions relevant to setting up a 360 performance review?

3. Angela Lacy, an African-American employee in your accounts receivable department, has filed a charge of discrimination, alleging she was unfairly passed over for promotion and regularly receives smaller pay increases than do employees who perform less well (she alleges). You have to go to your boss, the VP of HR, and explain what elements of your HR system can be used in your legal defense. What things do you hope you did in setting up and administering your systems to counter this discrimination charge?

4. Assume that you had one employee fall into each of the cells in Exhibit 11.13 (25 employees in the company). How much would base salary increase in dollars if the current average salary in the company is $15,000? (Assume that ratings are randomly distributed by salary level; you can use $15,000 as your base salary for calculation in each of the cells.)

Sample Appraisal Form: Pfizer Pharmaceutical

PERFORMING FOR RESULTS

Reaching for the future

District Manager/Regional Manager Capabilities

District Manager Baseline Capability Assessment

Employee Name:	Self Assessment: [ ]
Title:	(Select one)
	Manager Assessment: [ ]
District:	Manager's Name:

I. Strategic Capability Assessment	Unacceptable / Needs Improvement	Stage I	Stage II	Stage III	Stage IV	Comments
1. Leadership						
2. Recruiting and Selection						
3. People Development						
4. Strategic Perspective						

Capabilities Cross-Reference Table

II. Core Behaviors Assessment	U	NI	S	RO	A	Comments
1. Planning & Organizing						
2. Impact						
3. Job Knowledge						
4. Problem Analysis						
5. Communication Ability						
6. Facilitation Skills						
7. Judgment						

8. Flexibility						
9. Political Savvy/Protocol						
10. Sensitivity						
11. Teamwork						

III. Employee Comments

Employee Signature:	Date:
Supervisor Signature:	Date:

	Key
U	"Unacceptable"
NI	"Needs Improvement"
S	"Sometimes"
RO	"Routinely"
A	"Always"

District Manager Strategic Capabilities

Outlined below are four strategic capabilities for the District Manager (DM) role.

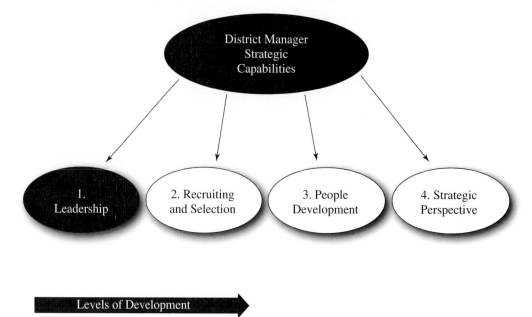

District Manager Strategic Capabilities (*Continued*)

Outlined below is the *Leadership* strategic capability continuum for the DM role.

1. Leadership

	Stage I	Stage II	Stage III	Stage IV
Descriptor	*Is learning to manage the district, and is becoming involved in the TACU process.*	*Coordinates district activities for the division and participates in the TACU process (e.g., completes the business plan.)*	*Successfully leads and manages own representatives while actively contributing to the TACU process.*	*Emerges as a leader within the region, division, and TACU. Is willing to take on reasonable risk to push representatives/TACU district/region towards more forward thinking.*
Leads implementation of sales strategy and tactics	• Provides direction to representatives regarding what work activities are important (e.g., communicates district standards to representatives).	• Ensures representatives are following through on work activities that need to be executed in the territory (e.g., physician calls, sample drops, computer data entry, etc.).	• Ensures that representatives understand how their activities affect district, regional, state, and U.S. Pharmaceuticals' objectives (e.g., regularly reviews territory, district, and regional results to reinforce line-of-sight).	• Takes a lead role in implementing and inspiring a vision of success for the district, region, and TACU (e.g., works with TACU members to clearly define outcomes based on what is best for the customer and Pfizer and develops innovative approaches that are adopted across U.S. Pharmaceuticals lines).

Note: DMs will be expected to maintain demonstration/mastery of behaviors from prior stages.

District Manager Strategic Capabilities (*Continued*)

Outlined below is the *Leadership* strategic capability continuum for the DM role.

1. Leadership (continued)

	Stage I	Stage II	Stage III	Stage IV
		• Implements the tactical aspects of targeted account selling.	• Designs and manages a full targeted account selling process, including copromotes, government relations, CECs, Specialty, LMMs, and MSLs.	• Understands the politics at work in district, region, and U.S. Pharmaceuticals (e.g., among local community leaders, employer groups, corporate affiliations, MCOs, medical groups, and deans of schools) and applies this understanding to developing targeted account selling strategies.
Leverages internal/ external relationships to deliver value	• Attends TACU meetings. • Focuses primarily on issues related to own products or division at TACU meetings.	• Suggests agenda items for TACU discussions.	• Advocates the TACU as a strategic advantage in the selling process.	• Optimizes the value of the TACU and LAT processes as critical elements in meeting U.S. Pharmaceuticals' strategic objectives.

Note: DMs will be expected to maintain demonstration/mastery of behaviors from prior stages.

District Manager Strategic Capabilities (*Continued*)

Outlined below is the *Leadership* strategic capability continuum for the DM role.

1. Leadership (continued)

Stage I	Stage II	Stage III	Stage IV
• Pays attention to other DMs' successes to learn management and leadership techniques and approaches. • Discourages or confronts the exchange of negative disrespectful comments.	• Actively networks with DMs from other districts to learn from their successes.	• Works seamlessly with copromote partners. Regularly engages in activities to strengthen copromote relationships to maximize their benefits (e.g., openly shares resources, knowledge, and experience to facilitate representative/DM mastery of market issues).	• Encourages and facilitates collaborating with CECs, MSLs, MSMs, Headquarters, and other field force members (e.g., identifies opportunities where a pooling of resources will increase the likelihood of success, matches up field force members who would benefit from collaboration).
• Often focuses on individual contributors but is beginning to encourage a team approach (e.g., encourages representatives to coordinate business plan, goals, speakers, and call cycles).	• Recognizes and encourages a team approach to achieving results (e.g., acknowledges a representative's support of a priority copromote selling effort).	• Focuses on growing Pfizer's market share and profitability [e.g., adopts a customer-focused (versus division-focused) selling approach].	

Note: DMs will be expected to maintain demonstration/mastery of behaviors from prior stages.

District Manager Strategic Capabilities (*Continued*)

Outlined below is the *Leadership* strategic capability continuum for the DM role.

1. Leadership (continued)

	Stage I	Stage II	Stage III	Stage IV
Raises performance in the field and develops high-performing teams	• Holds self to the same standards as representatives (e.g., is always punctual, files reports on time, willingly performs details, etc.). • Closely manages representative activities.	• Leads by example—personally demonstrates the core behaviors, skills, knowledge, and traits that representatives need to be successful. • Understands the principles of situational leadership and how it can improve performance (e.g., acknowledges individual differences but tends to rely on one preferred leadership style/approach). • Imparts a sense of responsibility among team members (e.g., requires representatives to assess their contributions and impact on district results, does not micro-manage or under manage representatives, etc.).	• Raises performance of representatives by setting high performance standards that are perceived by representatives as being challenging but achievable. • Applies the principles of situational leadership (e.g., uses multiple leadership styles and adapts approach to individual needs/circumstances).	• Raises performance of the field beyond division, TACU, district, and regional lines. • Sought out by peers for advice on developing high-performing teams. • Recognized by representatives, peers, RM, and Sales VP as a situational leadership role model as measured by IMDI, EQ, 360 Degrees, and Situational Leadership surveys.

Note: DMs will be expected to maintain demonstration/mastery of behaviors from prior stages.

District Manager Strategic Capabilities (*Continued*)

Outlined below is the *Leadership* strategic capability continuum for the DM role.

1. Leadership (continued)

	Stage I	Stage II	Stage III	Stage IV
Manages conflicts and makes tough decisions to position the district for success	• Learning to surface and manage conflicts when dealing with individual representatives and at the TACU level (e.g., points out when representatives are making excuses).	• Does not wait until problems arise before addressing performance issues (e.g., addresses significant work activity performance shortfalls early).	• Recognizes opportunities to improve policies and/or practices and takes action to do so. • Makes tough decisions within an appropriate time frame and with the appropriate documentation (e.g., places a representative on final probation after several performance discussions and demonstrates to the representative how to correct his/her behaviors).	• Sought out by peers, Headquarters, and sales leadership for advice, counsel, and assistance regarding business, customer, market, and people issues (e.g., is recommended by RM or Sales VP for various advisory panels).

Note: DMs will be expected to maintain demonstration/mastery of behaviors from prior stages.

District Manager Strategic Capabilities (*Continued*)

Outlined below is the *Leadership* strategic capability continuum for the DM role.

1. Leadership (continued)

	Stage I	Stage II	Stage III	Stage IV
Capitalizes on the benefits of diversity (field force and customers)	• Understands that representatives and customers have individual needs and styles and respects these differences.	• Helps representatives respect and understand individual differences. • Hires diverse candidates to complement the current field force (e.g., works with minority recruiters to select top talent).	• Adapts management style to respond to individual and customer needs/styles. • Utilizes a diverse set of skills and perspectives to enhance the overall effectiveness of the team.	• Recognizes and draws on individual backgrounds, experiences, and strengths to optimize district performance. • Is considered to be a role model by representatives, peers, and RM for his/her commitment to using diversity to increase effectiveness (e.g., helps others develop relationships with minority recruiting centers). • Assesses individuals' backgrounds and strengths and matches them to specific initiatives to optimize district performance.

Note: DMs will be expected to maintain demonstration/mastery of behaviors from prior stages.

District Manager Strategic Capabilities

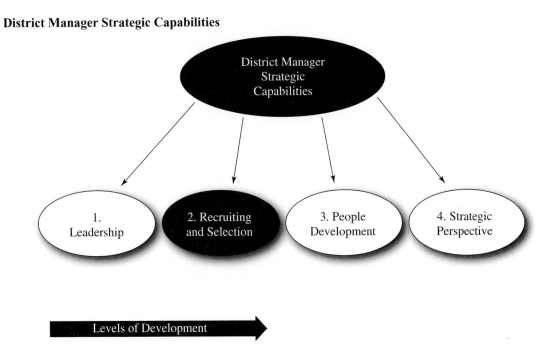

District Manager Strategic Capabilities (*Continued*)

Outlined below is the *Recruiting and Selection* strategic capability continuum for the DM role.

2. Recruiting and Selection

	Stage I	Stage II	Stage III	Stage IV
Descriptor	*Participates actively in the process of learning, and establishing systems for, the selection process.*	*Sources and selects qualified candidates for the representative position on a continual basis.*	*Consistently sources and selects top-performing representatives that are committed to pursuing a career in pharmaceutical sales.*	*Consistently sources and selects top-performing representatives that evolve into top candidates who are eligible for additional responsibilities within Pfizer.*
Plans for hiring needs	• Begins to interview candidates for the representative role as positions open up.	• Builds an active file of candidates for the representative position.	• Anticipates hiring needs and takes a proactive approach to recruiting. • Actively trains IHRs to screen candidates for the representative position and asks RMs for trainees.	• Effectively anticipates vacant positions within the district and acts to ensure minimal elapsed time to fill vacancies (e.g., anticipates turnover and minimizes the learning curve for new hires).
Sources high-caliber and diverse candidates	• Is beginning to establish a system for sourcing candidates.	• Uses personnel and employee referrals, and also identifies external resources to source qualified candidates for the representative position. • Recruits candidates who represent the diverse customer landscape.	• Cultivates strong relationships with key candidate sources (e.g., universities, military bases, recruitment sources for diverse candidates, etc.). • Shares candidates with mirrored DMs (e.g., considers regional, not just district, hiring needs).	• Cultivates relationships with individuals who identify and recommend high-caliber candidates (e.g., business school deans, reputable professors, recruiters, etc.).

Note: DMs will be expected to maintain demonstration/mastery of behaviors from prior stages.

District Manager Strategic Capabilities (*Continued*)

Outlined below is the *Recruiting and Selection* strategic capability continuum for the DM role.

2. Recruiting and Selection (continued)

	Stage I	Stage II	Stage III	Stage IV
Fills positions efficiently	• Is generally aware of what capabilities he/she is looking for when selecting top candidates	• Is decisive when selecting individuals from a pool of candidates (e.g., is clear on the capability profile he/she is selecting for and identifies which candidates fit this profile).	• Displays a sense of urgency in filling vacant positions with highly qualified candidates. • Sells Pfizer during the interview process.	• Convinces highly sought-after candidates that Pfizer is the employer of choice (e.g., makes compelling cases to persuade top candidates to join Pfizer over other organizations using a variety of resources such as career development, the career ladder, and training).
Selects candidates based upon predictors of success	• May focus initially on personality and intuition but is beginning to key into predictors of success when selecting candidates. • Is learning to screen out unqualified candidates early in the interview process.	• Assesses candidates' abilities to succeed based on capability profiles for successful representatives and screens out unqualified candidates.	• Selects candidates that have complementary capabilities with current representatives. • Is open to hiring representatives that have a diverse set of experiences.	• Analyzes the requirements for success in individual territories and recruits and selects based on this knowledge.

Note: DMs will be expected to maintain demonstration/mastery of behaviors from prior stages.

District Manager Strategic Capabilities (*Continued*)

Outlined below is the *Recruiting and Selection* strategic capability continuum for the DM role.

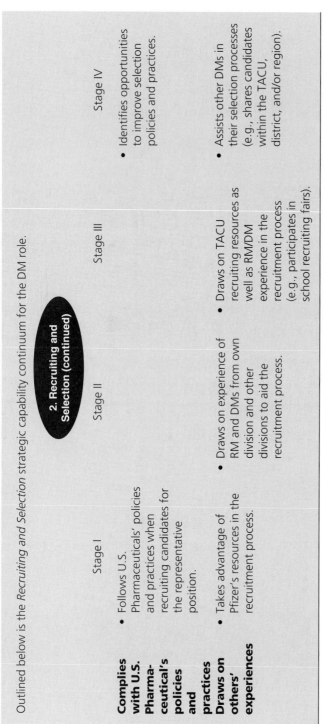

	Stage I	**2. Recruiting and Selection (continued)** Stage II	Stage III	Stage IV
Complies with U.S. Pharmaceutical's policies and practices	• Follows U.S. Pharmaceuticals' policies and practices when recruiting candidates for the representative position.			• Identifies opportunities to improve selection policies and practices.
Draws on others' experiences	• Takes advantage of Pfizer's resources in the recruitment process.	• Draws on experience of RM and DMs from own division and other divisions to aid the recruitment process.	• Draws on TACU recruiting resources as well as RM/DM experience in the recruitment process (e.g., participates in school recruiting fairs).	• Assists other DMs in their selection processes (e.g., shares candidates within the TACU, district, and/or region).

Note: DMs will be expected to maintain demonstration/mastery of behaviors from prior stages.

District Manager Strategic Capabilities

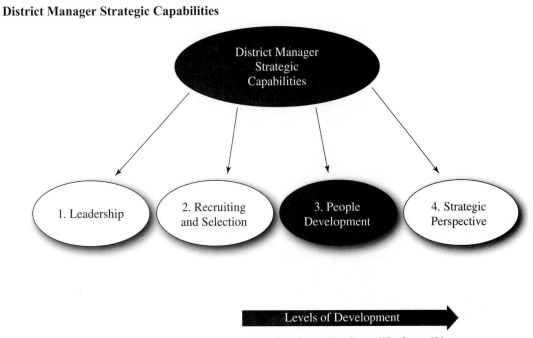

District Manager Strategic Capabilities (*Continued*)

Outlined below is the *People Development* strategic capability continuum for the DM role.

3. People Development

	Stage I	Stage II	Stage III	Stage IV
Descriptor	*Aids representatives' development*	*Develops representatives into consistent contributors.*	*Accelerates representatives' sales development through individualized field coaching (i.e., situational leadership).*	*Consistently develops individuals into top performing representatives that evolve into exemplary candidates for more senior sales (or sales management) roles.*
Provides coaching, training, and other opportunities to help individuals grow	• Coaches representatives as needs arise (e.g., initiates coaching based on an identified need and suggests trainings, self-education, and on-the-job activities). • Often focuses first on selling skills and core behaviors when providing feedback and coaching to representatives, but is beginning to incorporate other aspects of performance.	• Coaches representatives to improve performance in their current role. • Uses representatives' business plan and/or previously identified goals as a coaching tool when in the field.	• Coaches representatives to improve current and long-term performance. • Works with representatives on an ongoing basis to identify opportunities for learning that address their immediate and longer-term individual development needs (e.g., suggests tapes, University of Pfizer courses, POA workshop roles, coaching from others, etc.).	• Assesses common current training needs as well as potential training needs for the future (e.g., suggests additions to University of Pfizer curriculum, etc.). • Works with RMs and Headquarters to develop new learning tools and activities to help representatives and DMs acquire the skills they need to be successful.

Note: DMs will be expected to maintain demonstration/mastery of behaviors from prior stages.

District Manager Strategic Capabilities (*Continued*)

Outlined below is the *People Development* strategic capability continuum for the DM role.

3. People Development (continued)

	Stage I	Stage II	Stage III	Stage IV
Provides coaching, training, and other opportunities to help individuals grow (continued)	• Provides some developmental feedback to representatives (e.g., reviews the field coaching guide or contact report with representatives after a day in the field, provides feedback to representatives at the mid-year and annual reviews, etc.).	• Helps representatives develop custom action plans to address their development needs (e.g., prepares tailored, written field trip coaching guides after riding in the field with representatives).	• Coaches representatives to develop their own work styles, skill sets, and formulas for success. • Consistently encourages increased representative autonomy (e.g., supports representatives as they confront issues and accept ownership of their actions). • Helps representatives assume increasing levels of leadership responsibilities. • Effectively models how representatives should give and seek out constructive feedback. • Incorporates personal experience and other representative experience (where appropriate) into coaching sessions.	• Serves as an advocate for top-performers (e.g., involves high performers in task forces). • Cultivates representatives and helps them advance their careers (e.g., creates development and advancement opportunities for representatives to give them opportunities to demonstrate the highest stages on the representative strategic capability continuums).

Note: DMs will be expected to maintain demonstration/mastery of behaviors from prior stages.

District Manager Strategic Capabilities (*Continued*)

Outlined below is the *People Development* strategic capability continuum for the DM role.

3. People Development (continued)

	Stage I	Stage II	Stage III	Stage IV
Provides coaching, training, and other opportunities to help individuals grow	• Generally aware of basic differences in representative capabilities and is beginning to tailor coaching to these differences.	• Recognizes basic differences in representative capabilities and coaches representatives accordingly (e.g., helps representatives develop custom action plans to address their development needs).	• Accurately assesses representative strengths and development needs and customizes coaching approach to accommodate individual needs (i.e., situational leadership). • Demonstrates an ability to improve a representative's performance through persistence and skillful management (e.g., regularly evaluates representatives, performance against their development plans during field rides, gives and follows up on developmental assignments).	• Helps people realize their own potential (e.g., communicates the strengths of promotable representatives to RMs, gives credit to individuals rather than taking it for himself/herself, etc.).
	• Is learning to separate the person from the behaviors when providing feedback.	• Focuses on behaviors— not the person—when providing feedback.	• Emphasizes representatives' strengths and positive behaviors when providing feedback.	• Teaches representatives to assess their own performance by helping them identify their personal strengths and development needs (e.g., conducts regular POA workshops on professional development).

Note: DMs will be expected to maintain demonstration/mastery of behaviors from prior stages.

District Manager Strategic Capabilities (*Continued*)

Outlined below is the *People Development* strategic capability continuum for the DM role.

3. People Development (continued)

Provides strong career development opportunities (continued)

- Has a basic understanding about the career development program for representatives (and self).

- Helps representatives identify opportunities within the career development program to develop skills that will strengthen their ability to impact results and advance their careers.

- Identifies and provides opportunities for representatives to diversify their skill sets (e.g., calling on different types of customers, assuming greater responsibility at POA meetings, mentoring a new hire, sharing best practices, etc.).
- Identifies representatives' career/development goals (e.g., promotional/career aspirations) and helps representatives develop plans to achieve these goals.
- Recognizes the benefits of helping others succeed.

- Recognizes top performers and accelerates their development by providing increasingly challenging account opportunities and increased decision latitude (e.g., increased role in POA planning and execution).
- Coordinates career development planning with long-term succession planning.

- Exposes top-performing representatives to what it is "really like" to be a DM, IHR, or Specialty Representative (e.g., invites high-performing representatives to be his/her "shadow" for a day in the office, asks representatives to cover

Note: DMs will be expected to maintain demonstration/mastery of behaviors from prior stages.

District Manager Strategic Capabilities (*Continued*)

Outlined below is the *People Development* strategic capability continuum for the DM role.

3. People Development (continued)

	Stage I	Stage II	Stage III	Stage IV
Provides strong career development opportunities				him/her during vacations, prepares representatives for ARM slots, has representatives lead parts of POA meetings). • Demonstrates a strong track record of cultivating balanced high-performing representatives (e.g., regularly grooms representatives that get promoted). • Encourages top-performing representatives to apply for Headquarter internships, guest training, etc. • Helps representatives identify and capitalize on opportunities to exceed expectations.
Manages performance based on capabilities and results	• Performance feedback may focus primarily on GAR results but is beginning to include other aspects of performance (e.g., capabilities) as well.	• Focuses on both capabilities and results in measuring representative performance.	• Effectively and routinely communicates capability and results requirements (and the implications of exceeding or not meeting them) to representatives.	

Note: DMs will be expected to maintain demonstration/mastery of behaviors from prior stages.

District Manager Strategic Capabilities (*Continued*)

Outlined below is the *People Development* strategic capability continuum for the DM role.

3. People Development (continued)

	Stage I	Stage II	Stage III	Stage IV
	• Holds representatives accountable for results.	• Verbally communicates low-performance messages to focus representatives' attention on the issues; documents incidents in personnel files.	• Recognizes and appreciates representatives' future potential for driving sales and results (e.g., does not write off representatives with low GAR without assessing their capabilities and potential to learn/develop first).	• Facilitates representatives' ability to recognize and learn from others' strengths by creating mentoring within and outside the district (e.g., implements mentorship or "Shadow for A Day" programs).
			• Helps representatives identify role models (e.g., DMs, experienced/ successful representatives, etc.) to learn from (e.g., identifies specific mentors for different capability development needs).	• Emerges as a mentor to other DMs and representatives outside of his/her divisional responsibility.
Encourages sponsorships and mentor relationships	• Supports sponsorships or mentor relationships.	• Facilitates and initiates representative-representative mentor relationships within the district and across divisions (e.g., encourages and supports representatives coaching one another).		

Note: DMs will be expected to maintain demonstration/mastery of behaviors from prior stages.

District Manager Strategic Capabilities

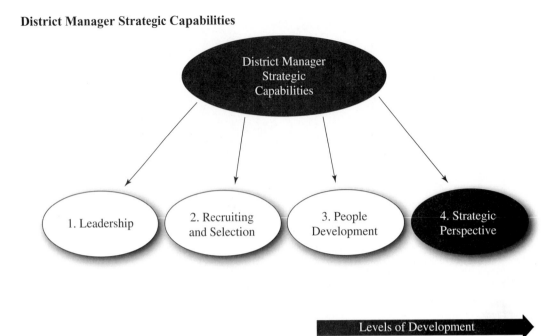

District Manager Strategic Capabilities (*Continued*)

Outlined below is the *Strategic Perspective* strategic capability continuum for the DM role.

4. Strategic Perspective

	Stage I	Stage II	Stage III	Stage IV
Descriptor	*Is developing a standard selling approach for the district.*	*Focuses on following a standard selling approach across the customer landscape.*	*Understands the customer landscape and develops customized selling strategies*	*Helps representatives, fellow DMs, and TACU members collaborate with customers to identify their specific business needs and demonstrate how Pfizer can deliver long-term value.*
Evaluates customer landscape, and develops a business plan to optimize field force effectiveness (continued)	• Keeps up-to-date with changes in the customer landscape (e.g., reviews internal sales reports, local business journals, etc.). • Makes sure that representatives follow the established guidelines regarding how to approach customers.	• Recognizes the implications of changes in the customer landscape for selling strategies. • Monitors representative activities to ensure that representatives are meeting customer needs (e.g., ensures that representatives complete the steps necessary to strengthen customer relationships and grow key accounts, works with representatives to analyze sales territories on a monthly basis).	• Brings customers, RAMs, LMMs, and CECs into POAs to discuss changing market trends. • Involves representatives in developing district business plans, drawing on their knowledge of specific accounts and physicians.	• Leads TACU's, representatives', and U.S. Pharmaceuticals' understanding of the long-term impact of various customer segments and their influence on long-term market and sales potential for Pfizer.

Note: DMs will be expected to maintain demonstration/mastery of behaviors from prior stages.

District Manager Strategic Capabilities (*Continued*)

Outlined below is the *Strategic Perspective* strategic capability continuum for the DM role.

4. Strategic Perspective (continued)

	Stage I	Stage II	Stage III	Stage IV
Evaluates customer landscape, and develops a business plan to optimize field force effectiveness		• Develops a structured business plan for the district (e.g., prioritizes key accounts, develops strategies for penetrating key accounts, etc.). • Balances selling efforts for different customers based on analyses of near-term sales potential. • Uses business plans to monitor performance throughout the year (e.g., reviews representative business plans on a quarterly basis). • Supports POA/RM regional strategies.	• Considers changing customer needs in the business planning process and works with TACU members to adapt selling strategies and representative tactics accordingly. • Integrates competitive intelligence into the business planning and TACU processes. • Collaborates with other TACU members and non-Pfizer copromote partners (e.g., Parke-Davis) to prioritize customers and contributes to the development of the TACU business plan. • Works with copromote partner to customize POA strategies to his/her local market.	• Encourages regular strategic account profiling at the TACU/cluster level to assess current and future customer segmentation and diversity, growth opportunities, Pfizer offerings, and their implications on sales. • Evaluates and deploys innovative strategies (e.g., market pull-throughs, customer goodwill programs, employer coalitions, state lobbying efforts, different allocation of resources, etc.) to enhance profitability and overall field force effectiveness. • Influences and contributes to regional and district POA strategy development. • Empowers successful tenured representatives to seek out new customers and implement strategies that optimize sales.

Note: DMs will be expected to maintain demonstration/mastery of behaviors from prior stages.

District Manager Strategic Capabilities (*Continued*)

Outlined below is the *Strategic Perspective* strategic capability continuum for the DM role.

4. Strategic Perspective (continued)

	Stage I	Stage II	Stage III	Stage IV
Develops selling skills and presentations for high customer impact	• Ensures that representatives' selling presentations support POS strategies and convey accurate information.	• Helps representatives develop standardized sales presentations for standard customer situations (e.g., reviews all sales presentations and identifies inconsistencies/areas for improvement, etc.).	• Helps representatives build customized selling presentations for strategic accounts that focus on meeting specific customer needs (e.g., targeted account selling). • Teaches representatives how to ask the right questions to assess customer needs. • Communicates to representatives how the selling message changes based on copromotes or organization pull-through.	• Asks the right questions to encourage representatives to identify situations where increased selling expertise may be required in the selling process (e.g., knows when to introduce CECs, SGRs, specialty representatives, or other subject experts to the customer). • Tailors selling approach for diverse customer groups.
	• Encourages representatives to use current goodwill programs.	• Helps representatives understand how goodwill programs can strengthen key customer relationships.	• Helps representatives collaborate with customers to tailor goodwill programs to address their specific needs.	• Works with RMs, TACU members, Headquarters representatives, and representatives to develop innovative selling approaches, such as goodwill programs, that respond to key customer and U.S. Pharmaceuticals challenges and focus on leveraging U.S. Pharmaceuticals expertise.

Note: DMs will be expected to maintain demonstration/mastery of behaviors from prior stages.

District Manager Strategic Capabilities (*Continued*)

Outlined below is the *Strategic Perspective* strategic capability continuum for the DM role.

4. Strategic Perspective (continued)

	Stage I	Stage II	Stage III	Stage IV
Targets influential contacts in customer organizations and cultivates key relationships to build influence	• Understands the necessity and value of developing strong relationships with key players in customer organizations.	• Draws on personal contacts in customer organizations and creates opportunities for representatives to build relationships with these contacts (e.g., introduces representatives to his/her personal network of key influencers).	• Works with representatives and TACU members to identify whom to target in accounts that are critical to the success of the district.	• Sought after by peers and RM as a reliable source for innovative selling strategies. • Positions Pfizer as the premier pharmaceuticals company in the minds of key influencers in customer organizations.
	• Personally calls on key accounts.	• Coordinates territory activities to ensure that important accounts receive appropriate exposure.	• Works with representatives to develop/maintain strong relationships with key influencers in the community (e.g., shares relationships and key contacts in medical groups and hospital networks with representatives).	• Sought after by representatives and other DMs for counsel and assistance in gaining access to key influencers in customer organizations.

Note: DMs will be expected to maintain demonstration/mastery of behaviors from prior stages.

District Manager Strategic Capabilities (*Continued*)

Outlined below is the *Strategic Perspective* strategic capability continuum for the DM role.

4. Strategic Perspective (continued)

	Stage I	Stage II	Stage III	Stage IV
Analyzes data to build knowledge and identify market opportunities	• Reviews key sales reports (e.g., Sherlock data).	• Encourages representatives to participate in VHO initiatives. • Analyzes therapeutic class and sales detail reports to understand the market and customer landscape (e.g., interprets trends in market data to syndicate throughout the district). • Analyzes district sales on a monthly basis and communicates sales strategies based on market share analyses.	• Cultivates strong relationships at key healthcare organizations in the community (e.g., with CIGNA, leading teaching hospitals, etc.) by organizing speaker dinners and other activities that translate into sales results. • Keeps up to date with local, regional, and national healthcare trends (e.g., subscribes to local business journals, consumer advocacy publications, etc.) and uses this knowledge to anticipate and plan for changes in the district.	• Works closely with volunteer health organizations (VHOs) to continue to build a strong, positive image for Pfizer (e.g., serves on the Board of Directors or advisory panels). • Envisions future data and their relevance to the changing healthcare landscape.

Note: DMs will be expected to maintain demonstration/mastery of behaviors from prior stages.

District Manager Strategic Capabilities (*Continued*)

Outlined below is the *Strategic Perspective* strategic capability continuum for the DM role.

4. Strategic Perspective (continued)

Stage I	Stage II	Stage III	Stage IV
• May rely primarily upon instinct to make decisions but is beginning to test instinct against market data.	• Knows how relevant data were gathered and the strengths and limitations of the data.	• Uses relevant data to challenge one's own thinking and that of the TACU (e.g., uses appropriate data to enhance and improve ideas rather than to confirm them).	• Identifies specific appropriate data that will be important in the future.
• Is generally aware of what sources of data are most important.	• Demonstrates an ability to select and prioritize the most important sources of data at TACU meetings.	• Analyzes data across divisional and geographical territories and districts to develop an even stronger understanding of market dynamics.	• Finds new ways to look at and apply data to capitalize on opportunities (e.g., draws on LMMs and MSLs to generate specific market data for the district and TACU).
	• Updates representatives on district sales trends on a monthly basis using the Sherlock Analyzer, weekly market share data, or TCR reports.	• Shares new data and/or market knowledge when collaborating with other TACU members.	

Note: DMs will be expected to maintain demonstration/mastery of behaviors from prior stages.

District Manager Strategic Capabilities (*Continued*)

Outlined below is the *Strategic Perspective* strategic capability continuum for the DM role.

4. Strategic Perspective (continued)

Allocates resources for the highest impact

- Is generally aware of return on investment when allocating resources to the field.

- Establishes appropriate criteria for allocating resources and funds that ensure sufficient return on investment.

- Combines past experience, knowledge of market dynamics, representative input, and analysis of all available data to develop effective resource allocation methods.
- Builds a strong business case to support requests for additional funding from the regional office, Regional Council, and/or Headquarters for important district initiatives.
- Requires representatives to build a strong business case (including expected return-on-investment) to justify resource allocation.

- Develops and implements strategies with TACU members to make the best use of combined resources.

District Manager Core Behaviors

Outlined below are the core behaviors for the District Manager (DM) role.

Core Behavior	Examples
1. Planning & Organizing *Plans and organizes activities and projects in a manner which will help achieve or exceed established goals.*	• Manages time effectively so that all high-priority activities are completed • Prepares complete and accurate sales reports • Maintains organized and up-to-date records (e.g., personnel files) • Responds promptly to all types of requests (e.g., electronic mail, voice mail, FedEx, UPS, etc.) • Uses technology to improve effectiveness (e.g., electronic mail, voice mail, Sherlock, etc.) • Prepares in advance for all meetings

2. Impact
 	
Makes a strong, professional impression. Projects an air of confidence that commands respect/attention and inspires trust.
	• Demonstrates strong/good:
	  –Presence
	  –Appearance
	  –Demeanor
	  –Speech
	  –Enthusiasm for the job and company
	  –Poise under pressure
	  –Ability to overcome adversity
	  -Persistence
	  –Self-discipline/self-control (in all work-related situations)
	• Displays integrity
	• Inspires trust
	• Accepts responsibility and accountability
	• Keeps an open mind and remains nonjudgmental
	• Role models a strong work ethic

3. Job Knowledge
 	
Demonstrates a strong understanding of how to fulfill all aspects of the DM role in a manner that will support long-term district success.
	• Demonstrates strong:
	  –Selling skills
	  –Knowledge of policies regarding starter administration, regulatory and legal compliance, marketing, and promotion of products
	  –Technical knowledge
	  –Product and disease state knowledge
	  –Ability to manage expenses and budgets

District Manager Core Behaviors (*Continued*)

Outlined below are the core behaviors for the District Manager (DM) role.

Core Behavior	Examples

–Ability to learn and acquire new skills
–Customer and competitive landscape (and specific customer account) knowledge
–Basic training skills to provide new hires with the tools/skills that they need to succeed (e.g., setting up representatives' cars and offices, developing territory management itineraries, monitoring task execution)
–Computer skills

4. Problem Analysis
Uses a logical approach in identifying issues and evaluating possible solutions.

- Demonstrates business and financial awareness
- Creates an atmosphere where issues are openly addressed before they evolve into problems
- Applies strong analytical and quantitative abilities when analyzing sales reports, manuals, and plans to identify and resolve business issues (i.e., sorts out key trends)
- Adopts a consistent, logical approach to address issues that:
  –Focus on controllables versus noncontrollables (e.g., willingly abandons ideas that are impractical)
  –Explore alternatives
  –Result in appropriate, practical, and implementable business solutions
- Follows a consistent method regarding when to:
  –Intervene and resolve problems versus
  –Coach others to resolve their own problems
- Remains level-headed when confronted with difficult or emotionally charged problems
- Draws on appropriate technology and available resources to help solve problems
- Takes into account all relevant background information when tackling challenging problems/issues
- Teaches representatives how to analyze market data and develop their analytical abilities
- Demonstrates understanding of district healthcare market dynamics and constituents (e.g., Managed Care, Employer Groups, PBMs, etc.) when determining the best solution to a problem

District Manager Core Behaviors (*Continued*)

Outlined below are the core behaviors for the District Manager (DM) role.

Core Behavior	Examples
5. Communication Ability *Listens and responds appropriately to various individuals' needs and social styles in a logical, coherent, and articulate manner.*	• Provides clear and succinct messages in all communications • Writes effectively (e.g., writing is clear, easy to understand, and compelling) • Is able to present to all audiences (including customers, representatives, business associations, customer advocacy groups, and senior U.S. Pharmaceuticals stakeholders) in a variety of circumstances/formats • Is articulate and persuasive • Seeks to understand (and be understood by) others • Listens closely to messages and strives to grasp the meaning and importance behind them • Manages two-way communication between Headquarters and the field to ensure that representatives focus on the most important information and that important field issues are communicated to Headquarters • Willingly shares appropriate and helpful information with representatives and peers • Uses the appropriate mode of communication to address specific issues (e.g., discusses performance appraisals in person versus over electronic mail) • Demonstrates timeliness in all communications
6. Facilitation Skills *Effectively leads a group through a process or meeting.*	• Is able to facilitate groups independent of audience seniority or level of influence • Demonstrates the ability to field and answer questions in an open forum • Engages audiences in productive and comprehensive discussions (e.g., ensures that everyone participates in POA meetings)
7. Judgment *Makes thoughtful and fair decisions based on relevant information.*	• Is a good judge of character and reads people well • Has a fair and equitable approach to managing representatives and other district employees • Makes sound decisions based on concrete facts (not opinions or emotions) • Considers all possible legal/political implications on the field force before making critical decisions or public statements (e.g., in recruiting/selection, public relations, etc.)
8. Flexibility *Willingly recognizes the need for change and modifies behavior to accommodate changing conditions and plans.*	• Deals with ambiguity; does not need a "road map" to forge ahead and break new ground • Changes position/course of action when persuaded by compelling facts or different opinions • Willing to respond to changes in the work environment or the market • Adjusts to others' work styles and leverages others' strengths to improve effectiveness • Adapts behavior to different personality styles, as appropriate • Seeks new challenges to take on/tackle

District Manager Core Behaviors (*Continued*)

Outlined below are the core behaviors for the District Manager (DM) role.

Core Behavior	Examples
9. Political Savvy/Protocol *Fulfills responsibilities in a manner that is consistent with U.S. Pharmaceuticals' chain of command and helps foster strong Headquarters/field relations.*	• Maintains poise in the face of adversity • Supports Headquarters (e.g., on pricing/product positioning), RMs, and the regional team both publicly and privately • Knows chain of command (benefits and limitations) • Keenly aware of Headquarters/field dynamics • Identifies the best channel/approach to use to access resources (i.e., observes protocol) • Works effectively across district, regional, TACU, and U.S. Pharmaceuticals lines
10. Sensitivity *Behaves in a manner that will enhance interpersonal relationships and optimize the productivity of the employees and/or group.*	• Balances individual representative needs with district, regional, and U.S. Pharmaceuticals priorities • Considers others' feelings and the ramifications of actions and decisions • Focuses on individuals' behaviors and results versus nonperformance-related personal perspectives and orientations • Understands and tries to respond to representatives' work/life balance needs, as appropriate • Creates an environment for open communications (e.g., open door policy, willingness to speak to representatives over the weekend, etc.) • Displays empathy toward representatives, as appropriate
11. Teamwork *Demonstrates the ability and willingness to work well with others and to draw upon others' resources and experience.*	• Willingly collaborates with others to achieve shared goals and build a strong team • Respects others' ideas and opinions • Openly acknowledges and recognizes representatives, other DMs, and Headquarters personnel for their efforts and contributions to the district, region, and U.S. Pharmaceuticals • Routinely shares ideas, new information, experience, and resources with fellow DMs, field force members, copromote partners, and Headquarters • Actively participates in TACU meetings to improve overall district, region, and U.S. Pharmaceuticals performance • Is responsive to others' needs • Cooperates effectively with the entire U.S. Pharmaceuticals team

Part Four

Employee Benefits

Dig three holes in the ground, one small, one medium size, and one large. In the first, bury $13,064. In the second, put $19,991. And in the largest hole, put $18,308. Leave the money in these holes as very expensive fertilizer for your geraniums. Why these amounts, you ask? Why bury them in the backyard, you ask? Well, those dollar amounts are what is spent on a full-time employee's benefits in, respectively, a small, medium, and large company in one year.[1] Burying the money in the backyard is our way of saying it's not clear the money is any worse off in the ground than invested in employee benefits. A bit harsh? An exaggeration, you say! Think about what we know that is fact—not faith—in the benefits area. Which of the issues covered in the pay model (Exhibit IV.1), for example, can we answer with respect to benefits? Does effective employee benefit management facilitate organization performance? The answer is unclear. We do know that benefit costs can be cut, and this affects the bottom line (admittedly an important measure of organization performance). But what about other alignment and management efforts? Do they complement organization strategy and performance? We don't know. Or do employee benefits impact upon an organization's ability to attract, retain, and motivate employees? Conventional wisdom says employee benefits can affect retention, but there is no definitive research to support this conclusion. A similar lack of research surrounds each of the other potential payoffs to a sound benefits program.

Employee benefits cost about $1 trillion today. Is it any wonder, then, that firms are increasingly paying attention to this reward component? It represents a labor cost with no apparent returns.

Compounding this concern is the ever-present entitlement problem. Employees perceive benefits as a right, independent of how well they or the company performs. Efforts to reduce benefit levels or eliminate parts of the package altogether would meet with employee resistance and dissatisfaction.

Assuming that organizations must find ways to control the costs of benefits wherever possible, this chapter focuses on identifying ways to maximize the returns from benefit expenditures. As a first step in this direction, Chapter 12 identifies issues organizations should face in developing and maintaining a benefit program. A model of the benefit determination process also is presented to provide a structure for thinking about employee benefits.

Chapter 13 provides a summary of the state of employee benefits today. Hopefully this will provide the groundwork for the innovative and effective benefit packages of tomorrow.

Exhibit IV.1   The Pay Model

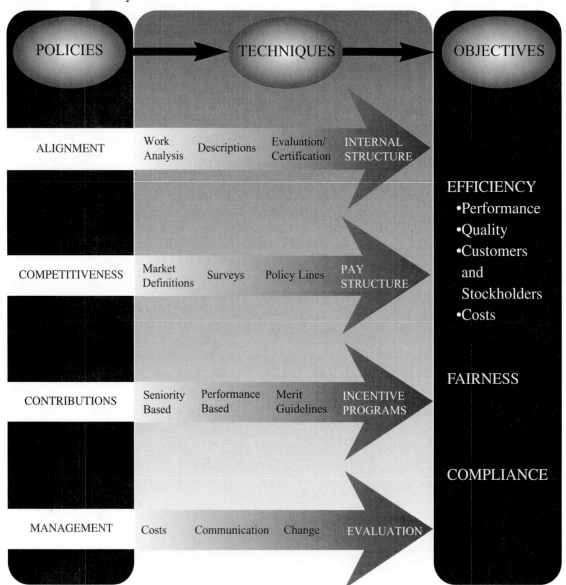

Chapter Twelve

The Benefit Determination Process

What can you do with a trillion dollars? Help balance the budget? Buy two used copies of this book? Well, the answer is, You can cover the cost of employee benefits in the United States today. It's hard to believe that employee benefits cost this much. Especially when we take a look at what used to pass as benefits in the not-too-distant past:

- A carriage shop published a set of rules for employees in 1880 that stated, in part: "Working hours shall be from 7 A.M. to 9 P.M. every day except the Sabbath. . . . After an employee has been with this firm for five years he shall receive an added payment of five cents per day, provided the firm has prospered in a manner to make it possible. . . . It is the bounden duty of each employee to put away at least 10 percent of his monthly wages for his declining years so he will not become a burden upon his betters."

- In 1915, employees in the iron and steel industry worked a standard 60 to 64 hours per week. By 1930 that schedule had been reduced to 54 hours.

- It was not until 1929 that the Blue Cross concept of prepaid medical costs was introduced.

- Prior to 1935 only one state (Wisconsin) had a program of unemployment compensation benefits for workers who lost their jobs through no fault of their own.

- Before World War II very few companies paid hourly employees for holidays. In most companies employees were told not to report for work on holidays and to enjoy the time off, but their paychecks were smaller the following week.[1]

In comparison to these "benefits" from the past, today's reality seems staggering. Consider the kinds of things that are common in companies that made the *Fortune* magazine list of "100 Best Companies to Work for in America." These companies recognize the importance of taking care of employees' needs as a key factor in attracting and retaining the best employees. A first-class benefit plan includes some mix of the following benefits: education reimbursement and employee training; on-site child care services, financial counseling, and concierge services; retirement benefits; and noncostly benefits such as casual-dress policies.[2] Some examples from specific companies include:[3]

Container Store: This retail box store ranks second on the best employer list for a second straight year. Amongst benefits offered are domestic partner benefits, free yoga classes at distribution centers, chair massages, and a 100 percent match for 401(k) for up to 4 percent of salary.

JM Smucker: Not only does Smucker make great jam and ice cream toppings, but it is a great employer too. Smucker offers such added benefits as health care for retirees and their spouses, on-site stop-smoking classes, and unlimited paid time off for volunteer work in the community

Wegmans Food Markets: Bob and Danny Wegman treat their employees right! Employees of this supermarket chain receive time off to volunteer and to care for sick pets. They are especially proud of the paid-time-off program for the mentoring of school children, which has helped more than 1,000 kids graduate from high school.

Clearly these firms would argue that these extra services are important benefits of employment, perhaps making attraction, retention, and motivation of employees just that much easier. But the truth is, we don't know if even ordinary benefits have positive payoffs. Until we can clearly identify the advantages of employee benefits, we need to find ways to control their costs or at least slow their growth. Exhibit 12.1 illustrates the rapid rise in employee benefit costs, moving from about 25 percent of payroll costs in 1959 to almost 40 percent today.[4]

Employee benefits are that part of the total compensation package, other than pay for time worked, provided to employees in whole or in part by employer payments (e.g., life insurance, pension, workers' compensation, vacation).

As Exhibit 12.1 illustrates, employee benefits can no longer realistically be called "fringe benefits." As an example, visualize a $20,000 car rolling down the assembly line at General Motors. A cost accountant would tell you that $1,200 of this cost is due to worker health insurance alone. Compare it to the cost of all the steel for the same car—$500—and the impact is evident. Now compare it to health insurance costs as low as $100 for foreign

[1]R. McCaffery, *Managing the Employee Benefits Program* (New York: American Management Association, 1972), pp. 1–2.

[2]S. Bates, "Benefit Packages Nearing 40 Percent of Payroll," *HRMagazine,* March 2003, pp. 36–38.

[3]*www.fortune.com/fortune/bestcompanies,* visited June 5, 2003.

[4]S. Bates, "Benefit Packages Nearing 40 Percent of Payroll," *HRMagazine,* March 2003. pp. 17–22.

**EXHIBIT 12.1
Changes in
Benefit Costs
over Time**

	1959	1969	1990	1998	2001
Percentage of Payroll	24.7	31.1	38.4	37.2	39

Source: U.S.
Chamber of
Commerce,
Annual Benefit
Surveys; and
S. Bates,
"Benefit
Packages
Nearing
40 Percent of
Payroll,"
HRMagazine,
March 2003.

automakers in their U.S. factories (with their younger, healthier workers and hardly any re-tirees), and the global implications of benefit costs are all too frightening.[5]

Over one 20-year period (1955–1975), employee benefit costs rose at a rate almost four times greater than employee wages or the consumer price index.[6] A similar compari-son for the period 1963–1987 showed that the rate of growth had slowed (benefit costs rose twice as fast as wage costs). And a still later comparison, for the period 1993–1999, shows the cost of benefits as actually stabilizing at about $14,700 per full-time employee. Even though the cost of benefits is rising more slowly, there are signs on the horizon of serious problems. Health care costs alone are rising this year about 15 percent, more than six times the rate of general inflation.[7] And pension costs, with so many companies using their stocks to finance payouts to pensioners, are in deep trouble with the declining stock market. Both of these benefit options are only expected to cause more problems as baby boomers age, retire, and face mounting health problems.

WHY THE GROWTH IN EMPLOYEE BENEFITS?

Wage and Price Controls

During both World War II and the Korean War, the federal government instituted strict wage and price controls. The compliance agency charged with enforcing these controls was relatively lenient in permitting reasonable increases in benefits. With strict limitations on the size of wage increases, both unions and employers sought new and improved bene-fits to satisfy worker demands. This was the catalyst for growth in pensions, health care coverage, time off, and the broad spectrum of benefits virtually unthinkable before 1950.

Unions

The climate fostered by wage and price controls created a perfect opportunity for unions to flex the muscles they had acquired under the Wagner Act of 1935. Several National Labor Relations Board rulings during the 1940s freed unions to negotiate over employee benefits. With little freedom to raise wages during the war, unions fought for the intro-duction of new benefits and the improvement of existing benefits. Success on this front during the war years led to further postwar demands. Largely through the efforts of unions, most notably the autoworkers and steelworkers, several benefits common today were given their initial impetus: pattern pension plans, supplementary unemployment compensation, extended vacation plans, and guaranteed annual wage plans.[8]

[5]Rebecca Blumenstein, "Seeking a Cure: Auto Makers Attack High Health-Care Bills with a New Approach," *Wall Street Journal,* December 9, 1996, p. A1.

[6]John Hanna, "Can the Challenge of Escalating Benefits Costs Be Met?" *Personnel Administration* 27(9) (1977), pp. 50–57.

[7]J. Catanese, "Cutting Health Care Costs," *Waste Age,* December, 2002, pp. 61, 64.

[8]R. McCaffery, *Managing the Employee Benefits Program* (New York: American Management Association, 1983).

Employer Impetus

Many of the benefits in existence today were provided at employer initiative. Much of this initiative can be traced to pragmatic concerns about employee satisfaction and productivity. Rest breaks often were implemented in the belief that fatigue increased accidents and lowered productivity. Savings and profit-sharing plans were implemented (e.g., Procter & Gamble's profit-sharing plan was initiated in 1885) to improve performance and provide increased security for worker retirement years. Indeed, many employer-initiated benefits were designed to create a climate in which employees perceived that management was genuinely concerned for their welfare. Notice, though, these supposed benefits were taken on faith. But their costs were quite real: Without hard data about payoffs, employee benefits slowly became a costly entitlement of the American work force.

Cost Effectiveness of Benefits

Another important and sound impetus for the growth of employee benefits is their cost effectiveness in two situations. The first cost advantage is that most employee benefits are not taxable. Provision of a benefit rather than an equivalent increase in wages avoids payment of federal and state personal income tax. Remember, though, recurrent tax reform proposals continue to threaten the favorable tax status granted to many benefits.

A second cost-effectiveness component of benefits arises because many group-based benefits (e.g., life, health, and legal insurance) can be obtained at a lower rate than could be obtained by employees acting on their own. Group insurance also has relatively easy qualification standards, giving security to a set of employees who might not otherwise qualify.

Government Impetus

Obviously the government has played an important role in the growth of employee benefits. Three employee benefits are mandated by either the state or federal government: workers' compensation (state), unemployment insurance (federal), and social security (federal). In addition, most other employee benefits are affected by such laws as the Employee Retirement Income Security Act (ERISA affects pension administration) and various sections of the Internal Revenue Code.

THE VALUE OF EMPLOYEE BENEFITS

Exhibit 12.2 shows the relative importance employees attached to different types of benefits across four different studies.[9]

[9]This table was compiled from four different sources. Some of the reward components rated in some of the studies were not traditional employee benefits and have been deleted from the rankings here. The four sources were "Employees Value Basic Benefits Most" (Aon survey), *Best's Review* 103(4) (2002), pp. 1527–1591; "The Future Look of Employee Benefits" (Hewitt Associates survey), *Wall Street Journal,* September 8, 1988, p. 23; Kermit Davis, William Giles, and Hubert Feild, *How Young Professionals Rank Employee Benefits: Two Studies* (Brookfield, WI: International Foundation of Employee Benefit Plans, 1988); Kenneth Shapiro and Jesse Sherman, "Employee Attitude Benefit Plan Designs," *Personnel Journal,* July 1987, pp. 49–58.

**EXHIBIT 12.2
Ranking of
Employee
Benefits.**

Note: x = not
rated in this
study.

	Study			
	1	**2**	**3**	**4**
Medical	1	1	3	1
Pension	2	3	8	3
Paid vacations and holidays	3	2	x	2
Sickness	4	x	5	8
Dental	5	x	6	6
Long-term disability	7	x	7	9
Life insurance	8	x	4	x

In general, the four studies reported in Exhibit 12.2 show fairly consistent results. For example, medical payments regularly are listed as one of the most important benefits employees receive. These rankings have added significance when we note that over the past two decades health care costs are the most rapidly growing and the most difficult to control of all the benefit options offered by employers.[10] In 2003 health care costs are projected to be $6,295, up $839 since 2001.[11] These costs would not seem nearly so outrageous if we had evidence that employees place high value on the benefits they receive. Unfortunately, there is evidence that employees frequently are not even aware of, or undervalue, the benefits provided by their organization. For example, in one study employees were asked to recall the benefits they received. The typical employee could recall less than 15 percent of them. In another study MBA students were asked to rank the importance attached to various factors influencing job selection.[12] Presumably the large percentage of labor costs allocated to payment of employee benefits would be easier to justify if benefits turned out to be an important factor in attracting good MBA candidates. Of the six factors ranked, employee benefits received the lowest ranking. Opportunity for advancement (1), salary (2), and geographic location (3) all ranked considerably higher than benefits as factors influencing job selection. Compounding this problem, these students also were asked to estimate the percentage of payroll spent on employee benefits. Slightly less than one-half (46 percent) of the students thought that benefits comprised 15 percent or less of payroll, and 9 out of 10 students (89 percent) thought benefits accounted for less than 30 percent of payroll. Only 1 in 10 students had a reasonably accurate (39 percent of payroll) or inflated perception of the magnitude of employee benefits.[13]

[10]Mary Fruen and Henry DiPrete, *Health Care in the Future* (Boston: John Hancock, 1986); Conference Board, "Health Plan Increases" (HRM update), New York, May 1988; Kintner and Smith, "General Motors Provides Health Care Benefits to Millions"; Health Research Institute, "1985 Health Care Cost Containment Survey," Walnut Creek, CA; North West National Life Insurance Co., "Ten Ways to Cut Employee Benefit Costs," 1988.

[11]J. Catanese. "Cutting Health Care Costs," *Waste Age*, December 2002, pp. 61–64.

[12]M. L. Williams and E. Newman, "Employees' Definitions of and Knowledge of Employer-Provided Benefits," paper presented at Academy of Management meetings, Atlanta, GA. 1993; Richard Huseman, John Hatfield, and Richard Robinson, "The MBA and Fringe Benefits," *Personnel Administration* 23(7) (1978), pp. 57–60.

[13]Ibid.

The ignorance about the value of employee benefits inferred from these studies can be traced to both employee attitude and option design problems. Looming largest is the attitude problem. Benefits are taken for granted. Employees view them as a right and have little comprehension of, or concern for, employer costs.[14]

One possible salvation from this money pit comes from recent reports that employees are looking not necessarily for more benefits but rather for greater choice in the benefits they receive.[15] In fact, up to 70 percent of employees in one study indicated they would be willing to pay more out of pocket for benefits if they were granted greater choice in designing their own benefit package. We do know, in support of this, that the perceived value of benefits rises when employers introduce choice through a flexible benefit package.[16] Maybe better benefit planning, design, and administration offer an opportunity to improve benefit effectiveness. Indeed, preliminary evidence indicates employers are making serious efforts to educate employees about benefits, with an outcome of increased employee awareness.[17] The simple act of writing in an employment ad, for example, that benefits are generous leads to applicants' focusing on this characteristic and relying more heavily on it in job choice. Some experts speculate that a key element in reward attractiveness (and benefits in this example) may be their visibility. Not only do we have to plan and design effective benefit programs; we also need to communicate their value to employees.

KEY ISSUES IN BENEFIT PLANNING, DESIGN, AND ADMINISTRATION

Benefits Planning and Design Issues

What do you want, or expect, the role of benefits to be in your overall compensation package?[18] For example, if a major compensation objective is to attract good employees, we need to ask, "What is the best way to achieve this?" The answer is not always, or even frequently, "Let's add another benefit."

Recently, a casino opened up in the Niagara Falls area. The Seneca Indians own this casino, and they need to fill thousands of entry-level jobs. The wages for a blackjack dealer are $4 per hour plus tips. The combination of the two exceeds minimum wage, but not by much. How do we attract more dealers, and other applicants, given these low

---

[14]J. Sammer, "New hope for controlling health care costs," *Business Finance,* 9(6), 2003, p. 57.

[15]Employee Benefit Research Institute, *America in Transition: Benefits for the Future* (Washington, DC: EBRI, 1987).

[16]D. M. Cable and T. A. Judge, 1998. "Pay Preferences and Job Search Decisions: A Person-Organization Fit Perspective," *Personnel Psychology* 47 (1994), pp. 317–348.

[17]Carol Danehower and John Lust, "How Aware Are Employees of Their Benefits?" *Benefits Quarterly* 12(4), pp. 57–61.

[18]Burton Beam, Jr., and John J. McFadden, *Employee Benefits* (Chicago: Dearborn Financial, 1996).

wages? One temptation might be to set up a day care center to attract more mothers of preschool children. Certainly this is a popular response today, judging from all the press day care centers are receiving. A more prudent compensation policy would ask the question: "Is day care the most effective way to achieve my compensation objective?" Sure, day care may be popular with working mothers, but can the necessary workers be attracted to the casino using some other compensation tool that better meets needs? If we went to compensation experts in the gaming industry, they might say (and we would be impressed if they did): "We target recruitment of young females for our entry-level jobs. Surveys of this group indicate day care is an extremely important factor in the decision to accept a job." If we heard this kind of logic, it would certainly illustrate the kind of care firms should use before adopting expensive benefit options. However, keep in mind that, this is a casino. We think it is unlikely that applicants would apply because it is a family-friendly work environment, with great family benefits.

As a second example, how do we deal with undesirable turnover? We might be tempted to design a benefit package that improves progressively with seniority, thus providing a reward for continuing service. This would only be the preferred option, though, if other compensation tools (e.g., increasing wages, introducing incentive compensation) were less effective.

In addition to integrating benefits with other compensation components, the planning process also should include strategies for ensuring external competitiveness and adequacy of benefits. Competitiveness requires an understanding of what other firms in your product and labor markets offer as benefits. Firms conduct benefit surveys much as they conduct salary surveys. Either our firm must have a package comparable to that of survey participants or there should be a sound justification of why deviation makes sense for the firm.

In contrast, ensuring that benefits are adequate is a somewhat more difficult task. Most organizations evaluating adequacy consider the financial liability of employees with and without a particular benefit (e.g., employee medical expenses with and without medical expense benefits). There is no magic formula for defining benefit adequacy.[19] In part, the answer may lie in the relationship between benefit adequacy and the third plan objective: cost of effectiveness. More organizations need to consider whether employee benefits are cost-justified. All sorts of ethical questions arise when we start asking this question. How far should we go with elder care? Can we justify a $250,000 operation that will likely buy only a few months more of life? Companies face these impossible questions when designing a benefit system. And more frequently than ever before, companies are saying no to absorbing the cost increases of benefits. A recent survey shows that only 32 percent of employers are willing to absorb cost increases, down from over 50 percent just two years earlier.[20]

Cybercomp

Benefitslink, at *www.benefitslink.com/index.shtml,* provides a wealth of information about types of benefits, a message board for interacting in discussions with others interested in benefits, and an "ask the expert" question-and-answer column.

---

[19]Ibid.

[20]Eighth annual Watson Wyatt/WBGH Survey, *www.watsonwyatt.com.*

EXHIBIT 12.3
Contingent
Worker
Benefits
Compared to
Full-Time
Workers

Source: National
Compensation
Survey 2000.
Bureau of Labor
Statistics,
www.bls.gov
visited
September 29,
2003.

	Full Time	Part Time
Holidays	87%	39%
Vacations	91	39
Short Term Disability	39	12
Long Term Disability	31	4
Life Insurance	65	11
Retirement	55	18
Medical	61	13
Dental	35	6
Vision	21	4

Benefit Administration Issues

Four major administration issues arise in setting up a benefit package: (1) Who should be protected or benefited? (2) How much choice should employees have among an array of benefits? (3) How should benefits be financed?[21] And (4) are your benefits legally defensible?[22]

The first issue—who should be covered—ought to be an easy question. Employees, of course. But every organization has a variety of employees with different employment statuses. Should these individuals be treated equally with respect to benefits coverage? Exhibit 12.3 illustrates that companies do indeed differentiate treatment based on employment status. The dollar value of benefits is much lower, even when we factor in the difference in hours worked, for part-timers than for full-time employees.

As a second example, should retired automobile executives be permitted to continue purchasing cars at a discount price, a benefit that could be reserved solely for current employees? In fact, a whole series of questions need to be answered:

1. What probationary periods (for eligibility of benefits) should be used for various types of benefits? Does the employer want to cover employees and their dependents immediately upon employment or provide such coverage only for employees who have established more or less permanent employment with the employer? Is there a rationale for different probationary periods with different benefits?

2. Which dependents of active employees should be covered?

3. Should retirees (as well as their spouses and perhaps other dependents) be covered, and for which benefits?

4. Should survivors of deceased employees (and/or retirees) be covered? If so, for which benefits? Are benefits for surviving spouses appropriate?

5. What coverage, if any, should be extended to employees who are suffering from disabilities?

---

[21]Ibid.

[22]E. Parmenter, "Employee Benefit Compliance Checklist," *Compensation and Benefits Review,* May/June 2002, pp. 29–39.

EXHIBIT 12.4
Possible
Options in a
Flexible
Benefit
Package

*AE = average
earnings.

	Package			
	A	**B**	**C**	**D**
Health	No	No	Yes	Yes
Dental	No	No	No	Yes
Vision	No	Yes	Yes	Yes
Life insurance	1 × AE*	2 × AE	2 × AE	3 × AE
Dependent care	Yes	No	No	No
401(k) savings	No	Yes	No	No
Cash back	Yes	No	No	No

6. What coverage, if any, should be extended to employees during layoffs, leaves of absence, strikes, and so forth?

7. Should coverage be limited to full-time employees?[23]

The answers to these questions depend on the policy decisions regarding adequacy, competition, and cost effectiveness discussed in the last section.

The second administrative issue concerns choice (flexibility) in plan coverage. In the standard benefit package, employees typically have not been offered a choice among employee benefits. Rather, a package is designed with the average employee in mind, and any deviations in needs simply go unsatisfied. The other extreme (discussed in greater detail later) is represented by "cafeteria-style," or flexible, benefit plans. Under this concept employees are permitted great flexibility in choosing the benefit options of greatest value to them. Picture an individual allotted x dollars walking down a cafeteria line and choosing menu items (benefits) according to their attractiveness and cost. The flexibility in this type of plan is apparent. Exhibit 12.4 illustrates a typical choice among packages offered to employees under a flexible benefit system. Imagine an employee whose spouse works and already has family coverage for health, dental, and vision. The temptation might be to select package A. An employee with retirement in mind might select option B with its contributions to a 401(k) pension plan. Exhibit 12.5 summarizes some of the major advantages and disadvantages of flexible benefits.

Even companies that are not considering a flexible benefit program are offering greater flexibility and choice. Such plans might provide, for example, (1) optional levels of group term life insurance; (2) the availability of death or disability benefits under pension or profit-sharing plans; (3) choices of covering dependents under group medical expense coverage; (4) a variety of participation, cash distribution, and investment options under profit-sharing, thrift, and capital accumulation plans.[24]

The level at which an organization finally chooses to operate on this choice/flexibility dimension really depends on its evaluation of the relative advantages and disadvantages

[23]Ibid.

[24]Karen Lee, "Full Plate: Employers Are Offering a Soup to Nuts Array of Non-traditional Benefits to Increase Flexibility and Choice for Their Workers," *Employee Benefit News,* October 2000; Kenneth Shapiro, "Flexibility in Benefit Plans," *1983 Hay Compensation Conference Proceedings* (Philadelphia: Hay Management Consultants, 1983).

EXHIBIT 12.5 Advantages and Disadvantages of Flexible Benefit Programs

Advantages

1. Employees choose packages that best satisfy their unique needs.
2. Flexible benefits help firms meet the changing needs of a changing work force.
3. Increased involvement of employees and families improves understanding of benefits.
4. Flexible plans make introduction of new benefits less costly. The new option is added merely as one among a wide variety of elements from which to choose.
5. Cost containment: Organization sets dollar maximum; employee chooses within that constraint.

Disadvantages

1. Employees make bad choices and find themselves not covered for predictable emergencies.
2. Administrative burdens and expenses increase.
3. Adverse selection: Employees pick only benefits they will use; the subsequent high-benefit utilization increases its cost.
4. Subject to nondiscrimination requirements in Section 125 of the Internal Revenue Code.

of flexible plans, noted in Exhibit 12.5.[25] Many companies cite the cost savings from flexible benefits as a primary motivation. Companies also offer flexible plans in response to cost pressures related to the increasing diversity of the work force. Flexible benefit plans, it is argued, increase employee awareness of the true costs of benefits and, therefore, increase employee recognition of benefit value.[26]

A key consideration in the continued popularity of flexible benefit plans may well be the increased scrutiny by the Internal Revenue Service. Section 125 of the Internal Revenue Code outlines a series of requirements a company must meet in setting up a flexible benefit package.[27] The most important of these restrictions is a nondiscrimination clause; that is, a plan may not give significantly higher benefits to highly compensated executives relative to average employees. In fact, the average benefits for nonhighly compensated employees must equal or exceed 75 percent of the average benefits for highly compensated executives.

The third administrative issue involves the question of how to finance benefit plans. Alternatives include:

1. Noncontributory (Employer pays total costs.)
2. Contributory (Costs are shared between employer and employee.)
3. Employee financed (Employee pays total costs for some benefits—by law the organization must bear the cost for certain benefits.)

[25]Melissa W. Barringer and George T. Milkovich, "A Theoretical Exploration of the Adoption and Design of Flexible Benefit Plans: A Case of Human Resource Innovation," *Academy of Management Review* 23 (1998), pp. 306–308; Commerce Clearing House, "Flexible Benefits," Chicago, 1983; American Can Company, "Do It Your Way," Greenwich, CT, 1978; L. M. Baytos, "The Employee Benefit Smorgasbord: Its Potential and Limitations," *Compensation Review,* First Quarter 1970, pp. 86–90; "Flexible Benefit Plans Become More Popular," *Wall Street Journal,* December 16, 1986, p. 1; Richard Johnson, *Flexible Benefits: A How to Guide* (Brookfield, WI: International Foundation of Employee Benefit Plans, 1986).

[26]EBRI, *Employee Benefits Research Institute Databook on Employee Benefits* (Washington, D.C., Employee Benefits Research Institute, 1995).

[27]Johnson, *Flexible Benefits: A How to Guide.*

In general, organizations prefer to make benefit options contributory, reasoning that a "free good," no matter how valuable, is less valuable to an employee. Furthermore, employees have no personal interest in controlling the cost of a free good. And with the cost of benefits rising considerably more than other goods and services, employers are increasingly turning to ways for cutting their costs.[28]

Finally, benefits have to comply with hundreds of arcane sections of the tax code and other "devils" designed to turn any benefit administrator's hair gray. Because there are so many rules and regulations, benefit administrators should develop a compliance checklist and regularly conduct audits to ensure that they are complying with the avalanche of new and existing requirements.[29]

COMPONENTS OF A BENEFIT PLAN

Exhibit 12.6 outlines a model of the factors influencing benefit choice, from both the employer's and the employee's perspective. The remainder of this chapter briefly examines each of these factors.

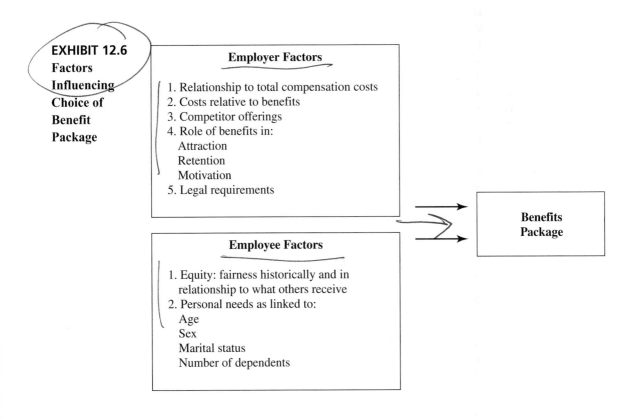

EXHIBIT 12.6
Factors Influencing Choice of Benefit Package

Employer Factors

1. Relationship to total compensation costs
2. Costs relative to benefits
3. Competitor offerings
4. Role of benefits in:
   Attraction
   Retention
   Motivation
5. Legal requirements

Employee Factors

1. Equity: fairness historically and in relationship to what others receive
2. Personal needs as linked to:
   Age
   Sex
   Marital status
   Number of dependents

Benefits Package

[28]F. Hansen, "The Cutting Edge of Benefit Cost Control," *Workforce*, March 2003, pp. 36–42.

[29]E. Parmenter, "Employee Benefit Compliance Checklist," *Compensation and Benefits Review*, 34(3) (2002), pp. 29–39.

Employer Preferences

As Exhibit 12.6 indicates, a number of factors affect employer preference in determining desirable components of a benefit package.

Relationship to Total Compensation Costs

A good compensation manager considers employee benefit costs as part of a total package of compensation costs. Frequently employees think that just because an employee benefit is attractive, the company should provide it. A good compensation manager thinks somewhat differently: "Is there a better use for this money? Could we put the money into some other compensation component and achieve better results?" Benefit costs are only one part of a total compensation package. Decisions about outlays have to be considered from this perspective.

Costs Relative to Benefits

A major reason for the proliferating cost of benefit programs is the narrow focus of benefit administrators. Too frequently the costs/advantages of a particular benefit inclusion are viewed in isolation, without reference to total package costs or forecasts of rising costs in future years. To control spiraling benefit costs, administrators should adopt a broader, cost-centered approach. As a first step, this approach would require policy decisions on the level of benefit expenditures acceptable both in the short and the long runs. Historically, benefit managers negotiated or provided benefits on a package basis rather than a cost basis. The current cost of a benefit would be identified, and if the cost seemed reasonable, the benefit would be provided for or negotiated with employees. This failed to recognize that rising costs of this benefit were expected to be born by the employer. The classic example of this phenomenon is health care coverage. An employer considering a community-based medical plan like Blue Cross during the early 1960s no doubt agreed to pay all or most of the costs of one of the Blue Cross options. As costs of this plan skyrocketed between the '60s and the '90s, the employer was expected to continue coverage at the historical level. In effect, the employer became locked into a level of coverage rather than negotiating a level of cost. In subsequent years, then, the spiraling costs were essentially out of the control of the benefit manager.

A cost-centered approach would require that benefit administrators, in cooperation with insurance carriers and armed with published forecasts of anticipated costs for particular benefits, determine the cost commitments for the existing benefit package. Budget dollars not already earmarked may then be allocated to new benefits that best satisfy organizational goals. Factors affecting this decision include an evaluation of benefits offered by other firms and the competitiveness of the existing package. Also important is compliance with various legal requirements as they change over time (Chapter 13). Finally, the actual benefit of a new option must be explored in relation to employee preferences. The benefits that top the list of employee preferences should be evaluated in relation to current and future costs. Because future cost estimates may be difficult to project, it is imperative that benefit administrators reduce uncertainty.

If a benefit forecast suggests future cost containment may be difficult, the benefit should be offered to employees only on a cost-sharing basis. Management determines what percentage of cost it can afford to bear within budget projections, and the option is offered to employees on a cost-sharing basis, with projected increases in both employer and employee costs communicated openly. In the negotiation process, then, employees or union representatives can evaluate their preference for the option against the forecasted cost burden. In effect, this approach defines in advance the contribution an employer is willing to make. And it avoids the constraints of a defined benefit strategy that burdens the employer with continued provision of that defined benefit level despite rapidly spiraling costs.

Competitor Offerings

Benefits must be externally equitable, too. This begs the question, What is the absolute level of benefit payments relative to important product and labor market competitors? A policy decision must be made about the position (market lead, market lag, or competitive) the organization wants to maintain in its absolute level of benefits relative to the competition. One of the best strategies for determining external equity is to conduct a benefit survey. Alternatively, many consulting organizations, professional associations, and interest groups collect benefit data that can be purchased. Perhaps the most widely used of these surveys is the annual benefit survey conducted by the U.S. Chamber of Commerce.[30]

Role of Benefits in Attraction, Retention, and Motivation

Given the rapid growth in benefits and the staggering cost implications, it seems only logical that employers would expect to derive a fair return on this investment. In fact, there is at best only anecdotal evidence that employee benefits are cost-justified. This evidence falls into three categories.[31] First, employee benefits are widely claimed to help in the retention of workers. Benefit schedules are specifically designed to favor longer-term employees. For example, retirement benefits increase with years of service, and most plans do not provide for full employee eligibility until a specified number of years of service have been reached. Equally, the amount of vacation time increases with years of service, and employees' savings plans, profit-sharing plans, and stock purchase plans frequently provide for increased participation or benefits as seniority increases. By tying these benefits to seniority, it is assumed that workers are more reluctant to change jobs.

There is also some research to support this common assumption that benefits increase retention. Two studies found that higher benefits reduced mobility.[32] More detailed follow-up studies, though, found that only two specific benefits curtailed employee turnover: pensions and medical coverage.[33] Virtually no other employee benefit had a significant impact on turnover.

---

[30]U.S. Chamber of Commerce, Employee Benefits annual surveys, Washington, D.C.

[31]Donald P. Crane, *The Management of Human Resources,* 2d ed. (Belmont, CA: Wadsworth, 1979); J. Foegen, "Are Escalating Employee Benefits Self-Defeating?" *Pension World* 14(9) (September 1978), pp. 83–84, 86.

[32]Olivia Mitchell, "Fringe Benefits and Labor Mobility," *Journal of Human Resources* 17(2) (1982), pp. 286–298; Bradley Schiller and Randal Weiss, "The Impact of Private Pensions on Firm Attachment," *Review of Economics and Statistics* 61(3) (1979), pp. 369–380.

[33]Olivia Mitchell, "Fringe Benefits and the Cost of Changing Jobs," *Industrial and Labor Relations Review* 37(1) (1983), pp. 70–78; William E. Even and David A. MacPherson, "Employer Size and Labor Turnover: The Role of Pensions," *Industrial and Labor Relations Review* 49(4) (July 1996), p. 707.

We've been assuming here that turnover is bad and stability is good. In fact, there are times when turnover may be good—something we may not want to discourage. For example, at one time or another 3 Americans in 10 have stayed in a job they wanted to leave simply because they could not give up their health care coverage.[34] This "job lock" probably is not a desirable outcome for employers.

Employee benefits also might be valued if we could prove they increase employee satisfaction. Unfortunately, today only 50 percent of workers consider their benefits adequate. This is down from 83 percent in the early 1980s.[35] The lowest satisfaction marks go to disability, life, and health insurance.[36] Why have satisfaction ratings fallen? One view holds that benefit satisfaction falls as cost-cutting companies attempt to reduce coverage and also shift more of the costs to employees.[37] A second view is more pessimistic, arguing that benefit plans fail to meet either employer or employee needs. In this view, simply pumping more money into benefits is inappropriate. Rather, employers must make fundamental changes in the way they approach the benefit planning process. Companies must realize that declining satisfaction with benefits is a result of long-term changes in the work force. Ever-increasing numbers of women in the labor force, coupled with increasing numbers of dual-career families and higher educational attainments, suggest changing values of employees.[38] Changing values, in turn, necessitate a reevaluation of benefit packages.

Finally, employee benefits also are valued because they may have an impact on the bottom line. Although supporting evidence is slim, there are some glimmers of potential. For example, employee stock ownership plans (Chapter 10), according to some reports, improve company productivity.[39] Presumably, owning stock motivates employees to be more productive. After all, part of the reward returns to them in the form of dividends and increased stock value. Similar productivity improvements are reported for employee assistance programs (e.g., alcohol and drug treatment programs for employees), with reports of up to 25 percent jumps in productivity after their implementation.[40] This finding suggests there may be some payoff to so called work/life benefits, those that increase employee perceptions of a company's caring attitude. Things like day care, elder care, on-site fitness centers, and weight loss programs foster a perception that the company cares about its employees. And in one well-constructed research study, this caring attitude led to greater worker involvement in suggesting ways to improve productivity and in helping others with their work.[41] Maybe benefits can pay off; we just need to better document this.

---

[34]New York Times and CBS poll, as reported in *Human Resource Management News* (Chicago: Remy Publishing, 1991).

[35]Christopher Conte, "Flexible Benefit Plans Grow More Popular as Companies Seek to Cut Costs," *Wall Street Journal,* March 19, 1991, p. A1.

[36]*Wall Street Journal,* April 30, 1985, p. 1.

[37]George Dreher, Ronald Ash, and Robert Bretz, "Benefit Coverage and Employee Cost: Critical Factors in Explaining Compensation Satisfaction," *Personnel Psychology* 41 (1988), pp. 237–254.

[38]Ibid.

[39]"ESOPs Key to Performance," *Employee Benefit News,* no. 5, 1987, p. 16.

[40]Lynn Densford, "Bringing Employees Back to health," *Employee Benefit News* 2 (February 1988), p.19.

[41]S. Lambert, "Added Benefits: The Link between Work-Life Benefits and Organizational Citizenship Behavior," *Academy of Management Journal,* 43(5) (2000), pp. 801–815.

EXHIBIT 12.7   Impact of Legislation on Selected Benefits

Legislation	Impact on Employee Benefits
Fair Labor Standards Act 1938	Created time-and-a-half overtime pay. Benefits linked to pay (e.g., social security) increase correspondingly with those overtime hours.
Employee Retirement Income Security Act 1974	If an employer decides to provide a pension (it is not mandated), specific rules must be followed. Plan must vest (employee has right to both personal and company contributions into pension) after five years' employment. Pension Benefit Guaranty Corporation, as set up by this law, provides worker some financial coverage when a company and its pension plan go bankrupt.
Tax reforms—1982, 1986	Permit individual retirement accounts (IRAs) for eligible employees. Established 401(k) programs, a matched-contribution saving plan (employer matches part or all of employee contribution) that frequently serves as part of a retirement package.
Health Maintenance Act 1973	Required employers to offer alternative health coverage (e.g., health maintenance organizations) options to employees.
Discrimination legislation (Age Discrimination in Employment Act, Civil Rights Act, Pregnancy Disability Act, various state laws)	Benefits must be administered in a manner that does not discriminate against protected groups (on basis of race, color, religion, sex, national origin, age, pregnancy).
Consolidated Omnibus Budget Reconciliation Act (COBRA) 1984	Employees who resign or are laid off through no fault of their own are eligible to continue receiving health coverage under employer's plan at a cost borne by the employee.
Family Medical Leave Act (1993)	Mandates 12 weeks of leave for all workers at companies that employ 50 or more people.

Legal Requirements

Employers obviously want a benefit package that complies with all aspects of the law. Exhibit 12.7 shows part of the increasingly complex web of legislation in the benefit area. Greater details on the three legally mandated benefits (workers' compensation, social security, and unemployment insurance) are provided in Chapter 13.

Absolute and Relative Compensation Costs

Any evaluation of employee benefits must be placed in the context of total compensation costs. Cost competitiveness means the total package must be competitive—not just specific segments. Consequently, decisions on whether to adopt certain options must be considered in light of the impact on total costs and in relationship to expenditures of competitors (as determined in benefit surveys such as the Chamber of Commerce survey mentioned earlier in this chapter).

Employee Preferences

Employee preferences for various benefit options are determined by individual needs. The benefits perceived to best satisfy individual needs are the most highly desired. In part these needs arise out of feelings of perceived equity or inequity.

Equity

To illustrate the impact of equity, consider the example of government employees working in the same neighborhood as autoworkers. Imagine the dissatisfaction with government holidays that arises when government employees leave for work every morning, knowing that the autoworkers are home in bed for the whole week between Christmas and New Year's Day. The perceived unfairness of this difference need not be rational. But it is, nevertheless, a factor that must be considered in determining employee needs. Occasionally this comparison process leads to a "bandwagon" effect, in which new benefits offered by a competitor are adopted without careful consideration, simply because the employer wants to avoid hard feelings. This phenomenon is particularly apparent for employers with strong commitments to maintaining a totally or partially nonunion work force. Benefits obtained by a unionized competitor or a unionized segment of the firm's work force are frequently passed along to nonunion employees. While the effectiveness of this strategy in thwarting unionization efforts has not been demonstrated, many nonunion firms would prefer to provide the benefit as a safety measure.

Personal Needs of Employees

One way to gauge employee preferences is to look at demographic differences. The demographic approach assumes that demographic groups (e.g., young versus old, married versus unmarried) can be identified for which benefit preferences are fairly consistent across members of the group. Furthermore, it assumes that meaningful differences exist between groups in terms of benefit preferences.

There is some evidence that these assumptions are only partially correct. In an extensive review of employee preference literature, Glueck traced patterns of group preferences for particular benefits.[42] As one might expect, older workers showed stronger preferences than younger workers for pension plans.[43] Also, families with dependents had stronger preferences for health/medical coverage than families with no dependents.[44] The big surprise in all these studies, though, is that many of the other demographic group breakdowns fail to result in differential benefit preferences. Traditionally, it has been assumed that benefit preferences ought to differ among males versus females, blue collar versus white collar, and married versus single. Few of these expectations have been born out by these studies. Rather, the studies have tended to be more valuable in showing preference trends that are characteristic of all employees. Among the benefits available, health/medical and stock plans are highly preferred benefits, while such options as early retirement, profit sharing, shorter hours, and counseling services rank among the least preferred options. Beyond these conclusions, most preference studies have shown wide variation in individuals with respect to benefits desired.

The weakness of this demographic approach has led some organizations to undertake a second and more expensive empirical method of determining employee preference: sur-

[42]William F. Glueck, *Personnel: A Diagnostic Approach* (Plano, TX.: Business Publications, 1978).

[43]Ludwig Wagner and Theodore Bakerman, "Wage Earners' Opinions of Insurance Fringe Benefits," *Journal of Insurance,* June 1960, pp. 17–28; Brad Chapman and Robert Otterman, "Employee Preference for Various Compensation and Benefits Options," *Personnel Administrator* 25 (November 1975), pp. 31–36.

[44]Stanley Nealy, "Pay and Benefit Preferences," *Industrial Relations,* October 1963, pp. 17–28.

EXHIBIT 12.8   Questionnaire Format for Benefit Surveys

Employee Benefit Questionnaire

1. In the space provided in front of the benefits listed below indicate how important each benefit is to you and your family. Indicate this by placing a "1" for the most important, and "2" for the next most important, etc. Therefore, if life insurance is the most important benefit to you and your family, place a "1" in front of it.

Importance		Improvement
	Dental insurance	
	Disability (pay while sick)	
	Educational assistance	
	Holidays	
	Life insurance	
	Medical insurance	
	Retirement annuity plan	
	Savings plan	
	Vacations	

Now, go back and in the space provided after each benefit, indicate the priority for improvement. For example, if the savings plan is the benefit you would most like to see improved, give it a "1," the next a priority "2," etc. Use the blank lines to add any benefits not listed.

2. Would you be willing to contribute a portion of your earnings for new or improved benefits beyond the level already provided by the Company?
   ❑ Yes   ❑ No

If yes, please indicate below in which area(s):

❑ Dental insurance   ❑ Medical insurance
❑ Disability benefits   ❑ Retirement annuity plan
❑ Life insurance   ❑ Savings plan

Source: Pfizer Corporation.

veying individuals about needs. One way of accomplishing this requires development of a questionnaire on which employees evaluate various benefits. For example, Exhibit 12.8 illustrates a questionnaire format.

A third empirical method of identifying individual employee preferences is commonly known as a *flexible benefit plan* (also called a *cafeteria-style plan* or a *supermarket plan*). As previously noted, employees are allotted a fixed amount of money and permitted to spend that amount in the purchase of benefit options. From a theoretical perspective, this approach to benefit packaging is ideal. Employees directly identify the benefits of greatest value to them, and by constraining the dollars employees have to spend, benefit managers are able to control benefit costs. NCR has adopted a variant on flexible benefits that is part of its "customer-oriented" benefit push. Employees who wish can actually exchange some of their base salary for greater coverage on desired benefits, as illustrated in Exhibit 12.9.

EXHIBIT 12.9   Administering the Benefits Program

A. Costs. Please modify this "base" benefit package into another which you would most prefer, bearing in mind that selecting different levels will impact your cash pay (see box to right).

Base Benefit Package	$11,460
Chosen Benefit Package	$11,460
Change in cash pay	$0

ALTERNATIVE LEVELS

FEATURE					
Medical Plan	Opt Out −$4,800	Traditional-Basic Current A Base	HMO −$800	Traditional-Enhanced +$1,000	PPO +$1,300
Long-Term Disability Plan	Opt Out −$840	50% of Your Salary Current A Base	60% of Your Salary +$240	70% of Your Salary +$480	
Life Insurance	None A Base	1 Times Your Salary +$240	2 Times Your Salary Current +$480	3 Times Your Salary +$720	4 Times Your Salary +$960
401(k) Plan	None −$1,800	3% Match 5-Year Vesting +$1,200	6% Match 5-Year Vesting Current A Base	6% Match 1-Year Vesting $900	10% Match No Vesting $2,400
Paid Parental/Family Leave	None Current −$180	3-Day Leave A Base	12-Week Leave 1/2 Salary +$540	12-Week Leave Full Salary +$1,800	

Source: "Employee a Customer" by Lynn Gaughan and Jorg Kasparek, NCR Corp., and John Hagens and Jeff Young, *Workspan*, September 2000, pp. 31–37.

ADMINISTERING THE BENEFIT PROGRAM

The job description for an employee benefit manager at Warner Brothers, shown, in Exhibit 12.10 indicates that administrative time is spent on three functions requiring further discussion: (1) communicating about the benefits program, (2) claims processing, and (3) cost containment.[45]

Employee Benefit Communication

Much of the effort to achieve benefit goals focuses on identifying methods of communication. The most frequent method for communicating employee benefits today is probably still the employee benefit handbook.[46] A typical handbook contains a description of all benefits, including levels of coverage and eligibility requirements. To be most effective, the benefit manual should be accompanied by group meetings and videotapes.[47] While some organizations may supplement this initial benefit discussion with periodic refreshers (e.g., once per year), a more typical approach involves one-on-one discussions between the benefit administrator and an employee seeking information on a particular benefit. In recent years the dominance of the benefit handbook is being challenged by personalized benefit statements generated by computer software programs specially designed for that

EXHIBIT 12.10 Job Description for Employee Benefit Manager at Warner Brothers

Source: *jobsearch. monster.com,* June 16, 2003.

Warner Bros. Entertainment Inc. seeks a Manager of Employee Benefits for the Compensation and Benefits department. Position acts as an Employee advocate for health, welfare, and retirement issues such as claims or questions requiring special handling, specialty referrals, and/or problem solving. Administrates for UCLA Executive Health program, Executive Medical Reimbursement program, and Flexible Spending Account Plans. Acts as liaison for Executive Appeals committee and the Emergency Allocations Committee. Position has major involvement in Special Projects such as Open Enrollment and Special Open Enrollment. Develops and maintains programs and communications designed to keep employees informed about company benefit programs and any changes by utilizing quarterly newsletter, intranet website, and Company-wide memos. Performs and completes benefit surveys as required. Investigates services/facilities to better serve the WB population. Performs eligibility audits, handles daily eligibility issues and customer service issues. Acts as a major liaison with MIS for resolution of systems issues. Interfaces with various HR partners/functions (e.g., generalists, International, Service Centers, Finance, Accounting, Legal) including composing and delivering written and verbal presentations to all levels of employees and management. Serves as resource to administrative Service Center on a regular basis for the ongoing improvement of standards, policies, and procedures related to benefits administration; coordinates and relays information and updates. Keeps abreast of federal, state, and local benefit laws and regulations.

[45]McCaffery, *Managing the Employee Benefits Program.*

[46]See "Towers Perrin Survey Finds Dramatic Increase in Companies Utilizing the Web for HR Transactions: Two- to Threefold Increase Compared to 1999 Survey," *www.towers.com/towers/news,* visited October 20, 2000; Towers, Perrin, Forster, and Crosby, "Corporate Benefit Communication . . . Today and Tomorrow," 1988.

[47]Ibid.

EXHIBIT 12.11 Typical Benefits Objectives

Objective	Respondents Indicating This Is a Primary Objective (in Percents)*
1. Increase Employee Understanding of Plan Objectives	82
2. Increase Employee Appreciation of the Benefits Program	81
3. Increase Employee Knowledge of the Cost of Providing Benefits	41
4. Obtain Employee Cooperation in Controlling Benefit Costs	36
5. Encourage Employee Responsibility for Own Financial Security	16
6. Maintain the Company's Commitment to Open Employee Communications	16

*Multiple responses permitted
Source: Towers, Perrin, Forster and Crosby (1988), "Corporate Benefit Communication . . . Today and Tomorrow."

purpose. These tailor-made reports provide a breakdown of package components and list selected cost information about the options.[48]

Despite this and other innovative plans to communicate employee benefit packages, failure to understand benefit components and their value is still one of the root causes of employee dissatisfaction with a benefit package.[49] We believe an effective communications package must have two elements. First, an organization must spell out its benefit objectives and ensure that any communications achieve these objectives. Exhibit 12.11 outlines typical benefit objectives.

Second, an effective communications package should match the message with the appropriate medium. Technological advances have made tremendous improvements in employee benefit communication. In the last several years, a new medium has emerged for communicating benefits—the *intranet*. In today's corporations, benefit administrators are aiming to maintain communication with employees in a timely, consistent, and accurate manner, and many are selecting an intranet as their chosen avenue of communication.[50] An intranet is an internal organizational online web through which all forms of communication within the organization can be streamlined. Advantages of an intranet include employee access to benefit information 24 hours a day, 7 days a week without added cost; employee's ability to directly post changes to their accounts without completing lengthy paperwork; and an increased ease of updating information.[51]

Employers are increasingly posting their employee benefit handbook components on their intranets.[52] This change is beneficial to employers because of the decreased cost and increased ease of making revisions in the employee benefit handbook components. More

[48]Ibid.

[49]"Yoder-Heneman Creativity Award Supplement," *Personnel Administration* 26(11) (1981), pp. 49–67.

[50]S. Smith, "New Trends in Health Care Cost Control," *Compensation and Benefits Review*, January/February 2002, pp. 38–44; B. Ambrose, "Leveraging Technology via Knowledge Portals," *Compensation and Benefits Review*, May/June 2001, pp. 43–46; Frank E. Kuzmits, "Communicating Benefits: A Double-Click Away," *Compensation and Benefits Review* 61 (September/October 1998).

[51]Ibid.

[52]Jonathan A. Segal, "Don't Let the Transmission of Bits of Data Bite You in Court," *HRMagazine* 45 (June 2000).

than 100,000 employees at IBM get benefit communications and enrollment data through the intranet, at expected savings of $1 million per year. Joining IBM in this intranet-based enrollment process are such organizations as Lucent and Continental Airlines. Experts say "e-benefits" are a huge trend waiting to reinvent human resource practices.[53]

Benefit administration over the Internet is also growing at a rapid pace. One report suggests that perhaps as many as 80 percent of the Fortune 1000 companies will utilize at least some form of Internet-based employee benefit application.[54] A wide range of applications will be offered, from online benefit information to annual benefit enrollment processing, personal data changes, 401(k) changes, and complete employee self-service.[55]

Another example of the recent advances in benefit communication is the streamlined call center operation that Kelloggs Company launched in 1999.[56] The call center decreased costs by as much as $105 million while improving service levels and maintaining close employee interaction. At a cost equal to approximately one-fifth of its paper-based predecessor, which required that specialists be located at every Kelloggs facility in the United States and Canada, the call center allows users to access benefit plan information, download and print documents, and retrieve basic information regarding Kelloggs' benefit vendors. Annual cost savings of this system equal $500,000. Kelloggs anticipates that the future technological initiatives will include setting up kiosks, which will be web-enabled personal computers that allow employees to access the information they presently access over the telephone and to contact specialists over the Internet in live chat rooms.

Claims Processing

As noted by one expert, claims processing arises when an employee asserts that a specific event (e.g., disability, hospitalization, unemployment) has occurred and demands that the employer fulfill a promise of payment.[57] As such, a claims processor must first determine whether the act has, in fact, occurred. If the answer is yes, the second step involves determining if the employee is eligible for the benefit. If payment is not denied at this stage, the claims processor calculates the payment level. It is particularly important at this stage to ensure coordination of benefits. If multiple insurance companies are liable for payment (e.g., working spouses covered by different insurers), a good claims processor can save from 10 to 15 percent of a claims cost by ensuring that the liability is jointly paid.[58]

[53]Stephanie Armour, "Workers Just Click to Enroll for Benefits," *USA Today,* November 8, 2000, p. B1.
[54]Scott Carver, "Making Internet Benefits Enrollment Work for You," *Employee Benefits Journal* 24(4) (December 1999), pp. 40–42.
[55]S. Simon and W. Mattle, "Rethinking Online Benefits," *Compensation and Benefits Review,* March/April 2002, pp. 80–84; "Towers Perrin Survey Finds Dramatic Increase in Companies Utilizing the Web for HR Transactions: Two- to Threefold Increase Compared to 1999 Survey," *www.towers.com/towers/news,* visited October 20, 2000.
[56]Judith N. Mottl, "Cereal Killer," *Human Resources Executive,* May 2000 pp. 74–75.
[57]Bennet Shaver, "The Claims Process," in *Employee Benefit Management,* ed. H. Wayne Snider, Warren, Gorham and Lamont, New York, NY 1997. pp. 141–152.
[58]Thomas Fannin and Theresa Fannin, "Coordination of Benefits: Uncovering Buried Treasure," *Personnel Journal,* May 1983, pp. 386–391.

Cost Containment

Increasingly, employers are auditing their benefit options for cost containment opportunities. The most prevalent practices include:

1. Probationary periods—excluding new employees from benefit coverage until some term of employment (e.g., 3 months) is completed.
2. Benefit limitations—it is not uncommon to limit disability income payments to some maximum percentage of income and to limit medical/dental coverage for specific procedures to a certain fixed amount.
3. Copay—requiring that employees pay a fixed or percentage amount for coverage.
4. Administrative cost containment—controlling costs through policies such as seeking competitive bids for program delivery.

So prevalent is the cost issue today that the terminology of cost containment is becoming a part of every employee's vocabulary. Exhibit 12.12 provides definitions of some common cost containment terms.

Probably the biggest cost containment strategy in recent years is the movement to outsourcing. By hiring vendors to administer their benefits programs, many companies, such as GTE and Tenneco, claim greater centralization, consistency, and control of costs and benefits.[59] Other companies, like Digital Equipment Corporation, outsource so that they may focus on their core businesses, "leaving benefits to the benefits experts."[60]

EXHIBIT 12.12 Basic Primer of Cost Containment Terminology

Deductibles: An employee claim for insurance coverage is preceded by the requirement that the first $x dollars be paid by the claimant.

Coinsurance: A proportion of insurance premiums are paid by the employee.

Benefit cutbacks: Corresponding to wage concessions, some employers are negotiating with employees to eliminate employer contributions or reduce them to selected options.

Defined contribution plans: Employers establish the limits of their responsibility for employee benefits in terms of a dollar contribution maximum.

Defined benefit plans: Employers establish the limits of their responsibility for employee benefits in terms of a specific benefit and the options included. As the cost of these options rises in future years, the employer is obligated to provide the benefit as negotiated, despite its increased cost.

Dual coverage: In families where both spouses work there is frequently coverage of specific claims from each employer's benefit package. Employers cut costs by specifying payment limitations under such conditions.

Benefit ceiling: Employers establish a maximum payout for specific claims (e.g., limiting liability for extended hospital stays to $150,000).

---

[59]G. McWilliams, "ACS Finds Profits in Business Outsourcing," *Wall Street Journal,* May 3, 2001, p. B5; E. Scott Peterson, "From Those Who've Been There . . . Outsourcing Leaders Talk about Their Experiences," *Benefits Quarterly,* 6(1) (First Quarter 1997), pp. 6–13.
[60]Ibid.

Your Turn

Lightning Industries

Lightning Industries manufactures lamps for residential homes. The president of the company, Lewis Jacobs, is convinced that he must get concessions from the workers if Lightning is to compete effectively with increasing foreign competition. In particular, Jacobs is displeased with the cost of employee benefits. He doesn't mind conceding a competitive wage increase (maximum 3 percent), but he wants the total compensation package to cost 3 percent less. The current costs are shown in Exhibit 1.

Your assistant has surveyed other companies that are obtaining concessions from employees. You also have data from a consulting firm that indicates employee preferences for different forms of benefits (Exhibit 2). Based on all this information, you have two possible concession packages that you can propose, labeled "Option 1" and "Option 2" (Exhibit 3).

1. Cost out these packages given the data in Exhibits 1 and 2 and the information obtained from various insurance carriers and other information sources (Exhibit 4).
2. Which package should you recommend to Jacobs? Why?
3. Which of the strategies do you think will require less input from employees in terms of their reactions?

EXHIBIT 1   Current Compensation Costs

Average yearly wage	$26,769
Average hourly wage	$13.12
Dollar value of yearly benefits, per employee	$8,923
Total compensation (wages plus benefits)	$35,692
Daily average number of hours paid	8.0

Benefits (by Category)	Dollar Cost/Employee/Year
1. Legally required payments (employer's share only)	$2,141.00
a. Old-age, survivors, disability, and health insurance (FICA) taxes	$1,509.00
b. Unemployment compensation	$292.00
c. Workers' compensation (including estimated cost of self-insured)	$311.00
d. Railroad retirement tax, railroad unemployment and cash sickness insurance, state sickness benefits insurance, etc.	$29.00
2. Pension, insurance, and other agreed-upon payments (employer's share only)	$3,124.00
a. Pension plan premiums and pension payments not covered by insurance-type plan (net)	$1,460.00
b. Life insurance premiums; death benefits; hospital, surgical, medical, and major medical insurance premiums; etc. (net)	$1,427.00
c. Short-term disability	$83.00
d. Salary continuation or long-term disability	$57.00
e. Dental insurance premiums	$51.00
f. Discounts on goods and services purchased from company by employees	$27.00
g. Employee meals furnished by company	$0
h. Miscellaneous payments (compensation payments in excess of legal requirements, separation or termination pay allowances, moving expenses, etc.)	$24.00
3. Paid rest periods, lunch periods, wash-up time, travel time, clothes-change time, get-ready time, etc. (60 minutes)	$727.00
4. Payments for time not worked	$2,769.00
a. Paid vacations and payments in lieu of vacation (16 days average)	$1,558.00
b. Payments for holidays not worked (9 days)	$973.00
c. Paid sick leave (10 days maximum)	$172.00
d. Payments for state or national guard duty; jury, witness, and voting pay allowances; payments for time lost due to death in family or other personal reasons, etc.	$66.00
5. Other items	$157.00
a. Profit-sharing payments	$0
b. Contributions to employee thrift plans	$71.00
c. Christmas or other special bonuses, service awards, suggestion awards, etc.	$0
d. Employee education expenditures (tuition refunds, etc.)	$40.00
e. Special wage payments ordered by courts, payments to union stewards, etc.	$ 46.00
Total	$8,923.00

EXHIBIT 2   Benefit Preferences

Benefit Type or Method of Administering	Importance to Workers	Benefit Type or Method of Administering	Importance to Workers
Pensions	87	Paid rest periods, lunch periods, etc.	55
Hospitalization	86	Dental insurance	51
Life insurance	79	Christmas bonus	31
Paid vacation	82	Profit sharing	21
Holidays	82	Education expenditures	15
Long-term disability	72	Contributions to thrift plans	15
Short-term disability	69	Discount on goods	5
Paid sick leave	70	Fair treatment in administration	100

Note: 0 = unimportant; 100 = extremely important.

EXHIBIT 3
Two Possible Packages for Cutting Benefit Costs

Option 1	
Implement Copay for Benefit	**Amount of Copay**
Pension	$300.00
Hospital, surgical, medical, and major medical premiums	350.00
Dental insurance premiums	75.00

Reduction of Benefit

Eliminate 10-minute paid break (workers leave work 10 minutes earlier)
Eliminate one paid holiday per year
Coordination with legally required benefit; social security coordinated
with Lightning Industries pension plan

Option 2

Improved claims processing:
    Unemployment compensation
    Workers' compensation
    Long-term disability
Require probationary period (one year) before eligible for:
    Discounts on goods
    Employee meal paid by company
    Contributions to employee thrift plans
Deductible ($100 per incident):
    Life insurance, death benefits, hospital, etc.
    Dental insurance

Copay	**Amount of Copay**
Hospital, surgical, medical and major medical premiums	$350.00

EXHIBIT 4

Analysis of Cost Implications for Different Cost-Cutting Strategies: Lightning Industries

Cost-Saving Strategy	Savings as Percent of Benefit-Type Cost
Copay	**Dollar-for-dollar savings equal to amount of Copay**
Deductible ($100 per incident):	
Life insurance premiums, death benefits, hospital, etc.	10%
Dental insurance	15
Require probationary period before eligible (one year):	
Discount on goods and services	10
Employee meals furnished by company	15
Contributions to employee thrift plans	10
Improved claims processing:	
Unemployment compensation	8
Workers' compensation	3
Long-term disability	1
Coordination with legally required benefits:	
Coordinate social security with Lightning pension plan	15

Summary

Given the rapid escalation in the cost of employee benefits over the past 15 years, organizations would do well to evaluate the effectiveness of their benefit adoption, retention, and termination procedures. Specifically, how do organizations go about selecting appropriate employee benefits? Are the decisions based on sound evaluation of employee preferences balanced against organizational goals of legal compliance and competitiveness? Do the benefits chosen serve to attract, retain, and/or motivate employees? Or are organizations paying billions of dollars of indirect compensation without any tangible benefit? This chapter has outlined a benefit determination process that identifies major issues in selecting and evaluating particular benefit choices. The next chapter catalogs the various benefits available and discusses some of the decisions confronting a benefit administrator.

Review Questions

1. Jim Drake, the CEO of Allied Industries, just read an article in the *Wall Street Journal* that said employee benefits cost employers, on average, about 39 percent of payroll. He did the math and figures benefits are costing Allied over $10,000 per employee. He calls you into his office and asks why he shouldn't get rid of all employee benefits, fire his benefit manager and administrator, and with the savings give everyone a $10,000 pay increase. Why might this be a really bad idea? Does it have any merits as an idea?

2. You live in Buffalo, New York, where population declines are the most evident sign of decay in this self-styled "gateway to the East." The average age of your 600-person work force is 43. Turnover is low, and the want-ad page is just that—one page. Not much is happening on the job front. How do these facts influence your decisions about designing an employee benefit program?

3. As HR director at Crangle Fixtures, your bonus this year is based on your ability to cut employee benefit costs. Your boss has said that it's okay to shift some of the costs over to employees (right now they pay nothing for their benefits) but that he doesn't want you to overdo it. In other words, at least one-half of your suggestions should not hurt the employee's pocket book. What alternatives do you want to explore, and why?

4. You are the CEO of a small plumbing supply company in Olean, New York. You want to do right by your employees in the benefits you offer, but you don't know what that means. How might you go about finding out what your employees need and want? How does the fact that the company is small affect the way you gather this information?

5. Describe how a flexible benefit program might increase worker satisfaction with benefits at the same time that costs are being reduced.

Benefit Options

Chapter Outline

At times the number of benefit options and choices can be quite overwhelming. Even trained human resource professionals can err in their evaluation of a benefit package. For example, one study asked both college graduates and human resource professionals to rank 11 different benefits, equated for costs to a company. The HR professionals' role was to estimate the graduates' responses. Surprisingly, at least to the recruiters, the college graduates placed high value on medical and life insurance, company stocks, and pensions. Lesser importance was placed on holidays and scheduling conveniences (e.g., flextime, four-day workweek). The recruiters systematically underestimated the value of most of the top benefits and overestimated the value of the leisure and work-schedule benefits. Just so this never happens to you in your professional career, below is a compilation of employee benefit preferences (5 is high value, 1 low).[1]

[1]Aon survey, "Employees Value Basic Benefits Most," *Best's Review,* 103(4) (2002).

1. Medical Insurance	4.62
2. Paid vacation and holidays	4.48
3. Employer-paid pension	4.43
4. Retirement savings plan	4.36
5. Prescription-drug card	4.34
6. Dental insurance	4.30
7. Ability to choose benefits that best meet your needs	4.28
8. Sick leave and short-term disability	4.24
9. Long-term disability insurance	4.20
10. Preventive/wellness coverage	4.11

Our goal in this chapter is to give you a clearer appreciation of employee benefits. We begin with a widely accepted categorization of employee benefits in Exhibit 13.1. The U.S. Chamber of Commerce issues an annual report based on a nationwide survey of employee benefits.[2] This report identifies seven categories of benefits in a breakdown that is highly familiar to benefit plan administrators. These seven categories will be used to organize this chapter and illustrate important principles affecting strategic and administrative concerns for each benefit type.

Exhibit 13.2 provides data from both the private sector (both small and large firms) and the public sector on employee participation in selected benefit programs.[3] Notice the high rate of participation for such common benefits as life and health insurance and pension plans in all except small firms. Only for legally required benefits (social security, workers' compensation, and unemployment insurance) is the participation rate higher.

Exhibit 13.2 shows that a greater percentage of employees are covered in the private sector. The one major exception is pension coverage: Typically, state and local government employees are more likely to have some form of retirement coverage than their private sector counterparts.

LEGALLY REQUIRED BENEFITS

Virtually every employee benefit is somehow affected by statutory or common law (many of the limitations are imposed by tax laws). In this section the primary focus is on benefits that are required by statutory law: workers' compensation, social security, and unemployment compensation.

---

[2]U.S. Chamber of Commerce, *Employee Benefits,* 2003 edition (Washington, DC: Chamber of Commerce, 2003).

[3]U.S. Department of Labor, "Employee Benefits Survey", data.bls.gov/labjava/outside.jsp?survey=eb, retrieved September 23, 2002.

EXHIBIT 13.1   **Categorization of Employee Benefits**

Type of Benefit

1. Legally required payments (employers' share only)
    a. Old-age, survivors, disability, and health insurance (employer FICA taxes) and railroad retirement tax
    b. Unemployment compensation
    c. Workers' compensation (including estimated cost of self-insured)
    d. State sickness benefit insurance
2. Retirement and savings plan payments (employers' share only)
    a. Defined benefit pension plan contributions (401(k) type)
    b. Defined contribution plan payments
    c. Profit sharing
    d. Stock bonus and employee stock ownership plans (ESOPs)
    e. Pension plan premiums (net) under insurance and annuity contracts (insured and trusted)
    f. Administrative and other costs
3. Life insurance and death benefits (employers' share only)
4. Medical and medical-related benefit payments (employers' share only)
    a. Hospital, surgical, medical, and major medical insurance premiums (net)
    b. Retiree hospital, surgical, medical, and major medical insurance premiums (net)
    c. Short-term disability, sickness, or accident insurance (company plan or insured plan)
    d. Long-term disability or wage continuation (insured, self-administered, or trust)
    e. Dental insurance premiums
    f. Other (vision care, physical and mental fitness benefits for former employees)
5. Paid rest periods, coffee breaks, lunch periods, wash-up time, travel time, clothes-change time, get-ready time, etc.
6. Payments for time not worked
    a. Payments for or in lieu of vacations
    b. Payments for or in lieu of holidays
    c. Sick leave pay
    d. Parental leave (maternity and paternity leave payments)
    e. Other
7. Miscellaneous benefit payments
    a. Discounts on goods and services purchased from company by employees
    b. Employee meals furnished by company
    c. Employee education expenditures
    d. Child care
    e. Other

Workers' Compensation

What costs employers $756 billion a year and is a major cost of doing business? Answer: workers' compensation.[4] Even with the infusion of all this money, the system is still in trouble. For every one dollar insurers take in to cover workplace injuries and illnesses, including medical treatment, wage replacement benefits, and lost productivity, they pay out $1.21 to cover claims.[5] As a form of no-fault insurance (employees are eligible even if

---

[4]National Academy of Social Insurance, "Workers' Compensation: Benefits, Coverage and Costs, 2000 New Estimates," *www.nasi.org/usr_doc/nasi_wkrs_comp_6_26_02.pdf*, retrieved September 24, 2002.

[5]R. Gastel, "Workers' Compensation," *Insurance Information Institute*, July 2002, p. 1.

EXHIBIT 13.2 **Percentage Participation in Selected Benefits**

Benefit Type	Small Firms				Medium and Large Firms			State and Local Government		
	1990	1992	1994	1996	1991	1993	1997	1992	1994	1998
Paid holiday	81%	79%	80%	80%	92%	91%	89%	75%	73%	73%
Paid vacation	86	85	86	86	96	97	95	67	66	67
Paid sick leave	47	53	50	50	67	65	56	95	94	96
Sickness and accident insurance*	23	24	24	29	45	44	55	22	21	20
Long-term disability	14	13	14	22	40	41	43	28	30	34
Health insurance	67	64	62	64	83	82	76	90	87	89
Life insurance	57	54	54	62	94	91	87	89	87	89
Retirement	35	34	35	46	78	78	79	93	96	90
Defined benefit plan	12	12	9	15	59	56	50	87	91	90
Defined contribution plan	28	27	29	38	48	49	57	9	9	14

*"Sickness and accident insurance" was changed after 1994 to include paid sick leave and short-term disability. Paid sick leave now includes only plans that have an unlimited or specified number of days per year. Short-term disability now includes all insured, self-insured and state-mandated plans, which provide benefits for each disability, including unfounded plans that were reported as sick leave in 1994.

Source: U.S. Department of Labor, Bureau of Labor Statistics, data.bls.gov/labjava/outside.jsp?survey=eb, November 2002.

their actions caused the accident), workers' compensation covers injuries and diseases that arise out of, and while in the course of, employment. Benefits are given for:[6]

1. Permanent total disability and temporary total disability
2. Permanent partial disability—loss of use of a body member
3. Survivor benefits for fatal injuries
4. Medical expenses
5. Rehabilitation

Of these five categories, temporary total disability is both the most frequent type of claim and one of the two most costly (along with permanent partial disability).[7] The amount of compensation is based on fixed schedules of minimum and maximum payments. Disability payments are often tied to the employee's earnings, modified by such economic factors as the number of dependents. Exhibit 13.3 shows the average benefit payment for different injury categories in a randomly chosen state.

Some states provide "second-injury funds." These funds relieve an employer's liability when a preemployment injury combines with a work-related injury to produce a disability greater than that caused by the latter alone. For example, if a person with a known heart condition is hired and then breaks an arm in a fall triggered by a heart attack, medical

[6]Ronald G. Ehrenberg, "Workers' Compensation, Wages, and the Risk of Injury," in *New Perspectives in Workers' Compensation,* ed. John Burton (Ithaca, NY: ILR Press, 1988).
[7]Ibid.

EXHIBIT 13.3   Benefits by Type of Accident: New Hampshire

Type of Accident	Maximum Benefit Payment
Loss of arm at shoulder	$193,830
Loss of hand	174,447
Loss of leg at hip	129,220
Loss of foot	90,454
Loss of eye	77,532
Loss of ear	27,690

Source: *www.worker scompensation.com/new_hampshire/quickfacts/glance.htm,* retrieved May 29, 2003.

EXHIBIT 13.4   Commonalities in State Workers' Compensation Laws

Issue	Most Common State Provision
Type of law	Compulsory (in 47 states)
	Elective (in 3 states)
Self insurance	Self-insurance permitted (in 48 states)
Coverage	All industrial employment
	Farm labor, domestic servants, and casual employees usually exempted.
	Compulsory for all or most public sector employees (in 47 states)
Occupational	Coverage for all diseases arising out of and in the course of employment.
diseases	No compensation for "ordinary diseases of life"

Source: *www.ncci.com/media/downloads/PPDsurvey2.xls,* retrieved May 29, 2003.

treatments for the heart condition would not be paid from workers' compensation insurance; treatment for the broken arm would be compensated.

Workers' compensation is covered by state, not federal, laws. In the past decade over 30 states passed significant workers' compensation reforms, most of which target safety concerns.[8] As Exhibit 13.4 shows, in general the states have fairly similar coverage, with differences occurring primarily in benefit levels and costs. Some employers argue that they are being forced to uproot established businesses in states with high costs to relocate in lower cost states.[9]

Cybercomp
This website from the Department of Labor provides extensive information about legally required benefits and specific requirements for compliance:
www.dol.gov/dol/regs/main.htm.

Why these rapid cost increases? At least three factors seem to play a role.[10] First, medical costs continue to skyrocket. Over 30 percent of workers' compensation costs can be traced to medical expenses, and these costs continue to grow dramatically: Medical costs jumped 11.5 percent in 2001, following five years of increases averaging 7.5 percent.[11] Second,

[8]Gastel, "Workers' Compensation."
[9]R. Rodriguez, "The High Price of Doing Business," *Fresno Bee,* February 2, 2003, p. C1.
[10]Ronald G. Ehrenberg, "Workers' Compensation, Wages, and the Risk of Injury."
[11]A. Geddes Lippold, "The Soaring Costs of Workers' Comp," *Workforce,* 82(2) (2003), pp. 42–48.

some employees use workers' compensation as a surrogate for more stringent unemploy-ment insurance programs. Rising numbers of employees, fearing recession and possible layoffs, fake new illnesses or stall reporting back after existing illnesses. Third, the cost of replacing worker wages has risen steadily, at a rate averaging 6.6 percent annually.

Social Security

When social security was introduced in 1937, only about 60 percent of all workers were eligible.[12] Today, nearly every American worker is covered.[13] Whether a worker retires, becomes disabled, or dies, social security benefits are paid to replace part of the lost fam-ily earnings. Indeed, ever since its passage, the Social Security Act has been designed and amended to provide a foundation of basic security for American workers and their fami-lies. Exhibit 13.5, outlines the initial provisions of the law and its subsequent broadening over the years.[14]

The money to pay these benefits comes from the social security contributions made by employees, their employers, and self-employed people during working years. As contri-butions are paid in each year, they are immediately used to pay for the benefits to current beneficiaries. Herein lies a major problem with social security. While the number of re-tired workers continues to rise (because of earlier retirement and longer life spans), no corresponding increase in the number of contributors to social security has offset the costs. Combine the increase in beneficiaries with other cost stimulants (e.g., liberal cost-of-living adjustments), and the outcome is not surprising. To maintain solvency, there has been a dramatic increase in both the maximum earnings base and the rate at which that base is taxed. Exhibit 13.6 illustrates the trends in tax rate, maximum earnings base, and maximum tax for social security.

Several points immediately jump out from this exhibit. First, with the rapid rise in tax-able earnings, you should get used to paying some amount of social security tax on every dollar you earn. This wasn't always true. Notice that in 1980 the maximum taxable earn-ings were $25,900. Every dollar earned over that amount was free of social security tax. Now the maximum is over $85,000, and for one part of social security (Medicare) there is no earnings maximum.[15] If Tiger Woods makes 30 million next year, he will pay 7.65 percent social security tax on the first $87,000 and 1.45 percent (the health/Medicare portion) on all the rest of his income. For the super rich (even with royalties, textbook au-thors need not apply), this elimination of the cap is costly.

Second, remember that for every dollar deducted as an employees' share of social se-curity, there is a matching amount paid by employers. For an employee with income in the $70,000 or more range, this means an employer contribution of about $6,000. Be-cause social security is retirement income to employees, employers should decrease pri-vate pension payouts by a corresponding amount.

[12]Employee Benefit Research Institute, *Fundamentals of Employee Benefit Programs* (Washington, DC: EBRI, 1990).

[13]*www.ssa.gov/policy/docs/statcomps/supplement/2002/highlights.pdf,* visited May 15, 2003.

[14]Ibid; William J. Cohen, "The Evolution and Growth of Social Security," in *Federal Policies and Worker Status since the Thirties,* ed. J. P. Goldberg, E. Ahern, W. Haber, and R. A. Oswald (Madison, WI: Industrial Relations Research Association, 1976), p. 62.

[15]*www.ssa.gov/policy/docs/statcomps/supplement/2002/oasdi.pdf,* visited May 15, 2003.

EXHIBIT 13.5   Social Security through the Years

Original Provisions of the 1935 Law
Federal old-age benefit program Public assistance for the aged, blind, and dependent children who would not otherwise qualify for social security Unemployment compensation Federally funded state program for maternity care, crippled children's services, child welfare services Public health services Vocational rehabilitation services

Changes in the Law since 1935	
1939	Survivor's insurance was added to provide monthly life insurance payments to the widow and dependent children of deceased workers.
1950–1954	Old-age and survivor's insurance was broadened.
1956	Disability insurance benefits were provided to workers and dependents of such employees.
1965	Medical insurance protection was provided for the aged, and later (1973) for the disabled under age 65 (Medicare).
1972	Cost-of-living escalator was tied to the consumer price index—guaranteed higher future benefits for all beneficiaries.
1974	Existing state programs of financial assistance to the aged, blind, and disabled were replaced by SSI (supplemental security income) administered by the Social Security Administration.
1983	Effective 1984, all new civilian federal employees were covered. All federal employees covered for purpose of Medicare.
1985	Social Security Administration (SSA) became an independent agency administered by a commissioner and a bipartisan advisory board.
1994	Amendments were enacted imposing severe restrictions on benefits paid to drug abusers and alcoholics (together with treatment requirements and a 36-month cap on the payment of benefits).
1996	Contract with America Advancement Act of 1996 (CWAAA) was enacted, eliminating substance abuse as a disabling impairment. Substance abuse may no longer be the basis for a finding of disability.
2000	Depression-era limits on amount of money that workers age 65 to 69 may earn without having their social security benefits reduced were eliminated—retroactive to January 1, 2000. The rules governing individuals who take early retirement at age 62 and the status of workers age 70 and over were not changed by the new law.

EXHIBIT 13.6 **What Social Security Does to Your Paycheck**

	Employers and Employees Each Pay Amounts Shown						
	OASDI			Health		Total Contribution	
Year	Maximum Taxable Earnings	% OASI (Old Age Survivors)	% DI (Disability)	Maximum Taxable Earnings	% health	%	$
1980	$25,900	4.52	0.56	$25,900	1.05	6.13	1,587.67
1990	51,300	5.6	0.6	51,300	1.45	7.65	3,924.45
1995	61,200	5.26	0.94	No max	1.45	7.65	No max because of uncapped health care
1997–1999	Increases with market wage movement	5.35	0.85	No max	1.45	7.65	No max, uncapped health
2000+	Increases with market wage movement— $87,000 in 2003	5.3	0.9	No max	1.45	7.65	No max, uncapped health

Source: *www.ssa.gov/,* retrieved May 29, 2003.

Current funding levels produced a massive surplus throughout the 1990s. In 2001, the social security surplus was $160 billion.[16] Baby boomers are just now reaching their peak earnings potential, and their social security payments subsidize a much smaller generation born during the 1930s. There are now almost 3.5 workers paying into the system for each person collecting benefits. Within the next 40 years this ratio will drop to about 2 to 1.[17] Many experts believe this statistic foreshadows the collapse of social security as we know it. In anticipation of this possibility, Congress currently is debating different reform plans, falling into four categories: (1) increasing payroll taxes, (2) decreasing benefits, (3) using general revenues, or (4) having social security go straight to your own individual account and be earmarked for your own personal retirement (rather than going into a pooled fund used for subsidizing all retirees in general).[18]

[16]R. Barro, "Why the U.S. Economy Will Rise Again," *Business Week,* October 1, 2001, p. 20.
[17]Thomas H. Paine, "Alternative Ways to Fix Social Security," *Benefits Quarterly,* Third Quarter 1997, pp. 14–18.
[18]*www.ssa.gov/qa.htm,* visited May 15, 2003.

Benefits under Social Security

The majority of benefits under social security fall into four categories: (1) old age or disability benefits, (2) benefits for dependents of retired or disabled workers, (3) benefits for surviving family members of a deceased worker, and (4) lump-sum death payments. To qualify for these benefits, a worker must work in covered employment and earn a specified amount of money (about $780 today) for each quarter-year of coverage.[19] Forty quarters of coverage will insure any worker for life. The amount received under the four benefit categories noted above varies, but in general it is tied to the amount contributed during eligibility quarters. The average monthly retirement benefit rose from $571 in 1990 to $897 in early 2003.[20]

Unemployment Insurance

The earliest union efforts to cushion the effects of unemployment for their members (c. 1830s) were part of benevolent programs of self-help. Working members made contributions to their unemployed brethren.[21] With passage of the unemployment insurance law (as part of the Social Security Act of 1935), this floor of security for unemployed workers became less dependent upon the philanthropy of co-workers. Since unemployment insurance laws vary by state, this review will cover some of the major characteristics of different state programs.

Financing

In the majority of states, unemployment compensation paid out to eligible workers is financed exclusively by employers that pay federal and state unemployment insurance tax. The tax amounts to 6.2 percent of the first $7,000 earned by each worker.[22] All states allow for experience rating—charging lower percentages to employers that have terminated fewer employees. The tax rate may fall to almost 0 percent in some states for employers that have had no recent experience (hence the term "experience rating") with downsizing and may rise to 10 percent for organizations with large numbers of layoffs.

Coverage

All workers except a few agricultural and domestic workers are currently covered by unemployment insurance (UI) laws. These covered workers (97 percent of the work force), though, must still meet eligibility requirements to receive benefits:

1. You must meet the State requirements for wages earned or time worked during an established (one year) period of time referred to as a "base period." [In most states, this is usually the first four out of the last five completed calendar quarters prior to the time that your claim is filed.]
2. You must be determined to be unemployed through no fault of your own [determined under state law], and meet other eligibility requirements of State law.[23]

---

[19]Social Security Administration, "Understanding the Benefits," *www.ssa.gov/pubs/10024.html*, visited October 30, 2000.

[20]*www.ssa.gov/policy/docs/statcomps/oasdi_monthly/table2.pdf*, visited May 15, 2003.

[21]Raymond Munts, "Policy Development in Unemployment Insurance," in *Federal Policies and Worker Status since the Thirties*, ed. J. P. Goldberg, E. Ahern, W. Haber, and R. A. Oswald (Madison, WI: Industrial Relations Research Association, 1976).

[22]U.S. Department of Labor, *workforcesecurity.doleta.gov/uitaxtopic.asp*, visited May 15, 2003.

[23]*workforcesecurity.doleta.gov/unemploy/uifactsheet.asp*, visited May 15, 2003.

Duration

Until 1958 the maximum number of weeks any claimant could collect UI was 26 weeks. However, the 1958 and 1960–61 recessions yielded large numbers of claimants who exhausted their benefits, leading many states temporarily to revise upward the maximum benefit duration. The most recent modification of the benefit duration involves a complex formula that ensures extended benefits in times of high unemployment. Extended benefits will be paid when either of two conditions prevails: (1) when the number of insured unemployed in a state reaches 6 percent, or (2) when the unemployment rate is greater than 5 percent and at least 20 percent higher than in the same period of the two preceding calendar years and remains that way for 13 weeks.[24] For example, in 2002 a new add-on law was passed, the Job Creation and Worker Assistance Act of 2002, that will give people an additional 13 to 26 weeks of coverage, depending on the state in which they live.[25]

Weekly Benefit Amount

In general, benefits are based on a percentage of an individual's earnings over a recent 52-week period—up to the state maximum amount.[26] The most recent calculation of the average weekly unemployment insurance benefit was $211.75.[27]

Controlling Unemployment Taxes

Every unemployed worker's unemployment benefits are "charged" against the firm or firms most recently employing that currently unemployed worker. The more money paid out on behalf of a firm, the higher is the unemployment insurance rate for that firm. Efforts to control these costs quite logically should begin with a well-designed human resource planning system. Realistic estimates of human resource needs will reduce the pattern of hasty hiring followed by morale-breaking terminations. Additionally, a benefit administrator should attempt to audit prelayoff behavior (e.g., lateness, gross misconduct, absenteeism, illness, leaves of absence) and compliance with UI requirements after termination (e.g., job refusals can disqualify an unemployed worker). The government can also play an important part in reducing unemployment expenses by decreasing the number of weeks that people are unemployed. Recent research has shown that unemployment duration decreases by three weeks simply by stepping up enforcement of sanctions against fraudulent claims.[28]

Family and Medical Leave Act (FMLA)

The 1993 Family and Medical Leave Act applies to all employers having 50 or more employees and entitles all eligible employees to receive unpaid leave up to 12 weeks per year for specified family or medical reasons. To be eligible, an employee must have

[24]C. Arthur Williams, John S. Turnbull, and Earl F. Cheit, *Economic and Social Security*, 5th ed. (New York: Wiley, 1982).

[25]NOLO, *www.nolo.com/lawcenter/ency/article.cfm/objectID/1D277D46-0996-40C1-993704A9E3057017/catID/3D3D9B4B-C63B-4E74-BA5458D500BBF72A.*

[26]U.S. Department of Labor, *workforcesecurity.doleta.gov/unemploy/uifactsheet.asp,* November. 2002.

[27]"EBRI Facts," *www.ebri.org/facts/0202fact.htm,* February. 2002.

[28]"The Effect of Benefit Sanctions on the Duration of Unemployment," Center for Economic Policy Research Report #469, April 2002.

worked at least 1,250 hours for the employer in the previous year. Common reasons for leave under FMLA include caring for an ill family member or adopting a child. More state legislatures are now moving toward some form of paid family and medical leave for workers. California has signed a bill enacting an employee-paid disability benefit that would provide six weeks of paid leave to care for a sick family member or a new baby.[29]

Consolidated Omnibus Budget Reconciliation Act (COBRA)

In 1985 Congress enacted this law to provide current and former employees and their spouses and dependents with a temporary extension of group health insurance when coverage is lost due to qualifying events (e.g., layoffs). All employers with 20 or more employees must comply with COBRA. An employer may charge individuals up to 102 percent of the premium for coverage (100 percent premium plus 2 percent administration fee), which can extend up to 36 months (standard 18 months), depending on the category of the qualifying event.[30] The rising costs of the health insurance premiums (12.7 percent in 2002) cause major financing problems for the unemployed, with only one in every four workers who get laid off being able to afford the continued health insurance through COBRA. In 2001 Congress approved limited COBRA subsidies for displaced workers, to allow more unemployed to afford health insurance.[31]

Health Insurance Portability and Accountability Act (HIPAA)

The 1996 HIPAA is designed to (1) lessen an employer's ability to deny coverage for a preexisting condition and (2) prohibit discrimination on the basis of health-related status.[32] Perhaps the most significant element of HIPAA began in 2002, when stringent new privacy provisions added considerable compliance problems for both the HR people charged with enforcement and the information technology people delegated the task of building secure health information systems.

RETIREMENT AND SAVINGS PLAN PAYMENTS

Pensions have been around for a long, long time. The first plan was established in 1759 to protect widows and children of Presbyterian ministers. Fret not, today pension plans are widely available, as indicated by Exhibit 13.2. Total pension assets were almost $11 trillion in 2001.[33] Perhaps because of their prevalence, pension plans are a prime target for

---

[29]*Employee Benefit News,* November 2002, *web.lexis-nexis.com/universe/document?_m= f0b98fa6d631a36028b211b198777688&_docnum =2&wchp=dGLbVlb-1S1A1&_md5=cf85df0d5da0a29b169777139041cec0.*

[30]U.S. Department of Labor, *www.dol.gov/pwba/faqs/faq_consumer_cobra.html.*

[31]*Washington Post,* November 5, 2002, *web.lexis-nexis.com/universe/document?_m=1cd5d9c0bd98b992927dfc56fc5162fc&_docnum=5&wchp=dGLbV1 b-1S1A1&_md5=85b6735ae2bbdd907f5c39ffceda6e61.*

[32]E. Parmenter, "Employee Benefit Compliance Checklist," *Compensation and Benefits Review,* 34(3), pp. 29–39.

[33]Employee Benefit Research Institute, "EBRI Research Highlights: Retirement Benefits," Special Report SR-42, June 2003,

cost control. Owens-Corning, for example, decreased the cost of its retirement package by 20 percent. To make up for the decrease, Owens-Corning added a variable sum linked to profitability of the company. In good years the company pays more into pension funds; in bad years the 20 percent savings makes the company that much more competitive.[34]

Employees rank pensions in the top three of all benefits in terms of importance.[35] The importance of employer-provided retirement plans is evidenced by a recent study which showed that employees with employer-provided retirement plans are more likely to have sufficient savings for a comfortable retirement than those who do not have these plans.[36] Two generic types of pension plans are discussed below: defined benefit plans and defined contribution plans. As you read their descriptions, keep in mind that defined benefit plans may be a dying breed. Today 9 out of 10 new plans are defined contribution plans.[37] To understand why this rapid change is occurring, we have to explain the cost-saving distinctions between the two types of plans.

Defined Benefit Plans

In a defined benefit plan an employer agrees to provide a specific level of retirement pension, which is expressed as either a fixed dollar or a percentage-of-earnings amount that may vary (increase) with years of seniority in the company. The firm finances this obligation by following an actuarially determined benefit formula and making current payments that will yield the future pension benefit for a retiring employee.[38]

Defined benefit plans generally follow one of three different formulas. The most common approach (54 percent) is to calculate average earnings over the last 3 to 5 years of service for a prospective retiree and offer a pension that is about one-half this amount (varying from 30 to 80 percent) adjusted for years of seniority. The second formula (14 percent of companies) for a defined benefit plan uses average career earnings rather than earnings from the last few years; other things being equal, this reduces the level of benefit for pensioners. The final formula (28 percent of companies) commits an employer to a fixed dollar amount that is not dependent on any earnings data. This figure generally rises with seniority level.

Defined Contribution Plans

Defined contribution plans require specific contributions by an employer, but the final benefit that will be received by employees is unknown as it depends on the investment success of those charged with administering the pension fund.

There are three popular forms of defined contribution plans. A *401(k) plan,* so named for the section of the Internal Revenue Code describing the requirements, is a savings plan in which employees are allowed to defer income up to a $12,000 maximum (which increases by $1,000 a year from 2003 to 2006, with amounts indexed for inflation thereafter).[39] Employers typically match employee savings at a rate of 50 cents on the dollar.

[34] "Benefits Are Being Picked to Death," *Business Week,* December 4, 1995, p. 42.

[35] Aon survey, "Employees Value Basic Benefits Most," *Best's Review,* 103(4) (2002), pp. 1527–1534

[36] IOMA, "Managing 401(k) Plans," Institute of Management & Administration (IOMA), August 2000.

[37] John Kilgour, "Restructuring Retirement Income Plans," *Compensation and Benefits Review,* November/December, 2000, p. 2940.

[38] Employee Benefit Research Institute, "Fundamentals of Employee Benefit Programs," 1997, pp. 69–73.

[39] "EBRI Facts" *www.ebri.org/facts/1102fact.htm,* November 2002.

The second type of plan is an *employee stock ownership plan (ESOP)*. In a basic ESOP a company makes a tax-deductible contribution of stock shares or cash to a trust. The trust then allocates company stock (or stock bought with cash contributions) to participating employee accounts. The amount allocated is based on employee earnings. When an ESOP is used as a pension vehicle (as opposed to an incentive program), the employees receive cash at retirement based upon the stock value at that time. ESOPs have one major disadvantage, which limits their utility for pension accumulations. Many employees are reluctant to "bet" most of their future retirement income on just one investment source. If the company's stock takes a downturn, the result can be catastrophic for employees approaching retirement age. A classic example of this comes from Enron . . . yes, the same Enron linked to all the ethics problems. Under Enron's 401(k), employees could elect to defer a portion of their salaries. The employees were given nineteen different investment choices, one of which was Enron common stock. Enron matched contributions, up to 6 percent of an employee's compensation. Enron's contributions were made in Enron stock and had to be held until the employee was at least age 50. This feature resulted in 60 percent of the total plan value being in Enron stock in 2001. Guess what? When Enron's shares went through the floor in 2001–02, thousands of employees saw their retirement nest eggs destroyed. Recently, critics have argued that ERISA (see below) should limit the amount of 401(k) money that can be invested in a company's stocks.[40]

Finally, *profit sharing* can be considered a defined contribution pension plan if the distribution of profits is delayed until retirement. Chapter 10 explains the basics of profit sharing.

The advantages and disadvantages of the two generic categories of pensions (defined benefit and defined contribution) are outlined in Exhibit 13.7. Possibly the most important of the factors noted in Exhibit 13.7 is the differential risk borne by employers on the cost dimension. Defined contribution plans have known costs from year 1. The employer agrees to a specific level of payment that changes only through negotiation or some voluntary action. This allows for quite realistic cost projections. In contrast, defined benefit plans commit the employer to a specific level of benefit. Errors in actuarial projections can add considerably to costs over the years and make the budgeting process much more prone to error. Also, declines in the stock market have led to huge gaps in funding for companies that use stock to meet pension commitments. Perhaps for both these reasons,

EXHIBIT 13.7
Relative Advantages of Different Pension Alternatives

Defined Benefit Plan	Defined Contribution Plan
1. Provides an explicit benefit which is easily communicated.	Unknown benefit level is difficult to communicate.
2. Company absorbs risk associated with changes in inflation and interest rates which affect cost.	Employees assume these risks.
3. More favorable to long-service employees.	More favorable to short-term employees.
4. Employer costs unknown.	Employer costs known up front.

[40]"Poor Market Conditions Contribute to Decline in Retirement Plan assets," *Pension Benefits,* (January 2003), 12(1) p. 12.

defined benefit plans have been much less popular than defined contribution plans for new adoptions over the past 15 years.[41]

Not surprisingly, both of these deferred compensation plans are subject to stringent tax laws. For deferred compensation to be exempt from current taxation, specific requirements must be met. To qualify (hence it is labeled a "qualified" deferred compensation plan), an employer cannot freely choose who will participate in the plan. This requirement eliminated the common practice of building tax-friendly, extravagant pension packages for executives and other highly compensated employees. The major advantage of a qualified plan is that the employer receives an income tax deduction for contributions made to the plan even though employees may not yet have received any benefits. The disadvantage arises in recruitment of high-talent executives. A plan will not qualify for tax exemptions if an employer pays high levels of deferred compensation to entice executives to the firm unless proportionate contributions also are made to lower-level employees.

A hybrid of defined benefit and defined contribution plans has emerged in recent years. *Cash balance plans* are defined benefit plans that look like a defined contribution plan. Employees have a hypothetical account (like a 401[k]) into which is deposited what is typically a percentage of annual compensation. The dollar amount grows both from contributions by the employer and from some predetermined interest rate (e.g., often set equal to the rate given on 30-year treasury certificates.) For the past three years conversions to cash balance plans have been on hold until the Internal Revenue Service is convinced conversions don't adversely impact older workers.[42]

Individual Retirement Accounts (IRAs)

An IRA is a tax-favored retirement savings plan that individuals can establish themselves. That's right, unlike the other pension options, IRAs don't require an employer to set them up. Even people not in the work-force can establish an IRA. Currently, IRAs are used mostly to store wealth accumulated in other retirement vehicles, rather than as a way to build new wealth.[43]

Employee Retirement Income Security Act (ERISA)

The early 1970s were a public relations and economic disaster for private pension plans. Many people who thought they were covered were the victims of complicated rules, insufficient funding, irresponsible financial management, and employer bankruptcies. Some pension funds, including both employer-managed and union-managed funds, were mismanaged; other pension plans required long vesting periods. The result was a pension system that left far too many lifelong workers poverty stricken. Enter the Employee Retirement Income Security Act in 1974 as a response to these problems.

---

[41]"DC Plan Investing," *web.lexis-nexis.com/universe/document?_ma6476adeeb047de912030155ffac 2b28&_docnum=2&wchp=dGLbVtb-1S1A1&_md5=ba5118dab6537dc2e2f3c8e09736e825, June 2002*.

[42]S. Bernstein, "Cash Balance Plans: Cloud of Uncertainty Continues," *Compensation and Benefits Review,* May–June 2003, pp. 51–61.

[43]Employee Benefit Research Institute, "EBRI Research Highlights: Retirement Benefit," Special Report SR-42, June 2003.

ERISA does not require that employers offer a pension plan. But if a company decides to have one, it is rigidly controlled by ERISA provisions.[44] These provisions were designed to achieve two goals: (1) to protect the interest of 99 million active participants who are covered by 730,000 plans,[45] and (2) to stimulate the growth of such plans.

The actual success of ERISA in achieving these goals has been mixed at best. In the first two full years of operation (1975 and 1976) more than 13,000 pension plans were terminated. A major factor in these terminations, along with the recession, was ERISA. Employers complained about the excessive costs and paperwork of living under ERISA. Some disgruntled employers even claimed ERISA was an acronym for "Every Ridiculous Idea Since Adam." To examine the merits of these claims, let us take a closer look at the major requirements of ERISA.

General Requirements

ERISA requires that employees be eligible for pension plans beginning at age 21. Employers may require six months of service as a precondition for participation. The service requirement may be extended to three years if the pension plan offers full and immediate vesting.

Vesting and Portability

These two concepts are sometimes confused but have very different meanings in practice. *Vesting* refers to the length of time an employee must work for an employer before he or she is entitled to employer payments made into the pension plan. The vesting concept has two components. First, any contributions made by the employee to a pension fund are immediately and irrevocably vested. The vesting right becomes questionable only with respect to the employer's contributions. The Economic Growth and Tax Relief Reconciliation Act of 2001 states that the employer's contribution must vest at least as quickly as one of the following two formulas: (1) full vesting after three years (down from five years previously) or (2) 20 percent after two years (down from three years) and 20 percent each year thereafter, resulting in full vesting after six years (down from seven years). Other changes resulting from the Economic Growth and Tax Relief Reconciliation Act of 2001 include increased contributions allowed for employees and increased tax deduction limits.[46]

The vesting schedule an employer uses is often a function of the demographic makeup of the work force. An employer who experiences high turnover may wish to use the three-year service schedule. By so doing, any employee with less than three years' service at time of termination receives no vested benefits. Or the employer may use the second schedule in the hopes that earlier benefit accrual will reduce undesired turnover. The strategy adopted is, therefore, dependent on organizational goals and work-force characteristics.

---

[44]In 2001 the Economic Growth and Tax Relief Reconciliation Act of 2001 was passed. This act replaced some of the aspects of the original ERISA and came into effect for plans starting after December. 31, 2001.

[45]"PR Newswire," *web.lexis-nexis.com/universe/document?_m=15ac40870d11b1f647ab6604b388c 5b4&_docnum=1&wchp=dGLbVtb-1S1A1&_md5=b0cae533bccb033d21997ac9779 fbe56, September 2002.*

[46]*New York Law Journal,* June 2001, *web.lexis-nexis.com/universe/document?_ m=59941dd011dab 32da821e1837d7ae3b0&_docnum=4&wchp=dGLbVtb-1S1A1&_ md5=ef6c695b129b10 bad644acb8cb4d7b14.*

Portability of pension benefits becomes an issue for employees moving to new organizations. Should pension assets accompany the transferring employee in some fashion?[47] ERISA does not require mandatory portability of private pensions. On a voluntary basis, though, the employer may agree to let an employee's pension benefits transfer to the new employer. For an employer to permit portability, of course, the pension rights must be vested.

Pension Benefit Guaranty Corporation

Despite the wealth of constraints imposed by ERISA, the potential still exists for an organization to go bankrupt or in some way fail to meet its vested pension obligations. To protect individuals confronted by this problem, employers are required to pay insurance premiums to the Pension Benefit Guaranty Corporation (PBGC) established by ERISA. In turn, the PBGC guarantees payment of vested benefits to employees formerly covered by terminated pension plans. Until 2002, the PBGC had a $7.7 billion surplus. Bankruptcies of LTV, National Steel, and Bethlehem, among others, turned this surplus into a $3.6 billion deficit in recent periods.

How Much Retirement Income to Provide

The level of pension a company chooses to offer depends on the answer to five questions. First, what level of retirement compensation would a company like to set as a target, expressed in relation to pre-retirement earnings? Second, should social security payments be factored in when considering the level of income an employee should have during retirement? One integration approach reduces normal benefits by a percentage (usually 50 percent) of social security benefits.[48] Another feature employs a more liberal benefit formula on earnings that exceed the maximum income taxed by social security. Regardless of the formula used, about one-half of U.S. companies do not employ the cost-cutting strategy. Once a company has targeted the level of income it wants to provide employees in retirement, it makes sense to design a system that integrates private pension and social security to achieve that goal. Any other strategy is not cost-effective.

Third, should other postretirement income sources (e.g., savings plans that are partially funded by employer contributions) be integrated with the pension payment? Fourth, a company must decide how to factor seniority into the payout formula. The larger the role played by seniority, the more important pensions will be in retaining employees. Most companies believe that the maximum pension payout for a particular level of earnings should be achieved only by employees who have spent an entire career with the company (e.g., 30 to 35 years). As Exhibit 13.8 vividly illustrates, job hoppers are hurt financially by this type of strategy. In our example, a very plausible scenario, job hopping cuts final pension amounts in half.

Finally, companies must decide what they can afford. In the past year the press has printed dozens of stories about companies having a hard time funding their pension plans. Because many of these plans are financed with company stock, and because stock prices have been weak through the beginning of this decade, companies are in trouble. Textron

---

[47]Stuart Dorsey, "Pension Portability and Labor Market Efficiency: A Survey of the Literature," *Industrial and Labor Relations Review,* January 1, 1995.

[48]Burton T. Beam and John J. McFadden, Employee Benefit 5. (Chicago, IL: Dearborn Financial Publishing, 1992).

EXHIBIT 13.8 The High Cost of Job Hopping*

Career History	Years in Company	Percent of Salary for Pension		Salary at Company (Final)	Annual Pension
Sam					
Job 1	10	10%	×	$35,817	= $ 3,582
Job 2	10	10%	×	$64,143	= 6,414
Job 3	10	10%	×	$114,870	= 11,487
Job 4	10	10%	×	$205,714	= 20,571
Total pension					$42,054
Ann					
Job 1	40		×	$205,714	= $82,286
Total pension					$82,286

*Assumptions: (1) Starting Salary of $20,000 with 6 percent annual inflation rate. (2) Both employees receive annual increases equal to inflation rate. (3) Pensions based on 1 percentage point (of salary) for each year of service multiplied by final salary at time of exit from company.

Source: Federal Reserve Bank of Boston.

recently suspended its matching contribution on 401(k) plans, down from a 50-cent match on each dollar up to 10 percent of salary. Similar drops in the size of matching contributions were reported by Goodrich, Charles Schwab, and Prudential Securities.[49]

LIFE INSURANCE

One of the most common employee benefits offered by organizations (about 87 percent of medium to large private sector firms) is some form of life insurance.[50] Typical coverage would be a group term insurance policy with a face value of one to two times the employee's annual salary.[51] Most plan premiums are paid completely by the employer (79 percent of employers).[52] Slightly over 30 percent include retiree coverage.[53] About two-thirds of all policies include accidental death and dismemberment clauses.[54] To discourage turnover, almost all companies make this benefit forfeitable at the time of departure from the company.

[49]C. Dugas, "Companies Cut Back on Retirement Plan Benefits," *USA Today*, May 14, 2003, p. B1.

[50]U.S. Department of Labor, Bureau of Labor Statistics, *data.bls.gov/labjava/outside.jsp?survey=eb*, November 2002.

[51]U.S. Department of Labor, Bureau of Labor Statistics, *Employee Benefits in Medium and Large Private Establishments, 1997* (Washington, DC: U.S. Government Printing Office, 1999).

[52]Ibid.

[53]U.S. Department of Labor, Bureau of Labor Statistics, *data.bls.gov/servlet/SurveyOutputServlet?jrunsessionid=1038089771307188261*, November 2002.

[54]U.S. Department of Labor, Bureau of Labor Statistics, *data.bls.gov/servlet/SurveyOutputServlet?jrunsessionid=1038090092762172089*, November 2002.

Life insurance is one of the benefits heavily affected by movement to a flexible benefit program. Flexibility is introduced by providing a core of basic life coverage (e.g., $25,000). The option then exists to choose greater coverage (usually in increments of $10,000 to $25,000) as part of the optional package.

MEDICAL AND MEDICALLY RELATED PAYMENTS

General Health Care

Health care costs represented 5.9 percent of the gross national product in 1965 and 10.5 percent in 1983; they are expected to reach 18 percent by 2012.[55] One out of every seven dollars spent by Americans today is spent on health care.[56] In 2001 employers spent just under $400 billion on health benefits, constituting 43 percent of the total benefit spending (compared to 14 percent in 1960).[57] More costly technology, the increased number of elderly people, and a system that does not encourage cost savings have all contributed to the rapidly rising costs of medical insurance. In the past 10 years, though, employers have begun to take steps designed to curb these costs. After a discussion of the types of health care systems, these cost-cutting strategies will be discussed. Exhibit 13.9 provides a brief overview of the four most common health care options.

An employer's share of health care costs is contributed into one of six health care systems: (1) a community-based system, such as Blue Cross, (2) a commercial insurance plan, (3) self-insurance, (4) a health maintenance organization (HMO), (5) a preferred-provider organization (PPO), and (6) a point-of-service plan (POS).

Of these six, plans 1 through 3 (labeled "Traditional Coverage in Exhibit 13.9) operate in a similar fashion. Two major distinctions exist, however. The first distinction is in the manner payments are made. With Blue Cross the employer-paid premiums guarantee employees a direct service, including room, board, and necessary health services covered by the plan. Coverage under a commercial insurance plan guarantees fixed payment to the insured for hospital service, and the insured in turn reimburses the hospital. A self-insurance plan implies that the employer provides coverage out of its own assets, assuming the risks itself within state legal guidelines. To protect against catastrophic loss, the most common strategy for self-insurers is to have stop-loss coverage, with an insurance policy covering costs in excess of some predetermined level (e.g., $50,000). Exhibit 13.10 shows typical costs for three of the four generic types of plans.

The second distinction is in the way costs of medical benefits are determined. Blue Cross uses the concept of *community rating*. In effect, insurance rates are based on the medical experience of the entire community. Higher use of medical facilities and services

[55]K. Spors, "Health Spending Is Likely to Slow in Next Decade," *Wall Street Journal*, February 7, 2003, p. A2; U.S. Department of Health and Human Services, "Health Care Spending Growth Rates Stay Low in 1998—Private Spending Outpaces Public: Final Accounting of 1998," *www.hhs.gov/news/press/2000pres/20000110.html*, January 10, 2000, visited October 19, 2000; "Final Accounting of 1998 Health Spending," *Business and Health*, March 1, 2000.

[56]Ibid.

[57]"EBRI Facts" *www.ebri.org/facts/1002fact.pdf*, October 2002.

EXHIBIT 13.9   How Health Insurance Options Differ on Key Dimensions

Issue	Traditional Coverage	Health Maintenance Organization (HMO)	Preferred-Provider Organization (PPO)	Point-of-Service (POS) Plan
Who is eligible?	May live anywhere	May be required to live in HMO-designated service area	May live anywhere	May live anywhere
Who provides health care?	May use doctor and health care facility of patient's choice	Must use doctors and facilities designated by HMO	May use doctors and facilities associated with PPO; if not, may pay additional copayment/ deductible	Must choose HMO or PPO doctor at time service is needed
How much coverage on routine, preventive level?	Does not cover regular checkups and other preventive services; diagnostic tests may be covered in part or full	Covers regular checkups, diagnostic tests, other preventive services with low or no fee per visit	Same as with HMO if doctor and facility are on approved list; copayments and deductibles are assessed at much higher rate for those not on list	Same as HMO/PPO if network physicians used
Hospital care	Covers doctors and hospital bills	Covers doctors and hospital bills if HMO-approved hospital	Covers doctors and hospitals if PPO-approved.	Same as HMO/PPO if network physicians used; deductible otherwise

EXHIBIT 13.10   Average Employer Monthly Costs 2003

	25th Percentile	75th Percentile	% Change
Preferred-provider organization	$5,036	$6,935	9.10
Point-of-service plans	5,029	6,482	9.60
Health maintenance organization	4,480	5,944	10.50
Indemnity plan (traditional)			9.60
Cost by Type of Employee (50th Percentile), per month			
Active employee	$529		
Retiree under age 65	$688		
Retiree age 65 or older	$352		

Source: Percentage change data from S. Smith, "New Trends in Health Care Cost Control," *Compensation and Benefits Review,* January–February 2002, pp. 38–44; rest of data from "Strategies for Dealing with Rising Health-Care Costs," *HR Focus,* November 2002, pp. 6–7.

results in higher premiums. In contrast, insurance companies use a narrower, experience-rating base, preferring to charge each employer separately according to its medical facility usage. Under a self-insurance program, the cost of medical coverage is directly related to usage level, with employer payments going directly to medical care providers rather than to secondary sources in the form of premiums.

As a fourth delivery system, health maintenance organizations provide comprehensive benefits for a fixed fee. Health maintenance organizations offer routine medical services at a specific site. Employees make prepayments in exchange for guaranteed health care services on demand. By law employers of more than 25 employees are required to provide employees the option of joining a federally qualified HMO. If the employee opts for HMO coverage, the employer is required to pay the HMO premium or an amount equal to the premium for previous health coverage, whichever is less.

Preferred provider organizations represent a variation on health care delivery in which there is a direct contractual relationship between and among employers, health care providers, and third-party payers.[58] An employer is able to select certain providers who agree to provide price discounts and submit to strict utilization controls (e.g., strict standards on number of diagnostic tests that can be ordered). In turn, the employer influences employees to use the preferred providers through financial incentives. Doctors benefit by increased patient flow. Employers benefit through increased cost savings. And employees benefit through a wider choice of doctors than might be available under an HMO.

Finally, a point-of-service plan is a hybrid plan combining HMO and PPO benefits. The POS plan permits an individual to choose which plan to seek treatment from at the time that services are needed. POS plans, therefore, provide the economic benefits of the HMO with the freedom of the PPO. The HMO component of the POS plan requires office visits to an assigned primary care physician, with the alternative of receiving treatment through the PPO component. The PPO component does not require the individual to first contact the primary care physician but does require that in-network physicians be used. When POS plan participants receive all of their care from physicians in the network, they are fully covered, as they would be under a traditional HMO. Point-of service plans also allow individuals to see a doctor outside the network, for which payment of an annual deductible ranging between $100 and $5,000 is required.[59]

Health Care: Cost Control Strategies

There are three general strategies available to benefit managers for controlling the rapidly escalating costs of health care.[60] First, organizations can motivate employees to change their demand for health care, through changes in either the design or the administration of

[58]Milt Freudenheim, "H.M.O. Costs Spur Employers to Shift Plans," *New York Times,* September 9, 2000, p. A1; Craig Gunsauley, "Health Plan Almanac—Sellers' Market: Health Plans Struggle for Profitability as Underlying Costs Increase and Patients Demand Greater Access to Providers and Services," *Employee Benefit News,* April 15, 2000.

[59]Catherine Siskos, "Don't Get Sick," *Kiplinger's Personal Finance Magazine* 54 (July 2000) p. 80; Diana Twadell, "Employee Benefits Made Simple," *San Diego Business Journal, June 12, 2000.*

[60]S. Smith, "New Trends in Health Care Cost Control," *Compensation and Benefits Review,* January 2002, pp. 38–44; Regina Herzlinger and Jeffrey Schwartz, "How Companies Tackle Health Care Costs: Part I," *Harvard Business Review* July–August 1985, pp. 69–81.

health insurance policies. Included in this category of control strategies are (1) deductibles (the first x dollars of health care cost are paid by the employee); (2) coinsurance rates (premium payments are shared by the company and employee); (3) maximum benefits (defining a maximum payout schedule for specific health problems); (4) coordination of benefits (ensure no double payment when coverage exists under the employee's plan and a spouse's plan); (5) auditing of hospital charges for accuracy; (6) requiring preauthorization for selected visits to health care facilities; (7) mandatory second opinion whenever surgery is recommended; (8) Using intranet technology to allow employees access to online benefit information, saving some of the cost of benefit specialists.[61] The more questions answered online, the fewer specialists needed. Evidence suggests, though, that employees are tired of having benefit cost increases paid out of their own pockets. Look no further than General Electric, regularly viewed as an employer of choice, where workers are threatening to strike if they are asked to pay a larger copay on health care.[62] A final example in this category is the formation of personal care accounts (PCAs). This is a tool used by employers to salvage some control over health care costs while still providing health security to workers. Under a PCA an employer establishes a high deductible, say $2,000. Normally it would be a great hardship if the first $2,000 of an illness had to be borne by the employee. To lessen this impact, the employer sets up a PCA with $1,000 in it. Now the liability for the employee is only $1,000. Any money not used by the employee in a year can be rolled over to the next year, lessening further the size of the deductible coming out of the employee's pocket. Clearly this type of account creates an incentive to build a PCA "nest egg," benefiting both the company (lower health costs) and the employee.[63]

The second general cost control strategy involves changing the structure of health care delivery systems and participating in business coalitions (for data collection and dissemination). In this category falls the trend toward HMOs, PPOs, and POSs. Even under more traditional delivery systems, there is more negotiation of rates with hospitals and other health care providers. Indeed, one trend involves direct contracting, which allows self-insured companies or employer associations to buy health care services directly from physicians or provider-sponsored networks. Some experts contend that direct contracting can save 30 to 60 percent over fee-for-service systems.[64]

The final cost strategy involves promotion of preventive health programs. No-smoking policies and incentives for quitting smoking are popular inclusions here. But there is also increased interest in healthier food in cafeterias and vending machines, on-site physical fitness facilities, and early screening to identify possible health problems before they become more serious. One review of physical fitness programs found fitness led to better mental health and improved resistance to stress; there also was some evidence of increased productivity, increased commitment, decreased absenteeism, and decreased turnover.[65]

[61]B. Ambrose, "Leveraging Technology via Knowledge Portals," *Compensation and Benefits Review,* May/June 2001, pp. 43–46.

[62]"GE Workers Plan Strike over Benefit Cost-Shifting," *Business Insurance,* January 6, 2003, pp. 23–26.

[63]P. Fronstin, "Can Consumerism Slow the Rate of Health Benefit Cost Increase," EBRI Issue Brief No.246, July 2002.

[64]"Business & Health, March 1997," *Compensation and Benefits Review,* July/August 1997, p. 12.

[65]Nicholas A. DiNubile and Carl Sherman, "Exercise and the Bottom Line," *Physician and Sportsmedicine* 27 (February 1999) p. 37.

> **Cybercomp**
> The Health Insurance Association of America provides research about a wide variety of specific health related issues at its website, *www.hiaa.org/pubs/*.

Short- and Long-Term Disability

A number of benefit options provide some form of protection for disability. For example, workers' compensation covers disabilities that are work-related. Even social security has provisions for disability income to those who qualify. Beyond these two legally required sources, there are two private sources of disability income: employee salary continuation plans and long-term disability plans.

Many companies have some form of salary continuation plan that pays out varying levels of income depending on duration of illness. At one extreme is short-term illness covered by sick leave policy and typically reimbursed at a level equal to 100 percent of salary.[66] After such benefits run out, disability benefits become operative. Short-term disability (STD) pays a percentage of your salary for temporary disability because of sickness or injury (on the job injuries are covered by workers' compensation). STD coverage typically targets payouts of between one-half and two-thirds of your salary for a maximum of 26 weeks. The overall expenditure for disability insurance totaled $9.1 billion in 2001, up 8 percent from 2000. Long-term disability payments accounted for roughly 71 percent of that.[67] The benefit level is typically 50 to 67 percent of salary, and it may be multitiered.[68] For example, a long-term disability plan might kick in when the short-term plan expires, typically after 26 weeks.[69] Long-term disability is usually underwritten by insurance firms and provides 60 to 70 percent of predisability pay for a period varying between two years and life.[70] Estimates indicate that only about 35 percent of all U.S. businesses provide long-term disability insurance.[71] In those businesses, only 34 percent of employees elect the option. Only 29 percent of all household members record some type of disability-income coverage, compared with life insurance penetration of 75 percent and health insurance penetration of 76 percent.[72]

---

[66]Employee Benefit Research Institute, *Fundamentals of Employee Benefit Programs*.

[67]*Bestwire,* March 29, 2002, *web.lexis-nexis.com/universe/document?_m=07f2442e71e 096251c4a6bd2a6c05b7a&_docnum=5&wchp=dGLbVtb-1Sl1A1&_md5=852bd73d67226efa741d38124b1700d8.*

[68]Ibid.

[69]Ibid.

[70]Employee Benefit Research Institute, *Fundamentals of Employee Benefit Programs,* 5th ed. (Washington, DC: EBRI, 1997), p. 297.

[71]Employee Benefit Research Institute, *Fundamentals of Employee Benefit Programs, 1999.*

[72]*Bestwire,* "Conning Study Shows Disability Coverage Still Lags," June 5, 2002, *web.lexis-nexis.com/universe/document?_m=9ed8d46ee9d443865eb5f58785efdd36&_docnum=5&wchp=dGLbVt b-1S1A1&_md5=07566855504c617f82349c4aa9c7eac1.*

Dental Insurance

A rarity 30 years ago, dental insurance is now more prevalent, with about 50 percent of all employers providing some level of coverage.[73] In many respects dental care coverage follows the model originated in health care plans. The dental equivalent of HMOs and PPOs is standard delivery systems. For example, a dental HMO enlists a group of dentists who agree to treat company employees in return for a fixed monthly fee per employee.

Fortunately for all of us, dental insurance costs have not spiraled like other health care costs. At the start of the century, the typical cost for employee dental coverage was $219.[74] Annual cost increases are a modest (compared to medical expense growth) 6 percent. In part these relatively modest costs are due to stringent cost control strategies (e.g., plan maximum payouts are typically $1,000 or less per year) and an excess supply of dentists. As the excess turns into a shortage in the coming years, we may expect dental benefit costs to grow at a faster rate.[75]

Vision Care

Vision care dates back only to the 1976 contract between the United States Auto Workers and the Big Three automakers. Since then, this benefit has spread to other auto-related industries and parts of the public sector. Most plans are noncontributory and usually cover partial costs of eye examination, lenses, and frames.

MISCELLANEOUS BENEFITS

Paid Time Off during Working Hours

Paid rest periods, lunch periods, wash-up time, travel time, clothes-change time, and get-ready time benefits are self-explanatory.

Payment for Time Not Worked

Included within this category are several self-explanatory benefits:

1. Paid vacations and payments in lieu of vacation
2. Payments for holidays not worked
3. Paid sick leave
4. Other (payments for National Guard, Army, or other reserve duty; jury duty and voting pay allowances; payments for time lost due to death in the family or other personal reasons).

---

[73]T. Dolatowski, "Buying Dental Benefits," *Compensation and Benefits Review,* January/February 2002, pp. 45–48.
[74]U.S. Chamber of Commerce, "1999 Employee Benefits Survey," p. 10, p. 2000.
[75]T. Dolatowski, "Buying Dental Benefits."

EXHIBIT 13.11   Employees Receiving Leave Time Benefits

Employee Benefit	All Full-Time Employees	Professional, Technical, and Related Employees	Clerical and Sales Employees	Blue-Collar and Service Employees
Paid Time Off				
Holidays	80%	86%	91%	71%
Vacations	86	90	95	79
Personal leave	14	21	18	8
Funeral leave	51	60	60	42
Jury duty leave	59	74	68	47
Military leave	18	25	23	12
Sick leave(5)	50	66	64	35
Family leave	2	3	3	1

Source: Bureau of Labor Statistics, *www.bls.gov,* visited July 8, 2003.

In 1997, time off was the most frequently provided benefit to full-time employees in medium and large private sector companies.[76] With only few exceptions, full-time employees received paid vacations and 90 percent of employees received paid holidays.[77]

Judging from employee preferences discussed in the last chapter and from analysis of negotiated union contracts, pay for time not worked continues to be a high-demand benefit. Twenty years ago it was relatively rare, for example, to grant time for anything but vacations, holidays, and sick leave. Now many organizations have a policy of ensuring payments for civic responsibilities and obligations. Any outside pay for such civic duties is usually nominal, so companies often supplement this pay, frequently to the level of 100 percent of wages lost. There is also increasing coverage for parental leaves. Maternity and, to a lesser extent, paternity leaves are much more common than they were 25 years ago. Indeed, passage of the Family and Medical Leave Act in 1993 provides up to 12 weeks of unpaid leave (with guaranteed job protection) for the birth or adoption of a child or for the care of a family member with a serious illness. Exhibit 13.11 outlines the percentage of workers who receive different types of leave time.

The following sick policy, taken from Motley Fool's employee manual, shows just how far such policies have come:

Unlike other companies, The Motley Fool doesn't make you wait for six months before accruing vacation or sick time. Heck, if you're infected with some disgusting virus—stay home! We like you, but don't really want to share in your personal anguish. In other words, if you're bleeding out your eyes and coughing up a lung—don't be a hero! Stay home. Out of simple Foolish courtesy, we expect you to call your supervisor and let him or her know

[76]U.S. Department of Labor, Bureau of Labor Statistics, *Employee Benefits in Medium and Large Private Establishments, 1997* (Washington, DC: U.S. Government Printing Office, 1999).
[77]Ibid.

you won't be in. And yes, you will get paid. So, pop quiz: You're feeling like you're going to snap any moment if you don't take some personal time off, you've made a small deposit on an M-16 rifle and are scoping out local clock towers, BUT you've only been a paid Fool for a short time . . . what do you do, what *do* you do?[78]

Interestingly, paid time off is one of the areas where firms are trying to cut employee benefits. In 1980 every medium and large private employer offered at least one paid holiday per year. Now that number is 10 percent lower.

Child Care

Companies are increasingly offering child care services to their employees as a paid benefit. A recent report stated that 68 percent of full-time working women have children under the age of three. According to the report, working is not optional for these women—on average, they contribute 41 percent of their household's earnings. Recent studies show that 85 to 90 percent of employers are offering some form of child care benefits to their employees.[79] Dependant child care spending accounts were offered by 88 percent of the responding employers. Resource and referral services were offered by 42 percent of the employers, 13 percent offered sick or emergency child care programs, and 10 percent offered on-site day care centers.[80]

One fast-growing employee benefit is emergency child care. Companies can lose significant worker-hours as a result of last-minute child care dilemmas, and therefore more and more companies are offering this low-cost benefit. In 1997, 15 percent of large corporations were offering some form of emergency child care—an increase from just 8 percent in 1993.[81] Emergency child care services are generally offered either at child care centers at or near the workplace or through company-paid baby-sitters.[82]

Elder Care

With longer life expectancy than ever before and the aging of the baby-boom generation, one benefit that will become increasingly important is elder care assistance. Just one-third of the companies offering child care assistance to employees also offer elder care assistance.[83] The programs that are available are limited—many merely provide referral services.

---

[78]The Motley Fool, "The Fool Rules! A Global Guide to Foolish Behavior," (1997) p. 14.

[79] Bill Leonard, "Work/Life Benefits Become Key Weapon in 'War for Talent,'" *HR Magazine* 45 (8) (August 1, 2000), p. 27 (citing a Hewitt Associates work/life study).

[80]Bill Leonard, "Work/Life Benefits Become Key Weapon in 'War for Talent,'" *HR Magazine* 45 (8) (August 1, 2000), p. 27.

[81]Susan Adams, "Those Baby-Sitter Blues," *Forbes,* January 11, 1999, p. 70 (citing a 1997 Hewitt Associates study).

[82]M. Wiley and A. Curatola, "Tax Credit: Employer-Provided Child Care Expenses," *Strategic Finance,* January 2002, pp. 16–17.

[83]Jean Bisio, "The Age Boom," *Risk Management* 46 (2) (February 1, 1999), p. 22.

Domestic Partner Benefits

Domestic partner benefits are benefits that are voluntarily offered by employers to an employee's unmarried partner, whether of the same or opposite sex. The major reasons motivating U.S. corporations to provide domestic partner benefits include fairness to all employees regardless of their sexual orientation or marital status and the market competition and diversity that are evident in today's tight labor market. One study found that 18 percent of U.S. employees were employed by corporations that offered health benefits for domestic partners; 11 percent, by corporations that offered these benefits to same-sex couples; and 12 percent, by corporations that offered these benefits to unmarried partners of the opposite sex.[84] In designing these offerings, an employer must first identify what constitutes a domestic partner and whether the plan will be available to same-sex partners, opposite-sex partners, or both.[85]

Legal Insurance

Prior to the 1970s, prepaid legal insurance was practically nonexistent. Even though such coverage was offered only by approximately 7 percent of all employers in 1997, the percentage of companies offering legal-benefit plans is expected to triple during the early years of this century.[86] A majority of plans provide routine legal services (e.g., divorce, real estate matters, wills, traffic violations) but exclude provisions covering felony crimes, largely because of the expense and potential for bad publicity. Keep in mind, though, that most legal insurance premiums are paid by the employee, not the employer. Technically, then, this doesn't qualify as a traditional employee benefit.

BENEFITS FOR CONTINGENT WORKERS

Depending on what definition we use, contingent workers represent between 5 and 35 percent of the work force. Ninety percent of all employers use some contingent workers.[87] Contingent work relationships include working through a temporary help agency, working for a contract company, working on call, and working as an independent contractor. Both to reduce costs and to permit easier expansion and contraction of production/services, contracting offers a viable way to meet rapidly changing environmental conditions.

Contingent workers cost less primarily because the benefits offered are lower than those for regular employees. As Exhibit 13.12 shows, contingent workers regularly receive fewer benefits. This "benefit penalty" is less prominent in larger organizations.[88]

---

[84]"Domestic Partner Benefits," *Facts from EBRI,* Employee Benefit Research Institute, Washington, 2000.

[85]Ibid.

[86]David Schlaifer, *Legal Benefit Plans Help Attract and Retain Employees, HR Focus,* December 1999 pp. S7–S8.

[87]P. Allan, "The Contingent Workforce: Challenges and New Directions," *American Business Review,* June 2002, pp. 103–110.

[88]IOMA, "What Benefits Are Being Offered to Attract and Retain P/T Personnel?" *Managing Benefit Plans,* August 2002, p.3.

EXHIBIT 13.12   Benefits Received: Full-Time versus Contingent Employees

	Small Companies		Medium Companies		Large Companies	
	Full Time	Contingent	Full Time	Contingent	Full Time	Contingent
Vacation	98%	40%	100%	79%	100%	80%
Health Insurance	96	21	100	56	100	67
Holidays	97	48	100	77	100	67
Life Insurance	85	21	100	47	100	58
Pension	89	43	98	91	100	71
Sick leave	70	26	83	53	96	58

Your Turn   Romance Novels Inc.

Romance Novels Inc. (RNI), has a distribution center in Depew, a suburb of Buffalo, New York. Books are shipped there from the publisher, and orders are processed for all of the Northeast from this distribution center. In recent years RNI has been plagued by two problems that are becoming more serious. First, Amazon.com continues to prove a powerful competitor, particularly because it can process and ship a book order in a maximum of two days. RNI still has difficulty hitting this turnaround time but has managed to meet a three-day time line for all books. Second, RNI finds itself, as do many organizations in a tight labor market, increasingly dependent on contingent (temporary) workers. Approximately 25 percent of RNI's workers are "temps," and they are disproportionately placed in the pick-and-pack division, the division that competes with Amazon.com for Internet sales. Recent attitude surveys show that these workers feel no loyalty to the organization, and their performance and turnover rates demonstrate this (Exhibit 1). John Meindl, plant manager, has called you in to help solve these two, perhaps interrelated, problems. Given the information in Exhibits 1 through 4, make suggestions on what to do. Note: Meindl is unwilling, without persuasive arguments, to hire temps full-time. He feels it is important to retain flexibility to terminate quickly should there be an economic downturn.

EXHIBIT 1
Productivity, Quality, and Turnover Data, by Employment Status

	Pieces Shipped (per Hour)	Customer Complaints (per 1,000 Orders)	Annual Turnover(%)
Full-time workers	327	6.32	14
Contingent workers	287	6.68	43

EXHIBIT 2   Base Wage, Variable Compensation, and Benefit Expenditures, by Employment Status of Order Fillers

	Base Wage Average	Variable Compensation (%)	Benefits (% Payroll)	Seniority (Years)
Full-time workers	$8.85	max 4	33	6.5
Contingent workers	8.05	max 4	17	1.8

*All temps are hired as order fillers.

EXHIBIT 3   Performance Appraisal Form for Full-Time and Temporary Employees

	Scale				
	Well Below Average	Below Average	Average	Above Average	Well Above Average
	1	2	3	4	5
Quality of work					
Job knowledge					
Initiative					
Dependability					
Overall performance					

Current Situation

Interviews with supervisory staff and John Meindl disclose the following information:
- Contingent workers feel like second-class citizens.
- Kelly Services, the temp agency used by RNI, charges 10% per hour for every contingent (temporary) worker.
- New York State law and federal law require 17% benefits be paid for all employees (unemployment insurance, workers' compensation insurance, social security). While these benefit payments are made by Kelly Services (and no others!), they are in addition to the 10% per hour charge noted above. So, in effect, RNI bears the cost burden for legally mandated benefits.

EXHIBIT 4
Costs and
Ratings of
Benefits

John Meindl is thinking about extending some combination of the following benefits to contingent workers. Decide which benefits should be extended and whether they should be given to all contingent workers or be based on some factor such as seniority or performance. Meindl is not averse to trying merit-(performance-) based benefits. Indeed, the high-tech firm he came from was a pioneer in that area in the early 1990s.

Benefit	Cost per Hour	Cost for Level of Current Coverage of Full-Time Employees	Temporary Workers Rating of Benefit
Vacation days (5 max)	.03/day of vacation	.18	High
Life Insurance ($10,000)	.01/$1,000 insurance	.07	Low
401(k) contribution (max 5% match)	.01/1% match	.11	Medium
Sick days (5 max)	.03/day sick	.21	High

Your Proposal

Which of these benefits should be extended? You may give any combination of 0 to 5 days of vacation and/or sick days, any amount of insurance in $1,000 increments between 0 and $10,000, and any amount of match on 401(k) plans from 0 to 5%. Keeping in mind equity issues with full-time workers, rating of benefits, and goals of being competitive with Amazon.com, how do you want to allocate these benefits and in what proportions. Justify your answer. If you could change Meindl's mind about how to proceed, what recommendations would you make to him, and why?

Summary

Since the 1940s employee benefits have been the most volatile area in the compensation field. From 1940 to 1980 dramatic changes came in the form of more and better types of employee benefits. The result should not have been unexpected. Employee benefits are now a major, and many believe prohibitive, component of doing business. Look for this century to be dominated by cost-saving efforts to improve the competitive position of American industry. A part of these cost savings will come from tighter administrative controls on existing benefit packages. But another part, as already seen in the auto industry, may come from a reduction in existing benefit packages. If this does evolve as a trend, benefit administrators will need to develop a mechanism for identifying employee preferences (in this case "least preferences") and use them as a guideline to meet agreed-upon savings targets.

Review Questions

1. Your company has a serious turnover problem among employees with fewer than five years' seniority. The CEO wants to use employee benefits to lessen this problem. What might you do, specifically, in the areas of pension vesting, vacation and holiday allocation, and life insurance coverage in the effort to reduce turnover?

2. Assume you are politically foolhardy and decide to challenge your CEO's decision, in question 1, to use benefits as a major tool for reducing turnover. Before she fires you, what arguments might you try to use to persuade her? (Hint: Are there other compensation tools that might be more effective in reducing turnover? Might the changes in benefits have unintended consequences on more senior employees? Could you make a cost argument against such a strategy? Is turnover of these employees necessarily bad, and how would you demonstrate that this turnover isn't a problem?

3. Why are defined contribution pension plans gaining in popularity in the United States and defined benefit plans losing popularity?

4. Some people claim that workers' compensation and unemployment compensation create a disincentive to work. What does this mean? In your opinion is there any validity to this argument?

5. One of the authors of this book counsels companies he deals with that spending more money on employee benefits is like throwing dollars down a black hole. Assuming he isn't crazy (a huge leap of faith), what might be the basis of this argument?

Extending the System

We have now completed the discussion of three strategic policies in the pay model used in this book. The first, which focused on determining the structure of pay, dealt with internal alignment. The second was determining the pay level based on external competitiveness, and the third dealt with determining the pay for employees according to their performance. Strategic decisions regarding alignment, competitiveness, and performance are directed at achieving the objectives of the pay system. Specific objectives vary among organizations; helping achieve competitive advantage and treating employees fairly are basic ones.

We now extend the basic pay model to the strategic issue of execution. A number of employee groups require, because of their importance to strategic success, special consideration in the way we design their compensation packages. In fact, Chapter 14 is titled just that: "Compensation of Special Groups." Here we talk about employee groups that don't quite fit our basic model. Their special employment status, for reasons we will discuss in a moment, dictates the design of compensation administration programs that sometimes differ from the more traditional designs covered in Parts 1 to 4.

In Chapter 15 we look at compensation in unionized firms. Although less than 15 percent of the work force in the United States is unionized, the role of unions in wage determination extends far beyond this small group. Firms looking to remain nonunion often pay considerable attention to the way rewards are distributed to union employees. As we shall see, the role of a compensation person in a unionized organization is, indeed, different.

Our final extension of the system focuses on international employees. Different cultures, different laws, and different economies all can lead to different strategic and administrative decisions for international employees. If we are truly to embrace the globalization of business, the globalization of compensation must be a key ingredient.

EXHIBIT V.1 **The Pay Model**

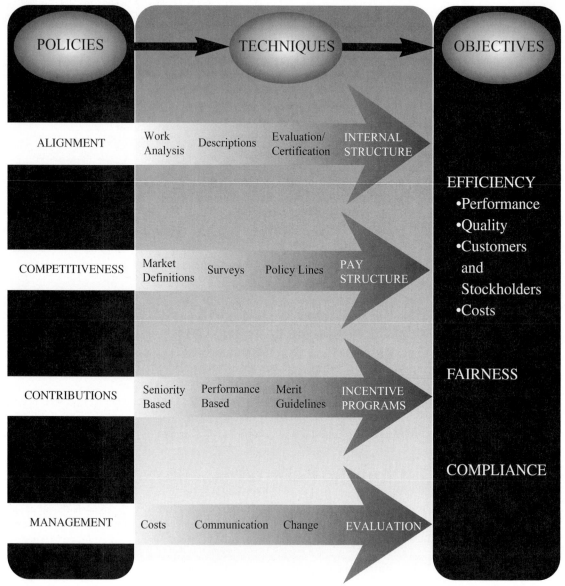

Compensation
of Special Groups

Chapter Outline

The country's in a bind, but I'm cheerful and I'm chipper,
As I slash employee wages like a fiscal Jack the Ripper.
And I take away their health care and never mind their hollers.
And pay myself a bonus of a couple of million dollars.

Mark Russell
Comedian

Mark Russell's satirical song is a reflection of our worst fears about pay: Injustice hits the common worker first. This chapter takes a look at groups that, for reasons we will discuss, receive compensation that is anything but common. Our goal is to show the logic of compensation practices for these special groups.

So far we have described compensation programs as if they were fairly uniform across all jobs in an organization: Jobs are analyzed; then job evaluation determines a job's internal worth; salary surveys give an indication of what other competitors pay for the job; discrepancies are reconciled; and provisions are made to recognize that variation in performance across individuals in the same job should be recognized with compensation differences. Not all jobs follow all these stages, though. Indeed, all we have to do is open a newspaper to see that some jobs and some people are singled out for special compensation treatment in an organization. Why will Bobby Holik, a fast-skating forward for the New York Rangers, make $45 million over the next five years? Why has Michael Eisner (chief executive officer, Walt Disney Company) received more than $700 million in compensation since 1996, during a period when Disney stock fell 22.6 percent?[1] Is the value of these jobs determined in the same way that compensation is determined for other jobs in a company? The answer is probably no. But why? To answer this question, it is useful to work backward. What jobs get special compensation treatment in a company? Are they basically the same kinds of jobs across companies? If they are the same kinds of jobs, are there any common characteristics the jobs share that would cause companies to devise special compensation packages?

WHO ARE SPECIAL GROUPS?

When we look at company practices with these questions in mind, a pattern begins to emerge. Special treatment, either in the form of add-on packages not received by other employees or in the form of compensation components entirely unique in the organization, tends to focus on a few specific groups. This chapter argues that special groups share two characteristics. First, special groups tend to be strategically important to the company. If they don't succeed at their jobs, success for the whole organization is in jeopardy. Second, their positions tend to have built-in conflict, conflict that arises because different factions place incompatible demands on members of the group.

As the first characteristic explains, the work these employees perform is central to the strategic success of the company. As an example, consider the contrast in compensation treatment for engineers in two different organizations. One is a high-technology firm with a strong research and development component. The other organization employs a few engineers, but their role is not central to the mission of the organization. A survey of this type of difference in employee composition and organizational strategy found that research and development organizations with heavy concentrations of engineers had evolved unique compensation systems that were responsive to the special needs of the engineering contingent. Organizations with a different focus and with fewer engineers merged this group's compensation with the standard package offered to other employees.

Exhibit 14.1 describes the nature of the conflicts faced by such special groups as supervisors, top management, boards of directors, scientists and engineers, sales personnel, and contingent workers. When both of these characteristics are present, we tend to find distinctive compensation practices adopted to meet the needs of these special groups.

COMPENSATION STRATEGY FOR SPECIAL GROUPS

Supervisors

Remember, supervisors are caught between the demands of upper management in terms of production and the needs of employees in terms of rewards, reinforcements and general counseling.[2] The major challenge in compensating supervisors centers on equity. Some incentive must be provided to entice nonexempt employees to accept the challenges of being a supervisor. For many years, the strategy was to treat supervisors like

[1]R. Blumenthal, "Disney Shareholders Reject Pay Review for Top Brass," *Barron's,* March 24, 2003, p. 10.
[2]P. Frost, "Handling the Pain of Others: The Hidden Role of Supervisors," *Canadian HR Reporter,* April 7, 2003, pp. 7–8.

EXHIBIT 14.1   Conflicts Faced by Special Groups

Special Group	Type of Conflict Faced
Supervisors	Caught between upper management and employees. Must balance need to achieve organization's objectives with importance of helping employees satisfy personal needs. If unsuccessful, either corporate profit or employee morale suffers.
Top management	Stockholders want healthy return on investment. Government wants compliance with laws. Executives must decide between strategies that maximize short-run gains at expense of long run versus directions that focus on long run.
Boards of directors	Face possibility that disgruntled stockholders may sue over corporate strategies that don't "pan out."
Professional employees	May be torn between goals, objectives, and ethical standards of their profession (e.g., should an engineer leak information about a product flaw, even though that information may hurt corporate profits) and demands of an employer concerned more with the profit motive.
Sales staff	Often go for extended periods in the field with little supervision. Challenge is to stay motivated and continue making sales calls even in the face of limited contact or scrutiny from manager.
Contingent workers	Play an important "safety valve" role for companies. When demand is high, more are hired; when demand drops, they are the first workers downsized. Employment status is highly insecure and challenge is to find low-cost ways to motivate.

lower-level managers. But in doing so, the existing job evaluation system sometimes left these supervisors making less money than the top-paid employees they supervised. As you might imagine, this created little incentive to take on the extra work involved. More recently organizations have devised several strategies to attract workers into supervisory jobs. The most popular method is to key the base salary of supervisors to some amount exceeding the top-paid subordinate in the unit (5 to 30 percent represents the typical size of the differential).

Another method for maintaining equitable differentials is simply to pay supervisors for scheduled overtime. Companies that do pay overtime are about evenly split between paying straight time and paying time and one half for overtime hours.

The biggest trend in supervisory compensation centers on increased use of variable pay. Slightly more than half of all companies now have a variable pay component for supervisors, up from 16 percent in prior years.[3]

Corporate Directors

A typical board of directors comprises 10 outside (the company) and 3 inside directors, each having a term averaging three years. Historically, directors frequently were given the role of "rubber stamping" decisions made by top management. Such boards were stacked with people affiliated in some way with the organization (e.g., retired corporate officers, suppliers, attorneys). Modern corporate boards have changed considerably. Approximately two-thirds of boards now include more outside directors than inside directors

[3]IOMA, *Pay for Performance Report,* May 2000, p. 6.

(e.g., CEO, corporate officers), and this move to more outside directors comes with a price—higher compensation. Almost 75 percent of the companies planning on increasing board pay this year will do so because of competition for talented outside directors.[4] Outside members now include unaffiliated business executives, representatives from important segments of society, and major shareholders. For example, Walter Mondale, vice president under Jimmy Carter, served on six boards of directors and was compensated $523,000 for his efforts.[5] The 200 largest industrial and service companies, plus the top 100 dot-coms, averaged $138,747 in total compensation of board members. Despite the intention to increase pay, total compensation still declined somewhat in year-to-year comparisons. The uncertainty in the stock market has led to increased base pay, less stock-based compensation, and an overall decline (exercised options in wildly increasing stock markets led to nice incentive-based packages—that has declined recently). Depending on the industry, recent figures suggest that total director compensation ranges from $40,000 to the low $50,000s.[6]

In addition to cash compensation, there is an increasing emphasis on director rewards that attempt to link to corporate performance. Shareholders are holding directors accountable for firm performance. Reflecting this trend of linking pay to performance, 61 percent of the compensation for directors in large companies is some form of stock.[7] This trend is increasing despite the lack of evidence that giving board members more shares of stock results in better firm performance.[8] The rest of the compensation is divided among annual retainers, committee chair fees, and board meeting fees. For example, each director receives almost $1,500 for each board meeting attended.[9]

Executives

How would you like to make $15.7 million per year? That is the average for chief executive officers (CEOs) in the 100 largest U.S. companies.[10] How does someone earn a compensation package like that? Well, consider Dennis Kozlowski. He made $82 million last year, enough to be near the top of the list of highly paid executives. At the same time, stock in his company slid 71 percent. And, oh, by the way, he has been accused of wholesale looting of his company.[11] If you and I had wages that rose as fast as those of CEOs, earnings of $25,000 in 1994 would be $138,000 today.[12] Is it any wonder that lofty executive pay packages are now the subject of public outrage. Exhibit 14.2 gives a brief history of how executive compensation climbed to such heights. Pay attention to the way the granting of stock options has gradually played a bigger role in executive compensation.

---

[4]*was.hewitt.com/hewitt/resource/newsroom/pressrel/2003/02-12-03.htm,* visited June 19, 2003.

[5]G. Strauss, "From Public Servant to Private Payday," *USA Today,* April 17, 2000, p. B1.

[6]IOMA, "Conference Board Reports Outside Director Pay Drops," *Report on Salary Surveys,* February 2002, p. 3.

[7]"2000 Director Compensation," *Pension Benefits,* November 2001, p. 12.

[8]C. Daily, "The Problem with Equity Compensation," *Journal of Business Strategy* 23(4) (2002), p. 28.

[9]"2000 Director Compensation," *Pension Benefits,* November 2001, p. 12.

[10]J. Useem, "Have They No Shame?" *Fortune,* April 28, 2003, pp. 56–64.

[11]Ibid.

[12]"Executive Pay," *Business Week,* April 19, 1999, p. 78.

EXHIBIT 14.2   Brief History of Executive Compensation

The Year	The Key Event
1974	Michael Bergerac cracks the $1 million mark when recruited to Revlon.
1979	Chrysler's Lee Iacocca takes $1 million plus 400,000 option shares.
1983	William Bendix of Bendix becomes the first executive to collect a huge golden parachute (contract clause for payment in a takeover leading to termination) of $3.9 million over five years.
1984	Congress tries to limit excessive golden parachutes but gives rise to unintended consequences—the rules actually lead to larger amounts.
1986	New law gives favorable tax treatment to stock option awards. Sizes increase.
1987	Lee Iacocca receives first megagrant of stock options: 820,000 option shares worth 15.3 times his salary and bonus that year.
1987	Junk bond expert Michael Milkin explodes through the $5 million mark in salary and bonus.
1987	Leon Hirsch of US Surgical gets even larger megastock option award, worth 126 times his salary and bonus.
1992	Securities and Exchange Commission rules CEO salaries must be disclosed more often in proxy statements. Easier availability of peer compensation data serves to drive up the standard.
1992	Michael Eisner of Walt Disney exercises low-cost stock options for pretax profit of $126 million.
1993	New tax law sets upper limit on tax-deductible executive compensation at $1 million but has unintended effect of raising bar to that level.
2000	Charles Wang, Computer Associates Intl. executive, cracks two-thirds of billion-dollar mark.
2003	Alfred Lerner, MBNA executive, is top-paid CEO, with $195 million, a drop from prior years, leading to speculation that furor over CEO pay is finally having an impact.

Source: *Business Week,* April 17, 2000, p. 100, April 23, 2003; and *Wall Street Journal,* April 11, 1996, p. R4.

EXHIBIT 14.3   Top Five Executives in Total Compensation (in millions)

	2002 Salary and Bonus	Long-Term Compensation	Total Pay
1. Alfred Lerner, MBNA	$9.0	$185.9	$194.9
2. Jeffrey Barbakow, Tenet Healthcare	$5.5	$111.1	$116.6
3. Millard Drexler, Gap	$2.5	$88.5	$91.0
4. Dennis Kozlowski, Tyco International	$4.0	$67.0	$71.0
5. Irwin Jacobs, Qualcomm	$1.8	$61.6	$63.3

Source: L. Lavelle, F. Jespersen, S. Ante and J. Kerstetter, "Executive Pay," *Business Week,* April 21, 2003.

Exhibit 14.3 shows the total compensation for the top five executives in the United States. Notice how most of these five, as is true for many highly paid executives, reap the greatest rewards from long-term incentives, usually by exercising stock options. Many critics argue that this level of compensation for executives is excessive.[13] And this phenomenon exists only in the United States. Wages in the European Union, for example, are much lower. Wages plus incentives for French CEOs, the highest-paid executives, average

[13]M. Langley, "Big Companies Get Low Marks for Lavish Executive Pay," *Wall Street Journal,* June 9, 2003, p. C1; Graef S. Crystal, *In Search of Excess* (New York: Norton, 1991).

about $2 million in a sample of the 300 largest European companies. U.K. salaries for CEOs are about 16 percent behind this, and other European executives fall even further behind.[14]

Cybercomp

For a union view of CEO wages, visit *www.aflcio.org/paywatch/*. This site is maintained by the AFL-CIO and is designed to monitor executive compensation. The Union view is that CEOs are overpaid and that monitoring is the first step to curbing excess.

Are the critics right? One way to answer the question is to look at the different ways executive compensation is determined and ask, "Does this seem reasonable?"

Possible Explanations for CEO Compensation

One approach to explaining why executives receive such large sums of money involves *social comparisons*.[15] In this view, executive salaries bear a consistent relative relationship to compensation of lower-level employees. When salaries of lower-level employees rise in response to market forces, top executive salaries also rise to maintain the same relative relationship. In general, managers who are in the second level of a company earn about two-thirds of a CEO's salary, while the next level down earns slightly more than half of a CEO's salary.[16] Much of the criticism of this theory, and an important source of criticism about executive compensation in general, is the gradual increase in the spread between executives' compensation and the average salaries of the people they employ. In 1980, CEOs received about 42 times the average pay of lower-level workers. Now top executives are paid 475 times the pay of the average factory worker.[17] As a point of reference, the corresponding differential in Japan is under 20.[18] Both these pieces of information suggest that a social comparison explanation is not sufficient to explain why executive wages are as high as they are.

A second approach to understanding executive compensation focuses less on the difference in wages between executive and other jobs and more on explaining the level of executive wages.[19] The premise in this *economic approach* is that the worth of CEOs, or their subordinates, should correspond closely to some measure of company success, such as profitability or sales. Intuitively, this explanation makes sense. There is also empirical support. Numerous studies over the past 30 years have demonstrated that executive pay

---

[14]P. Betts, "France Has the Fattest Cats," *Financial Times,* June 23, 2003.

[15]A. Henderson and J. Fredrickson, "Top Management Team Coordination Needs and the CEO Pay Gap: A Competitive Test of Economic and Behavioral Views," *Academy of Management Journal* 44(1) (2001), pp. 96–107; A. Simon, *Administrative Behavior,* 2d ed. (New York: Macmillan, 1957).

[16]Conference Board, *Top Executive Compensation:* (New York: 1996).

[17]"Executive Pay," *Business Week,* April 17, 2000, p. 110.

[18]R. Blumenthal, "The Pay Gap between Workers and Chiefs Looks like a Chasm," *Barron's,* September 4, 2000, p. 10. This comparison needs to be interpreted with some caution. One counterargument (the Hay Group, *Compflash,* April 1992, p. 3) notes that American companies are generally much larger than their foreign counterparts. When compared to like-size companies in other countries, the U.S. multiple is comparable to the international average.

[19]A. Henderson and J. Fredrickson, "Top Management Team Coordination Needs and the CEO Pay Gap: A Competitive Test of Economic and Behavioral Views," *Academy of Management Journal* 44(1) (2001), pp. 96–107.

bears some relationship to company success.[20] A recent article analyzing the results from over 100 executive pay studies found empirical evidence that firm size (sales or number of employees) is by far the best predictor of CEO compensation. Size variables are nine times better at explaining executive compensation than are performance measures. How big the firm is explains what the boss gets paid better than does how well he performs![21]

Some evidence contradicts this, though. Two studies combined both social comparison and economic explanations to try to better understand CEO salaries.[22] Both of these explanations turned out to be significant. Size and profitability affected level of compensation, but so did social comparisons. In one study, the social comparison was between wages of CEOs and those of the board of directors. It seems that CEO salaries rose, on average, 51 percent for every $100,000 more that was earned by directors on the board.[23] Recognizing this, CEOs sometimes lobby to get a board loaded with directors who are highly paid in their primary jobs.

A third view of CEO salaries, called *agency theory,* incorporates the political motivations that are an inevitable part of the corporate world. Sometimes, this argument runs, CEOs make decisions that aren't in the economic best interest of the firm and its shareholders. One variant on this view suggests that the normal behavior of a CEO is self-protective—CEOs will make decisions to solidify their positions and to maximize the rewards they personally receive.[24] As evidence of this self-motivated behavior, consider the following description of how executives ensure themselves high compensation.[25] The description comes from the experience of a well-known executive compensation consultant, now turned critic, who specialized for years in the design of executive compensation packages:

1. *If the CEO is truly underpaid:* A compensation consultant is hired to survey actual competitors of the company. The consultant reports to the board of directors that the CEO is truly underpaid. Salary is increased to a competitive or higher level.

2. *If the CEO is not underpaid and the company is doing well:* A compensation consultant is hired. Specific companies are recommended to the consultant as appropriate for surveying. The companies tend to be selected because they are on the top end in terms of executive compensation. The consultant reports back to the board that its CEO appears to be underpaid. Salary is increased.

[20]Ibid.; Marc J. Wallace, "Type of Control, Industrial Concentration, and Executive Pay," *Academy of Management Proceedings* (1977), pp. 284–288; W. Lewellan and B. Huntsman, "Managerial Pay and Corporate Performance," *American Economic Review* 60 (1977), pp. 710–720.

[21]H. L. Tosi, S. Werner, J. Katz, and L. Gomez-Mejia, "A Meta Analysis of CEO Pay Studies," *Journal of Management* 26(2) (2000), pp. 301–339.

[22]A. Henderson and J. Fredrickson, "Top Management Team Coordination Needs and the CEO Pay Gap: A Competitive Test of Economic and Behavioral Views," *Academy of Management Journal* 44(1) (2001), pp. 96–107; Charles O'Reilly, Brian Main, and Graef Crystal, "CEO Compensation as Tournament and Social Comparison: A Tale of Two Theories," *Administrative Science Quarterly* 33 (1988), pp. 257–274.

[23]Charles O'Reilly, Brian Main, and Graef Crystal, "CEO Compensation as Tournament and Social Comparison: A Tale of Two Theories," *Administrative Science Quarterly* 33 (1988), pp. 257–274.

[24]Kathryn M. Eisenhardt, "Agency Theory: An Assessment and Review," *Academy of Management Review* 14 (1989), pp. 57–74.

[25]Crystal, *In Search of Excess.*

3. *If the CEO is not underpaid and the company is doing poorly:* A compensation consultant is hired. The CEO laments with the consultant that wages are so low for top management that there is a fear that good people will start leaving the company and going to competitors. Of course, no one ever asks why the company is underperforming if it has such a good management team. Anyway, the result is that the consultant recommends a wage increase to avoid future turnover.

In each of these scenarios CEO wages rise. Is it any surprise that executive compensation is under close scrutiny by an outraged public and, more importantly, angry stockholders.[26]

Agency theory argues that executive compensation should be designed to ensure that executives have the best interests of stockholders in mind when they make decisions. The outcome has been to use some form of long-term incentive plan, most commonly stock options. A *Wall Street Journal*/Mercer survey of 500 firms found the use of long-term incentives rising for CEOs, from 62 percent of the package in 1998 to 68 percent in 2002.[27] In the simplest form, an executive is given the option to purchase shares of the company stock at some future date for an amount equal to the fair market price at the time the option is granted. There is a built-in incentive for an executive to increase the value of the firm. Stock prices rise. The executive exercises the option to buy the stock at the agreed-upon price. Because the stock price has risen in the interim, the executive profits from the stock sale.

Although this sounds like an effective tool for motivating executives, there are still many critics.[28] The major complaint is that stock options don't have a downside risk. If stock prices rise, the stock options are exercised. If stocks don't improve, or even decline, as was the case for much of the past four years, the executive suffers no out-of-pocket losses. Some argue that executive compensation should move more toward requiring that executives own stock, rather than just have options to buy it.[29] With the threat of possible financial loss and the hope of possible substantial gains, motivation may be higher. Others advocate linking stock options to executive performance. For example, if an executive doesn't lead his or her company to outperform other companies in the same industry, no stock options are granted.[30] Finally, there is growing recognition that the linkage between performance and pay is much more complex for executives than was previously thought. Current work focuses on firm risk, stock ownership versus stock options, and type of industry as possible additional factors explaining executive pay.[31]

[26]M. Langley, "Big Companies Get Low Marks for Lavish Executive Pay," *Wall Street Journal,* June 9, 2003, p. C1.

[27]IOMA, "A New Look at Long Term Incentive Plans for Execs," *Pay for Performance Report,* June 2003, pp. 1, 11.

[28]Nancy C. Pratt, "CEOs Reap Unprecedented Riches While Employees' Pay Stagnates," *Compensation and Benefits Review,* September/October 1996, p. 20.

[29]Ira T. Kay, "Beyond Stock Options: Emerging Practices in Executive Incentive Programs," *Compensation and Benefits Review* 23(6) (1991), pp. 18–29.

[30]IOMA, "Here's the Latest Thinking on How Organizations Can Solve the CEO Pay Problem," *Pay for Performance Report,* April 2003, pp. 1, 13.

[31]J. Miller, R. Wiseman, and L. Gomez-Mejia, "The Fit between CEO Compensation Design and Firm Risk," *Academy of Management Journal* 45(4) (2002) pp. 745–756; W. G. Sanders, "Behavioral Responses of CEOs to Stock Ownership and Stock Option Pay," *Academy of Management Journal,* 44(3) (2001), pp. 477–492; D. Balkin, G. Markman, and L. Gomez-Mejia, "Is CEO Pay in High-Technology Firms Related to Innovation? *Academy of Management Journal* 43(6) (2000), pp. 1118–1129.

The second trend in response to complaints about excessive executive compensation is increasing government regulation. In 1992 the Securities and Exchange Commission entered the controversy.[32] Stockholders are now permitted to propose and vote on limits to executive compensation. The 1993 Revenue Reconciliation Act limited employer deductions for executive compensation to $1 million and capped the amount of executive compensation used in computing contributions to and benefits from qualified retirement plans. Ironically, this very law may be contributing to the growth of executive compensation. The $1 million mark now serves as a new standard: Many executives who had been making less than $1 million are finding their pay quickly rising to this amount.

Components of an Executive Compensation Package

There are five basic elements of most executive compensation packages: (1) base salary, (2) short-term (annual) incentives or bonuses, (3) long-term incentives and capital appreciation plans, (4) employee benefits, and (5) perquisites.[33] Because of the changing nature of tax legislation, each of these at one time or another has received considerable attention in designing executive compensation packages. Exhibit 14.4 traces the trend in these components over time.

One obvious trend is apparent from these data. Companies are placing more and more emphasis on incentives at the expense of base salary. Such a change in emphasis signals the growing importance attached to making decisions that ensure profitability and survival of a company.

Base Salary   Although formalized job evaluation still plays an occasional role in determining executive base pay, other sources are much more important. Particularly important is the opinion of a compensation committee, composed usually of the company's board of directors or a subset of the board.[34] Frequently the compensation committee will

EXHIBIT 14.4   Breakdown of Executive Compensation Components

Compensation Component	1970s	1980s	1990s	Today
Base salary	60%	40%	33%	16%
Benefits	*	15	*	*
Perks	*	5	*	*
Short-term incentives	25	20	27	16
Long-term incentives	15	20	40	68

*Unreported.
Sources: IOMA, *Pay for Performance Report,* May 1998, p. 11, and June 2003, p. 12; various issues of the *Wall Street Journal;* Data from Towers, Perrin, Wyatt Co.; M. Bishko, "Compensating Your Overseas Executive, Part 1: Strategies for the 1990s," *Compensation and Benefits Review,* May–June 1990, pp. 22–30.

[32]Michelle Osborn, "SEC: Executive Pay Is an Issue for Shareholders," *USA Today,* 1994, p. B1.

[33]B. Ellig, *The Complete Guide to Executive Compensation* (New York: McGraw-Hill, 2002).

[34]C. Daly, J. Johnson, A. Ellstrand, and D. Dalton, "Compensation Committee Composition as a Determinant of CEO Compensation," *Academy of Management Journal* 41(2) (1998), pp. 209–220; H. Barkema and L. Gomez-Mejia, "Managerial Compensation and Firm Performance: A General Research Framework," *Academy of Management Journal* 41(2) (1998), pp. 135–148.

take over some of the data analysis tasks previously performed by the chief personnel officer, even going so far as to analyze salary survey data and performance records for executives of comparably-sized firms.[35] One empirical study suggests the most common approach (60 percent of the cases) of executive compensation committees is to identify major competitors and set the CEO's compensation at a level between the best and worst of these comparison groups.[36]

Bonuses Annual bonuses often play a major role in executive compensation and are primarily designed to motivate better performance. Most striking is the rapid rise in popularity of this type of compensation. Only 20 years ago just 36 percent of companies gave annual bonuses. Today bonuses are given to 90 percent of executives.

Long-term Incentive and Capital Appreciation Plans Long-term incentives now account for over one-half of total executive compensation, up from 28 percent a decade ago.[37] By far the most common long-term incentive remains the executive stock option. A stock option is the right (not obligation) to purchase a stated quantity of stock at a stipulated price (strike price) over a given period of time (exercise period) following certain eligibility (vesting) requirements.[38] Because many of the highest-reported executive pay packages can be traced to stock options, critics have focused on their use and abuse. One clear complaint is that stock options don't pay for performance of the executive. In a stock market that is rising on all fronts, executives can exercise options at much higher prices than the initial grant price—and the payouts are more likely attributed to general market increases than to any specific action by the executive. Efforts to counter such undeserved rewards are linked to the rise of other types of long-term incentives, some of which require that the executive "beat the market" or hit certain performance targets specifically linked to firm performance. For example, Citicorp CEO John Reed received 300,000 stock options at about $120 each. For those options to vest, Citicorp stock must reach $200 by the end of the year, an unlikely outcome given that the stock price is currently less than half that price.[39] Exhibit 14.5 identifies other types of long-term incentives and describes their main features. Clearly, in today's more turbulent stock market, stock options are not the "mother lode" they were in the 1990s. Options granted at one price quickly become poor motivational tools when the stock price drops far below that figure. Many companies now scramble to grant new options at lower prices, reflecting better the realities of a declining market.

Executive Benefits Since many benefits are tied to income level (e.g., life insurance, disability insurance, pension plans), executives typically receive higher benefits than most other exempt employees. Beyond the typical benefits outlined in Chapter 13, however, many executives also receive additional life insurance, exclusions from deductibles for health-related costs, and supplementary pension income exceeding the maximum limits permissible under ERISA guidelines for qualified (eligible for tax deductions) pension plans.

---

[35]B. Ellig, *The Complete Guide to Executive Compensation* (New York: McGraw-Hill, 2002).

[36]Daniel J. Miller, "CEO Salary Increases May Be Rational after All: Referents and Contracts in CEO Pay," *Academy of Management Journal* 38(5) (1995), pp. 1361–1385.

[37]IOMA *Pay for Performance Report,* June 2003, p.12, and May 1998, p. 11.

[38]B. Ellig, *The Complete Guide to Executive Compensation* (New York: McGraw-Hill, 2002).

[39]IOMA *Pay for Performance Report,* January 1999, p. 2.

EXHIBIT 14.5   Long-Term Incentives for Executives

Type	Description	Comments
Incentive stock options	Purchase of stock at a stipulated price, conforming with Internal Revenue Code (Section 422A).	No taxes at grant. Company may not deduct as expense.
Nonqualified stock options	Purchase of stock at a stipulated price, not conforming with Internal Revenue Code.	Excess over fair market value taxed as ordinary income. Company may deduct.
Phantom stock plans	Cash or stock award determined by increase in stock price at a fixed future date.	Taxed as ordinary income. Does not require executive financing.
Stock appreciation rights	Cash or stock award determined by increase in stock price during any time chosen (by the executive) in the option period.	Taxed as ordinary income. Does not require executive financing.
Restricted stock plans	Grant of stock at a reduced price with the condition that it may not be sold before a specified date.	Excess over fair market value taxed as ordinary income.
Performance share/ unit plans	Cash or stock award earned through achieving specific goals.	Taxed as ordinary income. Does not require executive financing.

Source: B. Ellig, *The Complete Guide to Executive Compensation (New York: McGraw-Hill, 2002).*

Of course, various sections of ERISA and the tax code restrict employers ability to provide benefits for executives that are too far above those of other workers. The assorted clauses require that a particular benefit plan (1) cover a broad cross-section of employees (generally 80 percent), (2) provide definitely determinable benefits, and (3) meet specific vesting (see Chapter 13) and nondiscrimination requirements. The nondiscrimination requirement specifies that the average value of benefits for low-paid employees must be at least 75 percent of the average value of those for highly paid employees.[40]

Executive Perquisites   Perquisites, or "perks," probably have the same genesis as the expression "rank has its privileges." Indeed, life at the top has its rewards, designed to satisfy several types of executive needs. One type of perk can be classified as internal, providing a little something extra while the executive is inside the company: a luxury office, an executive dining room, special parking. A second category comprises perks that are also company-related but are designed for business conducted externally: company-paid membership in clubs/associations and payment of hotel, resort, airplane, and auto expenses.

The final category of perquisites should be totally isolated from the first two because of its different tax status. This category, called *personal perks,* includes such things as low-cost loans, personal and legal counseling, free home repairs and improvements, personal

[40]Dennis Blair and Mark Kimble, "Walking through the Discrimination Testing Wage for Welfare Plans," *Benefits Quarterly* 3(2) (1987), pp. 18–26.

use of company property, and expenses for vacation homes.[41] Since 1978, various tax and regulatory agency rulings have slowly been requiring companies to place a value on perks.[42] If this trend continues, the taxable income of executives with creative perk packages may increase considerably. Examples of interesting perks are the following:

- The most famous perks profile in recent years belongs to the former CEO of GE, Jack Welch. Papers filed in his divorce case showed GE paying for an apartment for him on the Upper West Side of Manhattan, as well as all food, wine, laundry, and toiletry costs. Some of his recreational perks included floor-level seats at New York Knicks games, courtside seats at the U.S. Open, and satellite TV at his four homes. Mind you, this is all above and beyond compensation regularly reported to exceed $100 million.[43]
- W. J. Sanders, chairman of Advanced Micro Devices, gets a security guard who doubles as the chauffeur for his company-provided Mercedes Benz. Total cost of these since 1998? About $534,000.
- World Wrestling Federation chairman Vince McMahon gets $50,000 per year to cover cleaning costs.[44]

Exhibit 14.6 illustrates different types of perks and the percentage of companies that offer them.

Scientists and Engineers in High-Technology Industries

Scientists and engineers are classified as *professionals.* According to the Fair Labor Standards Act, this category includes any person who has received special training of a scientific or intellectual nature and whose job does not entail more than a 20 percent time allocation for lower-level duties.

The compensation of scientists and engineers focuses on rewarding them for their special scientific or intellectual training. Here lies one of the special compensation problems that scientists and engineers face. Consider the freshly minted electrical engineer who graduates with all the latest knowledge in the field. For the first few years after graduation this knowledge is a valuable resource on engineering projects where new applications of the latest theories are a primary objective. Gradually, though, this engineer's knowledge starts to become obsolete, and team leaders begin to look to newer graduates for fresh ideas. If you track the salaries of engineers and scientists, you will see a close resemblance between pay increases and knowledge obsolescence. Early years bring larger-than-average increases (relative to employees in other occupations). After 10 years increases drop below average, and they become downright puny in 15 to 20 years.

Partly because salary plateaus arise, many scientists and engineers make career changes such as moving into management or temporarily leaving business to update their technical knowledge. In recent years some firms have tried to deal with the plateau effect and also accommodate the different career motivations of mature scientists and engineers.

---

[41]Michael F. Klein, "Executive Perquisites," *Compensation Review* 12 (Fourth Quarter 1979), pp. 46–50.

[42]R. L. VanKirk and L. S. Schenger, "Executive Compensation: The Trend Is Back to Cash," *Financial Executive*, May 1978, pp. 83–91.

[43]M. Burger, "Executive Perks: How Much Is Enough?" *Potentials*, October 2002, p. 25.

[44]G. Strauss, "CEOs Rake in Big Perks on Top of Big Bucks," *USA Today*, May 1, 2001, pp. 1–2B.

**EXHIBIT 14.6
Popular
Perks
Offered to
Executives**

Source: Hewitt
Associates, 1990.

Perk	Companies Offering Perk
Physical exam	91%
Company car	68%
Financial counseling	64%
Company plane	63%
Income tax preparation	63%
First-class air travel	62%
Country club membership	55%
Luncheon club membership	55%
Estate planning	52%
Personal liability insurance	50%
Spouse travel	47%
Chauffeur service	40%
Reserved parking	32%
Executive dining room	30%
Home security system	25%
Car phone	22%
Financial seminars	11%
Loans at low or no interest	9%
Legal counseling	6%

The result has been the creation of dual-career tracks. Exhibit 14.7 shows a typical dual-career ladder.

Notice that dual ladders provide exactly that: two different ways of progressing in an organization, each reflecting different types of contributions to the organization's mission. The managerial ladder ascends through increasing responsibility for supervision or direction of people. The professional track ascends through increasing contributions of a professional nature that do not mainly entail the supervision of employees. Scientists and engineers have the opportunity at some stage in their careers to consider a management track or continue along the scientific track. Not only do dual tracks offer greater advancement opportunities for scientists and engineers, but maximum base pay in the technical track can approximate that of upper-management positions.

A second problem in designing the compensation package of scientists and engineers centers on the question of equity. The very nature of technical knowledge and its dissemination requires the relatively close association of these employees across organizations. In fact, scientists and engineers tend to compare themselves for equity purposes with graduates who entered the labor market when they did. Partially because of this and partially because of the volatile nature of both jobs and salaries in these occupations, organizations rely very heavily on external market data in pricing scientists' and engineers' base pay.[45] This has resulted in the use of maturity curves.

[45]Jo C. Kail, "Compensating Scientists and Engineers," in *New Perspectives on Compensation,* ed. David B. Balkin and Luis R. Gomez-Mejia (Englewood Cliffs, NJ: Prentice-Hall, 1987), pp. 247–281.

EXHIBIT 14.7
IBM Dual
Ladders

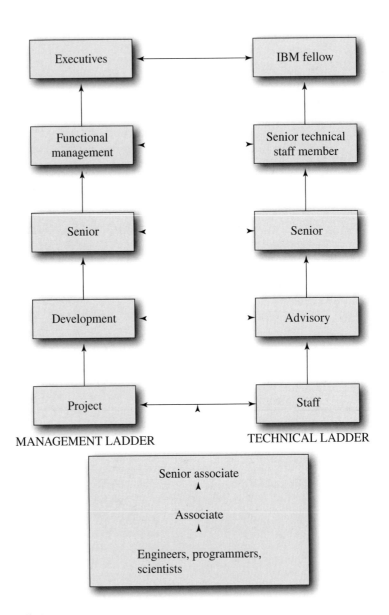

Maturity curves reflect the relationship between scientist/engineer compensation and years of experience in the labor market. Generally, surveying organizations ask for information about salaries as a function of years since the incumbent(s) last received a degree. This is intended to measure the half-life of technical obsolescence. In fact, a plot of this data, with appropriate smoothing to eliminate aberrations, typically shows curves that are steep for the first 5 to 7 years and then rise more gradually as technical obsolescence erodes the value of jobs. Exhibit 14.8 illustrates such a graph with somewhat greater so-

EXHIBIT 14.8
Maturity Curve: Years since Last Degree Relative to Salary

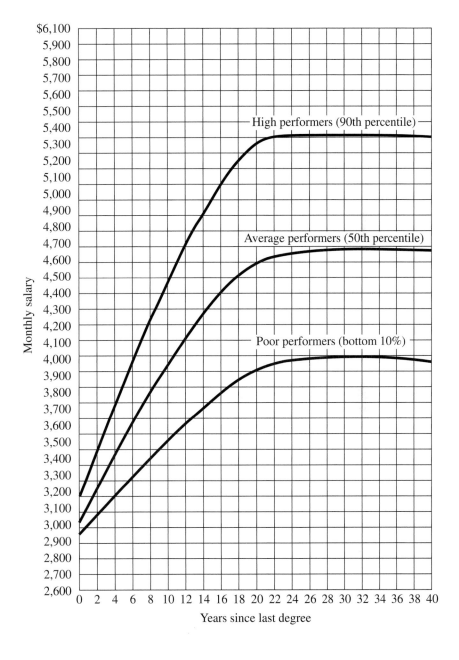

phistication built into it, in that different graphs are constructed for different levels of performance. To construct such graphs, the surveying organization must also ask for data broken down by broad performance levels. Notice in the illustration that the high performers begin with somewhat higher salaries and the differential continues to broaden over the first few years.

Scientists and engineers also receive compensation beyond base pay. In general, high-technology firms place a great emphasis on the use of performance-based incentives.[46] Common forms of incentives include profit sharing and stock ownership. Other incentives link payment of specific cash amounts to completion of specific projects on or before agreed-upon deadlines. Posthiring bonuses are also paid for such achievements as patents, publications, elections to professional societies, and attainment of professional licenses.

Finally, organizations have devoted considerable creative energy to development of perks that satisfy the unique needs of scientists and engineers. These perks include flexible work schedules, large offices, campuslike environments, and lavish athletic facilities. The strategic importance of these groups dictates that both mind and body be kept active.

Sales Forces

The sales staff spans the all-important boundary between the organization and consumers of the organization's goods or services. Besides the sales function, or even as part of selling, the sales staff must be sensitive to changing consumer tastes and provide rapid feedback to appropriate departments. Indeed, there is a growing trend toward linking sales compensation to customer satisfaction measures, with about one-third of all companies reporting use of such quality-based measures.[47] The role of interacting in the field with customers requires individuals with high initiative who can work under low supervision for extended periods of time. The standard compensation system is not designed for this type of job. As you might expect, there is much more reliance on incentive payments tied to individual performance. Thus, even when salespeople are in the field—and relatively unsupervised—there is always a motivation to perform. Exhibit 14.9 shows that sales employees at every organization level have some component of pay (usually a large one) that is incentive-based. For top-level sales representatives the incentive-based pay can be over 40 percent of total compensation.

EXHIBIT 14.9 **Sales Compensation Components**

Average Salary for Sales Employees			
Annual Revenue of Company	**Base Salary**	**Bonus plus Commision**	**Total Compensation**
Executive	$87,178	$35,721	$122,899
Top-level sales representative	78,483	60,976	139,459
Midlevel sales representative	49,144	28,035	77,179
Low-level sales representative	37,698	14,294	51,992
Average of all representatives	54,452	25,571	80,023

Source: C. Galea, "2002 Salary Survey," *Sales and Marketing Management,* May 1, 2003.

[46]George T. Milkovich, "Compensation Systems in High Technology Companies," in *New Perspectives on Compensation,* ed. Balkin & Gomez-Mejia, pp. 269–277.
[47]"Sales Compensation Is Increasingly Tied to Quality," *Compflash,* July 1995, p. 1.

Designing a Sales Compensation Plan

Seven major factors influence the design of sales compensation packages: (1) the nature of people who enter the sales profession, (2) organizational strategy, (3) market maturity, (4) competitor practices, (5) size of company, (6) economic environment, and (7) product to be sold.

People Who Enter the Sales Profession   Popular stereotypes of salespeople characterize them as being heavily motivated by financial compensation. One study supports this perception, with salespeople ranking pay significantly higher than five other forms of reward. In the study, 78 percent of the salespeople ranked money as the number-one motivator, with recognition and appreciation being ranked as the number-two motivator.[48] Promotional opportunities, sense of accomplishment, personal growth, and job security were all less highly regarded. These values almost dictate that the primary focus of sales compensation should be on direct financial rewards (base pay plus incentives).

Organizational Strategy   A sales compensation plan should link desired behaviors of salespeople to organizational strategy.[49] This is particularly true in the Internet age. As more sales dollars are tied to computer-based transactions, the role of sales personnel will change.[50] Salespeople must know when to stress customer service and when to stress volume sales. And when volume sales are the goal, which products should be pushed hardest? Strategic plans signal which behaviors are important. For example, emphasis on customer service to build market share or movement into geographic areas with low potential may limit sales volume. Ordinarily, sales representatives under an incentive system will view customer service as an imposition, taking away from money-making sales opportunities. And woe be to the sales supervisor who assigns a commission-based salesperson to a market with low sales potential. Salespeople who are asked to forgo incentive income for low-sales tasks should be covered under a compensation system with a high base pay and small incentive component.

Alternatively, an organization may want to motivate aggressive sales behavior. A straight commission-based incentive plan will focus sales efforts in this direction, to the possible exclusion of supportive tasks such as processing customer returns. Such incentive plans include both a statement about the size of the incentive and a discussion of the performance objective necessary to achieve the incentive. Typical performance measures include overall territory volume, market share, number of product placements in retail stores, number of new accounts, gross profit, percentage of list-price attainment (relative to other salespeople in the organization), consistency of sales results, expense control, productivity per square foot (especially popular in retail stores), and bad debt generated by sales.[51] Each measure, of course, corresponds to a different business goal. For exam-

[48]Charles Warner, "Recognition and Appreciation Is Vital for Salespeople," *www.charleswarner .us/recogsls.html,* retrieved April 10, 2003.

[49]Bill O'Connell, "Dead Solid Perfect: Achieving Sales Compensation Alignment," *Compensation and Benefits Review,* March/April 1996, pp. 41–48.

[50]B. Weeks, "Setting Sales Force Compensation in the Internet Age," *Compensation and Benefits Review,* March/April 2000, pp. 25–34.

[51]John K. Moynahan, *The Sales Compensation Handbook* (New York: AMACOM, 1991).

ple, an organization might use a volume measure such as number of units, orders, invoices, or cash received if the business goal is to increase sales growth. Alternatively, if the goal is profit improvement, the appropriate measurement would be gross margin on sales or price per unit. Percentage account erosion would be stressed if improved account retention became a major focus of attention, while customer satisfaction indices are increasingly popular because of greater emphasis on quality.

Market Maturity   As the market of a product matures, the sales pattern for that product will change, and companies need to adapt the compensation for their sales force accordingly. A recent study showed that with maturing markets, companies move toward a more conservative sales pattern, focusing even more on customer satisfaction and retention. This leads companies to employ more conservative, rather than aggressive, salespeople, who can comply with the companies' customer retention plans. In maturing markets, companies focus both on performance-based pay tied to customer satisfaction and on greater base salaries to retain conservative salespeople.[52]

Competitor Practices   In selecting an appropriate pay level, organizations should recognize that external competitiveness is essential. The very nature of sales positions means that competitors will cross paths, at least in their quest for potential customers. This provides the opportunity to chat about relative compensation packages, an opportunity which salespeople will frequently take. To ensure that the comparison is favorable, the organization should identify a compensation strategy that explicitly indicates target salaries for different sales groups and performance levels.

Size of Company   As Exhibit 14.10 shows, the total compensation for sales personnel varies with the size of the company. For executive sales staff the total compensation varies by as much as 50 percent; for normal sales staff, by as much as 44 percent.

Economic Environment   The economic environment also affects the way a compensation package is structured. In good economic climates with roaring sales, companies can afford to hire mid- and low-level sales personnel to capture the extra sales. In a recession environment, however, companies need to react to the decreasing level of sales by focusing more on the top-level performers and rewarding those that achieve high levels of sales despite the economic downturn. In the downturn of 2001 mid- and low-level performers' total compensation was down about 10 percent from the year before, while top performers increased their total compensation by an average of 9.3 percent. The difference in compensation is even greater when looking at the incentive part of total compensation. While base salaries rose for all levels of performance, incentive-based pay was up by 7.6 percent for top performers, but down by over 30 percent for mid- and low-level performers. About 30 percent of all managers reported a decrease in total head count, and only 34 percent reported an increase in head count.[53] For the economic recovery of 2003, 48 percent of managers expected an increase in sales force total compensation for that year, 2002, and less than 20 percent expected a decrease.[54]

[52]"Where Is Sales Compensation Heading in 2003?" *Workspan*, January 1, 2003.

[53]C. Galea, "2002 Salary Survey," *Sales and Marketing Management*, May 1, 2003.

[54]"Sales Pay Rising," *Sales and Marketing Management*, February 1, 2003.

EXHIBIT 14.10 **Sales Compensation Rises with Company Revenue**

Annual Revenue of Company	Total Compensation	
	Sales Executives	Sales Staff
Less than $1,000,000	$92,053	$69,081
$1,000,000–$9,999,999	103,759	70,289
$10,000,000–$49,999,999	124,611	75,868
$50,000,000–$249,999,999	127,597	82,289
$250,000,000–$999,999,999	138,903	85,169
$1 billion–$10 billion	142,839	95,240
More than $10 billion	138,490	99,897

Source: C. Galea, "2002 Salary Survey," *Sales and Marketing Management,* May 1, 2003.

Product to Be Sold The nature of the product or service to be sold may influence the design of a compensation system. For a product that, by its very technical nature, is difficult to understand, it will take time to fully develop an effective sales presentation. Such products are said to have high barriers to entry, meaning considerable training is needed to become effective in the field. Compensation in this situation usually includes a large base-pay component, thus minimizing the risk a sales representative will face and encouraging entry into the necessary training program. At the opposite extreme are products with lower barriers to entry, where the knowledge needed to make an effective sales presentation is relatively easy to acquire. These product lines are sold more often using a higher incentive component, thus paying more for actual sales than for taking the time to learn the necessary skills.

Products or services that sell themselves, where sales ability isn't as crucial, inspire different compensation packages than do opportunities where the salesperson is more prominent. Base compensation tends to be more important with easily sold products. Not surprisingly, incentives become more important when willingness to work hard may make the difference between success and failure. One recent study argues convincingly that setting sales targets or quotas is the most important, and most difficult, part of sales compensation. Several factors can help you determine whether your quotas are reasonable: (1) Can the sales force tell you explicitly how the quotas are set? (2) In periods when the company hits its performance target does 60 to 70 percent of the sales force hit quota? (3) Do high performers hit their target consistently? (4) Do low performers show improvement over time?[55]

Most jobs do not fit the ideal specifications for either of the two extremes represented by straight salary or straight commission plans. A combination plan is intended to capture the best of both these plans. A guaranteed straight salary can be linked to performance of nonsales functions such as customer service, while a commission for sales volume yields the incentive to sell. A plan combining these two features signals the intent of the organization to ensure that both types of activities occur in the organization.

[55]S. Sands, "Ineffective Quotas: The Hidden Threat to Sales Compensation Plans," *Compensation and Benefits Review,* March/April 2000, pp. 35–42.

Contingent Workers

Ninety percent of all U.S. employers hire contingent workers.[56] Let's define a contingent worker as anyone hired through a temporary-help agency, on an on-call basis, or as an independent contractor. Workers in the first two of these categories typically earn less than workers in traditional arrangements; those in the latter category earn more. For example, working through a temporary-help agency usually means low pay in administrative or day labor positions. In contrast, the wages for an independent contractor might be higher than those for a more permanently employed counterpart. Indeed, independent contractors often are people who have been downsized and then reemployed by the company. DuPont cut its work force by 47,000 during the 1990s. About 14,000 of these workers were subsequently hired as vendors or contractors.[57] Because the employment status of contingent workers is temporary and employee benefits are less or nonexistent, wages at times tend to compensate by being somewhat higher.

Why the move to contingent workers? Part of the answer may be cost savings. Employee benefit costs are about 50 percent less for contingent workers.[58] But sometimes wages are higher. The main reason for contingent workers may be the added flexibility such employment offers the employer. In today's fast-paced marketplace, lean and flexible are desirable characteristics, and contingent workers offer these options.

A major compensation challenge for contingent workers, as with all our special-group employees, is identifying ways to deal with equity problems. Contingent workers may work alongside permanent workers yet often receive lower wages and benefits for the same work. Employers deal with this potential source of inequity on two fronts, one traditional and one that challenges the very way we think about employment and careers. One company response is to view contingent workers as a pool of candidates for more permanent hiring status. High performers may be moved off contingent status and afforded more employment stability. Cummins Engine, for example, is famous for its hiring of top-performing contingent workers. The traditional reward of a possible "promotion," then, becomes a motivation to perform.

A second way to look at contingent workers is to champion the idea of boundaryless careers.[59] At least for high-skilled contingent workers, it is increasingly popular to view careers as a series of opportunities to acquire valuable increments in knowledge and skills. In this framework, contingent status isn't a penalty or cause of dissatisfaction. Rather, employees who accept the idea of boundaryless careers may view contingent status as part of a fast-track developmental sequence. Lower wages are offset by opportunities for rapid development of skills—opportunities that might not be so readily available in more traditional employment arrangements. Companies like General Electric that promote this reward—enhanced employability status through acquisition of highly demanded skills—may actually have tapped an underutilized reward dimension.

[56]P. Allan, "The Contingent Workforce: Challenges and New Directions," *American Business Review,* 20(2) (2002), pp. 103–110.

[57]Kim Clark, "Manufacturing's Hidden Asset: Temp Workers," *Fortune,* November 10, 1997, pp. 28–29.

[58]Ibid.

[59]Janet H. Marler, George T. Milkovich, and Melissa Barringer, "Boundaryless Organizations and Boundaryless Careers: A New Market for High Skilled Temporary Work," unpublished paper submitted to 1998 Academy of Management annual conference, Human Resource Division.

Your Turn

Compensation of Special Groups

You are the CEO of a 110-person consulting firm, Sierra Avo, that does high-level aeronautical engineering work for Boeing. You have 15 aeronautical engineers hired from the very best schools throughout the country. The problem is, six months ago you had 19 such engineers. Four have left recently, and rumors have it that some of the others are disgruntled. Exhibit 1 lists characteristics of the four engineers who left. The salaries of the remaining 15, and some other data you might find useful, are shown in Exhibit 2.

1. Do you see anything in the data that might explain why workers are leaving. Justify your arguments based on the reasoning given in the chapter for changes in scientist/engineer salaries. Do your arguments fit for Lance Welch also? If not, is there anything about current economic conditions that might explain his salary? Would you be surprised to hear he left for another job offer? Why?

2. Now that you've explained why people are leaving, should you change salaries to reduce the turnover? What are the economic arguments for not increasing wages?

3. Assume your company has created a two-track career path for engineers. On one path, senior engineers serve as managers who also specialize in client relations. How might this change the nature of your argument about wages?

EXHIBIT 1
Workers Who Left

Name	Degree	Years since Degree Received	Annual Salary	Performance Rating
Sam Lansing	B.S.	11	$61,000	Good
Naresh Rao	M.S.	10	$69,300	Excellent
Lance Welch	B.S.	1	$37,000	New (no rating)
Kim Lee	Ph.D	10	$87,238	Good

EXHIBIT 2
Workers
Who Remain

Employee	Highest Relevant Degree Received	Years since Degree Received	Annual Salary
1	B.S.	3	$ 39,000
2	M.S.	6	$ 58,800
3	M.S.	3	$ 50,400
4	Ph.D.	7	$ 95,900
5	B.S.	6	$ 48,000
6	Ph.D.	9	$ 105,300
7	M.S.	4	$ 53,200
8	Ph.D.	3	$ 77,100
9	B.S.	7	$ 51,000
10	Ph.D.	6	$ 91,200
11	M.S.	9	$ 67,200
12	M.S.	7	$ 61,600
13	Ph.D.	4	$ 81,800
14	B.S.	9	$ 57,000
15	B.S.	4	$ 42,000

Summary

Special groups are portrayed here as sharing two common characteristics: They all have jobs with high potential for conflict, and resolution of this conflict is central to the goals of the organization. Probably because of these characteristics, special groups receive compensation treatment that differs from the approach for other employees. Unfortunately, most of this compensation differentiation is prescriptive in nature, and little is known about the specific roles assumed by special groups and the functions compensation should assume in motivating appropriate performance. Future practice and research should focus on answering these questions.

Review Questions

1. What are the sources of monetary savings from hiring contingent workers? What equity problems can arise from hiring contingent workers, especially when they work alongside regular employees.

2. In recent years the newspapers have been full of stories about the excessive pay to CEOs. Assume you are a CEO trained in economics (you went to a good school, like SUNY Buffalo or Cornell). What arguments might you give in support of your compensation? Would LeBron James (number-one draft pick in the NBA for 2003) agree with these arguments?

3. From question 2, what might be the counterarguments from a critic of CEO compensation? (Be sure to include performance arguments and both internal and external equity arguments.)

4. Would you expect computer programmers to be treated as special groups (in the way defined in this chapter) in a company like Microsoft? If so, what special compensation practices might you expect for these programmers? Why?

5. A board of directors meets perhaps 12 times a year for a day (usually). How can we possibly justify to stockholders paying this group tens of thousands of dollars for this brief time period?

Chapter Fifteen

Union Role in Wage and Salary Administration

Chapter Outline

The Impact of Unions in Wage Determination

Union Impact on General Wage Levels

The Structure of Wage Packages

Union Impact: The Spillover Effect

Role of Unions in Wage and Salary Policies and Practices

Unions and Alternative Reward Systems

Lump-Sum Awards

Employee Stock Ownership Plans (ESOPs)

Pay-for-Knowledge Plans

Gain-Sharing Plans

Profit-Sharing Plans

Your Turn: General Technology

Many experts believe that unions are facing their most critical challenge of the last 50 years.[1] Between 1954 and 1987 union membership fell 50 percent.[2] The number of certification elections attempting to unionize a firm fell two-thirds, from a high of 8,799 in 1973 to about 3,000 in the late '90s. The win rate in these elections was almost 75 percent in the 1950s but has stabilized at less than 50 percent today (48 percent).[3] Today collective bargaining, except in the public sector, is not a major force. While 37 percent of firms in the public sector are unionized, the figure is only 8.5 percent in the private sector, and most of this concentration is in declining industries such as manufacturing.[4]

One popular explanation for this decline is that management is taking an increasingly hard stance against unions in general and union demands in particular.[5] A large portion of

[1]Jack Fiorito, "Human Resource Management Practices and Worker Desires for Union Representation," *Journal of Labor Research,* 22(2) (Spring 2001) pp. 335–354; Thomas A. Kochan, Harry C. Katz, and Robert B. McKersie, *The Transformation of American Industrial Relations* (New York: Basic Books, 1986), pp. 221–223.

[2]Kirkland Ropp, "State of the Unions," *Personnel Administrator* 32(7) (1987), pp. 36–41.

[3]Henry S. Farber, "Union Success in Representation Elections: Why Does Unit Size Matter?" *Industrial and Labor Relations Review* 54(2) (2001), pp. 329–348.

[4]Bureau of Labor Statistics, "Union Members in 2002,". *stats.bls.gov/news.release/union2.nr0.htm,* retrieved March 22, 2003; public sector union data come from *www.unionstats.com,* visited April 2, 2003.

[5]Gail McCallion, "Union Membership Decline: Competing Theories and Economic Implications," CRS report for Congress, August 23, 1993, p. 13.

this management opposition to unions is spurred by increasing pressure from both domestic and international competitors. Management more frequently resists wage increases that would give nonunion competitors, both domestic and foreign, a competitive price advantage. The end result of these competitive pressures is a declining union-nonunion wage differential. In fact, one study shows that a 10 percent rise in import share (a popular measure of international competition) has the effect of lowering the union wage differential (the difference between union and nonunion wages) by approximately 2 percent.[6]

Such competitive pressures, starting in the 1980s and continuing today, have triggered lower-than-normal wage increases in unionized firms and even some wage concessions. Although the statistics indicate a decline in unionism, some of the issues that are important cornerstones of unionization continue to be important for workers. Fully 63 percent of employees say they want to have more influence in workday decisions. If need be, 40 percent of workers would vote union to achieve their needs. When workplace relations are bad, when management is not trustworthy, when workers feel they have little influence over decisions affecting them, the workers show strong interest in joining a union. You want to invite a unionization effort? Show little concern for employees' welfare and be unwilling to share power—over 70 percent of workers who see management acting this way claim they would vote for a union.[7] This percentage supporting unionization is comparable to a figure reported 15 years earlier in a similar survey, and it suggests antiunion support may have bottomed out.[8]

THE IMPACT OF UNIONS IN WAGE DETERMINATION

Despite strong management efforts to lessen the impact of unions, they still assume an important role in wage determination. Even in a nonunion firm, the protective actions taken by compensation managers are influenced by external union activity. This section outlines four specific areas of union impact: (1) impact on general wage and benefit levels, (2) impact on the structure of wages, (3) impact on nonunion firms (also known as *spillover*), and (4) impact on wage and salary policies and practices in unionized firms. The chapter's concluding section focuses on union response to the changing economic environment of the 1980s and the alternative compensation systems that have evolved in response to these changes.

Cybercomp
These sites give detailed information about dozens of unions, including specifics of union contracts:

www.calstate.edu/LaborRel/contracts_html/contracts.shtml
atyourservice.ucop.edu/employees/policies/local_contracts/
www.iir.berkeley.edu/library/contracts/ (choose union or state)

[6]David A. Macpherson and James B. Steward, "The Effect of International Competition on Union and Non-Union Wages," *Industrial and Labor Relations* Review 43(4) (1990), pp. 434–446.
[7]Richard B. Freeman and Joel Rogers, *What Workers Want* (Ithaca, NY: ILR Press, 1999).
[8]R. Wayne Mondy and Shane Preameaux, "The Labor Management Power Relationship Revised," *Personnel Administrator,* May 1985, pp. 51–54.

Union Impact on General Wage Levels

Do unions raise wages? Are unionized employees better off than they would be if they were nonunion? Unfortunately, comparing what is to what might have been is no easy chore. Several measurement problems are difficult to overcome. The ideal situation would compare numerous organizations that were identical except for the presence or absence of a union.[9] Any wage differences among these organizations could then be attributed to unionization (a union wage premium). Unfortunately, few such situations exist. One alternative strategy that has been adopted is to identify organizations within the same industry that differ in level of unionization. For example, consider company A, which is unionized, and company B, which is not. Although they are in the same industry, it is still difficult to argue with assurance that wage differences between the two firms are attributable to the presence or absence of a union. First, the fact that the union has not organized the entire industry weakens its power base (strike efforts to shut down the entire industry could be thwarted by nonunion firms). Consequently, any union impact in this example might underestimate the role of unions in an industry where the percentage of unionization is greater. A second problem in measuring union impact is apparent from this example. What if company B grants concessions to employees as a strategy to avoid unionization? These concessions, indirectly attributable to the presence of a union, would lead to underestimation of union impact on wages.

Another strategy in estimating union impact on wages is to compare two different industries that vary dramatically in the level of unionization.[10] This strategy suffers because nonunionized industries (e.g., agriculture, service) are markedly different from unionized industries in the types of labor employed and their general availability. Such differences have a major impact on wages independent of the level of unionization and make any statements about union impact difficult to substantiate.

One source of continuing data on unionized and nonunionized firms is the Bureau of Labor Statistics. Between 1969 and 1985 the union wage premium more than doubled, from 17.6 to 35.6 percent.[11] In 2002 workers represented by unions had median weekly earnings of $740 compared to nonunion wages of $587, a 26 percent difference (32 percent difference in 1999).[12] Historically, union wages have experienced multiple-year upswings followed by multiple-year downswings. The 1950s were characterized by a widening of the union wage premium, followed by a constriction in the 1960s, an enlargement from 1969 to 1983, and in general a constriction from 1983 into the new millennium.[13] Since 1983, the nonunion sector has been securing larger wage increases than

[9]Allan M. Carter and F. Ray Marshall, *Labor Economics* (Homewood, IL: Irwin, 1982).

[10]Ibid.

[11]Michael L. Wachter and William H. Carter, "Norm Shifts in Union Wages: Will 1989 Be a Replay of 1969?" in *Brookings Papers on Economic Activity,* eds. William C. Brainard and George L. Perry (Washington DC: Brookings Institution, 1989), pp. 233–276.

[12]Bureau of Labor Statistics, "Union Members in 2002," *stats.bls.gov/news.release/union2.nr0.htm,* retrieved March 22, 2003.

[13]Bernt Pratsberg and James Ragan, Jr., "Changes in the Union Wage Premium by Industry," *Industrial and Labor Relations Review* 56(1) (2002), pp. 65–83; Wachter and Carter, "Norm Shifts in Union Wages: Will 1989 Be a Replay of 1969?"

the unionized sector, partially due to unions' acceptance of lump-sum payments in lieu of increases in base wage.[14] Of course, these differentials differ by industry. Some of the traditional union strongholds, such as construction (31.6 percent) and trucking (27.5 percent), enjoy much larger union-nonunion differentials than do less unionized segments such as services (13.3 percent) and utilities (11.8 percent).[15]

Perhaps the best conclusion about union versus nonunion wage differences comes from a summary analysis of 114 different studies.[16] Two important points emerged:

1. *Unions do make a difference in wages.* Union workers earn between 8.9 and 12.4 percent more than their nonunion counterparts.

2. *The size of the gap varies from year to year.* During periods of higher unemployment, the impact of unions is larger. During strong economies the union-nonunion gap is smaller. Part of the explanation for this time-based phenomenon is related to union resistance to wage cuts during recessions and the relatively slow response of unions to wage increases during inflationary periods (because of rigidities or lags introduced by the presence of multiyear labor contracts).

> **Cybercomp**
> These sites provide union employment and wage information:
>
> *www.unionstats.com*
> *http://stats.bls.gov/news.release/union2.nr0.htm*

Similar studies of union-nonunion wage differentials exist for employees in the public sector.[17] Union employees in the public sector earn, on average, about 16 to 19 percent more than their nonunion counterparts.[18] However, historically, this range masks some large variations in wage increases for different occupational groups in the public sector. The largest gains for public sector employees are reported for firefighters, with some studies reporting as much as an 18 percent wage differential attributable to the presence of a union. At the other extreme, however, teachers' unions (primarily affiliates of the National Education Association and the American Federation of Teachers) have not fared as well, with reported impacts generally in the range of 1 to 4 percent.[19]

In recent years, with low unemployment and reports of record profits, little mention is made of one old union nemesis: wage concessions, or wage cuts. Some experts claim that

---

[14]Fehmida Sleemi, "Collective Bargaining Outlook for 1995," *Compensation and Working Conditions* 47(1) (January 1995), pp. 19–39.

[15]Pratsberg and Ragan, "Changes in the Union Wage Premium by Industry."

[16]Stephen B. Jarrell and T. D. Stanley, "A Meta Analysis of the Union–Non-Union Wage Gap," *Industrial and Labor Relations Review* 44(1) (1990), pp. 54–67.

[17]David Lewin, "Public Sector Labor Relations: A Review Essay," in *Public Sector Labor Relations: Analysis and Readings,* eds. David Lewin, Peter Feuille, and Thomas Kochan (Glen Ridge, NJ: Thomas Horton and Daughters, 1977), pp. 116–144.

[18]Bureau of Labor Statistics, "Union Members in 2002," Table 4: Median weekly earnings of full time wage and salary workers by union affiliation, occupation, and industry," *stats.bls.gov/news .release/union2.t04.htm,* retrieved march 22, 2003.

[19]For a discussion on the reasons for this smaller public sector union impact, see Lewin et al., *Public Sector Labor Relations: Analysis and Readings.*

wage concessions are more prevalent in unionized firms and that this reduces the advantage union workers hold in wages, particularly during downturns in the economy. For example, in 1908 the glass-bottle blowers accepted a 20 percent wage cut in the hopes of fighting automation. During the 1930s concessions were a regular feature in the construction, printing, and shoe industries. Concessions were also made in the apparel and textile industries during the 1950s. Continuing today, terrorism has deeply affected wages in several industries, most notably the airline industry. Mechanics for American Airlines recently announced wage concessions of 17.5 percent to help keep troubled AMR, the parent company, afloat.[20] Similar concessions are expected from other unions to help United and Northwestern Airlines escape from post-9/11 woes.[21] Recent research suggests that concessions aren't solely, or even primarily, a tool used in unionized firms. Concessions are most likely in small firms, in high-wage-paying firms, and in firms where only a small portion of the work force is unionized.[22]

The Structure of Wage Packages

The second compensation issue involves the structuring of wage packages. One dimension of this issue concerns the division between direct wages and employee benefits. Research indicates that the presence of a union adds about 20 to 30 percent to employee benefits.[23] Whether because of reduced management control, strong union-worker preference for benefits, or other reasons, unionized employees also have a greater percentage of their total wage bill allocated to employee benefits. The most recent statistics show that benefits accounted for 34.4 percent of the total compensation package for union workers and 26.2 percent for nonunion employees.[24] Typically the higher costs show up in the form of higher pension expenditures or higher insurance benefits.[25] One particularly well controlled study found unionization associated with a 217 percent higher level of pension expenditures and 127 percent higher insurance expenditures.[26]

A second dimension of the wage structure issue is the evolution of two-tier pay plans. Basically a phenomenon of the union sector, two-tier wage structures differentiate pay based upon hiring date. A contract is negotiated which specifies that employees hired after a given target date will receive lower wages than their higher-seniority peers working on the same or similar jobs. From management's perspective, wage tiers represent a

---

[20]See website of the Transportation Workers Union, *www.twu.com/,* visited on March 31, 2003; Robert Gay, "Union Contract Concessions and Their Implications for Union Wage Determination," Working Paper 38, Division of Research and Statistics, Board of Governors of the Federal Reserve System, 1984.

[21]S. Carey, "UAL Flight Attendants Approve Pact," *Wall Street Journal,* April 30, 2003, p. A2.

[22]Linda A. Bell, "Union Wage Concessions in the 1980s: The Importance of Firm-Specific Factors," *Industrial and Labor Relations Review* 48(2) (January 1995) pp. 258–275.

[23]Bureau of Labor Statistics, "Employer Costs for Employee Compensation Summary," Table 7: Private industry, by region and bargaining status," *stats.bls.gov/news.release/ecec.nr0.htm,* retrieved March 28, 2003; Richard Freeman and James Medoff, *What Do Unions Do?* (New York: Basic Books, 1981).

[24]Bureau of Labor Statistics, "Employer Costs for Employee Compensation Summary," Table 7: Private industry, by region and bargaining status," *stats.bls.gov/news.release/ecec.nr0.htm,* retrieved March 28, 2003.

[25]Bureau of Labor Statistics, "Employer Costs for Employee Compensation Summary," Table 7: Private industry, by region and bargaining status," *stats.bls.gov/news.release/ecec.nr0.htm,* retrieved March 28, 2003.

[26]Loren Solnick, "Unionism and Fringe Benefits Expenditures," *Industrial Relations* 17(1) (1978), pp. 102–107.

viable alternative compensation strategy. Tiers can be used as a cost control strategy to allow expansion or investment or as a cost-cutting device to allow economic survival.[27] Two-tier pay plans initially spread because unions viewed them as less painful than wage freezes and staff cuts among existing employees. The tradeoff, however, bargained away equivalent wage treatment for future employees. Remember, this is a radical departure from the most basic precepts of unionization. Unions evolved and continue to endure, in part based on the belief that all members are equal. Two-tier plans are obviously at odds with this principle. Lower-tier employees, those hired after the contract is ratified, receive wages 50 to 80 percent lower than employees in the higher tier.[28] The contract may specify that the wage differential may be permanent, or the lower tier may be scheduled ultimately to catch up with the upper tier. Eventually the inequity from receiving different pay for the same level may cause employee dissatisfaction.[29] Consider the Roman emperor who implemented a two-tier system for his army in A.D. 217.[30] He was assassinated by his disgruntled troops shortly thereafter. Although such expressions of dissatisfaction are unlikely today, unions are much more reluctant to accept a two-tier structure and may view it as a strategy of last resort.[31]

A third dimension of the wage structure issue involves the relationship between worker wages and what their managers are paid in union and nonunion environments. Recent evidence suggests that the gap between these two groups is 23 percent smaller in unionized firms.[32] Interestingly this narrowing doesn't occur at the expense of lower or even constant wages for managers combined with higher union wages. Rather, managers in union firms receive higher wages than nonunion managers, perhaps as a bid to maintain internal equity. Apparently then, the narrowing of the gap arises because worker wages go up faster than manager wages in unionized firms.[33]

Union Impact: The Spillover Effect

Although union wage settlements have declined in recent years, the impact of unions in general would be understated if we did not account for what is termed the *spillover effect.* Specifically, employers seek to avoid unionization by offering workers the wages, benefits, and working conditions won in rival unionized firms. The nonunion management continues to enjoy the freedom from union "interference" in decision making, and the

---

[27]James E. Martin and Thomas D. Heetderks, *Two Tier Compensation Structures: Their Impact on Unions, Employers and Employees* (Kalamazoo, MI: Upjohn Institute for Employment Research, 1990).

[28]Mollie Bowers and Roger Roderick, "Two-Tier Pay Systems: The Good, the Bad, and the Debatable," *Personnel Administrator* 32(6) (1987), pp. 101–112.

[29]James Martin and Melanie Peterson, "Two-Tier Wage Structures: Implications for Equity Theory," *Academy of Management Journal* 30(2) (1987), pp. 297–315.

[30]"Two-Tier Systems Falter as Companies Sense Workers' Resentment," *Wall Street Journal,* June 16, 1987, p. 1.

[31]Fehmida Sleemi, "Collective Bargaining Outlook for 1995," *Compensation and Working Conditions* 47(1) (January 1995), pp. 19–39.

[32]Alexander J. Colvin, Rosemary Batt, and Harry Katz, "How High Performance Human Resource Practices and Workforce Unionization Affect Managerial Pay," *Personnel Psychology* 54(4) (2001), pp. 903–927.

[33]Ibid.

workers receive the spillover of rewards already obtained by their unionized counterparts. Several studies document the existence, although smaller as union power diminishes, of this phenomenon, providing further evidence of the continuing role played by unions in wage determination.[34]

Role of Unions in Wage and Salary Policies and Practices

Perhaps of greatest interest to current and future compensation administrators is the role unions play in administering wages. The role of unions in administering compensation is outlined primarily in the contract. The following illustrations of this role are taken from major collective bargaining agreements.

Basis of Pay

The vast majority of contracts specify that one or more jobs are to be compensated on an hourly basis and that overtime pay will be paid beyond a certain number of hours. Notice the specificity of the language in the following contract clause:

A. Overtime pay is to be paid at the rate of one and one-half (1 1/2) times the basic hourly straight-time rate.

B. Overtime shall be paid to employees for work performed only after eight (8) hours on duty in any one service day or forty (40) hours in any one service week. Nothing in this Section shall be construed by the parties or any reviewing authority to deny the payment of overtime to employees for time worked outside of their regularly scheduled work week at the request of the Employer.

C. Penalty overtime pay is to be paid at the rate of two (2) times the basic hourly straight-time rate. Penalty overtime pay will not be paid for any hours worked in the month of December.

D. Excluding December, part-time flexible employees will receive penalty overtime pay for all work in excess of ten (10) hours in a service day or fifty-six (56) hours in a service week.
   (Bargaining agreement between American Postal Workers Union, AFL-CIO, and U.S. Postal Service, original contract expired 11/2003, extended to 11/2005)

Further, many contracts specify a premium be paid above the worker's base wage for working nonstandard shifts:

Employees regularly employed on the second or third shift shall receive in addition to their regular pay for the pay period five (5) percent and ten (10) percent, respectively, additional compensation. (DaimlerChrysler and Auto Workers, 2003)

Alternatively, agreements may specify a fixed daily, weekly, biweekly, or monthly rate. In addition, agreements often indicate a specific day of the week as payday and sometimes require payment on or before a certain hour.

---

[34]Richard B. Freeman and Joel Rogers, *What Workers Want* (Ithaca, NY: ILR Press, 1999); David Neumark and Michael L. Wachter, "Union Effects on Nonunion Wages: Evidence from Panel Data on Industries and Cities," *Industrial and Labor Relations Review* 31(1) (1978), pp. 205–216.

Much less frequently, contracts specify some form of incentive system as the basis for pay. The vast majority of clauses specifying incentive pay occur in manufacturing (as opposed to nonmanufacturing) industries:

Section 7. Establishment of Labor Standards. The Company and the Union, being firmly committed to the principle that high wages can result only from high productivity, agree that the Company will establish Labor Standards that:

(a) Are fair and equitable to both the Company and the workers; and
(b) Are based on the working capacity of a normally qualified worker properly motivated and working at an incentive pace; and
(c) Give due consideration to the quality of workmanship and product required; and
(d) Provide proper allowances for fatigue, personal time, and normal delays, and
(e) Provide for payment of incentive workers based on the earned hours produced on-standard (except when such Employees are working on a Preliminary Estimate, etc.), and for each one per cent (1%) increase in acceptable production over standard, such workers shall receive a one per cent (1%) increase in pay over the applicable incentive rate.

The Company will, at its discretion as to the time and as to jobs to be placed on or removed from incentive, continue the earned-hour incentive system now in effect, and extend it to jobs in such other job classifications which, in the opinion of the Company, can properly be placed on incentive, with the objective of increasing productivity and providing an opportunity for workers to enjoy higher earnings thus made possible. The plan shall be maintained in accordance with the following principles.

(Maytag, Maytag and Admiral Products, and Auto Workers, 2001)

Occupation-Wage Differentials

Most contracts recognize that different occupations should receive different wage rates. Within occupations, though, a single wage rate prevails:

Occupation	Hourly Wage
Clerk typists	$ 7.30
Computer operators	10.05
Maintenance mechanics	12.30

Source: Negotiated agreement between District School Board of St. Johns County and St. Johns School Support Association, 2005.

Although rare, there are some contracts that do not recognize occupational/skill differentials. These contracts specify a single standard rate for all jobs covered by the agreements. Usually such contracts cover a narrow range of skilled groups.

Experience/Merit Differentials

Single rates are usually specified for workers within a particular job classification. Single-rate agreements do not differentiate wages on the basis of either seniority or merit. Workers with varying years of experience and output receive the same single rate. Alternatively, agreements may specify wage ranges. The following example is fairly typical:

Job Title	Years of Experience							
	None	**1**	**2**	**3**	**4**	**6**	**8**	**12**
Computer operators	$10.05	$10.30	$10.55	$10.80	$11.05	$11.55	$12.30	$14.05
QC inspector	12.30	12.55	12.80	13.05	13.30	13.80	14.30	16.30

Source: Negotiated agreement between District School Board of St. Johns County and St. Johns School Support Association, 2005.

The vast majority of contracts, as in the example above, specify seniority as the basis for movement through the range. *Automatic progression* is an appropriate name for this type of movement through the wage range, with the contract frequently specifying the time interval between movements. This type of progression is most appropriate when the necessary job skills are within the grasp of most employees. Denial of a raise is rare and frequently is accompanied by the right of the union to submit any wage denial to the grievance procedure.

A second strategy for moving employees through wage ranges is based exclusively on merit. Employees who are evaluated more highly receive larger or more rapid increments than average or poor performers. Within these contracts, it is common to specify that disputed merit appraisals may be submitted to grievance. If the right to grieve is not explicitly excluded, the union also has the implicit right to grieve.

The third method for movement through a range combines automatic and merit progression in some manner. A frequent strategy is to grant automatic increases up to the midpoint of the range and permit subsequent increases only when merited on the basis of performance appraisal.

Other Differentials

There are a number of remaining contractual provisions that deal with differentials for reasons not yet covered. A first example deals with different pay to unionized employees who are employed by a firm in different geographic areas. Very few contracts provide for different wages under these circumstances, despite the problems that can arise in paying uniform wages across regions with markedly different costs of living.

A second category where differentials are mentioned in contracts deals with part-time and temporary employees. Few contracts specify special rates for these employees. Those that do, however, are about equally split between giving part-time and temporary employees wages above full-time workers (because they have been excluded from the employee benefit program) or below full-time workers.

Vacations and Holidays

Vacation and holiday entitlements are among the clauses frequently found in labor contracts. They, too, use very specific language, as the following example illustrates:

26.01 Observance

The following holidays will be observed:
New Year's Day—First Day in January;
Martin Luther King, Jr.'s Birthday—Third Monday in January;
President's Day—Third Monday in February;
Memorial Day—Last Monday in May;
Independence Day—Fourth day of July;
Labor Day—First Monday in September;
Columbus Day—Second Monday in October;
Veterans' Day—Eleventh day of November;
Thanksgiving Day—Fourth Thursday in November;
Christmas Day—Twenty-fifth day of December;
Any other day proclaimed by the Governor of the State of Ohio or the President of the United States.

When a holiday falls on a Sunday, the holiday is observed on the following Monday. When a holiday falls on a Saturday, the holiday is observed on the preceding Friday. For employees whose work assignment is to a seven (7) day operation, the holiday shall be celebrated on the day it actually falls. A holiday shall start at 12:01 A.M. or with the work shift that includes 12:01 A.M.

26.02-Work on Holidays

Employees required to work on a holiday will be compensated at their discretion either at the rate of one and one-half (1½) times their regular rate of pay, or granted compensatory time at the rate of one and one-half (1½) times, plus straight time pay for the holiday. The choice of compensatory time or wages will be made by the employee.

(State of Ohio and Ohio Civil Service Employees Association (OCSEA) collective bargaining agreement, 2003)

Wage Adjustment Provisions

Frequently in multiyear contracts some provision is made for wage adjustment during the term of the contract. There are three major ways these adjustments might be specified: (1) deferred wage increases, (2) reopener clauses, and (3) cost-of-living adjustments (COLAs) or escalator clauses. A *deferred wage increase* is negotiated at the time of initial contract negotiations with the timing and amount specified in the contract. A *reopener clause* specifies that wages, and sometimes such nonwage items as pension and benefits, will be renegotiated at a specified time or under certain conditions. Finally, a *COLA clause,* as noted earlier, involves periodic adjustments based typically on changes in the consumer price index:

Section 4. Cost of Living Adjustment

A. Definitions

1. "Consumer Price Index" refers to the "National Consumer Price Index for Urban Wage Earners and Clerical Workers," published by the Bureau of Labor (1967 = 100) and referred to herein as the "Index."
2. "Consumer Price Index Base" refers to the Consumer Price Index for the month of October 2001 and is referred to herein as the "Base Index."

B.   Effective Dates of Adjustment
     Each employee covered by this Agreement shall receive cost-of-living adjustments, upward, in accordance with the formula in Section 4.C, below, effective on the following dates:
     —the second full pay period after the release of the January 2002 Index
     —the second full pay period after the release of the July 2002 Index
     —the second full pay period after the release of the January 2003 Index
     —the second full pay period after the release of the July 2003 Index

C.   The basic salary schedules provided for in this Agreement shall be increased 1 cent per hour for each full 0.4 of a point increase in the applicable Index above the Base Index. For example, if the increase in the Index from October 2001 to January 2002 is 1.2 points, all pay scales for employees covered by this Agreement will be increased by 3 cents per hour. In no event will a decline in the Index below the Base Index result in a decrease in the pay scales provided for in this Agreement.

(Bargaining agreement between American Postal Workers Union, AFL-CIO, and U.S. Postal Service, original contract expired 11/2003, extended to 11/2005)

UNIONS AND ALTERNATIVE REWARD SYSTEMS

International competition causes a fundamental problem for unions. If a unionized company settles a contract and raises prices to cover increased wage costs, there is always the threat that an overseas competitor with lower labor costs will capture market share. Eventually, enough market share means the unionized company is out of business. To keep this from happening, unions have become much more receptive in recent years to alternative reward systems that link pay to performance. After all, if worker productivity rises, product prices can remain relatively stable even with wage increases.

About 20 percent of all U.S. collective bargaining agreements permit some alternative reward system (e.g., lump sum, piece rate, gain sharing, profit sharing, skill-based pay).[35] Willingness to try such plans is higher when the firm faces extreme competitive pressure.[36] In the unionized firms that do experiment with these alternative reward systems, though, the union usually insists on safeguards that protect both the union and its workers. The union insists on group-based performance measures with equal payouts to members. This equality principle cuts down strife and internal quarrels among the members and reinforces the principles of equity that are at the very foundation of union beliefs. To minimize bias by the company, performance measures tend more often in unionized companies to be objective. Most frequently the measures rely on past performance as a gauge of realistic targets rather than on some time study or other engineering standard that might appear more susceptible to tampering.[37] Below we offer specific feedback about union attitudes toward alternative reward concepts.

[35]J. L. McAdams and E. J. Hawk, *Organizational Performance and Reward: 663 Experiences in Making the Link* (Scottsdale, AZ: American Compensation Association, 1994).

[36]L. B. Cardinal and I. B. Helbrun, "Union versus Nonunion Attitudes Toward Share Agreements," in *Proceedings of the 39th Annual Meeting of the Industrial Relations Research Association* (Madison, WI: IRRA, 1987), pp. 167–173.

[37]R. L. Heneman, C. von Hippel, D. E. Eskew, and D. B. Greenberger, "Alternative Rewards in Union Environments," *ACA Journal,* Summer 1997, pp. 42–55.

Lump-Sum Awards

As discussed in Chapter 10, lump-sum awards are one-time cash payments to employees that are not added to an employee's base wages. These awards are typically given in lieu of merit increases, which are more costly to the employer. This higher cost results both because merit increases are added on to base wages and because several employee benefits (e.g., life insurance and vacation pay) are figured as a percentage of base wages. Lump-sum payments are a reality of union contracts. For the past 10 years, a stable one-third of all major collective bargaining agreements in the private sector have contained a provision for lump-sum payouts.[38]

Employee Stock Ownership Plans (ESOPs)

An alternative strategy for organizations hurt by intense competition is to control base wages in exchange for giving employees part ownership in the company. For example, Southwest Airlines readily grants employee stock options as a key feature of its wage control strategy.[39]

Pay-for-Knowledge Plans

Pay-for-knowledge plans do just that: pay employees more for learning a variety of different jobs or skills. For example, the UAW negotiates provisions giving hourly-wage increases for learning new skills on different parts of the assembly process. By coupling this new wage system with drastic cuts in the number of job classifications, organizations have greater flexibility in moving employees quickly into high-demand areas. Unions also may favor pay-for-knowledge plans because they make each individual worker more valuable, and less expendable, to the firm. In turn, this also lessens the probability that work can be subcontracted out to nonunion organizations.

Gain-Sharing Plans

Gain-sharing plans are designed to align workers and management in efforts to streamline operations and cut costs. Any cost savings resulting from employees' working more efficiently are split, according to some formula, between the organization and the workers. Some reports indicate gain sharing is more common in unionized than nonunionized firms.[40] In our experience success is dependent on a willingness to include union members in designing the plan. Openness in sharing financial and production data, key elements of putting a gain-sharing plan in place, are important in building trust between the two parties.

While unions aren't always enthusiastic about gain sharing, they rarely directly oppose it, at least initially. Rather, the most common union strategy is to delay taking a stand until real costs and benefits are more apparent.[41] Politically, this may be the wisest choice

[38]Sleemi, "Collective Bargaining Outlook for 1995."

[39]"Southwest Air, Agents' Union Reach an Accord," *Wall Street Journal,* December 26, 2002.

[40]Heneman et al., "Alternative Rewards in Unionized Environments."

[41]T. Ross and R. Ross, "Gainsharing and Unions: Current Trends," in *Gainsharing: Plans for Improving Performance,* eds. B. Graham-Moore and T. Ross (Washington, DC: Bureau of National Affairs), pp. 200–213.

EXHIBIT 15.1   Union Perceptions of Gain Sharing

Advantages (% Agreement)	Disadvantages (% Agreement)
1. Increased recognition (95)	1. Management may try to substitute for wage increases (94)
2. Better job security (94)	2. Management can't be trusted (88)
3. More involvement in job activities (94)	3. Peer pressure to perform may increase (77)
4. More money (94)	4. Don't trust/understand bonus calculations (76)
5. More feeling of contributing to firm (86)	5. Union influence is undermined (66)
6. Increased influence of union (70)	6. Increased productivity may reduce need for jobs (64)

Source: T. Ross and R. Ross, "Gainsharing and Unions: Current Trends," in *Gainsharing: Plans for Improving Performance,* ed. B. Graham-Moore and T. Ross (Washington, DC: Bureau of National Affairs, 1990).

for a union leader. As Exhibit 15.1 illustrates, there are numerous possible costs and benefits to union members for agreeing to a gain-sharing plan. Until the plan is actually implemented, though, it is unclear what the impact will be in any particular firm.

Profit-Sharing Plans

Unions have debated the advantages of profit-sharing plans for at least 80 years.[42] Walter Reuther, president of the CIO in 1948 (which became the AFL-CIO in 1955) championed the cause of profit sharing in the auto industry. The goal of unions is to secure sound, stable income levels for the membership. When this is achieved, subsequent introduction of a profit-sharing plan allows union members to share the wealth with more profitable firms while still maintaining employment levels in marginal organizations. Introduction of a profit-sharing plan is particularly effective when union members participate in plan development.[43] We should note, though, that not all unions favor profit-sharing plans. As indicated by recent grumblings of employees at General Motors, inequality in profits among firms in the same industry can lead to wage differentials for workers performing the same work. Ford regularly distributes profit-sharing checks several times larger than what the employees at GM receive. Most General Motors employees would argue that the difference in payout cannot be traced to the fact that Ford employees work harder or smarter. In fact, the difference in profitability, the UAW argues, is due to management decision making. Therefore, the argument runs, workers should not be penalized for factors beyond their control.

[42]J. Zalusky, "Labor's Collective Bargaining Experience with Gainsharing and Profit Sharing," paper presented at the 39th Annual Meeting, December 1986, pp. 175–182; William Shaw, "Can Labor Be Capitalized?" *American Federationist* 17 (June 1910), p. 517.

[43]Dong-One Kim, "Determinants of the Survival of Gainsharing Programs," *Industrial and Labor Relations Review* 53(1) (1999), pp. 21–42

Your Turn

General Technology

THE COMPANY

General Technology (GT) is a producer of burglar alarm systems. To crack the international market, GT must comply with quality standards as set by the International Organization for Standardization (ISO). Compliance requires that all products and processes pass a series of 17 strict criteria, the so-called ISO 9000 audit.

THE UNION

The Technology Workers of America (TWA) organized GT's Buffalo division in 1979. In the last contract both parties agreed to have a three-person panel listen to all disputes between union and management concerning the proper classification of jobs.

YOUR ROLE

You are the neutral third party hired to hear the dispute described below. The union representative has voted in the union's favor, and the management rep has sided with management's position. You will break the tie. How do you vote and why? Some experts would argue that not enough evidence is presented here for you to make a decision. See if you can figure out what the logic was that led to this conclusion. Further, list what other information you would like to have and how that might influence your decision.

THE GRIEVANCE

A job titled "technical review analyst I" with responsibility for ISO 9000 audits is slotted as a tier 3 job.* Union believes that this job should be evaluated as a tier 4 job. Management contends that both this job and its counterpart in tier 4 (senior technical review analyst) should be graded in tier 3.

SUMMARY OF IMPORTANT POINTS IN THE UNION CASE

The union asserts, and management agrees, that the only difference historically between auditors classified as technical review analysts I (tier 3) and those classified as senior technical review analysts (tier 4) was the presence or absence of one task. That task was the performance of systems tests. Only tier 4 personnel performed this work, and this yielded the higher-tier classification. With the introduction of ISO 9000 audits, the systems test component of the tier 4 job was eventually phased out and both tier 3 and tier 4 auditors were asked to perform the ISO 9000 audit. The union and management agree that the systems test work previously performed by tier 4 employees was easier (and less valuable to the company) than the new ISO 9000 work now being performed. However, the union maintains that the added responsibility from the ISO 9000 audit, which involves about 150 hours of training, is sufficiently complex to warrant tier 4 classification. As partial support, the union provided a list of attendees to one ISO 9000 training session and noted that many of the attendees from other companies are managers and engineers, asserting this as evidence of the complexity involved in the audit material and the importance attached to this job by other firms.

* Tier 1 is the low end and tier 5 is the highest for all skilled craft jobs. Different evaluation systems are used for management and for clerical employees.

The union also presented evidence to support the assertion that tier 3 personnel performing ISO 9000 audits are doing work of substantially the same value as the old grade 310 work.[+] This grade, as agreed by both the union and the company, is equivalent to the new tier 4.

SUMMARY OF IMPORTANT POINTS IN MANAGEMENT CASE

Management's case includes four major points. First, management argues that a technical review analyst performing ISO 9000 audits has a job that is similar in complexity, responsibility, and types of duties to jobs previously classified as grades 308 and 309. Jobs in these old grades are now slotted into tier 3, per the contract.

Second, management presented evidence that many of the duties performed in the ISO 9000 audits were performed in a series of prior audits, variously labeled "Eastcore MPA," "QSA 1981," and "QPS 1982." This long and varied history of similar duties, management contends, is evidence that ISO 9000 does not involve higher-level or substantially different (and hence no more valuable) duties than have been performed historically.

Third, management presented both notes and a memorandum from W. P. Salkrist (the company job evaluation expert) in support of his argument that the audit job with ISO 9000 responsibilities should be classified as a tier 4 job. Prior to introduction of the ISO 9000 audit, neither the union nor management had found any reason to complain about the existing prior job evaluations of the tier 3 and tier 4 review analysts.

Fourth, management provided evidence that these jobs at other facilities, with other local contract provisions and conditions, were all classified into tier 3.[‡]

[+] The former job evaluation system broke jobs down into many more grades. As of the last contract, jobs are now classified into one of five tiers or grades.

[‡] Union strongly contests the introduction of this information. In the past, management has vehemently argued that conditions at other facilities should not be introduced because local contracts were negotiated, with different trade-offs being made by the different parties. Union believes that this same logic should now apply if a consistent set of rules is to evolve.

Summary

Other countries continue to make inroads in product areas traditionally the sole domain of American companies. The impact of this increased competition has been most pronounced in the compensation area. Labor costs must be cut to improve our competitive stance. Alternative compensation systems to achieve this end are regularly being devised. Unions face a difficult situation. How should they respond to these attacks on traditional compensation systems? Many unions believe that the crisis demands changing attitudes from both management and unions. Labor and management identify compensation packages that both parties can abide. Sometimes these packages include cuts in traditional forms of wages in exchange for compensation tied more closely to the success of the firm. We expect the beginning of the 21st century to be dominated by more innovation in compensation design and increased exploration between unions and management for ways to improve the competitive stance of American business.

Review Questions

1. In Chapter 9 we talk about 12 different rewards in an organization (compensation, benefits, social, security, status, work variety, workload, work importance, authority/control/autonomy, advancement, feedback, development opportunity). We usually think of the company as giving these rewards, in differing degrees. We could argue, though, that unions also fight to be the one employees perceive as "earning" these rewards for employees, by gaining them in bargaining sessions. Make the argument that unions are losing popularity because they aren't as good at obtaining these 12 rewards for workers as they used to be (or, perhaps, they never were good at obtaining some of the rewards). Which of the rewards is this particularly true for? How does international competition influence a union's ability to obtain rewards for workers?

2. If merit pay is supposed to increase individual equity and unions are very concerned about equity, why do unions frequently oppose merit pay for their membership?

3. The late 1990s and the beginning of the 21st century have enjoyed a rare combination of low unemployment and low inflation. Explain why this combination would make COLA clauses less likely to appear in union contracts than was true in the 1980s.

4. It is probably true that, if given a choice, unions would prefer to implement a skill-based pay system rather than some form of gain-sharing plan. Why?

International Pay Systems

Chapter Outline

Around the world, global competitive forces have changed the way people work and how they get paid. Toyota dismantled its seniority-based pay system for managers and replaced it with a merit-based system.[1] Toshiba offers stock awards, which were not even legal in Japan only a few years ago.[2] Deutsche Bank, Nokia, Seimens, and other European companies are experimenting with variable pay and performance-based (rather than personality-based) appraisal in their search for ways to improve productivity and control labor costs.[3] Global acquisitions of former competitors change pay systems. As part of its

---

[1] A. Harney, "Toyota Plans Pay Based on Merit," *Financial Times,* July 8, 1999, p. 20.

[2] Interviews with Toshiba managers, included in G. Milkovich, M. Bloom, and A. Mitra, "Research Report: Rethinking Global Reward Systems," working paper, Cornell University, 2000.

[3] Also see *Pay in Europe 2003, Remuneration Policy and Practices* (Surrey, England: Federation of European Employers, 2003), and the FEE's website at *www.euen.cok.uk;* Zhong-Ming Wang, presentation to Cornell University Global HRM Distance Learning seminar, Shanghai, China, March 2000; Conference Board, "Organizing for Global Competitiveness—Headquarters Design Report," No. 123399RR, and "The Country Subsidiary Design Report," No. 1180–97RR (New York: Conference Board, 1999).

takeover and restructuring of Tungsram Electric in Poland, General Electric changed the pay system from a rigid seniority-based one to a more flexible one with broad bands, market-based wage rates, and performance bonuses.

Sometimes the changes in pay are directly tied to cataclysmic sociopolitical change, as in China, Russia, and eastern Europe.[4] Central and government authorities had dictated pay rates in these communist command-and-control economies. Now these companies face the challenge of devising pay systems responsive to business and market pressures while maintaining a sense of social justice among the people. The Chinese situation is extraordinarily complex.[5] State-owned enterprises are being asked to become profitable. The only hope of profitability is to cut the massively bloated head count. Yet an army of unemployed people without social support threatens stability and even government survival. Some state-owned enterprises, such as Bao Gang, the country's largest steelmaker, have moved to more "market- and performance-based" systems, even though labor markets are just emerging in China. Shanghai Shenyingwanguo Security Company and Shanghai Bank have implemented job-based structures to help them retain key employees and increase pay satisfaction. Privatized enterprises, start-ups, and joint ventures with foreign firms use a variety of approaches. Most surprising of all is that some town-owned enterprises are using stock ownership as part of their employee compensation.[6] China may still be striving to become a worker's paradise, but the experimentation with compensation approaches might already qualify it as a pay pundit's paradise.

However, too much change and experimentation can have a dark side that threatens social unrest. There are reports from the Ukraine, Romania, and Russia of people going unpaid for months, without legal recourse.[7] In Russia, a friend maintains that "the most effective pay delivery system is a brown bag under the table."

[4]A. Puffer and S. Shekshnia, "Compensating Local Employees in Post-Communist Russia," *Compensation and Benefits Journal,* September–October 1994, pp. 35–42; D. Soskice, "Wage Determination: The Changing Role of Institutions in Advanced Industrialized Countries," *Oxford Review of Economic Policy* 6(4), pp. 36–61; D. Vaughan Whitehead, ed., *Paying the Price: Crisis in Central and Eastern Europe* (Geneva: ILO, 1999); L. Bajzikova, "Transition Process of HRM in the Slovak Republic," *Journal of International Human Resource Management,* no. 2, 2001; N. Zupan, "HRM in Slovenian Transitional Companies," presentation at CAHRS international conference, Berlin, June 2002.

[5]D. Dong, K. Goodall, and M. Warner, "The End of the Iron Rice Bowl," *International Journal of Human Resource Management,* April 2, 2000, pp. 217–236.

[6]Zhong-Ming Wang, presentation to Cornell University Global HRM Distance Learning seminar, Shanghai, China, March 2000; comments by Ningyu Tang, instructor in Shanghai for Global HRM Distance Learning seminar; Peter Nolan, "China and the Global Business Revolution, *Cambridge Journal of Economics* 26 (2002), pp. 119–137; Jing Zhou and J. J. Martocchio "Chinese and American Managers' Compensation Award Decisions," *Personnel Psychology* 54 (Spring 2001), pp. 115–145; National Bureau of Statistics, People's Republic of China, 2003; J. T. Landry, "Review of 'The New Chinese Empire and What It Means for the United States' by R. Terrill," *Harvard Business Review* 81 (7) (July 3, 2003); Zaohui Zhao, "Earnings Differentials between State and Non-State Enterprises in Urban China," *Pacific Economic Review* 7(1) (2002), pp. 181–197.

[7]G. T. Khulikov, "Ukraine Wage Decentralization in a Nonpayment Crisis," chap. 11 in *Pay the Price* (Geneva: ILO, 2000); R. Yokovlev, "Wage Distortions in Russia," chap. 9 in *Pay the Price* (Geneva: ILO, 2000); Muneto Ozocki, ed. *Negotiating Flexibility: The Role of the Social Partners and the State* (Geneva: ILO, 1999).

So it is a time of unprecedented global change. Or is it? Let's step back to gain some historical perspective:

> There is hardly a village or town anywhere on the globe whose wages are not influenced by distant foreign markets, whose infrastructure is not financed by foreign capital, whose engineering, manufacturing, and even business skills are not imported from abroad, or whose labor markets are not influenced by the absence of those who had emigrated or by the presence of strangers who had immigrated.[8]

This is not a description of the 21st century. Rather, it is from 100 years ago. In the late 1800s, trade barriers were being reduced, free trade was being promoted, and mass migration of people was underway. Thanks to transoceanic telegraphic cables, the speed of communication had increased dramatically, and investment capital flowed among nations. Yet by 1917 these global links had been replaced with a global war. Citizens became uncomfortable with the greater risks and uncertainty of globalization. Nations began to raise tariffs to protect domestic companies hurt by foreign competitors. Immigrants were accused of "robbing jobs." Historians conclude that "globalization is neither unique nor irreversible; it has and can again sow seeds of its own destruction."[9]

MANAGING VARIATIONS: THE GLOBAL GUIDE

Understanding international compensation begins with recognizing differences and similarities and figuring out how best to manage them. How people get paid around the world depends on variations in the factors in the global guide depicted in Exhibit 16.1. Four general ones are listed: *economic, institutional, organizational,* and *employee,* with subfactors. These factors have been discussed throughout the book; now they can be applied globally. But once we shift from a domestic to an international perspective, additional factors become important, too. Institutional factors, such as cultural traditions and political structures, and economic factors, such as differences in ownership of enterprises and the development of capital and labor markets, come into play. Further, social contracts and the role of trade unions must be considered. An example using the global guide illustrates its usefulness.

Consider the DaimlerChrysler situation discussed in Chapter 2. Prior to Daimler's acquisition of Chrysler, the pay for the top 10 Daimler executives equaled the pay of Chrysler's CEO alone. As little as 25 percent of Chrysler managers' total compensation was in the form of base pay, whereas Daimler managers' base pay accounted for up to 60 percent of their total compensation. The merged DaimlerChrysler adopted a Chrysler-like approach to executive compensation. Some have even claimed that the attractive pay was the reason Daimler executives were eager to acquire Chrysler!

---

[8]Kevin O'Rourke and J. G. Williamson, *Globalization and History: The Evolution of a 19th Century Atlantic Economy* (Cambridge, MA: MIT Press, 1999), p. 2.

[9]Kevin O'Rourke and J. G. Williamson, *Globalization and History: The Evolution of a 19th Century Atlantic Economy* (Cambridge, MA: MIT Press, 1999), chap. 14. Also see D. Rodrik, "Has Globalization Gone Too Far?" *California Management Review* 39(3) (Spring 1997); W. Keller, L. Pauly, and S. Reich, *The Myth of the Global Corporation* (Princeton, NJ: Princeton University Press, 1998); B. Kogut, "What Makes a Company Global?" *Harvard Business Review,* January–February 1999, pp. 165–170.

EXHIBIT 16.1   Guide to International Compensation

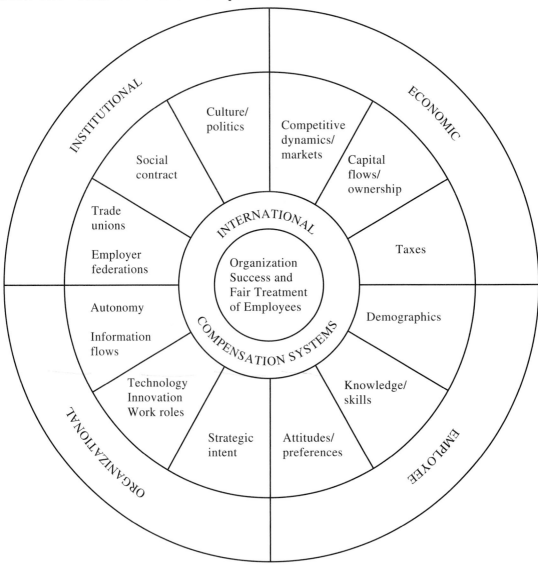

© George T. Milkovich.

The Daimler and Chrysler managerial pay systems are contrasted in Exhibit 16.2, using the factors in our global guide (Exhibit 16.1). At Daimler, the roots of today's pay system reach back to postwar Germany and efforts to rebuild an economy devastated by two world wars. Rather than companies' engaging in aggressive wage competition that risked inflation, trade union federations, employer associations, government agencies, and financial institutions participated in centralized negotiations. The result was industry-wide negotiated pay systems called *tariff agreements.* They included predictable annual increases, government-provided social welfare programs, and well-defined internal struc-

EXHIBIT 16.2   Applying the Global Guide

Pressures	Daimler	Chrysler
Economic		
Competitive markets	Moderately competitive	Highly competitive
Capital/ownership	Few shareholders	Many shareholders
Taxes	High taxes	Moderate taxes
Institutional		
Culture/politics	Centralized process	Decentralized process
Regulations	Strong government/ trade union involvement	Limited government involvement
Trade union/ employer federations	Tripartite-based social contract	Individual/employer-based social contract
Organizational		
Strategic intent	High margins/high-end vehicles	Lower-margin passenger vehicles, higher-margin SUVs, mini vans
Autonomy	Lower autonomy	Moderate autonomy
Work roles	Defined roles	More flexible roles
Employee		
Skill/knowledge	Continuous learning	On-the-job
Attitudes/behaviors	High commitment	Committed but contentious
Demographics	Older, experienced	Older, experienced
Total pay system		
	Sensitive to social contract; hierarchical; well-defined jobs	Aligned with strategy, sensitive to competitive markets
	Base and benefits; annual increase	Base/performance bonuses, stock ownership
	Focus on commitment and continuous learning	Focus on performance and cost control

tures. All companies competing in the same product markets (e.g., Daimler, Volkswagen, and Opel) used the same pay structures. Daimler could pay above these negotiated rates but had little reason to do so. Instead, it competed for employees based on its reputation as a place to work, its quality of training, and the like. As a result, managers were less likely to consider pay as an instrument of strategy. Instead, pay was a constraint determined outside the organization.

German tax policies and labor regulations supported this approach. A typical Daimler employee's marginal tax rate (percent tax on each additional euro earned) is 30 percent higher than a Chrysler employee's tax rate on an additional dollar's pay in the United States. As a result, the financial returns for working longer and harder in order to receive performance bonuses are significantly smaller at Daimler. Until very recently, broad-based stock options for employees were illegal. Daimler changed its plan in 2003 to award stock rather than options. Nevertheless, base salary and across-the-board pay increases (rather than performance bonuses and stock) remain the most common pay forms. In exchange for their higher taxes, Daimler employees receive generous welfare and unemployment payments, plus subsidized college and apprenticeship programs. As Exhibit 16.2 shows, centralized wage setting with predictable annual pay increases, concentrated financial ownership, and high taxes that support a wide social safety net still provide the context for the pay system at DaimlerChrysler's German locations.[10]

Now let us apply the global guide to Chrysler. Chrysler reflects the competitive dynamics in U.S. labor and product markets as well as the social contract in the United States, which places high value on individual choice. Pay setting is highly decentralized. Government's involvement is limited to ensuring conformance with minimum wage, tax, and discrimination laws. Chrysler's managerial pay system is arguably aligned with its business strategy, is sensitive to market conditions, and includes significant performance bonuses and stock ownership. The U.S. tax code supports the use of stock options. The pay system is considered a strategic tool intended to competitively attract, retain, and motivate managers and also support customer satisfaction and improve shareholder value (sound familiar?).

So the global guide serves as a tool kit. By examining each of the factors, we can increase our understanding of the variation in international pay practices. Five factors are particularly salient. These are variations in (1) social contracts, (2) cultures, (3) trade unions, (4) ownership and capital markets, and (5) managers' autonomy. While we separate the factors to clarify our discussion, they do not separate so easily in reality. Instead, they overlap and interact.

THE SOCIAL CONTRACT

Viewed as part of the social contract, the employment relationship is more than an exchange between an individual and an employer. It includes the government, all enterprise owners (sometimes acting individually and sometimes collectively through owner associations), and all employees (sometimes acting individually and sometimes in trade unions). The relationships and expectations of these parties form the social contract. As you think about how people get paid around the world, it will be clear that different people in different countries hold differing beliefs about the role of government, employees, unions, and employers. Understanding how to manage employee compensation in any country requires an understanding of the social contract in that country. Efforts to change employee compensation systems—for example, to make them more responsive to customers, encourage innovative and quality service, or control costs—require changing the expectations of parties to the social contract.

---

[10]Lowell Turner, ed., *Negotiating the New Germany: Can Social Partnership Survive?* (Ithaca, NY: Cornell University Press, 1998); Hugh Williamson, "IGMetall Is the Trend-Setter: What Happened in the Strike Will Have Far-Reaching Implications," *Financial Times,* July 2, 2003, p. 11; G. Thomas Sims and Christoper Rhoads, "Tough Times Humble German Labor," *Wall Street Journal,* July 1, 2003, p. A9; NCEO "Global Employee Ownership Plans Continue to Grow," *Employee Ownership Report* 22(2) (2002); Uta Harnischfeger, "DaimlerChrysler Mulls Removal of Options," *Financial Times,* July 10, 2003, p. 17.

Centralized-Localized Decision Making

Perhaps the most striking example of the social contract's effects on pay systems is in Exhibit 16.3, which contrasts the degree of centralization of pay setting among countries.[11] The United States, United Kingdom, Canada, Hong Kong, and Brazil use highly decentralized approaches with little government involvement. Japan, Singapore, Germany, Belgium, and Slovakia are moderately centralized by industry sector. Sweden, Denmark, and Austria use highly centralized approaches that create a national pay system.

CULTURE

Culture is defined as shared mental programming which is rooted in the values, beliefs, and assumptions held in common by a group of people and which influences how information is processed.[12] How critical is culture in managing international pay? Very important, according to some. The assumption that pay systems must be designed to fit different *national cultures* is based on the belief that most of a country's inhabitants share a

**EXHIBIT 16.3
Social
Contracts
and Pay
Setting**

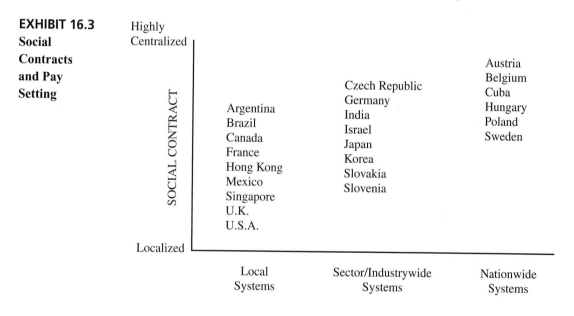

PAY-SETTING SYSTEMS

[11]Linda Bell and R. Freeman, "The Incentive for Working Hard: Explaining Hours Worked Differences in the US and Germany," NBER paper, 2000; R. Freeman and L. F. Katz, *Differences and Changes in Wage Structures* (Chicago: University of Chicago Press, 1994); Income Data Services, *Employment Europe 2000* (monthly newsletter).

[12]F. Trompenaars, *Riding the Waves of Culture: Understanding Diversity in Global Business* (Burr Ridge, IL: Irwin, 1995); H. C. Triandis, "Cross-Cultural Industrial and Organizational Psychology," in *Handbook of Industrial and Organizational Psychology,* eds. M. D. Dunnette and L. M. Hough (Palo Alto, CA: Consulting Psychologists Press, 1994), pp. 103–172; H. C. Triandis, *Individualism and Collectivism* (Boulder, CO: Westview Press, 1995).

national character. Therefore, the job of the global manager is to define the national characteristics that influence pay systems.

Typical of this thinking is the widely used list of national cultural attributes proposed by Hofstede (power distance, individualism–collectivism, uncertainty avoidance, and masculinity–femininity).[13] Advocates of this view believe that "it is crucial that companies adjust their compensation practices to the cultural specifics of a particular host country."[14] Accordingly, in nations where the culture emphasizes respect for status and hierarchy (high power distance, attributed to Malaysia and Mexico), hierarchical pay structures are appropriate. In low-power-distance nations (Australia and the Netherlands), egalitarianism is called for.[15]

Advice can get even more specific. Companies operating in nations with "collectivistic" cultures, such as Singapore, Japan, Israel, and Korea, should use egalitarian pay structures, equal pay increases, and group-based rather than individual-based performance incentives. Employers in the more "individualistic" national cultures, such as the United States, United Kingdom, and Hong Kong, should use individual-based pay and performance-based increases.

But such thinking risks stereotyping.[16] The question is not, What are the cultural differences among nations. Rather, the question is, Whose culture matters?[17] Any group of people may exhibit a shared set of beliefs. Look around your college or workplace; engineers, lawyers, accountants, and technicians may each share some beliefs and values. Employees of organizations may, too. Your school's "culture" probably differs from Microsoft's, Toshiba's, or the London Symphony Orchestra's. You may even have chosen your school because of its culture. However, you are likely part of many cultures. You

[13]G. Hofstede, "Cultural Constraints in Management Theories," *International Review of Strategic Management* 5 (1994), pp. 27–51.

[14]R. Schuler and N. Rogovsky, "Understanding Compensation Practice Variations across Firms: The Impact of National Culture," *Journal of International Business Studies* 29 (1998), pp. 159–178.

[15]L. R. Gomez-Mejia and T. Welbourne, "Compensation Strategies in a Global Context," *Human Resource Planning* 14 (1994), pp. 29–41; Sunny C. L. Fong and Margaret A. Shaffer, "The Dimensionality and Determinants of Pay Satisfaction: A Cross-Cultural Investigation of a Group Incentive Plan," *International Journal of Human Resource Management* 14(4), (June 2003), pp. 559–580.

[16]G. Milkovich and M. Bloom, "Rethinking International Compensation: From Expatriates and National Cultures to Strategic Flexibility," *Compensation and Benefits Review,* April 1998; L. Markoczy, "Us and Them," *Across the Board,* February 1998, pp. 44–48.

[17]F. Trompenaars, *Riding the Waves of Culture: Understanding Diversity in Global Business* (Burr Ridge, IL: Irwin, 1995); M. Bloom, G. Milkovich, and A. Mitra, "International Compensation: Learning from How Managers Respond to Variations in Local Host Contexts," *International Journal of Human Resource Management* special issue, 2003; Allen D. Engle, Sr., and Mark Mendenhall "Transnational Roles and Transnational Rewards: Global Integration in Executive Compensation," presentation at international HR conference, Limerick, Ireland, June 2003; Paul Evans, Vlado Pucik, and Jean-Louis Barsoux, *The Global Challenge* (New York: McGraw-Hill, 2002); G. Hundley and J. Kim, "National Culture and the Factors Affecting Perceptions of Pay Fairness in Korea and the U.S.," *International Journal of Organization Analysis* 5(4) (October 1997), pp. 325–341; L. Kim and G. Yi, "Transformation of Employment Practices in Korean Business," *International Studies of Management and Organizations* 28(4) (1998–99), pp. 73–83; G. Hofstede, "Cultural Constraints in Management Theories," *International Review of Strategic Management* 5 (1994), pp. 27–51; P. C. Earley and C. B. Gibson, "Taking Stock in our Progress on Individualism–Collectivism: 100 Years of Solidarity and Community," *Journal of Management* 24 (1998), pp. 265–304; David Landes, *Culture Matters: How Values Shape Human Progress* (New York: Basic Books, 2001).

are not only part of your university but also part of your family, your social/political/ interest groups, your region of the state or country, and so on. Cultures may be similar or different among all these categories.

Culture Matters, but So Does Cultural Diversity

Culture classifiers consider the United States a country of risk takers who rank high on the individualistic (rather than collectivistic) scale. In contrast, the country of Slovenia has been classified as more collectivistic and security-conscious (as opposed to risk taking).[18] Slovenia was the first country to break off from the former Yugoslavia. (How is that for taking a risk?) It has a population of less than 3 million and by most standards would be considered very homogeneous. So you would expect Slovenian managers to be very different from U.S. managers. However, a study found that Slovenian managers tended, on average, to be more risk taking and individualistic than U.S. managers. The most striking finding, as shown in Exhibit 16.4, was that the degree of variation among managers on cultural dimensions was virtually the same in both the Slovenian and the U.S. data. Thus, one can find risk-averse collectivists and risk-taking individualists in both nations.

So how useful is the notion of a national culture? In the absence of better data on variations such as those in Exhibit 16.4, it may offer a starting point. However, *it is only a starting point*. National culture can be thought of as the "average" in Exhibit 16.4. It provides some information about what kinds of pay attitudes and beliefs you are likely to find in an area. But overreliance on the "average" can seriously mislead. This point is critical for managing international pay. As the paleobiologist Stephen Jay Gould noted, "Failure to consider the 'full house' of cases plunges us into serious error again and again."[19] While Gould may not

EXHIBIT 16.4
Understanding the "Full House" of Variation within a Culture

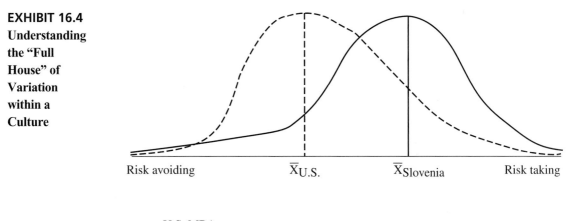

Risk avoiding $\overline{X}_{U.S.}$ $\overline{X}_{Slovenia}$ Risk taking

U.S. MBAs   – – – – – –

Slovenian MBAs   ————

[18]M. Bloom, G. Milkovich, and N. Zupan, "Contrasting Slovenian and U.S. Employment Relations: The Links between Social Contracts and Psychological Contracts" *CEMS Business Review* no. 2 (1997), pp. S95–S109.

[19]Stephen Jay Gould, *Full House: The Spread of Excellence from Plato to Darwin* (New York: Three Rivers Press, 1996).

have been talking about compensation, we can still extend his point to global pay. To claim that all organizations and people within Germany or within China use the same shared mindset ignores variations and differences within each nation. Considerable diversity among companies and people within any country exists. So keep in mind our basic premise in this chapter: The interplay among economic, institutional, organizational, and individual conditions within each nation or region, taken as a whole, forms distinct approaches to total comparisons. Understanding these factors in the global guide is useful for managing employee compensation. However, do not assume uniformity (the average) within a country. Understanding the full range of individuals within nations is important to managing international pay.

TRADE UNIONS AND EMPLOYEE INVOLVEMENT

As Exhibit 16.5 shows, Europe remains highly unionized: In Sweden, 91 percent of the work force belongs to unions; in the United Kingdom, 33 percent; and in Italy, 44 percent. Asia is less heavily unionized. Japan's unionization rate is 24 percent, and South Korea's is almost 13 percent. Although the exhibit might cause you to conclude that union power is declining, caution is in order. In some countries, workers' pay is set by collective agreements even though the workers may not be union members. In France, for example, 90 percent of workers are covered by collective agreements, but only 9 percent are union members.[20]

In addition to having higher rates of unionization, Belgium, Germany, and the European Union (EU) require the establishment of worker councils that must be involved in any changes to a pay plan. The European Union is trying to provide common labor standards in all its member countries. The purpose of standards is to avoid "social dumping," or the relocation of a business in a country with lower standards and labor costs. At present, hourly labor costs and productivity vary substantially among the EU countries. Often the higher labor costs are offset by greater productivity.[21]

Social legislation varies among European countries, as shown in Exhibit 16.6. Britain specifies the fewest requirements, with no minimum wage, no maximum hours, and no formal methods for employee participation. France and Germany have the most generous social insurance. Some writers predict the eventual "Europeanization" of pay determination.[22]

---

[20]H. Katz and Owen Darbishire, *Converging Divergences: Worldwide Changes in Employment Systems* (Ithaca, NY: Cornell University Press, 2000); George Boyer "Review Symposium: Converging Divergences: Worldwide Changes in Employment System," *Industrial and Labor Relations Review* 54 (2001).

[21]Christopher L. Erickson and Sarosh Kuruvilla, "Labor Costs and the Social Dumping Debate in the European Union," *Industrial and Labor Relations Review,* October 1994, pp. 28–47; K. Schwab, M. Porter, J. Sachs, A. Warner, and M. Levison, *The Global Competitiveness Report 2000,* World Economic Forum (Cambridge, MA: Harvard University Press, 2000).

[22]Chris Brewster and Hilary Harris, *International HRM: Contemporary Issues in Europe* (London: Routledge Press, 1999); P. Dowling and R. Schuler, *International Dimensions of Human Resource Management* (Boston: PWS Kent, 2000); Matthew F. Davis, "Global Compensation in the New Economy," *International HR Journal* 9(3) (Fall 2000), pp. 45–50; Mark Fenton-O'Creevy, "HR Practices: *Vive La Difference;* Part 7: Mastering People Management," *Financial Times,* November 26, 2001; Paul R. Sparrow, "International Rewards System: To Converge or Not To Converge?" in *International HRM: Contemporary Issues in Europe,* ed. Chris Brewster and Hilary Harris (London: Routledge Press, 1999).

EXHIBIT 16.5
Union
Density

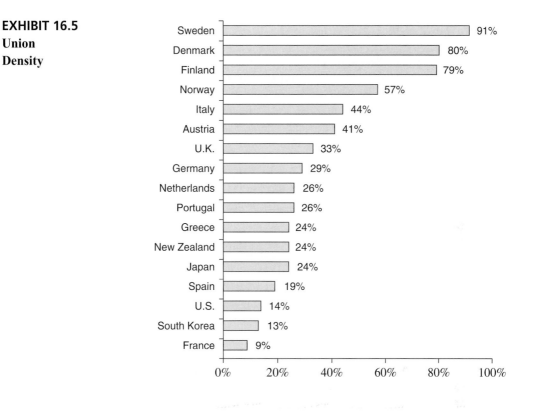

Sweden	91%
Denmark	80%
Finland	79%
Norway	57%
Italy	44%
Austria	41%
U.K.	33%
Germany	29%
Netherlands	26%
Portugal	26%
Greece	24%
New Zealand	24%
Japan	24%
Spain	19%
U.S.	14%
South Korea	13%
France	9%

0%   20%   40%   60%   80%   100%

EXHIBIT 16.6
Employment
Practices
Differ among
Nations

Source: Bureau
of Labor
Statistics;
International
Labor Office.

The Cost of an Employee

For an employer, the cost of social insurance as a percentage of salary is higher in France
than in some other places.

	The hourly cost of a production worker in manufacturing . . .	. . . is made up from the salary paid directly to the worker before deductions . . .	. . . and what an employer pays in social insurance and labor taxes.	What those extra costs are as a percentage of salary.
France	$17.97	$12.36	$5.61	45.4%
Germany*	$28.28	$20.94	$7.34	35.1%
United States	$18.24	$14.34	$3.90	27.2%
Japan	$19.37	$16.52	$2.85	17.3%
Britain	$15.47	$13.47	$2.00	14.8%

*Former West Germany

OWNERSHIP AND FINANCIAL MARKETS

Ownership and financing of companies differ widely around the world. These differences are important to understanding and managing international pay. In the United States, corporate ownership and access to capital is far less concentrated than in most other countries. Fifty percent of American households own stock in companies either directly or indirectly through mutual funds and pension funds.[23] Direct stock ownership is only a few mouse clicks away. In Korea, six conglomerates control a significant portion of the Korean economy, and the six are closely linked with specific families.[24] In Germany, the national Bundesbank and a small number of other influential banks have ownership interests in most major companies. These patterns of ownership make certain types of pay systems almost nonsensical. For example, linking performance bonuses to increased shareholder value or offering stock options to employees makes little sense in the large conglomerates in Germany, Korea, and Japan. However, ownership in small start-ups in the nations is outside the traditional channels, so these firms do offer stock options to attract new employees.[25] Recent tax law changes in these countries have made options more attractive, but the ownership of the major employers is slow to change.

The most vivid illustrations of the importance of ownership occur in China and in eastern Europe (Poland, Hungary, Slovenia, Czech Republic, and Slovakia), where a variety of forms are emerging. While state-owned enterprises still employ two-thirds of all workers in China, township enterprises, wholly privately owned enterprises, joint ventures with foreign companies, and wholly owned foreign enterprises (WOFEs) account for 50 percent of the profits. Chinese employees switching from government-owned enterprises to these newer organizations find that both the pay and the employer expectations (i.e., the social contract) are substantially different.[26] Individuals attracted to work in these various enterprises have different values and expectations. One study found that

---

[23]The website of the National Center for Employee Ownership (NCEO) has information and referrals concerning employee stock ownership plans (ESOPs) and other forms of employee ownership: *www.esop.org*. Worker Ownership around the world is discussed at *www.activistnet.org*.

[24]G. R. Ungson, R. J. Steers, and S. H. Park, *Korean Enterprises: The Quest for Globalization* (Boston: Harvard Business School Press, 1997).

[25]Lowell Turner, ed., *Negotiating the New Germany: Can Social Partnership Survive?* (Ithaca, NY: Cornell University Press, 1998); D. Soskice, "Wage Determination: The Changing Role of Institutions in Advanced Industrialized Countries," *Oxford Review of Economic Policy* 6(4), pp. 36–61; Wolfgang Streeck, *Social Institutions and Economic Performance: Studies of Industrial Relations in Advanced Capitalist Economies* (London: Sage, 1992).

[26]G. Breton, H. Lan, and Yuan Lu, "China's Township and Village Enterprises," *American Management Executive* 14(1) (February 2000), pp. 19–30; W. Van Honacher, "Entering China: An Unconventional Approach," *Harvard Business Review,* March–April 1992, pp. 130–140; Wei He, Chao C. Chen, and Lihua Zhang, "Rewards Allocation Preferences in Chinese State-Owned Enterprises: A Revisit after a Decade's Radical Reform," *Organization Science Special Issue: Corporate Transformation in the People's Republic of China,* in press; Helen Blair, Nigel Culkin, and Keith Randle, "From London to Los Angeles: A Comparison of Local Labour Market Processes in the US and UK Film Industries," *International Journal of Human Resource Management* 14(4) (June 2003), pp. 619–633; Marshall Meyer, Yuan Lu, Hailin Lan, and Xiaohui Lu, "Decentralized Enterprise Reform: Notes on the Transformation of State-Owned Enterprises," in *The Management of Enterprises in the People's Republic of China,* eds. Anne S. Tsui and Chung-Ming Lau (Boston: Kluwer Academic, 2002).

those working for local or town-owned enterprises prefer more performance-based pay than those working in federal-owned enterprises.[27] Many families find it makes sense to have one wage earner working at a safe but low-paying government enterprise and another wage earner working at a private enterprise where expectations and pay are high. So it is clear that ownership differences may influence what forms of pay make sense. It is very misleading to assume that every place is like home.

MANAGERIAL AUTONOMY

Managerial autonomy, an organizational factor in the global guide in Exhibit 16.1, refers to the degree of discretion managers have to make total compensation a strategic tool. It is inversely related to the degree of centralization discussed earlier. Thus, most U.S.- and U.K.-based organizations have relatively greater freedom to change employee pay practices than do most European companies. As already noted, the centralized pay setting found in European Union countries limits organizations' autonomy to align pay to business strategies and changing market conditions.[28] In contrast, in Singapore the National Wage Council issues voluntary guidelines (e.g., "Wage freezes for most companies," "Emphasize variable and performance-based pay"). Most government organizations adhere to these guides, while private organizations do so in varying degrees.[29]

> **Cybercomp**
> A good source of free information on labor laws throughout the world is the NATLEX database produced by the International Labor Organization (ILO): *natlex.ilo.org.*

Governments and trade unions are not the only institutions to limit managerial autonomy. Corporate policies often do so as well.[30] Compensation decisions made in the home-country corporate offices and exported to subunits around the world may align with the corporate strategy but discount local economic and social conditions. While IBM corporate in Armonk, New York, expects all its worldwide operations to "differentiate people on performance" with total compensation, some IBM units in Tokyo remain convinced that Japanese IBMers in Japan prefer more egalitarian practices. Nevertheless, managers are expected to comply with Armonk. Is IBM trying to attract the people in

---

[27]Jing Zhou and J. J. Martocchio, "Chinese and American Managers' Compensation Award Decisions," *Personnel Psychology* 54 (Spring 2001), pp. 115–145.

[28]Giuseppe Fajertag, ed., *Collective Bargaining in Europe 1998–1999* (Brussels: European Trade Union Institute, 2000). The European Trade Union Institute's website is at *www.etuc.org/etui/default.cf.*

[29]Hesan Ahmed Quazi and Sophia Lee, "A Study of Compensation Strategies of Organizations Operating in Singapore," Nanyang Business School, May 2003.

[30]K. Roth and S. O'Donnell, "Foreign Subsidiary Compensation Strategy: An Agency Theory Perspective," *Academy of Management Journal* 39(3) (1996), pp. 678–703; Ingmar Bjorkman and Patrick Furu, "Determinants of Variable Pay for Top Managers of Foreign Subsidiaries in Finland," *International Journal of Human Resource Management* 11(4) (August 2000), pp. 698–713; Paola Bradley, Chris Hendley, and Stephen Perkins, "Global or Multi-Local: The Significance of International Values in Reward Strategy," in *International HRM: Contemporary Issues in Europe* ed. C. Brewster and H. Harris (London: Routledge Press, 1999; J. Abowd and Michael Bognanno, "International Differences in Executive and Managerial Compensation," working paper, ILR School, Cornell University, Ithaca NY.

Japan who are seeking more performance-based pay and signal to others that IBM has a performance-based culture around the world? (Sounds like a research project to us.)

In sum, as the global guide depicts, international compensation is influenced by economic, institutional, organizational, and individual conditions.[31] Globalization really means that these conditions are changing—hence international pay systems are changing as well.

COMPARING COSTS

In Chapter 8 we discussed the importance of obtaining accurate information on what competitors pay in domestic markets. Similar comparisons of total compensation among nations can be very misleading. Even if wage rates appear the same, expenses for health care, living costs, and other employer-provided allowances complicate the picture. Outside the United States, many nations offer some form of national health care. An organization may pay for it indirectly through payroll taxes, but since all people in a nation share similar coverage, its value as part of total compensation is diminished. Consequently, comparing data in global and local markets around the world is a major challenge. Comparisons between a specific U.S. firm and a specific foreign competitor may be even more misleading. Accurate data are usually difficult to obtain. While consulting firms are improving their global data collection, much of their data is still from U.S. companies' operations in global locations. Other foreign and local-national companies' data are often not available. Thus, international data may be biased toward U.S. companies' practices.

Standard of Living: Basket of Goods versus Big Mac

If comparing total compensation is difficult, comparing living costs and standards is even more complex. The Bank of Switzerland uses a uniform basket of goods based on European consumer habits; the basket includes the prices of 137 items from clothing to transportation to personal care.[32] A woman shopping for a summer dress, jacket, skirt, shoes, and stockings will find Tokyo the most expensive place to shop ($1,760), whereas Manila ($130) and Bombay ($120) are best buys. Tokyo is equally expensive for a man. If he wants a blazer, shirt, jeans, socks, and shoes, he will need to come up with $1,050 to pay for a medium-priced outfit.

If your tastes don't run to summer dresses and blazers, the *Economist* takes a "Big Mac approach." Rather than pricing a complex basket of goods and services, the magazine uses the price of a Big Mac in different locations.[33] According to Exhibit 16.7, the average price of a Big Mac in the United States is $2.71 (average of four cities); in China, 9.90 yuan (US$1.20); in Canada, $3.20 (US$2.21); and in South Korea, 3,300 won (US$2.71).

---

[31]Christopher Brown-Humes, "Welcome to the Ways of the Market," *Financial Times,* November 12, 1999, p. 10.

[32]Daniel Kalt and Manfred Gutmann, eds., *Prices and Earnings around the Globe* (Zurich: Union Bank of Switzerland, 2000).

[33]"Big Mac Currencies," *Economist,* April 24, 2003.

EXHIBIT 16.7
The
Hamburger
Standard

Source: "Big
Mac Currencies,"
Economist April
23, 2003

	Big Mac Price	
	In Local Currency	**In Dollars**
United States	$2.71	2.71
Argentina	Peso 4.10	1.43
Australia	A$3.00	1.86
Brazil	*Real* 4.55	1.48
Britain	£1.99	3.14
Canada	C$3.20	2.21
Chile	Peso 1,400	1.95
China	Yuan 9.90	1.20
Czech Rep.	Koruna 56.57	1.96
Denmark	Dkr27.75	4.10
Egypt	Pound 8.00	1.35
Euro area	£2.71	2.97
Hong Kong	HK$11.50	1.47
Hungary	Forint 490	2.18
Indonesia	Rupiah 16,100	1.84
Japan	¥262	2.19
Malaysia	M$5.04	1.33
Mexico	Peso 23.00	2.18
New Zealand	NZ$3.95	2.21
Peru	New Sol 7.90	2.29
Philippines	Peso 65.00	1.24
Poland	Zloty 6.30	1.62
Russia	Rouble 41.00	1.32
Singapore	S$3.30	1.86
South Africa	Rand 13.95	1.84
South Korea	Won 3,300	2.71
Sweden	SKr30.00	3.60
Switzerland	SFr6.30	4.59
Taiwan	NT$70.00	2.01
Thailand	Baht 59.00	1.38
Turkey	Lira 3,750,000	2.34
Venezuela	Bolivar 3,700	2.32

So what does a Big Mac have to do with compensation? Companies use cost comparisons in adjusting pay for employees who transfer among countries. The objective is to maintain the same level of purchasing power.[34]

There are several ways to calculate purchasing power. A common approach is to divide hourly wages by the cost of a standard basket of goods and services. Another way is to calculate the working time required to buy a common item such as a 1-kilogram loaf of

---

[34]J. Abowd and M. Bognanno, "International Differences in Executive and Managerial Compensation," in *Differences and Changes in Wage Structures,* R. B. Freeman and L. Katz, eds. (Chicago: NBER, 1995), pp. 67–103.

bread: 7 minutes in London, 15 minutes in Tokyo, 27 minutes in Montreal, and 12 minutes in Chicago. Or to buy a Big Mac: 14 minutes in Chicago, 36 minutes in London, and 90 minutes in Mexico City. The Big Mac (plus fries) attains luxury status in Nairobi, Caracas, and Lagos; an employed person must toil three hours (Nairobi), four hours (Caracas), or almost two days (Lagos) to afford it. (Hold the fries.)

COMPARING SYSTEMS

We have made the points that pay systems differ around the globe and that the differences relate to variations in economic pressures, sociopolitical institutions, and the diversity of organizations and employees. In this section we compare several compensation systems. The caution about stereotyping raised earlier applies here as well. Even in nations described by some as homogeneous, pay systems differ from business to business. For example, two well-known Japanese companies, Toyota and Toshiba, have designed different pay systems. Toyota places greater emphasis on external market rates, uses far fewer levels in its structure, and places greater emphasis on individual-based merit and performance pay than does Toshiba. So as we discuss "typical" systems, remember that differences exist and that change in these systems is occurring everywhere.

The Total Pay Model: Strategic Choices

The total pay model used throughout the book guides our discussion of pay systems in different countries. You will recognize the basic choices, which seem universal:

- Objectives of pay systems
- External competitiveness
- Internal alignment
- Employee contributions
- Management

While the choices are universal, the results are not. We have noted that each nation has its own laws regulating pay determination.

NATIONAL SYSTEMS: COMPARATIVE MIND-SET

A national system mind-set assumes that most employers in a country adopt similar pay practices. Understanding and managing international compensation then consists mainly of comparing the Japanese to the German to the U.S. or other national systems.[35] This method may be useful in nations with centralized approaches (see Exhibit 16.4) or where homogeneous economic and cultural conditions exist (e.g., Sweden). Some even apply it

---

[35]Hugh Williamson, "IGMetall Is the Trend-Setter: What Happened in the Strike Will Have Far-Reaching Implications," *Financial Times,* July 2, 2003, p. 11; Bertrand Benoit, "German Executives May Be Forced to Publish Salaries," *Financial Times,* May 20, 2003, p. 6; Christopher Rhoads, "In Deep Crisis, Germany Starts to Revamp Vast Welfare State," *Wall Street Journal,* July 10, 2003, pp. 1, A5.

to regional systems, as in the "European Way," the "Asian Way," or the "North American Way."[36] We describe the Japanese and German national systems below. But please read this information with caution: The national or regional mind-set overlooks variations among organizations within each nation.

Japanese National System

Traditionally, Japan's employment relationships were supported by "three pillars":

1. Lifetime security within the company.
2. Seniority-based pay and promotion systems.
3. Enterprise unions (decentralized unions that represent workers within a single company).

Japanese pay systems tend to emphasize the person rather than the job (seniority and skills possessed rather than job or work performed) promotions based on supervisory evaluation of trainability, skill/ability levels, and performance rather than on performance alone (internal alignment over competitors' market rates) and employment security based on the performance of the organization and the individual (formerly lifetime security).

Japanese pay systems can be described in terms of three basic components: base pay, bonuses, and allowances/benefits.[37]

Base Pay

Base pay accounts for 60 to 80 percent of an employee's monthly pay, depending on the individual's rank in the organization. Base pay is not based on job evaluation or market pricing (as predominates in North America), nor is it attached to specific job titles. Rather, it is based on a combination of employee characteristics: career category, years of service, and skill/performance level.

Career   Five career categories prevail in Japan: (1) general administration, (2) engineer/scientific, (3) secretary/office, (4) technician/blue-collar job, and (5) contingent.

Years of Service   Seniority remains a major factor in determining base pay. Management creates a matrix of pay and years of service for each career category. Exhibit 16.8 shows a matrix for general administration work. Companies meet periodically to compare their matrixes, a practice that accounts for the similarity among companies. In general, salary increases with age until workers are 50 years old, when it is reduced. Employees can expect annual increases no matter what their performance level until age 50, although the amount of increase varies according to individual skills and performance.

Skills and Performance   Each skill is defined by its class (usually 7 to 13) and rank (1 to 9) within the class. Exhibit 16.9 illustrates a skill salary chart for the general administration career category. Classes 1 and 2 typically include associate (entry) and senior associate work;

[36]Duncan Brown, "The Third Way: The Future of Pay and Rewards in Europe," *WorldatWork Journal,* Second Quarter 2000, pp. 15–25.

[37]M. Yashiro, *Human Resource Management in Japanese Companies in the Future* (New York: Organization Resource Counselors, 1996); *International Benefit Guidelines* (New York: Mercer, 2000); H. Shibata "The Transformation of the Wage and Performance Appraisal System in a Japanese Firm," *International Journal of Human Resource Management,* no. 11, 2000, pp. 294–313; Toyo Keizai, *Japan Company Handbook,* Tokyo: Japan Labour Bureau, Summer 2001.

EXHIBIT 16.8
Salary and Age Matrix for General Administration Work in a Japanese Company

*Age 22 is typical entry with college degree.
†Monthly salary, converted to dollars.

Age*	Salary†	Age	Salary	Age	Salary	Age	Salary
		31	$1,900	41	$2,900	51	$3,800
22	$1,000	32	2,000	42	3,000	52	3,700
23	1,100	33	2,100	43	3,100	53	3,600
24	1,200	34	2,200	44	3,200	54	3,500
25	1,300	35	2,300	45	3,300	55	3,400
26	1,400	36	2,400	46	3,400	56	3,300
27	1,500	37	2,500	47	3,500	57	3,200
28	1,600	38	2,600	48	3,600	58	3,100
29	1,700	39	2,700	49	3,700	59	3,000
30	1,800	40	2,800	50	3,800	60	2,900

EXHIBIT 16.9 **Skill Chart for General Administration Work**

	Associate	Senior Associate	Supervisor		Manager	General Director	
	Class 1	Class 2	Class 3	Class 4	Class 5	Class 6	Class 7
Rank 1	$ 600	$1,600	$2,600	$3,100	$3,600	$4,500	$5,500
Rank 2	700	1,700	2,650	3,150	3,750	4,700	6,000
Rank 3	800	1,800	2,700	3,200	3,800	4,900	
Rank 4	900	1,900	2,750	3,250	3,900	5,100	
Rank 5	1,000	2,000	2,800	3,300	4,000		
Rank 6	1,100	2,100	2,850	3,350	4,100		
Rank 7	1,200	2,200	2,900	3,400			
Rank 8	1,300	2,300	2,950	3,450			
Rank 9	1,400	2,400	3,000	3,500			

2, 3, and 4, supervisor and managerial; 5, 6, and 7, managerial, general director, and so on. Employees advance in rank as a result of their supervisor's evaluation of their:

- Effort (e.g., enthusiasm, participation, responsiveness).
- Skills required for the work (e.g., analytical, decision making, leadership, planning, process improvement, teamwork).
- Performance (typical MBO-style ratings).

To illustrate how the system works, let us consider a graduate fresh from college who enters at class 1, rank 1. After one year, this new *salaryman* and all those hired at the same time are evaluated by their supervisors on their effort, abilities, and performance. Early in the career (the first three years) effort is more important; in later years abilities and performance receive more emphasis. The number of ranks an employee moves each year (and therefore the increase in base pay) depends on this supervisory rating (e.g., receiving an A on an appraisal form lets you move up three ranks within the class, a B moves you two ranks, and so on).

Theoretically, a person with an A rating could move up three ranks in class each year and shift to the next class in three years. However, most companies require both minimum and maximum years of service within each class. So even if you receive four A ratings, you would still remain in class 1 for the minimum of six years. Conversely, if you receive four straight D grades, you would still get promoted to the next skill class after spending the maximum number of years in class 1. On the one hand, setting a minimum time in each class helps ensure that the employee knows the work and returns value to the company. On the other hand, the system slows the progress of high-potential performers. And even the weakest performers eventually get to the top of the pay structure, though they do not get the accompanying job titles or responsibility.

The system reflects the traditional Japanese saying, "A nail that is standing too high will be pounded down." An individual employee will not want to stand out. Employees work to advance the performance of the group or team rather than themselves.

Under the traditional Japanese system, increases in annual base pay are relatively small (7 percent in our example of superior performance, compared to 10 to 12 percent for star performers in many U.S. merit systems), although they compound over time, just like conventional merit and across-the-board increases in the United States. However, since the Japanese system is so seniority-based, labor costs increase as the average age of the work force increases. In fact, a continuing problem facing Japanese employers is the increasing labor costs caused by the cumulative effects of annual increases combined with lifetime employment security. Early retirement incentives and "new jobs" with lower salaries are used to contain these costs.[38]

Bonuses

Bonuses account for between 20 and 40 percent of annual salary, depending on the level in the organization. Generally, the higher up you are, the larger the percent of annual salary received as bonus. Typical Japanese companies pay bonuses twice a year (July and December). The bonuses are an *expectable* additional payment to be made twice a year, even in bad financial times. They are not necessarily related to performance.

> **Cybercomp**
> U.S. consulting firms are entering the Japanese market to provide HR consulting services for firms in Japan. For example, the Unifi Tokyo office has an English website *(www.unifinetwork .co.jp/html/index_eng.htm)*. Go to this website to see how it describes Japanese pay systems.

[38]T. Kato, "The End of Lifetime Employment in Japan? Evidence from National Surveys and Field Research," *Journal of the Japanese and International Economies* 15 (2002), pp. 489–514; T. Kato and M. Rockell, "Experiences, Credentials, and Compensation in the Japanese and U.S. Managerial Labor Markets: Evidence from New Micro Data," *Journal of the Japanese and International Economies* 6 (1992), pp. 30–51; Vlado Pucik, "The Challenges of Globalization: The Strategic Role of Local Managers in Japanese-Owned U.S. Subsidiaries," paper presented at Cornell Conference on Strategic HRM, Ithaca, NY, October 1997; P. Evans, V. Pucik, and J. Barsoux, *The Global Challenge: Frameworks for International Human Resource Management* (New York: Irwin, 2002).

The amount of bonuses is calculated by multiplying employees' monthly base pay by a multiplier. The size of the multiplier is determined by collective bargaining between employers and unions in each company. Sometimes the multiplier may also vary according to an employee's performance evaluation. In a recent year, the average multiplier was 4.8 (2.3 in summer and 2.5 in winter) for white-collar workers. So an individual whose monthly base pay is $4,500 would receive a bonus of $10,350 in July and $11,250 in December.

According to the Japan Institute of Labour, for most employees (other than managers) bonuses are in reality variable pay that helps control the employer's cash flow and labor costs but are not intended to act as a motivator or to support improved corporate performance. Japanese labor laws encourage the use of bonuses to achieve cost savings by omitting bonuses from calculations of many other benefit costs (i.e., pension plan, overtime pay, severance pay, and early retirement allowances).

The timing of the bonuses is very important. In Japan both the summer festival and the new year are traditional gift-giving times; in addition, consumers tend to make major purchases during these periods. Employees use their bonuses to cover these expenses. Thus, the tradition of the bonus system is deeply rooted in Japanese life and is today considered an indispensable form of pay.

Benefits and Allowances

The third characteristic of Japanese pay systems, the allowance, comes in a variety of forms: family allowances, commuting allowances, housing and geographic differential allowances, and so on. Company housing in the form of dormitories for single employees or rent or mortgage subsidies is a substantial amount. Life-passage payments are made when an employee marries or experiences a death in the immediate family. Commuting allowances are also important. One survey reported that employees who took public transportation received about 9,000 yen (approximately $90) per month for commuting. Family allowances vary with number of dependents. Toyota provides about 17,500 to 18,000 yen ($175 to $180) a month for the first dependent and about 4,500 to 5,500 yen ($45 to $55) for additional dependents. Some employers even provide matchmaking allowances for those who tire of life in company dorms.

Legally Mandated Benefits Legally mandated benefits in Japan include social security, unemployment, and workers' compensation. Although these three are similar to the benefits in the United States, Japanese employers also pay premiums for mandated health insurance, preschool child support, and employment of the handicapped.

The lack of economic growth that Japan has been experiencing over the last decade, coupled with the nation's heavy emphasis on seniority-based pay, means that Japanese companies' labor costs have climbed faster than those of many of their global competitors. Faced with these pressures, many companies are trying to maintain *long-time* (rather than lifetime) employment and are looking for other ways to reward younger and more flexible employees. These younger employees, who have been paid relatively poorly under the seniority-based pay system, are finding the pay in non-Japanese firms operating in Japan more attractive. Their willingness to move is creating a more active labor market. U.S. firms are succeeding in hiring young Japanese workers by offering them more competitive base pay plus performance-based pay. In order to retain younger employees, Toyota,

Toshiba, and Mitsubishi are increasingly using the performance-based pay. As a result, more variation in pay systems has emerged among traditional Japanese companies.[39]

German National System

Traditional German pay systems are embedded in a social partnership between business, labor, and government that creates a generous *vater staat,* or "nanny state."[40] *Vergutung* is the most common German word for "compensation." Pay decisions are highly regulated; over 90 different laws apply. Different *tariff agreements* (pay rates and structures) are negotiated for each industrial sector (e.g., banking, chemicals, metals, manufacturing) by the major employers and unions. Thus, the pay rates at Adam Opel AG, a major car company, are quite similar to those at Daimler, Volkswagen, and any other German car company. Methods for job evaluation and career progression are included in the tariff agreements. However, these agreements do not apply to managerial jobs. Even small organizations that are not legally bound by tariffs tend to use them as guidelines.

Base Pay

Base pay accounts for 70 to 80 percent of German employees' total compensation depending on their job level. Base pay is based on job descriptions, job evaluations, and employee age. The tariff agreement applicable to Adam Opel AG, for example, sets the following *tariff groups* (akin to job families and grades):

Wage earners	8 levels (L2–L9)
Salary earners	6 office/administrative levels (K1–K6)
	6 technical levels (T1–T6)
	4 supervisory levels (M1–M4)

Exhibit 16.10 shows the rates established in the tariff agreement for the office and administration group (K1 to K6). The rates for K1 through K6 are a percent of the rate negotiated

[39]S. Strom, "In Japan, from Lifetime Job to No Job at All," *New York Times* Online, February 3, 1999; M. Bloom, G. Milkovich, and A. Mitra "International Compensation: Learning from How Managers Respond to Variations in Local Host Contexts," *International Journal of Human Resource Management,* special issue, 2003; Michiyo Wakamoto, "Leaving the Fold," *Financial Times,* April 22 2000, p. 18; Yoshio Yanadori and George Milkovich, "Minimizing Wage Competition? Entry-Level Compensation in Japanese Firms," working paper, Center for Advanced HR Studies, Ithaca, NY, 2003; T. Kato, "The End of Lifetime Employment in Japan? Evidence from National Surveys and Field Research," *Journal of Japanese and International Economies* 15 (2002), pp. 489–514; T. Kato and M. Rockell, "Experiences, Credentials, and Compensation in the Japanese and U.S. Managerial Labor Markets: Evidence from New Micro Data," *Journal of the Japanese and International Economies* 6 (1992), pp. 30–51; Hiromichi Shibata, "Wage and Performance Appraisal Systems in Flux: Japan-U.S. Comparison," *Industrial Relations* 41 (4) (2002); E. Gedajlovic and D. J. Shapiro "Ownership Structure and Firm Profitability in Japan," *Academy of Management Journal* 45 (2002), pp. 565–575; National Personnel Authority, *Current Status of Private Firms' Remuneration Systems,* 2001; Tokyo: Japan Labour Bureau, 2001 Nendo Saiyo Keikaku, *Nihon Keizai Shimbun* ("Recruiting Plan Survey"), fiscal year 2001 (in Japanese).

[40]We thank Thomas Gresch and Elke Stadelmann, whose manuscript, *Traditional Pay System in Germany* (Ruesselsheim, Germany: Adam Opel AG, 2001), is the basis for this section of the chapter.

EXHIBIT 16.10   Base Pay Rates for Office/Administrative Jobs in Adam Opel AG's Tariff Agreement

Tariff Group (Salaried Employees)	Job Examples	Percent of Corner Rate	Base Pay (in Euros, March 2000)
K1 (simple tasks)	Mail clerk	80–100	€1,149–1,437
K2 **(corner rate = salary for employees age 23–25)** (simple administration)	Receptionist **Typist**	85–120 **100**	€1,221–1,724 **€1,437**
K3 (general administration)	Secretary Clerk	100–140	€1,437–2,011
K4 (capable of independent work)	HR specialist	125–165	€1,796–2,370
K5 (capable of independent work *plus* specialized knowledge)	Senior specialist	165–190	€2,370–2,730
K6 (broader range of responsibility)	Supervisor	200–220	€2,874–3,160

for K2 (the "corner rate"). An HR specialist (K4) receives between 1,796 and 2,370 euros, depending on age (which is presumed to reflect professional experience).

Cybercomp
A number of web locations offer currency conversions to change euros into U.S. dollars, Canadian dollars, Hong Kong dollars, and any number of other currencies. Try *www.xe.net* or *www.globaldevelopment.org* over a period of several weeks to appreciate the complexity that currency conversion adds to managing compensation.

Bonuses

While there is a trend toward performance-based bonuses they have not been part of a traditional German pay system for unionized workers. However, Adam Opel AG's tariff agreement stipulates that an average of 13 percent of the total base wages must be paid as "efficiency allowances." Systems for measuring this efficiency are negotiated with the works councils for each location. In reality, the efficiency allowances become expected annual bonuses. Performance bonuses for managerial positions not included in tariffs are based on company earnings and other company objectives. Currently only about one-third of top executives receive stock options.

Allowances and Benefits

Germany's social contract includes generous social benefits. These nationally mandated benefits, paid by taxes levied on employers and employees, include liberal social security, unemployment protection, health care, nursing care, and other programs. Employer and employee contributions to the social security system can add up to more than one-third of wages. Additionally, companies commonly provide other benefits and services such as pension plans, savings plans, building loans, and life insurance. Company cars are always popular. The make and model of the car and whether or not the company provides a cell phone are viewed as signs of status in an organization. German workers also receive 30 days of vacation plus about 13 national holidays annually (compared to an average of 11 holidays in the United States).

Trends

Germany today is not all traditional manufacturing, machine tools, and Mercedes vehicles. It has over half of the top Internet companies in Europe. And nearly one in five German adults own stock—double the rate in the late 1990s. Many of the changes are the result of global competitive pressures and technological changes. However, the picture today is not as bright as it once was. An aging population, low birth rates, earlier retirement ages, and high pension and unemployment benefits are pushing up the costs of the social support system. Since 1970, the total number of pensioners and jobless increased by 80 percent in western Germany. But the number of workers, who together with employers finance the social support system, grew by just 4 percent in that time. A relatively inflexible labor market has slowed job creation, as employers are finding it easier to move to other EU countries. All these factors are causing a rethinking of the traditional German social contract and the resulting total compensation systems. Companies are asking for greater autonomy in negotiating tariff agreements to better reflect each company's economic conditions, the use of performance-based pay, and ways to link job security to company performance.[41]

Strategic Comparisons: Japan, Germany, United States

Japanese and German traditional systems reflect different approaches compared to U.S. pay systems. Exhibit 16.11 uses the basic choices outlined in the total pay model—objectives, internal alignment, competitiveness, contribution, and management—as a basis for comparisons. Both the Japanese and the German systems constrain organizations' use of pay as a strategic tool. German companies face pay rates, job evaluation methods, and bonuses identical to those of their competitors, set by negotiated tariff agreements. The basic strategic premise, that competitive advantage is sustained by aligning with business strategy, is limited by laws and unions. Japanese companies do not face pay rates fixed industrywide; rather, they voluntarily meet to exchange detailed pay information. However, the end result appears to be the same: similar pay structures across companies competing within an industry. In contrast, managers in U.S. companies possess considerable flexibility to align pay systems with business strategies. As a result, greater variability exists among companies within and across industries.

[41]George Boyer "Review Symposium: Converging Divergences: Worldwide Changes in Employment System," *Industrial and Labor Relations Review* 54 (2001); Wolfgang Streeck, *Social Institutions and Economic Performance: Studies of Industrial Relations in Advanced Capitalist Economies* (London: Sage, 1992).

EXHIBIT 16.11   Strategic Similarities and Differences: An Illustrated Comparison

	Japan	U.S.	German
Objectives	Long-term focus High commitment Egalitarian—internal fairness Flexible work force Control cash flow with bonuses	Short/intermediate focus High commitment Peformance—market—meritocratic Flexible work force Cost control; varies with performance	Long term High commitment Egalitarian—fairness Highly trained Cost control through tariff negotiations
Internal alignment	Person based: age, ability, performance determines base pay Many levels Small pay differences	Work based: jobs, skills, accountabilities Fewer levels Larger pay differences	Work based: jobs and experience Many levels Small pay differences
External competitiveness	Monitor age-pay charts Consistent with competitors	Market determined Compete on variable and performance-based pay	Tariff based Same as competitors
Employee contribution	Bonuses vary with performance only at higher levels in organization Performance appraisal influences promotions and small portion of pay increases	Bonuses an increasing percentage of total pay Increases based on individual, unit, and corporate performance	Tariff negotiated bonuses Smaller performance bonuses for managers
Advantages	Supports commitment and security Greater predictability for companies and employees Flexibility—person based	Supports performance—competitor focus Costs vary with performance Focus on short-term payoffs (speed to market)	Supports commitment and security Greater predictability for companies and employees Companies do not compete with pay
Disadvantages	High cost of aging work-force Discourages unique contributors Discourages women and younger employees	Skeptical workers, less security Fosters "What's in it for me?" No reward for investing in long-term projects	Inflexible; bureaucratic High social and benefit costs Not a strategic tool

The pay objectives in traditional German systems include mutual long-term commitment, egalitarian pay structures, and cost control through tariff agreements, which apply to competitors' labor costs too. Japanese organizations set pay objectives that focus on the long term (age and security), support high commitment (seniority-/ability-based), are also more egalitarian, signal the importance of company and individual performance, and encourage flexible workers (person-based pay). U.S. companies, in contrast, focus on the shorter term (less job security); are market-sensitive (competitive total pay); emphasize cost control (variable pay based on performance); reward performance improvement, meritocracy, and innovation (individual bonuses and stock, etc.); and encourage flexibility.

In Japan, person-based factors (seniority, ability, and performance) are used to set base pay. Market comparisons are monitored in Japan, but internal alignment based on seniority remains far more important. Job-based factors (job evaluation) and seniority are also used in Germany. Labor markets in Germany remain highly regulated, and tariff agreements set pay for union workers. So, like the Japanese system, the German system places much greater emphasis on internal alignment than on external markets.

Each approach has advantages and disadvantages. Clearly, the Japanese approach is consistent with low turnover/high commitment, greater acceptance of change, and the need to be flexible. U.S. firms face higher turnover (which is not always a disadvantage) and greater skepticism about change (i.e., what's in it for me?). U.S. firms encourage innovation; they also recognize the enormous talent and contributions to be tapped from work-force diversity. German traditional systems tend to be more bureaucratic and rule-bound. Hence, they are more inflexible. However, they also offer more predictability and stability for people. Both the Japanese and the German national systems face challenges from the high costs associated with an aging work force. Japan has taken very limited advantage of women's capabilities. The U.S. challenges include the impact of increased uncertainty and risk facing employees, the system's short-term focus, and employees' stress and skepticism about continuous change.

Cybercomp

Discussing national systems in other countries in the same detail as we do here for the Japanese and German systems would require another textbook. More information on these and other countries can be found easily on the web. Some useful websites for starting your search are provided by:

Economist Intelligence Unit (EIU):
countrydata.bvdep.com/ip (EIU country reports)
www.ebusinessforum.co (Ebusiness Forum)
Federation of European Employers:
www.euen.co.uk/condits.html (Report on Pay and Working Conditions across Europe)
Trak-it-Down: *www.trak-it-down.com/InterHR.htm* (list of international HR sites, updated regularly)

STRATEGIC MARKET MIND-SET

A global study of pay systems used by companies with worldwide operations identifies three general compensation strategies: (1) localizer, (2) exporter, and (3) globalizer.[42] These approaches reflect the company's business strategy.[43]

Localizer: "Think Global, Act Local"

If a localizer operates in 150 countries, it will have 150 different systems. The company's business strategy is to seek competitive advantage by providing products and services tailored to local customers. Localizers operate independently of the corporate headquarters. One manager in the study compared his company's pay system this way: "It's as if McDonald's used a different recipe for hamburgers in every country. So, too, for our pay system." Another says, "We seek to be a good citizen in each nation in which we operate. So should our pay system." The pay systems are consistent with local conditions.

Exporter: "One Size Fits All"

Exporters are virtual opposites of localizers. Exporters design a total pay system at headquarters and "export" it worldwide for implementation at all locations. Exporting a basic system (with some adjustments for national laws and regulations) makes it easier to move managers and professionals among locations (e.g., among European countries) without having to change how they are paid. It also communicates consistent corporatewide objectives. Managers say that "one plan from headquarters gives all managers around the world a common vocabulary and a clear message about what the leadership values." Common software used to support compensation decisions and deployed around the world makes uniform policies and practices feasible. However, not everyone likes the idea of simply implementing what others have designed. One manager complained that headquarters rarely consulted managers in the field: "There is no notion that ideas can go both ways. It's a one-way bridge."

Globalizer: "Think and Act Globally and Locally"

Similar to exporters, globalizers seek a common system that can be used as part of the "glue" to support consistency across all global locations. But headquarters and the operat-

---

[42]M. Bloom, G. Milkovich, and A. Mitra, "International Compensation: Learning from How Managers Respond to Variations in Local Host Contexts," *International Journal of Human Resource Management,* special issue, 2003. See also N. Napier and Van Tuan Vu, "International HRM in Developing and Transitional Economy Context," *Human Resource Management Review* 8(1) (1998), pp. 39–71.

[43]J. W. Walker, "Are We Global Yet?" *Human Resource Planning,* First Quarter 2000, pp. 7–8; R. Locke and K. Thelen, "Apples and Oranges Revisited: Contextualized Comparisons and Comparative Labor Policies," *Politics and Society* 23(2) (1996), pp. 337–367; Steve Gross and Per Wingerup "Global Pay? Maybe Not Yet!" *Compensation and Benefits Review,* 2000; H. Mehlinger and M. Krain, *Globalization and the Challenges of the New Century* (Bloomington, IN: Indiana University Press, 2000); M. Mendenhall and Gary Oddou, *Readings and Cases in International Human Resource Management* (Cincinnati: Southwestern College, 2000); J. S. Black, H. Gregerson, M. E. Mendenhall, and L. Stroh, *Globalizing People through International Assignments* (Reading, MA: Addison-Wesley, 1999); Daniel Yergin, "What Makes Global Firms Resilient?" *Harvard Business Review,* 7(14), July 2003.

ing units are heavily networked to shared ideas and knowledge. Managers in these companies said:

> "No one has a corner on good ideas about how to pay people. We need to get them from all our locations."

> "Home country begins to lose its meaning; performance is measured where it makes sense for the business, and pay structures are designed to support the business."

> "Compensation policy depends more on tax policies and the dynamics of our business than it does on 'national' culture. I suppose you could argue that tax policies reflect a country's dominant culture, but from where I sit it depends on the political aims of the ruling coalitions and our ability to effectively work with them. The culture argument is something politicians hide behind."

Cybercomp

Go to the Organization Resources Counselors' International website, *www.orcin.com*, to observe a state-of-the-art global market site. ORCI collects data from Azerbaijan, Belarus, and other central and eastern European locations as well as Latin America. How useful do you think its data would be for making pay decisions? What limitations exist? Compare the ORCI website with another consulting company's website. Critique each site.

All three of these strategic global approaches avoid matching national systems. Instead, they align the total pay system with the global business strategy. Even the localizer adapts to local (national) systems because such a pay system is aligned with the company's business strategy. If IBM, for example, is competing by integrating its solutions offered to customers around the world, then it is likely to use a globalizer approach. If Toshiba operates locally or nationally and emphasizes the differences among national markets, then it is likely to adopt a localizer approach. The challenge is for managers to rethink international compensation in the face of global competition and to align global pay with the way the business is aligned.

EXPATRIATE PAY

When multinationals decide to open facilities in an international location, one of the many decisions they face is the type of personnel to hire. International subsidiaries choose among a mix of:

- Expatriates ("expats": people who are citizens of the employer's base country; e.g., a Japanese citizen working for Sony in Toronto).
- Third-country nationals (TCNs: people who are citizens of neither the employer's base country nor the subsidiary's country; e.g., a German citizen working for Sony in Toronto).

- Local-country nationals (LCNs: people who are citizens of the country in which the subsidiary is located; e.g., a Canadian citizen working for Sony in Toronto).

Hiring LCNs has advantages. The company saves relocation expenses and avoids concerns about employees adapting to the local culture. Employment of LCNs satisfies nationalistic demands for hiring locals. Only rarely do organizations decide that hiring LCNs is inappropriate.

EXHIBIT 16.12   Why Expatriates Are Selected

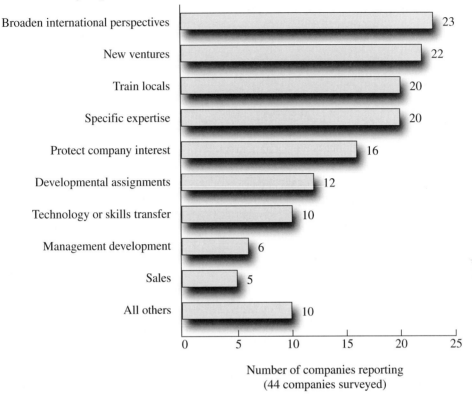

Number of companies reporting
(44 companies surveyed)

However, expats or TCNs may be brought in for a number of reasons.[44] The foreign assignment may represent an opportunity for selected employees to develop an international perspective; the position may be sufficiently confidential that information is entrusted only to a proven domestic veteran; or the particular skills required for a position may not be readily available in the local labor pool. Exhibit 16.12 catalogs a number of reasons for asking employees to take work assignments in another country.

Designing expatriate pay systems is a challenge. A company that sends a U.S. employee (base salary of $80,000) with a spouse and two children to London for three years can expect to spend $800,000 to $1,000,000. Obviously, the high cost of expatriate assignments must be offset by the value of the employee's contributions.[45]

[44]C. Reynolds, "Expatriate Compensation in Historical Perspective," *International Human Resource Journal,* Summer 1997, pp. 118–131; Geoffrey Latta, "Expatriate Policy and Practice: A 10 Year Comparison of Trends," *Compensation and Benefits Review,* 2000; C. Reynolds, "Global Compensation and Benefits in Transition," *Compensation and Benefits Review,* January/February 2000, pp. 27–37; J. Stewart Black and Hal B. Gregerson, "The Right Way to Manage Expats," *Harvard Business Review,* March–April 1999, pp. 52–62; Roger Heron, "The Cardinal Sins of Expatriate Policies," *Organization Resources Counselors: Innovations in International HR,* Fall 2001; Hilary Harris, "Strategic Management of International Workers," *Organization Resources Counselors: Innovations in International HR,* Spring 2002.

[45]*What It Costs to House Expatriates Worldwide* (New York: Runzheimer International, 2000); Steve Constantin and Charles Bell, "Linking a Global Work Force at Dow Chemical," *Workspan,* no. 3, 2002, 3 pp. 22–28.

EXHIBIT 16.13
Common Allowances in Expatriate Pay Packages

Financial Allowances	**Social Adjustment Assistance**
Reimbursement for tax return preparation	Emergency leave
Tax equalization	Home leave
Housing differential	Company car/driver
Children's education allowance	Assistance with locating new home
Temporary living allowance	Access to western health care
Goods and services differential	Club membership
Transportation differential	General personal services (e.g., translation)
Foreign service premium	Personal security (manager and family)
Household furnishing allowance	General culture-transition training (manager)
Currency protection	Social events
Hardship premium	Career development and repatriation planning
Completion bonus	Training for local-culture customs (manager)
	Orientation to community (manager and family)
Family Support	Counseling services
Language training	Rest and relaxation leave
Assistance locating schools for children	Domestic staff (excluding child care)
Training for local culture's customs (family)	Use of company-owned vacation facilities
Child care providers	
Assistance locating spousal employment	

Elements of Expatriate Compensation

Exhibit 16.13 is a shopping list of items that can make up expatriate compensation. The list includes everything from household furnishing allowances to language and culture training, spousal employment assistance, and rest and relaxation leaves for longer-term assignments. Usually such lists are organized into four major components: salary, taxes, housing, and allowances and premiums.

Salary

The base salary plus incentives (merit, eligibility for profit sharing, bonus plans, etc.) for expatriate jobs is usually determined via job evaluation or some system of "job leveling."[46] 3M applies a global job evaluation plan for its international assignments. Common factors describe different 3M jobs around the world. With this system, the work of a general manager in Brussels can be compared to the work of a manager in Austin, Texas, or in Singapore.

Beyond salaries and incentives, the intent of the other components is *to help keep expatriate employees financially whole and minimize the disruptions of the move.* This means maintaining a standard of living about equal to their peers in their home or base country. This is a broad standard that often results in very costly packages.

[46]Sherrie Webster Brown, "Spanning the Globe for Quality Pay Data," in *2003–2004 Survey Handbook and Directory* (Scottsdale, AZ: WorldatWork, 2002), pp. 95–100; Margaret A. Coil, "Salary Surveys in a Blended-Role World," in *2003–2004 Survey Handbook and Directory* (Scottsdale, AZ: WorldatWork, 2002), pp. 57–64.

Taxes

Income earned in foreign countries has two potential sources of income tax liability.[47] With few exceptions (Saudi Arabia is one), foreign tax liabilities are incurred on income earned in foreign countries. For example, money earned in Japan is subject to Japanese income tax, whether earned by a Japanese or a Korean citizen. The other potential liability is the tax owed in the employee's home country. The United States has the dubious distinction of being the only developed country that taxes its citizens for income earned in another country, even though that income is taxed by the country in which it was earned. Employers handle this through *tax equalization.*[48] The employer takes the responsibility of paying whatever income taxes are due to the host country and/or the home country. Taxes are deducted from employees' earnings up to the same amount of taxes they would pay had they remained in their home country.

This allowance can be substantial. For example, the marginal tax rates in Belgium, the Netherlands, and Sweden can run between 70 and 90 percent. So if a Swedish expatriate is sent to a lower-tax country, say, Great Britain, the company keeps the difference. If a British expatriate goes to Sweden, the company makes up the difference in taxes. The logic here is that if the employee kept the windfall from being assigned to a low-tax country, then getting this person to accept assignments elsewhere would become difficult.

Housing

Appropriate housing has a major impact on an expatriate's success. Most international companies pay housing allowances or provide company-owned housing. "Expatriate colonies" often grow up in sections of major cities where many different international companies group their expatriates.

Allowances and Premiums

A friend in Moscow cautions that when we take the famed Moscow subway, we should pay the fare at the beginning of the ride. Inflation is so high there that if we wait to pay until the end of the ride, we won't be able to afford to get off! Cost-of-living allowances, club memberships, transportation assistance, child care and education, spousal employment, local culture training, and personal security are some of the many service allowances and premiums expatriates receive.

The logic supporting these allowances is that foreign assignments require that the expatriate (1) work with less direct supervision than a domestic counterpart, (2) often live and work in strange and sometimes uncongenial surroundings, and (3) represent the employer in the host country. The size of the premium is a function of both the expected hardship and hazards in the host country and the type of job. An assignment in London will probably yield fewer allowances than one in Tehran, where Death to Americans Day is still a national holiday.

[47]Paul Bailey, "The Role of Cost of Living Data in Creating Cost-Effective Expatriate Assignments," *International Human Resource Journal* 9(4) (Winter 2001), pp. 27–30.

[48]C. Reynolds, "Expatriate Compensation in Historical Perspective," *International Human Resource Journal,* Summer 1997, pp. 118–131.

The Balance Sheet Approach

Most North American, European, and Japanese global firms combine these elements of pay in a *balance sheet approach*.[49] The name stems from accounting, where credits and debits must balance. It is based on the premise that employees on overseas assignments should have the same spending power as they would in their home country. Therefore, the *home country is the standard* for all payments. The objective is to:

1. Ensure mobility of people to global assignments as cost-effectively as feasible.
2. Ensure that expatriates neither gain nor lose financially.
3. Minimize adjustments required of expatriates and their dependents.

Notice that none of these objectives link to performance.

Exhibit 16.14 depicts the balance sheet approach. Home-country salary is the first column. A person's salary (based on job evaluation, market surveys, merit, and incentives) must cover taxes, housing, and goods and services, plus other financial obligations (a "reserve"). The proportions set for each of the components in the exhibit are *norms* (i.e., assumed to be "normal" for the typical expatriate) set to reflect consumption patterns in the home country for a person at that salary level with that particular family pattern. They are not actual expenditures. These norms are based on surveys conducted by consulting firms. Using the norms is supposed to avoid negotiating with each individual, although substantial negotiation still occurs.

Let us assume that the norms suggest that a typical manager with a spouse and one child, earning $84,000 in the United States, will spend $2,000 per month on housing, $2,000 on taxes, and $2,000 on goods and services and put away a reserve of $1,000 per month. The next building block is the equivalent costs in the host country where the assignment is located. For example, if similar housing costs $3,000 in the host country, the expatriate is expected to pay the same $2,000 paid in the United States and the company pays the employee the difference; in our example, the extra $1,000 per month. In the illustration, the taxes, housing, and goods and services components are all greater in the host country than in the home country. The expatriate bears the same level of costs (white area of right-hand column) as at home. The employer is responsible for the additional costs (shaded area). (Changing exchange rates among currencies complicates these allowance calculations.)

However, equalizing pay may not motivate an employee to move to another country, particularly if the new location has less personal appeal. Therefore, many employers also offer some form of financial incentive or bonus to encourage the move. The right-hand column in Exhibit 16.14 includes a relocation bonus. Four out of five U.S. multinational corporations pay relocation bonuses to induce people to take expatriate assignments.

[49]*International Total Remuneration,* certification course T9 (Scottsdale, AZ: WorldatWork, 2000); Cal Reynolds, "International Compensation," in *Compensation Guide,* ed. William A. Caldwell (Boston: Warren, Gorham and Lamont, 1998); Steve Gross and Per Wingerup, "Global Pay? Maybe Not Yet!" *Compensation and Benefits Review,* 2000; J. Boudreau, P. Ramstad, and P. Dowling, "Global Talentship: Toward a Decision Science Connecting Talent to Global Strategic Success," CAHRS Working Paper 02–21, Cornell, Ithaca, NY.

EXHIBIT 16.14
Balance Sheet
Approach

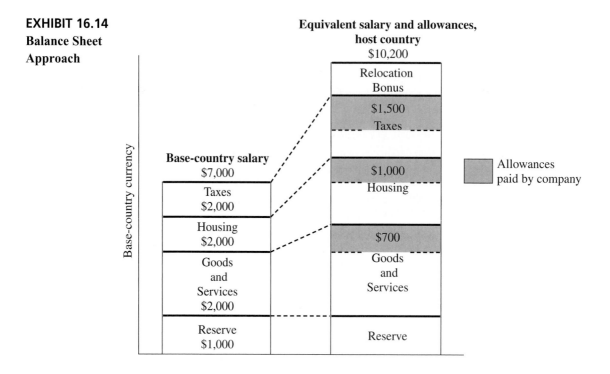

If gaining international experience is really one of the future competencies required by organizations, then the need for such bonuses ought to be reduced, since the expatriate experience should increase the likelihood of future promotions. Either the experience expatriates obtain is unique to each situation and therefore not transferable or companies simply do not know how to value it. Whatever the reason, research reveals that U.S. expatriates feel their U.S. organizations still do not value their international expertise.[50] So the rhetoric of the value of global competencies has yet to match the reality—hence the need for relocation incentives.

Alternatives to Balance Sheet Approach

Employers continue to explore alternatives to the balance sheet, due primarily to the cost. *Negotiation* simply means the employer and employee find a mutually agreeable package. The arrangements tend to be relatively costly (or generous, depending on your point of view), create comparability problems when other employees are asked to locate overseas ("but Mike and Sarah got . . ."), and need to be renegotiated with each transfer.

Another alternative, *localization,* ties salary to the *host* (local) *country's* salary scales and provides some cost-of-living allowances for taxes, housing, and dependents. The allowances tend to be similar to those under the balance sheet, but the salary can vary. The

[50]Richard A. Guzzo, Katherine A. Noonan, and Efrat Elron, "Expatriate Managers and the Psychological Contract," *Journal of Applied Psychology* 7(4) (1994), pp. 617–626; "Focusing on International Assignments," *ACA News,* July/August 1999; Steve Gross and Per Wingerup, "Global Pay? Maybe Not Yet!" *Compensation Benefits Review,* 2000.

downside is that individual salaries vary with the location (average rate for an engineer in Geneva is $55,000, compared to $41,300 in Rome and $32,000 in Bristol) rather than with the job or performance.

While the balance sheet approach ties salary to the home country, the *modified balance sheet* ties salary to a *region* (Asia-Pacific, Europe, North America, Central America, or South America). The logic is that if an employee of a global business who relocates from San Diego, California, to Portland, Maine, receives only a moving allowance, why should all the extras be paid for international moves of far less distance (e.g., from Germany to Spain)? In Europe, many companies no longer view European managers who work outside their home country as expats. Instead, they are Europeans running their European businesses. And the use of a common currency, the euro, makes this easier.

Another common modification is to decrease allowances over time. The logic is that the longer the employee is in the host country, the closer the standard of living should come to that of a local employee. For example, if Americans eat a $10 pizza twice a week in the United States, should they eat a $30 pizza twice a week in Tokyo, at the employer's expense? More typically, after a couple of months, the expatriate will probably learn where the nationals find cheaper pizza or will switch to sushi. The main purpose of the modified balance sheet seems to be to reduce costs; it pays little attention to performance, ensuring fairness, or satisfying preferences of expats.

The *lump-sum/cafeteria approach* offers expats more choices. This approach sets salaries according to the home-country system and simply offers employees lump sums of money to offset differences in standards of living. For example, a company will still calculate differences in cost of living, but instead of allocating them housing, transportation, goods and services, and so on, it simply gives the employee a total allowance. Perhaps one employee will trade less spacious housing for private schooling and tutors for the children; another employee will make different choices. We know of one expatriate who purchased a villa and a winery in Italy with his lump-sum allowance. He has been reassigned to Chicago but still owns and operates his winery.

Expatriate Systems → Objectives? *Quel dommage!*

Talk to experts in international compensation, and you soon get into complexities of taxes, exchange rates, housing differences, and the like. What you do not hear is how the expatriate pay system affects competitive advantage, customer satisfaction, quality, or other performance concerns. It does emphasize maintaining employee purchasing power and minimizing disruptions and inequities. But the lack of attention to improving performance or ensuring that the expatriate assignment is consistent with organization objectives is glaring.

Expatriate compensation systems are forever trying to be like Goldilocks's porridge: not too high, not too low, but just right. The expatriate pay must be sufficient to encourage the employee to take the assignment yet not be so attractive that local nationals will feel unfairly treated or that the expatriate will refuse any future reassignments. These systems also presume that expats will be repatriated to their home country. However, the relevant standard for judging fairness may not be home-country treatment. It may be the pay of other expats, that is, the expat community, or it may be local nationals. And how do local nationals feel about the allowances and pay levels of their expat co-workers? Very little research tells us how expats and those around them judge the fairness of expat pay.

Employee Preferences

Beyond work objectives, costs, and fairness, an additional consideration is employees' preferences for international assignments. For many Europeans, working in another country is just part of a career. Yet for many U.S. employees, leaving the United States means leaving the action. They may worry that expatriate experience sidetracks rather than enhances a career. Employees undoubtedly differ in their preferences for overseas jobs, and preferences can vary over time. Having children in high school or elderly parents to care for, divorce, working spouses, and other life factors exert a strong influence on whether an offer to work overseas is a positive or negative opportunity. Research does inform us of the following:

- 68 percent of expatriates do not know what their jobs will be when they return home.
- 54 percent return to lower-level jobs. Only 11 percent are promoted.
- Only 5 percent believe their company values overseas experience.
- 77 percent have less disposable income when they return home.
- Only 13 percent of U.S. expatriates are women. (Yet 49 percent of all U.S. managers and professionals are women.)
- More than half of returning expatriates leave their company within one year.[51] Unfortunately, while research does highlight the problem, it does not offer much guidance for designers of expat pay systems. Consequently, we are at the mercy of conjecture and beliefs.[52]

BORDERLESS WORLD → BORDERLESS PAY? GLOBALISTS

Many multinational corporations are attempting to create a cadre of globalists: managers who operate anywhere in the world in a borderless manner. They expect that during their career, they will be located in and travel from country to country. According to a former CEO of General Electric, "The aim in a global business is to get the best ideas from everyone, everywhere."[53] To support this global flow of ideas and people, some compa-

[51]"Expatriate Dual Career Survey Report" (New York: Windham International and National Foreign Trade Council, 1997); Garry M. Wederspahn, "Costing Failures in Expatriate Human Resources Management," *Human Resource Planning* 15(3), pp. 27–35; Michael S. Schell and Ilene L. Dolins, "Dual-Career Couples and International Assignments," *International Compensation and Benefits*, November–December 1992, pp. 25–29; Soo Min Toh and Angelo S. DeNisi, "Host Country National Reactions to Expatriate Pay Policies: A Model and Implications," *Academy of Management Review*, 28(4), 2003, pp. 606–621.

[52]Paul Evans, Vlado Pucik, and Jean-Louis Barsoux, *The Global Challenge* (New York: McGraw-Hill, 2002); Allen D. Engle, Sr., and Mark Mendenhall, "Transnational Roles and Transnational Rewards: Global Integration in Executive Compensation," presentation at international HR conference, Limerick, Ireland, June 2003; Meenal Chaukar, Jakub Sovina, and Charles Tyler, "Globalist Compensation," paper presented at Cornell University seminar on international compensation, Spring 2003.

[53]"The Global Company: Series on Global Corporations," *Financial Times*, November 7, 1995.

nies are also designing borderless or at least regionalized pay systems. One testing ground for this approach is the European Union. As our global guide points out, one difficulty with borderless pay is that base pay levels and the other components depend too much on differences in each nation's laws and customs about managerial pay.[54]

Focusing on expatriate compensation may blind companies to the issue of adequate rewards for employees who are seeking global career opportunities. Ignoring such employees causes them to focus only on the local operations and pay less attention to the broader goals of the global firm. It is naive to expect commitment to a long-term global strategy in which local managers have little input and receive limited benefits. Paradoxically, attempts to localize top management in subsidiaries may reinforce the gap in focus between local and global management.

Your Turn   Back to Classic Coke

1. Based on the description of Coca-Cola's worldwide business strategy in the accompanying *Financial Times* article (Exhibit 1) contrast what Daft means by "going global" versus "multi-local."
2. Which of the three international compensation strategies (globalizer, exporter, localizer) would you expect to find at Coca-Cola? Which would you recommend? Explain why.

On p. 533, Daft characterizes Coke's approach as "Think local, act local." Yet he quickly goes on to discuss Coke's global brand recognition. Coke is experiencing a classic case of trying to blend cohesiveness (global glue) and efficiencies by communicating clear strategies, policy, values, and standards across the globe while encouraging the flexibility and agility to be sensitive and leverage local conditions.

3. What does this mean for total compensation? What compensation decisions are global? Which are local? Why?
4. Select a specific policy, technique, and objective from the total pay model used in the book (e.g., external competitiveness or employee contributions). Use it to illustrate your answer to question 3.

[54]Paul Evans, Vlado Pucik, and Jean-Louis Barsoux, *The Global Challenge* (New York: McGraw-Hill, 2002); Allen D. Engle, Sr., and Mark Mendenhall, "Transnational Roles and Transnational Rewards: Global Integration in Executive Compensation," presentation at international HR conference, Limerick, Ireland, June 2003; Meenal Chaukar, Jakub Sovina, and Charles Tyler, "Globalist Compensation," paper presented at Cornell University seminar on international compensation, Spring 2003.

Coca-Cola's President Discusses the Company's Worldwide Business Strategy

[In the] 1980s we were "going global"—expanding geographically into many of the nearly 200 countries in which we do business today. Even though our historical strength came from operating as a "multi-local" business that for decades relied heavily on the insight of our local bottling partners, we knew that we had to centralise control to manage the expansion, and to ensure that our business operated cohesively.

We also encouraged consolidation among our bottling partners, equipping them to provide effective service to rapidly consolidating retailers, as well as creating capital structures substantial enough to weather the new global economic dynamics. That approach served its purpose very well, and we stuck with it. . . .

Globalisation had forced fundamental changes at a pace so rapid that many countries struggled to cope. And as globalisation accelerated, many national and local leaders understandably sought to ensure sovereignty over their political, economic and cultural destinies.

As a result, the very forces that were making the world more connected and homogeneous were simultaneously triggering a powerful desire for local autonomy and preservation of unique cultural identity.

So, as the century was drawing to a close, the world had changed course, and we had not. The world was demanding greater flexibility, responsiveness and local sensitivity, while we were further centralising decision-making and standardising our practices, moving further away from our traditional multi-local approach. We were operating as a big, slow, insulated, sometimes even insensitive "global" company; and we were doing it in a new era when nimbleness, speed, transparency and local sensitivity had become absolutely essential to success.

Consequently, you could say we got a taste of the 21st century before it arrived, making it obvious to us we had a lesson to learn. And what we learned was something simple, yet powerful: that the next big evolutionary step of "going global" now has to be "going local". In other words, we had to rediscover our own multi-local heritage. . . .

Because the world has changed so much, we do not have the luxury of merely turning back the clock to simpler days. We must lead a Coca-Cola business system that not only has the professional expertise, management systems and capital structures required for success in a globalised economy, but which is also able to act nimbly and with great sensitivity in every local community where our brands are sold.

That is why I have a mandate from our board of directors to create a new company and quickly change our behaviour. . . . In every community, we must remember we do not do business in markets, we do business in societies. The purpose was not simply to cut costs, or to try to save our way to prosperity. It was to begin to recreate the multi-local company that we need to be. Thus, in the first 100 days of our new management team, we specifically set out to remove the significant internal structural obstacles we had created for ourselves over the years, and thus to create optimal flexibility for our local operating units.

It was a painful decision to eliminate the jobs of good Coca-Cola professionals, but it was the most responsible choice for the long-term success of our company and our stakeholders around the world. We are moving quickly, and during the next few years you will see us following some clear principles to meet the demands of the 21st century:

- *Think local, act local.* Many people say Coca-Cola is the brand with the greatest worldwide relevance. We know instinctively, however, that the global success of Coca-Cola is the direct result of people drinking it one bottle at a time in their own local communities. So we are placing responsibility and accountability in the hands of our colleagues who are closest to those billions of individual sales.

   We will not abandon the benefits of being global. But if our local colleagues develop an idea or strategy that is the right thing to do locally, and it fits within our fundamental values, policies, and standards of integrity and quality, then they have the authority and responsibility to make it happen. Just as important, we will hold them accountable for the outcomes of that idea or strategy.
- *Focus as a pure marketing Company.* Disciplined focus is absolutely critical. All our success flows from the strength of our brands, and our ability to relate to people. . . .
- *Lead as model citizens.* In every community where we sell our brands, we must remember we do not do business in markets; we do business in societies. In Mozambique two weeks

ago, for example, I was extremely proud to see how our local colleagues and bottling partners all across southern Africa rallied together to provide much-needed support for the flood relief efforts. . . . They did it because they cared, and because they understood the implications for their own societies.

For two weeks this month, I travelled across Europe and southern Africa, talking with our people and with government, business and community leaders as well. As I listened during those conversations, I heard two consistent themes. First, our local people are ready to take on their shoulders the authority and accountability that naturally belongs to them. Second, the government, business and community leaders were very encouraging, openly sharing insights that will be helpful to us as we work hard to re-earn the status of model business citizens anywhere we might have taken steps backward.

So overall, we will draw on a long-standing belief Coca-Cola always flourishes when our people are allowed to use their insight to build the business in ways best suited to their local culture and business conditions.

We will, of course, maintain clear order. Our small corporate team will communicate explicitly the clear strategy, policy, values and quality standards needed to keep us cohesive and efficient. But just as important, we will also make sure we stay out of the way of our local people and let them do their jobs.

Source: Adapted from a *Financial Times* article by Douglas Daft, chairman and CEO of the Coca-Cola Company, March 27, 2000.

Summary

Studying employee compensation only in your neighborhood, city, or country is like being a horse with blinders. Removing the blinders by adopting an international perspective deepens your understanding of local issues. Anyone interested in compensation must adopt a worldwide perspective. The globalization of businesses, financial markets, trade agreements, and even labor markets is affecting every workplace and every employment relationship. And employee compensation, so central to the workplace, is embedded in the different political-socioeconomic arrangements found around the world. Examining employee compensation with the factors in the global pay model offers insights into managing total compensation internationally.

The basic premise of this book is that compensation systems have a profound impact on individual behavior, organization success, and social well-being. We believe this holds true within and across all national boundaries.

Review Questions

1. Rank the factors in the global guide according to your belief in their importance for understanding and managing compensation. How does your ranking differ from those of your peers? From those of international peers? Discuss how the rankings may change over time.

2. Distinguish between nationwide and industrywide pay determination. How do they compare to a business strategy–market approach?

3. Develop arguments for and against "typical" Japanese-style, "typical" German-style, and "typical" U.S.-style approaches to pay. Using the global guide, what factors are causing each approach to change?

4. Distinguish between global, workers, expatriates, local nationals, and third-country nationals.

5. In the balance sheet approach to paying expats, most of total compensation is linked to costs of living. Some argue that expatriate pay resembles a traditional Japanese pay system. Evaluate this argument.

6. Go back to Exhibit 16.4. What is meant by "the full house" or "variation within a culture"? Evaluate the concept's importance in understanding and managing global total compensation.

Managing the System

The last part of our total pay model is management. This means ensuring that the right people get the right pay for achieving objectives in the right way. We have touched on aspects of management already—the use of budgets in merit increase programs, the "message" that employees receive from their variable pay bonuses, communication and cost control in benefits, and the importance of employee involvement in designing the total compensation system.

Several important issues remain. The first, already noted in Chapter 16's global guide, is the significant role that government plays in managing compensation. Laws and regulations are the most obvious government intervention. In the United States, minimum-wage legislation, the Equal Pay Act, and Title VII of the Civil Rights Act, among others, regulate pay decisions. Legal issues in compensation in the United States are covered in Chapter 17.

Government is more than a source of laws and regulations, however. As a major employer, as a consumer of goods and services, and through its fiscal and monetary policies, government affects the supply of and demand for labor.

Chapter 18 covers several aspects of managing compensation: costs, communication, and change. One of the key reasons for being systematic about pay decisions is to manage the costs associated with those decisions. As Chapter 18 will show, a total compensation system is really a device for allocating money in a way that is consistent with the organization's objectives.

Communication and change are linked. What is to be communicated to whom is an important, ongoing issue. In addition to communication, the system must be constantly evaluated to judge its effectiveness. Is it helping the organization achieve the objectives? What information can help us make these judgments? If it is not doing what it should be doing, how do we change it? Any system will founder if it is ineffectively implemented, managed, and communicated.

Chapter 18 also discusses enterprise software that holds out the promise of helping users make pay decisions faster and smarter. The hope and hype surrounding the search for value gained from pay programs is discussed. Perhaps most critical of all, we look at ethics and the increasing importance of personal standards when no professional standards exist.

EXHIBIT VI.1 The Pay Model

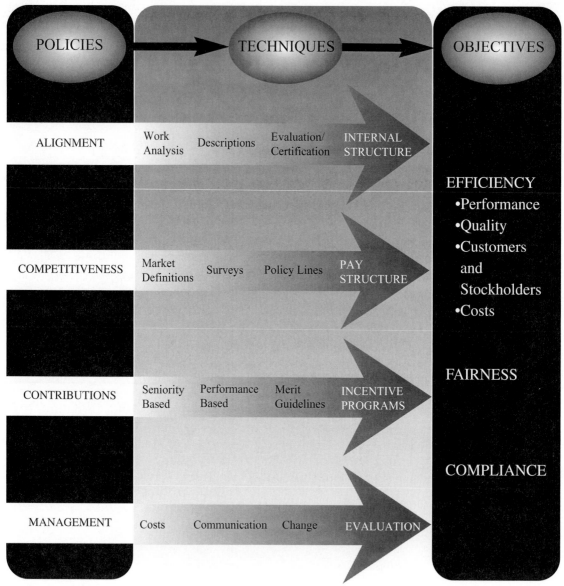

POLICIES	TECHNIQUES	OBJECTIVES
ALIGNMENT	Work Analysis — Descriptions — Evaluation/Certification — INTERNAL STRUCTURE	EFFICIENCY •Performance •Quality •Customers and Stockholders •Costs
COMPETITIVENESS	Market Definitions — Surveys — Policy Lines — PAY STRUCTURE	FAIRNESS
CONTRIBUTIONS	Seniority Based — Performance Based — Merit Guidelines — INCENTIVE PROGRAMS	COMPLIANCE
MANAGEMENT	Costs — Communication — Change — EVALUATION	

Government and Legal Issues in Compensation

Chapter Outline

A 1939 pay policy handbook for a major US corporation outlines this justification for paying different wages to men and women working on the same jobs:[1] . . .

> The . . . wage curve . . . is not the same for women as for men because of the more transient character of the former, the relative shortness of their activity in industry, the differences in environment required, the extra services that must be provided, overtime limitations, extra help needed for the occasional heavy work, and the general sociological factors not requiring discussion herein. Basically then we have another wage curve . . . for women below and not parallel with the men's curve.

The presumption that people should be paid different wages based on "general socio-logical factors" was still evident in the United States in the 1960s, in newspaper help-wanted ads that specified "perky gal Fridays" and in whites-only local unions. The 1960s civil rights movement and subsequent legislation ended such practices.

Are you thinking you have stumbled into a history class by mistake? Not so. These historical practices and subsequent legislation still affect pay decisions. However, legisla-tion does not always achieve what it intends. Nor does it always intend what it achieves. Consequently, *compliance* and *fairness* are continuing compensation issues.

In democratic societies, the legislative process begins when a problem is identified (not all citizens are receiving fair treatment in the workplace) and corrective legislation is proposed (the Civil Rights Act, Americans with Disabilities Act). If enough support de-velops, often as a result of compromises and tradeoffs, the proposed legislation becomes law. Employers, along with other stakeholders, attempt to influence the form any legisla-tion will take.

Once passed, laws are enforced by agencies through rulings, regulations, inspections, and investigations. Companies respond to legislation by auditing and perhaps altering their practices, perhaps defending their practices before courts and agencies, and perhaps again lobbying for legislative change. The laws and regulations issued by governmental agencies created to enforce the laws are a significant influence on compensation deci-sions throughout the world.

GOVERNMENT AS PART OF THE EMPLOYMENT RELATIONSHIP

The exact role that government should play in the contemporary workplace depends in part on one's political ideology. Some call for organizations and the government to act in concert to carry out a public policy that protects the interests of employees.[2] Others be-lieve that the best opportunities for employees are created by the constant change and re-configuring that is inherent in market-based economies; the economy ought to be allowed

---

[1]The job evaluation manual was introduced as evidence in *Electrical Workers (IUE) v. Westinghouse Electric Corp.,* 632 F.2d 1094, 23 FEP Cases 588 (3rd Cir. 1980), *cert. denied,* 452 U.S. 967, 25 FEP Cases 1835 (1981).

[2]Bruce Kaufman, ed., *Government Regulation of the Employment Relationship* (Ithaca, NY: Cornell University Press, 1998); Arthur Gutman, *EEO Law and Personnel Practices,* 2d ed. (Thousand Oaks, CA: Sage, 2000); Paul Osterman, Thomas A. Kochan, Richard M. Locke, and Michael J. Piore, *Working in America: A Blueprint for the New Labor Market* (Cambridge, MA: MIT Press, 2001).

to adapt and transform, undistorted by government actions.[3] All countries throughout the world must address these issues. However, different countries and cultures have different perspectives.

Governments' usual interests in compensation decisions are whether procedures for determining pay are fair (e.g., pay discrimination), safety nets for the unemployed and disadvantaged are sufficient (e.g., minimum wage, unemployment compensation), and employees are protected from exploitation (e.g., overtime pay, child labor restrictions). Consequently, company pay practices set the context for national debates on the minimum wage, health care, the security and portability of pensions, and even the quality of public education and the availability of training.

In addition to being a party to all employment relationships, government units are also employers and purchasers. Consequently, government decisions also affect conditions in the labor market.

Demand

In the United States, almost 18 million people are employed by local, state, and federal government units. A government also indirectly affects labor demand through its purchases (military aircraft, computer systems, paper clips) as well as its financial policy decisions. For example, lowering interest rates generally boosts manufacturing of everything from condoms to condominiums. Increased business activity translates into increased demand for labor and upward pressure on wages.

Supply

In addition to being an employer, government affects labor supply through legislation. Laws aimed at protecting specific groups also tend to restrict those groups' participation in the labor market. Compulsory schooling laws restrict the supply of children available to sell hamburgers or to assemble soccer balls. Licensing requirements for certain occupations (plumbers, cosmetologists, psychologists) restrict the number of people who can legally offer a service.

To see how regulations reflect a society, look at the U.S. compensation regulations in Exhibit 17.1. The exhibit shows how the issues have changed over time. An early emphasis was basic protection: Child labor was prohibited and overtime wage provisions were specified in the Fair Labor Standards Act. Prevailing-wage laws (Davis-Bacon and Walsh-Healey) specified government's obligations as an employer. The minimum wage has been periodically increased ever since its initial passage, and additional prevailing wage legislation continues to be passed. However, the main thrust of legislation shifted in the 1960s to emphasize civil rights. Since then we have continued to increase the scope of that legislation. More recently, legislation has dealt with issues in the changing contemporary workplace. The Worker Economic Opportunity Act exempts stock options from the calculation for overtime pay. The Sarbanes-Oxley Act is a response to recent accounting scandals.

This chapter will examine the most important U.S. regulations concerning wages. Because our society continues to wrestle with the issue of discrimination, we will go into

---

[3]*Keeping America Competitive* (Washington, DC: Employment Policy Foundation, 1994).

EXHIBIT 17.1 The Evolving Nature of U.S. Federal Pay Laws

1931	Davis-Bacon Act	Requires that mechanics and laborers on public construction projects be paid the "prevailing wage" in an area.
1936	Walsh-Health Public Contracts Act	Extends prevailing-wage concept to manufacturers or suppliers of goods for government contracts.
1938	Fair Labor Standards Act	Sets minimum wage, sets hours of work, and prohibits child labor.
1963	Equal Pay Act	Equal pay required for men and women doing "substantially similar" work in terms of skill, effort, responsibility, and working conditions.
1964	Title VII of Civil Rights Act	Prohibits discrimination in all employment practices on basis of race, sex, color, religion, national origin, or pregnancy.
1967	Age Discrimination Act	Protects employees age 40 and over against age discrimination.
1978	Pregnancy Discrimination Act	Pregnancy must be covered to same extent that other medical conditions are covered.
1990	Americans with Disabilities Act	Requires that "essential elements" of a job be called out. If a person with a disability can perform these essential elements, reasonable accommodations must be provided. Essential elements are specified as part of job evaluation.
1991	Civil Rights Act	Makes filing a lawsuit easier and more attractive.
1993	Family and Medical Leave	Requires employers to provide up to 12 weeks' unpaid leave for family and medical emergencies.
1997	Mental Health Act	Mental illness must be covered to same extent that other medical conditions are covered.
2000	Worker Economic Opportunity Act	Stock options and bonuses need not be included in calculating overtime pay.
2002	Sarbanes-Oxley Act	Executives cannot retain bonuses or profits from selling company stock if they mislead the public about the financial health of the company.

some depth on how pay discrimination has been defined and the continuing earnings gap between men and women and among racial groups.

FAIR LABOR STANDARDS ACT OF 1938

The Fair Labor Standards Act (FLSA) of 1938 covers all employees (with some exceptions, discussed later) of companies engaged in interstate commerce or in the production of goods for interstate commerce. In spite of its age, this law remains a cornerstone of pay regulation in the United States. The FLSA's major provisions are:

1. Minimum wage
2. Hours of work
3. Child labor

An additional provision requires that records be kept of employees, their hours worked, and their pay.

Minimum Wage

Minimum-wage legislation is intended to provide an income floor for workers in society's least productive jobs. When first enacted in 1938, the minimum wage was 25 cents an hour. It has been raised periodically; today it is $5.15. Almost as soon as it is increased, work begins on proposals for further increases. A current proposal would raise it by $1 an hour over two years.

Forty-three states have their own minimum wages to cover jobs omitted from federal legislation.[4] If state and federal laws cover the same job, the higher rate prevails. Nine states have minimums higher than the federal rate. The effect of raising the minimum wage may go beyond the number of people who actually are paid the minimum. As legislation forces pay rates at the lowest end of the scale to move up, pay rates above the minimum often increase in order to maintain differentials. This shift in pay structure does not affect all industries equally. The lowest rates paid in the software, chemical, oil, and pharmaceutical industries are already well above minimum; any legislative change has little direct impact on them. In contrast, retailing and service firms tend to pay at or near minimum wage to many clerks and sales persons. When legislation results in substantially higher labor costs for these firms, they may consider substituting capital for jobs (e.g., automated inventory control systems, paperless airline tickets) or reducing the number of jobs available.

Exhibit 17.2 shows the purchasing power of the federal minimum wage adjusted to the year 2003. The graph shows that for someone earning the minimum wage, changes in the rate have not kept pace with inflation. This decline in real purchasing power is the continuing argument in favor of raising the minimum wage or even indexing it to changes in the consumer price index.

Most economic studies associate a higher minimum wage with a disappearance of jobs, particularly for inexperienced and unskilled workers whose perceived value does not equal their actual cost. A widely quoted study in the 1990s declared the job loss to be minimal,[5] but other economists found fault with the methodology of the study.[6] The 1990s were a period of prolonged expansion of the U.S. economy. As a result, employers of minimum-wage workers were forced to pay above the minimum in order to attract sufficient employees during a period of record low unemployment levels. In this situation, raising the legal requirement made no difference.[7]

---

[4]"State Changes in Compensation Laws," *Compensation and Benefits Review,* November/December 2002, pp. 41–53.

[5]David Card and Alan Krueger, "Minimum Wages and Employment: A Case Study of the Fast Food Industry in New Jersey and Pennsylvania," *American Economic Review,* September 1994, pp. 772–793; Lawrence F. Katz and Alan B. Krueger, "The Effect of the Minimum Wage on the Fast-Food Industry," *Industrial and Labor Relations Review* 46(1) (October 1992), pp. 6–21.

[6]Finis Welch, Donald Deere, and Kevin Murphy, "Estimates of Job Loss with Increasing Minimum Wage," presentation at the meeting of the American Economic Association, Washington, DC, 1995; David Neumark and William Wascher, "The Effect of New Jersey's Minimum Wage Increase on Fast Food Employment: A Re-evaluation Using Payroll Records," NBER Working Paper 5224, August 1995, pp. 199–206.

[7]Don Bellante and Gabriel Picone, "Fast Food and Unnatural Experiments: Another Perspective on the New Jersey Minimum Wage," *Journal of Labor Research* 4 (Fall 1999), pp. 463–477; David Neumark, "Raising Incomes by Mandating Higher Wages," *NBER Reporter,* Fall 2002, pp. 5–9.

EXHIBIT 17.2
Real Value of
the Federal
Minimum
Wage,
1956–2003

Source: *Step Up,*
Not Out: The
Case for Raising
the Federal
Minimum Wage
for Workers in
Every State, EPI
Issue Brief 149.

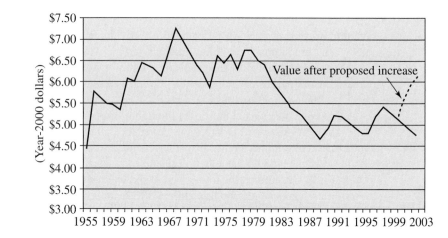

Minimum-wage discussion is also tied up in the social good of the people who are not faring well in the market economy. Some make the case that continuing a low minimum wage permits the continuation of boring, dead-end jobs that ought to be modernized. If employers are forced to pay higher wages, they will find it worthwhile to offer training to employees to increase their economic value. Marriott, for example, boasts of helping its low-wage cleaning staff apply for federal earned income tax credits. Marriott and others can get by paying minimum wages because of taxpayer-financed government benefit programs that exist to help low-income wage earners. While 30 percent of minimum-wage earners are young people who will work their way out of this category as their skills increase (thus becoming more valuable to employers), the other 70 percent are adults age 20 and over. Of the adult group, 45 percent work full-time and 40 percent are the sole wage earners in their households.

Minimum wages do create some jobs—for economists who have a field day studying whether a minimum wage destroys jobs or reduces poverty.[8] What is certain is that people working at or near the minimum wage who continue to work definitely do benefit from mandated minimum-wage increases, and other workers in higher-level jobs in the same companies may also benefit. Yet fewer workers will be hired or hours will be cut if the increased costs cannot be passed on to consumers or offset by increased productivity.

"Living Wage"

Rather than push for changes in national legislation, a more fruitful path has been to push for a "living wage" at local levels. Many cities have begun to enact such legislation, which provides for a minimum wage tailored to living costs in an area.[9] Sometimes the laws cover only city employees; other times they cover employers that do business with the city. Re-

[8]From "Not So Fair Pay," *Economist,* June 27, 1998, p. 80. Also see David Neumark, "Raising Incomes by Mandating Higher Wages," *NBER Reporter,* Fall 2002, pp. 5–9.

[9]D. Neumark and S. Adams, "Do Living Wage Ordinances Reduce Urban Poverty?" NBER Working Paper W606, March 2000; Dora L. Costa, "From Mill Town to Board Room: The Rise of Women's Paid Labor," *Journal of Economic Perspectives* 14(4) (2000); Greg Hundley, "Male/Female Earnings Differences in Self-Employment: The Effects of Marriage, Children, and the Household Division of Labor," *Industrial and Labor Relations Review* 54(1) (October 2000), pp. 95–114.

cent attempts have been made to cover all private sector employees in a municipality. Santa Fe passed an ordinance in 2003 that covers all employers with 25 or more employees. Supporters of the legislation pointed out that Santa Fe wages were 23 percent below the national average while the cost of living was 18 percent above the national average.[10]

Sometimes living wage laws cover only base wages, but more frequently they require health insurance, vacations, sick pay, job security, and provide incentives to unionize. Los Angeles's law covers 9,000 people whose employers receive benefits from tax abatements (e.g., restaurant workers in an area redeveloped with public funds), through service contracts (e.g., janitors who clean public buildings), or through leases at the Los Angeles airport (e.g., baggage handlers, wheelchair attendants). The aim is to increase the wages of the "working poor"—people who work full-time but do not earn enough to support their families. Because the wage that is mandated is based on an assessment of living costs in an area, the mandated amounts vary among cities. They may vary further depending on whether or not benefits are provided.

Hours of Work

The overtime provision of the FLSA requires payment at one-and-a-half times the standard for working more than 40 hours per week. The law's objective is to share available work by making the hiring of additional workers a less costly option than the scheduling of overtime for current employees. However, the workplace has changed a lot since the law was passed. Today, overtime pay is often the least costly option. Contemporary employers face (1) an increasingly skilled work force with higher training costs per employee and (2) higher fringe benefits, the bulk of which are fixed per employee. These factors have lowered the break-even point at which it pays employers to schedule longer hours and pay the overtime premium, rather than hire, train, and pay fringes for more employees.

Several amendments to increase the overtime penalty have been proposed over the years. These typically seek to increase the penalty, reduce the standard workweek to less than 40 hours, or repeal some of the exemptions.

Exemptions

The Wage and Hour Division of the Department of Labor, which is charged with enforcement of the FLSA, provides strict criteria that must be met in order for jobs to be exempt from minimum-wage and overtime provisions. Repeated amendments to the act, plus a changing workplace, have made the distinction between exempt and nonexempt jobs difficult to determine. In addition to exemptions for jobs in the transportation industry, where an eight-hour day is impractical logistically, there are exemptions for exectives, professionals, and administrators.

To be exempt, executives must:

- Primarily undertake management duties.
- Supervise two or more employees.
- Have control (or at least great influence) over hiring, firing, and promotion.
- Exercise discretionary powers.
- Devote at least 80 percent of their work hours to such activities.

[10]Santa Fe website: *www.santafelivingwage.org.*

Unscrupulous employers sometimes try to get around the overtime requirement by classifying employees as managers, even though the work of these "managers" differs only slightly from that of their co-workers.

To be an exempt professional, employees must:

- Do work requiring knowledge generally acquired by prolonged, specialized study, or engage in original and creative activity in a recognized artistic field.
- Consistently exercise discretion or judgment.
- Do work that is primarily intellectual and nonroutine.
- Devote at least 80 percent of their work hours to such activities.

However, contemporary workplace trends that increase employee discretion and omit specific details on duties blur the distinction between exempt and nonexempt.

What Time Is Covered?

Sometimes counting the hours of work becomes a contest. Exhibit 17.3 details what we mean. Occupational Safety and Health Administration legislation specifies the number of breaks that must be provided in an eight-hour workday. The Portal-to-Portal Act provides that time spent on activities before beginning the "principal activity" is generally not compensable. The original issue that inspired the Act was the time that miners were forced to spend traveling to and from the actual underground site where the mining was occurring. The law's most current application surrounds the use of "on-call employees" who must make themselves available to respond outside the usual workday.[11] Firefighters and other emergency personnel who are frequently on call for 24 hours a day are traditional examples. Today, with more businesses operating 24 hours a day, telecommunications and software services personnel must respond quickly to problems outside their regularly scheduled workday. In general, if employees can use this "on-call" time for their own purposes, there is no legal requirement to pay employees for such time, even if they are required to carry a beeper or must let their employer know where they can be reached. However, if they are required to stay on the employer's premises while on call, then they must be compensated for that time. Sometimes a flat rate is paid for the added inconvenience of being on call. These payments must be included when computing overtime pay.

What Income Is Covered?

FLSA specifies one and a half for overtime, but one and a half of what? As more employees became eligible for bonuses, there was an argument over whether bonus, gain-sharing, and stock option payments needed to be included for calculating overtime pay. A 1999 advisory from the Wage and Hour Division said they did. But the extra bookkeeping and calculations provided enough of a burden that employers simply did not offer these forms of pay to nonexempt employees. The Worker Economic Opportunity Act, a 2000 amendment to FLSA, allows stock options and bonuses to be exempt from inclusion in overtime pay calculations. Gifts or special-occasion bonuses have never needed to be included, because

---

[11]"Contingent Workers Fight for Fairness," National Alliance for Fair Employment, *www.fairjobs.org/report/,* 2000, Ray Cordelli, "Getting on Point about the Meaning of 'On Call,' " *HR Wire,* June 14, 1999, *www.hresource.com/hresources/sampleChapters/hrwirSampleChapter5.html;* N.E. Fried and Associates, "1994–95 Survey of Exempt and Non-Exempt On-Call Practices: Job Site vs. Home-Based" Dublin, OH, 1994.

**EXHIBIT 17.3
There's No
Such Thing
as a Free . . .**

Source:—
Canadian Press.
Item posted to
Internet by D.
Shniad.

Gainers Workers Must Pay to Use Bathroom
EDMONTON—Employees at Gainers Inc. are now docked pay for every bathroom break visit made outside of breaks and lunch hour under regulations brought in last week by company owner Burns Meats Ltd.

EDMONTON—Employees at Gainers Inc. are now docked pay for every bathroom break visit made outside of breaks and lunch hour under regulations brought in last week by company owner Burns Meats Ltd.

A notice posted in the meat-packing plant tells employees that abusing washroom visits has lowered productivity. If employees need to use the bathroom outside of breaks, they must report to a supervisor, who records the time of departure and return. The time is tabulated at the end of the week and pay cheques are deducted based on an employee's hourly wage.

"How can they charge you for going to the washroom?" asked one angry employee. The man said one worker at the plant had a kidney transplant and has to use the washroom often.

"Because of this system, he had to hold it in [between breaks] for a whole week. He went once for three minutes and was charged 43 cents."

Such washroom rules are rare but there is nothing in the Alberta employment standards code that requires a person to be paid when they don't work, said Kathy Lazowski, a public affairs officer with Alberta Labour.

they are at the employer's discretion rather than a pay form promised to employees if certain conditions are met.

Compensatory Time Off

The changing nature of the workplace and of pay systems has led to calls to reform FLSA to allow for more flexible scheduling and easier administration of variable pay plans.

Federal legislation has been proposed (but not yet passed) that would give employees and employers the option of trading overtime pay for time off. Rather than being paid overtime after 8 hours for a 10-hour workday, an employee would have the option of taking 2 or more hours off at another time. The employee would get more scheduling flexibility to attend to personal matters, and the employer would save money.

Child Labor

Generally, persons under 18 cannot work in hazardous jobs such as meat packing and logging; persons under 16 cannot be employed in jobs involving interstate commerce except for nonhazardous work for a parent or guardian. Additional exceptions and limitations also exist.

The union movement in the United States has taken a leading role in publicizing the extent of the use of child labor outside the United States to produce goods destined for U.S. consumers. A Your Turn exercise at the end of this chapter explores some of the issues surrounding child labor outside the United States.[12] Government guidelines help importers monitor the employment practices of subcontractors producing goods for the U.S. market.

The next group of laws set pay for work done to produce goods and services contracted by the federal government. These are called *prevailing-wage laws.*

---

[12]Douglas L. Kruse and Douglas Mahony, "Illegal Child Labor in the United States: Prevalence and Characteristics," *Industrial and Labor Relations Review* 54(1) (October 2000), pp. 17–40; Faraaz Siddiqi and Harry Anthony Patrinos, "Child Labor: Issues, Causes, and Interventions," Human Capital Development and Operations Policy Working Paper 56, *www.worldbank.org/html/extdr/hnp/hddflash/workp/wp_00056.html.*

PREVAILING WAGE LAWS

A *government-defined prevailing wage* is the minimum wage that must be paid for work done on covered government projects or purchases. If you have been to Boston within the past five years, you have seen "The Big Dig," Boston's government-financed project to put its freeways underground. A construction project of such magnitude attracts workers from a very wide area and distorts the labor market. Prevailing-wage laws prevent contractors from using their size to drive down wages. Contractors must determine the "going rate" for construction labor in an area. As a practical matter, the "union rate" for labor becomes the going rate. That rate then becomes the mandated minimum wage on the government-financed project.

Contractors object to this requirement because it frequently means that they have to match a wage rate which only a minority of area workers receive and which drives up the cost of government-financed projects.

A number of laws contain prevailing-wage provisions. They vary on the government expenditures they target for coverage. The main prevailing-wage laws include the Davis-Bacon Act, the Walsh-Healey Public Contracts Act, the Service Contract Act, and the National Foundation for the Arts and Humanities Act. A spate of new laws extends prevailing-wage coverage to new immigrants to the United States and to noncitizens who are working in the United States under special provisions. For example, the Nursing Relief for Disadvantaged Areas Act of 1999 allows qualified hospitals to employ temporary foreign workers as registered nurses for up to three years under a special visa program. The prevailing wage for registered nurses must be paid to these foreign workers. Similar acts target legal immigrants and farm workers.

Much of the legislation discussed so far was originally passed in the 1930s and 1940s in response to social issues of that time. While this legislation has continued to be extended up to the present, the equal rights movement in the 1960s pushed different social problems to the forefront. The Equal Pay Act and the Civil Rights Act were passed. Because of their substantial impact on human resource management and compensation, they are discussed at length below.

PAY DISCRIMINATION: WHAT IS IT?

Before we look at specific pay discrimination laws, let us address the more general question of how to legally define discrimination. The law recognizes two types of discrimination: access discrimination and valuation discrimination. The charges of discrimination and reverse discrimination that most often make the news involve *access discrimination:* the denial of particular jobs, promotions, or training opportunities to qualified women or minorities. The University of Michigan, for example, was accused of access discrimination for using differential standards among different racial groups to determine who is "qualified" for admission. Being a member of a minority group counted for 20 points, whereas the quality of the admission essay counted for 3 points. (Being an athlete also counted for 20 points.) In 2003, the Supreme Court ruled that while schools can take race into account for admission, this 20-point differential was illegal because it was applied in a mechanical way. However, the admission process for Michigan's law school was upheld because it was narrowly tailored and more flexible. Minority candidates for the law school were interviewed and their entire record was examined, in contrast to the routine addition of 20 points that the undergraduate school used. (The court did not address the issue of the preferred treatment for athletes or children of alumni or big donors.)

A second legally recognized interpretation of discrimination is *valuation discrimination,* which looks at the pay women and minorities receive for the jobs they perform. This is the more salient definition for our purposes. The Equal Pay Act makes it clear that it is discriminatory to pay minorities or women less than males when they are performing equal work (i.e., working side by side, in the same plant, doing the same work, producing the same results). This definition of pay discrimination hinges on the standard of *equal pay for equal work.*

Many believe that this definition of valuation discrimination does not go far enough. They believe that valuation discrimination can also occur when men and women hold entirely different jobs. For example, office and clerical jobs are typically staffed by women, and craft jobs (electricians, welders) are typically staffed by men. Is it illegal to pay employees in one job group less than employees in the other if the two job groups contain work that is not equal in content or results but is, in some sense, of comparable worth to the employer?

In this case, the proposed definition of pay discrimination hinges on the standard of *equal pay for work of comparable worth.* Existing federal laws do not support this standard. However, several states have enacted laws that require a comparable-worth standard for state and local government employees. The province of Ontario, Canada, has extended such legislation to the private sector.[13]

So two standards for defining valuation discrimination need to be considered: the already legally established standard of equal pay for equal work, and the more stringent standard of equal pay for work of comparable worth. For an understanding of the legal foundations of each, let us turn to the legislation and key court cases.

THE EQUAL PAY ACT

The Equal Pay Act (EPA) of 1963 forbids wage discrimination on the basis of gender under either of the following conditions:

- Employees perform equal work in the same establishment.
- Employees perform jobs requiring equal skill, effort, and responsibility under similar working conditions.

Pay differences between equal jobs can be justified by an *affirmative defense.* Differences in pay between men and women doing equal work are legal if these differences are based on any one of four criteria:

- Seniority.
- Merit or quality of performance.
- Quality or quantity of production.
- Some factor other than sex.

---

[13]Morley Gunderson, "The Evolution and Mechanics of Pay Equity in Ontario," *Canadian Public Policy* 28, suppl. 1 (2002).

These terms for comparison and permitted defenses seem deceptively simple. Yet numerous court cases have been required to clarify the act's provisions, particularly its definition of "equal."

Definition of Equal

The Supreme Court established guidelines to define equal work in the *Schultz v. Wheaton Glass* case back in 1970. Wheaton Glass Company maintained two job classifications for selector-packers in its production department: male and female. The female job class carried a pay rate 10 percent below that of the male job class. The company claimed that the male job class included additional tasks such as shoveling broken glass, opening warehouse doors, and doing heavy lifting that justified the pay differential. The plaintiff claimed that the extra tasks were infrequently performed and not all men did them. Further, these extra tasks performed by some of the men were regularly performed by employees in another classification ("snap-up boys"), and these employees were paid only 2 cents an hour more than the women. Did the additional tasks performed by some members of one job class render the jobs unequal?

The Court decided they did not. It ruled that the equal work standard required only that jobs be *substantially* equal, not identical. Additionally, in several cases where the duties employees actually performed were different from those in the job descriptions, the courts held that the *actual work performed* must be used to decide whether jobs are substantially equal.

Definitions of Skill, Effort, Responsibility, Working Conditions

The Department of Labor provides these definitions of the four factors.

1. *Skill:* Experience, training, education, and ability as measured by the performance requirements of a particular job.
2. *Effort:* Mental or physical—the degree of effort (not type of effort) actually expended in the performance of a job.
3. *Responsibility:* The degree of accountability required in the performance of a job.
4. *Working conditions:* The physical surroundings and hazards of a job, including dimensions such as inside versus outside work, heat, cold, and poor ventilation.

Guidelines to clarify these definitions have evolved through court decisions. For an employer to support a claim of *unequal* work, the following conditions must be met:

1. The effort/skill/responsibility must be substantially greater in one of the jobs compared.
2. The tasks involving the extra effort/skill/responsibility must consume a *significant amount* of time for *all* employees whose additional wages are in question.
3. The extra effort/skill/responsibility must have a *value commensurate* with the questioned pay differential (as determined by the employer's own evaluation).

Time of day (e.g., working a night shift) does not constitute dissimilar working conditions. However, if a differential for working at night is paid, it must be separated from the base wage for the job.

Factors Other than Sex

Of the four affirmative defenses for unequal pay for equal work, "a factor other than sex" has prompted the most court cases. Factors other than sex include shift differentials; temporary assignments; bona fide training programs; differences based on ability, training, or experience; and other reasons of "business necessity." A practice will not automatically be prohibited simply because wage differentials result. Rather, the practice must be evaluated for its business necessity and for whether reasonable alternatives exist.

Factors other than sex have been interpreted as a broad exception that may include business reasons advanced by the employer. *Kouba v. Allstate* was an early case that addressed the issue. Allstate Insurance Company paid new sales representatives a minimum salary during their training period. After completing the training, the sales reps received a minimum salary or their earned sales commissions, whichever was higher. The minimum salary during training needed to be high enough to attract prospective agents to enter the training program yet not so high as to lessen the incentive to earn sales commissions after training. Allstate maintained that the minimum salary needed to be calculated individually for each trainee and that the trainee's past salary was a necessary factor used in the calculation. But Allstate's approach resulted in women trainees generally being paid less than male trainees because women had held lower-paying jobs before entering the program. Allstate maintained the pay difference resulted from acceptable business reasons, a factor other than sex.

Lola Kouba didn't buy Allstate's arguments. She argued that acceptable business reasons were limited to "those that measure the value of an employee's job performance to his or her employer." But the court rejected Kouba's argument for a narrow definition of acceptable business reasons. It said that a company's business reasons for a practice must be evaluated for reasonableness. A practice will not automatically be prohibited simply because wage differences between men and women result. Notice that the court did not say that Allstate's business reasons were justified. It said only that Allstate's argument could not be rejected solely because the practice perpetuated historical differences in pay. Rather, Allstate needed to justify the business relatedness of the practice.[14]

The murkiness of "business necessity" persists, especially if it is part of "a pattern of economic disparity." That is what a group of female brokers at Merrill Lynch charged in their class action suit. They were concerned with how accounts from departing brokers, walk-ins, leads, and referrals were being distributed. They felt that the top men brokers were given the most promising accounts, while everyone else, including the 15 percent of brokers who were women, got the "crumbs." The women contended that Merrill Lynch discriminated against women in wages, promotions, account distributions, maternity leaves, and other areas. A negotiated settlement promised to establish a more open method for sharing leads and not to penalize brokers for time off in determining bonuses and production quotas. A similar lawsuit settling claims by women brokers at Salomon Smith Barney aims to make women constitute at least one-third of new trainees annually and to substantially increase the number of women and minorities in managerial positions.

---

[14]Fran D. Blau, Marianne A. Farber, and Ann E. Winkler, *The Economics of Women, Men, and Work,* 3d ed. (New York: Simon and Schuster, 1998); Michael E. Gold, "Towards a Unified Theory of the Law of Employment Discrimination," *Berkeley Journal of Employment and Labor Law,* February 2001.

All of these cases were settled out of court, so no legal clarification of a "factor other than sex" has ever been provided. It does seem that pay differences for equal work can be justified for demonstrably business-related reasons. But what is and is not demonstrably business-related has yet to be cataloged.

Reverse Discrimination

Universities seem to be hotbeds for claims of discrimination and reverse discrimination in pay systems, too. Several cases deal with allegations of reverse discrimination against men when pay for women is adjusted. In one case, the University of Nebraska created a model to calculate salaries based on estimated values for a faculty member's education, field of specialization, years of direct experience, years of related experience, and merit.[15] Based on these qualifications, the university granted raises to 33 women whose salaries were less than the amount computed by the model. However, the university gave no such increases to 92 males whose salaries were also below the amount the model set for them based on their qualifications. The court found this system a violation of the Equal Pay Act. It held that, in effect, the university was using a new system to determine a salary schedule, based on specific criteria. To refuse to pay employees of one sex the minimum required by these criteria was illegal.

So what does this have to do with compensation management in the United States? Viewed collectively, the courts have provided reasonably clear directions. The design of pay systems must incorporate a policy of equal pay for substantially equal work. The determination of substantially equal work must be based on the actual work performed (the job content) and must reflect the skill, effort, responsibility, and working conditions involved. It is legal to pay men and women who perform substantially equal work differently if the pay system is designed to recognize differences in performance, seniority, quality and quantity of results, or certain factors other than sex in a nondiscriminatory manner. Further, if a new pay system is designed, it must be equally applied to all employees.

But what does this tell us about discrimination on jobs that are *not substantially equal*—dissimilar jobs? Fifty-eight percent of all working women are not in jobs substantially equal to jobs of men, so they are not covered by the Equal Pay Act. Title VII of the Civil Rights Act extends protection to them.

TITLE VII OF THE CIVIL RIGHTS ACT OF 1964, CIVIL RIGHTS ACT OF 1991

Title VII prohibits discrimination on the basis of sex, race, color, religion, or national origin in any employment condition, including hiring, firing, promotion, transfer, compensation, and admission to training programs.[16] Title VII was amended in 1972 and 1978. The 1972 amendments strengthened enforcement and expanded coverage to include employ-

[15]William E. Becker and Robert K. Toutkoushian, "Measuring Gender Bias in the Salaries of Tenured Faculty Members," presentation to NBER Research Group on Higher Education, Cambridge, MA, October 1999; Mary Hampton, Carol Oyster, Leticia Pena, Pamela Rodgers, and John Tillman, "Gender Inequity in Faculty Pay," *Compensation and Benefits Review*, November/December 2000, pp. 54–59.

[16]29 U.S.C. § 206 (d) (1) (1970). Its coverage is broader, also. Employers, employment agencies, labor organizations, and training programs involving 15 or more employees and some 120,000 educational institutions fall under its jurisdictions.

ees of government and educational institutions, as well as private employers of more than 15 persons. The pregnancy amendment of 1978 made it illegal to discriminate based on pregnancy, childbirth, or related conditions.

Court cases have established two theories of discrimination behavior under Title VII: (1) disparate treatment and (2) disparate impact.

Disparate Treatment

Disparate or unequal treatment applies different standards to different employees: for example, asking women but not men if they plan to have children. Japanese female college students continue to report that recruiters ask them different questions than are asked of male college students. The mere fact of unequal treatment may be taken as evidence of the employer's intention to discriminate under U.S. law.

Disparate Impact

Practices that have a differential effect on members of protected groups are illegal, unless the differences are work-related. The major case that established this interpretation of Title VII is *Griggs v. Duke Power Co.*, which struck down employment tests and educational requirements that screened out a higher proportion of blacks than whites. Even though the practices were applied equally—both blacks and whites had to pass the tests— they were prohibited because (1) they had the consequence of excluding a protected group disproportionately and (2) the tests were not related to the jobs in question.

Under disparate impact, whether or not the employer intended to discriminate is irrelevant. A personnel decision can, on its face, seem neutral, but if its results are unequal, the employer must demonstrate that the decision is work-related.

The Civil Rights Act of 1991 reinforced the two standards of discrimination— disparate treatment and disparate impact. However, the two standards remain difficult to apply to pay issues, since pay differences are legal for dissimilar work. It is still not clear what constitutes pay discrimination in dissimilar jobs. Some legal scholars question whether this distinction even makes sense any longer.[17]

PAY DISCRIMINATION AND DISSIMILAR JOBS

In 1981, the Supreme Court, in *Gunther v. County of Washington,* determined that pay differences for dissimilar jobs may reflect discrimination. In this case, four jail matrons in Washington County, Oregon, claimed that their work was comparable to that performed by male guards. The matrons also were assigned clerical duties, because guarding the smaller number of female prisoners did not occupy all of the work time.

Lower courts said the matrons had no grounds because the jobs did not meet the equal work requirement of the Equal Pay Act. But the Supreme Court stated that a Title VII pay case was not bound by the definitions in the Equal Pay Act. While the Supreme Court did not say that Washington County had discriminated, it did say that a claim of wage discrimination could also be brought under Title VII for situations where the jobs were not the same. Unfortunately, the Court did not say what might constitute evidence of pay discrimination in

[17]Michael E. Gold, "Towards a Unified Theory of the Law of Employment Discrimination," *Berkeley Journal of Employment and Labor Law,* February 2001.

dissimilar jobs. The case was returned to a lower court for additional evidence of discrimination and was eventually settled out of court.

So if jobs are dissimilar and if no pattern of discrimination in hiring, promotion, or other personnel decisions exists, then what constitutes pay discrimination?[18] Courts have ruled on the use of market data (external competitiveness) as well as the use of job evaluation (internal alignment). We will look at both of these possible standards in turn.

Proof of Discrimination: Use of Market Data

In a landmark case regarding the use of market data, Denver nurse Mary Lemons claimed that her job, held predominantly by women, was illegally paid less than the city and county of Denver paid jobs held predominantly by men (tree trimmers, sign painters, tire servicemen, etc.). Lemons claimed that the nursing job required more education and skill. Therefore, to pay the male jobs more than the nurses' jobs simply because the male jobs commanded higher rates in the local labor market was discriminatory. She argued that the market reflected historical underpayment of "women's work." The court disagreed. The situation identified by *Lemons*—pay differences in dissimilar jobs—did not by itself constitute proof of intent to discriminate.

The courts continue to uphold use of market data to justify pay differences for different jobs. *Spaulding v. University of Washington* developed the argument in greatest detail. In this case, the predominantly female faculty members of the Department of Nursing claimed that they were illegally paid less than faculty in other departments. They presented a model of faculty pay comparisons in "comparable" departments that controlled for the effects of level of education, job tenure, and other factors. They asserted that any pay difference not accounted for in their model was discrimination.

But the courts have been dubious of this statistical approach. As the late Carl Sagan used to say, "Just because it's a light doesn't make it a spaceship." Far better to define discrimination directly, rather than concluding that it is "whatever is left." The judge in the *Spaulding* case criticized the statistical model presented, saying it "unrealistically assumed the equality of all master's degrees, ignored job experience prior to university employment, and ignored detailed analysis of day-to-day responsibilities." Without such data, "we have no meaningful way of determining just how much of the proposed wage differential was due to sex and how much was due to academic discipline." "Market prices," according to the judge, "are inherently job-related."

We wish we had as much confidence in "the market" as the judge did. As you recall from Chapter 8, a lot of judgment goes into the wage survey process.[19] Which employers constitute

[18]Orley Ashenfelter and Ronald Oaxaca, "The Economics of Discrimination: Economists Enter the Courtroom," *American Economic Review,* May 1987, pp. 321–325; Victor Fuchs, *Women's Quest for Economic Equality* (Cambridge, MA: Harvard University Press, 1988); B. F. Reskin and H. I. Hartmann, eds., *Women's Work, Men's Work: Segregation on the Job* (Washington, DC: National Academy Press, 1986).

[19]Sara L. Rynes and George T. Milkovich, "Wage Surveys: Dispelling Some Myths about the 'Market Wage,' " *Personnel Psychology,* Spring 1986, pp. 71–90; Marlene Kim, "Employers' Estimates of Market Wages: Implications for Wage Discrimination," working paper, Rutgers University, 1998; Charlie Trevor and Mary E. Graham, "Deriving the Market Wage: Three Decision Areas in the Compensation Survey Process," *WorldatWork Journal,* Fourth Quarter 2000, pp. 69–76; Judith K. Hellerstein, David Neumark, and Kenneth R. Troske, "Market Forces and Sex Discrimination," *Journal of Human Resources* 37(2) (Spring 2002), pp. 353–380.

the "relevant market"? Does the relevant market vary by occupation? Do different market definitions yield different wage patterns? Clearly, judgment is involved in answering these questions. Yet the courts have thus far neglected to examine those judgments for possible bias.

Proof of Discrimination: Jobs of Comparable Worth

A second approach to determining pay discrimination on jobs of dissimilar content hinges on finding a standard by which to compare the value of jobs. The standard must do two things. First, it must permit jobs with dissimilar content to be declared equal or "in some sense comparable."[20] Second, it must permit pay differences for dissimilar jobs that are not comparable. Job evaluation has been proposed as that standard.[21] If an employer's own job evaluation study shows that jobs of dissimilar content are of equal value to the employer, then isn't failure to pay them equally proof of intent to discriminate? That was the issue considered in *AFSCME v. State of Washington,* where the state commissioned a study of the concept of comparable worth (discussed later in this chapter) and its projected effect on the state's pay system. The study concluded that by basing wages on the external market, the state was paying women approximately 20 percent less than it was paying men in jobs deemed of comparable value to the state. The state took no action on this finding, alleging it could not afford to adjust wages, so the American Federation of State, County, and Municipal Employees (AFSCME) sued the state. The union alleged that since the state was aware of the adverse effect of its present policy, failure to change the policy constituted discrimination.

But an appeals court ruled that the state was not obligated to correct the disparity. Even though the state had commissioned the study, it had not agreed to implement the study's results. Therefore, the employer had not, in the court's view, admitted that the jobs were equal or established a pay system that purported to pay on the basis of comparable worth rather than markets. Rather than appeal, the parties settled out of court. The state revamped its pay system and agreed to make more than $100 million in "pay equity" adjustments.

So where does this leave us? Clearly, Title VII prohibits intentional discrimination, whether or not the employees in question hold the same or different jobs. Discrimination may be proved by direct evidence of an employer's intent (e.g., an overall pattern of behavior that demonstrates disparate treatment). However, Title VII rulings also make it clear that pay discrimination is not limited only to equal jobs; it may also occur in setting different rates for different jobs. It is also clear that the use of external market rates is not illegal. Consequently, simply demonstrating pay differences on jobs that are not equal is insufficient to prove discrimination.

What additional implications for the design and administration of pay systems can be drawn? These court decisions imply that pay differentials between dissimilar jobs will not be prohibited under Title VII if the differences can be shown to be based on the content of the work, its value to the organization's objectives, and the employer's ability to attract and retain employees in competitive external labor markets. The courts appear to recognize that "the value of a particular job to an employer is but one factor influencing the rate of compensation for a job." In the absence of new legislation, comparable worth is *not* the law of the land.

---

[20]H. Remick, ed., *Comparable Worth and Wage Discrimination* (Philadelphia: Temple University Press, 1984).

[21]*Job Evaluation: A Tool for Pay Equity* (Washington, DC: National Committee on Pay Equity, November 1987).

THE EARNINGS GAP

Earlier in this chapter we noted that legislation is the result of a concerted action to correct a problem in society. While the Equal Pay Act and Title VII have corrected some major problems, an earnings gap continues to persist between the sexes and between the races. The Bureau of Labor Statistics data in Exhibit 17.4 show that white women working full-time have a median weekly wage equal to approximately 75 percent of the weekly wage earned by men. Black males have a similar ratio to white males, but Hispanic males earn only 63 percent of the weekly wages of white males. The male-female gap is smaller among blacks (87 percent) and Hispanic-origin workers (88 percent). Exhibit 17.5 shows how the male-female wage gap has persisted over time. Although the size of the difference has fluctuated, the gap has been extremely persistent and always to the advantage of white males. What do we know about why that gap exists?

Some of the more important factors, shown in Exhibit 17.6, include the following:

1. Differences in the occupational attainment and the jobs held by men and women.
2. Differences in personal work-related characteristics and work behaviors.
3. Differences among industries and firms.
4. Differences in union membership.
5. The presence of discrimination.

Let us first examine some data and then some conflicting beliefs.

EXHIBIT 17.4
Wage
Comparisons

Data from U.S.
Department of
Labor.

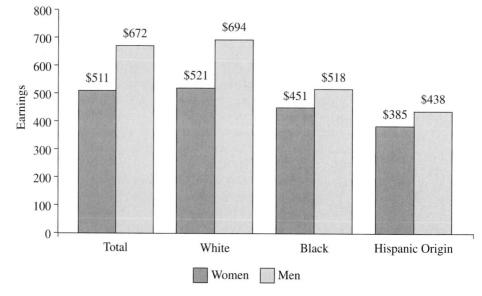

Median Usual Weekly Earnings of Full-Time Wage and
Salary Workers by Sex, Race, and Hispanic Origin, 2001 Annual Averages

EXHIBIT 17.5   Male-Female Wage Gap

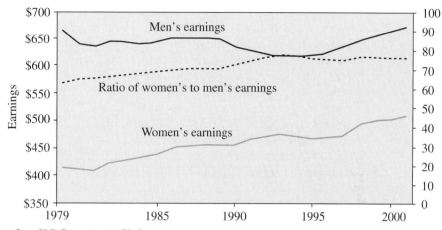

Data from U.S. Department of Labor.

EXHIBIT 17.6
Possible Determinants of Pay Differences

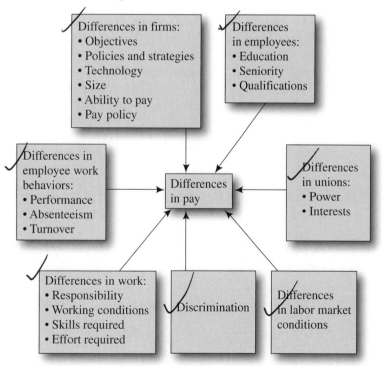

Source: George T. Milkovich, "The Emerging Debate," in *Comparable Worth: Issues and Alternatives,* ed. E. Robert Livernash (Washington, DC: Equal Employment Advisory Council, 1980).

Differences in Occupational Attainment

One of the most important factors in the pay gap is differences in jobs held by men and women. A variety of data illustrate these differences. In the early 1970s, 53 percent of women workers were in administrative support (including clerical) and service occupations, compared to only 15 percent of men. At that time, less than one in five managers were women; professional women were frequently employed in traditionally female professions, such as nurse, teacher, dietitian, or librarian. Women were also underrepresented in blue-collar jobs, including higher-paying precision production and craft occupations. Today, their numbers in administrative support and service jobs are down to 41 percent, and their numbers in managerial jobs are at parity with men. In 1960, almost half of the women who graduated from college became teachers, while today less than 10 percent do so. Occupational segregation is less of an issue today than it was in years past.[22]

However, evidence of increased levels of occupational attainment does not automatically mean that the wage gap will close. A study of women in science and engineering finds that even though they have already cleared the hurdles of misguided high school guidance counselors and/or lack of peer support or role models, women scientists and engineers are almost twice as likely to leave these occupations as are males.[23]

For a variety of reasons, a relatively small wage gap among younger cohorts (i.e., recent college graduates) tends to increase as the cohort ages. Perhaps women continue to be more likely to drop out of the labor force at some point for family reasons, or perhaps the barriers to continued advancement become more substantial at higher levels in the job hierarchy. A study of MBAs found that 10 to 15 years after graduation, in addition to a pay gap there is also a gender-based chasm in such subjective measures as career satisfaction, boss appreciation, and feeling of discrimination.[24] Fully 46 percent of the women said they had experienced discrimination; only 9 percent of the men said they had. The most common problem women reported was that less qualified men were chosen for promotions over them. Additionally, they felt that at higher levels discrimination had become more subtle and harder to prove. Clearly, many professional women and minorities believe they operate in less supportive work environments than their white male colleagues.[25]

[22]Francine D. Blau and Lawrence M. Kahn, "Swimming Upstream: Trends in the Gender Wage Differentials," *Journal of Labor Economics* 15(1) (1997), pp. 1–42; Kimberly Bayard, Judith Hellerstein, David Neumark, and Kenneth Troske, "New Evidence on Sex Segregation and Sex Differences in Wages from Matched Employee-Employer Data," NBER Working Paper 7003, Cambridge, MA, 1999; Mary E. Graham, Julie L. Hotchkiss, and Barry Gerhart, "Discrimination by Parts: A Fixed-Effects Analysis of Starting Pay Differences across Gender," *Eastern Economic Journal* 26(1) (Winter 2000), pp. 9–27.

[23]Anne E. Preston, "Why Have All the Women Gone? A Study of Exit of Women from the Science and Engineering Professions," *American Economic Review,* December 1994, pp. 1446–1462.

[24]Joy A. Schneer and Frieda Reitman, "The Importance of Gender in Mid-Career: A Longitudinal Study of MBAs," *Journal of Organizational Behavior* 15 (1994), pp. 199–207.

[25]F. Blau and L. Kahn, "Gender Differences in Pay," NBER Working Paper 7732, Cambridge, MA, June 2000; Alison M. Konrad and Kathy Cannings, "Of Mommy Tracks and Glass Ceilings: A Case Study of Men's and Women's Careers in Management," *Relations Industrielles* 49(2) (1994), pp. 303–333; Cheri Ostroff and Leanne Atwater, "Does WhomYou Work with Matter? Effects of Referent Group Gender and Age Composition on Managers' Compensation," *Journal of Applied Psychology* August 2003, pp. 725–740.

Differences in Personal Work-Related Characteristics

Differences in employee attributes and behaviors help explain part of the earnings gap. Work-related differences include experience and seniority within a firm, continuous time in the work force, education, and the like. Personal characteristics of questionable work-relatedness include obesity, height, and beauty. Yet empirical studies have found all of these factors related to pay differences.[26] Plain people earn less than average-looking people, who earn less than the good-looking. The "plainness penalty" is 5 to 10 percent. Short people earn less than tall people; each inch in height adds $789 to the annual pay packet.

Experience and Seniority

On average, male full-time workers put in 6 percent more hours per week than women full-time workers. By the time men and women have been out of school for 6 years, women on average have worked 30 percent less than men. After 16 years out of school, women average half as much labor market experience as men.[27] A study of middle-aged law school grads concluded that the women lawyers worked fewer hours—about 91 percent as long as men.[28] However, they were paid substantially (not proportionately) less; they earned only 61 percent of what men earned. Even with differences in work history accounted for, male lawyers continue to enjoy a considerable earnings advantage as well as a higher rate of earnings growth.

Women's record of work experience is continuing to grow closer to that of men, for several reasons. First, when a strong demand for employees exists, there are fewer barriers to women's entry. Additionally, as women see those above them receive promotions, they become more likely to invest in their own human capital via training, education, and experience to position themselves for such promotions. However, such "feedback effects" can also work in reverse: Small initial discriminatory differences in wages affect women's decisions about their own future, including their willingness to stay in the work force.[29]

[26]Tim Judge and Dan Cable, "A Meta-Analysis of the Relationship Between Height and Pay," *Journal of Applied Psychology* (in press); I. Saporta and J. J. Halpern, "Being Different Can Hurt: Effects of Deviation from Physical Norms on Lawyers' Salaries," *Industrial Relations* 41(3) (July 2002), pp. 442–466; Mark Roehling, "Weight-Based Discrimination in Employment: Psychological and Legal Aspects," *Personnel Psychology* 52 (1999), pp. 969–1016; John Cawley, "Body Weight and Women's Labor Market Outcomes," NBER Working Paper 7841, Cambridge, MA, August 2000; "The Right to be Beautiful," *Economist,* May 24, 2003, p. 9.

[27]Francine Blau and Marianne Ferber, "Career Plans and Expectations of Young Women and Men," *Journal of Human Resources* 26(4), 1998 pp. 581–607.

[28]Robert G. Wood, Mary E. Corcoran, and Paul N. Courant, "Pay Differences among the Highly Paid: The Male-Female Earnings Gap in Lawyers' Salaries," *Journal of Labor Economics* 11(3) (1993), pp. 417–441.

[29]Barry A. Gerhart and George T. Milkovich, "Salaries, Salary Growth, and Promotions of Men and Women in a Large, Private Firm," *Pay Equity: Empirical Inquiries* (Arlington, VA: National Science Foundation, 1989); Jane Waldfogel, "Understanding the 'Family Gap' in Pay for Women with Children," *Journal of Economic Perspectives* 12(1) (1998), pp. 157–170; Stephanie Boraas and William M. Rodgers III, "How Does Gender Play a Role in the Earnings Gap? An Update," *Monthly Labor Review,* March 2003, pp. 9–15.

Education

Currently, men and women graduate from college in nearly equal numbers. However, they still tend to choose different majors, although those differences are diminishing. College major is the single strongest factor affecting the income of college graduates.[30]

Combining Factors

Although many researchers studied the effects of differences in jobs and occupations and personal characteristics such as experience and education, few studies have looked at their effects on pay differences *over time*. One study controlled for education degree, college major, and prior experience. Males had a 12 percent *higher* starting salary than females. When all the variables were included, the current salary differential between male college graduates and female college graduates was less than 3 percent. The implication is that women received greater pay increases after they were hired than men did but differences in starting salary remain important and persistent contributors to gender-related pay differences.

A newer study used longitudinal data to compare pay differences between men and women who received an MBA degree and men and women who took the Graduate Management Admission Test but did not go on to receive the degree. Years later, the gender wage gap was lower among those who got the MBA than those who did not.[31] A study of veterinarians went even further, reasoning that men and women who become veterinarians are relatively similar on human capital and preference measures. Census data reveal a 15 percent gender gap in average earnings. But when productivity data are factored in (patients per hour and annual revenue produced), the gap narrows to 9 percent. The author suggests that women may make up this pay difference with other valued returns such as more flexibility in their work schedules.[32]

Another study looked at not only a combination of factors to explain pay differences but also at the combined effects of different areas of discrimination: in hiring, job assignment, and pay. While initial differences in treatment in each area may be small, when the effects are combined and projected ahead, they can become substantial. The authors of the study call for better measures to combine the effects of different types of discrimination.[33]

[30]Andrew M. Gill and Duane E. Leigh, "Community College Enrollment, College Major, and the Gender Wage Gap," *Industrial and Labor Relations Review* 54(1) (October 2000), pp. 163–181; Catherine J. Weinberger, "Race and Gender Wage Gaps in the Market for Recent College Graduates," *Industrial Relations* 37(1) (1998), pp. 67–84; John M. McDowell, Larry D. Singell, Jr., and James P. Ziliak, "Cracks in the Glass Ceiling: Gender and Promotion in the Economics Profession," *American Economic Review* 89(2) (1999), p. 392–396; C. Brown, and M. Corcoran, "Sex-Based Differences in School Content and the Male-Female Wage Gap," *Journal of Labor Economics* 15(3) (1997), pp. 431–465.

[31]M. Montgomery and I. Powell, "Does an Advanced Degree Reduce the Gender Wage Gap? Evidence from MBAs," *Industrial Relations* 42(3) (July 2003).

[32.] David M. Smith, "Pay and Productivity Differences between Male and Female Veterinarians," *Industrial and Labor Relations Review* 55(3) (April 2002), pp. 493–510.

[33]Mary E. Graham, Julie L. Hotchkiss, and Barry Gerhart, "Discrimination by Parts: A Fixed-Effects Analysis of Starting Pay Differences across Gender," *Eastern Economic Journal* 26(1) (Winter 2000), pp. 9–27; Stephanie Boraas and William M. Rodgers III, "How Does Gender Play a Role in the Earnings Gap? An Update," *Monthly Labor Review,* March 2003, pp. 9–15.

Differences in Industries and Firms

Other factors that affect earnings differences between men and women are the industries and the firms in which they are employed. The study of middle-aged lawyers revealed large differences between men and women lawyers in the types of firms that employed them. Men were much more likely than women to be in private practice, and they were twice as likely to practice in large firms (over 50 lawyers). In contrast, men were much *less* likely than women to be in the relatively low-paying areas of government and legal services. Clearly, these differences are related to pay: the most highly paid legal positions are in private-practice law firms, and the larger the law firm, the greater is the average rate of pay.[34]

Differences in the firm's compensation policies within a specific industry is another factor that accounts for some of the earnings gap. As noted in Chapters 7 and 8, some firms within an industry adopt pay strategies that place them among the leaders in their industry; other firms adopt policies that may offer more employment security coupled with bonuses and gain-sharing schemes. The issue here is whether *within an industry* some firms are more likely to employ women than other firms and whether that likelihood leads to earnings differences.

Within a firm, differences in policies for different jobs may even exist. For example, many firms tie pay for secretaries to the pay for the manager to whom the secretary is assigned. The rationale is that the secretary and the manager function as a team. When the manager gets promoted, the secretary also takes on additional responsibilities and therefore also gets a raise. However, this traditional approach breaks down when layers of management are cut. When IBM went through a major restructuring a few years back, it cut pay by up to 36 percent for secretaries who had been assigned to managerial levels that no longer existed. IBM justified the cuts by saying the rates were way above the market. Prior to the reduction, the highest base salary for a senior executive secretary was $70,000 plus overtime.

We also know that the size of a firm is systematically related to differences in wages. Female employment is more heavily concentrated in small firms. Wages of men in large firms are 54 percent higher than wages of men in small firms. The gap was 37 percent for women in small versus large firms. Other studies report that employees in some jobs can get a pay increase of about 20 percent simply by switching industries in the same geographic area while performing basically similar jobs.[35] Nevertheless, a recent study concludes that this pay premium associated with changing jobs is enjoyed only by white

[34]Robert G. Wood, Mary E. Corcoran, and Paul N. Courant, "Pay Differences among the Highly Paid: The Male-Female Earnings Gap in Lawyers' Salaries," *Journal of Labor Economics* 11(3) (1993), pp. 417–441; Donna K. Gunther and Kathy J. Hayes, "Gender Differences in Salary and Promotion for Faculty in the Humanities 1977–95," *Journal of Human Resources* 38(1) (Winter 2003), pp. 34–73.

[35]George F. Dreher and Taylor H. Cox, Jr., "Labor Market Mobility and Cash Compensation: The Moderating Effects of Race and Gender," *Academy of Management Journal* 43(5) (2000), pp. 890–900; J. M. Brett and L. K. Stroh, "Jumping Ship: Who Benefits from an External Labor Market Career Strategy?" *Journal of Applied Psychology* 82 (1997), pp. 331–341; G. F. Dreher and T. H. Cox, Jr., "Race, Gender, and Opportunity: A Study of Compensation Attainment and the Establishment of Mentoring Relationships," *Journal of Applied Psychology* 81 (1996), pp. 297–308; J. H. Greenhaus, S. Parasuraman, and W. J. Wormley, "Effects of Race on Organizational Experiences, Job Performance Evaluations, and Career Outcomes," *Academy of Management Journal* 33 (1990), pp. 64–86.

males. Women and minorities who were MBA graduates from five universities did not obtain the same pay increases as their white male classmates when they switched jobs.[36] The study authors speculate that the failure of women and minorities to receive a comparable premium is that they do not have the well-developed social networks that provide inside information on job opportunities. A weaker network may hurt them in the pay bargaining process, too.

To the extent that these differences in job setting are the result of an individual's preference or disposition, they are not evidence of discrimination. To the extent that these differences are the result of industry and firm practices that steer women and minorities into certain occupations and industries or lower-paying parts of a profession, they may reflect discrimination. At the minimum, they require thoughtful exploration.

Differences in Contingent Pay

Recently, a new and interesting approach was used to examine the gender earnings differential. Total pay was divided into base pay and contingent pay that varies with job performance. After controlling for individual characteristics (e.g., education and experience), occupation, and job level, approximately 34 percent of the unexplained pay gap was due to gender differences in performance-based pay.[37] If these differences occur *within* a firm, several possible explanations exist. Perhaps firms are not offering men and women equal opportunities to earn contingent pay; perhaps men and women are treated differently in the evaluations used to determine contingent pay; perhaps men and women differ substantially on performance.

However, if the differences are *across* firms, then perhaps women prefer less pay risk and choose those occupations and firms with less variable pay.[38] While their sample size did not permit the authors of the study to say if the differences were within or across firms, if the pay gap is the result of the way people select occupations and employers, then we need to understand how pay practices influence those choices.

Differences in Union Membership

Finally, we also know that belonging to a union will affect differences in earnings. Belonging to a union in the public sector seems to raise female wages more than it raises male wages. Little research has been devoted to studying the gender effect of union membership in the private sector.

Presence of Discrimination

Although we know that many factors affect pay and that discrimination may be one of them, we are not in agreement as to what constitutes evidence of discrimination. Although the earnings gap is the most frequently cited example, closer inspection reveals

[36]George F. Dreher and Taylor H. Cox, Jr., "Labor Market Mobility and Cash Compensation: The Moderating Effects of Race and Gender," *Academy of Management Journal* 43(5) (2000), pp. 890–900.

[37]Keith W. Chauvin and Ronald A. Ash, "Gender Earning Differentials in Total Pay, Base Pay, and Contingent Pay," *Industrial and Labor Relations Review,* July 1994, pp. 634–649.

[38]Marta M. Elvia and Mary E. Graham, "Not Just a Formality: Pay System Formalization and Sex-Related Earnings Effects," *Organization Science,* January 2002.

the weaknesses in this statistic. Unfortunately, many studies of the earnings gap have little relevance to understanding discrimination in pay-setting practices. Some studies use aggregated data—for instance, treating all bachelor's degrees as the same, or defining an occupation incorrectly (e.g., the U.S. Department of Labor categorizes Shaquille O'Neal as well as the basketball game timekeeper in the same occupation—"sports professional"). Another problem is that mere possession of a qualification or skill does not mean it is work-related. Examples of cab drivers, secretaries, and house painters with college degrees are numerous, depending on the overall economic conditions.

A standard statistical approach for determining whether discrimination explains part of the gap is to try to relate pay differences to the factors just discussed above (occupation, type of work, experience, education, and the like). The procedure typically used is to regress some measure of earnings on those factors thought to legitimately influence earnings. If the average wage of men with a given set of values for these factors is significantly different from the average wage of women with equal factors, then the standard statistical approach is to interpret the residual portion of the gap as discrimination. Unfortunately, in a sample limited to white males, such an approach explained only 60 to 70 percent of their earnings. So statistical studies, by themselves, are not sufficient evidence.[39] Nevertheless, a recent study using this approach arrived at a ratio of women's to men's wages of 88 percent based on data from a year in which the Bureau of the Census reported a 70 percent ratio.[40]

Cybercomp

The legality of giving preferences to members of one group in order to overcome the effects of historic discrimination against other members of that group continues to be a divisive issue in the United States. Many lawyers believe it is only a matter of time before cases on preferences reach the Supreme Court. You can track legal issues and read transcripts of Supreme Court decisions at *www. law.cornell.edu/*.

Many states have their own web pages that include their compensation legislation. What information is available from your state? Compare the extent of regulation in different regions of the United States. Are there any unique characteristics of your state that are addressed by state compensation legislation (e.g., unique industries, extent of unionization, etc.)?

Even if legitimate factors fully explain pay differences between men and women, discrimination still could have occurred. First, the factors themselves may be tainted by discrimination. For example, past discrimination against women in admission to engineering schools may have affected their earnings. Younger women may have decided against applying to engineering schools in the first place because of a perceived likelihood of future discrimination. High school guidance counselors or even peers may have steered them away from the necessary mathematics preparation. So measurable factors may underestimate the effects of past discrimination.

[39]Jerald Greenberg and Claire L. McCarty, "Comparable Worth: A Matter of Justice," in *Research in Personnel and Human Resources Management,* Vol. 8, eds. K. M. Rowland and G. R. Ferris (Greenwich, CT: JAI Press, 1990).

[40]F. Blau and L. Kahn, "Gender Differences in Pay," NBER Working Paper 7732, Cambridge, MA, June 2000.

In sum, statistical analysis needs to be treated as part of a pattern of evidence and needs to reflect the wage behaviors of specific firms. As one reviewer has written, "It is not the quantity of studies that is lacking; it is the quality."[41]

Global Gap

The wage gap between the sexes is fairly universal. However, in many countries, the size of the gap is smaller than in the United States. Yet women show more attachment to the labor force and there may be less occupational segregation in the United States than in Sweden, Australia, Germany, New Zealand, Belgium, France, Finland, and Italy. So what accounts for the narrower gap in these countries? One analysis concludes that the difference is the decentralized nature of wage decision making in the United States compared to the countries listed. In many countries, as the global guide in Chapter 16 suggests, rates negotiated by federations of employers and unions rather than individual companies and employees mean a narrower range of pay rates for each job, as well as smaller differences between jobs. In the United States, for most jobs, employers and individuals come to an agreement on the wage. Earlier chapters have emphasized the wide range of rates in the U.S. market for any job. More centralized wage decision making permits a pay gap to be closed by political/institutional fiat.[42] Multinational companies embedded in the fabric of different nations' social contracts face wide differences among countries in their approaches to closing the gap.

COMPARABLE WORTH

Why are jobs that are held predominantly by women, almost without exception, paid less than jobs held predominantly by men? Do job evaluation systems give adequate recognition to job-related contributions in those jobs held primarily by women? The state of Washington conducted a study that concluded that the job of a licensed practical nurse required skill, effort, and responsibility equal to that of a campus police officer. The campus police officer was paid, on average, one-and-a-half times what the state paid the licensed practical nurse.[43]

In Ontario, jobs that were deemed comparable based on numerical scores displayed a similar disparity in pay. A chief librarian made $35,050, while a dairy herd improvement

[41]Donald P. Schwab, "Using Job Evaluation to Obtain Pay Equity," in *Comparable Worth: Issue for the 80's,* Vol. 1 (Washington, DC: Equal Employment Advisory Council, 1980); Barry M. Goldman, "Toward an Understanding of Employment Discrimination Claiming: An Integration of Organizational Justice and Social Information Processing Theories," *Personnel Psychology* 54 (2001), pp. 361–386.

[42]Francine D. Blau and Lawrence M. Kahn, "Understanding International Differences in the Gender Pay Gap," NBER working paper, April 2001; Elizabeth Brainerd, "Women in Transition: Changes in Gender Wage Differentials in Eastern Europe and the Former Soviet Union," *Industrial and Labor Relations Review* 54(1) (October 2000), pp. 138–162; Christopher J. Ruhm, "The Economic Consequences of Parental Leave Mandates: Lessons from Europe," *Quarterly Journal of Economics* 113(1) (1998), pp. 285–317; Janet C. Gornick, Marcia K. Meyers, and Katherine E. Ross, "Supporting the Employment of Mothers: Policy Variation across Fourteen Welfare States," *Journal of European Social Policy* 7(1) (1997), pp. 45–70.

[43]Harry J. Holzer and David Neumark, "What Does Affirmative Action Do?" *Industrial and Labor Relations Review* 53(2) (January 2000), pp. 240–270; Sharon Toffey Shepela and Ann T. Viviano, "Some Psychological Factors Affecting Job Segregation and Wages," in *Comparable Worth and Wage Discrimination,* ed. H. Remick (Philadelphia: Temple University Press, 1984); Helen Remick, "Beyond Equal Pay for Equal Work: Comparable Worth in the State of Washington," in *Equal Employment Policy for Women,* ed. Ronnie Steinberg-Ratner (Philadelphia: Temple University Press, 1980), pp. 405–448; Laime Vaitkus, *The State of Gender-Based Pay Gaps in 2003* (New York: Institute of Management and Administration, 2003).

manager made $38,766. A computer operations supervisor made $20,193, while a forestry project supervisor made $26,947. A typist made $10,531, while a sailor made $14,097.[44] It is this type of wage difference between jobs judged in some sense to be comparable that is controversial. The notion of comparable worth says that if jobs require comparable skill, effort, and responsibility, the pay must be comparable, no matter how dissimilar the job content may be. (In Canada and the EU, comparable worth is called gender equity.)

Comparable-worth proponents continue to lobby for either new legislation or voluntary action on the part of employers that would include the comparable-worth standard. A lot of this political activity is occurring in state and local governments. This is not surprising, since over half of all women in the work force are employed in the public sector.

The Mechanics

Establishing a comparable-worth plan typically involves the following four basic steps:

1. *Adopt a single job evaluation plan for all jobs within a unit.* If employees are unionized, separate plans can be prepared for each bargaining unit and take precedence over previous agreements. The key to a comparable-worth system is a single job evaluation plan for jobs with dissimilar content.

2. *All jobs with equal job evaluation results should be paid the same.* Although each factor in the job evaluation may not be equal, if the total points are equal, the wage rates must also be equal.

3. *Identify general representation (percentages of male and female employees) in each job group.* Positions with similar duties and responsibilities that require similar qualifications, are filled by similar recruiting procedures, and are paid under the same pay schedule constitute a job group. Typically, a female-dominated job group is defined as having 60 percent or more female incumbents; a male-dominated job group has 70 percent or more male incumbents.

4. *The wage-to-job evaluation point ratio should be based on the wages paid for male-dominated jobs* since they are presumed to be free of pay discrimination.

These steps are based on the state of Minnesota's law that mandates comparable worth for all public-sector employees (e.g., the state, cities, school districts, libraries).

To understand the mechanics more clearly, consider Exhibit 17.7. The solid dots represent jobs held predominantly by women (i.e., female representation greater than or equal to 60 percent). The circles represent jobs held predominantly by men (i.e., greater than or equal to 70 percent men). The policy line (solid) for the women's jobs is below the policy line (dotted) for men's jobs. A comparable-worth policy uses the results of the single job evaluation plan and prices all jobs as if they were male-dominated jobs (dotted line). Thus, all jobs with 100 job points receive $600, all those with 200 points receive $800, and so on.

Market rates for male-dominated jobs are used to convert the job evaluation points to salaries. The point-to-salaries ratio of male-dominated jobs is then applied to female-dominated jobs.

[44]James Brooke, "Equity Case in Canada as Redress for Women," *New York Times,* November 19, 1999, p. A17; "Supreme Court Decision a Victory for Pay Equity and Human Rights," press release from Public Service Alliance of Canada, June 26, 2003.

EXHIBIT 17.7
Job
Evaluation
Points and
Salary

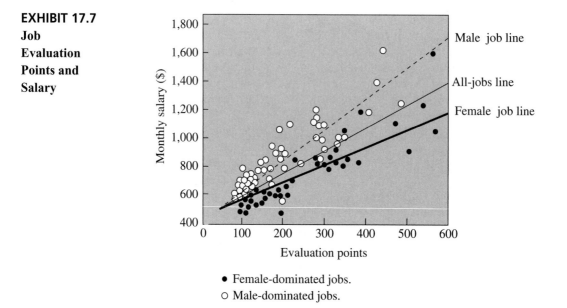

• Female-dominated jobs.
○ Male-dominated jobs.

However, a mandated job evaluation approach that specifies a hierarchy of jobs seems counter to the direction in which most organizations are moving today. A partner of Hay Associates observed:

> We, ourselves, do not know of a single case where a large and diverse organization in the private sector concluded that a single job evaluation method, with the same compensable factors and weightings, was appropriate for its factory, office, professional, management, technical, and executive personnel in all profit center divisions and all staff departments.[45]

People who advocate job evaluation as a vehicle for comparable worth credit the technique with more explanatory power than it possesses. Nevertheless, the comparable-worth debate lives on. The Office of Federal Contract Compliance Programs (OFCCP), the agency that oversees federal contractor compliance with hiring and promotion "goals" (some believe they are really "quotas"), has announced a new goal of its own: to develop a methodology to identify wage disparities so that the wage gap for protected groups can be closed. Most large employers have federal contracts of one size or another and thus are subject to such compliance reviews. Although, as already noted, the Equal Pay Act requires that men and women receive equal pay for jobs of substantially equal skill, effort, responsibility, and working conditions within the same establishment, the OFCCP plans to make such comparisons on the basis of nine broad occupational categories:

• Officials and managers
• Professionals
• Technicians

[45]Alvin O. Bellak, "Comparable Worth: A Practitioner's View," in *Comparable Worth: Issue for the 80's,* vol. 1. (Washington, DC: Equal Employment Advisory Council, 1980).

- Sales workers
- Office and clerical workers
- Craft workers
- Operatives
- Laborers
- Service workers

These are the categories the Bureau of Labor Statistics uses in its data reporting. The use of these occupational categories means that comparisons will almost certainly not meet the equal pay criteria, since each EEO occupational category includes jobs with substantially different skill, effort, responsibility, and working conditions. The broad nature of these categories limits their usefulness for pay decisions. Nevertheless, the practical result of such comparisons on the government's part will be a new and far broader interpretation of the Equal Pay Act.[46]

Union Developments

The amount of union support for comparable worth appears to be related to its effects on the union's membership. AFSCME and the Communication Workers of America (CWA) actively support comparable worth and have negotiated comparable-worth-based pay increases, lobbied for legislation, filed legal suits, and attempted to educate their members and the public about comparable worth. The public sector faces little competition for its services and is frequently better able to absorb a wage increase, since public employees are in a better position to pressure lawmakers than are taxpayers. This probably accounts for the relative success of public employees' unions in bargaining comparable-worth pay adjustments. But tradeoffs between higher wages and fewer jobs make unions in industries facing stiff foreign competition (e.g., the International Ladies' Garment Workers' Union and the United Steel Workers) reluctant to aggressively support comparable worth. The beauty of "equity adjustments," from a union's perspective, is that because they are a separate budget item, they do not appear to come at the expense of overall pay increases for all union members. Collective bargaining has produced more comparable-worth pay increases than any other approach.[47]

---

[46]Charles H. Fay and Howard W. Risher, "Contractors, Comparable Worth and the New OFCCP: *Déjà vu* and More," *Compensation and Benefits Review,* September/October 2000, pp. 23–33; Charles Fay and Howard Risher, "New OFCCP Survey: Comparable Worth Redux?" *Workspace,* July 2000, pp. 41–44.

[47]Unions are becoming more adept at using the web to share information. The AFSCME website has a section called "LaborLinks," and within that is a section called "Classification and Compensation." Here the AFSCME provides links to private wage survey sites such as salary.com, Wageweb, and the Executive Pay Watch, as well as links to BLS, DOT/ONET, and a few state and local government sites. In another section, it provides information on how to research companies using the web. Unite and the SEIU provide links to the BLS. The Steelworkers Union provides information on its wage policy statement. The UAW provides detailed information on its bargaining strategies and gains, all the way down to the locals. Most unions also have newsletters that provide helpful information, and you can search the old issues to find relevant information.

A Proactive Approach

Compliance with laws and regulations can be a constraint and/or an opportunity for a compensation manager. The regulatory environment certainly constrains the decisions that can be made. Once laws are passed and regulations published, employers must comply. But a proactive compensation manager can influence the nature of regulations and their interpretation. Astute professionals must be aware of legislative and judicial currents to protect both employers' and employees' interests and to ensure that compensation practices conform to judicial interpretation.

How can a compensation manager best undertake these efforts? First, join professional associations to stay informed on emerging issues and to act in concert to inform and influence public and legislative opinion. Second, constantly review compensation practices and their results. The fair treatment of all employees is the goal of a good pay system, and that is the same goal of legislation. When interpretations of what is fair treatment differ, informed public discussion is required. Such discussion cannot occur without the input of informed managers.

Your Turn   Conducting an OFCCP Audit

Your employer is considering bidding for several federal contracts, and your boss has asked you to determine whether your firm is in compliance with OFCCP regulations regarding compensation practices. Check out the OFCCP website, *www.dol.gov/esa/ofccp/index.htm,* and read through sections describing the OFCCP and its purpose, the legal regulations, special reports such as the "glass ceiling" initiative, and sections on equal pay, analyzing compensation data, and best compensation practices. You can also go to the U.S. Equal Employment Opportunity Commission's *Compliance Manual* on compensation discrimination at *www.eeoc.gov/docs/compensation.html.* You also might want to read some of the articles listed in the footnotes to this chapter.

1. Summarize for your employer the requirements for federal contractors regarding compensation.
2. Develop a recommendation for the steps you would take to determine whether or not your company is in compliance with the rules.
3. Discuss the types of actions your company might take if the OFCCP says it is not in compliance with the rules.
4. If you are using the FastCat case in *Cases in Compensation,* complete the OFCCP's "equal opportunity survey" for the 25 employees in Phase 3. Based on your analysis, what would you recommend to FastCat management.

Your Turn

Celebrity Sweatshops?

Rap music mogul Sean "P. Diddy" Combs recently found himself accused of exploiting Honduran workers in a sweatshop that turns out his Sean John line of clothing. The National Labor Committee (NLC) claims these workers are paid less than a dollar an hour, forced to work 11- to 12-hour daily shifts, are subjected to body searches, and are dismissed if they get pregnant.

Combs said that Sean John's compliance officer has already made five inspections of the plant in the past year and would launch another "zero tolerance" investigation. If any proof of wrongdoing was uncovered, the relationship with the subcontractor would be terminated immediately.

The subcontractor, American expatriate Steve Hawkins, says that the plant is air conditioned, employs a full-time nurse, has a doctor there each afternoon, and has a pharmacy that gives medicines to workers for free. Hawkins observes that his own grandmother was a sewing machine operator in North Carolina, and he likes to think he treats his workers the way he would have wanted his grandmother to have been treated.

Critics of the NLC accuse it of trying to smear celebrities (Kathie Lee Gifford, Liz Claiborne, P. Diddy) in order to undermine free trade agreements and protect union jobs in the United States. Whatever the motivation, the challenge is to ensure that foreign subcontractors adhere to legal expectations and appropriate social norms in their factories.

Apply what you have read in this chapter and the international chapter. Make four recommendations that would help ensure that the subcontractors meet the objectives in the compensation model used in the book.

Sources: Steven Greenhouse, "A Hip-Hop Star's Fashion Line Is Tagged with a Sweatshop Label," *New York Times*, October 28, 2003, p. 1B; "In Defense of P. Diddy," *Wall Street Journal*, November 4, 2003.

Summary

Governments around the world play varying roles in the workplace. Legislation in any society reflects people's expectations about the role of government. Beyond direct regulation, government affects compensation through policies and purchases that affect the supply of and demand for labor.

In the United States, legislation reflects the changing nature of work and the work force. In the 1930s, legislation was concerned with correcting the harsh conditions and arbitrary treatment facing employees, including children. In the 1960s, legislation turned to the issue of equal rights. Such legislation has had a profound impact on all of U.S. society. Nevertheless, discrimination in the workplace, including pay discrimination, remains an unresolved issue.

Pay discrimination laws require special attention for several reasons. First, these laws regulate the design and administration of pay systems. Second, the definition of pay discrimination and thus the approaches used to defend pay practices are in a state of flux. Many of the provisions of these laws simply require sound pay practices that should have been employed in the first place. Sound practices are those with three basic features:

1. They are work-related.
2. They are related to the mission of the enterprise.
3. They include an appeals process for employees who disagree with the results.

Achieving compliance with these laws rests in large measure on the shoulders of compensation managers. It is their responsibility to ensure that the pay system is properly designed and managed.

Should comparable worth be legally mandated? Not surprisingly, opinions vary. But by how much, if any, comparable-worth policy will diminish the earnings differential remains an unanswered question. The earnings differential is attributable to many factors. Discrimination, whether it be access or valuation, is but one factor. Others include market forces, industry and employer differences, and union bargaining priorities. Compensation managers need to constantly monitor pay practices to be sure that they are complying with regulations and are not discriminatory.

Is all this detail on interpretation of pay discrimination really necessary? Yes. Without understanding the interpretation of pay discrimination legislation, compensation managers risk violating the law, exposing their employers to considerable liability and expense, and losing the confidence and respect of all employees when a few are forced to turn to the courts to gain nondiscriminatory treatment.

Review Questions

1. What is the nature of government's role in compensation?
2. Explain why changes in minimum wage can affect higher-paid employees as well.
3. What is the difference between access discrimination and valuation discrimination?
4. Consider contemporary practices such as skill-competency-based plans, broad banding, market pricing, and pay-for-performance plans. Discuss how they may affect the pay discrimination debate.
5. What factors help account for the pay gap?
6. What kinds of proactive activities can an employer undertake to enhance the regulatory environment?

Chapter Eighteen

Budgets and Administration

Chapter Outline

At the request of the Missouri town where he lived, compensation consultant John Russell developed a salary plan for the city. He worked on it diligently and submitted the plan. Subsequently, he decided to run for the position of alderman on the city council and was elected. His salary program was then brought before the council for a vote. Russell voted against his own program. He explained his behavior by commenting, "I never realized how tight the budget was!"

Today, compensation managers need not share Russell's dilemma. They are business partners.[1] The financial conditions of the organization, the competitive pressures it faces, and budgeting are integral to managing compensation. The cost implications of actions

---

[1]John Boudreau and Peter Ramstad, "From 'Professional Business Partner' to 'Strategic Talent Leader': 'What's Next' for Human Resource Management," CAHRS Working Paper 02–10, Ithaca, NY.

such as updating the pay structure, increasing merit pay, or instituting gain sharing are critical for making sound decisions. Consequently, budgets are an important part of managing compensation.

Creating a compensation budget requires tradeoffs among the basic pay policies—how much of the increase in market rates should be budgeted according to employee contributions to the organization's success compared to automatic across-the-board increases. Tradeoffs also occur over short- versus long-term incentives, over pay increases contingent on performance versus on seniority, and over cash compensation compared to benefits.

Budgeting also requires understanding the potential returns gained from each compensation program. The returns might be productivity increases expected from a new gain-sharing or profit-sharing plan, the expected value added by giving greater merit increases to the top performers, or the value gained from attracting and retaining the best people. In the past, budgeting was all about costs. Expected returns were a matter of beliefs. But more objective analysis of the gains as well as the costs of compensation decisions is taking hold. More on this later.

Managers must decide the amount of financial resources to deploy toward compensation compared to staffing or training or other aspects of HRM. The human resource budget implicitly reflects the organization's human resource strategy. The budget becomes an important part of the human resource plan. Additionally, budgeting in the total organization allocates financial resources to human resources and/or technology, capital improvements, and the like. So from the perspective of a member of the city council, John Russell ended up making different resource allocation decisions than he might have made from the perspective of the compensation manager.

ADMINISTRATION AND THE TOTAL PAY MODEL

Without a formal pay system, each manager could pay whatever seemed to work at the moment. Total decentralization of compensation decision making would result in a chaotic array of rates. Employees could be treated inconsistently and unfairly. Managers could use pay to motivate behaviors that achieved their own objectives, not necessarily those of the organization.

This was the situation in the United States in the early 1900s. The "contract system" made highly skilled workers managers as well as workers. The employer agreed to provide the "contractor" with floor space, light, power, and the necessary raw or semifinished materials. The contractor hired *and* paid labor. Bethlehem Steel operated under such a contract system. Pay inconsistencies for the same work were common. Some contractors demanded kickbacks from employees' paychecks; many hired their relatives and friends. Dissatisfaction and grievances became widespread, resulting in legislation and an increased interest in unions.

Lest we pass the contract system off as ancient history dredged up by equally ancient professors, consider the current use of outsourcing. *Outsourcing* means that organizations secure a range of services from independent, external vendors. Payroll processing and benefit administration are two popular areas to outsource. The danger is that if everything is outsourced, then we are back to the organization as a network of individual contractors. Back to the future: In the early 1900s, individual contracting was common. Unfair treatment was common. Corruption and financial manipulations were part of the decentralized decision making. Some see parallels with today. To help avoid history repeating itself and to redeem HR (and compensation) vice presidents from the image of unindicted co-conspirators, compensation should be managed to achieve the objectives of the pay model: efficiency, fairness, and compliance. Properly designed pay techniques help managers achieve these objectives.[2]

Rather than being goal-directed tools, however, pay systems often degenerate into bureaucratic burdens whose administrators blindly follow the fads and fashions of the day. Techniques become ends in themselves rather than means of reaching objectives. Operating managers may complain that pay techniques are more a hindrance than a help. So any discussion of managing pay must again raise the questions: What does this technique do for us? How does it help us better achieve our objectives? Although it is possible to design a system that includes internal alignment, external competitiveness, and employee contributions, it will not achieve its objectives without competent management.

Although many pay administration issues have been discussed throughout the book, a few remain to be called out explicitly. These include (1) managing labor costs, (2) variable pay as a cost control, (3) value-added returns on compensation, (4) inherent controls, (5) communication, and (6) structuring the compensation function.

MANAGING LABOR COSTS

You already know many of the factors that affect labor costs. As shown in Exhibit 18.1,

$$\text{Labor costs} = \text{employment} \times \left(\text{average cash compensation} + \text{average benefit cost} \right)$$

Using this model, there are three main factors to control in order to manage labor costs: employment (e.g., number of employees and the hours they work), average cash

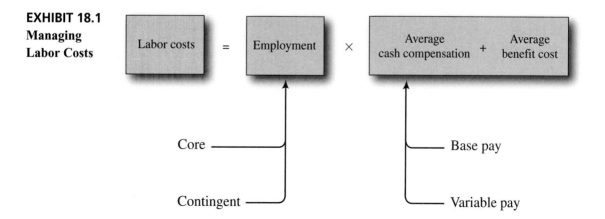

EXHIBIT 18.1
Managing Labor Costs

Labor costs = Employment × (Average cash compensation + Average benefit cost)

Core ———————— Employment ———————— Base pay

Contingent ———————— ———————— Variable pay

[2]Peter Capelli, *The New Deal at Work: Managing the Market-Driven Workforce* (Cambridge, MA: Harvard Business School Press, 1999).

compensation (e.g., wages, bonuses), and average benefit costs (e.g., health and life insurance, pensions). Cash and benefits have been this book's focus. However, if our objective is to better manage labor costs, then all three factors require attention.

Controlling Employment: Head Count and Hours

Managing the number of employees (head count) and/or the hours worked is the most obvious and perhaps most common approach to managing labor costs in the United States. Paying the same wages to fewer employees is less expensive. However, as part of their social contracts, many European countries have legislation that makes it very difficult to reduce head count. Managing labor costs is a greater struggle in such circumstances.

Announcements of layoffs and plant closings often have favorable effects on stock prices as investors anticipate improved cash flow and lower costs. However, it doesn't always work out that way. Adverse effects such as loss of trained employees, unrealized productivity, and lowered morale often translate into lower financial gains than anticipated.[3]

Many employers buffer themselves from layoffs by establishing different relationships with different groups of employees. As Exhibit 18.2 depicts, the two groups are commonly referred to as *core employees,* with whom a strong and long-term relationship is desired,

EXHIBIT 18.2
Core and Contingent Employees

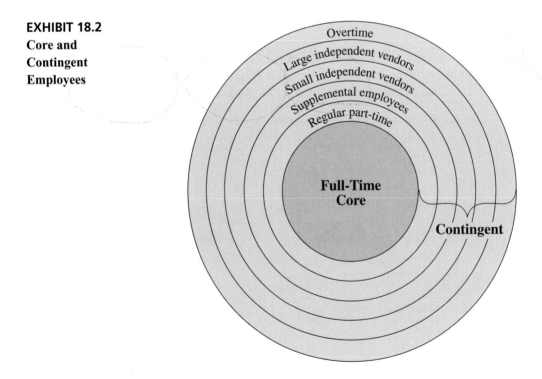

Overtime
Large independent vendors
Small independent vendors
Supplemental employees
Regular part-time

Full-Time Core

Contingent

[3]Wayne Cascio, *Responsible Restructuring: Creative and Profitable Alternatives to Layoffs* (San Francisco: Berrett-Koehler, 2002); Daniel Altman, "Downsizing Could Have a Downside," *New York Times,* December 26, 2002; David Leonhardt, "As Companies Reduce Costs, Pay Is Falling Top to Bottom," *New York Times,* April 26, 2003.

and *contingent workers,* whose employment agreements may cover only short, specific time periods. Rather than expand or contract the core work force, many employers achieve flexibility and control labor costs by expanding or contracting the contingent work force.[4] Hence, the fixed portion of labor costs becomes smaller and the variable portion longer. This variable portion can be expanded or contracted more easily than the core.

The splintered supply of nurses at St. Luke's Hospital, discussed in Chapter 7, illustrates the use of a variety of sources of contingent workers. As Exhibit 18.3 depicts, regular, pool, registry, and traveler nurses are paid differently. Some have benefits from St. Luke's, others have them from the contracting agencies, and still others must purchase their own benefits (pool nurses). The tradeoffs in managing costs involve balancing variation in patient loads, nurse-to-patient ratios, costs of the alternative sources, and quality of care.

Hours

Rather than defining employment in terms of number of employees, firms often do so on the basis of hours of work. For nonexempt employees in the United States, hours over 40 per week are more expensive (one-and-a-half times regular wage). Hence, another approach to managing labor costs is to examine paying for overtime hours versus adding to the work force. St. Luke's may not have to guarantee the contract nurses (pool, registry, or travelers) a specific number of hours; they are "on call."

The three factors—employment, cash compensation, and benefit costs—are not independent. Overtime hours require higher wages but avoid the cost of benefits for a new regular nurse. Other examples of interdependence are the retirement incentives that make early retirement attractive. Sweetened retirements drive head count down and usually affect the most expensive head count: older, more experienced employees. Hence, the average wage and health care costs for the remaining (younger) work force will probably be lowered too. Different nations regulate hours of employment differently. So in addition to understanding wage differences, other employment regulations must be monitored as well.

EXHIBIT 18.3 Splintered Supplies: St. Luke's Labor Cost Model

© George T. Milkovich.

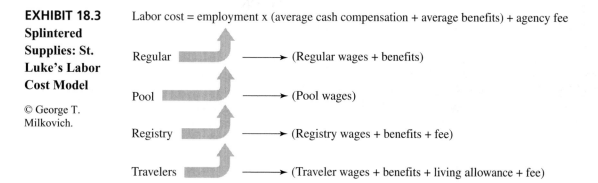

Labor cost = employment x (average cash compensation + average benefits) + agency fee

Regular → (Regular wages + benefits)

Pool → (Pool wages)

Registry → (Registry wages + benefits + fee)

Travelers → (Traveler wages + benefits + living allowance + fee)

[4]Janet H. Marler, Melissa Barringer, and George T. Milkovich, "Boundaryless and Traditional Contingent Employees: Worlds Apart," *Journal of Organization Behavior* 23 (2002), pp. 425–454.

Controlling Average Cash Compensation

Average cash compensation includes average salary level plus variable compensation payments such as bonuses, gain sharing, or profit sharing. Two approaches to help manage adjustments to average salary level are (1) *top down*, in which upper management determines pay and allocates it "down" to each subunit for the plan year, and (2) *bottom up*, in which individual employees' pay for the next plan year is forecasted and summed to create an organization salary budget.

CONTROL SALARY LEVEL: TOP DOWN

Top-down budgeting begins with an estimate from top management of the pay increase budget for the entire organization. Once the total budget is determined, it is then allocated to each manager, who plans how to distribute it among subordinates. There are many approaches to top-down budgeting in use. A typical one, controlling the planned pay-level rise, will be considered. A planned pay-level rise is simply the percentage increase in average pay for the unit that is planned to occur.

Exhibit 18.4 lists several factors that influence the decision on how much to increase the average pay level for the next period: how much the average level was increased this period, ability to pay, competitive market pressures, turnover effects, and cost of living.

Current Year's Rise

This is the percentage by which the average wage changed in the past year; mathematically:

Percent level rise =

$$100 \times \frac{\text{average pay at year-end} - \text{average pay at year beginning}}{\text{average pay at the beginning of the year}}$$

Ability to Pay

Any decision to increase the average pay level is in part a function of the organization's financial circumstances. Financially healthy employers may wish to maintain their competitive positions in the labor market or even share outstanding financial success through bonuses and profit sharing.

Conversely, financially troubled employers may not be able to maintain competitive market positions. The conventional response in these circumstances has been to reduce employment. Other options are to reduce the rate of increase in average pay by controlling adjustments in base pay and/or variable pay. Often as a last resort, firms decrease base wages (as well as variable pay). Other alternatives also exist. Look again at the cost

EXHIBIT 18.4
What Drives Level Rise?

Current year's rise Ability to pay Competitive market Turnover effects Cost of living	}	Percentage increase in average pay in plan year

model for St. Luke's and its splintered labor supply. The hospital can reduce costs by reducing the different sources of contract nurses.

Competitive Market Pressures

In Chapter 8, we discussed how managers determine an organization's competitive position in relation to its competitors. Recall that a distribution of market rates for benchmark jobs was collected and analyzed into a single average wage for each benchmark. This "average market wage" became the "going market rate." It then was compared to the average wage paid by the organization for its benchmark jobs. The market rates adjust differently each year in response to a variety of pressures.

Turnover Effects

Sometimes referred to as "churn" or "slippage", the *turnover effect* recognizes the fact that when people leave (through layoffs, quitting, retiring), they typically are replaced by employees who earn a lower wage. Depending on the degree of turnover, the effect can be substantial. Turnover effect can be calculated as annual turnover times planned average increase. For example, assume that an organization whose labor costs equal $1 million a year has a turnover rate of 15 percent and a planned average increase of 6 percent. The turnover effect is

$$.15 \times .06 = 0.9\%, \text{ or } \$9,000 \ (.009 \times \$1,000,000)$$

So instead of budgeting an additional $60,000 to fund a 6 percent increase, only $51,000 is needed. The turnover effect will also reduce benefit costs linked to base pay, such as pensions. Circuit City used the logic underlying the turnover effect when it matched its competitor Best Buy by laying off its more experienced and higher-paid salespeople and replacing them with less experienced, younger, and lower-paid associates.[5]

Cost of Living

Although there is little research to support it, employees undoubtedly compare their pay increases to changes in their costs of living. Unions consistently argue that increasing living costs justify increasing pay.

A Distinction

It is important to distinguish among three related concepts: the cost of living, changes in prices in the product and service markets, and changes in wages in labor markets. As Exhibit 18.5 shows, changes in wages in labor markets are measured through pay surveys. These changes are incorporated into the system through market adjustments in the budget and updates of the policy line and range structure. Price changes for goods and services in the product and service markets are measured by several government indexes, one of which is the consumer price index. The third concept, the cost of living, refers to the expenditure patterns of individuals for goods and services. The cost of living is more difficult to measure because employees' expenditures depend on many things: marital status,

[5]Carlos Tejada and Gary McWilliams, "New Recipe for Cost Savings: Replace Expensive Workers," *Wall Street Journal*, June 11, 2003, pp. 1, A12.

EXHIBIT 18.5 Three Distinct but Related Concepts and Their Measures

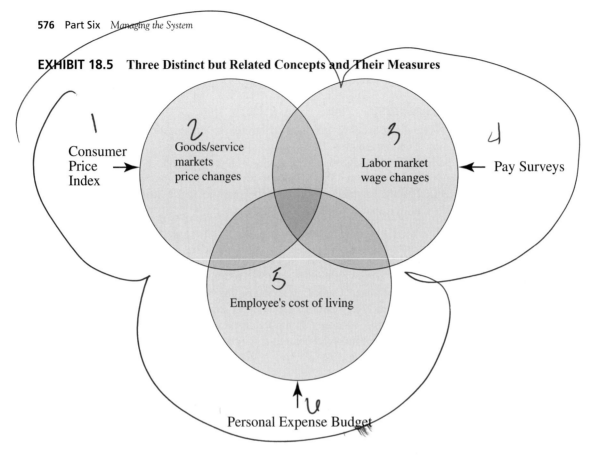

number of dependents and ages, personal preferences, and so on. Different employees experience different costs of living, and the only accurate way to measure them is to examine the personal expenditures of each employee.

The three concepts are interrelated. Wages in the labor market are part of the cost of producing goods and services, and changes in wages create pressures on prices. Similarly, changes in the prices of goods and services create the need for increased wages in order to maintain the same lifestyle.

The Consumer Price Index (CPI)

Many people refer to the CPI as a "cost-of-living" index, and many employers choose, as a matter of pay policy or in response to union pressures, to tie wages to it. However, the CPI does not necessarily reflect an individual employee's cost of living. Instead, it measures *changes in prices over time.* Changes in the CPI indicate only whether prices have increased more or less rapidly in an area since the base period. For example, a CPI of 110 in Chicago and 140 in Atlanta does not necessarily mean that it costs more to live in Atlanta. It does mean that prices have risen faster in Atlanta since the base year than they have in Chicago, since both cities started with bases of 100.

The CPI is of public interest because changes in it trigger changes in labor contracts, social security payments, federal and military pensions, and food stamp eligibility. Tying budgets or payments to the CPI is called *indexing*. The cost of living is included in Exhibit 18.4 as an influence on the percent increase in average salary level. It also may affect cost of benefits through health insurance coverage or pension costs tied to it.

> **Cybercomp**
> A simple inflation calculator at *www.westegg.com/inflation/* uses the consumer price index to adjust any given amount of data from 1800 on.
>   Most governments calculate some kind of consumer price index for their country. The web page for the U.S. Bureau of Labor Statistics provides many of these indexes (*stats.bls.gov*). They vary on how realistically they capture actual changes in prices.

A word of caution: If you decide to use the CPI rather than labor market salary surveys to determine the merit budget, you basically are paying for inflation rather than performance or market changes.

> **Cybercomp**
> A quicker way to compare living costs is to use the "relocation salary calculator" at *www.homefair.com.* Enter your salary, current city, and potential new city to see what salary you need in the new city based on cost-of-living differences. How accurate is this website's information?

Rolling It All Together

Let us assume that the managers take into account all these factors—current year's rise, ability to pay, market adjustments, turnover effects, changes in the cost of living, and geographic differentials—and decide that the planned rise in average salary for the next period is 6.3 percent. This means that the organization has set a target of 6.3 percent as the increase in *average* salary that will occur in the next budget period. It does not mean that everyone's increase will be 6.3 percent. It means that at the end of the budget year, the average salary calculated to include all employees will be 6.3 percent higher than it is now.

The next question is, How do we distribute that 6.3 percent budget in a way that accomplishes management's objectives for the pay system and meets the organization's goals?

Distributing the Budget to Subunits

A variety of methods exist for determining what percentage of the salary budget each manager should receive. Some use a uniform percentage, in which each manager gets an equal percentage of the budget based on the salaries of each subunit's employees. Others vary the percentage allocated to each manager based on pay-related problems, such as turnover or performance, which have been identified in that subunit.

Once salary budgets are allocated to each subunit manager, they become a constraint: a limited fund of money that each manager has to allocate to subordinates. Typically, merit increase guidelines are used to help managers make these allocation decisions. Merit increase grids help ensure that different managers grant consistent increases to employees with similar performance ratings and in the same position in their ranges. Additionally, grids help control costs. Chapter 11 provides examples of merit increase grids.

CONTROL SALARY LEVEL: BOTTOM UP

In contrast to top-down budgeting, where managers are told what their salary budget will be, bottom-up budgeting begins with managers' pay increase recommendations for the upcoming plan year. Exhibit 18.6 shows the process involved. Each of the steps within this compensation forecasting cycle is described here:

1. *Instruct managers in compensation policies and techniques.* Train managers in the concepts of a sound pay-for-performance policy and in standard company compensation techniques such as the use of pay increase guidelines and budgeting techniques. Communicate market data and the salary ranges.

2. *Distribute forecasting instructions and worksheets.* Furnish managers with the forms and instructions necessary to preplan increases. Most firms offer managers computer software to support these analyses. Exhibits 18.7 and 18.8 show the pay-planning and -forecasting information and current salaries Dell Computer Corporation provides managers.[6] Exhibit 18.7 shows summary information for all the employees supervised by Jean-Luc Picard. Adjustments for each individual are fed into the summary merit

**EXHIBIT 18.6
Compensation
Forecasting
and
Budgeting
Cycle**

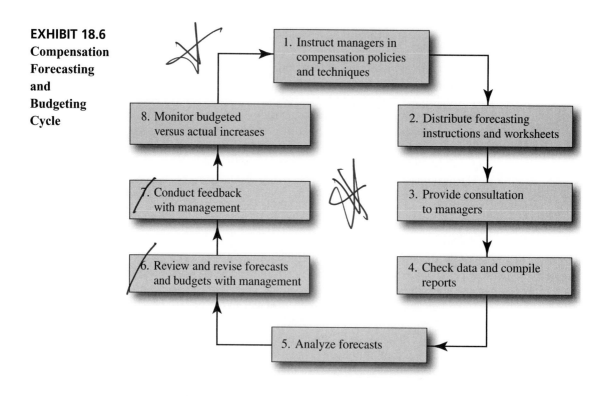

[6]John Watson, "Delivering Total Compensation Online at Dell," *ACA News* 42(4) (April 1999), pp. 14–19.

EXHIBIT 18.7 Summary Pay-Planning Data for Managers

Employee	Manager	Curr Grade	*Perf Rating	Current Salary	Merit %	Promo %	Equity %	Total %	New Salary	New% of Mid	FY00 Tgt%	FY99 Disc	FY99 Est Bonus
CRUSHER, BEV	PICARD,JE.	C3		$64,000					$64,000	71%		NA	NA
DATA, LC	PICARD,JE.	A5	(2)	$28,000					$30,240	103%	NA	NA	NA
LAFORGE, GEO	PICARD,JE.	C2		$56,000					$56,000	77%	NA		NA
RIKER, WILLIAM	PICARD,JE.	D3	(3)	$63,500					$67,945		35%	NA	
TROI, DEANNA	PICARD,JE.	C3		$61,500					$61,500	68%		NA	NA
WORF, L	PICARD,JE.	D3		$36,250					$36,250	71%	NA	NA	NA

	Merit		Promotion		Equity		Total		Executive Merit		FY99 Disc Bonus	FY99 Est Bonus
Budget	$00,000	0.00%	$00,000	0.00%	$00,000	0.00%	$00000	0.00%	$00,000	0.00%	$00,000	$0
Spent	$00,000	0.00%	$00,000	0.00%	$00,000	0.00%	$00000	0.00%	$00,000	0.00%	$00,000	$0
Available	$00,000	0.00%	$00,000	0.00%	$00,000	0.00%	$00000	0.00%	$00,000	0.00%	$00,000	$0

* A performance rating in parentheses indicates an unrecorded rating and New Hires are labeled 'N'. Average Ind Bonus Modifier: 100%

Source: John Watson, "Delivering Total Compensation Online at Dell," *ACA News* 42(4) (April 1999), pp. 14–19. Used with permission from WorldatWork (formerly American Compensation Association), *www.wordatworking.org.* © 1999 WorldatWork.

EXHIBIT 18.8 Individual Pay-Planning Data for Managers

Source: John Watson, "Delivering Total Compensation Online at Dell," *ACA News* 42(4) (April 1999), pp. 14–19. Used with permission from WorldatWork (formerly American Compensation Association), *www.wordatworking.org.* © 1999 WorldatWork.

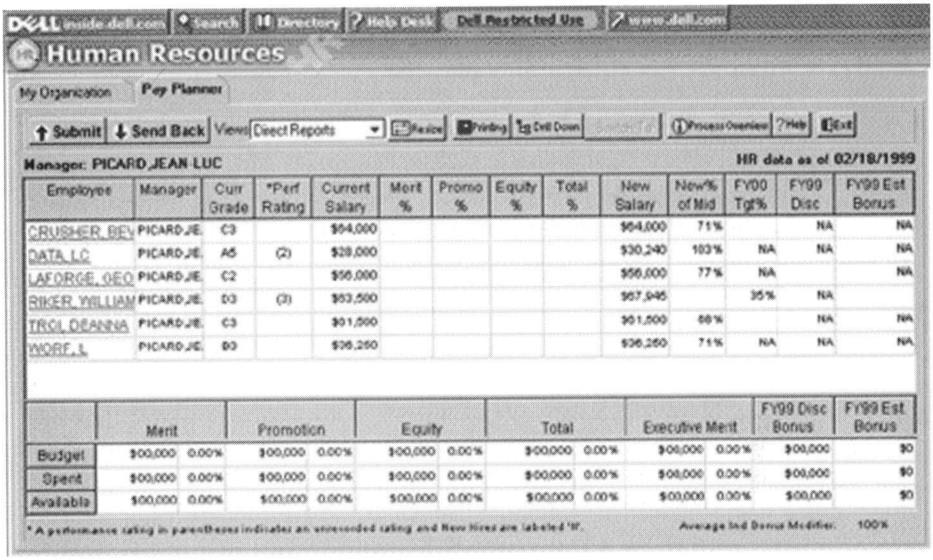

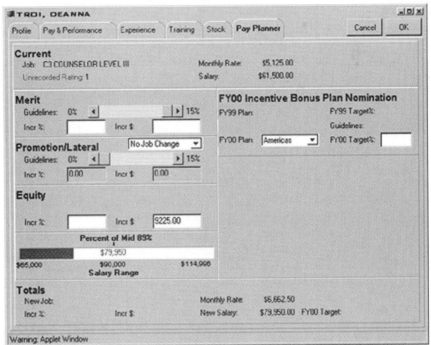

budget, promotion budget, equity adjustment budget, and so on, on this summary page. Captain Picard can submit his recommendations with a mouse click.

Exhibit 18.8 shows the depth of information that Captain Picard has on each individual to guide him in making his recommendations. Deanna Troi's performance rating history, past raises, training background, and stock allocations are all included. Guidelines for increases based on merit, promotion, and equity adjustments are provided, and all the worksheets are linked so that Picard can model pay adjustments for Troi and see the budgetary effects of those adjustments immediately.

Some argue that providing such detailed data and recommendations to operating managers makes the system too mechanical. How would you like your present instructor to look at your overall GPA before giving you a grade in this course? Pay histories however, ensure that managers are at least aware of this information and that pay increases for any one period are part of a continuing message to individual employees, not some ad hoc response to short-term changes.

3. *Provide consultation to managers.* Offer advice and salary information services to managers upon request. Dell's online approach makes it much easier to request and apply such guidance.

4. *Check data and compile reports.* Audit the increases forecasted to ensure that they do not exceed the pay guidelines and are consistent with appropriate ranges. Then use the data to feed back the outcomes of pay forecasts and budgets.

5. *Analyze forecasts.* Examine each manager's forecast, and recommend changes based on noted inequities among different managers.

6. *Review and revise forecasts and budgets with management.* Consult with managers regarding the analysis and any recommended changes. Obtain top-management approval of forecasts.

7. *Conduct feedback with management.* Present statistical summaries of the forecasting data by department, and establish unit goals.

8. *Monitor budgeted versus actual increases.* Control the forecasted increases versus the actual increases by tracking and reporting periodic status to management.

The result of the forecasting cycle is a budget for the upcoming plan year for each organization's unit as well as estimated pay treatment for each employee. The budget does not lock in the manager to the exact pay change recommended for each employee. Rather, it represents a plan, and deviations due to unforeseen changes such as performance improvements, and unanticipated promotions are common.

This approach to pay budgeting requires that managers plan the pay treatment for each of their employees. It places the responsibility for pay management on the managers. The compensation manager takes on the role of advisor to operating management's use of the system.[7]

[7]Ronald T. Albright and Bridge R. Compton, *Internal Consulting Basics* (Scottsdale, AZ: American Compensation Association, 1996); John Watson, "Delivering Total Compensation Online at Dell," *ACA News* 42(4) (April 1999), pp. 14–19.

MANAGING OR MANIPULATING?

Budgeting average compensation costs is increasingly complicated, for two reasons. First is the increased use of variable forms of pay (i.e., gain sharing, performance bonuses, and stock options). The second is the use of generally accepted accounting practices that permit earnings to be "managed."

Labor costs associated with performance-based pay are typically included in a budget process by estimating the anticipated profits and then the expected profit-sharing pool. Many organizations seek to ensure that these variable incentive plans are "self-funded"—the bonuses (increase in labor costs) are offset by productivity gains (output/costs).

However, controlling variable pay costs sometimes has a "smoke and mirrors" feel to it. At one organization's compensation strategy session, the chief financial officer observed that it was possible to "manage our reported earnings within several percentage points of the target. We can exceed analysts' and shareholder expectations by 1 to 10 percent." This was relatively easy for this company since about one-third of its earnings came from liquid investments in other companies. The remainder was revenue from its products and services. The implication of managing earnings for employees' profit-sharing payouts was not ignored, but clearly it was a secondary concern. Good-bye pay-for-performance strategy, hello managed earnings to "meet or slightly exceed analysts' expectations." The point is that measures of financial performance do not provide an immutable gold standard. They can be "managed."[8]

Ethics

Compensation managers need to become active players and become knowledgeable about the accounting practices used in their organizations. Unfortunately, some, though not all, compensation managers and consultants were silent during all the recent accounting malfeasance by their employers. Consequently, the performance metrics on which pay-for-performance plans depend were manipulated, often illegally. Here again, standards of conduct and ethical codes are absent. Manipulating measures on which variable pay is based is not the only area that presents an ethical dilemma for compensation managers. Misuse of surveys and statistics, repricing underwater options, benefit enhancements for senior management, escalating executive pay levels—all may force practitioners to take a hard look at what they are doing. Should they be advocates for employees or shareholders? Where do their loyalties lie?[9] Without a professional code of conduct, compensation managers must look to their own ethics—and our pay model, which calls for fair treatment of employees.

[8]Nancy Emmons, "Managed and Manipulated Earnings: Implications for Compensation Managers," working paper, ILR/Cornell University, 2000; Flora Guidry, Andrew J. Leon, and Steve Rock, "Earnings-Based Bonus Plans and Earnings Management by Business-Unit Managers," *Journal of Accounting and Economics* 26 (1999), pp. 113–142.

[9]Frederic W. Cook, "Compensation Ethics: An Oxymoron or Valid Area for Debate?" Featured speech at ACA International Conference Workshop, 1999; Alison Maitland, "How Do We Make the Company Do the Right Thing? We Delegate," *Financial Times,* July 10, 2003, p. 8.

INHERENT CONTROLS

Controls on managers' pay decisions come from two different aspects of the compensation process: (1) controls that are inherent in the design of the techniques, and (2) the formal budgeting process.

Think back to the many techniques already discussed: job analysis and evaluation, skill-competency-based plans, policy lines, range minimums and maximums, broad bands, performance evaluation, gain sharing, and salary increase guidelines. In addition to their primary purposes, these techniques also regulate managers' pay decisions by guiding what managers can and cannot do. Controls are embedded in the design of these techniques to ensure that decisions are directed toward the pay system's objectives. A few of these controls are examined below.

Range Maximums and Minimums

These ranges set the maximum and minimum dollars to be paid for specific work. The maximum is an important cost control. Ideally, it represents the highest value the organization places on the output of the work. With job-based structures, skills and knowledge possessed by employees may be more valuable in another job, but the range maximum represents all that the work produced in a particular job is worth to the organization. For example, the job of airline flight attendant is in a pay range with a maximum that is the highest an airline will pay a flight attendant, no matter how well the attendant performs the job.

Pressures to pay above the range maximum occur for a number of reasons—for example, when employees with high seniority reach the maximum or when promotion opportunities are scarce. If employees are paid above the range maximum, these rates are called *red-circle rates.* Most employers "freeze" red-circle rates until the ranges are shifted upward by market update adjustments so that the rate is back within the range again. If red-circle rates become common throughout an organization, then the design of the ranges and the evaluation of the jobs should be reexamined.

Range minimums are just that: the minimum value placed on the work. Often rates below the minimum are used for trainees. Rates below minimum may also occur if outstanding employees receive a number of rapid promotions and rate adjustments have not kept up.

Broad Bands

Broad bands are intended to offer managers greater flexibility compared to a grade-range design. Usually broad bands are accompanied by external market "reference rates" and "shadow ranges" that guide managers' decisions. Bands may be more about career management than pay decisions. From the perspective of managing labor costs, broad bands really don't play a role. Rather, the control is in the salary budgets given to managers. The manager has flexibility in pay decisions, as long as the total pay comes in under the budget.

Compa-Ratios

Range midpoints reflect the pay-policy line of the employer in relationship to external competition. To assess how managers actually pay employees in relation to the midpoint, an index called a *compa-ratio* is often calculated:

$$\text{Compa-ratio} = \frac{\text{average rates actually paid}}{\text{range midpoint}}$$

A compa-ratio of less than 1 means that, on average, employees in a range are paid below the midpoint. That is, managers are paying less than the intended policy. There may be several valid reasons for such a situation. The majority of employees may be new or recent hires; they may be poor performers; or promotion may be so rapid that few employees stay in the job long enough to get into the high end of the range.

A compa-ratio greater than 1 means that, on average, the rates exceed the intended policy. The reasons for this are the reverse of those mentioned above: a majority of workers with high seniority, high performance, low turnover, few new hires, or low promotion rates. Compa-ratios may be calculated for individual employees, for each range, for organization units, or for functions.

Other examples of controls designed into the pay techniques include the mutual sign-offs on job descriptions required of supervisors and subordinates. Another is slotting new jobs into the pay structure via job evaluation, which helps ensure that jobs are compared on the same factors. Similarly, an organizationwide performance management system is intended to ensure that all employees are evaluated on similar factors.

Variable Pay

The essence of variable pay is that it must be reearned each period, in contrast to conventional merit pay increases or across-the-board increases that are added to base pay each year and that increase the base on which the following year's increase is calculated.

Increases added into base pay have compounding effects on costs, and these costs are significant. For example, a $15-a-week take-home pay added onto a $40,000 base compounds into a cash flow of $503,116 over 10 years. In addition, costs for some benefits also increase. By comparison, the organization could use that same $503,000 to keep base pay at $40,000 a year and pay a 26.8 percent bonus every single year. As the example shows, the greater the ratio of variable pay to base pay, the more flexible the organization's labor costs. Apply this to the general labor cost model in Exhibit 18.1. The greater the ratios of contingent to core workers and variable to base pay, the greater the variable component of labor costs and the greater the options available to managers to control these costs.

A caution: Although variability in pay and employment may be an advantage for managing labor costs, it may be less appealing from the standpoint of managing fair treatment of employees. The inherent financial insecurity built into variable plans may adversely affect employees' financial well-being, especially for lower-paid workers, and subsequently affect their behaviors and attitudes toward customers and employers. Managing labor costs is only one objective for managing compensation.

Analyzing Costs

Costing out wage proposals is commonly done prior to recommending pay increases. It is also done in preparation for collective bargaining. For example, it is useful to bear in mind the dollar impact of a 1-cent-per-hour wage change or a 1 percent change in payroll as one goes into bargaining. Knowing these figures, negotiators can quickly compute the impact of a request for a 9 percent wage increase. Outside the bargaining session, commercial compensation software is available to analyze almost every aspect of compensation information. For example, software can easily compare past estimates to what actually occurred (e.g., the percentage of employees that actually did receive a merit increase and the amount). It can simulate alternate wage proposals and compare their potential effects. It can also help evaluate salary survey data and simulate the cost impact of incentive and gain-sharing options. However, trained compensation decision makers are still required to make decisions based on the results.

Analyzing Value Added

A decision to adopt a new compensation policy or to implement a new plan can be evaluated on its impact on costs. However, a handful of companies, supported by consultants and researchers, are also analyzing the value added (or return on investments) of these decisions.[10] Measuring the value gained from various programs is like the search for life on Mars: Both processes require an awful lot of assumptions, and both are susceptible to hope and hype.

Exhibit 18.9 illustrates the basic approach to assessing the value gained from installing a plan. The company in this exhibit is considering two actions:

1. Implement a bonus plan based on balanced scorecards for individual managers.
2. Increase the differentiation between top performers and average performers. (This decision is based on an analysis that suggested that the top 10 percent of employees improved returns by about 2 to 5 percent of their average salary.)

The exhibit shows the analysis of potential value added by these two options. The returns are grouped into four types: recruiting and retaining top talent, reducing turnover of top performers, revenue enhancement, and productivity gains. The logic, assumptions, measures, and estimates of gains are described in the exhibit. The cautious reader will immediately see that the assumptions are critical and based on best estimates and judgments.

The practice of analyzing the returns from compensation decisions is in its early stages. The promise is that it will direct thinking beyond treating compensation as only an expense to considering the returns gained as well. Analyzing potential gains provides information to make tradeoffs among alternative plans. Nevertheless, decision makers still must use their knowledge and judgment.

Making Information Useful—Compensation Enterprise Systems

Some organizations still have difficulty gathering information due to inefficient antiquated systems. A friend of ours e-mailed from Shanghai that "six months after we have acquired this operation from the government, I still cannot get an accurate headcount. I do not know how many people we actually employ or who should get paychecks!" That manager clearly needs more information. But most managers find themselves overwhelmed with too much information. The challenge is to make the information useful.

Compensation enterprise software transforms data into useful information and guides decision making. Many software packages that serve a variety of purposes are available.[11] Some of them support *employee self-service,* by which employees can access their

---

[10]Wayne Cascio, *Responsible Restructuring: Creative and Profitable Alternatives to Layoffs* (San Francisco: Berrett-Koehler, 2002); John Boudreau and Peter Ramstad, "Strategic Knowledge Measurement and Management," CAHRS Working Paper 02–17, Ithaca, NY; Helen De Cieri and John Boudreau, "Global Human Resource Metrics?" CAHRS Working Paper 03–07, Ithaca, NY; Jaap deJonge, *Watson Wyatt Human Capital Index* (New York: Watson Wyatt, 2003).

[11]Kadiri and Peoplesoft are two software companies whose software guides decision making. A useful guide on selecting HR software is James G. Meade, *The Human Resources Software Handbook* (San Francisco: Jossey-Bass/Pfeiffer, 2003). Also see Nona Tobin, "Can Technology Ease the Pain of Salary Surveys?" *Public Personnel Management* 31(1) (Spring 2002), pp. 65–77.

EXHIBIT 18.9   Illustration of Value-Added Analysis

Description of Value	Assumptions	Measure	Value Added	
			Low Estimate	**High Estimate**
Recruiting/Retaining Top Talent				
Increase pool of top people applying; increase percent accepting offers; decrease time to fill position	Top performers improve returns by 2% to 5% of average salary ($68,000)	Increase top talent yield ratios and turnover rates	Increases revenues by $1,400/top person	Improves revenues by $3,400/top person
Reduced Turnover/Replacement Costs				
Reduction of recruiting costs due to lower turnover of top performers	Reduction in turnover of one top performer results in a savings of $25,000 (based on an average salary of $68,000)	Savings of $25,000/top performer Productivity savings reflected in "loss of revenue" section	$100,000 for a reduction of four "resigned" top employees	$500,000 for a reduction of 10 "resigned" top employees
Revenue Enhancers				
Reduced loss of revenue due to faster time to fill key customer-facing (sales, technical support) and other key positions	Revenue will increase by some percentage (e.g., 5%) Head count remains constant	Revenue increase Assume current revenue of $2 billion	2% or $40 million	5% or $100 million
Greater revenue because of focus on revenue and customer goals as driven by the balanced scorecard				
Increased revenue because of stronger and longer-lasting customer relationships due to retention of key/top performers through market competitiveness and pay differentiation				
Productivity Gains				
Increased productivity by retaining top performers through significant pay differentiation and market-competitive base pay	Retaining and engaging more of the top employees results in significant productivity gains and revenue generation because top employees are 25% to 50% more productive than the average employee	Increased revenue (reflected in revenue gains-above) Head-count reduction (need fewer employees or grow slower)	A reduction in 10 head count results in a savings of $900,000 ($68,000 employee + benefit cost)	A reduction in 50 head count results in a savings of $4.5 million
Increased productivity of all employees because of greater perception of "internal alignment" and "market competitiveness" resulting from paying competitive with the market and common programs	Increasing the productivity of all results in increased revenue, customer satisfaction, or fewer head count			
	Terminating low-productivity employees and replacing them with high-productivity employees result in significant productivity gains and revenue generation	Head-count reduction because fewer top performers achieve the same results as more lower performers	A reduction in 1 head count results in a savings of $90,000	A reduction in 5 head count results in a savings of $450,000

personal information, make choices about which health care coverage they prefer, allocate savings between growth or value investment funds, access vacation schedules, or check out a list of child or elder care service providers. *Manager self-service,* illustrated by the Dell exhibits, helps managers pay their employees appropriately. *Communication portals,* designed for employees or managers, explain compensation policies and practices, answer frequently asked questions, and explain how these systems affect their pay.[12] Other compensation enterprise software *processes transactions.* It standardizes forms, performs some analysis, and creates reports at the click of the mouse. Its advantage is that all employees at all locations are on the same system.

While compensation software is proliferating, what remains a scarcer resource is the intellectual capital: the compensation knowledge and judgment required to understand which information, analyses, and reports are useful. Part of this intellectual capital includes analytical (read "statistical and math") skills. Another part is knowledge of the business. A shortage of this knowledge among compensation managers not only limits the usefulness of compensation software but also limits the contribution of compensation management beyond administering transactions.

Computers inevitably bring up the issue of confidentiality. If personal compensation data are accessible to employees and managers, privacy and security issues as well as ethical and legal issues emerge. Regulations vary around the world. The European Union has issued the Data Privacy Directive, which is significantly stronger than U.S. regulations.[13] Unauthorized users, both inside and outside the corporation, create a threat. The medical community is already adjusting to challenges created by new federal rules to protect patient privacy.

COMMUNICATION: MANAGING THE MESSAGE

Compensation communicates. It signals what is important and what is not. If you receive a pay increase for one more year of experience on your job, then one more year is important. If the pay increase is equal to any change in the CPI, then the CPI and its real meaning is important. If the increase is for moving to a bigger job or for outstanding performance, then a bigger job or outstanding performance is important. Changes in a pay system also send a powerful message. Microsoft's shift from stock options to grants tells everyone (current and future employees and stockholders) to expect lower risks and lower returns.

Earlier in this book, we stressed that employees must understand the pay system. Their understanding is shaped indirectly through the paychecks they receive and directly via formal communication about their pay, their performance, and the markets in which the organization competes. An argument for employee involvement in the design of pay systems is that it increases understanding. Two surveys are revealing. A Watson Wyatt survey of 13,000 employees reported that about only 35 percent of them understood the link between their job performance and the pay they receive. (Watson Wyatt failed to point out that perhaps there was no link! Perhaps the Dilbert cartoons about just showing up are

---

[12]Diane Palframan, *HR Technology Strategies* (New York: Conference Board, 2003).
[13]*www.privacilla.org/business/eudirective.html.*

correct.)[14] A second survey of 6,000 employees, done by WorldatWork, reported that pay plans are not well understood by managers and employees. Only about one-third say they understand how pay ranges are determined or have a reasonable idea of what their increase would be if they were promoted. Fewer than half understand how their own pay increases are calculated.[15]

Two reasons are usually given for communicating pay information. The first is that considerable resources have been devoted to designing a fair and equitable system that is intended to motivate effective performance and encourage productivity. For managers and employees to gain an accurate view of the pay system—one that perhaps influences their attitudes about it—they need to be informed.

The second reason is that according to some research, employees seem to misperceive the pay system. For example, they tend to overestimate the pay of those in lower-level jobs and to underestimate the pay of those in higher-level jobs. They assume that the pay structure is more compressed than it actually is. If differentials are underestimated, their motivational value to engage employees is diminished.

Further, there is some evidence to suggest that the goodwill engendered by the act of being open about pay may also affect perceptions of pay equity. Interestingly, the research also shows that employees in companies with open pay communication policies are as inaccurate in estimating pay differentials as those in companies in which pay secrecy prevails.[16] However, employers in companies with open pay policies tend to express higher satisfaction with their pay and with the pay system.

WorldatWork recommends a six-stage process of communication, shown in Exhibit 18.10.[17]

Step 1 is, not surprisingly, defining the objectives of the communication program. Is it to ensure that employees fully understand all the components of the compensation system? Is it to change performance expectations? Or is it to help employees make informed health care choices? While specifying objectives as a first step seems obvious, doing so is often overlooked in the rush to design an attractive brochure, website, or CD.

Step 2 is to collect information from executives, managers, and employees to assess their current perceptions, attitudes, and understanding of the subject. Information may be gathered through online opinion surveys and focus groups.[18] Information on current attitudes and perceptions is analyzed to identify problems (e.g., if the majority do not even know the value of their total compensation).

---

[14]"Growing Worker Confusion about Corporate Goals Complicates Recovery, Watson Wyatt WorkUSA Study Finds," Watson Wyatt news release, September 9, 2002.

[15]Robert L. Heneman, Paul W. Mulvey, and Peter V. LeBlanc, "Improve Base Pay ROI by Increasing Employee Knowledge," *WorldatWork Journal* 11(4) (Fourth Quarter 2002).

[16]Thomas A. Mahoney and William Weitzel, "Secrecy and Managerial Compensation," *Industrial Relations* 17(2) (1978), pp. 245–251; Julio D. Burroughs, "Pay Secrecy and Performance: The Psychological Research," *Compensation Review,* Third Quarter 1982, pp. 44–54; Ed Lawler III, "The New Pay," in *Current Issues in Human Resource Management,* ed. Sara L. Rynes and George T. Milkovich (Plano, TX: Business Publications, 1986), pp. 404–412.

[17]John A. Rubino, *Communicating Compensation Programs* (Scottsdale, AZ: American Compensation Association, 1997).

[18]George Milkovich and P. H. Anderson, "Management Compensation and Secrecy Policies," *Personnel Psychology* 25 (1972), pp. 293–302.

EXHIBIT 18.10 The Compensation Communication Cycle

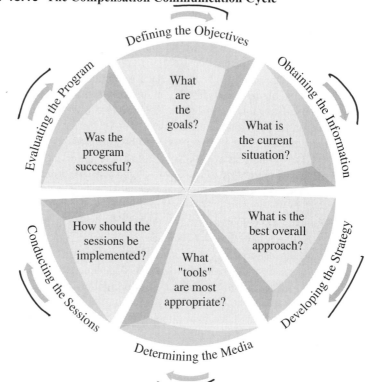

Source: Reprinted from ACA Building Block 4, *Communicating Compensation Programs: An Approach to Providing Information to Employees,* by John A. Rubino, CCP, with permission from the American Compensation Association (ACA), 14040 N. Northsight Blvd., Scottsdale, AZ 85260; telephone (602) 951-9191. fax: (602) 483-8352. © ACA.

Step 3 is a communication program that will convey the information needed to accomplish the original objectives. There is no standard approach on what to communicate to individuals about their own pay or that of their colleagues. Some organizations adopt a *marketing approach.* That includes consumer attitude surveys about the product, snappy advertising about the pay policies, and elaborate websites expounding policies and rationale. The objective is to manage expectations and attitudes about pay. In contrast, the *communication approach* tends to focus on explaining practices, details, and the way pay is determined. The marketing approach focuses on the strategy, values, and advantages of overall policies and may be silent on specifics such as range maximums, increase guides, and the like.

Steps 4 and 5 of the communication process are to determine the most effective media, in light of the message and the audience, and to conduct the campaign. Exhibit 18.11 recommends fine-tuning the message in terms of detail and emphasis, depending on the audience. Executives, for example, should be interested in how the compensation programs fit the business strategy. Managers need to know how to use the development and motivation aspects of the compensation program for the people they supervise. Employees may want to know the processes and policies as well as specifics about how their pay is determined. Exhibit 18.12 shows Dell's communication program delivered to employees

EXHIBIT 18.11   Conducting Formal Communication Sessions for Various Audiences

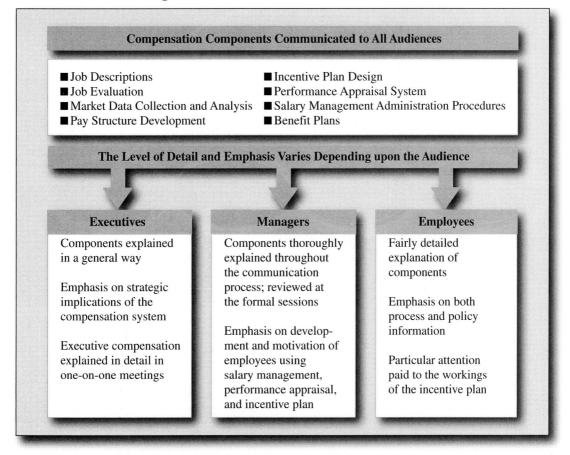

Source: Reprinted from ACA Building Block 4, *Communicating Compensation Programs: An Approach to Providing Information to Employees,* by John A. Rubino, CCP, with permission from the American Compensation Association (ACA), 14040 N. Northsight Blvd., Scottsdale, AZ 85260; telephone (602) 951-9191. fax: (602) 483-8352. © ACA.

via an intranet. The danger is overload—information is so detailed that employees get snowed under sorting through it.

Intended and Unintended Consequences

Step 6 of the communication process suggests that the program be evaluated. Did it accomplish its goals? Pay communication often has unintended consequences.[19] For example, improving employees' knowledge about pay may cause some initial short-term concerns. Over the years, employees may have rationalized a set of relationships between their pay and the perceived pay and efforts of others. Receiving accurate information may require that those perceptions be adjusted.[20]

[19.] Jeremy Handel, "Does It Matter If Employees Know about Pay?" 12(10) (2002).

[20.] John Case, "When Salaries Aren't Secret," *Harvard Business Review* Case Study, May 2001.

EXHIBIT 18.12 Communicating Employees via an Intranet

Source: John Watson, "Delivering Total Compensation Online at Dell," *ACA News* 42(4) (April 1999), pp. 14–19. Used with permission from WorldatWork (formerly American Compensation Association); *www.worldatwork.org.* © 1999 WorldatWork.

Cybercomp

One compensation manager reports having a great deal of difficulty with an employee who used the homefair website *www.homefair.com* to determine that he should receive a 30 percent pay differential to accompany his transfer from one office to another. In contrast, the manager's information showed a differential of around 12 to 15 percent. How can you judge the accuracy of information obtained on the web? How would you deal with the unhappy employee?

Say What?

If the pay system is not based on work-related or business-related logic, then the wisest course is probably to avoid formal communication until the system is put in order. However, avoiding *formal* communication is not synonymous with avoiding communication. Employees are constantly getting intended and unintended messages through the pay treatment they receive.

Many employers communicate the range for an incumbent's present job and for all the jobs in a typical career path or progression to which employees can logically aspire. Some also communicate the typical pay increases that can be expected for poor, satisfactory, and top performance. The rationale given is that employees exchange data (not always factual) and/or guess at normal treatment and that the rumor mills are probably incorrect. People do form expectations about pay. Managers can help create them or let the rumor mill do it for them. Improving employees' knowledge about their pay seems to be related to their work attitudes and behaviors.

Opening the Books

There are some who advocate sharing all financial information with employees.[21] For 15 years, employees at Springfield Remanufacturing, a rebuilder of engines, have been given weekly peeks at everything from revenues to labor costs. The employees, who own 31 percent of the company stock, and others argue that this "open-book" approach results in high commitment and an understanding of how to maintain competitiveness. Many employers don't share information with such gusto, but they are increasingly disclosing more to their employees. Some are even providing basic business and financial training to help employees better understand the information. Devotees of opening the books and providing financial training believe these methods will improve attitudes and performance, but there is no research to support this. With salary data available on the Internet (albeit often inaccurate and misleading), developing in-house compensation portals has appeal.

At the minimum, the most important information to be communicated is the work-related and business-related rationales on which pay systems are based. Some employees may not agree with these rationales or the results, but at least it will be clear that pay is determined by something other than the whims of their supervisors.

PAY: CHANGE AGENT IN RESTRUCTURING

Compensation often plays a singular role when organizations restructure. Strategic changes in the business strategy mean the compensation strategy must be realigned as well. Pay is a powerful signal of change; changing people's pay captures their attention.

Pay changes can play two roles in any restructuring. Pay can be a leading catalyst for change or a follower of change. Shifts from conventional across-the-board annual increases to profit sharing or from narrow job descriptions and ranges to broad roles and bands signal major change to employees. Microsoft's shift from its uniquely aggressive stock options to less risky stock awards illustrates the point. Microsoft used its change in the pay mix to communicate a shift from a "workaholic—get rich quick" to a "work hard—get paid well" approach. Whether this shift acts as a catalyst or a support is open to debate. As a catalyst it communicates change more strongly and vividly than any rhetoric could. It will help drive recruiting and retention. Yet it may be that Microsoft had already changed as an organization. Faced with murmuring employees (their options were underwater) and external conditions (a public debate over accounting for options) the shift in pay mix merely confirmed reality—that Microsoft had changed.

Whether pay is a leading catalyst for change or a follower of change, compensation managers must learn how to implement and manage change. Not only must they know the strategic and technical aspects of compensation; they also must know how to bargain, resolve disputes, empower employees, and develop teams. Being able to grab bullets in midflight doesn't hurt, either.[22]

[21]"Rethinking Ways to Present Financial Information to Employees," *Employee Ownership Report,* March/April 2000, pp. 7, 10.

[22]Michael Beer and Mitin Nohria, "Cracking the Code of Change," *Harvard Business Review,* May–June 2000, pp. 133–141; Dave Ulrich, "A New Mandate for Human Resources," *Harvard Business Review,* January–February 1998, pp. 125–134; Emily Lawson and Colin Price, "The Psychology of Change Management," *McKinsey Quarterly,* No. 2, 2003; Patrick M. Wright, Lee Dyer, and Michael G. Takla, *Execution: The Critical "What's Next?" in Strategic Human Resource Management* CAHRS Working Paper 99–11, Ithaca, NY.

STRUCTURING THE COMPENSATION FUNCTION

Compensation professionals seem to be constantly reevaluating where within the organization the responsibility for the design and administration of pay systems should be located. The organizational arrangements of the compensation function vary widely.

Centralization-Decentralization

An important issue related to structuring the function revolves around the degree of decentralization (or centralization) in the overall organization structure. *Decentralized* refers to a management strategy of giving separate organization units the responsibility of designing and administering their own systems. This contrasts with a *centralized* strategy, which locates the design and administration responsibility in a single corporate unit.

Some firms, such as 3M, Xerox, and IBM, have relatively large corporate staffs whose responsibility it is to formulate pay policies and design the systems. 3M calls its group the Total Compensation Resource Center. Administration of these policies and systems falls to those working in various units, who often are personnel generalists. Such an arrangement runs the risk of formulating policies and practices that are well tuned to overall corporate needs but less well tuned to each unit's particular needs and circumstances. The use of task forces, with members drawn from the generalists in the affected units, to design new policies and techniques helps diminish this potential problem.

Other, more decentralized organizations, such as Eaton and GE, have relatively small corporate compensation staffs (three or four professionals). Their primary responsibility is to manage the systems by which executives and the corporate staff are paid. These professionals operate in a purely advisory capacity to other organization subunits. The subunits, in turn, may employ compensation specialists. Or the subunits may choose to employ only personnel generalists rather than compensation specialists and may turn to outside compensation consultants to purchase the expertise required on specific compensation issues.

AES, an electric power company, has no compensation unit at all, nor any HR department either. Compensation functions are totally handled by teams of managers. Decentralizing certain aspects of pay design and administration has considerable appeal. Pushing these responsibilities (and expenses) close to the units, managers, and employees affected by them may help ensure that decisions are business-related. However, decentralization is not without dilemmas. For example, it may be difficult to transfer employees from one business unit to another. A pay system may support a subunit's objectives but run counter to the overall corporate objectives. The potential for pay discrimination increases.

Flexibility within Corporatewide Principles

The answers to these and related problems of decentralization can be found in developing a set of corporatewide principles or guidelines that all must meet. The principles may differ for each major pay technique. For example, GE's business units worldwide have the flexibility to design incentive plans tailored to each unique business unit's strategies and cultures. The only guidance is to ensure that the plans adhere to GE's basic beliefs, improve financial and business objectives, and maintain or enhance GE's reputation.

Keep in mind that the pay system is one of many management systems used in the organization. Consequently, it must be congruent with these other systems. For example, it may be appealing, on paper at least, to decentralize some of the compensation functions. However, if financial data and other management systems are not also decentralized, the pay system may not fit and may even be at odds with other systems.

Reengineering and Outsourcing

Six sigma is a process used to improve quality and ensure that value is added by each technique. For the compensation system, it involves changing the process of paying people. It means reshaping the compensation function to make it more client- or customer-focused.[23] Clients probably include employees, managers, and owners and perhaps even real customers of the organization. The basic question asked during reengineering is, "Does each specific activity (technique) directly contribute to our objectives (i.e., to our competitive advantage)?" If some added value isn't apparent, then the technique should be dropped. The next question, directed at pay activities that do contribute to achieving objectives, is, "Should we be doing the specific activity in-house, or can others do it more effectively? That is, should we outsource it?"

Outsourcing is a viable alternative in the compensation (and benefits) field as organizations struggle to cease doing activities that do not directly contribute to objectives. In a recent survey, about 33 percent of over 1,000 firms reported that they already outsourced major responsibilities for their pay (e.g., market surveys and structure design) and benefit administration.

Cost savings are the apparent major short-term advantage of outsourcing. All those compensation wonks can be laid off or retrained. Major disadvantages of outsourcing include less responsiveness to unique and specific employee-manager problems, less control over decisions that are often critical to all employees (i.e., their pay), and information leaks to rivals and competitors.[24]

CONTROLS AS GUIDELINES: LET (THOUGHTFUL) MANAGERS MANAGE

One of the major attacks on traditional compensation plans is that they often degenerate into bureaucratic nightmares that interfere with the organization's ability to respond to competitive pressures. Some recommend reducing the controls and guidelines inherent in any pay plan. Hence, banding eliminates or at least reduces the impact of range maximums and minimums. Replacing merit grids with bonuses eliminates the link between the pay increase and the employees' salary position in the range and performance rating. Replacing job evaluation with skill- or competency-based plans opens up the freedom to assign employees to a wider variety of work, regardless of their pay.

---

[23]Mark A. Youndt and Scott A. Snell, "Human Resource Configurations, Intellectual Capital, and Organizational Performance," CAHRS Working Paper 03–16, Ithaca, NY.

[24]Michael Skapinker, "Much to Question on Outsourcing," *Financial Times,* June 30, 2003, p. 4, *www.ft.com/managejune2003.*

Such approaches are consistent with the oft-heard plea that managers should be free to manage pay. Or, as some more bluntly claim, pay decisions are too important to be left to compensation professionals.

Yet permitting managers to be free to pay employees as they judge best rests on a basic premise: Managers will use pay to achieve the organization's objectives—efficiency, fairness, and compliance with regulations—rather than their own objectives. But the recent leadership scandals in some corporations and public agencies cause us to be cautious. Clearly, some balance between hidebound controls and chaos is required to ensure that pay decisions are directed at the organization's goals yet permit sufficient flexibility to respond to unique situations. Achieving the balance becomes part of the art of managing compensation.

A final issue related to pay design and administration is the skills and competencies required in compensation managers. The grandest strategy and structure may seem well designed, well thought out in the abstract, but could be a disaster if people qualified to carry it out are not part of the staff.

In view of the importance of a well-trained staff, both WorldatWork and the Society of Human Resource Managers (SHRM) have professional development programs to entice readers into the compensation field.[25] In addition, the websites in this chapter's appendix provide a lot more information.

Your Turn — Two Harbors Teachers

Public school teachers typically are paid according to salary schedules that include:

1. "Steps" that pay for accumulating experience.
2. "Lanes" that pay for extra college credits.

Steps and lanes operate to boost pay even if the local school board does not grant any across-the-board or cost-of-living increases.

Critics of such schedules say that they guarantee steadily climbing costs, even in times when a district's finances do not permit increases.

Exhibit 1 shows a simplified salary schedule at Two Harbors, a district that employs 100 teachers and whose enrollment is growing at about 3 percent a year.

Calculate the change in salary in year 2 under the following conditions:

1. Six teachers earning an average salary of $43,444 resign.
2. Nine teachers are hired at an average of $25,666.

---

[25]Schedules and course registration information are available from WorldatWork, 14040 N. Northsight Blvd., Scottsdale, AZ 85260 (*www.worldatwork.org*), and from Society of Human Resource Managers, 606 N. Washington Street, Alexandria, VA, 22314 (*www.shrm.org*).

EXHIBIT 1   Two Harbors Salary Schedule Showing Distribution of 100 Teachers

	B.A. Degree	B.A. and Credits	M.A. Degree	M.A. and Credits
Year One				
Total salaries for 100 teachers: $3,110,000				
Average salary: $31,100				
Step 5	7 teachers $29,000	18 teachers $33,000	14 teachers $36,000	11 teachers $41,000
Step 4	4 teachers $27,000	6 teachers $30,000	5 teachers $34,000	1 teacher $38,000
Step 3	6 teachers $25,000	4 teachers $28,000	3 teachers $31,000	1 teacher $35,000
Step 2	6 teachers $23,000	2 teachers $26,000	2 teachers $28,000	0 teachers $32,000
Step 1	8 teachers $22,000	1 teacher $24,000	1 teacher $26,000	0 teachers $28,000

Each step represents four years of service; the vertical columns show levels of college credits. In year 2, the faculty moves from an average of 3.86 steps to 3.93, and the proportion of teachers with master's degrees increases from 38 to 39 percent.

Summary

We have now completed the discussion of the pay management process. Management includes control: control of the way managers decide individual employees' pay as well as control of overall costs of labor. As we noted, some controls are designed into the fabric of the pay system (inherent controls, range maximums and minimums, etc.). The salary budgeting and forecasting processes impose additional controls. The formal budgeting process focuses on controlling labor costs and generating the financial plan for the pay system. The budget sets the limits within which the rest of the system operates.

We also noted that with the continuous change in organizations, compensation managers must understand how to manage change and be knowledgeable business partners.

Other aspects of management we examined in this chapter include the fair treatment of employees in communications and participation. The basic point is that pay systems are tools, and like any tools they need to be evaluated in terms of usefulness in achieving an organization's objectives.

Review Questions

1. How can employers control labor costs?
2. How does the management of the pay system affect pay objectives?
3. Why is the structure of the compensation function important?
4. Give some examples of how employers use inherent controls.
5. What activities in managing the pay system are likely candidates to be outsourced? Why?
6. Explain how employee communications and participation influence the effectiveness of the pay system.

Appendix **18**

Compensation Websites

CONSULTING FIRMS

Consulting Firms	WWW Address	What Does Website Offer?
Hay Group	*haygroup.com* *haypaynet.com*	• News releases, legislative and regulatory updates, and survey data • Hay PayNet allows organization to tap into Hay's customized compensation databases
Hewitt Associates	*www.hewitt.com*	• Provides press releases, full text articles, and brief items on laws, regulations, and federal agency activities
KPMG	*www.kpmg.com* *www.us.kpmg.com*	• Summaries of developments in benefit laws and short reports on KPMG survey results
Runzheimer International	*www.runzheimer.com*	• A Wisconsin-based management consulting firm that developed standards for the IRS • Information on salary differentials, living costs, and travel and moving benefits
Sibson & Company	*www.sibson.com*	• Case studies drawn from client experiences • Items on compensation design, organization development, etc.
Towers Perrin	*www.towersperrin.com*	• Information on international pay and benefits • New legislation, regulations, and new issues in major countries.
Watson Wyatt Worldwide	*www.watsonwyatt.com*	• Global news service, including reports and surveys from all over the world, from two-tier pay systems in Spain to performance pay in China and Vietnam. • Choice of five languages
William M. Mercer	*www.mercer.com*	• User can stop at Mercer's home page or go directly to its "Rewarding Employees" site with press releases, publication • Surveys on salaries, performance pay, assessment, compensation committees, and executive pay

EXECUTIVE COMPENSATION

Executive Compensation	WWW Address	What Does Website Offer?
Frederic W. Cook	*www.fredericwcook.com*	• Alert letter includes items on executive compensation issues and legislation • New publication ads
Securities and Exchange Commission	*www.sec.gov*	• Executive salaries and some executives' employment contracts

BROAD LISTING FOR COMPENSATION

Employee Compensation	WWW Address	What Does Website Offer?
WorldatWork	*www.worldatwork.org*	• Information on seminars and organization certification programs • Listings of publications
American Management Association	*www.amanet.org*	• Information about AMA's training programs, publications and other resources
BLS Covered Employment and Wages	*stats.bls.gov/cewhome.htm*	• Leads to large files for time-series data, all of which are downloadable.
BLS Occupational Compensation Survey	*stats.bls.gov/ocshome.htm*	• Leads to large files for time-series data, all of which are downloadable
BLS Economy at a Glance	*stats.bls.gov/eag.table.html*	• The latest data for employment, hours, earnings, productivity, the CPI, and the employment cost index
Bureau of Labor Statistics (BLS)	*www.bls.gov*	• The single largest source of data on salaries and wages, labor costs, employment, labor markets, benefits, workplace safety and health statistics, prices, and working conditions • All data are free and downloadable
Cornell University/ HR Executive	*www.workindex.com*	• Performs more targeted searches than Yahoo and Alta Vista • Compensation-related site listings include benefits, compensation, economic and business statistics, etc.
Society for HR Management	*www.shrm.org*	• HR news and wide range of links, including compensation and benefits • A number of links to private consulting firms and publishers

COMPENSATION LAWS AND REGULATIONS

Compensation Laws and Regulations	WWW Address	What Does Website Offer?
Family Medical Leave Act	*www.dol.gov/dol/esa/fmla.htm*	• This is DOL site for FMLA regulations • Guidance on compliance issues, plus toll-free number for assistance
National Labor Relations Board (NLRB) issues	*www.nlrb.gov*	• Weekly summaries, NLRB decisions, rules and regulations, and other information on labor relations
State Labor Department	e.g., website for New York State: *www.labor.state.ny.us/wages/man.htm*	• A number of states have websites for their labor department or employment agency with information on minimum wage, labor markets, and local wages
U.S. Department of Labor (DOL)	*www.dol.gov*	• Press releases, reports, forms, and compliance guidance

BENEFITS

Benefits	WWW Address	What Does Website Offer?
BenefitsLink	*benefitslink.com*	• Links to a number of benefit topics, plus legal updates on pensions, retirement plans, and FRISA, and a forum for benefit professionals to post questions and offer comments • References for benefit-related official federal government documents and a list of service providers
Employee Benefit Research Institute (EBRI)	*www.ebri.org*	• Lists of health care providers and links to other benefit and business websites • A list of links to other benefit sources on the web • EBRI reports on benefit issues
Health and Human Services Department	*www.healthfinder.gov*	• Links to more than 500 health information websites, plus news, publications, online journals, and toll-free numbers (from private and public sources)
Health Insurance Association of America	*www.hiaa.org*	• Press releases on health care legislation and a list of HIAA publications • Extensive collection of statistics on health insurance and health care
International Foundation of Employee Benefit Plans	*www.ifebp.org*	• Industry news • Reports on benefit issues • Full listing of IFEBP services and resources
National Committee for Quality Assurance	*www.ncqa.org*	• The NCQA is the major accreditation organization for managed care providers • Allows user to select a provider or a location and view the provider's performance ratings

PENSIONS AND RETIREMENT

Persions and Retirement	WWW Address	What Does Website Offer?
Association of Private Pension and Welfare Plans	*www.appwp.org/appwp*	• Information on legislation affecting pensions • Updates on current issues • Links to other websites
Pension Benefit Guarantee Corporation (PBGC)	*www.bpgc.gov*	• Information on pensions and ERISA, PBGC regulations, compliance guidance, and lists of underfunded pension plans
Social Security Administration	*www.ssa.gov*	• Basic social security and Medicare information for employers and employees

INTERNATIONAL INFORMATION

International Organizations	WWW Address	What Does Website Offer?
International Data Base	*www.census.gov/ipc/ www/idbnew.html*	• A computerized databank containing statistical tables or demographic and socioeconomic data for 227 countries and areas of the world
International Labour Organization	*www.ilo.org*	• This United Nations agency promotes social justice and human and labour rights
Latin American Network Information	*lanic.utexas.edu*	• Good starting place for information on Latin America, including economic information
China Online	*www.chinaonline.com*	• A news and analysis website that provides business information of China
Federal Statistical Office of Germany	*www.statistik.bund.de/e_ home.htm*	• Economic information on Germany, including monthly and quarterly economic reports
Asia Society	*www.asiasource.org*	• Covers many Asian countries: culture; business and economics; policy and government; society and history
Nikkeiren	*www.nikkeiren.or. jp/english/top.htm*	• The Japan Federation of Employers' Associations
International Reform Monitor	*www.reformmonitor.org*	• Information on social policy, labor market policy, and industrial relations in 15 countries

Glossary

ability An individual's capability to engage in a specific behavior.

ability to pay The ability of a firm to meet employee wage demands while remaining profitable; a frequent issue in contract negotiations with unions. A firm's ability to pay is constrained by its ability to compete in its product market.

access discrimination Discrimination that focuses on the staffing and allocation decisions made by employers. It denies particular jobs, promotions, or training opportunities to qualified women or minorities. This type of discrimination is illegal under Title VII of the Civil Rights Act of 1964.

across-the-board increases A general adjustment that provides equal increases to all employees.

adjective checklist An individual (or job) rating technique. In its simplest form, it is a set of adjectives or descriptive statements. If the employee (job) possesses a trait listed, the item is checked. A rating score from the checklist equals the number of statements checked.

Age Discrimination in Employment Act (ADEA) of 1967 (amended 1978, 1986, and 1990) Legislation that makes nonfederal employees age 40 and over a protected class relative to their treatment in pay, benefits, and other personnel actions. The 1990 amendment is called the Older Workers Benefit Protection Act.

agency theory A theory of motivation that depicts exchange relationships in terms of two parties: agents and principals. According to this theory, both sides of the exchange will seek the most favorable exchange possible and will act opportunistically if given a chance. As applied to executive compensation, agency theory would place part of the executive's pay at risk to motivate the executive (agent) to act in the best interests of the shareholders (principals) rather than in the executive's own self-interests.

all-salaried work force Pay approach in which not only exempt employees (exempt from provisions of the Fair Labor Standards Act), who traditionally are paid a salary rather than an hourly rate, but also nonexempt employees receive a prescribed amount of money each pay period that does not primarily depend on the number of hours worked.

alternation ranking A job evaluation method that involves ordering the job description alternately at each extreme. All the jobs are considered. Agreement is reached on which is the most valuable and then the least valuable. Evaluators alternate between the next most valued and next least valued and so on until the jobs have been ordered.

Americans with Disabilities Act Legislation that requires that reasonable accommodations be provided to permit employees with disabilities to perform the essential elements of a job.

appeals procedures Mechanisms are created to handle pay disagreements. They provide a forum for employees and managers to voice their complaints and receive a hearing.

balance sheet A method for compensating expatriates based upon the belief that the employee should not suffer financially for accepting a foreign-based assignment. The expatriate's pay is adjusted so that the amounts of the financial responsibilities the expatriate had prior to the assignment are kept at about the same level while on assignment—the company pays for the difference.

balanced scorecard A corporatewide, overall performance measure typically incorporating financial results, process improvements, customer service, and innovation.

base pay See base wage.

base wage The basic cash compensation that an employer pays for the work performed. Tends to reflect the value of the work itself and ignore differences in individual contributions.

basic pay policies Decisions on the relative importance of (1) internal alignment, (2) external competitiveness, (3) employee contributions, and (4) the management of the pay system. These policies form the foundation for the design and administration of pay systems and serve as guidelines for managing pay to accomplish the system's objectives.

Bedeaux plan Individual incentive plan that provides a variation on straight piecework and standard hour plans. Instead of timing an entire task, a Bedeaux plan requires determination of the time required to complete each simple action of a task. Workers receive a wage incentive for completing a task in less than the standard time.

behaviorally anchored rating scales (BARS)
Variants on standard rating scales in which the various scale levels are anchored with behavioral descriptions directly applicable to jobs being evaluated.

benchmark conversion   Process of matching survey jobs by applying the employer's plan to the external jobs and then comparing the worth of the external job with its internal "match."

benchmark (key) job   A prototypical job, or group of jobs, used as a reference point for making pay comparisons within or without the organization. Benchmark jobs have well-known and stable contents; their current pay rates are generally acceptable, and the pay differentials among them are relatively stable. A group of benchmark jobs, taken together, contains the entire range of compensable factors and is accepted in the external labor market for setting wages.

benefit ceiling   A maximum payout for specific benefit claims (e.g., limiting liability for extended hospital stays to $150,000).

best pay practices   Compensation practices that allow employers to gain preferential access to superior human resource talent and competencies (i.e., valued assets), which in turn influence the strategies the organization adopts.

BLS   See Bureau of Labor Statistics.

bonus   A lump-sum payment to an employee in recognition of goal achievement.

bottom-up approach to pay budgeting   Approach in which individual employees' pay rates for the next plan year are forecasted and summed to create an organization's total budget.

broad banding   Collapsing a number of salary grades into a smaller number of broad grades with wide ranges.

budget   A plan within which managers operate and a standard against which managers' actual expenditures are evaluated.

budgeting   A part of the organization's planning process; helps to ensure that future financial expenditures are coordinated and controlled. It involves forecasting the total expenditures required by the pay system during the next period as well as the amount of the pay increases. Bottom up and top down are the two typical approaches to the process.

Bureau of Labor Statistics (BLS)   A major source of publicly available pay data. It also calculates the consumer price index.

cafeteria (flexible) benefit plan   A benefit plan in which employees have a choice as to the benefits they receive within some dollar limit. Usually a common core benefit package is required (e.g., specific minimum levels of health, disability, retirement, and death benefits) plus elective programs from which the employee may select a set dollar amount. Additional coverage may be available through employee contributions.

capital appreciation plans   See long-term incentives.

career paths   The progressions of jobs within an organization.

cash balance plan   A defined benefit plan that looks like a defined contribution plan. Employees have a hypothetical account, (like a 401(k), into which is deposited what is typically a percentage of annual compensation. The dollar amount grows both from contributions by the employer and by some predetermined interest rate (e.g., often set equal to the rate given on 30-year treasury certificates).

central tendency   A midpoint in a group of measures.

central tendency error   A rating error that occurs when a rater consistently rates a group of employees at or close to the midpoint of a scale irrespective of the true score performance of ratees. Avoiding extremes (both high and low) in ratings across employees.

churn   See turnover effect.

Civil Rights Act of 1964   Legislation that prohibits, under Title VII, discrimination in terms and conditions of employment (including benefits) that is based on race, color, religion, sex, or national origin.

Civil Rights Act of 1991   Legislation that clarifies the standards for proving discrimination. Allows jury trials and damage awards.

claims processing   Procedure that begins when an employee asserts that a specific event (e.g., disablement, hospitalization, unemployment) has occurred and demands that the employer fulfill a promise for payment. As such, a claims processor must first determine whether the act has, in fact, occurred.

classification   Job evaluation method that involves slotting job descriptions into a series of classes or grades that cover the range of jobs and that serve as a standard against which the job descriptions are compared.

clone error   A rating error that occurs when a rater gives better ratings to individuals who are like the rater in behavior or personality.

coinsurance   Benefit option whereby employees share in the cost of a benefit provided to them.

commission   Payment tied directly to achievement of performance standards. Commissions are directly tied to a profit index (sales, production level) and employee costs; thus, they rise and fall in line with revenues.

compa-ratio   An index that helps assess how managers actually pay employees in relation to the midpoint of the pay range established for jobs. It estimates how well actual practices correspond to intended policy. Calculated as average rates actually paid /range midpoint.

comparable worth   A doctrine that maintains that women performing jobs judged to be equal on some measure of inherent worth should be paid the same as men, excepting allowable differences, such as seniority, merit, production-based pay plans, and other non-sex-related factors. Objective is to eliminate use of the market in setting wages for jobs held by women.

compensable factor   Job attributes that provide the basis for evaluating the relative worth of jobs inside an organization. A compensable factor must be work-related, business-related, and acceptable to the parties involved.

compensating differentials   Economic theory that attributes the variety of pay rates in the external labor market to differences in attractive as well as negative characteristics in jobs. Pay differences must overcome negative characteristics to attract employees.

compensation   All forms of financial returns and tangible services and benefits employees receive as part of an employment relationship.

compensation differentials   Differentials in pay among jobs across and within organizations, and differences among individuals in the same job in an organization.

compensation objectives   The desired results of the pay system. The basic pay objectives include efficiency, fairness, and compliance with laws and regulations. Objectives shape the design of the pay system and serve as the standard against which the success of the pay system is evaluated.

compensation at risk   *See* risk sharing.

compensation system controls   Basic processes that serve to control pay decision making. They include (1) controls inherent in the design of the pay techniques (e.g., increase guidelines, range maximums and minimums) and (2) budgetary controls.

competency   Basic knowledge and abilities employees must acquire or demonstrate in a competency-based plan in order to successfully perform the work, satisfy customers, and achieve business objectives.

competency analysis   A systematic process to identify and collect information about the competencies required for the person and the organization to be successful.

competency based   Compensation approach that links pay to the depth and scope of competencies that are relevant to doing the work. Typically used in managerial and professional work where what is accomplished may be difficult to identify.

competitive objective   The midpoint for each pay range. The pay-policy line that connects the various midpoints becomes a control device: Compensation must be managed to conform to these midpoints if the organization is to maintain the pay policy it has specified.

competitive position   The comparison of the compensation offered by one employer relative to that paid by its competitors.

compression   The existence of very narrow pay differentials among jobs at different organization levels as a result of wages for jobs filled from the outside (frequently these are entry-level jobs) increasing faster than the internal pay structure.

congruency   The degree of consistency or "fit" between the compensation system and other organizational components such as strategy, product-market stage, culture and values, employee needs, and union status.

Consolidated Omnibus Budget Reconciliation Act (COBRA)   Legislation that provides that employees who resign or are laid off through no fault of their own are eligible to continue receiving health coverage under the employer's plan at a cost borne by the employee.

consumer price index (CPI)   A measure of the *changes* in prices of a fixed market basket of goods and services purchased by a hypothetical average family. *Not* an absolute measure of living costs; rather, a measure of how fast costs are changing. Published by the Bureau of Labor Statistics, US Department of Labor.

content theories   Motivation theories that focus on what motivates people rather than on how people are motivated. Maslow's need hierarchy theory and Herzberg's two-factor theory are in this category.

contingency work force   A growing work force that includes flexible workers, temporaries, part-time employees, and independent contractors.

contingent employees   Workers whose employment is of a limited duration (part-time or temporary).

contributory benefit financing plans   Plans in which costs are shared between employer and employee.

contributory financing   Benefit option in which an employee benefit is partially paid for by the employee.

conventional job analysis methods   Methods (e.g., functional job analysis) that typically involve an analyst using a questionnaire in conjunction with structured interviews of job incumbents and supervisors. The methods place considerable reliance on analysts' ability to understand the work performed and to accurately describe it.

coordination of benefits   Process of ensuring that employer coverage of an employee does not "double pay" because of identical protection offered by the government (private pension and social security coordination) or a spouse's employer.

core employees   Workers with whom a long-term, full-time work relationship is anticipated.

cost containment   An attempt made by organizations to contain benefit costs, such as imposing deductibles and coinsurance on health benefits or replacing defined benefit pension plans with defined contribution plans.

cost of living   Actual individual expenditures on goods and services. The only way to measure it accurately is to examine the expense budget of each employee.

cost-of-living adjustments (COLAs)   Across-the-board wage and salary increases or supplemental payments based on changes in some index of prices, usually the consumer price index (CPI). If included in a union contract, COLAs are designed to increase wages automatically during the life of the contract as a function of changes in the CPI.

cost-of-living increase   See cost-of-living adjustments.

cost savings plans   Group incentive plans that focus on cost savings rather than on profit increases as the standard of group incentive (e.g., Scanlon, Rucker, Improshare).

CPI   *See* consumer price index.

culture   The informal rules, rituals, and value systems that influence how people behave.

Davis-Bacon Act of 1931   Legislation that requires that most federal contractors pay wage rates prevailing in the area.

deductibles   Employer cost-saving tool by which the employee pays the first *x* number of dollars when a benefit is used (e.g., hospitalization). The employer pays subsequent costs up to some predetermined maximum.

deferred compensation program   Pay approach that provides income to an employee at some future time as compensation for work performed now. Types of deferred compensation programs include stock option plans and pension plans.

defined benefits plan   A benefit option or package in which the employer agrees to give the specified benefit without regard to cost maximum. Opposite of defined contribution plan.

defined contribution plan   A benefit option or package in which the employer negotiates a dollar maximum payout. Any change in benefit costs over time reduces the amount of coverage unless new dollar limits are negotiated.

differentials   Pay differences among levels within the organization, such as the difference in pay between adjacent levels in a career path, between supervisors and subordinates, between union and nonunion employees, and between executives and regular employees.

differentiating Competencies   Factors that distinguish superior performance from average performance.

direct compensation   Pay received directly in the form of cash (e.g., wages, bonuses, incentives).

disparate (unequal) impact standard   Discrimination theory that outlaws the application of pay practices that may appear to be neutral but have a negative effect on females or minorities unless those practices can be shown to be business-related.

disparate (unequal) treatment standard   Discrimination theory that outlaws the application of different standards to different classes of employees unless the standards can be shown to be business-related.

dispersion   Distribution of rates around a measure of central tendency.

distributive justice   Fairness in the amount of reward distributed to employees.

double-track system   A framework for professional employees in an organization whereby at least two general tracks of ascending compensation steps are available: (1) a managerial track to be ascended through increasing responsibility for supervision of people and (2) a professional track to be ascended through increasing contributions of a professional nature.

drive theory   A motivational theory that assumes that all behavior is induced by drives (i.e., energizers such as thirst, hunger, sex) and that present behavior is based in large part on the consequences or rewards of past behavior.

dual-career ladders   Presence of two different ways to progress in an organization, each reflecting different types of contribution to the organization's mission. The managerial ladder ascends through increasing responsibility for supervision or direction of people. The professional track ascends through increasing contributions of a professional nature that do not mainly entail the supervision of employees.

dual coverage   In families in which both spouses work, the coverage of specific claims from each spouse's employment benefit package. Employers cut costs by specifying payment limitations under such conditions.

earnings-at-risk plans   *See* risk sharing.

efficiency pay objective   Compansation goal that involves (1) improving productivity and (2) controlling labor costs.

efficiency wage theory   A theory that explains why firms are rational in offering higher-than-necessary wages.

employee benefits   The parts of the total compensation package, other than pay for time worked, provided to employees in whole or in part by employer payments (e.g., life insurance, pension, workers' compensation, vacation).

employee contributions   Comparisons among individuals doing the same job for the same organization.

employee-pay-all financing   Benefit option in which an employee benefit is fully paid for by the employee.

Employee Retirement Income Security Act (ERISA) of 1974   An act regulating private employer pension and welfare programs. The act has provisions that cover eligibility for participation, reporting, and disclosure requirements; establish fiduciary standards for the financial management of retirement funds; set up tax incentives for funding pension plans; and establish the Pension Benefit Guaranty Corporation to insure pension plans against financial failures.

employee services and benefits   Programs that include a wide array of alternative pay forms ranging from payments for time not worked (vacations, jury duty) through services (drug counseling, financial planning, cafeteria support) to protection (medical care, life insurance, and pensions).

employer of choice   The view that a firm's external wage competitiveness is just one facet of its overall human resource policy and that competitiveness is more properly judged on overall policies. Challenging work, high-calibre colleagues, or an organization's prestige must be factored into an overall consideration of attractiveness.

entitlement   Employee belief that returns and/or rewards are due regardless of individual or company performance.

entry jobs   Jobs that are filled from the external labor market and whose pay tends to reflect external economic factors rather than an organization's culture and traditions.

Equal Employment Opportunity Commission (EEOC)   A commission of the federal government charged with enforcing the provisions of the Civil Rights Act of 1964 and the Equal Pay Act of 1963 as it pertains to sex discrimination in pay.

Equal Pay Act (EPA) of 1963   An amendment to the Fair Labor Standards Act of 1938 that prohibits pay differentials on jobs that are substantially equal in terms of skills, efforts, responsibility, and working conditions, except when they are the result of bona fide seniority, merit, production-based systems, or any other job-related factor other than sex.

equalization component   As a part of an expatriate compensation package, a form of equity designed to "keep the worker whole" (i.e., maintain real income or purchasing power of base pay). This equalization typically comes in the form of tax equalization, housing allowances, and other allowances and premiums.

equity theory   A theory proposing that in an exchange relationship (such as employment) the equality of outcome/input ratios between a person and a comparison other (a standard or relevant person/group) will determine fairness or equity. If the ratios diverge from each other, the person will experience reactions of unfairness and inequity.

ESOP (employee stock ownership plan)   A plan in which a company borrows money from a financial institution by using its stock as a collateral for the loan. Principal and interest loan repayments are tax-deductible. With each loan repayment, the lending institution releases a certain amount of stock being held as security. The stock is then placed into an employee stock ownership trust (ESOT) for distribution at no cost to all employees. The employees receive the stock upon retirement or separation from the company. TRASOPs and PAYSOPs are variants of ESOPs.

essay   An open-ended performance appraisal format. The descriptors used can range from comparisons with other employees to adjectives, behaviors, and goal accomplishment.

essential elements   The parts of a job that cannot be assigned to another employee. The Americans with Disabilities Act requires that if applicants with disabilities can perform the essential elements of a job, reasonable accommodations must then be made to enable the qualified individuals to perform the job.

exchange value   The price of labor (the wage) determined in a competitive market; in other words, labor's worth (the price) is whatever the buyer and seller agree upon.

executive perquisites (perks)   Special benefits made available to top executives (and sometimes other managerial employees). May be taxable income to the receiver. Company-related perks may include luxury offices, special parking, and company-paid membership in clubs/associations, hotels, resorts. Personal perks include low-cost loans, personal and legal counseling, free home repairs and improvements, and so on. Since 1978, various tax and agency rulings have slowly been requiring that companies place a value on perks, thus increasing the taxable income of executives.

exempt jobs   Jobs not subject to provisions of the Fair Labor Standards Act with respect to minimum wage and overtime. Exempt employees include most executives, administrators, professionals, and outside sales representatives.

exercise period   Time during which, or after which, an individual who has been granted stock options is permitted to exercise them.

expatriate colony   A section of a large city where expatriates tend to locate and form a community that takes on some of the cultural flavor of their home country. An example is the Roppongi section of Tokyo, where many Americans live while working in Japan.

expatriates   Employees assigned outside their base country for any period of time in excess of one year.

expectancies   Beliefs (or subjective probability climates) individuals have that particular actions on their part will lead to certain outcomes or goals.

expectancy (VIE) theory   A motivation theory that proposes that individuals will select an alternative based on how this choice relates to outcomes such as rewards. The choice made is based on the strength or value of the outcome and on the perceived probability that this choice will lead to the desired outcome.

experience rating   Rating system in which insurance premiums vary directly with the number of claims filed. An experience rating is applied to unemployment insurance and workers' compensation and may be applied to commercial health insurance premiums.

external competitiveness   The pay relationships among organizations; focuses attention on the competitive positions reflected in these relationships.

extrinsic rewards   Rewards that a person receives from sources other than the job itself. They include compensation, supervision, promotions, vacations, friendships, and all other important outcomes apart from the job itself.

face validity   The determination of the relevance of a measuring device on the basis of "appearance" only.

factor scales   Measures that reflect different degrees within each compensable factor. Most commonly five to seven degrees are defined. Each degree may be anchored by typical skills, tasks and behaviors, or key job titles.

factor weights   Measures that indicate the importance of each compensable factor in a job evaluation system. Weights can be derived through either a committee judgment or a statistical analysis.

Fair Labor Standards Act of 1938 (FLSA)   A federal law governing minimum wage, overtime pay, equal pay for men and women in the same types of jobs, child labor, and record-keeping requirements.

Family and Medical Leave Act of 1993   Legislation that entitles eligible employees to receive unpaid leave up to 12 weeks per year for specified family or medical reasons, such as caring for ill family members or adopting a child.

fat grades   The wide ranges of flexibility permitted in broad-band pay structures in defining job responsibilities. Fat grades support redesigned, downsized, or seamless organizations that have eliminated layers of managerial jobs. Employees may move laterally across a band in order to gain depth of experience.

Federal Insurance Contribution Act (FICA)   The source of social security contribution withholding requirements. The FICA deduction is paid by both employer and employee.

first-impression error   Rating error in which the rater develops a negative (positive) opinion of an employee early in the review period and allows it to negatively (positively) color all subsequent perceptions of performance.

flat rate   A single rate, rather than a range of rates, for all individuals performing a certain job. Ignores seniority and performance differences.

flexible benefit plan   Benefit package in which employees are given a core of critical benefits (necessary for minimum security) and permitted to expend the remainder of their benefit allotment on options that they find most attractive.

flexible benefits *See* cafeteria (flexible) benefit plan.

flexible compensation The allocation of employee compensation in a variety of forms tailored to organization pay objectives and/or the needs of individual employees.

forms of compensation The various types of pay, which may be received directly in the form of cash (e.g., wages, bonuses, incentives) or indirectly through series and benefits (e.g., pensions, health insurance, vacations). This definition excludes other forms of rewards or returns that employees may receive, such as promotion, recognition for outstanding work behavior, and the like.

forms of pay *See* forms of compensation.

functional job analysis (FJA) A conventional approach to job analysis that is followed by the U.S. Department of Labor. Five categories of data are collected: what the worker does; the methodologies and techniques employed; the machines, tools, and equipment used; the products and services that result; and the traits required of the worker.

gain-sharing (group incentive) plans Incentive plans that are based on some measure of group performance rather than individual performance. Taking data on a past year as a base, group incentive plans may focus on cost savings (e.g., the Scanlon, Rucker, and Improshare plans) or on profit increases (profit-sharing plans) as the standard for distributing a portion of the accrued funds among relevant employees.

Gantt plan Individual incentive plan that provides for variable incentives as a function of a standard expressed as time period per unit of production. Under this plan, a standard time for a task is purposely set at a level requiring high effort to complete.

general schedule (GS) A job evaluation plan used by the U.S. Office of Personnel Management for white-collar employees. It has 18 "grades" (classes). Most jobs are in 15 grades; the top 3 are combined into a "supergrade" that covers senior executives.

generic job analysis Generalized, less detailed data collection at a level used to write a broad job description that covers a large number of related tasks. The result is that two people doing the same broadly defined job could be doing entirely different, yet related, tasks.

geographic differentials *See* locality pay.

glass ceiling A subtle barrier that keeps women and minorities out of the very highest executive positions.

global approach Substitution of a particular skill and experience level for job descriptions in determining external market rates. Includes rates for all individuals who possess that skill.

group incentive plans *See* gain-sharing (group incentive) plans.

halo error Rating error in which an appraiser gives favorable ratings to all job duties based on impressive performance in just one job function. For example, a rater who hates tardiness rates a prompt subordinate high across all performance dimensions exclusively because of this one characteristic.

Halsey 50-50 method Individual incentive method that provides for variable incentives as a function of a standard expressed as time period per unit of production. This plan derives its name from the shared split between worker and employer of any savings in direct costs.

Hay system A point factor system that evaluates jobs with respect to know-how, problem solving, and accountability. It is used primarily for exempt (managerial/professional) jobs.

Health Maintenance Act Legislation that requires that employers offer alternative health coverage options (e.g., health maintenance organizations) to employees.

health maintenance organization (HMO) A nontraditional health care delivery system. HMOs offer comprehensive benefits and outpatient services, as well as hospital coverage, for a fixed monthly prepaid fee.

hierarchies (job structures) Jobs ordered according to their relative content and/or value.

high-commitment practices Factors such as high base pay, sharing successes only (not risks), guaranteed employment security, promotions from within, training and skill development, employee ownership, and long-term perspective. High-commitment practices are believed to attract and retain a high-committed work force that will become the source of competitive advantage.

hit rate The ability of a job evaluation plan to replicate a predetermined, agreed-upon job structure.

horn error The opposite of halo error; downgrading an employee across all performance dimensions exclusively because of poor performance on one dimension.

human capital theory An economic theory proposing that the investment one is willing to make to enter an occupation is related to the returns one expects to earn over time in the form of compensation.

hybrid policy   Pay plan that includes base pay set at or below competitive market rates *plus* performance-based bonuses that vary with the unit's profitability.

implicit employment contract   An unwritten understanding between employers and employees about their reciprocal obligations and returns; employees contribute to achieving the goals of the employer in exchange for returns given by the employer and valued by the employee.

implicit social contract   People's beliefs and expectations of the inputs they are expected to make to society and the outputs they are expected to get in return.

Improshare (IMproved PROductivity through SHARing)   A gain-sharing plan in which a standard is developed to identify the expected hours required to produce an acceptable level of output. Any savings arising from production of agreed-upon output in fewer-than-expected hours are shared by the firm and the worker.

incentive   Inducement offered in advance to influence future performance (e.g., sales commissions).

incentive stock options (ISO)   A form of deferred compensation designed to influence long-term performance. Gives an executive the right to pay today's market price for a block of shares in the company at a future time. No tax is due until the shares are sold.

increase guidelines   Inherent compensation system controls. They specify the amount and timing of pay increases on an organizationwide basis.

indirect compensation   Pay received in the form of services and benefits (e.g., pensions, health insurance, vacations).

individual-based systems   Systems that focus on employee rather than job characteristics. Pay is based on the highest work-related skills or competencies employees possess rather than on the specific job performed.

individual incentive plans   Incentive compensation that is tied directly to objective measures of individual production (e.g., sales commissions).

individual retirement accounts (IRAs)   Tax-favored retirement savings plans that individuals can establish themselves.

institutional theory   Theory that organizations base their practices to a large extent on what other organizations are doing.

instrumentality   The perceived contingency that an outcome (performing well) has another outcome (a reward such as pay).

integrated manufacturing strategies   Organization strategies designed to gain competitive advantage, such as just-in-time manufacturing, statistical quality control, and advanced technologies.

internal alignment   The pay relationships among jobs or skill levels within a single organization; focuses attention on employee and management acceptance of those relationships. It involves establishing equal pay for jobs of equal worth and acceptable pay differentials for jobs of unequal worth.

internal labor markets   The rules or procedures that regulate the allocation of employees among different jobs within a single organization.

internal pricing   Pricing jobs in relationship to what other jobs within the organization are paid.

interrater reliability   The extent of agreement among raters rating the same individual, group, or phenomena.

inventories   Questionnaires in which tasks, behaviors, and abilities listed. The core of all quantitative job analysis.

job analysis   The systematic process of collecting information related to the nature of a specific job. It provides the knowledge needed to define jobs and conduct job evaluation.

job-based systems   Systems that focus on jobs as the basic unit of analysis to determine the pay structure; hence, job analysis is required.

job class (grade)   A grouping of jobs that are considered substantially similar for pay purposes.

job cluster   A series of jobs grouped for job evaluation and wage and salary administration purposes on the basis of common skills, occupational qualifications, technology, licensing, working conditions, union jurisdiction, workplace, career paths, and organizational tradition.

job competition theory   Economic theory that postulates a "quoted" wage for a job irrespective of an individual's qualifications. Since the most qualified applicants will be hired first, later hires will be more costly because they will require more training or will be less productive.

job content   Information that describes a job. May include responsibility assumed and/or the tasks performed.

job description   A summary of the most important features of a job. It identifies the job and describes the general nature of the work, specific task responsibilities, outcomes, and the employee characteristics required to perform the job.

job evaluation   A systematic procedure designed to aid in establishing pay differentials among jobs within a single company. It includes classification, comparison of the relative worth of jobs, blending internal and external market forces, measurement, negotiation, and judgment.

job evaluation committee   Group that may be charged with the responsibility of (1) selecting a job evaluation system, (2) carrying out or at least supervising the process of job evaluation, and (3) evaluating the success with which the job evaluation has been conducted. Its role may vary among organizations, but its members usually represent all important constituencies within the organization.

job evaluation manual   Handbook that contains information on the job evaluation plan and is used as a "yardstick" in evaluating jobs. It includes a description of the job evaluation method used, descriptions of all jobs, and, if relevant, a description of compensable factors, numerical degree scales, and weights; may also contain a description of the available review or appeals procedure.

job family   A group of jobs involving work of the same nature but requiring different skill and responsibility levels (e.g., computing and account recording are a job family; bookkeeper, accounting clerk, and teller are jobs within that family).

job grade   *See* pay grade.

job hierarchy   A grouping of jobs based on their job-related similarities and differences and on their value to the organization's objectives.

job pricing   The process of assigning pay to jobs, based on thorough job analysis and job evaluation.

job structure   Relationship among jobs inside an organization, based on work content and each job's relative contribution to achieving the organization's objectives.

just wage doctrine   A theory of job value that posits a "just" or equitable wage for any occupation based on that occupation's place in the larger social hierarchy. According to this doctrine, pay structures should be designed on the basis of societal norms, customs, and tradition, not on the basis of economic and market forces.

key jobs   *See* benchmark (key) job.

knowledge analysis   The systematic collection of information about the knowledge or skills required to perform work in an organization.

knowledge blocks   The different types of knowledge or competencies required to perform work.

knowledge systems   Systems in which pay is linked to additional knowledge related to the same job (depth), e.g., scientists and teachers, or to a number of different jobs (breadth), e.g., technicians.

labor demand   The employment level organizations require. An increase in wage rates will reduce the demand for labor, other factors constant. Thus, the labor demand curve (the relationship between employment levels and wage rates) is downward-sloping.

labor supply   The different numbers of employees available at different pay rates.

lag pay-level policy   A wage structure that is set to match market rates at the beginning of the plan year only. The rest of the plan year, internal rates will lag behind market rates. Its objective is to offset labor costs, but it may hinder a firm's ability to attract and retain quality employees.

lead pay-level policy   A wage structure that is set to lead the market throughout the plan year. Its aim is to maximize a firm's ability to attract and retain quality employees and to minimize employee dissatisfaction with pay.

least squares line   In regression analysis, the line fitted to a scatter plot of coordinates that minimizes the squared deviations of coordinates around the line. This line is known as the *best-fit line.*

legally required benefits   Benefits that are required by statutory law: workers' compensation, social security, and unemployment compensation are required in the United States. Required benefits vary among countries. Companies operating in foreign countries must comply with host-country compensation and benefit mandates.

leniency error   Rating error in which the rater consistently rating someone higher than is deserved.

level of aggregation   The size of the work unit for which performance is measured (e.g., individual work group, department, plan, or organization) and to which rewards are distributed.

level rise   The percentage increase in the average wage rate paid. Calculated as:

$$100 \times \frac{\text{Average pay year end} - \text{average pay-year beginning}}{\text{Average pay at beginning of year}}$$

leveling   Weighting market survey data according to the closeness of the job matches.

lifetime employment   Most prevalent in Japanese companies, the notion of employees' staying with the same company for their entire career, despite possible poor performance on the part of either an employee or the company.

line of sight   An employee's ability to see how individual performance affects incentive payout. Employees on a straight piecework pay system have a clear line of sight—their pay is a direct function of the number of units they produce; employees covered by profit sharing have a fuzzier line of sight—their payouts are a function of many forces, only one of which is individual performance.

linear regression   A statistical technique that allows an analyst to build a model of a relationship between variables that are assumed to be linearly related.

living wage   Pay legislation in some U.S. cities that requires wages well above the federal minimum wage. Often applies only to city government employees.

local-country nationals (LCNs)   Citizens of a country in which a U.S. foreign subsidiary is located. LCNs' compensation is tied either to local wage rates or to the rates of U.S. expatriates performing the same job.

locality pay   Adjusted pay rates for employees in a specific geographic area that account for local conditions such as labor shortages, and housing cost differentials.

long-term disability (LTD) plan   An insurance plan that provides payments to replace income lost through an inability to work that is not covered by other legally required disability income plans.

long-term incentives   Inducements offered in advance to influence longer-rate (multiyear) results. Usually offered to top managers and professionals to get them to focus on long-term organization objectives.

low-high approach   Use of the lowest- and highest-paid benchmark job in the external market to anchor an entire skill-based structure.

lump-sum award   Payment of entire increase (typically merit-based) at one time. Because amount is not factored into base pay, any benefits tied to base pay do not increase.

lump-sum bonus   *See* lump-sum award.

managed care   Steps taken to contain health care and workers' compensation costs, such as switching to preferred provider organizations for health care delivery, utilization-review procedures, and medical bill audits.

management by objectives (MBO)   An employee planning, development, and appraisal procedure in which a supervisor and a subordinate, or group of subordinates, jointly identify and establish common performance goals. Employee performance on the absolute standards is evaluated at the end of the specified period.

managing compensation   The fourth dimension in the pay model: ensuring the right people get the right pay for achieving the right objectives in the right way.

marginal product of labor   The additional output associated with the employment of one additional human resource unit, with other factors held constant.

marginal productivity theory (MPT)   In contrast to Marxist "surplus value" theory, a theory that focuses on labor demand rather than supply and argues that employers will pay a wage to a unit of labor that equals that unit's use (not exchange) value. That is, work is compensated in proportion to its contribution to the organization's production objectives.

marginal revenue of labor   The additional revenue generated when the firm employs one additional unit of human resources, with other factors held constant.

market pay lines   Means of summarizing the distribution of market rates for the benchmark jobs under consideration. Several methods to construct the lines can be used: a single line connecting the distributions' midpoints (means or medians) or lines depicting the 25th, 50th, and 75th percentiles. Often the lines are fitted to the data through a statistical procedure, such as regression analysis.

market pricing   Setting pay structures almost exclusively through matching pay for a very large percentage of jobs with the rates paid in the external market.

maturity curve   A plot of the empirical relationship between current pay and years since a professional has last received a degree (YSLD), thus allowing organizations to determine a competitive wage level for specific professional employees with varying levels of experience.

merit pay   A reward that recognizes outstanding past performance. It can be given in the form of lump-sum payments or as increments to the base pay. Merit programs are commonly designed to pay different amounts (often at different times) depending on the level of performance.

merit pay increase guidelines Specifications that tie pay increases to performance. They may take one of two forms: The simplest version specifies pay increases permissible for different levels of performance. More complex guidelines tie pay not only to performance but also to position in the pay range.

Merrick plan Individual incentive plan that provides for variable incentives as a function of units of production per time period. It works like the Taylor plan, but three piecework rates are set: (1) high—for production exceeding 100 percent of standard; (2) medium—for production between 83 and 100 percent of standard; and (3) low—for production less than 83 percent of standard.

middle and top management Employees above the supervisory level who have technical and administrative training and whose major duties entail the direction of people and the organization. They can be classified as special groups to the extent the organization devises special compensation programs to attract and retain these relatively scarce human resources. By this definition, not all managers above the supervisory level qualify for consideration as a special group.

minimum wage A minimum-wage level for most Americans established by Congress as part of the FLSA of 1938.

motivation An individual's willingness to engage in some behavior. Primarily concerned with (1) what energizes human behavior, (2) what directs or channels such behavior, and (3) how this behavior is maintained or sustained.

multiskill systems Systems that link pay to the number of different jobs (breadth) an employee is certified to do, regardless of the specific job he or she is doing.

mutual commitment compensation A pay strategy that combines high wages with an emphasis on quality, innovation, and customer service. Based on the belief that high wages are essential to reinforce cooperation and participation and will provide a better living standard for all employees.

National Electrical Manufacturing Association (NEMA) system A point factor job evaluation system that evolved into the National Position Evaluation Plan sponsored by NMTA associates.

National Metal Trades Association (NMTA) plan A point factor job evaluation plan for production, maintenance, and service personnel.

need theories Motivation theories that focus on internally generated needs that induce behaviors designed to reduce these needs.

noncontributory financing Benefit option in which an employee benefit is fully paid for by the employer.

nonexempt employees Employees who are subject to the provisions of the Fair Labor Standards Act.

nonqualified deferred compensation plans A plan does not qualify for tax exemption if an employer who pays high levels of deferred compensation to executives does not make proportionate contributions to lower-level employees.

nonqualified stock options Form of compensation that gives an executive the right to purchase stock at a stipulated price; the excess over fair market value is taxed as ordinary income.

objective performance-based pay systems Pay approach that focuses on objective performance standards (e.g., counting output) derived from organizational objectives and a thorough analysis of the job (e.g., incentive and gain-sharing plans).

occupational diseases Diseases that arise out of the course of employment, not including "ordinary diseases of life," for which workers' compensation claims can be filed.

occupational safety and health act (OSHA) of 1970 Legislation designed to improve working conditions in industry, thereby reducing worker accidents and job-related illnesses.

on-call employees Employees who must respond to work-related assignments/problems 24 hours a day. Firefighters, SPCA humane officers, and other emergency personnel are traditional examples. Increasingly, this group includes technical workers such as software service personnel.

organizational culture The composite of shared values, symbols, and cognitive schemes that ties people together in the organization.

organizational values Shared norms and beliefs regarding what is socially, organizationally, and individually right, worthy, or desirable. The composite of values contributes to form a common organizational culture.

outlier An extreme value that may distort some measures of central tendency.

outsourcing The practice of hiring outside vendors to perform functions that do not directly contribute to business objectives and in which the organization does not have a comparative advantage.

paired comparison A ranking job evaluation method that involves comparing all possible pairs of jobs under study.

pay bands   Pay approach in which separate job classifications are combined into a smaller number of divisions, called *bands*. Created to increase flexibility.

pay discrimination   Descrimination usually defined as including (1) access discrimination, which occurs when qualified women and minorities are denied access to particular jobs, promotions, or training opportunities, and (2) valuation discrimination, which takes place when minorities or women are paid less than white males for performing substantially equal work. Both types of discrimination are illegal under Title VII of the Civil Rights Act of 1964. Some argue that valuation discrimination can also occur when men and women hold entirely different jobs (in content or results) that are of comparable worth to the employer. Existing federal laws do not support the "equal pay for work of comparable worth" standard.

pay equity   *See* comparable worth.

pay-for-knowledge system   A compensation practice whereby employees are paid for the number of different jobs they can adequately perform or the amount of knowledge they possess.

pay-for-performance plans   Pay that varies with some measure of individual or organizational performance, such as merit pay, lump-sum bonus plans, skill-based pay, incentive plans, variable pay plans, risk sharing, and success sharing.

pay grade   One of the classes, levels, or groups into which jobs of the same or similar values are grouped for compensation purposes. All jobs in a pay grade have the same pay range—maximum, minimum, and midpoint.

pay increase guidelines   The mechanisms through which performance levels are translated into pay increases and, therefore, dictate the size and time of the pay reward for good performance.

pay level   An average of the array of rates paid by an employer.

pay-level policies   Decisions concerning a firm's level of pay vis-à-vis product and labor market competitors. There are three classes of pay-level policies: to lead, to match, or to follow competition.

pay mix   Relative emphasis among compensation components such as base pay, merit, incentives, and benefits.

pay objectives   *See* compensation objectives.

pay plan design   A process to identify the pay levels, components, and timing that best match individual needs and organizational requirements.

pay-policy line   Representation of the organization's pay-level policy relative to what competitors pay for similar jobs.

pay ranges   The range of pay rates from minimum to maximum set for a pay grade or class. It puts limits on the rates an employer will pay for a particular job.

pay satisfaction   A function of the discrepancy between employees' perceptions of how much pay they should receive and how much pay they do receive. If these perceptions are equal, an employee is said to experience pay satisfaction.

pay structures   The array of pay rates for different jobs within a single organization; they focus attention on differential compensation paid for work of unequal worth.

pay techniques   Mechanisms or technologies of compensation management, such as job analysis, job descriptions, market surveys, job evaluation, and the like, that tie the four basic pay policies to the pay objectives.

pay-with-competition policy   Policy that tries to ensure that a firm's labor costs are approximately equal to those of its competitors. It seeks to avoid placing an employer at a disadvantage in pricing products or in maintaining a qualified work force.

PAYSOP (Payroll-Based Tax Credit Employee Stock Ownership Plan)   A form of TRASOP in which the tax credit allotted to plan sponsors who permit and match voluntary employee contributions is payroll-based, not investment-based.

pension benefit guaranty corporation (PBGC)   Agency to which employers are required to pay insurance premiums to protect individuals from bankrupt companies (and pension plans!), In turn, the PBGC guarantees payment of vested benefits to employees formerly covered by terminated pension plans.

pension plan   A form of deferred compensation. All pension plans usually have four common characteristics: They (1) involve deferred payments to a former employee (or surviving spouse) for past services rendered; (2) specify a normal retirement age, at which time benefits begin to accrue to the employee; (3) specify a formula for calculating benefits, and (4) provide for integration with social security benefits.

percentage pay range overlap   *See* range overlap.

performance-based pay   *See* pay-for-performance plans.

performance dimension training   Training that gives performance appraisers an understanding of the dimensions on which to evaluate employee performance.

performance evaluation (performance appraisal)   A process to determine correspondence between worker behavior/task outcomes and employer expectations (performance standards).

performance ranking   The simplest, fastest, easiest-to-understand, and least expensive performance appraisal technique. Orders employees from highest to lowest in performance.

performance share/unit plans   Cash or stock awards earned through achieving specific goals.

performance standard   An explicit statement of what work output is expected from employees in exchange for compensation.

performance standard training   Training that gives performance appraisers a frame of reference for making ratee appraisals.

perquisites (perks)   The extras bestowed on top management, such as private dining rooms, company cars, and first-class airfare.

personal care account (PCA)   A tool used by employers to gain some control over health care costs while still providing health security to workers. The employer establishes a high deductible paid by employees but cushions the blow by setting up a PCA to cover part of the deductible cost.

phantom stock plan   Stock plan in which an increase in stock price at a fixed future date determines the cash or stock award. It is called a phantom plan because the organization in question is not publicly traded. Stock price, therefore, is an illusion. The "phantom price" is derived from standard financial accounting procedures.

planned compa-ratio budgeting   A form of top-down budgeting in which a planned compa-ratio, rather than a planned level rise, is established to control pay costs.

planned level rise   The percentage increase in average pay that is planned to occur after considering such factors as anticipated rates of change in market data, changes in cost of living, the employer's ability to pay, and the efforts of turnover and promotions. This index may be used in top-down budgeting to control compensation costs.

planned level rise budgeting   A form of top-down budgeting under which a planned level rise, rather than a planned compa-ratio, is established as the target to control pay costs.

point (factor) method   A job evaluation method that employs (1) compensable factors, (2) factor degrees numerically scaled, and (3) weights reflecting the relative importance of each factor. Once scaled degrees and weights are established for each factor, each job is measured against each compensable factor and a total score is calculated for each job. The total points assigned to a job determine the job's relative value and hence its location in the pay structure.

policy line   A pay line that reflects the organization's policy with respect to the external labor market.

portability   Transferability of pension benefits for employees moving to a new organization. ERISA does not require mandatory portability of private pensions. On a voluntary basis, the employer may agree to let an employee's pension benefit transfer to an individual retirement account (IRA) or, in a reciprocating arrangement, to the new employer.

position analysis questionnaire (PAQ)   A structured job analysis technique that classifies job information into seven basic factors: information input, mental processes, work output, relationships with other persons, job context, other job characteristics, and general dimensions. The PAQ analyzes jobs in terms of worker-oriented data.

position description questionnaire (PDQ)   A quantitative job analysis technique.

preferred provider organization (PPO)   Health care delivery system in which there is a direct contractual relationship between and among employers, health care providers, and third-party payers. An employer is able to select providers (e.g., selected doctors) who agree to provide price discounts and submit to strict utilization controls.

Pregnancy Discrimination Act of 1978   An amendment to Title VII of the Civil Rights Act. It requires employers to extend to pregnant employees or spouses the same disability and medical benefits provided to other employees or spouses of employees.

prevailing-wage laws   Legislation that provides for a government-defined prevailing wage as the minimum wage that must be paid for work done on covered government projects or purchases. In practice, these prevailing rates have been union rates paid in various geographic areas.

procedural justice   Concept concerned with the process used to make and implement decisions about pay. It suggests that the way pay decisions are made and implemented may be as important to employees as the results of the decisions.

process theories Motivation theories that focus on how people are motivated rather than on what motivates people (e.g., drive, expectancy, and equity theories).

product market The market (or market segments) in which a firm competes to sell products or services.

professional employee An employee who has specialized training of a scientific or intellectual nature and whose major duties do not entail the supervision of people.

profit-sharing plan A plan that focuses on profitability as the standard for group incentive. These plans typically involve one of three distributions: (1) Cash or current distribution plans provide full payment to participants soon after profits have been determined (quarterly or annually); (2) deferred plans have a portion of current profits credited to employee accounts, with cash payments made at time of retirement, disability, severance, or death; and (3) combination plans incorporate aspects of both current and deferred options.

progression through the pay ranges Any of three strategies to move employees through the pay ranges: (1) automatic or seniority-based progression, which is most appropriate when the necessary job skills are within the grasp of most employees; (2) merit progression, which is more appropriate when jobs allow variations in performance; and (3) a combination of automatic and merit progression (e.g., employers may grant automatic increases up to the midpoint of the range and permit subsequent increases only when merited on the basis of performance appraisal).

psychological contracts Perceptions and beliefs on the part of individuals regarding the terms and conditions of the employment relationship. Psychological contracts differ from implied contracts insofar as they describe individual perceptions of mutual obligation not necessarily observable and verifiable by others.

purchasing power The ability to buy goods and services in a certain currency, determined by exchange rates and availability of goods. Companies must determine purchasing power when allocating allowances to expatriates.

qualified deferred compensation plan A deferred compensation program that qualities for tax exemption. It must provide contributions or benefits for employees other than executives that are proportionate to contributions provided to executives.

quantitative job analysis (QJA) Job analysis method that relies on scaled questionnaires and inventories that produce job-related data that are documentable, can be statistically analyzed, and may be more objective than other analyses.

range maximums The maximum values to be paid for a job grade, representing the top value the organization places on the output of the work.

range midpoint The salary midway between the minimum and maximum rates of a salary range. The midpoint rate for each range is usually set to correspond to the pay-policy line and represents the rate paid for satisfactory performance on the job.

range minimums The minimum values to be paid for a job grade, representing the minimum value the organization places on the work. Often, rates below the minimum are used for trainees.

range overlap The degree of overlap between adjoining grade ranges is determined by the differences in midpoints among ranges and the range spread. A high degree of overlap and narrow midpoint differentials indicate small differences in the value of jobs in the adjoining grades and permit promotions without much change in the rates paid. By contrast, a small degree of overlap and wide midpoint differentials allow the manager to reinforce a promotion with a large salary increase.

ranges *See* pay range.

ranking A simple job evaluation method that involves ordering the job descriptions from highest to lowest in value.

ranking format A type of performance appraisal format that requires that the rater compare employees against each other to determine the relative ordering of the group on some performance measure.

rater error training Training that enables performance appraisers to identify and suppress psychometric errors such as leniency, severity, central tendency, and halo errors when evaluating employee performance.

rating errors Errors in judgment that occur in a systematic manner when an individual observes and evaluates a person, group, or phenomenon. The most frequently described rating errors include halo, leniency, severity, and central tendency errors.

rating format A type of performance appraisal format that requires that raters evaluate employees on absolute measurement scales that indicate varying levels of performance.

recency error The opposite of first-impression error. Performance (either good or bad) at the end of the review period plays too large a role in determining an employee's rating for the entire period.

red-circle rates   Pay rates that are above the maximum rate for a job or pay range for a grade.

reengineering   Making changes in the way work is designed to include external customer focus. Usually includes organizational delayering and job restructuring.

regression   A statistical technique for relating present-pay differentials to some criterion, that is, pay rates in the external market, rates for jobs held predominantly by men, or factor weights that duplicate present rates for all jobs in the organization.

reinforcement theories   Theories such as expectancy and operant conditioning theory that grant a prominent role to rewards (e.g., compensation) in motivating behavior. They argue that pay motivates behavior to the extent merit increases and other work-related rewards are allocated on the basis of performance.

relational returns   The nonquantifiable returns employees get from employment, such as social satisfaction, friendship, feeling of belonging, or accomplishment.

relative value of jobs   The relative contribution of jobs to organizational goals, to their external market rates, or to some other agreed-upon rates.

relevant markets   Those employers with which an organization competes for skills and products/services. Three factors commonly used to determine the relevant markets are the occupation or skills required, the geography (willingness to relocate and/or commute), and employers that compete in the product market.

reliability   The consistency of the results obtained, that is, the extent to which any measuring procedure yields the same results on repeated trials. Reliable job information does not mean that it is accurate (valid), comprehensive, or free from bias.

reopener clause   A provision in an employment contract that specifies that wages, and sometimes such nonwage items as pension/benefits, will be renegotiated under certain conditions (changes in cost of living, organization, profitability, and so on).

reservation wage   A theoretical minimum standard below which a job seeker will not accept an offer, no matter how attractive the other job attributes.

resource dependency   The theory that internal pay structures are based on the differential control that jobs exert over critical resources.

restricted stock plan   Plan that grants stock at a reduced price with the condition that it not be sold before a specified date.

Revenue Act of 1978   Legislation that set up simplified pension plans, added tax incentives for individual retirement accounts (IRAs), and adjusted requirements for ESOPs. The act also provided that cafeteria benefit plans need not be included in gross income and reaffirmed the legality of deferring compensation and taxes due on it for an employee.

Revenue Reconciliation Act of 1993   Legislation that limits employer deductions for executive compensation to $1 million and caps the amount of executive compensation used to compute contributions to and benefits from qualified retirement plans.

reward system   The composite of all organizational mechanisms and strategies used to formally acknowledge employee behaviors and performance. It includes all forms of compensation, promotions, and assignments; nonmonetary awards and recognitions; training opportunities; job design and analysis; organizational design and working conditions; the supervisor; social networks; performance standards and reward criteria; performance evaluation; and the like.

risk sharing   An incentive plan in which employees' base wages are set below a specified level (e.g., 80 percent of the market wage) and incentive earnings are used to raise wages above the base. In good years an employee's incentive pay will more than make up for the 20 percent shortfall, giving the employee a pay premium. Because employees assume some of the risk, risk-sharing plans pay more generously than success-sharing plans in good years.

Rowan plan   Individual incentive plan that provides for variable incentives as a function of a standard expressed as time period per unit of production. It is similar to the Halsey plan, but in this plan a worker's bonus increases as the time required to complete the task decreases.

Rucker plan   A group cost savings plan in which cost reductions due to employee efforts are shared with the employees. It involves a somewhat more complex formula than a Scanlon plan for determining employee incentive bonuses.

salary   Pay given to employees who are exempt from regulations of the Fair Labor Standards Act and hence do not receive overtime pay (e.g., managers and professionals). Exempt pay is calculated at an annual or monthly rate rather than hourly.

salary continuation plans   Benefit options that provide some form of protection for disability. Some are legally required, such as workers' compensation provisions for work-related disability and social security disability income provisions for those who qualify.

salary sales compensation plan A plan whereby, the sales force is paid a fixed income not dependent on sales volume.

sales compensation Any form of compensation paid to sales representatives. Sales compensation formulas usually attempt to establish direct incentives for sales outcomes.

scaling Determining the intervals on a measurement instrument.

Scanlon plan A group cost savings plan designed to lower labor costs without lowering the level of a firm's activity. Incentives are derived as the ratio between labor costs and sales value of production (SVOP).

self-insurance System in which an organization funds its own insurance claims, for either health or life insurance or workers' compensation.

seniority increases Pay increases tied to a progression pattern based on seniority. To the extent performance improves with time on the job, this method has the rudiments of paying for performance.

severity error The opposite of leniency error. Rating someone consistently lower than is deserved.

shared choice An external competitiveness policy that offers employees substantial choice among their pay forms.

shirking behavior The propensity of employees to allow the marginal revenue product of their labor to be less than its marginal cost; to be lax.

short-term disability *See* workers' compensation.

short-term incentives Inducements offered in advance to influence future short-range (annual) results. Usually very specific performance standards are established.

short-term income protection *See* unemployment insurance.

sick leave Paid time when an employee is not working due to illness or injury.

signaling The notion that an employer's pay policy communicates to both prospective and current employees what kinds of behaviors are sought. Applicants may signal their likely performance to potential employees through their personal credentials such as experience or educational degrees.

simplified employee pension (SEP) A retirement income arrangement intended to markedly reduce the paperwork for regular pension plans.

single-rate pay system A compensation policy under which all employees in a given job are paid at the same rate instead of being placed in a pay grade. Generally applies to situations in which there is little room for variation in job performance, such as an assembly line.

skill analysis A systematic process to identify and collect information about the skills required to perform work in an organization.

skill based Compensation approach that links pay to the depth and/or breadth of the skills, abilities, and knowledge a person acquires/demonstrates that are relevant to the work. Typically applies to operators, technicians, and office workers where the work is relatively specific and defined. The criterion chosen can influence employee behaviors by describing what is required to get higher pay.

skill-based/global approach to wage survey An approach that does not emphasize comparison of pay for specific jobs. Instead, it recognizes that employers usually tailor jobs to the organization or individual employee. Therefore, the rates paid to every individual employee in an entire skill group or function are included in the salary survey and become the reference point for designing pay levels and structures.

skill-based pay system *See* pay-for-knowledge system.

skill blocks Basic units of knowledge employees must master to perform the work, satisfy customers, and achieve business objectives.

skill requirement Composite of experience, training, and ability as measured by the performance requirements of a particular job.

slippage *See* turnover effect.

social information processing (SIP) theory Theory that counters need theory by focusing on external factors that motivate performance. According to SIP theorists, workers pay attention to environmental cues (e.g., inputs/outputs of co-workers) and process this information in a way that may alter personal work goals, expectations, and perceptions of equity. In turn, this influences job attitudes, behavior, and performance.

social security What has become the federal old-age, survivors, disability, and health insurance system established by the Social Security Act of 1935. The beneficiaries are workers who participate in the social security program, their spouses, dependent parents, and dependent children. Benefits vary according to (1) earnings of the worker, (2) length of time in the program, (3) age when benefits start, (4) age and number of recipients other than the worker, and (5) state of health of recipients other than the worker.

special groups Employee groups for whom compensation practices diverge from typical company procedures (e.g., supervisors, middle and upper management, nonsupervisory professionals, sales, and personnel in foreign subsidiaries).

spillover effect The fact that improvements obtained in unionized firms "spill over" to nonunion firms seeking ways to lessen workers' incentives for organizing a union.

spillover error Rating error in which the rater continues to downgrade an employee for performance errors in prior rating periods.

splintered supply A labor supply that comes from multiple markets. Some employees may come from different global locations, may receive different pay forms, and may have varied employment relationships.

spot award One-time award for exceptional performance; also called a *spot bonus.*

standard hour plan Individual incentive plan in which rate determination is based on time period per unit of production and wages vary directly as a constant function of product level. In this context, the incentive rate in standard hour plans is set based on completion of a task in some expected time period.

standard rating scales Appraisal system characterized by (1) one or more performance standards being developed and defined for the appraiser and (2) each performance standard having a measurement scale indicating varying levels of performance on that dimension. Appraisers rate the appraisee by checking the point on the scale that best represents the appraisee's performance level. Rating scales vary in the extent to which anchors along the scale are defined.

statistical approach to factor selection A method that uses a variety of statistical procedures to derive factors from data collected through quantitative job analysis from a sample of jobs that represent the range of the work employees (or an employee group) perform in the company. It is often labeled *policy capturing* to contrast it with the committee judgment approach.

stock appreciation rights (SARs) Rights that permit an executive to receive all the potential capital gain of a stock incentive option (ISO) without having to purchase the stock; thus, they reduce an executive's cash commitment. Payment is provided on demand for the difference between the stock option price and the current market price.

stock purchase plan (nonqualified) A plan that is, in effect, a management stock purchase plan. It allows senior management or other key personnel to buy stock in the business. This plan has certain restrictions: (1) The stockholder must be employed for a certain period of time, (2) the business has the right to buy back the stock, and (3) stockholders cannot sell the stock for a defined period.

stock purchase plan (qualified) A program under which employees buy shares in the company's stock, with the company contributing a specific amount for each unit of employee contribution. Also, stock may be offered at a fixed price (usually below market) and paid for in full by the employees.

straight piecework system Individual incentive plan in which rate determination is based on units of production per time period; wages vary directly as a constant function of production level.

straight ranking procedure A type of performance appraisal format in which requires the rater compares or ranks each employee relative to each other employee.

strategy The fundamental direction of the organization. It guides the deployment of all resources, including compensation.

strike price Price an individual is permitted to buy a stock at by the company granting the stock.

subjective performance-based pay systems Pay approach that focuses on subjective performance standards (e.g., achieving agreed-upon objectives) derived from organizational objectives and a thorough analysis of the job.

success sharing An incentive plan (e.g., profit sharing or gain sharing) in which an employee's base wage matches the market wage and variable pay adds on during successful years. Because base pay is not reduced in bad years, employees bear little risk.

supplemental unemployment benefits (SUB) plan Employer-funded plan that supplements state unemployment insurance payments to workers during temporary periods of layoffs. Largely concentrated in the automobile, steel, and related industries.

surplus value The difference between labor's use and exchange values. According to Marx, under capitalism wages are based on labor's exchange value—which is lower than its use value—and thus provide only a subsistence wage.

SVOP (sales value of production) Concept that include sales revenue and the value of goods in inventory.

tariff agreements In some European countries, the wage rates negotiated by employer associations and trade union federations for all wage earners for all companies in an industry group.

task oriented Job descriptions that describe individual jobs in detail based on a prescribed set of duties.

tax equalization allowance A method whereby an expatriate pays neither more nor less tax than the assumed home-country tax on base remuneration.

Taylor plan Individual incentive plan that provides for variable incentives as a function of units of production per time period. It provides two piecework rates that are established for production above and below standard, and these rates are higher and lower than the regular wage incentive level.

team incentive Group incentive restricted to team members with payout usually based on improvements in productivity, customer satisfaction, financial performance, or quality of goods and services directly attributable to the team.

third-country nationals (TCNs) Employees of a U.S. foreign subsidiary who maintain citizenship in a country other than the United States or the host country. TCNs' compensation is tied to comparative wages in the local country, the United States, or the country of citizenship.

thrift savings plans Plans designed to help American workers meet savings goals. The most common plan involves a 50 percent employer match on employee contributions up to a maximum of 6 percent of pay.

Title VII of the Civil Rights Act of 1964 A major piece of legislation prohibiting pay discrimination. It is much broader in intent than the Equal Pay Act, forbidding discrimination on the basis of race, color, religion, sex, pregnancy, or national origin.

top-down approach to pay budgeting Also known as *unit-level budgeting,* an approach in which a total pay budget for the organization (or unit) is determined and allocated "down" to individual employees during the plan year. There are many kinds to unit-level budgeting. They differ in the type of financial index used as a control measure. Controlling to a planned level rise and controlling to a planned compa-ratio are two typical approaches.

topping out Situation in which employees in a skill-based compensation plan attain the top pay rate in a job category by accumulating and/or becoming certified for the top-paid skill block(s).

total cash Base wage plus cash bonus; does not include benefits or stock options.

total compensation The complete pay package for employees, including all forms of money, bonuses, benefits, services, and stock.

total returns All returns to an employee, including financial compensation, benefits, opportunities for social interaction, security, status and recognition, work variety, appropriate workload, importance of work, authority/control/autonomy, advancement opportunities, feedback, hazard-free working conditions, and opportunities for personal and professional development. An effective compensation system will utilize many of these returns.

total rewards *See* total returns.

tournament theory The notion that larger differences in pay are more motivating than smaller differences. Like prize awards in a golf tournament, pay increases should get successively greater as one moves up the job hierarchy. Differences between the top job and the second-highest job should be the largest.

transactional returns Cash and benefit forms of compensation, as contrasted with relational returns, which emphasize the sociopsychological returns.

turnover effect The downward pressure on average wage that results from the replacement of high-wage-earning employees with workers earning a lower wage.

two-tier pay plans Wage structures that differentiate pay for the same jobs based on hiring date. A contract is negotiated that specifies that employees hired after a stated day will receive lower wages than their higher-seniority peers working on the same or similar jobs.

underwater stock option A stock option with a market price lower than the original offer price. Fairly common during a market downturn, these options are of no value to someone who has received them as an incentive.

unemployment benefits *See* unemployment insurance.

unemployment compensation *See* unemployment insurance.

unemployment insurance (UI)   State-administered program that provides financial security for workers during periods of joblessness.

unequal impact   *See* disparate (unequal) impact standard.

unequal treatment   *See* disparate (unequal) treatment standard.

U.S. expatriates (USEs)   American citizens working for a U.S. subsidiary in a foreign country. Main compensation concerns are to "keep the expatriates whole" relative to their U.S.-based counterparts and to provide expatriates with an incentive wage for accepting the foreign assignment.

universal job factors   Factors that could theoretically be used to evaluate all jobs in all organizations.

use value   The value or price ascribed to the use or consumption of labor in the production of goods or services.

valence   The amount of positive or negative value placed on specific outcomes by an individual.

validity   The accuracy of the results obtained; that is, the extent to which any measuring device measures what it purports to measure.

valuation discrimination   Discrimination that focuses on the pay women and minorities receive for the work they perform. Discrimination occurs when members of these groups are paid less than white males for performing substantially equal work. This definition of pay discrimination is based on the standard of "equal pay for equal work." Many believe that this definition is limited and that valuation discrimination can also occur when men and women hold entirely different jobs (in content or results) that are of comparable worth to the employer. Existing federal laws do not support the "equal pay for work of comparable worth" standard.

variable pay   Pay tied to productivity or some measure that can vary with the firm's profitability.

vesting   A benefit plan provision that guarantees that participants will, after meeting certain requirements, retain a right to the benefits they have accrued, or some portion of them, even if employment under their plan terminates before retirement.

VIE theory   *See* expectancy (VIE) theory.

wage   Pay given to employees who are covered by overtime and reporting provisions of the Fair Labor Standards Act. Nonexempts usually have their pay calculated at an hourly rate rather than a monthly or annual rate.

wage adjustment provisions   Clauses in a multilayer union contract that specify the types of wage adjustments that have to be implemented during the life of the contract. These adjustments might be specified in three major ways: (1) deferred wage increases—negotiated at the time of contract negotiation, with the time and amount specified in the contract, (2) cost-of-living adjustments (COLAs) or escalator clauses, and (3) reopener clauses.

wage and price controls   Government regulations that aim at maintaining low inflation and low levels of unemployment. They frequently focus on "cost-push" inflation, limiting the size of pay raises and the rate of increases in prices charged for goods and services. Used for limited time periods only.

wage survey   The systematic process of collecting information and making judgments about the compensation paid by other employers. Wage survey data are useful in designing pay levels and structures.

Walsh-Healey Public Contracts Act of 1936   A federal law requiring certain employers holding federal contracts for the manufacture or provision of materials, supplies, and equipment to pay industry prevailing-wage rates.

work or task data   Information on the elemental units of work (tasks), with emphasis on the purpose of each task, collected for job analysis. Work data describe the job in terms of actual tasks performed and their output.

worker or behavioral data   Information on the behaviors required by the job. Used in job analysis.

workers' compensation   An insurance program, paid for by the employer, designed to protect employees from expenses incurred for a work-related injury or disease. Each state has its own workers' compensation law.

YSLD   Years since a professional has last received a degree.

zones   Ranges of pay used as controls or guidelines within pay bands that can keep the system more structurally intact. Maximums, midpoints, and minimums provide guides to appropriate pay for certain levels of work. Without zones employees may float to the maximum pay, which for many jobs in the band is higher than market value.

Name Index

Subject Index

Accountability, 131
Across the board wage component, 269
ADA. *See* Americans with Disabilities Act (ADA)
Adam Opel AG, 517
Administrative ease, 339
Advanced Micro Devices, 470
AES, 15, 17
Affirmative defense, 547–549
AFL-CIO, 69
AFSCME v. State of Washington, 553
Age Discrimination in Employment Act, 413, 540
Agency theory, 264, 265, 465
Alignment. *See* Internal alignment
Allowances
    financial allowances in international pay systems, 525–526
    housing allowances, 526
    overview of, 10
Allstate Insurance Company, 549
Alternation ranking procedure, 122, 334, 335
American Airlines, 115
American Federation of Teachers, 43, 484
American Management Association, 597
American Postal Workers Union, 487
American Steel and Wire, 140
Americans with Disabilities Act (ADA), 96, 540
Appeals/review procedures, 138, 172
Applebee's, 274
Appraisals. *See* Performance appraisals
Apriso, 201, 203–204
Argentina, 511
Asia Society, 599
Association of Private Pension and Welfare Plans, 599
AT&T, 273
Australia, 3, 504, 511
Austria, 3, 507
Authority, 268
Automatic progression, 489
Baker Tool Coating, 150–151
Bank of Switzerland, 510
Bao Gang, 498
BARS's. *See* Behaviorally anchored rating scales (BARS's)
Base pay, 7–8, 269, 467–468

Behavior motivation, 63
Behaviorally anchored rating scales (BARS's), 335–336, 341
Belgium, 506
Ben and Jerry's Homemade, 76
Benchmark jobs, 120–121, 226–227
Benefits
    administration of, 406–409, 416–420
    allowances, 10
    benefits packages, 427–438
    categorization of, 429
    child care, 451
    claims processing and, 419
    communication about, 417–419
    components of, 409–416
    for contingent workers, 452
    cost issues, 402, 410–411, 445–447
    definition of, 400
    design issues, 404–405
    disabilities and, 430–431, 448
    domestic partner benefits, 452
    elder care, 451
    employee benefit questionnaire, 415
    employee needs and, 414–415
    employer preferences and, 410–414
    external competitiveness and, 411
    fairness and, 414
    flexible benefits programs, 407–408, 415
    government role in, 402
    health care, 444–447, 449
    income protection and, 9–10
    labor costs and, 402, 410–411, 445–447
    legal insurance, 452
    legislation and, 413, 428–437
    life insurance, 443–444
    motivation and, 411–412
    overview of, 399–401
    paid time off, 449–451
    perquisites, 469–471
    ranking of, 403
    recruitment and, 411–412
    required benefits, 428–437
    retirement and savings plan payments, 437–443
    tax reforms and, 413
    unions, 401
    value of, 402–404
    wage and price controls and, 401
    websites for, 598
    work/life focus and, 10
    workers' compensation, 429–432
BenefitsLink, 598
Best Buy, 49, 244
"Best fit," 50–54. *See also* Fit
"Best practices," 50–54
Bethlehem Steel, 570
Bias, 173–175. *See also* Discrimination
Biomet, 79

BLS. *See* Bureau of Labor Statistics (BLS)
BMS. *See* Bristol-Myers Squibb (BMS)
Boards of directors, 461, 461–462
Boeing, 29
Bonuses, 468, 474
Boston Scientific, 18
Boston Survey Group, 223
Bottom-up budgeting, 578–580
Bourse markets, 189
Brazil, 511
Bristol-Myers Squibb (BMS), 9, 27–31, 45–46
British Royal Navy, 335
Brito v. Zia Company, 353–354
Broad banding, 247–250
Broad listing for compensation, 597
Brookings Institute, 92
Budget administration
    bottom-up budgeting, 578–580
    centralization-decentralization and, 591–593
    compa-ratios and, 582–583
    compensation communication and, 586–591
    controls, 582–586, 593–594
    cost analysis, 583–586
    ethics and, 581
    labor cost management, 571–574
    overview of, 569–570
    range and maximums and, 582
    restructuring and, 591
    top-down budgeting, 574–578
    total pay model and, 570–571
    variable pay and, 583
Bundesbank, 508
Bureau of Labor Statistics (BLS), 224, 483, 597
Burns Meats Ltd., 545
Business strategies
    compensation and, 31–34, 44
    cost cutter strategy, 34
    customer-focused business strategy, 34
    definition of, 31–32
    innovator strategy, 33–34
Cafeteria-style compensation, 261
Canada, 3, 511, 512
Carrier, 35
Cash balance plans, 440
Cash compensation, 7–9, 21. *See also* Compensation; Wages
Cats, 1–2
Central tendency errors, 331
CEO compensation. *See also* Managers; Special groups
    agency theory and, 465
    benefits, 468–470
    company performance and, 4